WRITER'S ENCYCLOPEDIA

WRITER'S ENCYCLOPEDIA

EDITED BY

KIRK POLKING
JOAN BLOSS AND COLLEEN CANNON

Writer's
Digest
Books

Cincinnati, Ohio

Writer's Encyclopedia. Copyright 1983 © Writer's Digest Books. Printed and bound in the United States of America. All rights reserved. No part of this book may be reproduced in any form or by any electronic or mechanical means including information storage and retrieval systems without permission in writing from the publisher, except by a reviewer who may quote brief passages in a review. Published by Writer's Digest Books, an imprint of F&W Publications, Inc., 1507 Dana Ave., Cincinnati, Ohio 45207. First edition.

90 89 88 87   6 5 4 3 2

Library of Congress Cataloging in Publication Data

Writer's encyclopedia.

    Bibliography: p.
    1. Authorship—Dictionaries. 2. Mass media—Dictionaries.
I. Polking, Kirk.
PN141.W75 1983   808'.02'0321   83-1058
ISBN 0-89879-253-3

Design by Charleen Catt Lyon

ACKNOWLEDGMENTS

Contributing Editors: Richard Balkin, Phyllis Ball, Kathryn Falk, Bill Francois, Victor Marton, Tom McCormack, Paul Nathan, Robert Orben, Miriam Phelps, Yuri Rasovsky, Hugh Rawson, Victor Schmalzer, John Tebbel.

Consulting Editors: Connie Achabal, Rose Adkins, John Brady, Bill Brohaugh, Anita Buck, Carol Cartaino, Bernadine Clark, Sally Davis, Henry Dorfman, Jean Fredette, Beth Franks, Don Herman, Jo Hoff, Nancy Kersell, Barb Kuroff, Dave Luppert, Bob Lutz, Mary Mangold, Leonard Meranus, Mert Neal, Richard Rosenthal, P.J. Schemenaur, W.B. Wallis, Howard I. Wells III, the editorial associates of Writer's Digest School and Writer's Digest Criticism Service, and the authors and friends of Writer's Digest Books.

CONTENTS

PREFACE

Writing is an art, a craft, a business. It is the persuasive power of advertising, the lyrics of a song, the pages of a novel we can't stop reading. And each writing specialty has its idioms to be mastered. This reference work brings together in one volume all the terms, techniques, procedures, and trade expressions you'll need to know, whether your interest is publishing, broadcasting, films, lecturing, the theater, advertising, or public relations.

Arranged in an easy-to-use A-Z format, the *Writer's Encyclopedia* is designed to be an experienced fellow writer, an editorial colleague, a marketing manager, a reference librarian, a knowledgeable teacher— available for instant consultation, no matter what your question.

In assembling the more than 1,200 entries in the *Encyclopedia*, we naturally drew on the material published in *Writer's Digest* and *Writer's Yearbook*, along with hundreds of references on specialized types of writing. We sought advice from the faculty of Writer's Digest School and the professional writers who work with the Writer's Digest Criticism Service. We wrote specialists in every field with questions as simple as "What are the ten most important words in your industry?" to more complex discussions of the economics of publishing. As any writer who has done research knows, the "experts" don't always agree, so we had to make a lot of judgment calls. The result is our best synthesis of all the sources we consulted.

There were a few trade expressions we couldn't track to their original source. "Over the transom," for example, has long been used in publishing to refer to unsolicited manuscripts; and while the architectural style of pre-airconditioning office doorways is well known, we never were able to pin down the first person who used the expression.

The copyediting expression "the Harvard comma" was disavowed by that university's English department, and the origin of "bastard title," referring to the half title page in books, was also unknown to the publishing archivists we consulted. (Any bibliophiles who care to set us straight on these terms for the next edition are invited to write the editors!)

Although the three primary editors of this encyclopedia are all women, and sensitive to the sexism that permeates language, we chose to use the traditional "he" for easier readability. Women writers are as prominent as men in each of the disciplines covered by this book, but we found the repeated use of "he or she" or the newer contractions awkward and distracting.

Since this encyclopedia is designed primarily for the professional writer, as opposed to the scholar or teacher of literature, it does not concentrate on the kind of literary terms that can be found in readers' encyclopedias or literary dictionaries. It does include every term we think writers in any staff or freelance capacity might want to look up. It does not include the biographies of classic or contemporary authors, but it does direct the reader to sources of such information. Since writing and writers are so heavily concerned with publication, we have included many publishing as well as strictly writing terms.

In creating this encyclopedia, the editors have tried to give the reader enough information for a general understanding of each topic; readers who want more detailed information on individual subjects will find additional sources listed at the end of some entries. These references are incorporated into the bibliography at the end of the book.

We have used numerous cross references throughout the encyclopedia to lead the reader to related information, or to help locate a topic that a reader might look up under a different subject heading. Whenever we could refer the reader to specific professional associations or other research sources, we have done so. Anyone who contacts any of the resources described in this encyclopedia is advised to enclose a self-addressed, stamped envelope with inquiries, since some of these organizations have only limited or volunteer staff.

Many charts, tables, script samples, tax forms, and other data that we thought would be of additional help to the reader are included in the Appendix. The subject matter in the Appendix is alphabetized by title on the contents pages for easy reference.

An encyclopedia—especially one about a major form of self-expression—has a personality all its own based on the needs of its readers as perceived by the editors. This book was created to respond to those anguished cries from writers who have hunted through hundreds of sources for scattered and specialized information and then written or phoned us and said, "I wish there were just *one* book I could use to find out things like this!" This book is also the result of impassioned debates among its editors on the kinds of information that should be included to best serve the professional writer. As you use this volume, we welcome any suggestions for topics that should be included in future editions, or comments on any entries in this edition.

Thomas Carlyle reminds us that "The best effect of any book is that it excites the reader to self-activity." The editors hope their *Writer's Encyclopedia* will excite its readers to the activity they love best—writing.

Kirk Polking
Joan Bloss
Colleen Cannon

AA. Acronym for *author's alteration*, which refers to text corrections or emendations made by the writer on galleys or page proofs. Typographical errors, known as printer's errors (PEs), are not counted as part of author's alterations. The author's contract indicates a percentage of the text that may be changed by the author, who must pay for any alterations made after that percentage has been reached. Also called *author's alts*. (*See: author's alteration clause*.)

A&R (artists' and repertoire) representative. Working either independently or on a record company staff, an A&R representative traditionally finds potential acts and matches artists with songs to be recorded. However, the duties in this position vary widely, and the A&R representative may also seek out artists, choose the engineer for each recording project, or find an appropriate studio, among other tasks.

In recent years, the number of musical groups that continuously record and compose together has increased. Since they know their own style and their music, such groups need little guidance from an A&R representative. In working with this kind of group, the latter typically serves to budget the album.

ABC. (*See: broadcast networks*.)

Abridged Readers' Guide to Periodical Literature. A shortened form of the *Readers' Guide to Periodical Literature*, this index lists magazines usually found in elementary school libraries, which are its primary subscribers. The *Abridged Readers' Guide* currently indexes 68 magazines. (*See:* Readers' Guide to Periodical Literature.)

Abridgment. A shortened form of literary work, in which the major themes of the original are kept. Books are abridged for the sake of faster and easier reading. The Reader's Digest Condensed Books are the most notable examples of abridgment; *The Reader's Digest Bible*, for instance, is 40% shorter than the 850,000-word Revised Standard Version. Although well-known passages have been left intact, the editors excised what they described as the "repetition, rhetoric and redundancy" of the complete work. (*See: abstract; pony.*)

Abstract. An abstract is a synopsis of a piece of nonfiction writing, such as an article, document, speech, or statement. It summarizes the main points of the publication in the same order that the writer has presented them. Abstracts are published with their respective articles (especially in scientific and professional journals) and in some indexes to periodicals.

Indexes that contain abstracts sometimes use the word *abstracts* in their titles instead of the word *index; Psychological Abstracts* is an example. (*See: periodicals, indexes to.*)

A/C (adult contemporary). A term used in the music business to refer to a particular category of popular music. Also known as *middle-of-the-road* and *easy listening* music, A/C songs are melodic and easy to listen to, as the name implies. They are composed for and performed at lower volumes and slower tempos than rock music. Most A/C songs have lyrics, but some are purely instrumental, such as *Chariots of Fire*, the theme from the movie of the same name.

Billboard, a trade magazine of the music industry, publishes weekly charts listing the titles of the 50 current bestselling singles in this category. Songs by artists as diverse as Simon and Garfunkel, Elton John, Stevie Wonder, and Dolly Parton have appeared on *Billboard*'s chart.

Academy of American Poets. This organization exists to "encourage, stimulate, and foster the production of American poetry." The Academy awards two annual $10,000 Fellowships to poets of proven merit, the Lamont Poetry Selection for a poet's second book, the Walt Whitman Award for a poet's first book, the Landon Translation Award, and more than 120 College and University Prizes around the country. Its New York City activities include poetry readings and literary walking tours. The Academy is located at 177 East 87th Street, New York NY 10028. (212) 427-5665.

Account executive. The advertising-agency contact person who acts as a liaison between the client and the agency's creative and media buyer departments.

In radio advertising, an account executive is a radio station representative who calls on the station's advertisers to service their accounts.

Accrediting Council on Education in Journalism and Mass Communication (ACEJMC). This organization accredits college and university journalism programs, and elicits cooperation between schools and industry for the advancement of journalism education. The Council publishes lists of ACEJMC-accredited programs and accrediting standards. ACEJMC conventions are held each April in New York City.

This organization was formerly called the American Council on Education for Journalism. ACEJMC is headquartered c/o Secretary-Treasurer Milton Gross, School of Journalism, University of Missouri, Box 838, Columbia MO 65205.

Acknowledgment page. The page of a book on which the author credits sources of assistance. Acknowledgments are customarily given to persons or institutions who have helped with research, writing, editing, or typing, and to sources of copyrighted material that have been quoted in the book. Some publishers now shy away from the overly personal, gushy acknowledgments popular in the past.

Acronym. A word formed from the initial letters of a proper name or a series of words referring to one thing. Examples of acronyms are *MASH*, for Mobile Army Surgical Hospital; *SASE*, for self-addressed, stamped envelope; and *ZIP* (as in ZIP code), for Zone Improvement Program. Writers generally use acronyms in this way: spell out the entire phrase initially, follow it with the acronym in parentheses, and use only the acronym thereafter. Two sources of standard acronyms are *New Acronyms, Initialisms and Abbreviations* and the *Trade Names Dictionary*, both of which are available in libraries.

Across the board. Refers to a radio program or commercial used five, six, or seven days a week that is scheduled to be broadcast at the same time every day.

Adaptation. This term refers to the process of rewriting a composition (e.g., novel, story, film, article, play) into a form suitable for some other medium, such as television or the stage. Since the copyright owner has the exclusive right to adapt his own work, anyone else wishing to adapt the material must get permission from the original owner or whomever he may have assigned the adaptation rights to. This is the basis for the sale (usually by his agent or publisher) of various subsidiary rights. (*See: rights for sale.*)

Addresses, sources of. In order to gather authoritative and current information, the writer must sometimes contact a person who is prominent in a given field. When a noted person's address is not directly available, librarians can often furnish directories that contain the necessary information, or an organization with which the person is affiliated will be able to supply an address.

A book author, for example, can be reached care of his publisher; a magazine writer, through the magazine(s) he writes for. The directory *Contemporary Authors* is another source of writers' addresses. Addresses of scientists are listed in *American Men and Women of Science* and *World Who's Who in Science*; similarly, addresses of artists and others who work in the field of art can be found in *Who's Who in American Art*. A university professor can usually be located at the university he is affiliated with; if his current affiliation is unknown, he may be listed in the *National Faculty Directory*.

To find the address of an attorney outside his own city, the writer should consult the *Martindale-Hubbell Law Directory*, which contains information on individual attorneys and law firms. (It is discussed in the

3

entry "lawyers, where to find," in this encyclopedia.) The address of a physician can be obtained from the *American Medical Directory* (published by the American Medical Association).

Clergymen can be located through the home offices of their respective denominations. Sports figures can be reached through the teams or professional sports organizations they play on or are associated with. A librarian can assist the researcher in finding directories of such organizations.

Freelancers who want to contact government offices, corporations, colleges, banks, national unions, transportation companies, media, and other business services will find 50,000 selected entries in the *National Directory of Addresses and Telephone Numbers*, published in paperback by W.C.C. Directories, Inc., New York. Of course, if the writer knows the city in which the expert is located, he can consult an out-of-town phone book, available in most large public libraries.

Celebrity Service, Inc., aids researchers in locating celebrities not listed in directories. (It is discussed in the entry "celebrity addresses" in this encyclopedia.) (*See: celebrity addresses; lawyers, where to find.*)

Adjective. An adjective is a word that in some way describes, qualifies, restricts, or changes the meaning of the noun or pronoun it modifies. Adjectives are a means of adding specific description and color to writing. The simplest way to use an adjective is to place it directly in front of the noun it modifies—the dented, red Volkswagen—but that's not always the most interesting way.

Vern Sneider described in *Writer's Digest* five variations of "the adjectival idea": 1) an adjective combined with a prepositional phrase, e.g., "Maria, *heavy with child*"; 2) the relative clause with relative pronoun and verbs understood, e.g., "it was an island, (that was) *unimportant except to its inhabitants*"; 3) the participial phrase, e.g., "Harry, *having completed four years of college*"; 4) the absolute phrase, e.g., "John (with) *a gun in his hand*"; and 5) the ablative absolute, e.g., "the whistle *having blown.*"

Many writers feel that it is more effective to use precise nouns, rather than rely on adjectives; overuse of adjectives is a common writing flaw.

Additional information: any handbook on English grammar and composition such as *Harbrace College Handbook* or *Essentials of English*.

Ad-lib. Music or spoken parts used extemporaneously in a radio or television program; elements that are used but are not indicated on the script.

Adult fiction. A novel or story in which the subject matter is often sexually explicit. (*See: erotica.*)

Advance. A sum of money that a publisher pays a writer(s) prior to the publication of a book. The advance represents at least partial compensation for the time and effort to be expended writing the book, and it usually reflects the publisher's expectation of the work's prospective sales as well. It is usually paid in installments, such as one-half on signing the contract; one-half on delivery of a complete and satisfactory manuscript. When royalties begin to accrue, the publisher withholds the amount of the advance paid to the author before making royalty payments to him.

The writer and/or his agent negotiates the advance against royalties, and its provisions are incorporated into the book contract. In the instance that an advance is actually larger than the royalties ultimately collected, the contract may specify that the advance is nonreturnable. The contract may also provide for protection against a publisher's trying to recoup all or part of the advance if for some reason he decides not to issue a book.

Advances vary with the type of book, the author's writing ability, his reputation, and the book idea itself. They may be nonexistent in some cases, as low as $500-$1,000 for a fledgling writer, or as much as $15,000 and up for a veteran in the field. The publisher sometimes figures the advance as a function of the price of the book times the royalty percentage times the estimated advance sale. Thus, an estimated 4,000-copy advance sale of a $13.95 book with a 10% of list price starting royalty might produce an advance offer to the author of a maximum of $5,600. A writer's advances generally rise from book to book, as his audience increases. (*See: book contract; book publishing economics.*)

Advance sale. This publishing term refers to the commitments to buy made by bookstores or wholesalers before the formal publication date of a particular book. To make advance sales, a publisher's representative supplies information on forthcoming books to buyers. Publishers also circulate direct-mail catalogs listing and describing forthcoming publications so that individual consumers can place orders in advance. Data from the very earliest advance sales, especially the orders placed by the major bookstore chains, help the publisher estimate the print order for a book.

Adventure story. A genre of fiction in which action is the key element, overshadowing characters, theme, and setting. (Even though *adventure story* is the name of the genre, the term refers to articles, novels, and nonfiction books as well.)

The conflict in an adventure story is almost always man against nature. Often a secondary plot that reinforces this kind of conflict is included. In Alistair MacLean's *Night Without End*, for example, the hero, while investigating a mysterious Arctic air crash, also finds himself dealing with espionage, sabotage, and murder.

In recent years, adventure novels have been less in demand than adventure stories, and novels and stories alike have begun to borrow elements from spy stories and war stories.

Papillon, by Henri Charrier, and *Annapurna*, by Maurice Herzog, are two examples of nonfiction adventure stories, while the aforementioned *Night Without End* is an adventure novel. Some publishers have produced series of books under such imprints as "Men of Action," "Hawk," "Destroyer," and other lines.

Men's, young adults', children's, religious, and women's magazines all publish adventure stories. *Fiction Writer's Market* lists editors' needs and payment rates for writers.

Advertiser control of media. Because advertisers provide a substantial portion of media revenue, they sometimes try to exert influence on the editorial aspects of media presentations. They might try to suppress a news story unfavorable to them or influence editors to give their products favorable treatment in magazines.

Most editors working in print media will vigorously defend their ideological independence from advertisers, although the industry has experienced occasional lapses.

Television producers, on the other hand, are placed under more pressure by their sponsors. Advertisers hire celebrities to advertise products on their own shows; ensure that their product, as opposed to a similar one, is used in the program; and may censor controversial characters and philosophies featured in teleplays. (*See: advertorial.*)

Advertising agencies' costs and profits. (See the Appendix to this encyclopedia.)

Advertising, copyrighted. Copyright protection for print-media advertisements can be obtained by placing the copyright notice (©, year, owner's name) on all copies of the ad. In addition, it may be registered at the U.S. Copyright Office. Unpublished material can be copyrighted, but publication generally precedes registration: two copies of the published ad are deposited with the Copyright Office together with the application for registration and the copyright registration fee.

Whether or not the advertisement is registered, the copyright notice is extremely important; its proper use cannot be overemphasized. Without such notice, the copyright may be rendered unenforceable. Under copyright law, any publication of material without a copyright notice places the material in the public domain.

Parts of an advertisement, such as original jingles, illustrations, photos, and copy, are eligible for copyright protection, as are many objects used in advertisements, such as original works of art, dolls, games, and maps.

Advertisers in the print media must place their own copyright notices on ads and not rely upon the overall copyright for the publication the ads appear in.

Anyone—a radio or television station or an advertiser who has the right to control a program's content—can be held responsible for copyright infringement when using the copyrighted material of others in an unauthorized fashion. (*See: copyright; copyright notice; Copyright, Register of.*)

Advertising copywriters. Writers whose purpose is selling products or services for clients through written or spoken copy. These writers prepare newspaper and magazine ads, brochures, billboards, radio and TV commercials, annual reports, and anything else that is used to sell a product or service.

Copywriters work for advertising agencies or for the advertising departments of companies. Copy

entory off entontory offtory

chiefs prefer applicants with liberal arts/English backgrounds and retail or marketing research experience. Desirable personality traits include: an ability to get along with others, a spirit of inventiveness, and the discipline to work long hours under pressure.

Freelance copywriters develop their own clients by contacting people and organizations that advertise. Department stores, catalog houses, shopping centers, art studios, printing companies, and political campaigns afford opportunities for copywriters. Sample copy presented to these advertisers to solicit their business should deal with the merchandise or service they offer and should be slanted to reflect their particular advertising "image" (e.g., institutional copy for banks and hotels would be different from the action words and catchy headlines for sportswear).

Salary scales for ad copywriters vary with company size and the availability of competent writers. Beginning copywriters in small ad agencies currently expect an annual salary of $15,000-$18,000; those in large agencies, $20,000 and up. Successful freelance copywriters work to gain the confidence of steady clients. Some employers hire by the day or the hour, and capable writers should be able to get at least $20/hr. Those with experience may choose to quote a price for a job before accepting it.

One advantage of copywriting for advertising may well be the growth and flexibility it offers the writer. Freelancers often work at home, sometimes during their spare time from other employment. They can move from one ad job to another with relative ease once they establish a portfolio. Though advertising copywriters get no bylines of their own, they are known and have visibility within the advertising community they serve.

Additional information: *Standard Directory of Advertisers*; *Standard Directory of Advertising Agencies*.

Advertising freelance services. Freelance writers and editors can take advantage of several methods of advertising without purchasing ads in publications. Direct-mail brochures can be sent to any printers, businesses, or agencies that the freelancer perceives as prospective clients. A résumé and a portfolio are effective means of introducing work to a client in person. Similarly, copies of articles can be sent to acquaintances or associates, such as librarians, editors, and professors, to keep them current on a writer's career.

The writer can obtain a listing in a directory such as *Literary Market Place* or *Working Press of the Nation*. Another method of direct advertising is to post business cards or other notices at suitable locations.

Finally, speaking for organizations is a way many writers make themselves known. (*See: business cards; speechwriting; stationery.*)

Advertorial. Advertising presented in such a way as to resemble editorial material. Even though it may contain the same kind of information that might have been written as an editorial feature in a magazine, it is paid for by an advertiser, and the word "advertising" usually appears in small type at the top of each page.

The Association of Business Publishers has guidelines for the use of special advertising supplements.

Advice columns. Besides the well-known personal advice columns of twin sisters Ann Landers and Abby Van Buren, there are numerous other specialized advice columns in U.S. newspapers. A list of those columns, their authors, and the syndicates that handle them appears in the *Editor and Publisher Syndicate Directory*, described in this encyclopedia. Freelancers who have an idea for a specialized advice column usually try for sales to their local and regional papers before approaching a national syndicate. (*See:* Editor and Publisher Syndicate Directory; *self-syndication; syndicated column.*)

Affiliate. A local radio or TV station that has a contract with a network to carry certain programs.

AGAC/The Songwriters Guild. Made up both of published and aspiring songwriters, this 50-year-old association provides a number of services to its members: The AGAC Uniform Popular Songwriters Contract, the Royalty Collection Plan, the Copyright Renewal Service, a group medical and life insurance plan, contract review, estates administration, and the AGAC Foundation for music scholarships and workshops. It publishes a periodic newsletter.

The former names of the Guild were the Songwriters Protective Association, and then the American Guild of Authors and Composers. Recently the name was expanded to AGAC/The Songwriters Guild. The Guild meets annually. Its headquarters are at 40 W. 57th Street, New York NY 10019. The West Coast branch is located at 6430 Sunset Boulevard, Suite 317, Hollywood CA 90028; the Nashville branch is locat-ed at 50 Music Square West, Suite 207, Nashville TN 37203.

Agents, comedians'. A writer interested in submitting gag material to a well-known comedian should first try contacting him through a club at which or a TV show on which he's appearing. If that doesn't work, the writer must approach the comic through a personal manager. The National Conference of Personal Managers, located at 7060 Hollywood Boulevard, Suite 1212, Hollywood CA 90028, or The Conference of Personal Managers East, 1650 Broadway, New York NY 10019, may be able to provide information on which personal manager represents which comedian. (*See:* Variety.)

Agents, literary. Writers' business representatives. As marketing experts in the publishing field, they sell book outlines or manuscripts, negotiate royalty advances, and contract terms for writers. They know what publishers are buying and which books are selling; therefore, they can often speed up the purchase of material. They know editors' tastes and serve as liaisons between them and authors with appropriate ideas.

Agents earn their money by deducting commissions from the manuscripts they sell. Commission rates on U.S. material range from 10%-15%. When a U.S. agent deals with a foreign agent on the writer's behalf, the commission is at least 20%. Agents represent writers in any kind of literary output, but generally do not handle poetry, verse, articles, short stories, cartoons, or fillers because of the low commissions they generate. Most agents do not charge reading and evaluation fees if they consider a work salable. Some agents specializing in handling the beginning writer's work, however, charge fees for reviewing manuscripts, since their opportunities for commissions on sales are so much more limited.

There are many ways to find an agent. The most direct approach is to query by mail. Query letters should contain an outline of the project and the qualifications of the writer. (Complete manuscripts should not be sent to an agent at this point.) Since it is not unusual for an agent's client list to be sixty authors to whom he is already responsible, an agent may not be interested in taking on another client unless the project is compelling. A self-addressed, stamped envelope should accompany the request for the agent's consideration of the proposed work.

Lists of agents are published in the annual directories *Writer's Market* and *Literary Market Place*. Some agents advertise their services in writers' magazines. In addition, editors, writer-friends, and teachers can often recommend suitable agents. (*See: Independent Literary Agents Association, Inc., Society of Authors' Representatives.*)

Agents, television. The television business is unlike publishing in that a writer interested in breaking into television writing usually approaches producers through an agent; most television producers will not consider unsolicited manuscripts from a writer. Television agents, like literary agents, work on a commission (10%-15% on domestic sales).

Names of agents who have regular contact with television producers

are maintained in the files of the Writers Guild of America, West, 8955 Beverly Boulevard, Los Angeles CA 90048. Agents willing to work with previously unproduced writers are listed in *Writer's Market*. (*See: agents, literary.*)

AKA. Acronym for *also known as*. It is used in connection with writers' pen names, and sometimes appears in bibliographies of a writer's works, for example, Erle Stanley Gardner (aka A.A. Fair). (*See: pen name.*)

All rights. Some magazines buy all rights to the articles, stories, and poems they acquire from freelancers. They indicate this policy either in their listings in *Writer's Market* or on the checks they issue for manuscripts. Magazines with this policy will, in some cases, return all but first North American serial rights to the author on request.

Under the old copyright law, a publisher was presumed to have bought all rights to a manuscript unless the author and the publisher agreed otherwise. Under the new law, which went into effect in 1978, the publisher is presumed to have bought only one-time rights unless the author and the publisher have agreed otherwise.

A work-for-hire agreement, which concerns assigned rather than unsolicited work, includes the purchase of all rights; the writer has no power to negotiate future rights when such an agreement has been made. The purchase of all rights without such an agreement, on the other hand, usually concerns unsolicited work, the rights to which may someti nes be regained by the author, as mentioned above. Listings in *Writer's Market* indicate editors' policies on rights. (*See: copyright; rights to manuscripts; work made for hire.*)

Alpha Epsilon Rho—The National Broadcasting Society. An honorary society made up of 17,000 men and women in radio and television. Most members are college or university students majoring in broadcasting. They represent all aspects of this field, including advertising, news, public relations, writing, directing, and announcing. Activities of the organization include broadcast production competitions and annual conventions; it also presents awards and scholarships.

Alpha Epsilon Rho—The National Broadcasting Society publishes the monthly *Signals* and an annual directory. It was formerly known only as Alpha Epsilon Rho. The headquarters of the Society are located at the College of Journalism, University of South Carolina, Columbia SC 29208.

Alternate (or alternate selection). In book club offerings, a book that, though not a main selection, is called to the special attention of the club's membership. A book club's catalogue sometimes promotes more than one alternate.

The first time an alternate selection is offered, it is featured—given special treatment in the book club's bulletin. In later months, it becomes part of the backlist of alternate selections, and so is given a short descriptive entry in the bulletin. Like a main selection, an alternate means additional sales for the author. (*See: book club selection; book clubs; selection [or main selection].*)

Alternative weekly. (*See: newsweekly.*)

American Academy & Institute of Arts & Letters. The National Institute of Arts & Letters was established in 1898 to further literature and the fine arts in the United States. The American Academy of Arts & Letters, founded by the Institute in 1904, is a self-perpetuating group of fifty members chosen for special recognition in literature, art, and music. Eminent foreign artists, writers, and composers are elected as honorary members.

The Institute encourages excellence in the arts by conferring a number of awards and honors for works meriting praise. Many of the awards have been established in memory of a distinguished practitioner of a particular craft: for example, the Sue Kaufman Prize for First Fiction; the Marjorie Peabody Waite Award, given to an older writer for continuing achievement; and the Witter Bynner Poetry Prize. Other awards have been established to recognize achievement in other fields, such as the Award of Merit Medal given to an outstanding novelist, poet, or dramatist. The Academy also sponsors fellowships—for example, the Rome Fellowship in literature at the American Academy in Rome.

Some of the awards are accompanied by cash prizes and/or medals. Most of them may not be applied for but are awarded by decision of the Academy members. Further details of the awards are given in the annual *Literary Market Place*. Recipients of the various awards are listed in recent editions of *Literary and Library Prizes*.

American Book Awards. Formerly called the National Book Awards, the American Book Awards are given annually by the Association of

American Publishers to living American authors for the year's best books in several categories to promote "reading and literacy." Three awards in the amount of $10,000 each are presented for fiction, nonfiction and a first novel. Two runners-up in each category are awarded $1,000 each. Nominees are announced in October and awards given in November each year. Judging is by a panel of eleven authors, critics, librarians, booksellers, editors, and publishers. "Best" books are sometimes those which have appeared on bestseller lists during the award period.

Literary Market Place details submission dates and contact persons for more information about the American Book Awards. (*See: National Book Critics Circle.*)

American Book Trade Directory. This directory, available in most public libraries, lists bookstores in the U.S. and Canada by state and city. It lists, in addition to the address, phone number, and name of owner (or manager), the types of books and other products carried by bookstores. The directory also includes the names and addresses of book and magazine wholesalers, national distributors of paperbacks, and other book trade information. Writers who self-publish their books use the Annual to find stores that are likely prospects for their work.

American Booksellers Association (ABA). An organization of 5,500 retail bookstores whose goals are to facilitate bookstore operations; educate members in their trade, through seminars and workshops; foster greater numbers of book sales; and sustain harmonious relations between booksellers and publishers.

The ABA publishes the weekly *Newswire*, the monthly *American Bookseller*, the biennial *Sidelines Directory*, the biennial *Basic Book List*, and *A Manual on Bookselling: How to Open and Operate Your Own Bookstore* (3rd edition), which is distributed by Crown Publishers. It convenes annually and is the largest publishing-related meeting of the year, attended by foreign as well as domestic publishers, packagers, and agents.

ABA headquarters are located at 122 E. 42nd Street, New York NY 10168. (*See:* Basic Book List.)

American Dialect Society (ADS). This group, founded in 1889, is made up of scholars who study not only the English language in North America, but also languages that influence or are influenced by English in this region. The Society has research committees that report on new words, proverbial sayings, regionalisms and linguistic geography, non-English dialects, and usage.

Membership currently comprises 400 individuals and 300 institutions. Persons interested in the goals and activities of the organization are qualified to join; members must pay dues, however.

The ADS holds an annual meeting and other, regional meetings. Its publications include *American Speech*, published quarterly; *Publication of the American Dialect Society* (PADS), published occasionally; and *Newsletter of the American Dialect Society* (NADS), published in January, May, and October.

This organization sponsors the five-volume *Dictionary of American Regional English* (DARE). The Society's publications are sources for half the dictionary's content.

While fiction writers are always cautioned to use dialect sparingly, the use of an apt word or phrase to pinpoint a certain section of the country can add flavor and credibility to a work. Writers with questions about regionalisms, for example, may find the Society's research helpful. The Society's headquarters are c/o the English Department MacMurray College, Jacksonville IL 62650. (*See:* Dictionary of American Regional English *(DARE).*)

American Guild of Authors and Composers. See AGAC/The Songwriters Guild.

American Library Association (ALA). A 38,000-member organization of libraries, library trustees, individual librarians, and other individuals interested in libraries.

According to the American Library Association, the Association is "an organization with the overarching objective of promoting and improving library services and librarianship. The priorities are access to information, legislation/funding, intellectual freedom, public awareness, and personnel resources."

ALA's committees include Instruction in the Use of Libraries, Intellectual Freedom, Professional Ethics, Publishing, and Research. It publishes *Booklist*, semimonthly; *American Libraries*, 11 times per year; *Choice*, 11 times per year; books; and pamphlets.

The Association holds an annual convention and an annual midwinter meeting. The address of ALA is

50 E. Huron Street, Chicago IL 60611. (*See:* Booklist.)

American Medical Writers' Association (AMWA). Members of this organization are medical writers, editors, publishers, administrators, audiovisualists, and pharmaceutical and public relations professionals concerned with effective communication about medicine and allied sciences. The Association publishes a newsletter, a journal, a membership directory, and a freelance directory. Awards for medical books and medical films are given; a conference is held annually. The address of the AMWA is 5272 River Road, Suite 410, Bethesda MD 20816.

American Society of Indexers (ASI). The 400 members of ASI strive to encourage communication concerning developments in the field and to stimulate members to improve their professional capacities. Besides indexers, members include librarians, editors, publishers, and organizations that employ indexers.

Committees of the group include Education, Getting Started as an Indexer, Indexer Economics, and Indexer-Publisher Relations.

The organization presents an annual award with the cooperation of the H.W. Wilson Co. ASI holds a meeting each spring and fall and sponsors other seminars, workshops, or tours. Publications include *The Indexer*, a journal published in affiliation with the Society of Indexers (England); the ASI newsletter; and the *Register of Indexers*, a list of indexers available for freelance assignments.

The address of the ASI is 235 Park Avenue S., 8th Floor, New York NY 10003.

American Society of Journalists and Authors (ASJA). The ASJA is a nationwide organization of more than 600 independent nonfiction writers. It encourages high standards of nonfiction writing, takes a strong stand against practices denigrating the freelance writer's professional status, holds educational conferences and meetings, offers awards for outstanding accomplishments, and examines issues that concern the freelance writer and the reading public. ASJA publishes a monthly newsletter for its members, a "Code of Ethics and Fair Practices" (reprinted in the Appendix to this encyclopedia), an annual membership directory, and books on writing.

The American Society of Journalists and Authors was formerly called the Society of Magazine Writers. ASJA is located at 1501 Broadway, Suite 1907, New York NY 10036. (*See: Dial-a-Writer; and ASJA position papers in the Appendix to this encyclopedia.*)

American Society of Magazine Editors (ASME). The 400 members of ASME are senior editors on magazines. The organization presents national magazine awards, sponsors a magazine internship program, holds seminars and luncheons, and publishes an occasional newsletter for members. ASME convenes annually. Its address is 575 Lexington Avenue, New York NY 10022.

American Society of Magazine Photographers (ASMP). (Formerly the Society of Photographers in Communications.) Established in 1944, this organization comprises more than 3,500 members worldwide. General members have had at least three years' experience following their first published work; they are involved in advertising, documentary photography, and photojournalism.

Freelancers may wish to inquire if there is an ASMP photographer in their area to recommend to an editor on an article idea for which they're not equipped to provide illustrations themselves. The address of the American Society of Magazine Photographers (ASMP) is 205 Lexington Avenue, New York NY 10016.

American Society of Newspaper Editors (ASNE). The membership of this group is made up of 860 daily newspaper editors in the U.S. and Canada, who hold such positions as managing editor, executive editor, associate editor, and editorial page editor. Committees include Freedom of Information and Press-Bar. The organization meets annually.

ASNE publishes the *Bulletin of ASNE* nine times per year, and *Problems of Journalism—ASNE Proceedings* annually. The mailing address of the ASNE is Box 551, 1350 Sullivan Trail, Easton PA 18042.

American Society of Picture Professionals (ASPP). The Society's 600 members are persons who work with still pictures: photographers, agents, picture researchers, editors, librarians, curators, and historians. To qualify for membership an individual must have two years' experience in working with still pictures, and be recommended by two members or submit a résumé. The Society publishes a membership directory and a quarterly newsletter. The organization has local chapters in San Francisco, Boston, Chicago, and Washington, D.C.; all chapters hold monthly meetings with speakers.

The ASPP has an annual photo show in New York each fall.

The organization would refer a writer in search of photo materials either to a photographer or to a photo-researcher. The address of the ASPP is Box 5283, Grand Central Station, New York NY 10063.

American Translators Association (ATA). This international organization of 1,700 members advocates improvement of professional standards and encourages professional training. Its members are categorized as follows: *active* (citizens or permanent residents of the U.S. who are professional translators or interpreters or who work in related fields), *associate* ("individuals who are interested in the objectives of ATA but who are not eligible for active membership"), *student* (full-time students at accredited institutions; must be 30 years of age or under), *institutional*, *corporate*, and *sustaining*. According to the pamphlet "Guide to ATA," the "ATA actively discourages anyone from joining it primarily to obtain employment or freelance assignments."

The monthly *Chronicle*, the *ATA Professional Services Directory*, and *Translator Training Guidelines* (a curriculum for university-level training) are its publications.

Awards presented by the ATA are the Alexander Gode Medal, for "outstanding achievement in the profession"; the Lewis Galantiere Prize, for literary translation; the Distinguished Service Plaque, for "outstanding and dedicated service to the American Translators Association"; and the Academic Programs Fund, given to a student or group of students.

The American Translators Association convenes annually to exchange ideas and to discuss common problems. Its headquarters are at 109 Croton Avenue, Ossining NY 10562.

American Writers Congress. This was a four-day gathering of American writers in New York during October 1981. It was organized by The Nation Institute as a forum for the common grievances and concerns of writers. The three major topics addressed were an increase in literary censorship brought about by the influence of the political right; the increasing presence of conglomerates in the publishing, movie, and television industries; and a worldwide comparison of writers' unions. It was the first step in an effort to form a national writers' union of all types of writers in the U.S. (*See: writers' unions.*)

Anecdote. A short narrative revealing a curious, amusing, or insightful incident that illustrates a point or reinforces an idea. Anecdotes frequently contain dialogue, provide explicit detail, and sometimes incorporate plays on words or humorous endings. It is a glimpse of life that is often used to "humanize" a topic.

An anecdote may be biographical, or it may result from the writer's observation. It is used in virtually all article writing, in addition to being salable in itself as a filler.

Here, for example, is an anecdote as it appeared in a column by Robert Sylvester in the New York *Sunday News*:

The other day a truck, a cab, and a private car managed to ram each other at Fifth Avenue and 48th

Street. The three drivers were using some pretty strong language. A newcomer to the onlookers' circle asked: "Anybody hurt?"

"Not yet," said another bystander.

Ready examples of anecdotes are available in any issue of *Reader's Digest* in departments titled, "Life in These United States," "Humor in Uniform," "Campus Comedy," and "All in a Day's Work."

Angle. In television and motion picture scripts, a designation of camera position used to highlight a dramatic scene. It could be either straight forward or an oblique camera angle. The expression *angle on* is used to indicate the major subject of the scene the camera should emphasize. Both terms are typed all in caps when used in scripts.

Annotation. Notes that explicate or augment a text. Ancient or reconstructed or symbolically dense literature is frequently published in annotated editions, e.g., Chaucer, Shakespeare, collections of folk tales, translations of classics or of national literature, Joyce, and the poetry of Pound and Eliot.

An annotated bibliography briefly describes and/or evaluates the listed works to better aid the reader in researching a topic.

Announcement. In radio advertising, another word for *commercial* or *spot*.

Annual report. The financial statement published at the end of each fiscal year by a corporation or institution. They often contain corporate histories, executive profiles, and other information for which freelance writers are sometimes employed. (*See: seasonal jobs for writers.*)

Anonymity of sources. Confidentiality between newsperson and certain sources is important to the media's function of gathering and disseminating news: if a reporter reveals a source, he risks losing the confidence of the person who was his source, as well as his reputation among potential sources.

The court trial represents a common situation in which reporters are asked to reveal their sources of information. Although no federal law protects writers from such requests, some states have *shield laws*, or laws that give reporters the right to keep their sources confidential. However, shield law privileges apply to freelance writers only in some states. (*See: attribution; free press vs. fair trial; shield laws.*)

Additional information: *Law and the Writer.*

Antagonist. The primary character in a story or novel with whom the hero or heroine is in conflict. (*See: protagonist.*)

Anthology. A collection of selected writings by various authors, or a gathering of works by one author.

A freelancer who sells a publisher on an anthology becomes the editor of the collection. As such, he usually includes an introduction highlighting the purpose of the work. Upon a publisher's acceptance of the writer's proposal for a new anthology, a contract is written outlining the term of cash advances, royalty schedules, and permission fees. Royalty schedules depend on whether the book is retailed as hardbound or paperback and on the permission fees, which are negotiated between the publisher and the editor.

Permission must be secured to use previously copyrighted material in an anthology. Before the new copyright law took effect in 1978, most copyrights were held by the magazine in which the work originally appeared. Now, they may be owned by either the original author or the publisher, depending on what rights were sold by the author. Books, of course, are usually copyrighted in the name of the author, so reprint requests on work in books would be sent to the author, in care of the publisher. Reprint fees depend on the original author's reputation and the source of the original publication. Materials in uncopyrighted U.S. government journals are available for reprint without cost. (Since the government itself sometimes may pick up copyrighted material for reprint, the author/editor should be on the lookout for copyright notices. If there are none, the material is in the public domain.)

Upon receipt of permission to use copyrighted materials, the anthologist selects a consistent method of indicating which materials in the collection have been previously copyrighted, usually on an "Acknowledgments" page preceding the table of contents. The anthology may be copyrighted in the name of the publisher or the author/editor, depending on the type of book and the terms of the contract.

The contents of the anthology may be arranged in a number of ways, depending on the subject matter and the editor's view of how the reader would use the book. It may be chronological (for textbooks), alphabetical (by author), categorical, or organized in any other reasonable way.

Anticlimax. The part of a novel, story, or play that follows the resolution of the climax. Its purpose is usually merely to satisfy the reader's curiosity regarding subsequent events in the characters' lives. The reader's interest level drops sharply from the climax to the anticlimax, which is usually a letdown for most readers. (*See: climax; story line, diagram of.*)

Antihero. An antihero, or nonhero, is a protagonist that lacks traditional heroic qualities such as strength, valor, and nobility of mind and spirit. Found primarily in modern fiction, drama, and cinema, an antihero is not ordinarily an admirable or heroic figure: he might even be a coward, a clod, or a crook. Nevertheless, an antihero is generally likeable because, while he might not live by society's values, he is true to the personal moral code that he has established. The comic strip character Charlie Brown is something of an antihero, as is the hardboiled, coarse, but streetwise Sam Spade character in Dashiell Hammet's *The Maltese Falcon*. The protagonists in many of Kurt Vonnegut's novels are antiheroes; Woody Allen is adept at creating engaging antiheroes in his films. (*See: protagonist.*)

Article. A nonfictional prose composition that appears in a magazine or newspaper. (Articles printed in newspapers are often called *feature stories* to distinguish them from straight news.)

A successful article begins with an

idea that may come from almost anywhere—a friend, an item in a newspaper, an observation. The writer mulls over the idea, does some market research to determine what, if anything, has recently been written about the subject, then hones the idea into a *theme*—the precise subject of an article. While a theme may be a complex one, it is very important that the writer think it through and find a sufficiently narrow aspect of it to discuss in proper depth; this is the *peg* of the article. (The peg determines not only how extensively the writer will treat the topic, but also where he will market the article—and vice versa. An article on liverworts, for example, marketed to a local Sunday magazine rather than to *Smithsonian*, not only would require a regional peg, but also would have to be written in much simpler language and briefly explain even basic natural processes to a less sophisticated readership.)

After finding a solid peg, the writer researches the piece, both at the library for background and by conducting interviews. (Research may also uncover a more promising peg; the writer should be alert for this.) He then begins to organize his material into an article.

Most articles have a four-part structure. The *lead*, or opening paragraph, is crucial to capturing reader interest; a good lead clearly sets forth the problem or situation the article deals with and demonstrates (directly or indirectly) why the reader should read the piece. If the lead has not directly stated the theme or explained the reader's stake in the piece (for instance, if the lead were an anecdote), then the next *theme* paragraph must do so. Succeeding paragraphs, the *body* of the article,

develop the theme using quotes and anecdotes (and sometimes statistics) where appropriate. The *conclusion* should relate back to the lead in some way, by concluding the opening anecdote, by answering questions raised at the beginning, or by summarizing the main points of the article.

If the article demands extensive research, some magazine editors may request the author's bibliography so that the research department can verify the facts presented in the article. (*See: essay; feature.*)

Article rejection terms. When rejecting an article, the editor may indicate the piece lacks "authority." By that, he may mean: 1) the writer used only material from previously published sources instead of interviewing original sources himself; 2) statements that are apparently opinion are not documented; 3) the article lacks or contains too few quotes from experts; or 4) conclusions presented in the article do not arise logically from the previous statements.

Other editors might say that an article is "flat." By this they usually mean the article lacks dialogue, local color, anecdotes, moving passages of forceful argument, or proper pacing and flow of ideas.

Another article rejection term might be the article is too "slight." This usually means that the treatment of the subject is too general, or without any meaty new angles to make it different from other articles on the subject.

Arts review. A critical reaction to a popular or classical cultural event. Some forms of art that are typically reviewed are concerts, plays, films, records, and exhibits. A review should be constructed from the critic's personal, analytical reaction, although audience response may also be mentioned in the piece.

A reviewer must be informed about the art form he writes about, because a good review gives insight into, as well as an account of, a performance or exhibit. By the same token, preparation for the specific event to be reviewed is necessary. The critic can read a play script or book before attending a play or movie; similarly, a critic should be knowledgeable about other records or concert performances by an artist.

In a newspaper review, certain facts, such as time, place, dates, and credits are often placed in the first paragraph; the decision as to which facts are necessary and where they are placed, of course, varies with the editor.

An arts review of a play, film, etc., mentions the plot, but should refrain from revealing the outcome if that is essential to enjoying the work. The reviewer also evaluates the plot, the interpretation of the theme, and the technical skill displayed. In the case of a live performance, the critic can sometimes meet the performers and directors in order to ask questions and to take photos to accompany his piece.

Arts reviews are used by newspapers and magazines. For an assignment, a writer should query a newspaper editor. (A weekly, because it is less likely to have a staff person handling reviews and imposes less deadline pressure, is a better place to start than a daily.) Payment for a review in a weekly ranges from $5-$15; in a daily, from $10-$50. In addition, the reviewer usually receives tickets to the event.

National trade magazines specializing in the arts use reviews from different parts of the U.S.; a writer querying such a magazine will include sample summary reviews of a month's events in his area. Payment for this type of work is about $15 for a beginner, and up to $50 for an experienced correspondent.

Records and related printed material are supplied free of charge by record companies, but a reviewer who requests them must prove that he has published work in this field. The contact for review copies of new records is the promotion and publicity department of a record company. (*See: book review; criticism; drama criticism; restaurant review.*)

ASCAP. (*See: performing rights organizations.*)

Aside. A speech, or perhaps just a line, in a play in which a character reveals his thoughts aloud. When an aside is delivered, other characters are on stage besides the speaker; the audience understands that for the purposes of the drama, the other characters do not hear the speaker's aside. The technique is not used very often in contemporary drama. (*See: soliloquy.*)

Assignment, writing on. Writing on assignment is almost always done by writers who have already established a reputation with particular editors. The magazine requests that a freelance writer do a story on a subject it has conceived. It also sets a word length, a focus, a fee, and a kill fee.

Beginning writers rarely get assignments; however, a beginner in a unique situation, such as that of having access to a celebrity, may sometimes obtain an assignment from a magazine. Unlike the established writer, the beginner must usually submit his assigned work on speculation with no guarantee of a purchase.

Professional freelance writers may write on assignment, of course, not only for magazines, but for businesses, book publishers, and others as well. (*See: kill fee; on spec.*)

Associated Business Writers of America (ABWA). A subsidiary of The National Writers Club. This group serves as a link between writers specializing in business and editors of business magazines. NWC/ABWA holds periodic workshops. Its publications include newsletters and market reports, published monthly; the official publication, *Authorship*, published six times annually; and an annual directory. The ABWA's address is 1450 S. Havana, Suite 620, Aurora CO 80012.

Associated Press (AP). Established in 1848, the Associated Press is the oldest international news service, with a staff of 2,600 reporters, photographers, editors, technicians, and administrative staff in more than 200 bureaus worldwide, engaged in the gathering and distribution of world, national, regional, and state news. The AP is a nonprofit cooperative owned by its American newspaper members. AP supplies information and photographs via satellite, wire, ocean cable, landline, and radio to some 10,000-15,000 newspapers and broadcasters around the world. AP Radio Network in Washington is the audio arm of this news company.

As a cooperative news service, the AP has the right to reprint any local news stories or photographs that originate with member papers. In the case of a freelance story rewritten and published by the AP, the writer of the original receives no additional payment from the news organization. When a story is copyrighted, however, AP makes reprint arrangements before running the story. The Associated Press does not routinely use freelance material, however.

The Associated Press convenes annually. Its headquarters are located at 50 Rockefeller Plaza, New York NY 10020. (*See: United Press International.*)

Associated Writing Programs. An association of colleges and universities that offer undergraduate and graduate programs in creative writing. The Association publishes a newsletter, an annual anthology of student work, and a catalog describing 256 writing programs in the United States and Canada.

The Association's purposes include enhancing the quality of literary education and helping writers and teachers get jobs. Students who want to major in creative writing can find appropriate colleges in the geographical areas of their choice by writing the program.

Its current headquarters are at the Department of English, Old Dominion University, Norfolk VA 23508.

Association for Education in Journalism and Mass Communications (AEJMC). An organization of 1,800 college and university professors, professionals, and students, whose goals are to improve techniques in teaching journalism, and the overall quality of journalism itself. The AEJ conducts research on and stays abreast of enrollment in journalism programs. In addition, it maintains a list of persons seeking teaching positions, as well as a list of positions open in the field.

Publications of the Association include *Journalism Abstracts* (published annually), and *Journalism Educator, Journalism Monographs, Journalism Newsletter,* and *Journalism Quarterly,* all published quarterly. Committees include AEJ-American Newspaper Publishers Association Cooperative on Journalism Education, Journalism Language Skills, Professional Freedom and Responsibility, Publications, Research, Status of Women in Journalism Education, and Teaching Standards.

The AEJMC meets annually. Its headquarters are located at the University of South Carolina, College of Journalism, Columbia SC 29208.

Association of American Publishers (AAP). The more than 300 members of this organization publish trade books, textbooks, reference books, and books for a general audience, as well as teaching materials.

AAP operates a library of materials on book publishing and presents the Curtis G. Benjamin Award for creative publishing. In addition, it publishes the *AAP Newsletter.*

Committees within the Association include Copyright, Education for Publishing, Freedom to Read, International Freedom to Publish, New Technology, and Postal.

The group's seven divisions, based on members' interests and areas of greatest sales volume, are general publishing, college, school, professional and scholarly, mass paperback, direct marketing/book club, and international.

AAP holds a spring annual meet-

ing and a fall divisional meeting. Its offices are located at One Park Avenue, New York NY 10016; and 2005 Massachusetts Avenue, N.W., Washington DC 20036.

Association of American University Presses (AAUP). A group of scholarly publishers operating at colleges and universities, AAUP exists to assist and counsel its members, conduct research, inform the public through public information programs, act as a medium through which members can exchange information, and manage workshops and seminars. It is active in soliciting funds in the form of grants from foundations, in order to keep university presses in existence. The Association currently has 80 members and 5 affiliate members.

AAUP publishes *Exchange,* a quarterly newsletter; an annual directory; books; and handbooks. Its committees include Books, Catalogs, and Ads; Copyright; Education and Training; Marketing; and Systems and Information Technology.

The Association convenes annually in June. Its headquarters are located at One Park Avenue, New York NY 10016. (*See: university press.*)

Association of Editorial Businesses (AEB). Companies that specialize in editorial services, such as writing, editing, proofreading, indexing, and research, belong to this organization. The AEB, which was established in 1980, exists to uphold professionalism, to improve standards in editorial quality and in business dealings, to conduct research, and to educate its members and the public. It publishes a newsletter and a membership directory and meets monthly.

The AEB's headquarters are located % Laura Horowitz, 4600 Duke St., Alexandria, VA 22304.

Association of Independent Video and Filmmakers, Inc. (*See: videotape.*)

As-told-to article or book. This term refers to a ghostwritten, first-person narrative, for which the writer is given an "as told to" or "with" joint byline; or credit on the acknowledgment page. This technique lends itself to at least three types of accounts: the dramatic personal experience, the opinion on some matter of public interest by an authority, and the commentary or personal revelation by a celebrity.

One of the best idea sources for possible co-authors of as-told-to articles and books is the newspaper or newsmagazine. A writer "sells" the idea to the subject and together they settle the financial arrangements. If the two write and sell an article, the subject may get the public recognition while the author gets the check from the publication. Or they may split 50/50. In the case of a book, the split of advance and royalties varies. The writer (sometimes with the help of an agent or literary lawyer) often negotiates in writing the sharing of proceeds to suit their particular situation, depending on which person—the subject or the writer—contributes more to the salability of the project. Some professional writers prefer to get 75% of the advance and take less than 75% of the royalties, in case the book does not sell as well as expected and to cover their work on the book "up front."

After completing the manuscript, the writer obtains a signed release from the subject giving permission for publication. (*See: ghostwriting.*)

Atmosphere. A term describing the overall effect or mood of a piece of writing. It is a combination of setting, descriptive details and dialogue (if any). It includes both physical and psychological details and is achieved not only by the choice of words but also by the pacing of sentences. A successfully evoked atmosphere heightens the reader's emotional response.

For example, the bleak setting of Arthur Miller's *Death of a Salesman* and the emphasis on familial allegiance in Mario Puzo's *The Godfather* create atmosphere for those works.

Attribution. A term that refers to the writer's or reporter's stating the source of a direct quote.

Attribution is important because it lends credibility to a story. However, whether or not to use a speaker's actual name in attribution can cause a dilemma for the writer when his material pertains to personal or controversial subjects, or when the interviewee has designated particular bits of information as "not for attribution."

A method of solving the writer's problem is to print the direct quote while using a descriptive phrase or a professional title to name the source. For example, certain information about news in Washington might be attributed to "a prominent White House aide." (*See: off the record.*)

Auction (of a manuscript). Publishers sometimes bid for the acquisition of a book manuscript that has excellent sales prospects. Before such an auction, which is private, takes place, the author's agent submits the manuscript simultaneously to various publishers. Publishers' bids are for the amount of the author's advance, plus other considerations such as guaranteed dollar amounts to be used for advertising and promotion, royalty percentages, agreement for the publisher to take smaller shares of paperback revenue, and the like.

In recent years, runaway bidding on some blockbuster books has resulted in considerable financial success for some authors. However, when a publisher pays an extremely high advance for one author's book, he has few funds for promotional and other expenses for others' books, which can cause those works to suffer.

This practice was begun by literary agent Scott Meredith in about 1950 when, armed with a book his agency considered particularly strong, he phoned and saw many publishers about it rather than just one publisher, giving them a two-week bidding deadline. All publishers at that time had the strict policy of considering submissions only on an exclusive basis, but Meredith felt that this policy was protective for publishers but very unfair for writers, who sometimes had to wait through years of slow readings and rejections, getting through only a handful of publishers and perhaps never reaching the firm ready to buy the manuscript.

A number of publishers flatly refused to consider the manuscript if other publishers were also considering it. Other publishers, however, agreed to read the manuscript if that was the only way they were going to get to see it, and in time the literary auction became established practice in the field. Today, virtually all "hot" books—books by major authors, and unusual or unusually good books by new or newer authors—are auctioned. The title of that first auctioned book? Unfortunately, neither Scott Meredith nor his staff can remember, since, says Meredith, "the first time we tried an auction, I had no idea I was doing anything historic."

Today, of course, book publishers themselves auction books to paperback houses and book clubs.

Audiovisual communication. Audiovisual communication is writing for the voice and ear as well as the eye. Its format may be motion pictures, video and slide tapes, filmstrips, audio cassettes or whatever new forms technology brings us. Its purpose, like writing for print, is to entertain and/or inform.

The audiovisual communicator faces challenges different from those of conventional writers. He strives to achieve a balance between copy and visuals. His script persuades the viewer to his point of view not just with dialogue or narration, but also with lighting, camera angles, music, sound effects (or silence)—all of the nonverbal techniques that are largely emotional in appeal.

A typical script is divided into two columns, one labeled "picture" or "video," in which the writer indicates everything the viewer will see. This includes a description of the scene, camera directions, etc. The other column, labeled "sound" or "audio," contains the words spoken in narration or dialogue plus indications of sound effects, music, etc. A sample AV script format is found in the Appendix to this encyclopedia.

AV markets include business, industry, government, education, medicine, religion—virtually any group with a motive and the money to reach an audience. Before querying a potential AV producer, the writer should find out the company's current needs and previous productions as described in the "Scriptwriting" chapter of *Writer's Market* and the producer's current catalog.

Before beginning a script, the writer consults with the client, who outlines the purpose, the budget, and the target audience.

Payment rates for audiovisual writers vary. While the Writers Guild of America has established rates for theatrical and TV material, payment for nontheatrical AV filmscripts usually depends on the producers and clients. The going rates are listed in the "Scriptwriting" section of *Writer's Market* and vary from a flat fee to a percentage of the production cost. (*See: film writing, nontheatrical; screenwriting.*)

Audiovisual Market Place (AVMP). This directory refers the writer to organizations and services connected to the audiovisual industry, which comprises films, slide-tape programs, audio cassettes, etc. The largest of the directory's sections, "Producers, Distributors and Services," has both geographic and classified listings for writers seeking contacts in the AV field. Other sections of the directory of particular interest to writers are "Periodicals" and "Reference Books."

A cross-index section contains the names of persons and organizations listed in the book.

Listings in *Audiovisual Market Place*

include names, addresses, telephone numbers, names of personnel, and descriptive data about the companies and services.

Authorized biography. An authorized biography is an account of a person's life, written with the subject's complete cooperation. Such cooperation involves in-depth interviews, anecdotes from family, friends (and sometimes enemies), and access to personal records/correspondence. If the subject is dead, authorization comes from his family or the executor of his estate.

When writing an authorized account, the biographer secures the subject's approval before the work is published. In addition, the writer sometimes shares with him the byline, advance, and royalties. Some authorized biographies are simply puffery and are panned by critics for lack of objectivity. (*See: biography; unauthorized biography.*)

Author's alteration clause. This book contract clause spells out the amount of changes (in terms of a percentage of the typesetting cost) an author is allowed to make on galleys or page proofs. Usually, if the author makes changes totaling more than 10% of the cost of typesetting, charges for the overage are deducted from future royalties. (*See: AA.*)

Author's copies. An author usually receives about ten free copies of his own hardcover book from the publisher; more from a paperback firm. He can obtain additional copies at a price that has been reduced by an author's discount. (*See: author's discount.*)

Author's discount. A reduction in cost of a book—usually by 40% of the retail price—given to the author of that book. An author may wish to buy books from the publisher and sell them, at a profit, to individuals and groups to which the publisher may not have easy access but the author does—as, for example, when he is a frequent lecturer at various conventions or workshops related to the book's topic. This provision, however, must be covered by the contract, and when large quantities of books are involved, better discounts are possible. Author's discounts on textbooks may average 20%-25% rather than 40%. (*See: author's copies.*)

Authors Guild. A national professional organization made up of over 6,000 book authors and magazine writers. It is involved in such issues as free speech, copyright, and taxes, and has represented the writer in such matters before Congress and in the courts. The Guild also provides writers with information about publishers' contract provisions for advances, royalties, subsidiary rights, etc.

Applicants for membership to the Guild are generally required to have published either one book at an established American house, within seven years of their application or three fiction or nonfiction pieces in a general circulation magazine within the previous 18 months of their application for membership.

The Guild meets every February in New York City. Its committees include the Book Contract Committee and the Children's Book Committee,

and it publishes a bulletin five times per year.

All Authors Guild members also belong to the Authors League of America, which comprises the Authors Guild and the Dramatists Guild. The Guild headquarters are located at 234 W. 44th Street, New York NY 10036. (*See: Authors League of America.*)

Author's information forms. After signing with a book publisher, an author may be asked to complete two or more forms: one provides the publisher with his social security number for tax purposes, while another questionnaire seeks promotion information on the author (such as education and career accomplishments), and on the book's subject matter. The publisher uses this information to write book jacket copy and send publicity releases to the author's home town newspapers and college alumni publications, and to any professional organization newsletters or other publications related to the author's background. Authors should take great care to provide as much good descriptive copy about the book and as many sales and publicity leads as possible.

Authors League of America. This 13,000-member professional organization comprises the Authors Guild's 6,000 book authors and magazine writers and the Dramatists Guild's 7,000 playwrights. The Guilds publish and distribute (to members only) the *Dramatists Guild Quarterly* and *Newsletter* and the *Authors Guild Bulletin* which, along with other printed materials, provide information on contract terms, copyright, libel, and other legal and professional matters affecting writers. The ALA's headquarters are located at 234 W. 44th Street, New York NY 10036. (*See: Authors Guild; Dramatists Guild.*)

Author's tour. (*See: book-promotion tour; promotion by author.*)

Autobiography. A book-length account of a person's life written by the subject himself. An autobiography is usually set down in the form of narrative recollections of those people and events in his life that the writer considers interesting. Some celebrities' autobiographies really *are* written by the subject—*Lauren Bacall By Myself*—while others are opportunities for professional writer-collaborators, such as *The Times of My Life* by Betty Ford and Chris Chase.

Persons who are not well known and who want to publish an autobiography must have either an exceptionally unusual or fascinating life or fine writing style, or both, to interest a commercial publisher. (*See: biography.*)

Autographing party. An autographing party is a promotional device that is provided by publishers, usually to authors of books with bestseller potential. The author appears at bookstores or book departments and autographs each copy of his book, as it is sold, for individual customers.

It is unlikely that an autograph party would be held for a book by a new author, since the publisher's profit would not justify the cost. However, an author may decide to promote his book independently of the publisher; in such a case, he could take it upon himself to arrange a local autographing party through a bookstore or department store chain. (*See: promotion by author; publishing party.*)

Availability list. In radio advertising, a list maintained by the traffic manager; it indicates the amount of time that can be sold.

Avant-garde. A kind of writing in which the subject matter or style shows a break from tradition. *Avant-garde*, which literally means *foreguard* in French, is often used to refer to experimental writing.

As a noun, this term applies to the group of persons in a field (such as writers or artists) whose work is unconventional. (*See: magazine, alternative.*)

Aviation/Space Writers Association (AWA). This 1,450-member organization is made up of writers and editors involved in books, newspapers, magazines, radio, television, and public relations for and about the aviation/space industry. The AWA presents annual awards for writing, public relations, public affairs, company communications, visual communications, and helicopter heroism. Its publications include a newsletter published 10 times per year, and a manual containing a membership list. An annual meeting/news conference is held.

The headquarters of the AWA are located at 1725 K St. N.W., Suite 1412, Washington DC 20006. (*See: Council of Writers Organizations.*)

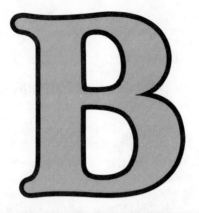

Back matter. (*See: book manuscript preparation and submission.*)

Background information, books of. Nonfiction writers who need statistical or factual data to support their arguments can find such information in the *Information Please Almanac* and similar one-volume almanacs, *The Statistical Abstract of the United States*, and in references such as *Facts on File*, which deals with news events indexed by subject, person, and country. While reference books provide factual information, encyclopedias, travel books, magazines, newspapers—almost anything— can provide the writer with background information.

When writing a book set in Rome, for example, the writer who wants to add authenticity to the fiction may find detailed background in a travel guide. A writer doing a nonfiction piece on breast cancer would want to get background information from publications about breast cancer, medical journal reports, and recent magazine articles on the subject.

Reference books of facts are just a starting place to look for background information on a subject. (*See: period-*

icals, indexes to.)

Backlist. The publishing term for a group of previously published books that are still in print a year after publication. Backlist books are available from the publisher, but not usually from bookstores except on special order; some independent bookstores, however, do carry backlist titles.

The ABA *Basic Book List* includes those backlist books that continue to sell well enough to be carried by bookstores.

Backstory. The fictional biography of the part of a character's life that preceded the events the audience sees in a television production or motion picture, or hears in a radio drama.

Basic Book List. An annual publication of the American Booksellers Association listing books with sales records. The *Basic Book List* recommends titles in various categories which might complete a bookseller's stock, balance his inventory, or fill a void in a subject area. Though the list is designed to assist booksellers, it may also be used by writers as an adjunct to bestseller lists, to get a feel for the books that sell consistently in certain subject areas.

The *Basic Book List* is compiled by a panel of booksellers who update, revise, and expand the previous year's list, and consider title and category suggestions submitted by other booksellers. It is available in some public libraries, some bookstores, and from the American Booksellers Association.

Bay Area Writing Project (BAWP). This program for teachers of writing was founded at the University of California, Berkeley, in 1974 and has influenced other universities throughout the U.S. to establish similar programs. In conjunction with BAWP, the programs are known as the National Writing Project Network.

BAWP exists to instruct teachers how to teach writing. Participants, who teach in colleges, secondary schools, and elementary schools, gather during the summer for a five-week session. The program consists of presentations by the students (teachers), small group discussions, exposure to new ideas and to research findings, and writing. To be eligible, teachers must submit recommendations and prove that they have had successful teaching experience. Those who attend receive a stipend and college credit. After the summer session, teachers take part in a follow-up program during the school year; they are paid for acting as consultants to school districts.

Some assumptions underlying the philosophy of the program are that most teachers are unaware of the knowledge that exists in the field of teaching writing, that teachers have not been adequately prepared to teach writing, and that anyone who teaches writing must write himself.

BAWP publishes monographs written by teacher-consultants. A list of publications, as well as information on how to obtain them, is available from the Publications Department, Bay Area Writing Project, 5635 Tolman Hall, University of California, Berkeley CA 94720. (*See: National Writing Project.*)

Beat. In a motion picture, television, or radio script, a one-count pause in the action or in a character's speech.

Berne Union. (*See: International Copyright Convention.*)

Best Books for Children: Preschool Through the Middle Grades. A guide to children's fiction and nonfiction books, which is aimed at librarians and used to begin collections, to add to or judge existing collections, to help children to choose books, and to compile bibliographies and reading lists. The majority of books described in this volume are those written for children in preschool through the sixth grade, but some can be used by junior high school students as well. They are books intended for pleasure reading as well as those designed to fit into a school curriculum.

It is useful to writers of children's books in showing them the existing competition in selected subject matter. For example, a writer who had a book idea in mind for an animal story aimed at an elementary school child, would find this entry under "Land Animals": 8373. Berrill, Jacquelyn. *Wonders of How Animals Learn* (5-7). Illus. by author.

1979, Dodd $5.95. Animal intelligence and various learning processes are described in this account.

The directory contains approximately 13,000 entries, divided into 34 sections, many of which contain subsections. Examples of section headings are "Books for Beginning Readers," "Mythology," "The Arts and Language," "Folklore," "Personal Development," and "The Sciences."

Entries contain such data as title, author, and illustrator of the book; grade levels for which the book is appropriate; publication date; publisher; cost; information on the book's format, i.e., *LB* for library binding or *paper* for paperback, and an annotation.

Best Books for Children was begun in 1959 as a series of annual books. In 1978, it took on its present subtitle, changed format, and became a hardbound volume. The third edition of the revised version was published in 1985.

The best markets. Beginning writers frequently ask the editors of Writer's Digest Books what is the "best" market to write for. For beginners, nonfiction represents by far the largest *numbers* of markets since magazines contain predominately articles, these days, not stories. Obviously the larger circulation magazines *pay* more but demand a higher level of professionalism and experience. Smaller circulation magazines pay less but there are fewer writers competing for the editors' checks.

Nonfiction books, too, are usually easier than novels to sell, for a new writer.

Writing for films and television is lucrative but usually demands residence in the areas of film production and specialized skills.

There is no one answer to the question of "best" markets. Many novelists never earn more royalties than their advances, while others are millionaires. Some film and television writers hunger to have their names on a book, even though their annual freelance income far surpasses that of the average book author. Some writers see the runaway success of a genre like romance novels but don't have the fiction skills necessary to write them.

Each writer must serve an apprenticeship of both finding his own voice and learning about the marketplace through trial and error submissions. A new architect doesn't get his first job as designer of a skyscraper office/hotel/retail shops complex; there are no shortcuts for the writer either. There are Cinderella stories of previously unknown writers who became overnight successes, but investigation usually uncovers a long period of development that preceded that sudden fame.

Bestseller lists. Lists which appear in *Publishers Weekly*, the *New York Times Book Review Section*, and the book pages of local newspapers are compiled from sales figures reported by bookstores, bookstore chains, wholesalers and distributors. They don't usually report sales of Bibles, cookbooks, and other specialized books. A good summary of the year's bestselling hardcover, trade paperback, and mass market paperback sales appears in the annual statistics issue of *Publishers Weekly*, which is published in March each year.

Bibliography. Most publishers of general interest trade books prefer a bibliography and appendix to footnotes for citing sources used in book research. Textbook formats, on the other hand, are more likely to include footnotes.

In one style for writing bibliographic entries suggested by the University of Chicago Press's *The Chicago Manual of Style*, the components are listed in the following order: name of author (with last name first), title of book (set in italics), city of publication, publishing company, date of publication (year only). The following example demonstrates the proper form, including punctuation, according to *The Chicago Manual of Style*: Provost, Gary. *Make Every Word Count*. Cincinnati: Writer's Digest Books, 1980.

The book *Words Into Type* suggests the following order for bibliographic references to articles: author's name (surname first), the title of the article (in quotation marks), publication title (in italics), the volume number, date of issue, and page number. Example: Childe, V. Gordon. "War in Prehistoric Societies." *Sociological Review*, Vol. XXXIII (1941), pp. 126-38.

Persons who write or edit scientific books or journals should note that these publications usually have a different system than publications related to the humanities. They should query the particular editors they work with about methods of citing sources.

Bilingual edition. A book that is printed—either wholly or partially—in two different languages. When a single publisher produces such editions, the author and the translator usually share the royalties. (*See: translation rights.*)

Bimonthly. Referring to something that takes place once every two months such as a magazine published bimonthly.

This word is sometimes confused with *semimonthly*, which refers to a publication issued twice a month. (*See: biweekly; semimonthly.*)

Biographical novel. A life story documented in history and transformed into fiction through the insight and imagination of the writer. This type of novel melds the elements of biographical research and historical truth into the framework of a novel complete with dialogue, drama, and mood. A biographical novel resembles historical fiction, save for one aspect: characters in a historical novel may be fabricated and then placed into an authentic setting; characters in a biographical novel have actually lived.

There are several identifying characteristics that distinguish the biographical novel. First is the writer's choice of a subject he values and whose life is naturally traversed with the substance of a novel—e.g., recurring themes, human conflicts, triumphs, and defeats. Another distinction is the writer's painstaking study of the human condition and everyday life of the subject and his time. Finally, the biographical novel unfolds as if it were happening at this moment. Perhaps the classic example of a biographical novel is Irving Stone's *Lust for Life*, the story of Vincent Van Gogh.

Biographical references. The standard references for biographical research that are available in most public libraries include: *Biography Index*, which refers the reader to books and periodicals containing biographical material; *Marquis Who's Who Publications/Index to All Books*, which covers the persons listed in most of the Marquis directories such as *Who's Who in America*, *Who Was Who in America*, and specialized directories such as *Who's Who in Finance and Industry*; and *Current Biography*, with articles on prominent persons in national and international affairs. Other sources include the *International Who's Who*, *Webster's Biographical Dictionary*, and *American Men and Women of Science. Biography News* is a monthly publication that contains material from American newspapers about persons prominent in the news.

Writers interested in looking up their favorite authors can refer to volumes such as: *Author Biographies, Twentieth Century Authors, Contemporary Authors*, and *Journalist Biographies Master Index*. (*See: writers, biographical directories of.*)

Biography. An account of a person's life (or the lives of a family or close-knit group) written by someone other than the subject(s). The work is set within the historical framework (i.e., the unique economic, social, and political conditions) existing during the subject's life.

A biography can detail the lives of persons living or dead. Its subjects are people who inspire, repel, attract, or intrigue.

A biography may take several forms. The traditional or narrative biography begins with a subject's birth and proceeds chronologically through his life. Or it may open with some dramatic or character-revealing episode and later bring in his early life. A life story may also take a topical format, in which various aspects of the subject's life are detailed in designated chapters. Finally, a biography may be written in essay form, wherein the author writes in the first person and includes his own comments about the subject.

Characteristics of the modern biography include an opening scene or statement establishing the subject's prominence or suggesting a reason for the biography, suppositions about the subject's subconscious life, and probes into the subject's personality.

The average length of an adult biography runs from 300-400 manuscript pages. (*See: authorized biography; autobiography; collective biography; juvenile biography; memoir; unauthorized biography.*)

Biweekly. Referring to something that takes place once every two weeks such as a magazine published biweekly. This word is sometimes confused with *semiweekly*, which refers to a publication issued twice a week. (*See: bimonthly; semiweekly.*)

Black humor. A kind of humor that concentrates on social issues and social outcasts. It is somber and destructive in tone. Black humor comments on societal problems through grotesque and nightmarish means.

Bruce Jay Friedman, editor of the anthology *Black Humor*, describes this form as one that goes beyond satire. He holds that since the modern world contains elements of the absurd, satire is no longer the province of the novelist, but rather of the journalist; out of the fiction writer's groping for new territory black humor evolved.

Black humor is found in all media. The Evelyn Waugh novel *The Loved One* is a classic example of black humor, as is the Emmeline Grangerford segment in *The Adventures of Huckleberry Finn*. Some playwrights and filmmakers deal exclusively in black humor—Brendan Behan and Sam Shepard, in *The Hostage* and *Buried Child*, respectively, are just two of many dramatists who rely on the form, and filmmaker John Waters has acquired a large cult following with movies like *Pink Flamingos* and *Female Trouble*. Even artists and cartoonists—such as Edward Gorey, Charles Addams, and Gahan Wilson—have developed distinctive black-humor styles.

Black writers. Although over the centuries the nature of race relations in the U.S. has kept unknown numbers of black writers from being published, blacks have nevertheless made invaluable contributions to American literature. The struggle against racial prejudice and the resultant economic, political, and social disadvantage has given rise to a rich and powerful black literature; while most black writers have never been commercially successful, many have received critical acclaim, and proponents of black literature have rediscovered—and in some cases republished—the work of fine black writers of the past.

One of the most important black forms is the autobiography. Frederick Douglass's 1845 narrative of his life as a slave and escape to the North helped popularize the Abolitionist movement. Other black writers and political figures who have published influential autobiographical works include Booker T. Washington, James Baldwin, Richard Wright, Malcolm X, Eldridge Cleaver, and Gwendolyn Brooks.

Around the turn of the last century, Paul Lawrence Dunbar was one of the most widely read poets in America; Charles W. Chestnutt achieved critical success among the literary realists, but failed to find a popular audience and gave up literature. The Harlem Renaissance of the 1920s and 30s sparked admiration for black art forms among blacks and educated whites alike; the best-known Harlem writers included Countee Cullen, Claude McKay (who wrote *Home to Harlem*, the first bestseller by a black writer), Zora Neale Hurston, and Langston Hughes. In the 1940s, Richard Wright published *Native Son* and *Black Boy*.

The struggle for black civil rights in the 1950s was in part fueled by, and helped produce important black literature. Gwendolyn Brooks received the first Pulitzer Prize awarded to a black for her second book of poems, *Annie Allen*. In 1952, Ralph Ellison published *Invisible Man*, widely regarded as the finest novel of the postwar era. James Baldwin produced his first novel, *Go Tell It on the Mountain*, and his first collection of essays, *Notes of a Native Son*, and went on to become the most successful black writer of the 50s and 60s.

It was in the late 50s and early 60s that a number of important black plays were first produced: Lorraine Hansberry's *A Raisin in the Sun* (1958); Ossie Davis's *Purlie Victorious* (1961); in 1964, Baldwin's *Blues for Mister Charlie* and LeRoi Jones's *Dutchman*, two spectacularly angry plays, were produced within months of each other.

Among the most important contemporary black writers are poet/novelist Ishmael Reed, poet/playwright Ntozake Shange, and fiction writers Alice Walker, Toni Cade Bambara, and Toni Morrison.

Bleed. Printed copy or an illustration that, to attract the reader's attention, reaches to one or more edges of the page.

Bleeds are found more often in books and magazines than in newspapers. According to the number of edges on the page where material bleeds, an illustration or print copy is called a one-, two-, three-, or four-side bleed. *Bleed* can be used as a verb or noun: printing or an illustration *bleeds*, the designer *bleeds* an ad, and printing or an illustration that bleeds is called a *bleed*.

Blind writers' resources. The National Library Service for the Blind and Physically Handicapped, a division of the Library of Congress, lends talking books (on discs and cassette), braille reading materials, and braille and large-print music to print-handicapped persons. Novels,

nonfiction books, and general interest magazines are available, as is information on handicap conditions. Reading materials are distributed and returned by postage-free mail.

Talking Book Topics and *Braille Book Review*, two bimonthly magazines published by the Library of Congress, announce the latest reading materials produced for visually and physically handicapped readers. Persons interested in borrowing the Service's material must complete an application and have it signed by a physician or other professional working in a school, hospital, nursing home, rehabilitation center, or other institution. Applications are available from the National Library Service for the Blind and Physically Handicapped, Library of Congress, Washington DC 20542, and may be submitted either to the Library of Congress or to a regional or subregional library. (A list of regional and subregional libraries can be obtained from the Library of Congress.)

Blockbuster. A book that is a commercial success. *Blockbuster* is defined differently by different publishers, depending on the size of the latter. To a large publishing house, a blockbuster is a book with hardcover sales in the hundred thousands and paperback reprints in the millions, that is placed on national bestseller lists, and for which other subsidiary rights are sold. Another publishing term for *blockbuster* is *big book*. Blockbuster books like *Noble House*, by James Clavell, and *Princess Daisy*, by Judith Krantz, have made their authors millionaires.

Blurb. The copy on paperback book covers or hardcover book dust jackets. Blurbs can either give information about the book and the author or promote the book by featuring testimonials from book reviewers or well-known persons in the book's field.

In fields other than publishing, *blurb* sometimes refers to any overstated advertisement or publicity release.

The word *blurb* was first used in 1907 by humorist Gelett Burgess. The jacket of his book *Are You a Bromide?* carried a picture of a young woman (which was customary for novels of that period) and textual matter mentioning "Miss Belinda Blurb."

BMI. (*See: performing rights organizations.*)

Book club selection. For a book sold through a book club, the royalty is usually 10% of the book club list price. If the book is a premium (a book offered at a low price to recruit new members), the royalty is 5% of the club's list price. Royalties are usually split 50/50 by author and publisher on net sums received. Similarly, the advance varies according to the size of the club and whether the book is offered to members as a main or an alternate selection.

One large book club reports that its selections are chosen on the basis of entertainment/interest (as perceived by in-house editors) and members' response to previous books offered in the same category. (*See: book clubs.*)

Book clubs. A book club offers books on selected subjects to its members at a discounted price; it purchases such books from the publisher at a special price—in some cases at cost plus a royalty. Large clubs may print their own editions from duplicates of the publisher's films.

Acceptance by a major book club is a very positive factor for an author, since it brings the book to a large number of people throughout the country at the same time, but even selection by a small book club can enhance his royalties. The usual contract between author and publisher stipulates a 50/50 split of proceeds from book club sales.

The sale of book club rights is almost invariably made by the publisher. Book club selection usually comes about in one of two ways. The publisher may send advance galleys of a book to the club; or the club director, having read about forthcoming publication of a title he feels would interest his members, may request them from the publisher.

Larger book clubs usually print special editions for their members. Some clubs print cheaper editions; others print editions equal in quality to the publisher's. Smaller clubs may simply request the publisher to add a number of copies to his printing.

An advance for a large book club's main selection averages $85,000; a medium-sized club, from $5,000-$10,000; a large book club's alternate selection yields an advance of from $10,000-$25,000. But an author's royalties can vary from as little as $100 from a small specialized book club to five or six figures if the book is a major book club selection.

Book contract. A legal agreement between author and publisher defining their commitments and establishing the financial terms of their partnership, including the advance, rights, and royalties from the manuscript accepted for publication.

The typical publisher's contract is a standard form that allows for some of the terms, as well as the author's name and the book's title, to be filled into blanks. Many contracts mention the approximate length of the book (number of words) if it has not yet been fully written or if expansion has been requested by the editor.

The specific terms of a contract vary from publisher to publisher, depending on whether the author is a first-time writer or an established professional; whether the author has an agent or not; the topic; the publisher's estimate of the book's sales potential; and other factors. The usual royalty payment for hardcover books is 10% of the retail price on the first 5,000 copies; 12½% on the next 5,000 copies; and 15% thereafter. Advances vary by type of book, author's reputation, and sales prospects for the book. The book is copyrighted in the name of the author by the publisher.

Most contracts grant the publisher exclusive distribution of the book in a designated territory (e.g., the United States, the world), and for a defined period of time (usually as long as the book remains in print). The sale of subsidiary rights is also provided for. In any case, the author's share of the subsidiary rights is usually no less than 75% on foreign editions, 50% on paperback and book club sales, and 90% on TV and movie sales.

Changes in book contracts may be negotiated by the author himself or with the help of an agent or lawyer. The Authors Guild, a professional organization offering guidance on the financial matters of writers, makes available to its members a sample contract designed to educate writers to the legalese of the book contract. This sample also provides recommendations on contract terms to seek that would be ideal for the author.

Book distribution. Major book publishers have their own salesmen calling on bookstores and wholesalers, e.g., Baker & Taylor, Ingram, and ship books directly to stores. Smaller companies hire independent book salesmen to represent them and contract with book distributing companies and wholesalers to ship to bookstores. A list of such publishers' representatives, wholesalers, and distributors appears in *Literary Market Place*. A list of hardcover book and paperback wholesalers, set up geographically, appears in *The American Book Trade Directory*, which also lists geographically all bookstores in the U.S. and Canada and describes the types of books they carry.

When ordering books from a distributor, a buyer, such as a bookstore, must allow several weeks between the time the order is placed and the time delivery can be made. This fact is significant for teachers ordering books for classes, and for authors who receive inquiries about the availability of their books.

Book distribution by author. An author who self-publishes a book and wishes to distribute it to trade bookstores, schools, or libraries will find lists of wholesalers and sales representatives for hardcover and paperback books in *Literary Market Place* and *The American Book Trade Directo-*

ry, available in most libraries. There are also some helpful sections on book distribution in the various books about self-publishing. For the titles of such books, check the *Subject Guide to Books In Print* under the category "Publishers and Publishing."

Book editor. (*See: book publishing jobs*.)

Book indexing. A book author is expected to provide his own index or have the cost of its preparation deducted from his royalties. When the author does not provide his own index, publishers often delegate this task to freelancers. The freelancer who seeks an indexing job usually must be located in the same general area as the publisher.

Freelancers looking for indexing jobs should consult *Literary Market Place*, an annual directory available at most libraries, which lists book publishers in the United States and Canada cross-indexed by geographic region. Another section in this directory, "Editorial Services," presents an opportunity for freelancers to announce their services to publishers and printers. (*See: index; indexing*.)

Book Industry Study Group, Inc. (BISG). This is a not-for-profit association of firms and individuals representing various sectors of the book trade. Incorporated in 1976, the group includes publishers, manufacturers, suppliers, wholesalers, retailers, librarians, and others engaged in the development, production, and dissemination of books. The Group promotes and supports research in and about the book industry. Its members share

data and work to develop information useful to all segments of the industry. BISG publishes annual research reports on book industry trends in its aim to increase readership, improve book distribution, and expand members' markets.

Information specifying membership criteria, dues, and current activities of BISG is available by contacting its Managing Agent at 160 Fifth Avenue, New York NY 10010.

Book jacket and paperback cover copy. A freelance writer can make $60-$75 and up writing cover copy for books.

A paperback copy assignment, for example, usually consists of three segments: front cover, back cover, and inside first page. The latter two generally require a summary of content written in the same tone as the book itself. A typical back cover of a novel may offer a brief description of the main characters and their motivations; the back cover or inside first page of a nonfiction paperback often highlights the book's features in some creative manner. Writing copy for the front cover may prove even more challenging, since the writer has only about 15 words in which to capture the browser's interest.

A freelancer interested in writing cover copy begins by querying various publishing houses to find out which ones use freelancers. (Most New York publishing houses require that the freelancer live in New York City.) An editor may offer a writer with no related experience a book on speculation, in which case the writer will be paid for the assignment only if the copy is used. In other cases, an editor may ask the writer to rework copy that's already been written: the writer may not be paid for this work, but if it is acceptable, it may lead to future cover copy assignments.

Before starting, the cover copy writer should ask the editor for copies of readers' reports of the book and sample jackets of other books in the same line, both of which will provide the writer with key words and ideas for cover copy. Generally, a freelancer can work faster on creating copy for nonfiction books, since, although he must read the whole book, much of the key material he'll need is in the table of contents. (*See: blurb; sell copy.*)

Book manuscript preparation and submission. A book manuscript comprises three parts: front matter, text, and back matter. The front matter includes the title page (the author's name and address should be typed three inches below the title), frontispiece, table of contents, list of illustrations, list of tables, list of abbreviations, dedications, preface or foreword, acknowledgments, and introduction. Lower-case Roman numerals placed in the upper right corner number all front matter pages except the introduction, which is numbered with the text.

The text is numbered with Arabic numerals in the upper right corner of each page beginning with the first page of the introduction. Margins on all sides of the text should measure at least one inch. The manuscript should be typed double-spaced, with a new ribbon, on a regular (not fancy script) typewriter using a standard weight paper. Editors do not like the erasable bond since it is hard to edit on such a slick surface. At the beginning of each chapter, one-third of the page is left blank above the title; the chapter number is indicated on its first page in upper-case Roman numerals placed upper center. Each chapter begins on a new page. Major subheads are centered; minor subheads are placed flush left with the margin. In the upper left margin of every text page the author's last name, a shortened form of the book's title, and a chapter number should be typed. Book pages are numbered consecutively from beginning to end, not chapter by chapter. The phrase "The End" is typed three spaces below the last line of text.

A book's back matter consists of all or some of the following sections: appendices, footnotes, bibliography, glossary, and index(es). Like the text and the front matter, these sections should be typed double-spaced; the margins equal those in the text.

A book manuscript should be mailed in a box, with no staples or other fasteners on the manuscript itself.

An author usually receives a faster reply from a publisher if he submits an outline and only three sample chapters, as opposed to an entire manuscript. (Authors of nonfiction write only enough of a book to be able to market it, finishing a work once they're under contract.) Book editors prefer to see the first three chapters of a book instead of three chapters that have been chosen at random. Most editors prefer a query letter, without any of the author's work, on the first communication; most fiction editors would rather receive an entire novel.

Listings in the book publishers section of *Writer's Market* provide details on manuscript submission, i.e., preferences in the types of manuscripts sought, and whether they can be submitted directly or must come through a literary agent. Of course the author should always include postage and a self-addressed envelope or label for the return of his manuscript. (*See: manuscript preparation and submission; nonfiction books, marketing.*)

Book producer (book packager). An entrepreneur whose function is to engage writers, designers, and editors to create a book and deliver it either as a manuscript or "ready for printing" to a publisher who markets it.

Book producers are likely to package certain kinds of books: how-to and reference books that call on the talents of many experts, books whose impact depends greatly on graphic layout, and novels that originate in paperback.

Book producers may think of an idea for a book or book series, or they may work up a detailed outline of a subject presented to them. They usually contract with a veteran writer and sell the publication rights for an advance. Many, if not most, packaged books are done for a flat fee. Royalties are sometimes paid, but scales vary widely. They are almost always less than the standard 10%-12 1/2%-15%. Usually, the royalty from the publisher is included in the unit price per copy agreed upon by packager and publisher. The writer then has a separate contract with the packager.

The producer is usually acknowledged on the title or copyright page of the book.

There are currently over 100 book producers in the United States, most of them small enterprises in the Northeast. About 20% of them have banded together as the American Book Producers Association. Among the best-known packagers in the trade is Lyle Kenyon Engel, who contracted with John Jakes for the first books in the Kent Family Chronicles, published by Jove Publications.

Book promotion. The job of devising strategies for selling books. Book promotion is a joint project between publisher and author. A publisher's duties usually include advertising a book by sending review copies and press releases to book reviewers and—where budgeted—planning the author's tours.

The best advertising is word-of-mouth by satisfied buyers/readers, but giving a book exposure via television, radio, and newspaper feature interviews with the author builds an audience not only for a specific book, but often generates a following for the author himself. Other face-to-face promotional tools include authors' visits to bookstores and speeches to special-interest groups. Author input—his contacts, suggested avenues of promotion, etc.—is most helpful to the publisher, as the author is usually much more expert in his field than the publisher is. (If fact, marketing suggestions from the author in his original book proposal and/or his track record in the past on interview shows, may have helped sway the publisher toward acceptance.)

Books are also effectively promoted through book club sales (over 100 clubs in the United States); some newspaper advertising is used, too, usually with the publisher and the bookseller splitting the cost. Posters, bookmarks, circulars, and other promotion and advertising theoretically are allocated a percentage (usually 10%) of the book's projected net sales income. (In practice, some authors' books get more; other authors', less.) Reviews of specialized books in publications for readers who are prospective buyers of the book are useful, and if a book has a news angle, a promotional press conference may be arranged.

If a book is self-published, the writer may hire a publicist or handle a promotion campaign himself. He may also solicit the help of friends and/or place ads (with order form coupons) in targeted publications. He also identifies local and regional organizations that might welcome a personal introduction to his book through a speaking engagement. (*See: autographing party; book clubs; mid-list books; promotion by author; talk shows.*)

Book Publisher Reader's Report. (See the sample in the Appendix to this encyclopedia.)

Book publishing economics. (See the Appendix to this encyclopedia.)

Book publishing, history of. Although civilized man and woman attempted to record information as early as 3500 B.C., when the Sumerians wedged cuneiform inscriptions onto clay tablets, it was the Romans, teaching slaves to work as copyists, who increased production of rolls so that as many as 1,000 copies of a popular work could be produced and distributed throughout their world.

The format of modern books can be traced to the *codex*, a flat manuscript made up of several folded sheets of parchment or vellum (dried animal skin) and bound on one side. Dating from the first century A.D., the codex remained the typical book of the Middle Ages, during which monks wrote, lettered, and circulated codex books, primarily with other monks for scholarly use.

John Dessauer notes in the "The Past is Prologue" chapter of *Book Publishing: What It Is, What It Does*, that two vital developments in the 15th century—the introduction of linen paper and the invention of movable type—resulted in widespread printing and distribution of books. "By 1500 books were paginated and title pages listed publishers' imprints and dates of publication much as they do today. In 1501 Aldus Manutius designed the first small book which thereafter replaced the large and awkward codex." An estimated 1,000 printers had published about 30,000 editions of different books before the end of the 15th century in western Europe. Some nine million volumes were in existence.

According to Dessauer, modern publishing began in the 18th century when the general population of the western world began to recognize and appreciate the knowledge to be gained from books. Several of the great encyclopedias, including the English *Britannica*, were founded during this century, and many countries established circulating libraries around this period, which made books more accessible to the public. The British Copyright Act of 1710 weakened the power of the monopolistic printers of the time, and enabled authors to negotiate for more favorable financial terms.

Many of today's active American publishing houses were founded during the 19th century, including John Wiley and Sons (1807), Harper

38

& Row (1817), Houghton, Mifflin (1832), G.P. Putnam's Sons (1838), Rand McNally (1856), and Doubleday (1897). J.B. Lippincott was founded even earlier (1792).

It was the post-World War II period—characterized by an educational boom and general prosperity of the country—that determined the shape and character of the contemporary publishing industry. The post-World War II period brought a boom in the modern paperback book industry, which had been originated by Pocket Books in 1939, and the emergence in the 1950s of the "quality" trade paperback industry (serious nonfiction and literary classics) which served the needs of the ever-increasing student enrollments at the elementary, high school, and college levels.

The 60s saw continued growth in the industry: many publishing houses were acquired by corporations seeking to diversify or expand the market for other related products; many more new bookstores opened, new book clubs were established to cater to specialized consumer interests, and mass paperback sales increased. More people than ever bought books.

The general economic recession in the mid-1970s hit the book publishing industry particularly hard, however, with rising operating expenses creating higher book prices and causing unit sales to fall off when general consumers, libraries, and schools could not afford to keep up with the rapidly rising cost of books.

The result was another round of mergers in the late 1970s. Lewis A. Coser, Charles Kadushin, and Walter W. Powell comment on this trend in *Books: The Culture and Commerce of Publishing* noting the mergers of soft-cover and hardcover houses, the formation of film company/book publishing combines, and other media mergers.

Coser, Kadushin, and Powell point out that "multimedia mergers in trade publishing have created an environment in which books, films, and even television programs, are viewed as constituent parts of a media package" and writers would do well to keep that in mind.

There are currently over 1,500 book publishing companies in the United States; more than 12,000 when all the small presses are included. New York, Boston, Philadelphia, and Chicago have long been the hubs of publishing; in recent years, the West Coast has increased its role as a publishing locale.

Book publishing companies and their vital statistics (i.e., addresses, what they publish, number of titles, etc.) are listed in the annual *Writer's Market* and *Literary Market Place*. The *U.S. Book Publishing Yearbook and Directory* contains an overview of the current state of the publishing industry. In addition, the *Publishers' Trade List Annual* is a reference of current backlisted books of publishing companies, policies of book publishers, and their related products. (*See: paperbacks, history of.*)

Additional information: *Book Publishing: What It Is, What It Does; Books: The Culture and Commerce of Publishing; History of Book Publishing in the United States.*

Book Publishing House Organization Chart. (See the Appendix to this encyclopedia.)

Book publishing jobs, editorial. Editorial titles and functions vary significantly from one publishing house to another, depending on the size and type (i.e., trade publisher, paperback house, university press, textbook publisher) of the organization. In general, the larger the publishing house, the more differentiated and specialized the editorial functions. In smaller publishing organizations, editorial positions are often less clearly defined, and editors may have a variety of duties and responsibilities.

In a medium-sized publishing house there is a fairly standard set of editorial positions that is adapted by larger and smaller houses, depending on their specific needs. The Editor-in-Chief or Chief Editor (sometimes called the Executive Editor or Editorial Director) is primarily an executive rather than an editor in the traditional sense. He is responsible for coordinating and supervising all of the organization's editorial activities and functions. Duties are largely managerial: delegating work to the editorial staff, conducting staff meetings, and taking responsibility for editorial budget, policy-making, and personnel management. The Editor-in-Chief also works closely with the publisher and marketing department of the organization to create new book ideas and other publishing projects.

Senior Editors are experienced staff members who work closely with authors and their agents in contracting books and other publishing projects. Senior Editors are also very involved in creating and proposing ideas for new books and other publishing projects. A Senior Editor may have the title of Acquiring or Sponsoring Editor. (A separate entry for "editor, acquisitions" is included in this encyclopedia.)

The Managing Editor or Produc-

tion Editor is a liaison between the editorial and production departments of a publishing organization. He is responsible for coordinating a manuscript through all phases of production—copyediting, design, and manufacture—to bound book. This position is discussed in more detail in the "editor, production" entry in this encyclopedia.

The people who do substantive editing of manuscripts are known by various titles: Associate Editors, Assistant Editors, Developmental Editors. Depending on their specific position in the publishing house, these editors may be involved in reading and reporting on incoming manuscripts, doing in-depth editing and rewriting of manuscripts, and preparing the final revision of a manuscript to send to the copyeditor.

Editorial Assistants, often novices in the business, perform clerical and routine editorial duties such as typing, filing, and opening and routing mail. In addition to basic clerical duties, however, many editorial assistants are assigned to work directly with copy, taking on editing and rewriting responsibilities. The distinction between editors and editorial assistants is thus sometimes blurred.

Other positions in publishing are held either by full-time staff members or freelancers, depending on the size of the publishing house. Copyeditors polish the style, grammar, and spelling of manuscripts, and are responsible for composition matters such as typeface style and consistency of design. Proofreaders check printed copy against original, noting every letter, word, and symbol. Although proofreading usually means checking for typographical and spelling errors, proofreaders are often asked to query editors on questionable points that may have slipped by previous readers.

Unlike the preceding two jobs, indexing is almost always performed by a freelancer working outside the company. This job is discussed further under "book indexing" in this encyclopedia.

To qualify for the jobs described above, one generally needs a college degree. While most editors have an English, journalism, or liberal arts degree, a background in these areas is not required. Many textbook publishers, for example, seek editors with educational or teaching backgrounds in the type of books they publish: science, math, political or social science, etc. One survey revealed that, in hiring editors, publishers are not as interested in educational background as they are in evidence of curiosity and intelligence in a candidate, since editorial positions involve primarily on-the-job training. As John Dessauer notes in *Book Publishing: What It Is, What It Does*: "Although a number of academic programs throughout the country offer courses on book publishing, most of the education and training given to employees in the industry is imparted on the job."

Customarily, jobs in publishing provide lower pay than do those in other business fields; what they offer instead, is prestige and psychic rewards. Starting salary at a New York firm, for example, is currently $9,000-$11,000. According to *The American Almanac of Jobs and Salaries*, Assistant Editors may receive anywhere from $11,700-$15,500, while Associate Editors make between $10,800 and $25,000. The median salary for a Production Editor is $21,000, and Senior Editors fall into the $25,000-$50,000 range with a higher percentage at the lower end of the spectrum. Freelance copyeditors, proofreaders, and indexers usually receive an hourly rate for assignments.

Newcomers to the publishing industry are often required to begin at clerical jobs, regardless of educational background. (*See: book indexing; continuing education; copyeditor; editing, freelance; editor, acquisitions; editor, content; editor, production; editors; indexing.*)

Book publishing jobs, publicity. The publicity department of a publishing organization offers job opportunities for individuals with writing skills. Since the goal of the publicity department is to secure media coverage for the publishing house's books and other products, publicists are primarily responsible for creating press releases describing books and their authors, and developing special feature stories about books and authors, intended for distribution to newspapers, magazines, and broadcast media. In some publishing houses, the publicity department is responsible for writing the copy that appears on a book's dust jacket.

In addition to these duties, members of the publicity department also send out review copies of new publications, arrange radio and television appearances for authors, coordinate authors' promotional tours and autographing parties, and perform related promotional duties such as creating book catalogs, book ads, etc. The publicity department serves a public relations function as well, sending out press releases about the company's activities, sometimes preparing annual reports, and keeping up to date a complete biographical file of authors and book reviews for use by critics, students, and writers.

Publicists in the book publishing industry are generally paid between $10,000 and $21,500, depending on the size and locale of the publishing house and the specific duties involved in the job. (*See: autographing party; book promotion; book publishing jobs, editorial; promotion by author.*)

Book review. An analytical, evaluative account of a work, usually by a person qualified to comment on its literary merit and/or subject matter. The review conveys an opinion and supports that critical judgment with evidence from the book's content. In the case of nonfiction, the review considers aspects such as the accuracy of the facts, the organization of the information, and the completeness of the bibliography and index. For fiction, the review comments on plot development, the unity of theme, the credibility of the characters, and the effect of the whole work on the reader. Book reviews may also contain the following: some background information about the author, a comparison of the book to others in the field, and an appraisal of the book in terms of the author's intended purpose.

Book reviews appear in general interest newspapers and magazines as well as professional journals. Payments vary: compensation may range from only a copy of the book reviewed to fees of $25-$100 and more in the case of larger circulation magazines and newspapers. (*See: arts review; criticism.*)

Book reviews, indexes to. For reviews of books on general topics, the researcher should consult the *Book Review Digest* or *Book Review Index. Readers' Guide to Periodical Literature*, in volumes from 1976 on, lists book reviews in a separate section at the end of the book. *The New York Times Index* and *Popular Periodicals Index* both list book reviews within the text, under the category "book reviews."

There are also indexes that list reviews of books in specialized fields. (They are discussed under "periodicals, indexes to" in this encyclopedia.)

If a book review was written too recently to have been catalogued in an index, it is best to consult a recent issue of a magazine with a book review department, such as the *New York Times Book Review, New York Review of Books*, and *Times Literary Supplement. (See: book review; periodicals, indexes to.)*

Book revision for second edition (terms). The contract between author and book publisher generally has a revision clause, a built-in provision regarding subsequent editions. Therefore, the author is usually obligated to do a revision, or have its cost—if done by another writer for a flat fee—deducted from his royalties on the new edition. Whether a new advance is offered depends on whether the revision involves an excessive amount of work, and whether the book needs revising very frequently.

In the case of a second author's revising of the published work of another—for example, an author who is asked by a publisher to revise a book of a deceased author—the author who does the revision faces two alternative methods of payment: either a flat fee or the publisher may offer a percentage of the royalties due the original author. This would depend on the amount of work involved, and what kind of agreement can be negotiated between the freelancer and the original author or his heirs.

Bookkeeping. (*See: recordkeeping.*)

Booklist. *Booklist* is a semimonthly trade magazine for librarians published by the American Library Association (ALA). In addition to reviews of books for both adults and young people, the magazine also reviews films, recordings, reference books, and U.S. government publications.

One of its regular features is a column reviewing first novels, through which the fiction writer can discover which publishers publish what kinds of novels. *Booklist* is available in most libraries; its publisher's address is American Library Association, 50 E. Huron Street, Chicago IL 60611.

Book-promotion tour. Publishers sometimes send authors on promotional tours that include personal and/or media appearances. Only authors who have reached celebrity status or whose books are projected blockbusters are sent on such tours. Some self-promotion tips for authors are given in books on self-publishing, which are listed in *Subject Guide to Books In Print* under the category "Publishers and Publishing."

Books Published 1971 vs 1981 by Subject/Format. (See the Appendix to this encyclopedia.)

Books, tapes of. Cassette tapes of books can be listened to when driving, working, or otherwise occupied so that reading is impossible. Regular trade publishers which are now offering books on cassettes include Bantam, Random House, Simon and Schuster, Warner Publishing, Books on Tape, Inc., P.O. Box 7900, Newport Beach CA 92660; Listen for Pleasure, 417 Center St., Lewiston NY 14092; and Norwood Industries, 3828 South Main Street, Salt Lake City UT 84115.

Bookstore directories. (*See:* American Book Trade Directory.)

Bound proofs. (*See: preliminary edition.*)

Brand name author. A well-known author who has acquired a large following. The term is often associated with authors of certain types of fiction—mysteries, gothics, science fiction, etc. Any brand name author's book is likely to be a good seller, since readers search out new books by a writer whose style they admire.

British spelling and usage. George Bernard Shaw once remarked that America and England are two nations divided by a common language, and American writers need to keep those differences in mind when writing for publications in

Great Britain. As examples, some British spellings are colour, practise, civilisation, cheque (the document), and theatre. In England, a mechanical device used to transport persons or objects from one level to another is called a *lift*, while in America, it is known, of course, as an *elevator*. To the British, *holiday* means what *vacation* means to Americans.

The *Oxford English Dictionary*, available in most libraries, is a source of British spellings of English words, as is *Brewer's Dictionary of Phrase and Fable*, which defines words, idioms, and phrases used in the English language. One of the most recent books Americans might find useful is *Britishisms: A Dictionary of Words, Idioms and Phrases Characteristic of British English*, by Lawrence Holofcener.

Broadcast networks. Television and radio networks are groups of stations over which programs are broadcast simultaneously. They can assist the writer doing research by providing transcripts of and other information about their programs.

The American Broadcasting Company (ABC) can be reached at 1330 Avenue of the Americas, New York NY 10019.

CBS, Inc. (the Columbia Broadcasting System) is located at 51 W. 52nd Street, New York NY 10019. The address of the National Broadcasting Co., Inc. (NBC) is 30 Rockefeller Plaza, New York NY 10112.

Writers may contact National Public Radio (NPR) at 2025 M Street, N.W., Washington DC 20036; and the Public Broadcasting Service (PBS), by writing Public Broadcasting Service, 475 L'Enfant Plaza, S.W., Washington DC 20024.

Turner Broadcasting System Inc., a cable system, is located at 1050 Techwood Drive, Atlanta GA 30318.

The Mutual Broadcasting System is at 1755 S. Jefferson Davis Highway, Arlington VA 22202. (*See: transcripts of broadcasts.*)

Broadcasting directories. *Broadcasting/Cablecasting Yearbook* gives details on the ownership and operation of radio, television, and cable TV stations throughout the U.S. and Canada. It is arranged geographically by state and by city, and includes additional information on program producers, market areas, etc. It is published by *Broadcasting* Magazine, 1735 De Sales Street, N.W., Washington DC 20036.

Names of staff personnel at radio and television stations throughout the country are included in Volume 3 of *Working Press of the Nation*, and a new directory of *Cable* (TV) *Contacts* is being produced. Both directories are described in detail under their titles in this encyclopedia.

Directories of programs featuring authors as guests are published by companies such as *New England Talk Show Directory*, 5 Auburn Street, Framingham MA 01701, and a nationwide directory, *TV Publicity Outlets*, P.O. Box 327, Washington Depot CT 06794.

Radio and television programs that feature book reviews and/or author interviews are also listed in *Literary Market Place*, described under its title in this encyclopedia. (*See:* Cable Contacts; *directories;* Literary Market Place; Working Press of the Nation.)

Broadcasting, Museum of. A museum located in New York City that contains cassette recordings of 10,000 radio programs and 6,000 television programs. The collection represents the U.S. and foreign countries, and contains material produced during the past 60 years. Writers who live within commuting distance of Manhattan may find the archives useful in communicating the flavor of a certain time in visual and audio form, as opposed to a backdated newspaper account.

In the Museum's library, a card catalogue indexed by title, subject, date, network, cast members, and production staff gives users access to cassette tapes. The tapes are viewed at consoles on videocassette players; they are not lent by the library. Tapes are available for an hour at a time, and are distributed on a first-come, first-served basis.

Museum visitors may also view programs in the MB Theater and the Videothèque, which screen programs and stage exhibits for large groups.

In addition, the Museum maintains a reference library of books and periodicals, a collection of 2,400 radio scripts, and the NBC Radio archives, which hold recordings of radio programs.

The Museum of Broadcasting is located at 1 E. 53rd Street, New York NY 10022.

Business and industry as it employs writers. Persons seeking full-time writing jobs may wish to look to business and industry, which employ them in advertising, public relations, sales, training, company publications, handbook/manual, and speechwriting work.

In this kind of work, the writer serves as a link between the company and its dealers or customers and the public. He can be either a generalist or a specialist, and his education, experience, and interests should guide him in selecting where he will work.

To approach a corporation, one should write to its personnel manager, enclosing a résumé and writing samples with the letter. (*See: advertising copywriters; company publication; financial writing; ghostwriting speeches; public relations [PR] representative; technical writing.*)

Business cards. A writer's business card can help him obtain new clients when he makes personal calls on local prospects, or remind present clients of his availability. Business cards should display the writer's name, address, telephone number, and an indication of his services, e.g., "freelance writer" or "editorial services." A freelance writer may create a company name for his business and include it as well.

In some cases, e.g., if a writer works as a stringer for a publication, the publisher may provide the writer with business cards. Independent writers may have cards designed professionally and/or printed by a quick-print service. (*See: stationery.*)

Business side of writing. Writers tend to concentrate on creating and too often ignore administrative details. But freelance writers are essentially small businesspersons, and that role demands the management of many sides of an enterprise. (Of course, an independently wealthy writer or a writer who has attained considerable financial success can hire an accountant, a secretary, or other assistants, but the majority of writers, especially early in their careers, are one-person operations.)

Financial matters usually left to an employer are the freelancer's own responsibility. For example, he must deduct federal, state—and sometimes city—taxes from his income, save for his retirement, and pay social security tax. Similarly, insurance fees are paid out of a freelancer's own income, not by an employer. In some areas, the writer must obtain a license to operate a small business.

Devising personal and business budgets can be complicated by the fact that the freelancer's income is irregular, but these administrative tasks, though time consuming, are necessary to the freelancer's success.

Keeping records of expenses is essential for figuring tax deductions, as well as for collecting reimbursements from publishers on assignments involving travel, for example. (*See: recordkeeping; taxes.*)

Business writing. A term that includes the copy found in business magazines, in-house publications, speeches, annual reports, newsletters, position papers, press releases, catalogues, and brochures and pamphlets used in public relations, advertising, and fundraising. Business writing is clear, accurate, and usually positive. Its purpose is to get a message across quickly and economically.

The craft of business writing is applicable not only to business and industry but also to nonprofit institutions such as churches and hospitals, as well as community associations and professional societies. Though businesses often have their own writing staffs, freelancers who can meet pressing needs may be welcomed. Freelance business writers know the background of the company or organization they write for; they know the group's objectives and their intended audience. Because the words of business writing are often closely tied with a graphic presentation of the message, knowledge of layout, photography, typography, and printing are extra pluses for a freelance business writer.

Payment depends on the availability of good business writers, specific market needs, size of the company, and scope of the assignment. Rates generally range from $100-$200/day; for smaller projects the beginning business writer can expect $10-$50/hr. Current average rates for specific business writing assignments (speeches, catalogues, etc.) are listed in *Writer's Market* in the section "How Much Should I Charge?"

There are several organizations representing business writers, including Associated Business Writers of America (ABWA), International Association of Business Communicators (IABC), and the Industrial Communication Council (ICC). These business writers' groups are described, under their names, in this encyclopedia.

Additional information: *Directory of Corporate Affiliations; Dun & Bradstreet Reference Book of Corporate Managements; Standard & Poor's Register of Corporations, Directors and Executives.*

Byline. Most magazines publish an author's name with his article or story or poem, and in some small publications, this may be his only "payment." But any such pieces—along with paid-for, bylined publications—are useful additions to the

46

writer's portfolio in gaining recognition among editors and readers.

A well-established, prolific writer may occasionally have more than one article in the same issue of a publication, and in that case, he usually uses a pseudonym with one of the pieces.

Writers are not given bylines for two types of work: 1) confession stories that are published as intimate disclosures by the story's central character; and 2) research work that the writer sells in the form of notes rather than a finished article, the latter of which is assigned to a staff writer. (*See: as-told-to article or book; pseudonym.*)

Cable Contacts. A new directory listing major market cable systems, satellite networks, independent producers, news services, and multiple system operators. It includes guest/information/product usage on the various cable systems, plus technical requirements (such as kinds of tape for submissions), subscriber figures, and program placement opportunities. The directory contains approximately 800 pages and is published annually in October by Larimi Communications Associates, Ltd., 151 E. 50th Street, New York NY 10022. (*See:* Broadcasting/Cablecasting Yearbook.)

Caldecott Medal. This award is offered annually by the American Library Association to honor the artist who has illustrated what they consider to be the most significant American picture book for children published in the preceding year. Established in 1938, the Caldecott Medal was the first award created with the purpose of giving recognition to a book's illustrator. The award is named for the famous nine-teenth-century English illustrator Randolph Caldecott who, together with his wife and a colleague, began a new era of picture books for young people.

Publishers send a copy of each of their books published for children to the ALA's Association for Library Service to Children, whose committee makes the choice.

The award itself is a bronze medal presented at the annual ALA conference, usually in June. The face of the medal carries a reproduction of an original Caldecott illustration; the reverse side is an illustration of "four and twenty blackbirds baked in a pie" and an inscription, "For the most distinguished American picture book for children."

A list of the prize-winning books appears in *Literary and Library Prizes.*

Camera. A valuable accessory for writers, the camera has many potential uses: as an effective instrument for increasing not only the likelihood of an actual sale, but also for increasing the fee an editor will pay; and as a way to take fast, accurate fiction research notes, e.g., showing how a person looks or details of a setting. A camera may also be used to tell a story mostly with pictures, accompanied by minimal text.

Though the choice of camera equipment is a personal one, the basic outfit for a freelance writer usually begins with a 35mm single-lens-reflex camera equipped with a "normal" 50mm lens. A flash unit, collapsible tripod, and an equipment bag to carry them in complete the basic requirements. Depending on the writer's taste and expertise, as well as on the current rate of inflation, the total cost of a basic system may range from $300-$700. From this starter outfit, the writer's collection of equipment grows with his experience. (A wide-angle lens and a telephoto lens are valuable additions to any system.)

To supplement the instruction book that comes with a camera, salespersons in camera or department stores can usually provide basic hands-on instruction at the time of (and after the) purchase. Often, such stores also sell beginners' books in photo-taking, which can be helpful.

Camera and equipment descriptions and price ranges are available in such magazines as *Modern Photography* and *Popular Photography*. Places to sell individual photos or photo series are detailed in *Photographer's Market*.

Canadian Authors Association (CAA). The CAA exists "to work for protection of Canadian writers and other artists producing copyrightable material; to act as a spokesman before Royal Commissions and official enquiries; and to sponsor a system of awards, and otherwise

encourage work of literary and artistic merit."

Active members are writers of books, plays, short stories, articles, poetry, television, radio scripts, and other forms, who have produced "a sufficient body of work." Associate members are beginning writers and other persons who have an interest in Canadian literature. All members belong to the national Association and have the option of joining one of 16 branches, which sponsor speeches by authors and panel discussions. The CAA holds an annual meeting. Members receive a subscription to the *Canadian Author and Bookman*, a quarterly magazine.

This organization strives for reform of copyright laws, tax laws, and book contracts. It publishes a guide to Canadian markets for writers.

Although membership is open to anyone, only Canadian writers are eligible for awards. The Vicky Metcalf Award is presented annually by the CAA to a children's writer. It consists of $1,000. In addition, the CAA Awards, sponsored by Harlequin Enterprises Limited, are presented, in the categories of prose fiction, prose nonfiction, poetry, and drama. A CAA Award is a silver medal and $5,000.

The Canadian Authors Association is located at 151 Bloor Street W., Suite 480, Toronto, Ontario, Canada M5S 1T3.

Cap. An abbreviation for *capital*, used by proofreaders to indicate that a letter or letters printed in lower case should be capital letters. *Cap.* is written in the margin on galleys or page proofs, and accompanies the symbol of three parallel lines underscoring the erroneous letter. (The symbol is shown in the chart of proofreading symbols in the Appendix to this encyclopedia). *(See: l.c.)*

Caption (cutline). Explanatory text that accompanies a photograph or illustration. Composing captions for pictures is an important part of the writer/photojournalist's responsibility when submitting material for publication. A good caption complements the photograph, forming a visual unit that is understandable independent of the body text. In submissions, photo quality is paramount, but captions may also influence an editor (and the subsequent magazine reader) to read the accompanying article.

Captions for pictures in news articles consist of identifying the who-what-where-why-how of the photograph. Captions for photographs in magazines and books must not only identify the photo subject, but also induce the reader to want to read the magazine article or the book text it accompanies.

When prints are submitted for publication, captions (including picture credits) are often typed on separate pieces of paper and taped to the back of each one. Other photojournalists number the photographs and provide a separate caption sheet, keyed to the numbers. Caption length may range from one to hundreds of words, depending on the publication's style.

It is important not to write on the backs of photos with pencils or ball point pens (the marks go right through and can be seen on the other side) and not to paperclip anything to photos, another common way of damaging them. Stiff cardboard, of course, should protect the photos in the mailing package.

Careers in writing. The various opportunities for careers in writing fields such as advertising, magazines, newspapers, public relations, publishing, radio, teaching, and television are discussed throughout this encyclopedia.

It is important to note that although persons in all fields of writing have some skills in common, most writers have particular personality traits that make them more suitable for one field than another.

For example, the kind of personality needed by an advertising copywriter who is a great idea generator and a facile writer is different from that required by a nonfiction book writer who can organize a mass of research material and over a protracted period of time write a well-thought-out, but highly readable book.

The publications *Toward Matching Personal and Job Characteristics* and the *Occupational Outlook Handbook*, which can be used in career decisions, are available in the government and business departments of most public libraries. They detail job requirements, working conditions, and special personal qualifications needed beyond education in the field. *(See: jobs for writers; writers, characteristics of.)*

Cart. A shortened form of *cartridge;* a tape loop similar to an 8-track tape, used by radio stations to store commercials, PSAs, etc., one advertiser's commercials per cartridge. On a broadcast cartridge, when a commercial has been played, the tape automatically recycles itself to the beginning of that spot, or stops at the beginning of the next spot on the cartridge.

Cartoon. A drawing or sketch, usually intended to be humorous, that satirizes or comments on a person, situation, or subject of popular interest. In form, a cartoon usually consists of a line drawing and a caption (gag line) that work together to express an idea. (Some cartoons make a point without a caption, however.) Cartoons rely on the spontaneous reactions of their readers; readership studies show that they rank near the top of the list of what people read in magazines and newspapers. The successful cartoonist is tuned in to current events. He knows the editorial slant of a particular publication, and he understands its readers.

There are many cartoon types, each requiring a different perspective. The *political cartoon* presents an issue—often through caricature—in such a way that the reader quickly grasps the artist's opinion on the issue. The *gag cartoon*—the kind most often found in magazines—often jokes about social trends or plays on trendy phrases or catchwords; some gag cartoonists specialize in situation-pictures without words. *Comic-strip* cartoonists use panel drawings and balloon dialogue to set up and deliver their jokes and commentary.

Freelance cartoonists have many potential markets for their work. The annual *Artist's Market* lists specific magazines, newspapers, greeting card companies, book publishers, ad agencies, etc., that solicit cartoons. (The annual *Writer's Market* lists cartoonists who solicit gag ideas on which they can base cartoon drawings—and for which they pay a commission to the writer when the cartoon sells.) In the magazine market, the cartoonist earns from $5 to more than $100 per cartoon. A few magazines pay only in contributor's copies. (*See: comics writing; gag writing.*)

Category fiction. A term used to include all the various labels attached to types of fiction. Category tags name popular fiction writing as mystery, spy, suspense, western, Gothic, religious, historical, science fiction, etc. Category publishing houses include: Harlequin (romance), Greenleaf Classics (erotica) and large paperback publishers such as Avon, Bantam, and Pocket Books (which publish books in several categories) among the many others listed in *Fiction Writer's Market*. (*See: fiction.*)

CATV writing. Writing for programs distributed on a community antenna television system. Cable TV began in 1949-50 as a way—via a cable of electrically conducting wires—to bring television service to communities outside the reach of broadcast signals. Because the cable construction minimizes electrical interference from outside sources, it soon spread to other communities that wanted to receive more stations and obtain better reception from the regular stations. There are currently over 4,700 cable systems in the United States.

Cable television is not now primarily an originator of programming; rather, it augments and supplements the offerings of commercial television. CATV systems, however, represent *potential* markets for generalist writers, playwrights, poets, juvenile specialists, cartoonists, feature writers, and ad writers. CATV managers (directors of original programming) may be receptive to writers' local interest ideas, news, and features geared to a well-defined audience. In addition, the Federal Communications Commission has established provisions for government, private, and public access channels for which writers may be needed.

The *Broadcasting/Cablecasting Yearbook*, available in most libraries, lists location, ownership, and management of every system in the U.S. Yellow Pages directories also pinpoint local cable networks. (*See: broadcasting directories;* Cable Contacts.)

CBS. (*See: broadcast networks.*)

Celebrity addresses. Some well-known persons' home or business addresses are available through *Who's Who* or other biographical directories. Writers may also reach celebrities through Celebrity Service, Inc., 171 W. 57th Street, New York NY 10019. This firm provides the name and telephone number of a celebrity's personal manager, agent, or press agent; at present, the writer pays $10 per name. Celebrity Service, Inc., also publishes the biennial *Celebrity Service International Contact Book.* (*See: research sources, directories of.*)

Censorship, literary. Most censorship in the United States concerns publications for use in schools, and alleged pornography in books for the mass market. According to a report by the American Library Association, reports of books having been removed or threatened to be removed from libraries averaged 100 per year in the early 1970s, 300 per year in the late 1970s, and approxi-

mately 1,000 per year in the early 1980s.

Although censorship has always existed to some degree, the criteria for proposing that books be banned seem to shift with societal trends. In the late 1960s and early 1970s, racism, sexism, and other forms of discrimination were considered objectionable; in the 1980s, it is material alleged to be anti-American, antifamily, or obscene that is challenged. While educators traditionally have chosen books for use by schoolchildren for their literary value and for their handling of controversial topics in what they consider to be a tasteful manner, some conservative lobbying groups emerged in the early 1980s as opponents of certain works of literature.

Pornography can be defined as "obscene material," but *obscenity* has an alterable legal meaning, depending on evolving court rulings. The most recent court decision, in the case *Miller* vs. *California*, states that obscenity is determined by (a) whether "the average person, applying contemporary standards, would find that the work, taken as a whole, appeals to the prurient interest . . . (b) whether the work depicts or describes, in a patently offensive way, sexual conduct specifically defined by the applicable state law, and (c) whether the work, taken as a whole, lacks serious literary, artistic, political, or scientific value."

In addition, by this ruling, local standards replaced national standards as the criteria for judging whether a book, film, or play is obscene.

P.E.N. and the Author's Guild are two of several writers organizations that speak out against censorship by sponsoring lectures and readings and involving themselves in court cases by filing friend-of-the-court briefs. (*See: freedom of the press.*)

Additional information: *Law and the Writer.*

Census Bureau, Department of Commerce. The Bureau of the Census in the U.S. Department of Commerce is the primary agency of the federal government engaged in the collection and publication of general-purpose statistics. It takes the national censuses of population, housing, agriculture, retail and wholesale trade, service industries, manufacturers, mineral industries, transportation, construction industries, and governments. The Bureau also conducts monthly, quarterly, and annual surveys on some of the same subjects. An inquirer may learn from the Bureau, for instance, which cities in the United States have the highest crime rates, or what the country's annual growth rate of coal consumption is. The Bureau can provide information about the number of single-parent households in the U.S., or the employment statistics for U.S. psychologists. These are just a few examples of the wealth of statistical information the Census Bureau makes available.

The Bureau publishes an average of 2,000 titles a year. Among the more popular is the *Statistical Abstract of the United States,* an annual summary of American social, economic, and political data. This reference volume is available at any library; it may also be purchased from the Government Printing Office (GPO).

The Bureau also publishes "Telephone Contacts for Data Users," a list of names and phone numbers of individual analysts in each subject area. The list can be obtained free from the Customer Services Branch (DUSD), Bureau of the Census, Washington DC 20233. (*See: Ombudsman, Office of, U.S. Department of Commerce.*)

cf. Abbreviation for the Latin word *confer,* which translates to *compare.* Used in footnotes and text material, *cf.* points out a related subject to the reader, for example, "Most researchers agree that alcohol can adversely affect the unborn child (cf. alcoholism)."

Chain magazine publishers. (*See: magazine publishers, multiple.*)

Character. The unique set of traits and features that form the nature of a fictional person. For example, the *character* of Falstaff is the blend of physical attributes, feelings, thoughts, and actions that readers recognize as distinctly his.

Characters that the reader will remember start with a basis of reality. The writer takes a trait, the mannerisms, or perhaps the appearance of someone he has known and adds to and embellishes them from his imagination. Sometimes a character is a composite. Often a character reflects the writer's own background or fantasies.

The character's motivation, the "why" of his behavior, is revealed through his dialogue and actions. He is the sum total of everything that has happened to him in his fictional life: a character with flesh and blood and genuine emotions who brings the validity of truth to a work of fiction.

Writer Damon Knight, in *Creating*

Short Fiction, advises the following background exercises for creating characters: writing biographical sketches of them; writing a scene that would give the reader insight into a character; and writing a scene that involves two of the story's characters who are similar to each other, pointing out their differences. In the story itself, Knight suggests describing a character from the viewpoint of another character or of two different characters, and showing a character in a scene that includes part of his daily routine.

Knight offers the following advice on inventing original characters: "Each time you write a scene from the viewpoint of one of your characters, imagine yourself inside that person's head. Exactly what is that person seeing right now—what is she hearing? What other sensations is she aware of? What is she thinking? Remembering? What impulses does she suppress? What does she notice while another person is speaking? What is her mood? Is she elated, depressed, or what?"

Character change. Every short story or novel necessarily involves a change in the central character. Just as real-life persons do, fictional characters undergo change as a result of their experiences. At the end of a story, the writer may show that a character is in a different situation or has a different attitude, but the alteration within the fictional person is always brought about as the logical result of his experience. (*See: consequence, a sense of; incident.*)

Characterization. The process of creating an image of a person in drama, fiction, or narrative poetry in such a way that the reader believes in his authenticity. Characterization—the consistent evolution of a character—both generates plot (conflict) and results from it.

The writer uses various methods of character development. He may give the reader a picture of a person by describing his appearance, manners, and mood. Or he may let a character "speak for himself" in the form of dialogue. The writer may cultivate a character's nature by showing what he does and how he acts; in the same vein, he may indicate to the reader how the character reacts to people and situations around him. Finally, the writer may portray a character's effect on others in the story.

The writer achieves a successful characterization when the fictional person becomes so credible that he exists as a real person for the reader. (*See: character.*)

Chases' Calendar of Annual Events. A reference booklet that lists and describes events and observances of each day of the year; each day's events are listed alphabetically under the date heading. Entries cover events worldwide; national and religious holidays are included, as well as famous birthdays, traditional holidays, festivals, fairs, promotional events, week-long and month-long observances, and other happenings. Some listings give the name and address of a contact who can supply further information on the event or observance; the booklet also contains a general cross-index by subject.

A sample of listings in the 1982 Calendar includes "Great Seal of the United States: Bicentennial" (January 28); "National Wildlife Week" (March 14-20); "Birthday of the First

Adhesive Postage Stamp" (May 6); "Pennsylvania Bed Making Championships" (September 22); and "Liszt, Franz: Birthday" (October 22).

Writers may find this directory helpful in inspiring ideas for seasonal articles.

Chase's Calendar of Annual Events is published by Best Publications, 180 N. Michigan Ave., Chicago IL 60601. (*See: seasonal material.*)

Check contract. A statement endorsed on the back of a publisher's check in payment to an author, indicating what rights are being purchased to an article, story, or poem in a magazine. (While a copyright is the property of the author, he sells the contractual rights to use his manuscript in certain ways to a publisher.) An author who endorses a check contract may be simultaneously signing a legal contract.

In the case in which a previous agreement concerning rights has been made in correspondence between publisher and author, and the endorsement runs counter to that agreement, the author may endorse the check but cross out the publisher's notation. In this way, he is not bound by unagreed-to obligations imposed by the check contract.

If the endorsement carries a message to the effect that any alteration of it voids the check, then the author has no choice but to return the check, remind the publisher (with a photocopy of their previous agreement), and request that a new check be issued showing the correct rights bought. (*See: rights to manuscripts.*)

Children as writers. A number of magazines solicit articles, poems, stories, and drawings from young people. Some child writers begin their careers by being published in special children's sections of newspapers and magazines, then branch out into magazines that suit their interests.

Editors agree that articles written by children need original ideas, slants, and attention to grammar. They also suggest that the young writer develop persistence and a thick skin, and find a family member or friend to serve as a critic, attributes that are essential to writers of all ages.

Publications that contain sections created by children include *Alive! for Young Teens,* the *Christian Science Monitor, Highlights for Children, Scholastic Scope,* and *Wee Wisdom Magazine. Tigers and Lambs* and *Stone Soup* are magazines consisting entirely of work by children. Also, *Seventeen, Straight,* and *Tiger Beat* sometimes accept material written by teenagers. Each of these magazines has individual editorial needs and submission requirements. With material written by children, it is often necessary to include a statement from a parent or teacher attesting to its originality.

Writer's Market, in the section "Juvenile," lists additional magazines written for children.

Children's Book Council (CBC). This association of publishers of children's books works with groups in other fields through joint committees to create children's book programs. The CBC sponsors an annual Children's Book Week in November, and supports an examination library that contains reference works and children's trade books published during the past three years. Beginning in 1983, the CBC sponsored *Everychild: The American Conference*, a national meeting about books and other media, that also includes exhibits of materials.

This organization publishes annotated bibliographies of children's books, available free for a 6½x9½-inch SASE. These lists include "Children's Choices," compiled annually and based on schoolchildren's voting on books selected by publishers; "Outstanding Science Trade Books for Children"; and "Notable Children's Trade Books in the Field of Social Studies." When requesting these publications, envelopes should be coded as follows: *Att'n.: Children's Choices* for "Children's Choices," *NSTA* for the list of science books, and *NCSS* for the list of social studies books. (A request for all three lists must include first-class postage for two ounces.) "Writing Books for Children and Young Adults" and two annually revised lists—the "Members List" of editors' names and "Members' Publishing Programs" featuring brief descriptions of each publisher's list—are other publications of the CBC that may be obtained for an SASE. The address of the Children's Book Council is 67 Irving Place, New York NY 10003.

Children's Media Market Place (CMMP). A biennial directory that lists organizations and individuals in various categories of communications for children. Listings include names, addresses, and telephone numbers of personnel, as well as a description of the audience, services, and products of the company, agency, or group.

CMMP contains sections on book publishers, periodical publishers (which include "Periodicals for Chil-

dren," "Periodicals for Professionals & Parents," and "Review Journals & Services"), book clubs, bookstores, audiovisual producers, agents, television and radio stations, and distributors of television programs. The sections "Public Library Coordinators of Children's & Young Adult Services," "State School Media Officers," and "Examination Centers" deal with individuals and organizations that select books for public libraries and school libraries. Also included in the book are a section on federal grants, a calendar of events, and a bibliography of works about children's media.

The section "Names & Numbers Index to Children's Media Sources" lists individuals, companies, and other organizations.

Children's theater. The term used to refer to plays written to entertain young people. Full-length dramas written for children's theater usually have performance times of an hour or longer (but not too much longer). Dramatized fairy tales (*The Wizard of Oz*, *The Snow Queen*) and original scripts (modern comedies, historical sagas) written for children are not usually intended to be acted by young people.

The children's theater playwright knows his young audience well. He uses vivid language, lively stage behavior, attention-getting devices, and dialogue that neither preaches nor moralizes. He attempts to grip his audience's attention at the outset of the play. He states and restates ideas/themes understandable by children, but never underestimates the depth of perception they may have.

The children's playwright submits his script, along with specific costume or prop needs and unique staging requirements, to producers. Multiple submissions of plays to amateur and touring companies, college experimental groups, contests, and church organizations are common. Some beginning playwrights allow amateur productions of their work for limited fees to gain exposure for their work.

When a play has been successfully produced, the playwright may submit it (along with its reviews) to a play publisher who, on accepting the work, markets it—usually through a catalog. *Writer's Market* offers information on producers and publishers that solicit plays for young audiences as well as producers of films and AV materials for children. *Songwriter's Market* identifies markets for musicals. (*See: play royalties; plays for young actors.*)

City magazine. A regional publication reflecting the people, services, institutions, and unique environment of a metropolitan area. City magazines are generally upbeat publications willing to look analytically at a city's many themes. Though some "citymags" began as chamber-of-commerce-type publications, whose "boosterism" articles discussed only the best and brightest aspects of the city, the most successful are now independent operations free of the restraints of public relations.

City magazines share similar philosophies because of their common denominator—people and cities. They are not strictly news, business, or local interest journals; rather, they are periodicals offering in-depth pieces on the background, significance, and effect of area happenings. They also present life-

styles, distinct personalities, and local-color situations that might otherwise go unnoticed. Because they are not usually in competition with each other, city magazines frequently copy and imitate each other's ideas and formats.

They are published mainly for the middle- and upper-class, well-educated, sophisticated reader interested in various aspects of life in the city. Writers must know the particular demographics of their readership and tackle subjects appealing to them. Current popular offerings include service articles, exposés, how-to's, community calendars, columns—even pieces that take on a popular urban cause, such as neighborhood safety.

The city magazine represents a potentially fruitful market for freelancers. (There are currently more than 200 city magazines nationwide, most of them supported by populations of one million or more. Smaller cities, if they are both diverse and booming, may provide suitable ground for a magazine.) Because local newspapers are usually in competition with city magazines for advertising, stories, and readers, newspaper staff writers are not generally permitted to write for area city magazines; moreover, city magazines usually carry few staff writers of their own.

Payment for articles depends on the magazine's profitability, its size, management, budget, and talent pool. For major features writers may earn $100-$500. For shorter articles and columns the price is usually about half the major feature rate. Most city magazines do not pay by the word. *Writer's Market* highlights potential markets and their requirements.

Classical music. Established, formal, elegant, and precise musical art forms. Throughout history, different styles of classical music have predominated, such as the work of J.S. Bach of the baroque period (1600-1750), Wolfgang Amadeus Mozart of the classical period (1750-1820); Felix Mendelssohn of the romantic period (1820-1920); and Arnold Schoenberg and Igor Stravinsky of the twentieth century.

Cliché. A trite word or phrase that lacks originality or impact because of frequent and prolonged use. Clichés clutter a manuscript and should be avoided, except when used deliberately as sarcasm or as a revealing commentary through the dialogue of a particular character.

"Cool as a cucumber" and "green with envy" are examples of clichés.

Climax. The climax, as the result of all the events that have preceded it, is the most intense point in the story line of a fictional work. (A novel or a play may contain more than one climax; however, a short story may include only one.)

A climax represents the peak of emotional response from the reader as well as the turning point in the story's action. It always follows a crisis, but when time elapses between the two occurrences, the event is called an *anticlimax* instead of a climax. (*See: crisis.*)

CLIO awards. These awards of the advertising industry were named for Clio, one of the muses of Greek mythology, who is described as "the proclaimer and glorifier of great accomplishments and deeds." They are given annually for best U.S. TV, radio, cable TV, print, packaging de-

sign, and specialty advertising, and for best international TV/cinema, radio, print, and packaging design. The best entries receive CLIO statuettes; the finalists, certificates.

Criteria for judging are effectiveness of communication of sales message, appeal and/or taste, and use of production techniques. In 1982, 215 statuettes were awarded out of 12,815 entries. The competition is open to all ads in all media introduced between January 1 and January 31 of a given year. Entry deadline is February 1. CLIO Awards are presented in New York City in June.

Inquiries may be addressed to CLIO Awards, 336 E. 59th Street, New York NY 10022; the office can be reached by phone at (212) 593-1900.

Clip. In journalistic terms, a sample of a writer's published work, usually from a newspaper or magazine. Editors often indicate that *clips* or *clippings* should be mailed or presented in person when applying for a job.

A clip can also be a piece cut out of a newspaper or magazine for any other reason. For example, freelance writers may keep files of clips for article ideas and research. (*See: tearsheet.*)

Clip art. Camera-ready drawings on various subjects. Clip art firms sell booklets of clip art to editors of small publications, publicists at nonprofit organizations, and others who need inexpensive illustrations. Clip art firms include companies like Dynamic Graphics, Inc., 6000 N. Forest Park Drive, Peoria IL 61614; and

Volk Clip Art, Inc., Pleasantville NJ 08232.

Some current subscription prices are $168 per year and $29.50 per month. (*See: copyright-free art.*)

Clipping services. These firms employ persons to read thousands of U.S. newspapers and magazines and clip items for writers or publishers on selected subjects.

While some publishing companies provide copies of reviews to authors whose books they publish (and may hire a clipping service for this purpose), some authors prefer to engage a service on their own for a certain book, or to collect newspaper or magazine clippings on a subject they're researching that's in the news.

Costs for the service are usually a set fee plus an additional amount for each clip provided. Current charges at one major national firm, for example, are $129 per month for three months' service plus 66¢ per clipping.

Many such firms are listed in the Manhattan Yellow Pages telephone directory under "Clipping Bureaus."

Close shot. In a motion picture or television script, this direction indicates that the camera should emphasize an actor or object by singling him or it out to fill the screen. When an extremely close shot is needed, the term *tight shot* is used. Both terms are typed all in caps when used in a script. (*See: close-up.*)

Close-up. A camera direction indicating that the subject is seen at close range. In a close-up of a person, only the head or the head and shoulders are in view. *Close-up* can be abbreviated *CU*. A related camera direction is *extreme close-up* or *XCU*. Both terms are typed all in caps when used in scripts. (*See: close shot.*)

Co-author. When more than one writer is an author of a book, the multiple bylines appear on the text and the jacket, and the royalties usually are shared proportionate to the individual authors' contributions to the salability of the book. When a writer works with a subject or expert who is not a writer, the division of royalty income again depends on how much each party contributed to the book. (*See: as-told-to article or book; collaboration.*)

Coins, illustrations of. Coins of the U.S. and foreign countries that are represented in photographs, illustrations, motion pictures, or slides, "may be used for any purpose including advertising," according to the U.S. Department of the Treasury. (*See: money, illustration of; stamps, illustration of.*)

Collaboration. In the writing field, this term refers to the act of working with one or more persons in a joint enterprise involving research and writing. The writer may collaborate with various people: another writer, an editor, illustrator, technical person, photographer, celebrity, or musician.

Both fiction and nonfiction can be written as collaborative efforts. Writing in this way succeeds when careful planning accompanies the choice of a partner. Collaborators share similar motivations for the work, feel comfortable with brainstorming sessions, and are willing to give and take in writing, revising, editing, and marketing. In the case of the co-written manuscript, writers generally share the workload and agree to an equitable split of the income and title page credits according to what percentage of the work's salability depends on each person's contributions.

Three categories of collaboration are especially appropriate for nonfiction. (1) The as-told-to manuscript is ghostwritten in the first person, with the writer getting an as-told-to byline. Income is often split 50-50, but this is negotiable depending on the creative contributions of each party to the salability of the work. (2) The ghostwritten work exists where the writer does the job of telling someone's story, usually for a set fee, and with no accompanying credits. Books by politicians and stage personalities are often ghostwritten. (3) The anthology is collated by a writer acting as an editor, who gets contributors to write chapters for the work or himself secures reprint permissions for published material. Fees for the contributors are deducted from the publisher's advance to the author or paid from a publisher's fund set up for that purpose; the writer/editor gets the royalties.

Whatever the collaborative agreement or genre of writing, the collaborators draw up a contract providing for division of the rights and income from the work. More complex contracts give attention to the effect that disability or death of one of the collaborators would have on the work and whether/how to progress with the project. Several forms of collaboration contracts are described in *Entertainment, Publishing, and the Arts: Agreement and the Law*. (*See: anthology; as-told-to article or book; ghostwriting; musical*.)

Collective biography. A volume of biographical sketches of individuals in similar professions, related persuasions, or parallel life circumstances. Example: *Winners on the Tennis Court*, by William S. Glickman. The successful collective biography knits the individual accounts together in a meaningful way by suggesting common threads among the lives of the profiled persons.

Writers who would like to see which publishers are currently producing biographies can refer to the book publishers section of *Writer's Market* and the "biography" category of the *Subject Guide to Books in Print*. (*See: biography*.)

Colloquial language. (*See: dialogue; informal writing style*.)

Colophon. The term *colophon* is sometimes used interchangeably with *logo* as the publisher's identifying mark or symbol on the book's title page, jacket, and binding. It can also be a brief description or discussion of some or all of the elements of a high-quality book's design and production: the designer, typeface, printer, printing process, and paper stock.

For example, the colophon to *The Lone Pilgrim*, a collection of stories by Laurie Colwin, credits the typesetter, the printer, and the designer, and gives the following note on the type: "The text of this book was set in Intertype Garamond, a modern rendering of the type first cut by Claude Garamond (1510-1561). Garamond was a pupil of Geofroy Tory and is believed to have based his letters on the Venetian models, although he introduced a number of important differences, and it is to him we owe the letter that we know as 'old style.' He gave to his letters a certain elegance and a feeling of movement that won for their creator an immediate reputation and the patronage of Francis I of France."

This type of colophon is usually located at the back of a book. (*See: logo.*)

Color in writing. (*See: local color.*)

Columbia Journalism Review. (*See: media reviewers.*)

Column. A short newspaper or magazine piece that deals specifically with a particular field of interest, or broadly with an issue or circumstance of far-reaching scope. A good column is written clearly and succinctly. Columns appear with by-lines on a regular basis (daily, weekly, etc.) and usually run 350-500 words in newspapers. They may be written exclusively for one newspaper or magazine; they may be marketed by a syndicate; or they may be self-syndicated by the writer.

Columns generally fall into two types. The first is the column written by an expert in a particular subject area. From education and/or experience the writer knows a topic and is able to come up with new slants and fresh approaches to inform interested readers about his specialty. Columns dealing with subjects such as gardening, business, child care, and fitness are currently popular.

The second kind of column is written by a person expert in the observation of humans and their activities. This writer views the routine and the ordinary with a keen perspective. His or her columns may be humorous or serious and usually appeal to mass audiences.

Beginning writers are more likely to find success in writing and selling a special-interest column than in attempting to write columns in the style of Art Buchwald or Erma Bombeck. Publishers and editors of weekly and daily newspapers, county tabloids, and independent newsletters are receptive to "focused" columns likely to generate and sustain interest among their unique readerships.

Local newspaper column rates currently range from 80¢ per column-inch to $5 for a weekly publication and from $7.50 to $25 or more for dailies, depending on their circulation. *Writer's Market* details rates for local, syndicated, and self-syndicated columns. (*See: self-syndication; syndicated column.*)

Column-inch. In a printed publication, the area whose boundaries are the width of the column and one inch of depth. This measurement is used in selling advertisements, and is also used by some small newspapers as a guideline for paying correspondents.

Comedy writing. This category includes special material composed of gags and routines written to be performed by a comedian. Comedy writing begins with a premise or theme, such as the financial dilemmas of an oil sheik. This subject is developed into a routine, a four- to five-minute bit with appropriate gags. Its purpose is to amuse an audience. Subjects for comedy material range from the absurd to the unexpected, from the ungarnished to the pompous; there is very little that cannot be slanted to make people laugh. Successful comedy writing is visual in that it conjures amusing images in the minds of an audience.

Comedy material is geared to the style and practice of a comedian. The comedy writer submits his work to a market, i.e., comedian, who he feels is best suited to delivering it successfully. The freelance comedy writer usually contacts "big-name" comics and entertainers through clubs where they appear or through the television networks on which they perform. However, would-be comedy writers use whatever means they can to bring their work to the attention of comedians. One, who worked as a tailor in a shop in the Manhattan theater district, started out leaving gags in the pockets of suits left at the shop by well-known comedians. Trade papers like *Variety* and *Show Business* may also reveal who a well-known comic's personal or theatrical manager is. Writers looking for comics in smaller cities may be able to contact them by phone when they appear in town at a night club or hotel. If no comedians routinely perform in an area, comedy material may be sold to local disc jockeys, TV personalities, and newspapers.

Producers of TV situation comedies and variety shows also need comedy material. Sitcom producers look for comedy plots and situations in which to put their characters; variety show producers want sketches and monologues for their stars. Both sitcoms and variety shows, however, are usually written by staff writers, not freelancers.

Rates for freelance comedy writers vary according to the popularity and income of the comedian. Night club performers currently pay $10-$50 for each gag; $500 and up per minute for routines. New comics offer only slim rates to writers for five-minute rou-

tines, but some comedians pay $5,000 and more for a five-minute stint from an established comedy writer. (*See: gag writing; humor.*)

Additional information: *How to Write and Sell Your Sense of Humor.*

Come-to-realize story. A short story in which the main character's learning or changing occurs entirely within his mind. This kind of story cannot be dramatically effective because the character never takes action as a result of his new insight. Because of this weakness, come-to-realize stories are often rejected by editors.

For example, such a story may end when a newly successful young pianist (the main character) realizes that without the untiring encouragement of the self-sacrificing mother he has all but forgotten, he would be nothing. He feels deep remorse and resolves to write his mother at once. This ending lacks drama because it's all mental, but the story could be effective if the pianist were to *do something*. He may telephone his mother, for example, even though it's 2:00 a.m. where she lives, confess his neglect, and tell her he's sending air fare (which the reader knows he can ill afford) for her to join him for his Vienna debut. (*See: character change; short story.*)

Comic relief. A literary device in which a humorous scene or comment is injected into a work that is generally serious. Although it is used in fiction, comic relief is especially associated with drama: it serves to release the audience's tension brought about by previous scenes, and to amplify the tragic elements of the story.

Comic relief is used in *Hamlet* to relieve the feeling of doom created by Ophelia's and Polonius's deaths, and Hamlet's despondent state. Just after the audience learns of Ophelia's drowning, a comic scene is inserted in which two clowns exchange witticisms as they dig the young woman's grave.

In the contemporary drama *The Night of the Iguana*, Tennessee Williams uses comic relief in the persons of the German family who are residents at the same hotel as the hero. By what they wear, how they act, and what they say, the characters always bring a laugh and momentarily slow the play's pace.

Comics writing. This job involves creating and writing copy for stories told in a comics/graphic art technique—an extremely versatile technique used for advertising, for instructional material, for educational material and other non-fiction, and for fiction of all sorts—action-adventure stories, fantasy, science fiction, humor, westerns, horror, drama, romance, etc.

Comics reach all ages and levels effectively, and are properly considered a communications medium in their own right. Like television and motion pictures, comics are a visual medium; however, comics can be absorbed at the reader's own pace, and material can be reread and reviewed easily and conveniently.

Comics writers have a number of unique devices at their disposal. Smooth-bordered "balloons" indicate that the words enclosed are spoken; scalloped balloons indicate thoughts. (A "pointer" on the side or bottom of the balloon identifies which character is speaking or think-ing.) Captions enclosed in ruled boxes provide whatever narration is needed to augment the illustrations. Whether a comics writer's work is a short vignette, a series of multi-panel strips, or a book-length project, he must succeed in covering a lot of ground in a small space and in only two or three sentences at a time.

A writer interested in creating comic book scripts submits a plot idea to the editor. If it is approved, he is assigned to submit a synopsis of 3-20 pages for the editor's appraisal. At this stage, the editor sometimes requests that the writer make corrections. (If, for certain reasons, the project is abandoned, a kill fee may be involved.)

Then the *penciler* takes over, interpreting the story in drawings. He spends from one to four weeks at this task, after which his work (called the *pencils*) is submitted to the editor. The writer then receives the drawings so that he can *script* the pages by typing the dialogue and captions for them (on a separate sheet), and indicating where on each page the copy is to be placed.

The editor then rechecks the work; the writer may be asked to make revisions. If he lives a considerable distance from the publisher, he may not see the copy after this stage, because of the time involved in sending it back and forth.

The next step, lettering the copy and drawing borders around the panels, is the job of a *letterer*. Then the drawings are *inked*—traced over with India ink—either by the penciler (who drew them originally) or by yet another person, an *inker*. Coloring, proofreading, and designing the cover are the final steps to producing a comic book.

An alternate method involves the

writer, upon approval of his plot, creating a "full script," which includes all dialogue, captions, and descriptions of the required pictures on a panel-by-panel basis. The full script, once approved by the editor, is sent on to the artist, letterer, etc., for completion of the comic.

Payment for comics averages $35-$50 a page—although some well-established, steady contributors to some comic companies receive more per page and earn $20,000-$100,000 (plus) a year. All of the major comic book publishers—such as DC Comics, Inc. and Marvel Comics—are in the New York area; their addresses are in the Manhattan telephone book.

Comment song. A kind of song in a musical that provides commentary on (or opinion of) the action of the story. A well-known comment song is "Sunrise, Sunset," from *Fiddler on the Roof.* (*See: musical.*)

Commission person. An independent salesperson of books, sometimes also called a publisher's rep. This type of salesperson is used by some small publishing houses, from which he receives a commission rather than a salary. A commission person may be engaged by several different publishers at once. Some work with assistants, and others work alone.

The work of a commission person involves travel to bookstores that is usually regional. A list of Publishers Representatives appears in the directory *Literary Market Place.*

Commissioned writing. (*See: assignment, writing on.*)

Committee of Small Magazine Editors & Publishers (COSMEP). COSMEP is an association of publishers of small magazines and books. Its 1,200 members strive to increase the promotion and distribution of their publications. COSMEP sponsors an exhibit service, publishes a monthly newsletter, and convenes annually. Their headquarters can be reached at P.O. Box 703, San Francisco CA 94101.

Comp. Abbreviation for *complimentary copy.* An author receives a certain number of comps of his own book from his publisher.

Publishers sometimes supply other authorities on the book's subject with comps so that they can review the book or provide testimonial quotes for advertising copy. Authors do not receive royalties on these comp copies or the copies sent to book reviewers.

Magazine publishers usually maintain a complimentary subscription list for their regular advertisers, prospective advertisers, regular correspondents, and contributing editors. (*See: author's copies; pre-publication review.*)

Company publication. This is an institutional publication taking one of two forms. One, the *internal*, is designed primarily to promote good employee relations within a company. The second, an *external*, is published for dealers, distributors, and/or stockholders to keep them informed about a company's progress. A company publication may be produced as a general notice, letter, newsletter, newspaper, magazine, or annual report.

Company publications are also known as *house organs*, but the latter term is not preferred by editors.

Freelance writers can serve as contributors to or editors of company publications. However, many businesses depend on their own staff members to produce these publications. The section "Company Publications" in *Writer's Market* outlines needs of editors and payment to writers. (*See: business writing.*)

Complaints against publishers. The writer's grievance most often filed at Writer's Digest Books is publishers' failure to return manuscripts (even when an SASE has been enclosed). Another common complaint is that the publisher has neglected to respond to a query letter. In addition, a publisher's failure to carry out a promise of payment is an increasing writer's concern, according to the editor of *Writer's Market*. (See the summary of types of complaints in the Appendix to this encyclopedia.)

For writers who have been unsuccessful in getting responses to their own follow-up letters to the editor and/or the publisher, *Writer's Market* operates a complaint service dealing with grievances against the organizations listed in the directory. The editors are prepared to intercede for the writer in two areas only: 1) cases in which a promised payment for accepted material has not been delivered or has been delivered only in part, and 2) cases in which the writer has received no report on solicited material. Writers must enclose both SASE and photocopies of correspondence that verify their claims. The service can solve approximately 50% of the writer-publisher conflicts brought to its attention, according to an estimate by the *Writer's Market* editor.

In cases of possible mail fraud, the writer is referred to the U.S. Postmaster. Similarly, when other kinds of legal problems are involved, the writer is referred to a legal service such as Volunteer Lawyers for the Arts or the attorney general of the state in which the publisher does business. (*See: editorial ethics; Volunteer Lawyers for the Arts.*)

Composite character. With this device, a nonfiction writer combines the experiences and attitudes of several real persons into one character. He creates a composite either to protect individual identities or to avoid having numerous persons make similar comments. In such cases, of course, he mentions this fact in his covering letter to the editor, who should, of course, alert the reader to the use of the device.

Among the earliest examples of this new journalism technique was an article about prostitution written by *New York* magazine writer Gail Sheehy, in which the hustler she called Redpants was actually a composite of the many hustlers she interviewed over several weeks.

Computerized typing equipment. (*See: word processor.*)

Conceit. A particularly striking or imaginative extended image or metaphor found most often in poetry, especially in Elizabethan verse and the work of the seventeenth-century metaphysical poets. Robert Frost's poem "Departmental," in which a community of ants is treated as a bureaucracy, is a modern conceit. (*See: metaphor.*)

Concept. A general statement regarding a screenplay or teleplay. It is usually created before the outline or treatment is written. A concept, which is a general idea about a situation or a character in a story, is more vague and less developed than a premise, which indicates the story's beginning, middle, and resolution. (*See: premise; screenwriting; television script; television writing.*)

Condensation and copyright law. (*See: adaptation.*)

Confession. The confession is a first-person story in which the narrator is involved in an emotional situation that encourages sympathetic reader identification, concluding with the affirmation of a morally acceptable theme. The basic story themes of love, anger, or fear, based on everyday problems, are intended primarily for female readers ranging in age from pre-teen to senior citizen, although there is a small male readership as well. Published for the most part without a byline, confession stories give the writer the advantage of anonymity, especially with regard to writing freely about personal problems. While following basic story structure, confessions are generally introspective episodes written with sincerity, rather than tongue-in-cheek sophistication. Confessions run from 1,500-12,000 words long, the greatest demand being for 5,000- to 6,000-word stories.

Confessions are written in one of two structural formats. The formula confession begins with the narrator facing, or about to face, an identifiable problem that has arisen through some character flaw or "wrong" attitude—sufficiently motivated to insure reader sympathy. The viewpoint character muddles through obstacles en route to an emotionally satisfying solution. This "sin-suffer-repent" format is still used in the standard confession, but it is less melodramatic than in the original stories of sixty years ago; today the narrator profits from her experience and reaches new maturity.

The non-formula story deals with a narrator struggling to solve a problem that has occurred through no fault of her own. In either confession format, the "lesson learned" and consequent growth in human understanding are meant to stimulate growth in the reader.

Confessions can also be classified by subject matter. One common type of confession is in the *family problem* category. There is also the *inspirational* story, in which the narrator overcomes some handicap, and the *documentary*, which explores a problem (often medical) or dispels a myth with up-to-date, authoritative information. The *tabloid* confession is usually a frank sexual account that does not depend on reader identification. The *romance* story emphasizes dating and courtship, rather than sex. There is also room for humor, the supernatural, and suspense writing in the confession writer's craft.

Currently about twenty confession magazines are on the stands, averaging eight or nine stories an issue. Rates usually run from 3¢ to 5¢ per word, paid on publication. Both *Writer's Market* and *Fiction Writer's Market* give details on submission requirements. (*See: first person short story.*)

Conflict. Conflict is one of the prime ingredients of fiction. It usually represents some obstacle to the main character's goals; in order for the reader to be concerned about the resolution of the conflict, that resolution must have consequence for the main character.

Any conflict in fiction can be defined by one of five themes. Although we're using the traditional expression "man"—obviously, all these themes apply to either men or women. *Man against himself* can be manifest in a character's conflicting emotions, which sometimes involves a battle with the conscience. Many of Henry James's protagonists—for instance, John Marcher in "The Beast in the Jungle"—live in such inner turmoil. The conflict of *man against man* can take either a psychological or physical form; it places a goal or the well-being of the main character in jeopardy because of another character. In *Wuthering Heights*, for example, Heathcliff is in conflict with practically every other character.

When a writer places *man against environment*, something in the character's societal surroundings—a city, a government, a social class—causes the conflict; the American naturalistic writers of the late nineteenth and early twentieth centuries—Theodore Dreiser and Stephen Crane, for example—were preoccupied with this problem. Similarly, natural surroundings can threaten a character; in this type of conflict—*man against nature*—the opposition to the protagonist can be either a natural setting or a natural disaster. Jack London's "To Build a Fire" is a classic story of conflict with nature.

A fictional situation may also place *man against the machine*. Since machines do not possess volition, there are few pure examples of such conflict, but the Frank Norris muckraking novel *The Octopus*, which deals with the sprawling prewar American railway system, can be read as man versus technology. (*See: climax; crisis; plot.*)

Conflict of interest. This is an issue of ethics that confronts newspaper editors and reporters, as well as freelance writers. Its basic cause is the simultaneous need to serve readers and to maintain associations with other businesses.

Conflict of interest can occur when a reporter or newspaper uses information obtained in the gathering of news for his/their own benefit, or suppresses or distorts news for his/their own or someone else's benefit. When a newspaper reporter moonlights at a public relations job, for example, or writes speeches for political candidates, what he is doing in his second job—promoting products or people—may interfere with his fair and accurate reporting of the news in his first job. Other conflicts involve a newsperson's appearance in commercials; a reporter's writing about a news event he was somehow involved in; journalists' working for the CIA; and a newspaper's including or omitting copy to satisfy advertisers.

For freelancers, conflict of interest is presented by some freebies and junkets (typically offered to writers on travel, food, and cosmetics, who must attempt objective reporting despite the financial support of the supplier). On the other hand, a magazine, for example, may be backing a political candidate and so refuse to publish a negative story about him. That may not be "objective," but the magazine is under no obligation to be so. Its editors can pick and choose what they want to publish, what slant they want to take, etc., whereas a newspaper is expected to print the news—unslanted and in its entirety, with no angles concealed. (*See: press trip.*)

Conglomerates—book publishers. In recent years, some book publishers have been purchased by companies unrelated to publishing, thereby joining conglomerates. Although some corporate owners grant a certain amount of autonomy to publishers, others subject them to restrictions that may prove harmful to beginning authors. For example, a publishing house that is part of a conglomerate may be less likely to gamble on a first novel.

On the other hand, as Dean Koontz points out in *How to Write Best-Selling Fiction,* conglomerate takeovers in the past 15 years have strongly influenced publishers' advertising and marketing techniques, so that some books are exposed to a much larger audience than they were in the past. This situation can, of course, increase the writer's income.

Literary Market Place listings for book publishers indicate if they are a subdivision of a parent company, which may be either another publishing firm or a corporation unrelated to publishing. (*See: book promotion; magazine publishers, multiple.*)

Additional information: *How to Write Best-Selling Fiction.*

Congressional Directory. This volume, available in most libraries, furnishes the names and addresses of all current members of Congress, along with details on committee assignments, federal agencies, members of the judiciary, foreign representatives and consular offices in the United States, and other data. Of particular interest to writers are the names of all reporters or photographers (and the publications and broadcast media they represent) who are accredited to the press galleries in Congress. Representatives of consumer and specialized magazines are included, as well as newspapers, wire services, radio and television networks, and station representatives. (*See: press galleries.*)

Consent. (*See: libel.*)

Consequence, a sense of. *Esquire*'s fiction editor Rust Hills reminds fiction writers that "Whatever happens must happen to someone and must have consequence to him. A lot can happen in a story or novel—a man can be shot by another man or go crazy in the jungle—but if there is no sense of the consequence of these events to someone, then they might as well go unrecounted; they are artistically pointless." Fiction writers need always examine their stories to see that the conflicts faced and resolved by their characters leave readers with this sense of consequence. (*See: conflict; plot.*)

Consulting. Writers who have developed specialties can serve as consultants to businesses, educational institutions, and other organizations that produce their own films, books, and other materials. A consultant's big advantage to a company is objectivity: he is freer to criticize and suggest changes than an employee is, and he can concentrate solely on his task without taking the time to become part of an operation. A consultant does not have to go to staff meetings, which enables him to produce relatively more than staffers in the same amount of time. A consultant also need not be concerned with office politics, or with internal advancement.

The usual qualifications for a consultant, according to Consultant Richard A. Stemm, include a combination of formal education, practical experience, and seasoning; and the ability to maintain a mental storehouse of information and experiential knowledge.

Stemm advises the would-be full-time consultant to prepare for a consulting career one or two years before he actually begins a practice. Preparation consists of becoming acquainted with the necessary jargon and with jobs at all levels in the field, reading trade journals, and attending meetings of professional organizations.

Experts disagree on the best approach. Some say marketing consulting services through indirect means is preferable to directly approaching a prospective client. A consultant can make his name known through articles in trade journals, and giving seminars and speeches. He can also contact professional acquaintances for leads. As his experience increases, the consultant is likely to receive referrals.

On the other hand, the direct approach of advertising in trade journals is also recommended.

A consultant's fees are based on the comparable amount he is capable of earning as an employee. Since he must earn enough to cover insurance and other benefits that would be paid an employee by a corporation, he increases the hourly rate he is capable of receiving by 2½-3 times. Expenses required by the consultant to travel out of town or spend the night in a motel are paid for by the client, but the cost of commuting to and from the client's office (when the distance is 50 miles or less) is paid for by the consultant. Billing procedures vary, and many consultants request that part of the total fee be paid in advance.

The *Consultants and Consulting Organizations Directory* lists individuals and organizations in 135 fields. Names, addresses, phone numbers, and descriptions of services are included in the listings, which are cross-referenced by geographic location, subject, names of persons, and names of companies. Specialist writer-consultants who want to be listed should contact the publisher (Gale Research Company, Book Tower, Detroit MI 48226) regarding eligibility requirements.

Consumer magazines. Those publications aimed at the reader of general interest, sport, hobby, or other specialized consumer interest material; as opposed to magazines aimed toward business, professional, and trade interests.

Contest writing. This term is usually applied to the short, original entries that are submitted in competition for prize and profit. Contest writing usually involves composing prose or rhyme, often in response to a request for a product-praising statement, jingle, slogan, name, or caption. It uses parodies, analogies, and take-offs on current speech as well as triad constructions (Our apples are *selected* for their flavor, *inspected* for their quality and *protected* for your pleasure), to make a point or sell a product.

Contest writers understand the particular requirements of various games and respond with the necessary research to produce concise, fluent, catchy entries. They vie for prizes of money, vacations, or product samples. Participants equip themselves with the tools of the literary trade—standard dictionary, thesaurus, rhyming dictionary. They recognize that judges often look for timely, topical writing.

Contest announcements appear in newspapers, magazines, company publications, even in grocery stores. Several publications of interest to contest writers are listed in *The Newsletter Yearbook Directory*, and books on how to be successful in contest writing are listed under "Rewards (Prizes, Etc.)" in the *Subject Guide to Books In Print*.

The National Contesters Association (NCA) represents persons interested in contest writing. It sponsors an annual meeting and publishes a bulletin for members. Information can be obtained from President Jesse Long, 406 Hamilton Road, Knoxville TN 37920, for a self-addressed, stamped envelope. (*See: contests, writing.*)

Contests, writing. While "contest writing" usually refers to the short statements or jingles composed for prizes or money, there are other contests open to writers working in a variety of literary forms. The directory *Gadney's Guide to 1500 International Contests, Festivals and Grants in Film and Video, Photography, TV-Radio Broadcasting, Writing, Playwriting and Journalism* is one such detailed compilation. Four individual directories of *How to Enter and Win Fiction Writing Contests, Film Contests, Nonfiction/*

Journalism Contests, and Video and Audio Contests by Alan Gadney have been published by Facts on File Publications. Other sources are the "Contests and Awards" section of *Fiction Writer's Market* , and "Prize Contests Open" in *Literary Market Place.*

Literary contests offer writers an incentive (prestige, money) and a self-imposed deadline by which to produce a specific manuscript that may also have other marketing potential after the contest is over.

Some literary prizes are awarded by sponsoring organizations and cannot be competed for directly by the writer. Many of these are listed in the directory *Literary and Library Prizes*. Information on major literary awards such as the Nobel or Pulitzer Prize is provided in the individual entries in this encyclopedia.

Continuing education. Writers and professionals in writing-related fields have several options available for keeping abreast of their fields once they have completed their formal college education. (A good liberal arts background is a given for any writer.)

In addition to local universities which may offer classes in professionally related topics, professional organizations offer periodic educational workshops, seminars, and conferences. American Women in Radio and Television; Public Relations Society of America; Society of Professional Journalists, Sigma Delta Chi; and Women in Communications, Inc., are a few such organizations.

Folio: The Magazine for Magazine Management sponsors an annual conference for practitioners in magazine and book publishing. In addition, courses such as Harvard's Radcliffe Publishing Procedures Course and others throughout the country are described in Petersen's *Guide to Book Publishing Courses.* Some programs, such as the Nieman Fellowships in Journalism at Harvard, are specifically designed for working professionals who want to take a year's leave of absence and return to the university for a period of intensive study in their specialty.

Of course, in addition to courses specifically related to careers in writing, freelance writers also seek information and education in new areas of interest about which to write, whether it's a trip to Spain related to a historical novel, or a course in computers for a nonfiction book. (*See: correspondence courses for writers; publishing, courses in.*)

Continuity. Commercials and other spoken parts of a radio program. Also refers to the spoken part of a commercial.

Contributing editor. A person who writes for a magazine on a continuous basis is sometimes called a contributing editor of the magazine and is so listed on the masthead. A contributing editor is an expert on a subject of special interest to readers of the magazine he writes for. Usually a contributing editor is an author who has written a number of articles on a freelance basis for a magazine, and whom the editor has chosen because he perceives a need in his audience for this writer's knowledge. He may write a regular column for

an agreed-on fee or submit ideas for and be given a specific number of article assignments annually.

Contributor's copies. An author's copies of his own work (such as a book) or of the issue of a publication in which his work appears, sent by some publishers either as partial payment or full payment. Literary/little magazines and small presses often pay only in contributor's copies.

Co-op copy. Radio advertising for a store in which a manufacturer's name is mentioned; the spot is paid for partly by the store and partly by the manufacturer. (*See: cooperative [co-op] advertising.*)

Cooperative (co-op) advertising. Although it could be for any product or service, as it applies most frequently to writers it is a form of print advertising in which a publisher's book is featured in an ad for a particular bookstore. The publisher pays a lower rate for cooperative advertising than he would pay for his own ad, since co-op ads are charged the retail rate (applied to bookstores) rather than the higher national rate (applied to publishers). The publisher and bookstore owner arrange between themselves the way to divide the total cost of the ad; the publisher pays his share of the cost to the bookstore rather than to the newspaper or magazine. In addition, the publisher often supplies a camera-ready ad free to the bookstore. Unfortunately for the average writer, a lot of this co-op advertising goes to the bestselling titles for which the bookstores have large inventories, rather than to a first novel or a mid-list book. (*See: mid-list books.*)

Cooperative publishing. (*See: co-publishing; poetry book publishing.*)

Coordinating Council of Literary Magazines (CCLM). This organization provides grants to noncommercial literary magazines that have published at least three issues and have been publishing for at least one year. It sponsors annual regional workshops in conjunction with its annual meeting of editors and writers. CCLM publications include the CCLM *Newsletter*, the CCLM *Catalog of Literary Magazines*, the CCLM *Catalog of Undergraduate Literary Magazines*, and *A Guide to Organizing and Exhibiting at Bookfairs*.

CCLM maintains a 12,000-volume library of literary magazines and small press publications that is open to the public five days a week. Its headquarters are at 2 Park Ave., Suite 1809, New York NY 10016.

Co-publishing. Publication of a book by two publishers (often a hardcover and a paperback publisher; but could also include a U.S. and foreign publisher, a publisher and a foundation, etc.). The term also refers to an agreement, usually underscored by a contract, in which both a book publisher and an author pay for publishing costs and receive profits. Small publishing houses are likely to work under this system.

One advantage of co-publishing is that the author has some influence in the production and promotion of his book. The disadvantage is that he must contribute not only the creative product but a financial investment as well. (*See: self-publishing.*)

Copyeditor. Copyediting positions are found in book, magazine, journal, and newspaper publishing. A copyeditor corrects faulty grammar, spelling, and punctuation in a manuscript, and improves readability when necessary. He checks to see that the work conforms to the publisher's style, and that specifications for typefaces and type sizes are correct. (*See: editing, freelance; editor, content.*)

Copyfitting. A magazine editor's job that involves calculating how many magazine column-inches a typed manuscript will take up once it is typeset; or, conversely, how much typed copy is needed to fill a fixed amount of magazine space.

Various systems for copyfitting exist, including the em system, the square-inch method, and the character-count method. The character-count method is considered the most accurate for magazine and advertising copy, and will be explained here.

To use this system, the editor must know how many characters occupy a typeset line; to find that figure, he consults a *type book*—a system of charts devised by typesetting machine manufacturers for use by printers, editors, and art directors. Type books give the correct character count per *pica* (the standard unit of measure for magazine layout; six picas equal an inch) for every type size a particular typeface is available in.

To find what amount of magazine space a manuscript will fill, the editor first determines the total number of typed characters in the manuscript (each space between words counts as one character). He does this by measuring the line width—pica typewriters type 10 characters per inch; elite typewriters, 12—and either totaling the individual line counts, or finding the average line count and multiplying it by the number of lines in the manuscript. The editor then divides the resultant figure by the number of characters per typeset line (as determined from the chart in the type book) to get the number of typeset lines the copy will occupy.

In facing the other problem—i.e., finding how much copy must be written to fill a given area—the editor simply reverses the process. He divides the depth of the space to be filled (measured in *points*: 12 points per pica) by the depth of each line (also in points; usually one or two points greater than the type size) to get the number of lines of typeset copy that will fill the space. He multiplies the number of lines by the character count (which he finds in the type book) to get the total character count for the area, then divides by the average number of characters in a typewritten line to get the number of typed lines the copy must be.

While copyfitting is a complicated process to describe, in practice it is relatively simple. An experienced editor can quickly gauge manuscript length and estimate how many column-inches it will be, typeset. Absolute precision in word count is seldom necessary, since magazine layout can usually be adjusted to allow for a little more or less copy.

Copyright. A proprietary right designed to give the creator of a work the power to control that work's reproduction, distribution, and public display or performance, as well as its adaptation to other forms.

Teachers, students, and others may excerpt parts of copyrighted material for nonprofit use, in some cases, without infringing on copyrights. (This provision of the copyright law is outlined under the heading "fair use" in this encyclopedia.)

The law considers literary works, musical works, and dramatic works to be copyrightable. Derivative works, or modifications of existing works, are also copyrightable; this includes translations, dramatizations, fictionalizations, screenplays, abridgments, and condensations. Compilations, such as magazines or anthologies, are also copyrightable material. U.S. government publications are not copyrightable; however, a freelancer may be able to obtain copyrights on work produced for the government under a grant or contract, i.e., when the writer is not a regular employee of the government. Titles, ideas, jokes, and other items are *not* copyrightable. (See entry on "public domain" in this encyclopedia.)

One change brought about by the Copyright Revision Act of 1976 (which became effective January 1, 1978) is that statutory copyright exists in a work as soon as it is created in tangible form, even if it has not been published, and whether or not it has been registered with the U.S. Copyright Office. (However, even though an unregistered work is copyrighted, registration is required before a writer can bring an infringement suit.) Under the original law, a literary work had to be published in order to be protected under statutory law; it was protected under common law between the time it was created and the time it was published.

Registration is accomplished through the U.S. Copyright Office, which supplies the registrant with the appropriate application form. The registration fee is currently $10; sometimes a group of works by the same author can be registered for a single fee. A work need not be published in order to secure copyright registration.

Copyright notice, consisting of the symbol © and/or the word *copyright* (or an abbreviation of it), the copyright owner's name, and the year of publication, must be placed on all copies of a work that are intended to be distributed to the public. The owner can lose the copyright for neglecting to include the notice, but he has some lawful recourse. (This subject is discussed further in the entry "copyright notice.") An author's individual copyright notice is especially important when his copyrighted work appears in an uncopyrighted publication. But when a piece copyrighted by an author appears in a copyrighted publication— a magazine, for example—without the individual's copyright notice, and the publication does not own the copyright to the individual piece, the writer is still usually protected.

The owner of a copyright may transfer his copyright or any part of it to another party. For example, the copyright owner may transfer only the right to translate his work to one individual, and only the right to abridge his work to another. For works copyrighted after January 1, 1978, the copyright owner may, 35 years after the transfer took place, regain the rights he has transferred. Publication rights may be regained at the earlier of these two dates: 35 years after the date of publication, or

40 years after the date of execution of the grant. Termination of a grant must occur within the five-year period that begins at the end of the specified terms.

Copyright protection lasts for the duration of the owner's life plus the 50 years following his death. On collaborative works, the life of the last surviving owner determines the term of copyright, i.e., protection lasts 50 years following the death of the last surviving collaborator. On anonymous works, pseudonymous works, and works made for hire, the copyright expires either 75 years after the work's first publication or 100 years after its creation, whichever is reached first. The term of copyright was revised with the latest law, so those works protected under statutory law as of December 31, 1977 (i.e., covered under the previous law *and published*), retain their original term of protection, 28 years. These works must be reregistered before December 31st of the 28th year for future copyright protection; the new law increases the second term to 47 years. (It was previously 28 years.) Works that were not copyrighted prior to January 1, 1978 (and therefore covered under common law), now are protected for a term of the author's life plus the following 50 years; however, the law stipulates that coverage will be in effect until at least December 31, 2002, and if the work is published on or before that date, copyright protection lasts until at least December 31, 2027. In 1983 the oldest book that might still be in copyright would be dated 1908. In 1986, the oldest book possibly still in copyright would be dated 1911.

When a freelance writer creates a work made for hire, the buyer of the work is also obtaining the copyright.

When a writer works for an organization as an employee and produces creative works as part of his job, the copyright to those works belongs to the employer.

An amendment to the new copyright law also, as of July, 1982, extended the manufacturing clause until July, 1986. This provision limits the number of copies of certain kinds of works that can both be manufactured abroad and enjoy copyright protection in the U.S. (*See: copyright notice; Copyright, Register of; fair use; infringement of copyright; international copyright; International Copyright Convention; public domain; work made for hire.*)

Copyright Clearance Center. With limited exception, the copyright act of 1978 requires that individuals and institutions wishing to photocopy copyrighted materials must obtain permission to do so from copyright owners. In response to this act, the Association of American Publishers (AAP) established the Copyright Clearance Center to serve as a centralized agency responsible for recording eligible photocopying, granting permission to use registered materials, collecting fees, and processing royalty payments. The 1,800 members of the CCC include photocopy users (e.g. libraries, research institutes, universities, and others who regularly use or distribute photocopy material—as opposed to the single individual who makes one copy for his own use); and copyright owners such as publishers and authors.

The widespread use of photocopying equipment and the increasing development in photocopying technology make it difficult for the CCC to monitor the photocopying of copyrighted materials. The Center estimates that it receives reports of only six percent of the photocopying activity for which permission from copyright owners is required. This type of copyright infringement affects not only publishers' earnings, but consequently authors' incomes. The CCC cannot accomplish its established goal—to distribute the full earnings amount to which each publisher-member is entitled—until the reporting volume level rises.

To strengthen its effectiveness, the CCC is attempting to broaden publisher participation in the organization, and to educate and inform the public about copyright law requirements regarding photocopy use. CCC publications include two quarterly catalogs, *Guide to CCC-Participating Document Delivery Services* and *Publishers' Photocopy Fee Catalog*, and two semiannual volumes, *Directory of Registered Publishers* and *Directory of Registered Users*.

The address of the Copyright Clearance Center is 27 Congress Street, Salem MA 01970. (*See: copyright; fair use.*)

Copyright notice. The law requires that a copyright notice appear on all copies of a copyrighted work that are destined for public distribution. Copyright notice consists of the copyright symbol ©, used internationally, (or the word "copyright" or the abbreviation "Copr."), the year the work was first published, and the copyright owner's name. It usually is published on the reverse of the title page of a book and on the contents page of a magazine.

If the copyright notice has been omitted from copies of a work, the copyright is still valid, according to law, under the following conditions: 1) notice is absent from "a relatively small number" of the copies made available to the public; 2) the work is registered within five years after publication and the owner makes a "reasonable effort" to place the copyright notice on copies distributed in the United States; or 3) the owner stipulated that notice be included before distribution but his instructions were disregarded by another.

While a copyright exists for works created on or after January 1, 1978 from the moment of creation, the year stated in the copyright notice is generally the year of publication of the work.

The law regards a work as having no copyright notice if: 1) the notice includes a date that is more than one year later than the year of first publication, or 2) either a name or a date has been omitted from the notice.

Copyright page. (*See: copyright notice.*)

Copyright, Register of. The U.S. Copyright Office can inform the writer of current fees for copyright registration and for copyright search, a procedure that determines whether or not a work has been registered with the Office. It can also provide the writer with applications for copyright registration. The copyright office can be reached at Register of Copyright, Copyright Office, Library of Congress, Washington DC 20559, phone (202) 287-8700.

Forms on which application for registration is made are coded by category of creation. A new form, Form SE, is used by those who wish to register a serial, such as a magazine or newspaper; Form TX is used to register literary work other than drama, as well as non-dramatic works to be included in serials and to which the author, rather than the publisher, owns the copyright (see sample copyright form in the Appendix to this encyclopedia); Form PA registers a work of the performing arts; with Form GR/CP, a writer applies for registration of a group of pieces intended for periodicals. Form RE is used to renew registration; Form CA, for a supplementary registration. For a list of free copyright circulars, also see the Appendix in this encyclopedia. (*See: copyright; copyright notice.*)

Copyright-free art. Examples of art in the styles of different historical periods are compiled into books and sold to editors and publishers. Such illustrations can be used in advertisements, brochures, books, and magazines.

Editors of small magazines, company publications, and other publications with limited budgets may find such sources a money-saver.

One source of copyright-free art is Dover Publications, Inc., 180 Varick Street, New York NY 10014, which publishes books of old illustrations, borders, ornaments, etc. Another company that produces books of specialized art subjects on gummed repro paper (which can be cut out and pasted down as camera-ready art) is Graphic Products Corp., Rolling Meadows IL 60008. (*See: clip art.*)

Correspondence courses for writers. Writers may participate in organized study by means of courses conducted through the mail that are designed to provide them with incentives to write and deadlines to keep. Home study courses allow motivated students to further their training in a convenient alternative to the classroom.

There are two main sources for learning through the mail. Some universities offer correspondence courses for writers on both credit and non-credit bases. In addition to writing courses, studies in English, literature, cartooning, and photography are available. Other correspondence courses are offered by privately-operated schools, which frequently advertise in issues of *The Writer* and *Writer's Digest*. They teach students how to write for specific commercial markets, e.g., newspapers, magazines. The instructors, who ideally are themselves published writers, critique student work on assignments.

Good candidates for correspondence courses are disciplined individuals who work independently and with minimal guidance. They accept the fact that no home study course guarantees future success as a published writer. They choose a specific writing course for its purpose and subject matter; they consider its costs, length of time to complete, quality of instructional material, and the credentials of the instructor.

Education expenses—whether for a college class or a home study course—incurred for improving an individual's performance in a trade or profession are tax deductible. (*See: Associated Writing Programs.*)

Correspondent. (*See: stringer.*)

Council of Writers Organizations. This is a group comprising the following writers' organizations: the American Society of Journalists and Authors, Associated Business Writers of America, Aviation/Space Writers Association, Dance Critics Association of America, Eastern Ski Writers, Editorial Freelancers Association, Garden Writers of America, The I.B.W. (business writers), International Motor Press Association, Media Alliance, Mystery Writers of America, National Association of Science Writers, National Book Critics Circle, Outdoor Writers Association of America, Science Fiction Writers of America, Society of American Travel Writers, Travel Journalists Guild, United States Ski Writers Association, Washington (DC) Independent Writers, and Writers Guild of America, East.

While each organization remains a separate entity, the 21 groups work collectively on certain research projects to aid writers, such as insurance, taxation, magazine rates, book contracts, and copyrights. The Council also shares research and information among its members.

The address of the Council of Writers Organizations is care of the American Society of Journalists and Authors, 1501 Broadway, Suite 1907, New York NY 10036.

Council of Writing Program Administrators. This professional organization was established to address the needs of and disseminate knowledge among U.S. and Canadian college and university writing program administrators.

The Council publishes a journal three times per academic year; its focus is the professional interests of Council members, which are specialized in that they relate to a combination teaching-administrative objective. Information on the journal can be obtained from the English Department, University of Louisville, Louisville KY 40292. (*See: Associated Writing Programs.*)

Counterplot. (*See: subplot.*)

Cover letter. A letter accompanying a completed manuscript. A cover letter is especially useful as a reminder when submitting finished material that has been requested by an editor. It is not necessary when there has been no previous correspondence and the manuscript must be judged on the writing style itself, as in the case of fiction or humor.

The cover letter may request an editor's response within a reasonable length of time if the topic is timely. No rates or fees should be mentioned in the letter, since most publications' rates are listed in *Writer's Market*. No biographical information about the writer is included unless the manuscript requires credentials by the author in a specific area of expertise.

Editors generally discourage writers from submitting letters with completed unsolicited manuscripts.

Creativity. Creativity can be described as the potential of human beings to be inventive and original.

Scientists and lay people alike have long grappled with an explanation of the creative process. What is generally accepted is the belief that every person is creative to some degree, and in some capacity. Whereas intelligence is an individual's capacity to learn and reason, creativity goes beyond the acquisition of knowledge or skill to the development and expression of a unique point of view. Though there is no clear-cut, established relationship between creativity and intelligence, it is fairly certain that creativity does

not require a high I.Q.—nor does a high I.Q. guarantee creativity. Rather, the potential for original and imaginative response—creativity—is present in every person having some measure of intellectual ability.

Creativity may be nurtured and cultivated. It is like a muscle that atrophies without exercise. It may be fostered at any stage of life so long as the individual is able to transcend his previous exposure to the trite and the stereotyped. Creativity germinates in a creative atmosphere—that is, a setting, circumstance or situation in which a person is free to apply his energy and enthusiasm to perceiving relationships around him and being conscious of his life experience. For some people, a creative atmosphere might be reading a book; for others, it might be a quiet walk or the noise of a big city. Establishing a creative environment is as essential to writers and other artists as possessing the techniques and disciplines of their craft.

The process of creativity may often result in some end product—a written work, a piece of sculpture, a song. The work is in fact "creative" if the process produces a unique result that communicates with its audience on an emotional as well as an intellectual level.

Credit line. The name of the photographer or illustrator or company or institution that supplied a photograph, diagram, chart, or artwork to a magazine or book. The name is usually typeset alongside the published illustration or printed with the page number on an acknowledgments page. When a writer obtains illustration material from a business or institution, credit lines may be required and are usually indicated on the back of the photograph, drawing, etc. Writers should call such requirements to the attention of the editor.

Crime writing. This term refers to nonfiction accounts, published in detective magazines, of real crimes that detail how they were committed and ultimately solved. The true crime story is neither an unsolved nor an open-shut case. (For legal reasons, most editors will not consider a story until the suspect is indicted.) It is usually a crime filled with false clues and suspects, mysterious leads, suspenseful sleuthing, and sexual encounters. The detective work represents the bulk of the story. Most true crime stories are murders (often with female killers or victims), but intricate cases of rape, kidnapping, assault, and robbery are potential articles. They are timely, chronological tales that may include colorful biographical sketches of the protagonists.

The stuff of crime writing is found in the news. Crime writers use police detectives, autopsy findings, coroner's inquest reports, and newspaper clippings to find out what happened and to build their accounts accordingly. Besides covering the five W's and H of newspaper writing, true crime stories add action and human emotion to the facts. Though their movement is fast paced and suspenseful, the stories never veer from the truth. (Crime writers keep all verifying documents, as they are asked to submit them to the editor with the completed manuscript.)

Crime writing sells best if it is accompanied by pictures. It is common for a story to appear with as many as eight 8x10 photographs.

They may be taken by the writer himself, obtained from newspaper photo files, or gathered from the detective on the case. Pictures of the main officer on the case, the suspect and victim, the scene of the crime, and any significant equipment or weapons used in the crime add to the reality of the story.

There are about a dozen magazines devoted specifically to this genre, as well as general interest and men's magazines that buy true crime stories. *Writer's Market* lists magazines and their submission requirements. Though many crime story magazines have regular staff writers, freelancers may provide accounts of intriguing crimes committed close to their homes. A detailed query letter on the case should precede any actual manuscript submission. Magazines that buy true crime stories usually try to buy all rights to them.

Crisis. In fiction, the word *crisis* refers to part of the plot that represents a turning point. A crisis arises from a conflict, the forces of which take action to effect a turning point. The result of a crisis is a climax, which refers to the degree of emotion elicited from the reader.

A novel can contain a series of crises, but a short story contains only one. In a short story, the major character experiences a crisis in two steps: the dark moment/black moment, and the moment of revelation, the latter of which results in a change in the character. (*See: character change; climax; dark moment/black moment.*)

Criticism. This term applies to a piece written to analyze a work of art. Criticism is distinguished from the arts review in several ways. It is written in a more scholarly tone by a writer who is well versed in the particular art form he writes about. Criticism is usually published in some magazines and journals; it would be inappropriate in a newspaper, since most of the general public is not interested in such in-depth analysis. By the same token, newspaper reviews necessarily display a different style; lofty language and too much profundity serve only to alienate the newspaper reviewer's readers.

While a review is an account of a performance or work, often providing subjectivity through an audience reaction, criticism depends on the writer's educated perspective for reaction and judgment. Criticism, in contrast to the arts review, discusses the particular work in relation to the art form it reflects.

Karl Shapiro wrote that ". . . a good work of criticism is a work of art about another work of art." A critique can, indeed, stand on its own literary merits. The criticism of George Bernard Shaw, for example, is still read today. His criticism of music has been compiled in *Shaw's Music: The Complete Musical Criticism.* (*See: arts review; book review; drama criticism; restaurant review.*)

Criticism of manuscript. An evaluation of a written work by a person who, through experience and knowledge of the marketplace, has acquired expertise to judge it objectively. Valuable criticism comes from editors and writers skilled in pointing out strengths and weaknesses in fiction and nonfiction technique. The art of receiving criticism is tied up with being able to distinguish between helpful comments from professionals, and well-meaning but useless or possibly harmful comments from other people who may read the manuscript—and then using the significant remarks accordingly.

Some firms that offer criticism services for writers advertise in *Writer's Digest.* (*See: self-criticism.*)

Cumulative Book Index: A World List of Books in the English Language (CBI). This publication lists books published in the English language; its scope is worldwide. Published monthly except August, it has been in existence since 1928. Issues are accumulated annually.

Listings in this index are categorized by author, title, and subject. (*See:* National Union Catalog.)

Customs reminders for writers. Persons returning to the United States from abroad are charged a duty on items purchased in foreign countries. The total value of items purchased is assessed in the U.S., and an exemption is granted, the amount of which depends on the country the person has traveled to. Limitations are placed on imports of cars, pets, and products bearing certain trademarks.

Foreign-made equipment such as cameras, typewriters, and tape recorders taken abroad could be taxed upon the traveler's return to the U.S. To avoid this situation, the writer should be able to provide proof—such as a sales slip—that he purchased it before leaving the U.S.; or he can obtain a form from U.S. Customs before leaving the country to cover this problem.

More information on customs can be obtained from the Department of the Treasury, U.S. Customs Service, Washington DC 20229.

Writer-photographers are also cautioned about the possibility of airport x-ray machines fogging their film. They can usually have airport security personnel hand-check their equipment, thus avoiding the risk of such damages.

Cut to. An editing direction. In motion pictures or television, the shift from one scene to another without using a fade or a dissolve. Also, *cut*. (*See: dissolve; fade in; fade out.*)

Cutline. (*See: caption [cutline].*)

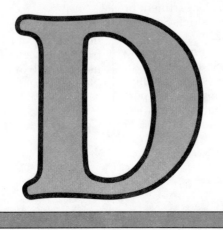

Dance Critics Association (DCA).
Members of DCA are full-time and
freelance dance critics and others interested in dance writing, such as
teachers, historians, and publicists.
Voting members, associate members, and student members make up
its ranks.

The DCA's committees include
Critics' Training and Publications. It
publishes the quarterly *DCA Newsletter*, and pamphlets such as "Copyright for Newspaper and Magazine
Writers," "Training Opportunities
for Dance Critics," and "Research
Sources for Dance Writers."

DCA's annual conference, usually
held in New York City in June, features talks by prominent persons in
the field, films, and workshops. According to DCA, the conference provides "a chance for critics and other
interested people from across the
country to meet together and explore ways to be more effective in
their profession."

The address of the Dance Critics
Association is 127 W. 83rd St., New
York NY 10024. (*See: Council of Writ-
ers Organizations.*)

Dark moment/black moment. This
forms a part of the short story structure. At the beginning of the crisis,
the protagonist experiences a *dark
moment* (also called *black moment*)
when his problem has increased to
such proportion that he can conceive
of no solution for it; moreover, the
conflict action in the crisis forces the
central character to make a decision
that resolves the problem. This decision at the end of the crisis leads to
the character change. (*See: character
change; crisis.*)

Data bases. Data bases are a relatively new method of doing research.
They have been used in science and
industry since the mid-fifties and by
academic and public libraries since
the early seventies.

A data base is a collection of specialized information that is stored in
a computer. Depending on the type
of information it contains, a data
base is labeled either "numeric" or
"bibliographic." Numeric data bases
lead the researcher to numbers and
statistics, and bibliographic data
bases lead him to citations and/or

summaries of textual material.

Compustat II (Standard and Poor's Compustat Services, Inc.), for example, is a numeric data base that houses financial information on industrial companies, banks, and utilities. Included are balance sheets, trading data, statements of income, sources of funds, and uses of funds. An example of a bibliographic data base is *Educational Resources Information Center* (ERIC), which cites documents in the field of education.

In general, three types of establishments house data bases: libraries, corporations, and government agencies. Data bases in academic and public libraries are accessible to the freelance writer, but some data bases controlled by government and industry contain classified information and are therefore closed to the public. Some government information, however, is a matter of public record.

To utilize a data base, the researcher can proceed in one of two ways. He can request that a librarian do a computer search. The result of such a search is a printout containing references to books or periodicals or other information sources pertaining to his research topic. When using this procedure it is important for the researcher to state the topic as specifically and clearly as possible in order to avoid a more complex—and therefore more expensive—search than is needed. For example, the writer may be researching learning disabilities, but may be interested in that subject only insofar as it relates to children under 12 years of age in American public schools. The data base would probably contain many other aspects of the topic "learning disabilities," and if the information input

into the computer were not qualified according to the writer's needs, the majority of the resulting sources would be irrelevant to the writer's project.

The library charges the researcher for a computer search: fees generally range from $15-$40 but can be lower or higher, depending on the library and how much computer time is used and how many sources are found.

Alternatively, the researcher can learn what information is housed in a particular data base by perusing its index, which is usually a set of bound volumes. For example, *Resources in Education* is a group of indexes to materials compiled by ERIC. The researcher may check its title index, subject index, or institution index, then obtain a microfiche version of the document at the library or a printed version from a document reproduction service.

A computer search is faster and more complete than a manual one. It can research a topic more specifically, i.e., combine qualifying factors to avoid uncovering irrelevant material, as discussed above. In addition, some data base material is unavailable in printed form; the researcher may only obtain it, in those cases, through a computer search.

The researcher who is unfamiliar with the data base may consult an index that lists the data bases themselves. One such index is *Computer Readable Data Bases: A Directory & Sourcebook*, which contains a subject index and a name index. Another index, the *Directory of Online Databases*, contains a name index.

Examples of data bases available in some libraries are *Economic Abstracts International, Federal Index, New York Times Information Bank, Na-*

tional Institute of Mental Health, and *Psychological Abstracts.*

The Directory of Federal Statistical Data Files, categorized by agency and subject matter, refers the reader to statistical data files of federal departments and agencies. (*See: U.S. government as a resource.*)

Additional information: *Writer's Resource Guide.*

Daybook. A book in which each page corresponds to a day of the month; used by radio advertising copywriters.

DBA. Acronym for *doing business as.* Sometimes used in connection with a writer's pen name. A writer, for example, may notify his local postmaster and bank manager that he is doing business as _____ , his pen name, so that he will safely receive any mail and be able to cash checks in that business name.

Deadline. A specified date and/or time that an article or news story must be turned in to the editor. The writer's deadline is important in the editor's production schedule, which involves a copyeditor, a typesetter, a printer, and other personnel.

In magazine work, a writer has more time between deadlines than he has in newspaper or broadcast newswriting. Short deadlines, of course, require working under pressure, and not all writers can endure the stress of working both quickly and accurately.

Freelance writers learn, with experience, to schedule several projects at once and have them conform to different deadlines. When the freelance writer must miss a dead-line, he should inform the editor as soon as he is aware that he needs more time for the project.

Dedication. A brief inscription in a nonfiction book or novel expressing the author's affection or respect for a person or persons, who may or may not be directly related to the subject matter of the book. Dedications usually appear on the right-hand page directly opposite the reverse side of the title page. The dedication page is one of several preliminary pages the writer prepares after a book has been accepted for publication.

Defamation. (*See: libel.*)

Delta Kappa Alpha. An honorary fraternity of professional and student filmmakers, which exists to encourage association among students and between students and professionals. This organization holds seminars to which professional cinematographers, directors, and editors contribute; it also inducts selected professionals as honorary members.

Delta Kappa Alpha publishes a newsletter three to four times per year. Its committees include the Banquet Committee, Casting Files Committee, Film Festival Committee, Screenings Committee, Special Programs Committee, and Student Films Committee.

Delta Kappa Alpha can be reached at the Division of Cinema Television, USC, University Park, Los Angeles CA 90089.

Dénouement. French for "an untying." The *dénouement* of a novel or story follows the climax; it represents the unraveling of the complexities of a plot, and the clarifying of the story's details and misunderstandings.

Derivative works (and copyright). A derivative work is one that has been translated, adapted, abridged, condensed, annotated, or otherwise produced by altering a previously created work. Derivative works can take many forms, including plays, motion pictures, and revised versions of books.

Before producing a derivative work for publication, it is necessary to secure written permission from the author or the copyright owner of the work on which the new piece will be based. If the original work is in the public domain, however, as in the case of those works first published more than 75 years ago or published in an uncopyrighted periodical, permission from the author is not necessary. (*See: adaptation; copyright; novelization; tie-in.*)

Description. The art of showing the reader how a person, place, or thing looks, tastes, feels, sounds, smells, or acts. It is more than the amassing of details; it is bringing something to life by carefully choosing and arranging words and phrases to produce the desired effect. Here's an example, from John Steinbeck's *Of Mice and Men*:

On the sand banks the rabbits sat as quietly as little, gray, sculptured stones. And then from the direction of the state highway came the sound of footsteps on crisp sycamore leaves. The rabbits hurried noiselessly for cover. A stilted heron labored up into the air and pounded down river.

Description cannot be objective; it always delivers a specific and intentional graphic message to the reader within the context of the work in which it appears.

Detective story. The phrase "detective story" is used by the editors of fact-crime magazines to mean a nonfictional account of a true crime. The term *detective fiction* is used by some mystery magazines to refer to stories in which detectives play a central role. Among book publishers, *novel of suspense* and *thriller* are synonymous, and this type of story may contain elements of mystery, romance, and adventure. (*See: adventure story; mystery story; romance novel.*)

Deus ex machina. This term, meaning "a god from the machine," originated in Greek drama, in which playwrights sometimes introduced a god to resolve a problem so that the play could end. These intervening gods descended onto the stage by means of a mechanical device.

Today, *deus ex machina* is used to refer to any unlikely, contrived, or trick resolution of a plot in any type of fiction. Critics—and readers—generally object to this technique, which is commonly used by beginning writers.

Dial-a-Writer. The American Society of Journalists and Authors (ASJA) maintains a writer referral service that can provide experts on a wide variety of subjects—the arts, business and finance, education, health and medicine, and many more. Dial-a-Writer will locate professionals to write articles, books, scripts, speeches, annual reports, promotional materials, etc., almost anywhere in the U.S. and overseas.

Writers interested in being referred by Dial-a-Writer must be members of ASJA. Information on membership can be obtained from ASJA, 1501 Broadway, Suite 1907, New York NY 10036, (212) 398-1934. (*See: American Society of Journalists and Authors.*)

Dialect. The language of a particular geographic region, social class, or ethnic group is referred to as dialect. Dialect is often used in fiction as a means of characterization. The way a person speaks (i.e., the words he uses, the accent he has, the sentence structure and speech patterns he employs) tells the reader something about his status in life. Dialect helps portray a character's individuality and makes him real and believable. Dialect can clarify the regional setting for a fictional work. For example, "My cah is pahked at the hahbuh" puts the speaker's home within fifty miles of Boston. Dialect may also establish a date or time period for a piece of writing. "Dig it! We've got us one heavy scene . . ." can only suggest the psychedelic sixties.

To succeed, dialect should be neither so contrived and complicated as to be distracting, nor so sporadic and subtle that it fails to create a consistent, distinct flavor for a character or an entire work. Usually the writer sets the stage by having his characters use certain words or phrases which, in combination with his other narration, give the reader a picture of the dialect involved. There may be limited phonetic spellings in these introductory passages. Once the characterization is established, dialogue can be typed normally and it is the speech patterns that convey the image to the reader.

The use of dialect is difficult to accomplish successfully. Most writers, particularly beginners, would do well to avoid this fictive device. (*See: dialogue;* Dictionary of American Regional English (DARE); *idiom.*)

Dialogue. An essential element of fiction, dialogue consists of conversations between two or more people. Every bit of it has a purpose that contributes to the effect of the total work. A great many stories are told essentially through dialogue. The writer may use dialogue to move the plot along. It may serve to distinguish one character from another, or one locale from another. Dialogue may effectively provide the reader with information pertinent to the understanding of the plot. It does not interrupt the story to tell the reader something; it is, in fact, an integral part of the story itself. In addition, it adds color and life to a work. And, from a purely cosmetic point of view, dialogue on a page is more attractive to the reader's eye than solid paragraphs of narration.

Dialogue captures the quirks and peculiarities of characters' speech patterns. It should be appropriate to the speakers and the setting of the action.

The writer uses dialogue to provoke humor, prompt understanding, establish tension, or stir emotion more convincingly through the characters' words than through his own. Dialogue conveys a lot of information in a brief amount of time and space. Written dialogue is a compression of "real" conversation because it eliminates most of the nonsense syllables, repetition, pauses, audible sighs, and chitchat that occur in actual talk, using only enough to simulate concisely the flavor of the speaker. Like all fictional elements, dialogue creates an illusion of reality.

Beginning writers sometimes try too hard to find substitutes for the verb "said," when that is usually the best choice, except where the verb can be eliminated entirely in short passages where the reader clearly understands who is speaking. (*See: dialect.*)

Dictionary. A book containing the words of a language, profession, discipline, or special interest, arranged alphabetically. Depending on their purpose and scope, dictionaries may supply spellings, pronunciations, meanings, origins, and examples of word usage.

Dictionaries differ in approach. "Descriptive" volumes reflect current language practice; they do not attempt to establish standards of usage. *Webster's Third New International Dictionary* is a descriptive work. "Prescriptive" dictionaries, on the other hand, attempt to dictate word usage by labeling certain words or phrases as "slang" or "vulgar." *The American Heritage Dictionary* and *Random House Dictionary* use a prescriptive approach.

Depending on the writer's needs and his pocketbook, he has several other choices to make regarding a dictionary. "Unabridged" dictionaries of the English language are comprehensive works, usually with more than 250,000 entries. *The Oxford English Dictionary* is an outstanding example of an unabridged dictionary. "Abridged" dictionaries are taken from the larger edition by the same publisher and contain between 130,000 and 150,000 entries. The "pocket" dictionary comprises concise entries of only commonly used words. "Pronouncing" dictionaries indicate only spelling, pronunciation, and syllabification of frequently used words.

Two specialty dictionaries a writer might like to refer to are: *The Dictionary of American Slang* and *The Dictionary Catalogue*, which is a comprehensive list of thousands of dictionaries in the sciences, humanities, and social sciences.

Dictionary revisions are usually made every ten years. Editors add newly coined words and new meanings of old words, and delete those words and meanings considered obsolete. Writers may wish to check the copyright dates in a dictionary before purchase.

A Dictionary of American Idioms. This reference book, arranged in dictionary form, furnishes the meanings of more than 4,000 idioms used in American English.

Entries are arranged in alphabetical order. Within each entry, every meaning of the same idiom is preceded by a different number. The entry information includes variations on the idiom, its part of speech, definition(s), notes on usage, cross-references to synonymous and antonymous idioms, its etymology, and other idioms derived from the entry-heading idiom. Each entry contains a sentence using the idiom, followed by a sentence that conveys the same meaning without using the idiom.

The words *slang, informal, formal, literary, vulgar, substandard, nonstandard, archaic,* and *Southern* (or other terms denoting geographic regions) indicate situations/places in which each idiom is used. (*See: idiom.*)

Dictionary of American Regional English (DARE). This reference work will be published in five volumes by the Belknap Press; the first volume appeared in 1983.

DARE entries concentrate on the spoken language of specific regions and social groups of the U.S. They provide such information as the region in which a word is used; its origin; characteristics of persons who use the word, such as age, sex, race, and education level; and actual quotes from a resident of a particular region using the word. Besides the entries, the DARE includes maps that indicate regions in which a word is used. (See examples of regional English on a map in the Appendix to this encyclopedia.) DARE was compiled using 1,002 questionnaires and informal conversations with 2,752 individuals in local communities in all 50 states. In process since 1965, this work was produced at the University of Wisconsin; Chief Editor is Frederic G. Cassidy. Cassidy.

A fiction writer whose work is set in a particular locale may find research into speech patterns helpful.

Diet for writers. The sedentary activities that make up the bulk of a writer's working hours (thinking, typing, writing, filing, reading) rarely burn up more than 60-80 calories per hour. On the other hand, an active person who walks (about three to four miles per hour) in the same amount of time burns 400-600 calories. To counter the effects of hours spent without physical exertion, some writers may exercise; others stick to coffee or tea.

Nevertheless, many writers are snackers. They munch while they work and may easily take in more calories than they expend. Just as people vary in the amounts of fuel they need, foods too, generate differing amounts of energy. The "calorealities" of some favorite nibbles are: one apple, 70 calories; 12 fluid ounces of beer, 150 calories; one candy bar with nuts, 275 calories; one cup of ice cream, 255 calories; one ounce of cheddar cheese, 115 calories; an average martini, 160 calories.

Coupling the information about calorie intake with the statistics on energy output, writers may determine their individual diet formulas designed to maintain optimum body weight.

Dingbat. A printer's name for any typographical ornament. Also called a *flubdub*. Stylized ornaments are available in hundreds of different shapes and sizes for the type page.

Dingbats have been added for design purposes to many of the pages in this encyclopedia.

Dinner theater. This term describes a production staged in a restaurant where patrons sit at a table and pay one price for dinner and a show. The U.S. has approximately 125 dinner theaters, which seek light, humorous plays designed to appeal to audiences who are interested primarily in entertainment rather than thought-provoking drama.

Plays produced in these theaters are realistic, but not too profound; they neither offend the audience nor offer it great insights. Dinner-theater productions are characterized by comic plots that are exaggerated but believable, and sex that is implied but never shown on stage. Profanity, if used at all, is mild.

The physical structure of dinner

theaters presents singular limitations to the playwright. The full- or three-quarter-arena stages of most dinner theaters can pose logistical problems, and because most stages are less than 20 feet square, crowd scenes cannot be accommodated. Also, the entire theater is likely to be small, so loud noises (such as gunfire) that startle an audience should be avoided.

The following organizations maintain lists of dinner theaters: the American Dinner Theatre Institute, P.O. Box 2537, Sarasota FL 33582; and the Foundation for Extension and Development of the American Professional Theatre (FEDAPT), 165 W. 46th Street, Suite 310, New York NY 10036.

Direct marketing/direct response. These two terms are used to include not only direct-mail advertising, but also any interactive system that uses one or more advertising medium to effect a measurable response and/or transaction at any location. This could include coupon ads in magazines, television ads using a toll-free number or a regular call-in telephone number, and any two-way electronic advertising/ordering system, such as the Warner-Amex QUBE cable television system.

Direct-mail advertising. Advertising sent to potential customers through the U.S. mail. Direct-mail advertising touts products and services and is also used to generate leads for salesmen, raise funds, etc. Successful direct-mail copy appeals to basic human wants, describes a credible benefit of the product or service, and impels the reader to some direct, immediate action—such as filling out an order card or enclosing a check.

Industrial firms, businesses such as retailers, and fundraising organizations all rely heavily on this technique, as do mail-order companies that sell exclusively by catalogue. While large companies and mail-order firms have their own direct-mail advertising copywriting staffs, smaller businesses use freelance copywriters to create their sales letters, brochures, order cards, etc. Even large companies use freelancers for major pieces.

Earnings for freelance direct-mail ad writers vary with the size of a company and the market for a product or service. Copywriters, for example, may earn from $30-$300 per page for catalogue copy or $25-$100 per hour, depending on the market. Veteran freelancers who create a basic mailing package of letter, brochure, response card, and outer envelope design earn from $3,000-$10,000 from magazine publishers and other clients. Freelancers whose clients are smaller publishers may earn $300 and up for direct-mail packages.

The Yellow Pages lists countless goods and services that may be potential clients for freelance direct-mail copywriters. Companies that do much of that writing for clients and may also use freelancers are listed under "Advertising—Direct Mail." Trade journals such as *Advertising Age* frequently carry classified ads seeking direct-mail copywriters. Many of the companies that use direct mail to promote their products and services are members of the Direct Marketing Association, 6 E. 43rd Street, New York NY 10017. (*See: direct marketing/direct response.*)

Directories. Two general sources to consult are *The Directory of Directories* and *The Guide to American Directories*, but there are many specialized directories nonfiction writers will find useful; some of these are mentioned in other entries in this encyclopedia under "biographical references"; "business writing"; "science writing"; and "U.S. government, research on." (*See: directories, writer-related.*)

Directories, writer-related. Directories related to the writing field include the *Media Personnel Directory* and *Magazine Industry Market Place*, which list major editorial and business personnel in magazine publishing; and the *Directory of American Poets and Fiction Writers*, which is useful to writers who want to obtain lecture or workshop engagements at colleges and with arts councils. *Working Press of the Nation* is a five-volume set of print- and broadcast-media-related directories; it is described in this encyclopedia under its title. Newspaper personnel are listed in the *Editor and Publisher International Year Book*, and broadcast employees are detailed in the *Broadcasting/Cablecasting Yearbook*. (*See:* Literary Market Place; Magazine Industry Market Place; Working Press of the Nation; *writers, biographical directories of.*)

Disc jockey. The host of a radio recorded music program; also, an announcer.

Disco. Dance-oriented music that is usually composed in 4/4 time with 130 beats per minute.

Dissertations as research sources. Dissertations, often unpublished,

can be sources of article or book reference material. A writer has access to these works through *Dissertation Abstracts International*, an international directory of abstracts of dissertations, which are arranged in two sections: humanities and social sciences, and sciences and engineering.

This publication is indexed by keyword and author and is published monthly. The researcher can find *Dissertation Abstracts International* in most libraries, but may have to contact a university to obtain a dissertation itself, or buy a copy from University Films International of any dissertation abstracted in DAI.

Dissolve. A motion picture or television editing direction indicating that one scene should fade away at the same time a new scene fades in. In a dissolve, both scenes overlap each other for a moment. It can be written as *dissolve to*. Both terms are typed all in caps when used in scripts.

Distribution rights. (*See: book contract.*)

Distributor. A business that buys books from a publisher and resells them to wholesalers, jobbers, retail outlets, or individual consumers. (*See: book distribution.*)

Division (publisher's). Major publishing corporations may produce not only trade books but also lines of books for schools and colleges, as well as reference books and specialized books for professionals. Since each division of a corporation may be responsible for a separate line of books, the writer should be sure he will be dealing with the appropriate division before approaching a publisher. The major divisions of publishing corporations are detailed in *Literary Market Place*. (*See: magazine publishers, multiple; conglomerates—book publishers; trade books.*)

Documentary. A documentary is a nonfiction film in which real people "play" themselves. Its subject matter may be anything from the drilling of oil to the children of migrant workers. Motion picture and television documentaries either film actual events or recreate situations based on research, factual evidence, and information about a subject. Private organizations, large companies, and foundations often sponsor the production of documentary films to inform the public or influence their attitude about a certain person, event, or social condition.

Though a documentary may or may not have an actual script or narration, much writing is done before it is ready for production. A writer composes a proposal (like a 2- to 3-page query letter) for a producer to present to a sponsor, convincing the sponsor that a particular idea for a documentary is good, that the producer knows just what kind of film is needed, and that he can do the job best. If the proposal is accepted, the writer does a treatment (an outline of the film based on research) and ultimately a script—a blueprint for the film—describing a series of "master scenes" as they would be seen by the audience. The writer may also be involved in detailing a shooting script describing actual shots and camera angles, and finally a narration script after the film has been shot.

As with all audiovisual writing, drawing up documentary scripts is a cooperative venture in which the writer depends on other professionals to bring his work to life. He creates a series of visual images that tell a story, and the director and producer develop the means to take an audience through the revelation process during which a subject unfolds before them. (*See: audiovisual communication.*)

Donut. A radio commercial consisting of a jingle sung at the beginning, a *hole* in the middle where instrumental music is played and copy is read, and more singing at the end.

Double spotting. In broadcasting, using two commercials in the same break, sometimes back to back with nothing intervening.

Down and under. In a radio commercial script, a direction to reduce the volume and music to a background level so that the announcer's voice can be heard.

Drama criticism. An evaluation of a drama written by a reviewer, who gives the reader an idea of the topic of a play and offers an opinion on the success of its execution. The reviewer attempts to discover the intended effect of the work and comments on the form and style of the performance. As an expert in the techniques and conventions of drama, he analyzes actors, sets, lighting, makeup, costume, and direction. The reviewer loves theater, and therefore, applauds the superior and chastises the second rate.

Drama criticism both teaches and entertains. Ideally, criticism is informative to both those who have and those who have not seen a performance. It shares one informed reviewer's insights and reactions to what happened on stage. As a kind of feature writing, drama criticism strives to be well written and readable. It does not "talk down" to its readers, nor does it give evaluative comments without supportive evidence from the production. Good drama criticism does not depend heavily on plot summary, and it never gives away an ending, if the surprise is essential to enjoying the play.

Drama criticism appears both in daily and weekly newspapers and national magazines. Though some large publications have their own reviewing staffs, there are opportunities for freelance drama critics. Performances worthy of review take place in cities across the country, and local newspapers may welcome a drama "correspondent" to provide reviews of regional performances. In this case, writers should contact the editor of the publication. Magazines may pay little to beginning reviewers, but writers who have proved their worth may earn $50 and more per review. Information on potential magazine markets for drama criticism and related drama features, and the rates they pay, are available in the "Theater, Movie, TV and Entertainment" section of the annual *Writer's Market*. (*See: playwriting*.)

Dramatic agent. Some agencies specialize in material for theatrical, motion picture, and television presentation. An author who wishes to be represented by such an agent uses the same technique as he does to secure a literary agent—by recommendation of a writer already represented by the agent, or by his own letter outlining the publishing and production credits he's already obtained on his work and offering to submit scripts for examination. The dramatic agent's commission is usually 10%-15%—the same as that of a literary agent—and he negotiates for possible production with theatrical and film producers. (*See: agents, literary; agents, television*.)

Dramatic convention. A contrivance of playwriting and staging that the audience understands is to be taken for reality. Some common dramatic conventions are the *monologue* (in real life, people do not speak so coherently at such length), the *aside* (in which a character gives vital information to the audience, while the other characters onstage are understood not to hear)—even the stage itself (which obviously is not really a battlefield, or a garret). (*See: aside*.)

Dramatic irony. Dramatic irony refers to the theatrical device in which the audience is made aware of information unknown to some or all of the characters in the play. This information may be about the real identity of a character, his actual intentions, or the probable outcome of the play's action. Dramatic irony may be described as putting into a speaker's (character's) mouth words that have for the audience a meaning not intended by the speaker. It depends for effect on the contrast between what the character says or believes and the play's or film's true state of affairs.

Irony based on misunderstanding or partial knowledge is common to both tragedy and comedy. A classic example is Sophocles' tragedy *Oedipus Rex*, in which Oedipus seeks throughout the play to discover and punish the murderer of his father, only to find that he himself is guilty of the crime. Dramatic irony in a tragedy is also called *tragic irony* or *Sophoclean irony*. Dramatic irony in comedy is particularly common in plots involving mistaken identities, such as Shakespeare's *A Comedy of Errors*.

A second type of dramatic irony results when a character's remarks early in a play prove to have quite another meaning later on. After the murder of Duncan in Shakespeare's *Macbeth*, for example, Lady Macbeth says to her husband, "A little water clears us of this deed," yet during the sleepwalking scene, she says that all the waters of the ocean won't cleanse the stain of blood from her hand. (*See: irony.*)

Dramatic rights. A type of subsidiary rights to a copyrighted created work. They belong to the author unless transferred to someone else. Such rights are usually optioned from a script or book by a director or producer and usually handled by the author's agent, or by his publisher on his behalf.

Dramatic rights, television rights, and *motion picture rights* are often offered at a percentage of the total price as an option to buy for a specific period of time. The idea is then brought to the attention of individuals or organizations in the industry—actors, directors, studios, or television networks—for possible production.

A chart showing the variety of "Rights for Sale" an author has on his work is shown in the Appendix to this encyclopedia.

Dramatis personae. Literally, "characters of the play." An archaic term

for the cast of characters; a modern playwright would not use it unless he meant to be tongue-in-cheek.

Dramatists Guild. A division of the Authors League of America, Inc., this organization includes playwrights, lyricists, and composers as members. Active-member status is reached by those who have had a play produced in a Broadway or Off-Broadway theater; associate members have written at least one play; and subscriber members are nonwriters who have an interest in theater.

The Guild sponsors seminars on the business and creative aspects of playwriting, as well as symposia on various aspects of the theater. The latter are led by noted professionals such as Edward Albee and Stephen Sondheim.

Members of the Guild have access to its reference library of materials on plays, playwriting, and the theater. They may also participate in a health insurance plan. In addition, the organization advises members on business topics, copyright, agents, contracts, options, dealings with producers, motion pictures, and taxes.

The seven Dramatists Guild contracts are considered the world's most comprehensive contracts for playwrights. They cover the areas of first-class dramatic plays, first-class dramatico-musical works, off-Broadway dramatic plays, off-Broadway dramatico-musical works, stock tryout productions, review productions, and collaborations.

The Minimum Basic Production Contract for playwrights is negotiated between the Dramatists Guild and the League of New York Theaters and Producers. According to its stipulations, the playwright receives 5% in royalties on the first $5,000 of box office sales, 7½% in royalties on the next $2,000 of sales, and 10% in royalties for the sales above $7,000. (These royalty figures apply to first-class productions, i.e., those staged on Broadway or in other large houses.)

This association publishes the *Dramatists Guild Newsletter*, issued 10 times per year, and the *Dramatists Guild Quarterly.*

The Dramatists Guild Headquarters are located at 234 W. 44th St., New York NY 10036. (*See: Authors League of America.*)

Dramatists Sourcebook. This directory lists nonprofit professional theaters in America to which playwrights, composers, lyricists, and librettists may submit their work. The *Sourcebook* also lists contests and awards, fellowships and grants, conferences and festivals, workshops and residencies, and other services for those who create new material for the stage; it is published by the Theatre Communications Group, Inc., 355 Lexington Avenue, New York NY 10017.

Drugs and writers. Narcotics such as opium, milder drugs such as marijuana and hashish, and such social drugs as alcohol, coffee, and even chocolate effect at least temporary physiological and psychological changes in their users. With respect to writers, two categories of drugs deserve mention: those used to relieve the tensions associated with the creative process, and those taken in an attempt to enhance the process itself.

Writers intensely engaged in their craft may feel stress and anxiety from its demands and pressures and may seek an escape. The substance most commonly used to "tune out" writers' troubles is alcohol, and indeed, writers have long been characterized as drinkers. Some well-known writers have written about their experiences with alcohol, a drug that dulls the senses and disorients mental faculties. Presently, there is no evidence to suggest that writers use alcohol to stimulate their creative output; rather, drinking may be one way to numb the doubts writers sometimes have about the merit of their work and/or to escape actually doing it. What may begin as a social exercise or a way to relax, if unchecked, can lead to blackouts, personality changes, and depression resulting in little or no creative yield at all.

But through the ages, writers have sought ways to heighten their creative potential, and more than a few have experimented with various drugs. In the 1840s, for example, a group of Parisian writers and artists frequently gathered to use them. These French romantics, including Baudelaire, Dumas, and Gautier, sought new ways of enhancing their perceptions of the outside world. They, along with others like English essayist Thomas DeQuincey, who wrote "Confessions of an Opium Eater," vividly described their drug experiences and composed artistic works while under the influence. They felt that their powers of association and gifts for fantastic detail were elevated during these periods and that they realized great expansions of consciousness. Although drugs played havoc with the writers' bodies, writers in the era of the 1960s used LSD and similar drugs in attempts to deepen their awareness.

The use of amphetamines, marijuana, tobacco, and the caffeine stimulants found in coffee, cola, and chocolate may produce similar but less striking effects. The highs reported by marijuana users and scientific reports confirming that moderate smoking of the drug does not cause changes in the physical structure of the brain make it attractive. Smoking tobacco may temporarily improve creativity and give writers a spurt of energy, but it may also quell underlying symptoms of stress. Some evidence regarding coffee intake suggests that after 200-300 milligrams of caffeine (2 cups of coffee=about 200 milligrams of caffeine), the onset of boredom slows, and a rested, healthy individual may experience motor and mental efficiencies above his normal levels. On the other hand, in some persons, even smaller amounts of the stimulant may generate nervousness, sweaty palms, insomnia, and ulcers. In fact, caffeine may actually increase stress levels. Writers—like anyone else—who take drugs to stimulate their senses and "tune in" to their environment risk side effects and potential addiction. (*See: lifestyle of the writer—impact on the person; stress and the writer.*)

Dub. In the radio business, a tape copied from a master tape, sometimes for another station; means *duplicate.*

Dummy. The physical plan for a publication, such as a magazine, book, or newspaper. Dummies are constructed at various levels of sophistication, the simplest being a group of blank pages the size and format of the publication, and the most elaborate a printed blueprint of the publication, called a *positive blue dummy.* The purpose of the more elaborate dummy is to show the position of and the area occupied by each piece of copy, illustration, photograph, and heading.

An entrepreneur also will use as a dummy a printed sample or section of a proposed new magazine containing articles, stories, and advertisements (just as they would appear if the effort got off the ground) to solicit investors and potential advertisers.

Dust jacket copy. Copy describing the book, typically prepared by the editor. Writing it is an important job because later promotion pieces as well as some reviews are likely to be written out of it. (*See: blurb.*)

E

Eastern Ski Writers (ESW). The 325 members of ESW write about both the sporting and the business aspects of skiing. The group meets every two months and holds seminars concerning the writing and skiing industries once per year. ESW is a division of the United States Ski Writers Association and can be contacted through the USSWA at Seven Kensington Rd., Glens Falls NY 12801.

Easy Listening Formula (ELF). A gauge of listening comprehension, the ELF was developed by Dr. Irving Fang, an expert in determining the "learnability" levels of television news reports. It is designed to make broadcasters and writers aware of the various degrees of language complexity in their presentations. The formula consists of counting each syllable above one, per word, in any one sentence. For example, Dr. Fang found that Walter Cronkite's scripts had an easy-listening score of less than 12. That meant no sentence had more than 12 two-or-more-syllable words, and was easily understood by the average listener. The most readable newspaper he tested, the *Christian Science Monitor,* also averaged less than 12. Writers who are writing speeches and/or broadcast copy could use the Easy Listening Formula to keep their sentences from becoming too complex and difficult to listen to and understand. (*See: readability formulas.*)

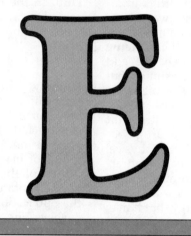

Edgar Awards. This group of awards was established in 1945 by the Mystery Writers of America, Inc., to recognize outstanding contributions to various categories of mystery, crime, and suspense writing. The Edgar Allan Poe Awards consist of ceramic statuettes of Poe, known as "Edgars." They are awarded annually for the best first mystery novel by an American and the best mystery novel published in America. Edgars are also awarded in such categories as best juvenile mystery novel, best mystery short story, and best mystery motion picture, among others. More information on the Edgar prizes is available from the Mystery Writers of America, Inc., 150 Fifth Avenue, New York NY 10011.

Editing. Editing is the art of generating and selecting, compiling, and revising literary, photographic, or audiovisual material and making it suitable for publication/production. Editors are the "gatekeepers" of publishing. They solicit and read manuscripts and decide what is publishable. Newspaper and magazine editors may write captions, choose which Letters to the Editors to print, send potentially libelous manuscripts to the company lawyer, and confer with writers and art directors to meet deadlines and stay within budget. Book editors often have many of the same responsibilities, in addition to their duties surrounding new acquisitions and new authors on publishers' lists.

Editing is the skill of knowing what works for an audience, and an editor's primary responsibility is to see that a piece or an entire publication does just that. Whatever his specific duties, he maintains a commitment to his readership. He accepts appropriate material and rejects the rest. On accepting a manuscript, an editor discusses with the writer any significant changes to be made and shows him alterations via the copyedited manuscript or the galley proofs. Ideally, the writer-editor relationship is based on mutual respect for accuracy and good writing. (*See: copyeditor; editor, acquisitions; editor, content; editor, production.*)

Editing, freelance. There are basically three types of freelance editing opportunities available: proofreading, copyediting, and content editing.

A proofreader is responsible for comparing printer's proofs against the original material for the purpose of identifying and correcting errors in the typeset copy. This job requires familiarity with the standard proofreading symbols, as well as with the basic rules of grammar and spelling. Proofreading is painstaking and often tedious; nevertheless, it is an important job that demands both speed and accuracy. Upon accepting a proofreading assignment, the freelancer should ask for an estimate of how long the job should take or how much work he is expected to complete within a specified time. Of the three types of freelance editing opportunities, proofreading pays the least, usually $6-$9 per hour. The fee for a straight proofreading assignment is generally fixed by the publishing house or other client, and is not ordinarily negotiable. Although proofreading may not pay exceptionally well, the job does provide the freelancer with training and experience that can lead to more responsible editorial positions.

Copyediting, a job that pays more than proofreading does, also involves more responsibilities. The copyeditor prepares a manuscript to be typeset, reviewing the material to make sure the text reads well and makes sense. He corrects spelling and grammatical errors; verifies proper names, certain facts, and cited references; makes sure that all the manuscript pages and auxiliary material (tables, charts, graphs, etc.) are there; and generally makes the book consistent with the publishing house's own style. The job often requires that the copyeditor recognize and correct factual errors as well as grammatical and style problems; many publishing houses seek copyeditors who have knowledge or experience in a certain field to work on a specific project. The average rate of pay for copyediting is $6-$9 per hour; an experienced copyeditor with specialized knowledge in a subject—e.g., scientific, or technical—may be able to command a higher rate.

Content editing is an opportunity that writer/editor Elizabeth L. Dugger calls "the pearl of editing services." A content editor is responsible for analyzing and organizing a manuscript, determining what information should be added or deleted to improve and enhance the text. A content editing assignment is ordinarily offered to a freelancer only after he has worked with a publisher on several other projects and has earned the staff editor's trust. This freelance job pays very well compared to proofreading and copyediting assignments: $7-$15 per hour, and up.

In order to gain the experience needed to become a regular proofreader or copyeditor for a major publishing house, the writer interested in freelance editing may begin with local proofreading jobs. Commercial printers and typesetting firms, for example, usually proofread the copy they've typeset in order to minimize the number of PEs (printer's errors) before returning it to the customer's proofreader. These firms, listed in the Yellow Pages under "Typesetting" (or those firms found under "Printing" that advertise typesetting services) often require part-time proofreading help. Schools, social service groups, government agencies, and other community organizations that publish brochures, pamphlets, and other printed materials are also likely to require a proofreader from time to time.

A solid résumé bearing editing or proofreading credits may lead to freelance editing assignments with major publishing firms. It is not uncommon for large publishing companies in New York, Boston, and Chicago to work by mail on specialized books with freelance editors throughout the U.S. The freelancer who submits a résumé and engaging cover letter to a major publisher will probably receive back an editing test designed to measure background knowledge, ability to recognize and correct factual and grammatical errors, and familiarity with editing symbols. His performance on the test, as well as his specialized knowledge and areas of expertise, will determine whether the publishing house offers him a freelance editing assignment.

Freelance editing opportunities are regularly listed in the classified section of the trade publications *Editor & Publisher* and *Publishers Weekly*. Occasionally a freelancer may find an opportunity for a freelance editing position advertised in the classified portion of his local newspaper. A writer may use either of these avenues to advertise his own freelance editing services as well.

Besides providing additional income, freelance editing allows a writer to make contacts in the publishing field that may prove valuable in getting the writer's own work published. Some writers, however, feel that editing work saps energy from their own writing and seek out non-writing-related employment.

(*See: copyeditor; editor, content; proofreading.*)

Additional information: *The Complete Guide To Editorial Freelancing; Jobs for Writers.*

Editor. (*See: contributing editor; copyeditor; editing; editing, freelance; editor, acquisitions; editor, content; editor, production; magazine personnel.*)

Editor, acquisitions. An editor responsible for originating and/or acquiring new publishing projects. An acquisitions editor seeks out authors to write books based on ideas conceived by the editorial and marketing personnel. He also meets regularly with writers and literary agents who have presented book ideas to the company and who may likely contract with the company on future titles.

After a publisher accepts a book proposal, the acquisitions editor works out a contract with the author or agent, seeking—within the policy and monetary guidelines established by the company and with respect to the author's desires—a compromise acceptable to both parties. As the book idea is developed, the acquisitions editor works with the author to make the final product the most salable and attractive property possible. The exact duties of an acquisitions editor vary from company to company. In some, the emphasis is more on acquisition; in others, the acquisition editor will edit as well, overseeing the book's progress from start to finish.

An acquistions editor working for a paperback publisher also deals with other publishing companies, negotiating reprint rights to some of their books.

Editor & Publisher (E&P). A weekly trade journal for the newspaper industry. Each issue includes industry news and articles on the editorial, advertising, production, and business aspects of the newspaper field. Special annual sections of the journal are devoted to journalism awards and syndicates. E&P also publishes a *Yearbook*, listing details on each of the newspapers in the U.S., Canada, and foreign countries, along with related information on associations, foreign correspondents, journalism schools, etc. Another of E&P's annual publications is its *Market Guide*, giving statistical information on the market areas served by the daily newspapers in the U.S. and Canada. The address of *Editor & Publisher* is 11 W. 19th St., New York NY 10011. (*See:* Editor & Publisher Syndicate Directory; *journalism awards.*)

Editor & Publisher Syndicate Directory. This annual directory contains alphabetical listings of syndicates that provide columns, cartoons, and comic strips to newspapers. Each listing includes the name and address of a syndicate, as well as one or more persons to contact. The directory is cross-indexed by titles of features, the writers and artists who create them, and subject matter.

Writers who have an idea for a syndicated column should first check this directory (which is probably available in their local newspaper office or public library) to see what competition there is for their proposed subject matter. The Directory is published by *Editor & Publisher*, a trade magazine for newspapers, located at 11 W. 19th St., New York NY 10011.

Editor, content. Also called the *developmental* or *substantive editor*, the content editor is responsible for seeing that a book's completed manuscript remains true to its outline and fulfills the publisher's goals for the book. The content editor makes sure that everything that should be included is, and that extraneous material is deleted. He evaluates the manuscript to determine whether material is presented in the best possible order, and challenges the author on cloudy explanations, vague assumptions, faulty logic, and potential legal problems. He also is concerned with making sure that the material is written and presented in the way it was envisioned: e.g., in formal or informal style, with a light or serious slant, anecdotally or straight to the point. Since the editor is the person who knows the book best, he is its leading advocate (and the author's) within the publishing house. The content editor usually is responsible as well for selecting and placing any illustrations that appear in the book. Some content editors may also acquire books. (*See: copyeditor; editor, acquisitions.*)

Editor, production. The production editor—sometimes called the *managing editor*—is a liaison between a publisher's editorial and production departments. He is usually responsible for conducting a manuscript through all phases of production to bound book—from copyediting through design, typesetting, and on through manufacture. The production editor assumes the complex task of coordinating editorial and production schedules, keeping a manuscript moving smoothly through the process with the fewest possible delays. The position of production editor is a difficult one: because he is seldom supervising just one book, the job requires that he juggle a number of schedules at once, coordinating several manuscripts simultaneously.

The job requires a general knowledge of the entire publishing process; the skill to assign, coordinate, and supervise various freelance personnel; and the ability to work cooperatively with three departments—art, editorial, and production—to ensure that a book is published on schedule. (*See: book publishing jobs, editorial; copyeditor; editing, freelance; editor, content.*)

Editorial ethics. Editorial ethics are guidelines pertaining to the business behavior expected by freelancers of the editors they deal with. Rooted in consideration and mutual respect, editorial ethics are standards for maintaining good writer-editor relationships. For instance, editorial ethics command that an editor will not rewrite a work without the author's permission, nor will he take one author's idea and assign it to another writer. Editorial ethics call for reimbursing a writer for time spent on an assigned story in the event that an editor cancels plans to use it, and reporting on submitted queries or manuscripts within a reasonable time.

Writers follow complementary ethical guidelines in their dealings with editors. The American Society of Journalists and Authors publishes a Code of Ethics and Fair Practices in its membership directory of freelancers. (It is reprinted in the Appendix to this encyclopedia.) Other professional organizations have similar codes of ethics for their membership. (*See: ethics for writers; kill fee; reporting time on manuscripts; steal my idea?*)

Editorial Freelancers Association (EFA). This organization exists to advance professionalism, to exchange information and support, and to furnish benefits to its members. Activities include seminars and training workshops.

The EFA's 500 members work part-time and full-time in capacities such as editor, writer, indexer, and proofreader.

The Association publishes a bimonthly newsletter and an annual membership directory. The newsletter contains news of past and future Association activities, features and tips related to freelancing, book reviews, and classified advertising. The address of the EFA is 175 Fifth Avenue, Suite 1101, New York NY 10010. (*See: Council of Writers Organizations.*)

Editorial rewriting. Editors usually make changes in submitted manuscripts for greater clarity, smoother flow, or to accommodate space restrictions, but it is customary for them to send the altered manuscript or the galley proof to the author for approval. This practice avoids changes that obliterate points an author was trying to make. It also reflects the recognition that, because the author's byline is on the piece, he has the right to know how his work will appear in print.

A good editor does not rewrite for the sake of his own intellectual exercise: he strives for a clear, interesting and concise presentation of the author's ideas. (*See: editorial ethics.*)

Editors. An editor's exact job description and title vary from publication to publishing house, depending on size and available personnel. Editors of small operations may easily do as much writing as they do editing. On the other hand, editing responsibilities on large publications are usually divided among several staffers.

There are many kinds of editing jobs in the publishing world. For example, copyeditors check manuscripts for grammatical details, factual errors, and consistent writing style. Content editors are more concerned with clarifying ambiguities and correcting conceptual problems in a manuscript, as well as possible libel or other legal problems. Current rates for freelance content and copyeditors, some magazine editors, and in-house company publications editors are listed in the "How Much Should I Charge?" section of the annual *Writer's Market*. Current staff salaries of magazine editors are given in the chart, "Magazine Editorial Salaries and Responsibilities" in the Appendix to this encyclopedia.

Book publishing, too, offers freelance and editorial staff opportunities for editors. Acquisitions editors, for example, contact agents and scan magazines, newspapers, and publishers' catalogs in search of ideas and possible authors to add to a publisher's list. Assistant editors may read manuscripts and write synopses and recommendations for

Writer's Encyclopedia

action. Further details on freelance book editing are given in *Jobs for Writers*. (*See: editing; editorial ethics; reporting time on manuscripts; writer's guidelines.*)

Editors' filler services. These come in two forms: 1) a subscription to a camera-ready newsletter of editorial copy and cartoons, or 2) a newsletter detailing brief articles and photographs that can be requested for free use as filler. The latter are paid for by the client whose product or service is mentioned in the feature.

Filler services are offered by public relations firms that prepare the features and notify editors of their availability by periodically mailing a tabloid magazine filled with features and accompanying photographs, fillers, cartoons, puzzles, and clip art. In the free versions, the editor requests certain features, indicates whether his publication is printed letterpress or offset, and specifies whether he wants mats or glossy proofs (with photographs newspaper screened) for reproduction in his publication. Subjects may be recipes, health or medical advice, home maintenance tips, or any other news or seasonal feature.

Some fillers include mention of a specific product. For example, a short feature "Prescription: Fun for Sickbed Blues" includes a drawing of a child in bed with his teddy bear playing at taking Teddy's temperature; the lead of the article includes this copy: "Toy Manufacturers of America, Inc. (TMA), the industry trade association, offers these suggestions for dealing with the special play problems of the bedridden child. . . ." The article goes on not only to give advice about dealing with sick children, but to make a plug for certain types of toys at the same time. For example, "Through play, a child may often act out (and thus relieve) fears. Dramatic play can be encouraged with doctor, nurse, or paramedic kits."

Editors who would like to be put on the mailing list to receive notices of these free features can contact firms like: Derus Media Service, 8 W. Hubbard Street, Chicago IL 60610; and North American Precis Syndicate, Inc., 201 E. 42nd Street, New York NY 10036. Subscription fillers are available from Fillers for Publications, 1220 Maple Avenue, Los Angeles CA 90015. (*See: clip art; copyright-free art.*)

Editor-writer correspondence. Besides selling an editor on an article idea (the query letter) and submitting manuscripts (the cover letter), writers encounter other situations in which they must write an editor regarding their work.

Gary Turbak described some of the kinds of letters written to editors by freelancers in a *Writer's Digest* article. Besides query letters and cover letters (which are described in separate entries in this encyclopedia), another type of letter is written in response to an assignment or go-ahead (instructions to write a piece on speculation). This brief letter, the *confirmation of assignment/go-ahead*, simply lets the editor know that the writer does indeed plan to write the piece, acknowledges the editor's response to the query, and mentions a deadline, either by confirming one suggested by the editor or proposing a different one.

A brief letter is also in order when the writer discovers that he will not be able to meet an agreed-upon deadline. In this kind of letter, the *deadline postponement letter,* the writer merely informs the editor that he will need more time than he had anticipated and gives the editor the date that he can expect to receive the manuscript.

The *jog letter* serves to remind an editor (or jog his memory) about a submitted piece of work in a case in which a response from the editor is long overdue. In the jog letter, the writer is careful to omit evidence of any impatience or anger he may be feeling, and to convey a businesslike impression. He explains to the editor what has happened in the past regarding his manuscript and asks to be informed of the status of same. Turbak points out that the jog letter can also be used to inquire about query letters, photos, and late payment.

The *demand letter* is the writer's recourse when more than one jog letter brings no response. The tone of this kind of letter is businesslike, but the writer is less tactful and more direct than in previous inquiries. Turbak suggests writing to others higher up in the organization after one demand letter to the editor brings no results.

Writers who have submitted material to a magazine on speculation and have been unable to get a reply from the editor after several jog inquiries should send one more certified letter indicating that, since the writer has not heard from the editor, the writer is formally *withdrawing his manuscript* from consideration and resubmitting another original elsewhere.

Sometimes a writer needs to explain in detail the kinds of rights he is selling, e.g., reprint rights. This method is especially valuable when dealing with those who may not be familiar with the provisions of each kind of manuscript rights. The writer's *granting rights letter,* therefore, may be the only written evidence of which rights were sold. (*See: cover letter; go-ahead; query.*)

Education for journalism. The classic educational debate among those in the field (who are, of course, future employers of today's students) concerns the value of a journalism degree as opposed to a liberal arts degree. Proponents of journalism degrees hold that concentration on writing skills and early exposure to the working world of the media are the foremost educational elements needed, while advocates of liberal arts degrees believe that general knowledge and basic composition skills are the ideal qualities of a beginning journalist. Schools that are accredited by the American Council on Education for Journalism (ACEJ) prepare their students for the varying expectations of employers in that they require each student majoring in journalism to earn a specified number of credits outside the journalism department, thus exposing them both to journalistic practice and knowledge of other disciplines.

Education for writers. The lifelong study and experiences that contribute to the development of a writer. Writers' educations may consist of formal university study, local creative writing courses, continuing education programs, weekend seminars, correspondence courses, and the countless informal lessons of living. Perhaps the only absolute of a writer's education is that it never ends.

Organized programs afford the writer opportunities to learn fundamental writing techniques, to polish style, and to act on the insights of constructive criticism. They also teach discipline and perseverance. Writing classes or conferences may provide an opportunity for sharing experiences as well as instruction.

But out of the unstructured, casual learning situations that arise from the writer's being alert to life, also come the nuances of successful stories, articles, and books. (*See: Associated Writing Programs; continuing education; correspondence courses for writers; writing courses.*)

Educational Press Association of America (EDPRESS). Editors of education publications make up this 600-member group, whose activities include editorial workshops and annual meetings. The Association publishes a monthly newsletter, an annual membership roster, *The Idea Book*, *The Book of Lists for the Education Editor*, and other materials to aid the educational editor.

EDPRESS awards one Golden Lamp Award annually "to a publication which shows excellent and significant achievement in the field of educational journalism," and several other awards under the categories "Editorial," "Graphics," and "Graphics-Editorial." The competition is open to "publications, institutions, or individuals with paid-up EDPRESS memberships." EDPRESS is located at the Communications Department, Glassboro State College, Glassboro NJ 08028.

800 numbers. Freelancers who want to find out if a company or institution they want to call long distance has a free "800" number can dial 1-800-555-1212 to reach the toll-free number information operator.

In searching for the toll-free number of a federal or state office that serves consumers, the writer may find useful "Direct Contacts for Consumers," a booklet published jointly by the U.S. government and the American Telephone and Telegraph Company. This publication, which contains 150 listings, may be obtained free for a self-addressed postcard from the Consumer Information Center, Pueblo CO 81009.

Electronic journalism. This term refers to writing news programs, features, and documentaries for radio and television. With the expansion of both cable and low-power television stations, newly licensed by the Federal Communications Commission, potential exists for increased writing/reporting opportunities. Current references on the how-to's of the subjects can be located in the *Subject Guide to Books In Print* under categories such as "Journalism—Handbooks, Manuals, etc.," "Radio Journalism," "TV Broadcasting of News," "TV Production and Direction," and related topics.

Electronic text. One of several terms (others are videotext, rotatext, teletext and intertext) that refer to the technology of electronic distribution of printed news and information via a television screen. Dr. Ralph Lowenstein, Dean of the College of Journalism and Communications at the University of Florida at Gainesville, suggests that since this is a text-via-video medium, the word "videotext" is the most apt generic term.

The University of Florida is the

first university in the nation to establish an electronic text center to experiment with this new technology and build an educational curriculum around it.

El-hi. A book-publishing term that refers to texts or other books suitable for supplementary reading both in elementary school and in high school. (*See: stories in textbooks; textbook publishing.*)

Ellipsis. An omission in a text. Ellipses can be made in composition, but such use is usually limited to poetry in which a word or two must be left out to keep the meter correct. More often, ellipses are made in quotation for the sake of clarity and brevity; omissions up to an entire paragraph in length are permissible.

In quoting another work, ellipses must always be indicated by the use of *ellipsis points*: three dots for any omission within the body of a sentence, four dots for an omission including the period at the end of a sentence or anything longer than a sentence.

Here is a passage from Anthony Trollope's *Doctor Thorne*, first in its entirety, then as it might read with ellipses.

He felt rather sick at heart when Mr. Baker got up to propose the toast as soon as the servants were gone. The servants, that is, were gone officially; but they were there in a body, men and women, nurses, cooks, and ladies'-maids, coachmen, grooms, and footmen, standing in the two doorways to hear what Master Frank would say. The old housekeeper headed the maids at one door, standing boldly inside the room; and the butler controlled the men at the other, marshalling them back with a drawn corkscrew.

He felt rather sick at heart when Mr Baker got up to propose the toast . . . . The servants . . . were gone officially; but they were there in a body . . . standing in the two doorways to hear what Master Frank would say. The old housekeeper headed the maids at one door . . . and the butler controlled the men at the other, marshalling them back with a drawn corkscrew.

The writer should refer to a good style book, such as *The Chicago Manual of Style*, for the more intricate aspects of ellipsis use.

Em. The square measurement of any size of type, so named because in conventional typefaces the capital M approximates that measure. For example, in 12-point type an em is 12 points; in 8-point type, 8 points. (There are 12 points to a *pica*; 6 picas to 1 inch.)

Editors, proofreaders, and designers most frequently use the em to measure indents—paragraph indents, for instance, may be one, two, three (or more) ems wide, depending on the design; lists are indented by ems from the margin.

Dashes are referred to as *em-dashes* or *en-dashes*, depending on their width—an en-dash (or hyphen width) is half as wide as an em-dash.

Emotion in writing. In fiction writing, an author elicits an emotional response from the reader through the situations in which he places the characters. Stories and novels not only relate what happens, they make the reader vicariously experience the events so that he can respond emotionally to them. The emotional responses of the characters also help convey emotions to the reader. Among the strongest emotions experienced by human beings (and therefore fictional characters), are the primary emotions of love, happiness, hope, compassion, courage, pain, hunger, hate, anger, grief, fear, and greed. The secondary emotions, which are less powerful, include a sense of humor, loyalty, gratitude, pride, curiosity, self-pity, loneliness, jealousy, vanity, timidity, inferiority, envy, suspicion, revenge, guilt, shame, and boredom. How the emotion is expressed varies with the type of fiction, but the ability to smoothly integrate an emotional quality into writing is characteristic of the successful short story writer or novelist. Beginning writers often neglect this aspect in their work.

The reader's empathy should be aroused in the first paragraph; from that point on, an emotional undertone should be present, according to writer Omer Henry. He suggests that although plot, character, and theme are essential to a good story, emotion is the element that retains the reader's attention.

Emotion in writing is important in some types of nonfiction as well as in fiction. Here is an excerpt from a "Drama in Real Life" *Reader's Digest* piece about a mother and son caught in a flash flood:

Then Helen spotted a telephone pole about a yard away. "Grab that, Rowdy," she panted, "and hold tight! Whatever happens, hang on to that pole and don't let go!"

Helen herself was feeling very weak. Suddenly her torn left hand lost its grip on the fence. The current swiftly carried her away. There was time only to scream once more, "Stay where you are, Rowdy! Hold on, whatever you do!"

Horrified, the little boy saw his mother vanish into the dark, heard her receding screams.

"Stay where you are!" she had said. But Rowdy couldn't obey. He let go of the telephone pole and, spinning in the current, dog paddled frantically after his mother.

"Mom!" he cried. "Mom, where are you?" But there was only darkness and the roar of the water rushing him along.

The writer should avoid confusing sentimentality, which tends to foster a one-dimensional, unrealistic view of life, with emotion. (*See: empathy.*)

Empathy. The condition of being able to identify with another person's feelings. A writer must have empathy toward his characters in order to make them seem real to readers.

Author Colleen L. Reece evokes her own ability to empathize with her characters by recalling an experience in which she felt the same emotion she imagines the character would feel. Sometimes she instills in her characters emotions that were expressed by someone she knows and she can identify with. In Reece's technique, author and character usually do not face the same situation, but rather the same principle: Reece cites the examples of confronting prejudice and of being pressured to betray personal values.

Reece's philosophy shows her awareness of the need for empathy: "Every character I create includes a small part of myself, no matter how minute. It may only be a passing thought, a fleeting moment, a quick flash of insight or temper. Yet it is that very part most needed to make those characters alive, real, lovable, or despicable." (*See: emotion in writing.*)

Employment searches by writers. Writers seeking editorial or staff writing positions can refer to the trade magazines of specific writing fields such as *Advertising Age* and *Editor & Publisher* (for newspapers) which carry classified ads for writing and editorial opportunities. Most carry "situation wanted" ads as well.

In major publishing centers such as New York, Chicago, or Los Angeles, there are also specialized employment agencies that exist to help writers and editors secure staff positions in their fields. They are listed under "Employment Agencies" in the Yellow Pages telephone directory.

The annual *Literary Market Place* lists agencies specializing in the placement of book publishing personnel, as does *Magazine Industry Market Place* for magazine employees.

In smaller cities, local and regional chapters of professional communications organizations such as the Public Relations Society or Women in Communications are a good source of job leads.

Encyclopedia. An encyclopedia is a book or set of books containing alphabetically arranged articles/entries on numerous topics covering either many branches of knowledge or several aspects of one subject field. An encyclopedia's primary purpose is the clear, accurate presentation of facts. In addition, contemporary encyclopedias may use

cross-references to help readers explore concepts further; they may use statistical charts and illustrations and art reproductions to enhance the text; they may include color photographs and striking visuals to establish a rapport with readers. Many American encyclopedias are designed for use as curriculum-related references. Freelance writers use them as reference tools, for checking historical facts, dates, etc.

Encyclopedias contain some of the same elements as dictionaries, textbooks, atlases, and statistical manuals. General encyclopedias cover all important fields of knowledge and address lesser topics according to the needs and interests of the intended readers. There are currently more than 30 general encyclopedias published in the United States varying in reading level, number of pages, and volumes. (The *Encyclopaedia Britannica* and *World Book Encyclopedia* are general works.) Special encyclopedias—often only one volume, rather than multivolume—confine their coverage to specific fields, subjects, and viewpoints: for example, the *Encyclopedia of Sports* and the *New Catholic Encyclopedia.*

Both general and specialized encyclopedias may contain entries written by specialists in a particular discipline or by staff writers. Specialists' articles are usually signed. Alphabetical arrangements of entries may be determined in at least two ways. Word-by-word arrangements place entries according to the first word in the title; for example, "On Wisconsin" would come before "onomatopoeia." The letter-by-letter method uses the complete title of the entry to determine its placement order; in this case, "onomatopoeia" would precede "On Wisconsin."

Encyclopedias are continually revised (representing freelance opportunities for writers and editors), and many publishers issue annual or quarterly supplements. As a tool of writers and readers, encyclopedias must be carefully examined. Their authoritativeness, accuracy, objectivity, clarity, style, quality, physical format, and recency are important considerations prior to use or purchase. The American Library Association has published a guide, "Purchasing an Encyclopedia," which is available in most libraries.

Endings, story. There are many ways to end a short story, and even more ways to label different types of story endings. There are, however, certain elements required of a good story ending, regardless of the type of conclusion a writer chooses.

The ending of a story must, first of all, be satisfying to the reader. It honestly and fairly answers the question(s) the author posed at the beginning of the narrative. A good ending leaves the reader feeling that the story could have ended no other way.

Second, the ending must be logical: it must develop naturally from the characterization and events of the story. Even if the story solution is a surprise, the surprise must have been foreshadowed earlier in the story and not be dependent on some newly introduced character or amazing coincidence to provide the twist.

The ending of a story must be consistent with the mood, atmosphere, and subject matter of the piece. A light, humorous narrative about a young woman's adventures as she moves into her first apartment should not end with her brutal murder at the hands of a psychopathic

killer. Similarly, the writer who creates a somber atmosphere throughout a piece should maintain that serious mood at the end; even though the conclusion may promise better days ahead, an abrupt shift from gray skies to blue may weaken the intended effect of the story.

A good ending *gives* the reader something, whether it be a surprise, an emotional charge, or an idea to reflect on—in other words, a good ending provokes a reaction from the reader. A story should end on an important note and not be allowed to ramble on or be dragged out to an anticlimax.

Finally, a story's conclusion should show that the viewpoint character has passed through an experience that has changed him somehow, as well as proved the theme of the story.

Every story ending should fulfill these fundamental requirements; within these basic rules however, a variety of approaches exist. In the *summary* ending, all the threads of a story are neatly tied up into a happy (or unhappy) ending. In the *reversal* ending, the protagonist undergoes a reversal of some character trait. The *twist* or *surprise* ending sometimes involves a gimmick. The *periscope* ending offers the reader a brief glimpse of what the future holds for the characters in a story, while the *reader's choice* leaves the reader to supply his own ending, once the problem has been developed dramatically.

Fiction editors agree that a weak

ending will inevitably ruin a story's chances of acceptance, despite a brilliant beginning, skillful characterization, and a strong plot. The ending is the part of a story that will stay with the reader, the part that he will remember after he has closed the book or magazine. It is important that a writer spend as much time on the ending of a story as he does on the beginning and middle.

The ending of a story should be clear in a writer's mind before he sits down at the typewriter. Katherine Anne Porter once remarked, "If I didn't know the ending of a story, I wouldn't begin. I always write my last line, my last paragraphs, my last page first." (*See: plant; plot; falling action; surprise ending.*)

Entertainment columns. In small newspaper operations, all reviews (theater, music, cinema, dance, art, books, food, etc.) are sometimes written by one person. Because a small newspaper has limited space and a low budget, this job is likely to be given to a freelance writer. At a weekly or suburban paper, for example, pay may be only a byline to begin with, but it gives the freelancer exposure and experience. Some writers prepare sample reviews to give the editor an example of their writing style, and request an opportunity to do some reviews on assignment. (*See: arts review; book review; drama criticism; restaurant review.*)

Epilogue. A section added at the end of some novels, long poems, plays, and teleplays, often dealing with what happens to the characters after the actual conclusion of the story; it is not part of the plot. John Irving's epilogue to *The World According to Garp*, for example, briefly describes each of the characters' lives, until their deaths. These events all take place after Garp's death, which marks the end of the story. The climax/resolution takes place before the epilogue appears.

In a stage play, the epilogue can be a speech recited by an actor. In a teleplay, the epilogue, or *tag*, follows the climax and ties together any loose ends that may have been left. (*See: television writing.*)

Epiphany. A term first used by Joyce to describe the abrupt revelation of an event's or thing's essential significance; also, a work or portion of a work in which such a revelation takes place. The concept of the epiphany grew fashionable in the 1960s and 70s, when readers found epiphanies everywhere; it is considered more accurate, however, to restrict the term's use to Joyce's works. The 15 stories that make up *Dubliners*, for example, are all epiphanies.

Erotica. *Erotica, adult fiction,* and *men's fiction* are terms often used by publishers to refer to fiction writing on sexual topics.

This category of literature is concerned with different aspects of physical lovemaking and attraction, which can be conveyed through allusions, settings, situations, and other descriptive techniques. Its content is not always related to prurient interests, although pornography is one sub-species of erotica.

Publishers that seek erotica indicate their preferences in the listings in *Fiction Writer's Market* and *Writer's Market.*

Essay. A short, literary, nonfiction composition (usually prose) in which a writer develops a theme or expresses an idea.

Coined in 1580 to describe the personal reflections of the French writer Montaigne, this literary form survives in several different types of articles in today's magazines and newspapers. It has been expanded to include descriptive, narrative, argumentative, satiric, historical, and humorous pieces. Formal essays are generally serious, logically developed, and intended to persuade or inform. Informal essays, whose topics and tones are practically boundless, are frequently known as personal, light, and familiar essays. They are well-polished writings that tend to suggest much more than they actually say.

Essays are usually subjective—a revelation of the writer's own thoughts and feelings, but some more objective versions are used in some newspapers and magazines. In his book *Articles and Features*, Roy Paul Nelson describes the information essay—an extension of the news story, in which the writer is a detached reporter "teaching" his audience with facts—and the interpretive essay, which uses evidence and facts to stress the whys of an issue and offer new perspectives on it.

A number of magazines solicit opinion essays on topics of interest to their readers, and others use inspirational essays which deal (without being preachy) with uplifting personal experiences. The humorous essay is usually light and witty and treats as subject matter the trials and irritations common to the readers of the magazine to which it is submitted.

Publications listed in the "General Interest" section of *Writer's Market* often solicit essay material.

Establishing shot. A camera shot that affords a view of a large area; it is often used at the beginning of a film or television program to help set the scene. When used in a script, the term is typed all in caps. (*See: television script terms.*)

Establishing song. In a musical, a song that presents the setting or the general context for the story. It can perform its function in a *production number*, which uses a large group of performers, or a *soft opening*, a quiet song often sung solo. "Magic to Do," from *Pippin*, is a production number; "Try to Remember," from *The Fantasticks*, is a soft opening. (*See: musical.*)

et al. Abbreviation for *et alii*, which is Latin for "and others." It is used in footnotes to refer to a work by more than three authors; however, it is always preceded by the name of the author listed first on the published work. It is typed in lower case letters (et al.) in a manuscript.

Ethics for writers. A code of conscientious professional behavior for writers. Though ethics by their nature are subject to interpretation and translation and writers by *their* nature are diverse, complex personalities, certain rudimentary standards reflecting the ideals of the profession do exist. They are not laws, but guidelines, followed for the sake of professional and personal integrity, dealing with writers' actions toward their readers and editors.

The code of ethics relating to readership is based on truth. It takes effect when an idea for a novel, an article, or even a filler is born. It dictates that a writer know his subject. It necessitates that he track down accurate information and complete the homework needed to produce a credible piece of fiction or nonfiction that is his own and not plagiarized from others. He doesn't mix fact and fiction. In following this ethical code, the nonfiction writer investigates opposing views and checks story corroborations. He honors interviewees' requests for anonymity and does not quote information given "off the record." The fiction writer narrates from a point of view appropriate for his theme. He strives to create a worthy literary work for his intended audience.

In writers' professional behavior toward editors, the bulk of the standards involve consideration and regard. A writer submits neatly typed material; the act of submitting a piece verifies its authenticity, if nonfiction, and confirms complete fabrication, if fiction. He sends manuscripts appropriate for a given market, having previously studied its needs. He encloses sufficient postage and an envelope for return of a manuscript or a query reply. If given an assignment he is honest about his expenses, meets his deadline, or notifies his editor in advance of reasons for possible delay. If he fails to complete a book manuscript through his own fault, he returns the advance or has the sum deducted from his royalties on other books. (*See: conflict of interest; editorial ethics; press trip; simultaneous submission.*)

Ethnic fiction. Stories and novels whose central characters are black, Native American, Italian-American, Jewish, Appalachian, or members of some other specific cultural group. Ethnic fiction usually deals with a protagonist caught between two conflicting ways of life: mainstream American culture and his ethnic heritage. Except for black and Jewish writers—who can draw on a large body of work in their respective traditions and now often write in experimental forms—ethnic fiction tends to be conventional in form; the ground it breaks is in subject matter.

It is difficult for nonwhite ethnic writers to find a commercial publisher, since publishers feel that ethnic concerns tend not to be the concerns of the general American book buying and reading public. There are exceptions, of course—Toni Morrison's *Tar Baby* achieved respectable sales. For the most part, though, the action in ethnic fiction is with small and independent presses and literary/little magazines, many of which have a regional or cultural focus. In addition to the nonprofit and low-profit publishers, though, commercial ethnic magazines such as *Ebony Jr.*, *Essence*, *Attenzione*, and *Greek Accent* accept ethnic fiction.

MELUS, the Journal of the Society for the Study of the Multi-Ethnic Literature of the United States, prints scholarly criticism and analysis of ethnic literature. The Society's editorial offices are located at the Department of English, McMicken Hall, University of Cincinnati, Cincinnati OH 45221.

Exercise for writers. Physical and mental activity apart from that involved in the process of writing are essential to effective creativity and production. Writers spend hours seated at the typewriter in painstaking discipline. As a result, backs tense; necks kink. Mental processes also cloud, and temporary writer's block may ensue. Physical exercise often provides an outlet for pent-up tensions. Not only does the activity of jogging, lifting weights, jumping rope, playing tennis, or dancing recharge the fatigued body, but exercise also relieves some of the chemical imbalances resulting from stress.

There are other exercises writers use to combat mental fatigue: one is progressive muscle relaxation. The writer focuses attention on specific muscle tightness and then alternates between tensing and relaxing those areas. Other writers exercise through yoga and deep breathing practices. Some merely remove themselves from the writing mode: they go shopping, call a friend, work on the car, or fly a kite. Chances are good that they will be refreshed physically and mentally when they return to the keys. (*See: diet for writers.*)

Exhibit. In publishing, *exhibit* has two meanings. Most commonly, it means a display at a book industry convention, but it can also refer to charts or illustrations used in the appendix of a book.

Expenses (editorial reimbursement). In most cases, writers are reimbursed by publications for costs incurred in completing an article assigned to them. Though many magazines pick up the tab for story-related expenses, a writer should get approval and verification before assuming that he will be reimbursed. An editor's willingness to pay for travel expenses, for example, may depend on an editorial budget and the importance of the writing project to the magazine. Writers should keep all receipts for reimbursement or tax deduction purposes.

In the case of expenses run up in writing a book, the writer receives an advance against royalties to help finance the project. Writers are expected to cover the costs of travel, extensive research, long-distance interviews, photocopying, art work production, secretarial help, etc., out of this advance. However, a writer may sometimes be able to make arrangements with his publisher (if he lives in the same city, for example) to get photocopying done, use the WATS line, etc., to help defray some of these expenses. Occasionally, depending on the project and the expected costs, a publisher will agree to create a budget, separate from the royalty advance, to cover research or other expenses. This probably happens most often in the case of artwork (the publisher might ask the author to supply rough drawings but convert them into reproduction copy at the publisher's expense). The publisher may also pay all or some of the permissions fees for reproducing photos or artwork.

Experimental fiction. Setting and strong characterization are basic elements of experimental fiction. This form depends largely on the revelation of a character's inner being that elicits an emotional response from the reader. Helen Hinckley Jones, writer and writing instructor, says of the experimental short story: "This isn't so much a story of *doing* as a story of *being*."

Other prominent characteristics of experimental fiction are style, structure, symbol, and narrative technique. Experimental fiction can be unplotted, although the absence of a plot is not a necessary feature; when a plot is used, however, it is subordinate to the other, aforementioned elements.

What is experimental in one age can become cliché in the next; in its day, *Moby Dick* was an experimental work that virtually no one understood. Some of the most important experimental writers of the past few decades are Alain Robbes-Grillet, John Barth, and Thomas Pynchon; probably the most influential experimentalist today is Argentine writer Jorge Luis Borges.

Except for the most important writers, who are published in prestige editions, experimental fiction is published primarily in university quarterlies and in little magazines. (*See: mainstream fiction.*)

"Experts"—how to find them. Writers sometimes need to contact authorities for verification, explanation, and update of research collected in writing an article or book. Public and university libraries often have comprehensive works suggesting individuals as subject-matter experts. Helpful sources include: *American Men and Women of Science* and the *Directory of American Scholars*, a four-volume set listing authorities by their expertise in the fields of history, English, languages, and philosophy, religion, and law. A master *Biographical Index* records individuals appearing in the many Marquis "Who's Who" publications. In addition, hundreds of reference directories, such as Wasserman's *Encyclopedia of Business Information Sources*, are listed in the *Directory of Directories. Speakers and Lecturers: How to Find Them* has a useful subject cross-index of topics on which these persons could be contacted.

Other library materials writers may use in pursuit of authorities include general and specific periodical indexes (e.g., the *Reader's Guide to Periodical Literature* and *Psychological Abstracts*, respectively) where names of authors of recently published articles may be found who could be written in care of the publication. Writers may also refer to the *Writer's Resource Guide*, which provides the names of contact persons, addresses, and telephone numbers of various information-dispensing centers in government, industry, education, and the arts.

Local authorities may be identified by contacting schools, libraries, newspapers, and chambers of commerce that often compile lists of referral and resource people within their own community. Businesses listed in the Yellow Pages of the telephone directory may also be sources of local "experts."

Writers contacting experts usually enclose a photocopy of whatever statement, theory, or research finding they need verification or updating on, with a covering letter asking the expert to respond at his convenience, in an enclosed stamped envelope addressed to the writer. Normally no payment is involved, since the expert wants to be sure any statement attributed to him is accurate and current.

In the case of specialized nonfiction books, the publisher may absorb the cost of having the manuscript vetted (checked for factual accuracy) by an outside expert. If not, the author may be required to pay this cost, which could vary from around fifty to several hundred dollars—depending on the complexity of the book, whether the author knows a local expert he can trust with the job, and other factors. (*See: directories.*)

Exposé. An exposé is a revelation of documented facts intended to expose wrongdoing, injustice, or foul play. Honest, legitimate exposés appear in newspapers and magazines and in book forms as products of careful investigative reporting. They are contrasted with the sensational stories in "gossip" publications.

Exposés are public disclosures that take on many shapes. They may be personality sketches, accounts of company practices, or reports of government waste. They sometimes grow out of a writer's own experience or awareness of contradictions surrounding a subject or situation. They are usually written in straightforward, objective fashion. But they may also be successfully treated in a light, sarcastic, or even cynical way. In fact, exposés of this type may have a better chance of reaching a large audience than do the hard-hitting accounts. Some editors may be reluctant to endorse a highly discrediting piece for fear of the unfavorable impact it could have on readership and advertisers.

Exposés have long served to influence social reform and public policy. To do so, they must be fairly written and free of libel and malicious intent. They must attribute controversial comments to at least loosely defined sources. Exposé writers often seek help from government regulatory agencies (through the provisions of the Freedom of Information Act), chambers of commerce, and professional societies in verifying facts and tracking down statistics. The National Better Business Bureau, for example, is a valuable checkpoint in unearthing material for exposés dealing with products, services, and companies. Because of the inflammatory nature of some exposé material, writers must be ready to defend critical pieces (both to readers and editors) with unconditional evidence. Depending on the nature of the exposé, they may choose (for business or personal safety reasons) to withhold their identity from the public by using a pseudonym. Editors are generally cooperative about pseudonyms if the exposé is timely and well-documented. Exposés currently in demand include reports of consumer fraud.

Two well-known American exposés are Upton Sinclair's *The Jungle*, about the meat-packing industry in Chicago, and Woodward and Bernstein's probe of the Watergate affair, *All the President's Men*. (*See: investigative reporting; magazine article, types of; pen name.*)

Exposition. The technique of communicating information—in nonfiction writing, by explaining something to the reader in a news story or magazine article; in fiction, by skillfully relating details about events, characters, or situations that have taken place before a story started and that the audience must know to understand the story.

Exposition can be presented in fiction through narration, dialogue, or action. Writers skilled at this technique insert exposition subtly, so that the reader or viewer doesn't recognize it as exposition.

Exterior. In a motion picture or television script, this term indicates an outdoor scene; it is followed by more specific information about the location, sometimes describing in detail how it looks. Typed all in caps in a script, *exterior* is abbreviated *ext.* (*See: television script terms.*)

Fable. A story written in either prose or verse that intends to teach a lesson or a truth about living. Fables often use personified animals or objects as characters, in contrast to parables, in which the characters are human beings. The major character in a fable discovers a universal truth after undergoing a single experience; this truth, or moral, is usually presented at the end of the story, in the form of a platitude rather than as an implicit theme. The fable writer, or fabulist, intends to impress the moral upon the reader's memory. "Don't count your chickens before they're hatched" is the moral of Aesop's fable "The Milkmaid and Her Pail."

Fables existed before the printed word as folk tales that were recounted orally. Hundreds of fables have been attributed to the Greek slave Aesop, who lived between 620 and 560 B.C. Two hundred of his tales were gathered in about 320 B.C. to make up the earliest known collection. During the medieval period, Latin translations of Aesop's fables were used as textbooks in schools. "The Crow and the Pitcher," "The Lion and the Mouse," "The Hare and the Tortoise," and "The Town Mouse and the Country Mouse" are some of Aesop's fables. Other ancient fable collections include *The Panchatantra* and *The Jatakas*, both from India. *The Panchatantra* was written about 200 B.C. Structured in verse, these stories are much more elaborate than Aesop's are. *The Jatakas*, a huge collection of stories about the reincarnation of Buddha, dates at least as far back as the fifth century A.D.

Jean de La Fontaine, a seventeenth-century Frenchman, was the master of the French fable. His tales, written in verse, include "The Fox and the Crow," "The Grasshopper and the Ant," and "The Frog Who Would Be an Ox."

Adaptations of fables are published today as single stories, such as "The Monkey and the Crocodile" by Paul Galdone, and as modern versions of traditional stories, such as "The Black Sheep" by Jean Merrill. Some authors have adapted collections of fables, as shown in

Louis Untermeyer's *Aesop's Fables,* intended for young children; other authors, such as James Thurber, have created *Fables For Our Times.* (*See: parable; proverb.*)

Fact sheet. An outline used by an announcer during ad-libbed broadcast commercials.

Faction. The term for works that are presented as fiction but that use actual persons and events in their story lines. The *roman á clef* ("novel with a key") is a form of faction in which famous persons and events are used and are not heavily disguised.

The novels by Arthur Hailey about the hotel business, international airports, and the automobile business (*Hotel, Airport, Wheels,* etc.) were often called "faction" by his publisher. A recent novel that incorporated historical figures into the story line was E.L. Doctorow's *Ragtime.*

Facts on File. (*See: periodicals, indexes to; research aids/techniques.*)

Fade in. An editing direction for motion pictures or television, used to indicate that the image begins all in one color and the scene gradually comes up full. Used at the beginning of most screenplays; this direction is typed all in caps in a script. (*See: television script terms.*)

Fade out. An editing direction for motion pictures or television, used to indicate that the scene fades away to black. This direction is typed all in caps in a script. (*See: television script terms.*)

Fair comment. Some authors of what might otherwise be libelous comments have a defense against lawsuit under the *fair comment privilege.* Fair comment requires the following criteria: 1) It must be clear that the libelous comment is an opinion, not a statement of fact. 2) The opinion must be fair. 3) There must be no malice. 4) The opinion must rest on facts.

The fair comment defense is a concern of writers of columns, reviews, letters to the editor, and other articles of a critical nature.

The average citizen can sue for libel a person he feels has damaged his reputation. A film reviewer, on the other hand, who writes that a certain director has produced less than his best work in a certain film, is usually protected under the fair comment privilege from a lawsuit for libel. (*See: libel.*)

Fair use. The amount of copyrighted material that may be quoted—especially for the purposes of criticism, comment, news reporting, teaching, or research—without infringing a copyright. Fair use is usually determined by these four factors: 1) the purpose and character of the use—for example, commercial or nonprofit educational; 2) the nature of the copyrighted work; 3) the amount used in proportion to the copyrighted work as a whole; and 4) the effect on the market value of the copyrighted work.

A book reviewer, for example, may quote a passage from a novel in order to illustrate what he is criticizing; or a teacher may reprint a poem from a book, under certain conditions, in order to discuss its merits and/or faults with his class. Teachers and writers may wish to write for a free copy of "Reproduction of Copyrighted Works by Educators and Librarians," Circular R21, from the Copyright Office, Library of Congress, Washington DC 20559, which contains the "Agreement on Guidelines for Classroom Copying . . ." among other guidelines on fair use.

There is no specific number of words, lines, or notes that can safely be taken without permission although writers and editors have established some "rules of thumb" which, until they are challenged in court, serve as guidelines. For example, quoting four lines from a 200-line poem is not expected to require permission, whereas four lines from an eight-line poem would. Quoting 100-250 words from a trade book without permission seems a common practice, whereas university presses may allow up to 500 words quoted without permission. Acknowledging the source of the copyrighted material does not substitute for obtaining permission when the material quoted goes beyond the fair use guidelines. (*See: copyright; permissions.*)

Fair use of broadcast materials. As this encyclopedia goes to press, the courts have not yet decided in the suit of Walt Disney Productions against Sony, manufacturer of the Betamax videocassette recorder, for copyright infringement. Nor has Congress completed its study of whether, and/or how, royalties might be assessed against the manufacturers of VCR equipment, blank tapes and related equipment (and ultimately the consumer) whose buyers are using them to tape copyrighted programs off the air.

Guidelines have been established, however, for off-air recording of broadcasts for educational purposes by nonprofit institutions. The guidelines define *broadcast programs* as "television programs transmitted by television stations for reception by the general public without charge."

Basic limitations are: 1) the recorded program may be retained by the institution for no more than 45 days after recording; 2) the program may be used only once by individual teachers during the first 10 school days in the 45-day retention period; 3) the remaining 35 days is for teacher evaluation purposes only; and 4) the off-air recording must include the copyright notice on the program. The complete guidelines were published in the October 14, 1981 *Congressional Record*, pp. E4750-E4752. (*See: copyright.*)

Fairy tale. A genre of children's fiction characterized by magic, personified animals and objects, and such imaginary beings as wizards, fairies, ogres, gnomes, and witches. A fairy tale can be written as a traditional story, such as *Cinderella*, by John Fowles; a variation on the traditional tale, such as *Nibble Nibble Mousekin: A Tale of Hansel and Gretel*, by Joan W. Anglund; or an original, contemporary story, such as *Mary Poppins*, by Pamela L. Travers.

The structure of a fairy tale is similar to that of the short story in that it has a beginning, a middle that rises to a climax, and a conclusion in which the conflict is resolved. But fairy tales, unlike most contemporary stories, are often begun and ended with statements from a narrator. A piece might begin with "Long ago and far away. . ." and end with "And now the joy began in earnest. I wish you had been there too."

Many fairy tales contain maxims, themes, or religious messages, which have endured for centuries.

Characters are often stereotypical: they clearly embody good or evil.

A storytelling feeling is evident in classic fairy tale style, because many of these stories were recited for generations before being written down; even the published versions are characterized by naturalistic dialogue and economy in description. Verse is an element of some fairy tales.

Classic fairy tale anthologies include Hans Christian Andersen's *Fairy Tales; Tales of Long Ago with Morals* (also known as *Tales of Mother Goose*), by Pierre Perrault d' Armancour (also attributed to Charles Perrault, his father); and *Grimms' Popular Stories*, by Jacob and Wilhelm Grimm. Contemporary versions of some classic fairy tales are *The Blue Fairy Book*, by Andrew Lang, and *The Brocaded Slipper*, by Lynette Vuong (a collection of five Vietnamese counterparts of such Western fairy tales as Cinderella, Thumbelina, etc.).

Whether juvenile magazines use fairy tales (and which type if they do) varies by publication. *Writer's Market* listings provide editors' guidelines regarding fairy tales. (*See: fantasy in children's literature.*)

Falling action. In literature—especially drama—the part of the story that takes place after the climax. The falling action usually consists of a *reversal*, which indicates a change in the characters' situation, and a *resolution*, or unraveling of plot complications. The latter is also known as the *dénouement*. (*See: dénouement; rising action.*)

False plant. Information that has nothing to do with the conclusion or resolution of a conflict in a short story or novel is called a *false plant*. Usually found in mystery stories, the false plant's purpose is to throw the reader off the track; it is often referred to as a "red herring." A false plant, for example, might be the introduction of a character who seems to have a good motive, the means, and the opportunity for murder—even though he turns out not to be the real murderer. Erle Stanley Gardner's Perry Mason novels made frequent use of false plants to challenge the reader.

Dangling plants—information introduced and then never referred to again in the story—are annoying to both editors and readers. A satisfactory false plant is brought to a conclusion before the story ends. Although the information may be misleading, it is nevertheless adequately explained somewhere in the story. (*See: plant; plot.*)

Fan magazine writing. Colorful portrayals of the lives of motion picture and TV personalities are found in fan magazines. Fan magazine writing, geared for a readership of teenagers and young adult women, depicts stars as "real" people with universal experiences, both triumphant and dismal.

Writing for fan magazines may fall into one of two categories: the exclusive and the angled story. *Exclusives* usually involve personal interviews with stars, and therefore are generally written by magazine staffers or correspondents. *Angled* stories, on the other hand, may be submitted by freelancers who hit on a timely new slant for an article about a currently popular star.

Because of the volatile lives that many celebrities lead, fan magazine writers often concentrate on aspects of stars' lives not likely to change quickly. They write of celebrities' long-term marriages, children, health, and religious experiences. Usually running between 1,500 and 3,000 words, angled stories are filled with quotes and anecdotes available from news clipping and library files. The actual story line in angled pieces is almost secondary to grabbing the reader's interest with a catchy title and showing her yet one more glimpse of a star's personal life.

Successful fan magazine writing comes from knowing the movie magazine field. Publications such as *Variety* and *TV Guide* give writers reliable information about which stars are currently "hot."

Fan magazine markets and their specific submission requirements and payment rates are listed in the "Theater, Movie, TV and Entertainment" section of *Writer's Market*.

Fantasy in children's literature. If fantasy is introduced in a children's story, it must be on a separate plane from reality, according to Claudia Lewis, educator and author of *Writing for Young Children*. She points out that the two worlds may be juxtaposed, as when a character awakens from a dream, but that one world may not be evidenced in the other—for example, a character's bringing back a material possession from a dream or a fantasy world is unacceptable to most editors. In some stories, such as A.A. Milne's *Winnie the Pooh*, reality and fantasy coexist but only seem to be in conflict with each other. In Milne's story, while Christopher Robin appears to be a real boy, the fact that he lives alone in a treehouse helps the reader realize that Christopher is partially fantastic—and so he is believable when

conversing with animals.

In some juvenile stories, the author can shift to a fantasy setting credibly if he transports the characters near the start of the piece, before readers are accustomed to the realistic scene.

Lewis contends that fantasy is ineffective when an author violates the reader's sense of logic: she gives the example of a personified train whose lights fail because of its emotional state, but then are repaired mechanically by an engineer.

Freelancers submitting fantasy to children's magazine editors should research each editor's own preferences and prejudices by reading specific requirements in *Writer's Market*.

Farm writing. Emphasizing informative articles dealing with the business of farming, farm writing reflects the many changes in the industry resulting from automation, scientific research, and the trend toward larger farms. "Down home" farm tales of the early 1900s have been replaced with business management and profitability articles intended for farming entrepreneurs.

Most successful farm writers have at least a general understanding of agricultural terms. They frequently contact local agricultural colleges and land-grant universities to learn about particular farm commodities, crops, and breeds of livestock. Armed with that knowledge, they are better able to focus and specialize their writing for a unique farm readership.

Knowing the farm audience and potential markets is perhaps the most crucial element in writing successful farm material. The readership is generally persons 25-55 years old with college backgrounds and/or extension course work in some aspect of agriculture, managing a farm yielding a six-figure income. This clientele reads farm magazines for technical advice, information about industrial suppliers, agribusiness organizations, and pending farm legislation.

The writing reflects a farm viewpoint (not an urban one) and translates technical and business data into clear, readable prose substantiated with research and interviews.

In addition, there are some opportunities for feature articles dealing with rural life, health care, and transportation in general interest and farm life magazines. *Writer's Market* lists publications according to their farm speciality, such as "Crops and Soil Management" and "Dairy Farming," to assist writers in querying magazines with appropriate material.

Feature. The newspaper term for a piece of nonfiction intended to involve, teach, or amuse the reader by giving him information of human interest rather than news. Features may use some of the conventions of fiction, including plot, symbolism, character, and dialogue. They are colorful pieces that deal with real events, innovations, trends, issues, and processes, placing an emphasis on the people involved.

Feature writing is not concerned so much with formula (as in the pyramid structure of "hard" news writing) as it is interested in impact. The gamut of subject matter and writing style employed by feature writers is nearly endless, as "feature" becomes an umbrella term for many literary structures. Personality sketches, narratives, interview pieces, essays, exposés, how-to's,

columns, miniature anthologies, and reviews may all be considered features.

Ideas for writing features come from having a keen news sense, an awareness of human interests, and a healthy curiosity. A successful feature story's coverage must be suited to its news value. Its tone and slant must be appropriate to the article's intended effect. For example, features that grow out of a slumping economy reflect the anxiety and despair of the individuals who are most affected.

Besides local newspapers as potential outlets for feature writing, the annual *Writer's Market* lists thousands of magazine markets for freelance articles. (*See: article.*)

Federal Communications Commission (FCC). A U.S. government agency that regulates privately owned radio and television stations, and telephone and telegraph operations. Established by the Communications Act of 1934, the Commission is composed of four members and one chairman who are appointed by the President of the U.S. and serve a seven-year term.

The FCC has the power to issue, revoke, and alter licenses. A license is granted to a broadcaster on the basis of "public interest, convenience, or necessity."

Some requirements of broadcasters, according to FCC regulations, are that call letters must be announced, sponsors must be identified, and equal time to political parties must be given.

Federal Information Center Program, General Services Administration. Writers seeking information or "experts" in virtually any subject area can contact the Federal Information Center Program of the General Services Administration, a primary source of assistance for individuals with questions or problems related to the Federal government. Experienced and knowledgeable about the wide range of services provided by the hundreds of different departments, agencies, and programs of the Federal government, the numerous laws and regulations it administers, and the multitude of publications and periodicals available, the FIC staffs can either answer a question within minutes or refer the caller to specific agencies, departments, or individuals considered authorities in a particular field.

Federal Information Centers currently operate in 37 cities throughout the United States. Residents of 41 other cities have direct access to the nearest FIC via local telephone tielines. Statewide, toll-free 800 telephone service is available in Florida, Iowa, Kansas, Missouri, and Nebraska.

Many FICs have staff specialists who speak languages other than English. In addition, every center makes available to callers government publications on consumer information, energy conservation, and a variety of other topics.

Federal Information Centers are listed under the heading "U.S. Government" in the white pages of the telephone directory, and a list of FIC addresses and telephone numbers appears in the Appendix to this encyclopedia. (*See: Census Bureau, Department of Commerce; Library of Congress; Ombudsman, Office of, U.S.*

Department of Commerce; United States Government Manual.)

Fees. Fees for one-time editorial/writing jobs vary according to many factors, including the client, the reputation and experience of the writer, and the geographic area. The list of suggested fees provided in "How Much Should I Charge?" in *Writer's Market* can guide the writer in establishing fees. The article also includes advice on choosing jobs and setting fees. (*See: book publishing economics [in the Appendix]; full-time freelancing, economics of; magazine publishing economics.*)

Additional information: *Jobs for Writers.*

Feet. (*See: verse.*)

Fellowships. (*See: scholarships, fellowships, internships.*)

ff. Abbreviation for *folios.* It appears as lower case letters (ff) in indexes and footnotes after the first page number of the subject being referenced, when the subject is discussed on a considerable number of pages that are consecutive or in proximity. The abbreviation *ff.* connotes "and the following."

Fiction. This term refers to literary work created in the writer's imagination and designed to entertain readers. Although it is a work of imagination, it may incorporate large amounts of factual material—and in many genres, e.g., the historical novel and many modern suspense-thrillers—the appeal of the story resides as much in the factual background as in the imaginative narrative. The term *fiction* is generally applied to novels and short stories, but its ingredients are found in other genres, including poetry, drama, film, folklore, and fairy tale. The earliest known *written* fiction, some say, is the Egyptian story "The Two Brothers," which dates from around 3200 B.C.

Fiction is an illusion of reality woven from concrete sensations and pertinent observations of the human experience. It is usually built on a character searching for a solution to a problem. The fiction writer's story, presented from a specific viewpoint, grows out of an appropriate setting where believable characters and significant, complicating events are developed through vivid narration and incisive dialogue; the suspense and action of fiction is directed toward the resolution of the initiating problem. Though novels and short stories employ constructions unique to themselves and frequently differ in length, depth, and impact, they share these common elements that distinguish them as fictional works. Although formats change, the art of storytelling never seems to go out of vogue.

There are many molds for fiction writing, but traditionally, the writer plots a main character against at least one of three adversaries: nature, another character or characters, or himself. From the writer's creativity science fiction, westerns, mysteries, erotica—all works of fiction—are fashioned.

Mainstream fiction (the kind that usually makes the bestseller list) uses conventional storytelling devices, such as exposition, mood, and a series of conflicts leading to a crisis and finally a climax. It may also consist of a story in which characterization may overshadow plot and the story "problem" pivots on the unusual.

Conversely, experimental fiction is more interested in the form and structure of the work as a literary composition and less concerned with developing a dramatic story line. Experimental fiction writers concentrate on literary style, narrative technique, and symbolism to achieve a unified work.

Though fiction currently represents about 7.2% of the title output of the commercial book publishing world, the potential market for stories and novels is growing with the proliferation of small, independent publishing houses and literary/little magazines. In addition, specialized magazines continue to offer outlets for fiction material. *Fiction Writer's Market* is a reference book with up-to-date listings of fiction publishing markets, their terms, and payment rates. It also carries articles on fiction writing composed by professionals in the art. (*See: category fiction; literary fiction vs. commercial fiction.*)

Fiction, indexes to. Writers who want to look up a specific short story or novel have several research sources available. Fictional works may be located through specialized indexes, which are either general or specific in category. Two standard indexes of general fiction are the *Fiction Catalog* and the *Short Story Index*. The *Fiction Catalog* lists both novels and anthologies of short stories, while the *Short Story Index* lists short stories that have appeared in anthologies—whether of a single author or several.

References to fiction in the detective and mystery categories are included in *A Catalogue of Crime*, arranged by author, and *The Bibliography of Crime Fiction, 1749-1975*, arranged by author, title, and series.

Who Done It? is an index referring the reader to mystery fiction by subject, movie adaptation, setting, sleuth, anthologies, and awards.

Historical fiction is indexed by time period in *World Historical Fiction Guide*.

The two-volume *Science Fiction and Fantasy Literature* leads the researcher to works of science fiction. Volume 1 is indexed by author, title, series, and awards, and Volume 2 lists works by contemporary science fiction authors. References in *Science Fiction Story Index* are listed by story title, but the book also has an index to authors. The *Science Fiction Book Review Index*, which lists book reviews of science fiction works, is indexed by author of book, and includes a title index.

Fiction terms. (*See: adult fiction; adventure story; antagonist; anticlimax; antihero; atmosphere; character; climax; conflict; crisis; dark moment; description; dialogue; emotion in writing; empathy; endings, story; erotica; ethnic fiction; experimental fiction; fairy tale; fantasy in children's literature; first novels; first person viewpoint; flashback; flashforward; flat character; foil; foreshadowing; formula story; gimmick; gothic; imagery; interior monologue; legend; literary fiction vs. commercial fiction; mainstream fiction; motivation; mystery story; myth; narrator; nonfiction novel; novel writing; novelization; novels for young people; novels, marketing; occult; picaresque; plot; popular fiction; protagonist; roman à clef; romance novel; romantic suspense novel; round character; scene; science fiction; second level story; setting; short stories for young people; short story; short-short story; stock character; story line; stream of consciousness; subplot; symbolism;* theme; third person viewpoint; viewpoint.)

Fiction Writer's Market. This annual directory lists publishers who accept fiction from freelance writers; it includes literary magazines, commercial periodicals, small press, and commercial book publishers. The directory also lists writing competitions and author's agents.

The 1,200 listings for publications include addresses and telephone numbers of the firms, the name of the person to whom manuscripts should be sent, the types of fiction needed by the publisher, the preferred method of contacting the publisher, the amount of payment (and/or the terms of payment), and advice from the publisher to the writer.

In addition to the market listings, *Fiction Writer's Market* contains more than forty instructional articles on novel writing, short story writing, and the elements of fiction. (*See: Writer's Market.*)

Fictionalizing nonfiction material. This technique is used to disguise the identity of a quoted source in an article. Fictionalization is used as a means of protecting the source, the writer, and the publication from lawsuits. In highly personalized or controversial accounts, the writer informs readers that the character/subject has been masked. He may use an alternate first name or a first name and last initial for identification. In addition, the writer may paraphrase one or more quotes to protect the anonymity of a source who uses a habitual expression. Another instance of fictionalization occurs when the writer inserts his own opinion by crediting it to a nondescript "observer" in the piece to avoid openly editorializing about an issue.

In addition to fictionalizing people, a writer may also use a generic rather than a specific name for a locale—e.g., "a small Midwestern farm town"—or a group—e.g., "a local fraternal organization" instead of the Rockford, Iowa, Rotary Club.

The great danger of fictionalizing nonfiction lies in jeopardizing the writer's and the article's or book's credibility. Therefore, a writer attempts to maintain a balance between attribution to "real" names and anonymous people. In any case, the editor should be informed about the writer's use of fictionalization and the reasons for it. (*See: composite character; faction; new journalism; nonfiction novel; symbolic quote.*)

Fictitious names. When a work of fiction is based on a true incident, the author should give fictitious names to the characters, as well as change the setting, their occupations, etc., in order to avoid risking a lawsuit for invasion of privacy. The changes should be substantial enough that the real identity of the fictionalized character is not obvious. Author Gwen Davis Mitchell learned that lesson the hard way when she was sued by Dr. Paul Bindrim in connection with her novel *Touching.*

Fictitious names are also sometimes given to persons mentioned in nonfiction articles (e.g., "Susan Smith—not her real name—is one of the more than 50 teenagers to appear before the County School Board in connection with . . . .") to protect a source's privacy and/or to prevent the reporter/writer from losing a future source. (*See: privacy, invasion of.*)

Fifty Common Errors in Writing. (See the Appendix to this encyclopedia.)

Fifty Most Misspelled Words. (See the Appendix to this encyclopedia.)

Figures of speech. Writing techniques that furnish the writer with a nonliteral means of conveying images. Figures of speech include hyperbole, irony, metaphor, metonymy, onomatopoeia, paradox, personification, and simile.

When used effectively, figures of speech are appropriate to the characters and the setting of a story. A skillful writer uses them selectively and in moderation. (*See: hyperbole; imagery; irony; metaphor; metonymy; onomatopoeia; paradox; personification; simile.*)

Filler. A filler is a short, nonfiction item used by an editor to "fill" a column or page. The hallmark of filler material is its variety of subject matter. Fillers succeed more often because of their spontaneity than deep literary merit. They are informative morsels of writing that generate an instant reaction/rise from intended readers. They may be jokes, light verse, little-known historical facts, clever epigrams, word puzzles, helpful hints, crazy definitions— even distinctive photographs tied into the interests of a unique readership.

A popular filler with some editors is the humorous sign, such as this one mentioned in *Reader's Digest*: "Notice at Everglades National Park: 'Fishing in this area reserved for the birds.' " (Any issue of *Reader's Digest* carries a variety of fillers at the ends of articles.)

Ideas for fillers come from folklore

and proverbs, from signs of a season and political shenanigans, from typographical errors and overheard conversations. Fillers may also be news clippings transformed into "newsbreaks"—short tidbits, not otherwise covered in a particular publication, but interesting for the acknowledgment of some technological breakthrough, medical advance, or significant development.

Fillers appear in countless publications: newspapers, general and special-interest magazines, newsletters. Radio announcers and disc jockeys use them on their shows. Writers select potential filler markets according to the type of material they use and the characteristics of their readers/audience. Each filler is typed double-spaced, on an 8½x11-inch sheet of paper with the writer's name and address in the upper left corner of the page. If the filler is a clipping, the publication name and date of issue is also included. *Writer's Market* lists hundreds of publications seeking fillers and specifies their individual payment schedules (usually a flat rate). (*See: potboiler.*)

Film Table. Words per frame of 8mm, 16mm, and 35mm film. (See the Appendix to this encyclopedia.)

Film writing, nontheatrical. Certain public relations, industrial, scientific, and documentary movies are produced for selected audiences rather than for use in commercial theaters. When the idea for a nontheatrical film is "sold" to a sponsor, the script is usually written in four stages. The first is a synopsis, a brief step-by-step outline of the plot and main action of the film. The second phase is the treatment, a fully developed narrative covering all the principal situations and some key passages of dialogue. The bulk of the research is done in writing the treatment; this is the key to a good script. Equipped with background information, the film writer uses his imagination and organizational skills to determine what will be covered, in how much detail, and in what order. From the treatment a first draft that breaks down the action into sequences and numbered scenes evolves. Finally, the screenplay, also known as the master *shooting script* or *scenario*, is written as a detailed, two-column shooting outline. Generally, all visuals, including scene description and camera directions, are grouped into one column, and all corresponding audio portions, including narration, music, sound effects, and dialogue, are placed in the other. As literature, the script, like other manuscripts designed for the ear, does not usually stand too well on its own; rather, its merits lie in how effectively it serves as a blueprint for the multifaceted efforts involved in producing a film. (See the sample audiovisual film script included in the Appendix to this encyclopedia.)

Film writing as a freelance venture is most often done for an independent sponsor such as the armed forces, various government agencies, boards of education or educators' associations, or business and industry. Writers land film contracts by locating producers who are investigating particular market needs and using their own expertise and reputation to propose and "sell" an idea to a potential backer. Both producer and writer consult with a client, who outlines a purpose, budget, and target audience.

Business Screen/Back Stage and *Audio-Visual Communication*, business trade magazines, and basic periodicals of films, audiovisuals, and television, contain ads and nontheatrical film reviews and discuss equipment and new trends in the film writing industry. They are also an excellent source for locating potential film sponsors. In addition, local film producers are frequently listed in the Yellow Pages of the telephone directory, under "Motion Picture Producers."

Payments for nontheatrical film writing vary depending on the sponsor, but working for a production company currently yields the writer between 5% and 12% of the film's production cost. If, for example, production cost is $1,500 per release-minute, the writer would earn from $25-$180 per minute of film. *Writer's Market* lists current rates for film writers in its "How Much Should I Charge?" and audiovisual sections. (*See: audiovisual communication; screenwriting.*)

Film writing, theatrical. (*See: screenwriting.*)

Films. (*See: screenwriting.*)

Financial writing. This category comprises articles related to business management, economics, finance, and case histories of successful businesses. Financial writing is one rib of the business writing umbrella. It is clearly written and packed with verified facts, slanted for business professionals and other interested individuals. It may put the "human element" into

business analysis; prepare reports for investment houses, managements, political decision makers; try to provide money-making ideas; or suggest profitable ventures for its readers.

The financial writer has a basic business "sense"—acquired through formal education, practical experience, or informal study. Knowledge of the stock market is a common foundation; the writer then develops a financial specialty, since editors often look for writers who can add depth and focus to their work. A financial writing specialty may take any of several forms, including coverage of an industry (steel, oil), a profession (international business, banking), a discipline (accounting, investing, marketing), a category of investment items (precious gems, wines), or a geographical area (the Southwest, Canada). Writers keep current in their field by regularly reading industry publications, union newspapers, *The New York Times*, and the *Wall Street Journal*. They gather accurate economic information from government offices, public relations agencies, and professional societies associated with their writing specialty.

Financial writing appears in national and regional business magazines, newspapers, and various trade magazines, where articles aim at informing readers about the state of their industry. Editors usually welcome technical articles on the latest developments in the field and case histories showing how successful members of the trade operate for efficiency and profit. *Writer's Market* lists specific outlets for financial writing in its "Business Management" and "Business and Finance" sections. (*See: business writing.*)

First amendment. (*See: freedom of the press.*)

First draft, revising and rewriting. The first draft of an article or story is the first typed version of the manuscript from beginning to end. There is no specific number of drafts that can be said to result in a good manuscript; different writers complete their work by different methods. Some do several rewritten drafts of each manuscript, while others consider the first draft with minor revisions the final copy.

Although there are no set rules regarding manuscript revision, certain standard methods are widely used by writers. For example, it can be helpful to set aside the first draft for a day or more before rereading it, and to reread it in a different location from the one in which it was written. Rereading the drafts aloud to oneself or to another person can uncover poor or weak spots. Many writers have a tendency to reread the first draft, page by page, as it is written. This time-consuming method of revision is not as efficient as the alternate method suggested above, but some writers work best this way. Anyone who reads a page at a time should not forget at the end to go through the whole manuscript one more time. Focusing on one page at a time may result in small repetitions or contradictions from page to page; the writer needs to step back, figuratively, and look at everything all at once.

In editing his own work, much of an author's revision is accomplished through deletion and condensation. First, the author eliminates redundancies, irrelevances, too-obvious statements, and unnecessary words and circumlocutions. Next, he assesses the logical order of the remaining elements of the work. Some writers, for example, color-code their first draft with a highlighting pen to emphasize the major elements of an article and to make sure the structure best serves the point they're trying to make. The author's next step is to add any necessary new information. Checking word choice should be the emphasis the next time he reads through; during this part of the revision, he looks for imprecise verbs and weak nouns needing too many modifiers. The final stage of revision finds the author concentrating on consistency of tense, verb agreement, and other grammatical points, as well as punctuation and spelling.

Some changes needed in the first draft can be prevented by completing all necessary research before beginning to write. Some retyping can be avoided by a judicious use of scissors and tape when reorganizing earlier drafts. (*See: criticism of manuscript; self-criticism.*)

First novels. While there are approximately 2,000 novels published each year, only 100-200 on the average are by previously unpublished authors.

Although first novels represent less than one percent of the new books published annually, publishers still seek out the best prospects from the manuscripts they receive because the beginning novelist who shows promise today is likely to generate income with subsequent works.

In general, first novels receive little promotion and few reviews. Advances may range from only a few hundred dollars in the case of those publishers selling mainly to libraries, to a few thousand dollars. Since they're not promoted or reviewed, most first novels don't yield enough income to pay back the advance to the publisher. The *median* print order on a first novel is 4,500 copies. More optimistic results for both author and publisher are possible with genre fiction—romance novels, science fiction, mysteries.

The beginning writer who intends to submit a novel for publication can consult publications that will direct him to publishers who handle first novels. In addition to the directory *Fiction Writer's Market*, *Booklist* and *Library Journal* are two such publications. Both these magazines review first novels, and the *Library Journal* carries interviews with novelists who have recently been published for the first time. See book publishing economics in the Appendix to this encyclopedia. (*See:* Booklist.)

First person short story. The fictional account of an event, told as if it really happened. The story may, and frequently does, have a basis in a personal experience; the fiction writer has the privilege of bending the truth, adding, combining, or eliminating characters, and altering background and actual character traits. He exaggerates to build drama and suspense, and shapes the conclusion into what he thinks should have happened. He tells something of importance that—for better or for worse—has changed the character. The lesson—the character growth—may be subtle, but it is there.

First person stories are used in every genre, from the confession to the detective, from the general to the literary. The writing style varies with each field.

Writers sometimes confuse the first person short story with the *per-*

sonal experience article. (*See: personal experience.*)

First person, use in nonfiction. Although most magazine articles are written in the third person, a few article types lend themselves to narration in the first person. Many authors of personal experience, inspirational, nostalgia, and humor pieces write in the first person for greater personal identification with the reader. Many of the listings in *Writer's Market*—such as those in the "Sports: Hunting and Fishing" category—specify whether the editors prefer or prohibit first-person material.

First person viewpoint. The manner of writing that makes use of the pronoun "I" and thus lets the reader experience events through the viewpoint either of the main character in a piece of fiction or through the nonfiction writer himself. Writing from the "I" viewpoint has certain advantages. In the confession story, for example, designed for intense reader identification, the narrator can easily reveal her emotions—"I discovered that my husband was lying to me for the first time."

In nonfiction, personal experiences, inspiration, nostalgia, and humor pieces often work best when told in the first person.

Writer's Market listings specify whether the editors prefer or prohibit first-person material.

First printing vs. first edition. Writers sometimes confuse these two terms. There may be several printings of a first edition. But once a book is revised it becomes a second edition; it, too, may go several printings before it is revised again. The number of printings of a particular edition is usually shown on the copyright page.

First reader. The first person at a publishing house to read a book proposal or manuscript. Procedures vary widely from publisher to publisher, but usually an unsolicited, unagented manuscript (which most manuscripts are) is put in the *slushpile*. A junior editor or editorial assistant pulls a manuscript out of the pile, reads it, and prepares a brief report summarizing the book, appraising its potential market and suitability for the publisher, and recommending either rejection or further consideration. A book recommended for consideration moves on to a more senior editor— sometimes, at a small house, the editor-in-chief.

First serial rights. (*See: rights to manuscripts.*)

First vs. second serial rights. (*See: rights to manuscripts.*)

First works, contests for. Publishing companies and other organizations offer contests exclusively for writers who have not yet been published in a particular genre. Such contests may be for novels, poetry, or scholarly articles. The annual directories, *Fiction Writer's Market*, in its "Contests and Awards" chapter, and *Literary Market Place*, in its "Prize Contests Open" category, detail submission requirements and furnish the names and addresses a writer needs to enter these contests. (*See: contests, writing.*)

Flashback. A fictive device in which a scene is interjected into the narration to relate events or situations that occurred prior to those just presented or before the work opened. It is relevant information adding to the reader's understanding of the story twists and characters' motivations: flashbacks dip into the past to give meaning to the present. Because fiction often opens on a dramatic high note, a flashback may also be a necessary way of explaining how the story got to the opening point.

Flashback, to be effective, must be inserted into a story without interrupting its continuity and mood. Its association with the elements of the tale is organic, growing naturally out of the present action. In a short story, flashback may take the form of a one- or two-sentence glimpse into a character's memory. (For example: "The sparkling pearl on her finger took me back to the oceanside where we had scavenged for oysters.") In a novel, it could be a highly theatrical incident brought to the foreground by a conversation, action, or emotional response by the character to some surrounding. It may take shape as a dream sequence or a character's reverie in response to a question about his past. In some cases, the flashback technique may compose much of the work itself, e.g., Tillie Olsen's novella *Tell Me a Riddle*.

Shorter fictional works (and especially children's literature) usually take fewer glances into the past, to avoid confusing the reader by frequent juggling of time sequences. In novels, however, flashbacks may be incorporated throughout the book into episodes that stir interest and provoke insight. In any case, the skill of using flashback rests in balancing the present with only those telling events of the past that give the story credence.

Flashforward. A fictive technique, generally employed at the end of a story or novel, that provides an inkling as to what will happen or how the characters will handle themselves in the future. The conclusion of *Gone with the Wind* uses flashforward, through the following lines of dialogue, spoken by Scarlett: "I'll think of it all tomorrow, at Tara. I can stand it then. Tomorrow, I'll think of some way to get him back. After all, tomorrow is another day." (*See: false plant; flashback; plant.*)

Flat character. A flat character is a fictional person the writer has described with only one distinguishing trait; the flat character can be a major character in a short story or a minor character in a novel. Sometimes such a minor character does not participate significantly in the main plot and is just used as a foil. But if an editor has criticized a *main* character as "flat," the author should consider reconstructing the character in greater depth, with plausible motivations, and a stronger change in his situation to produce a better semblance of reality. (*See: round character.*)

Fog Index. This readability formula was designed by the late Robert Gunning, an American writer, editor, and writing consultant. It is used to measure the level of reading skill that a reader needs to be able to understand a given piece of writing. Using this method, one considers length of sentences and of words to determine the complexity of a passage. A writer might wish to calculate the Fog Index of a publication he wants to write for, to see if his style conforms.

The Fog Index can be calculated in three steps. First, the average sentence length (the total number of words divided by the number of sentences) is determined. (Each complete thought, or *independent clause*, contained in a compound sentence is considered a separate sentence.) Then, the number of hard words is found: this step is accomplished by finding the number, per 100 words, of words having at least three syllables. Proper names, compounds formed from short, easy words, and verb forms whose suffixes give them three syllables, should be omitted from this count (even though they may have three or more syllables).

The Fog Index of the passage is determined by adding the average sentence length to the percentage of hard words and multiplying that sum by .4. The resulting numeral represents the school grade level that corresponds to the reading skills necessary to understand the piece.

This entry, for example, contains 13.6% hard words; 18.6 words is its average sentence length. The sum of these two figures multiplied by .4 yields 12.8 as the Fog Index. (*See: readability formulas.*)

Foil. In fiction, a foil is a contrasting person or thing that makes another seem better or more notable. Foils are often flat characters (the meek, understanding butler who worships his powerful master) or stock characters (the villain of a gothic romance). In the mystery, the foil usually plays a reversal role, appearing to be something he is not. (*See: character; flat character.*)

Folio. The most current use of *folio* is to mean page numbers, but it also designates a book's title, chapter titles, and page numbers—or a magazine's or newspaper's name, date, and page numbers—that run in the top or bottom margin of each page.

Folio also means a sheet of paper folded to form four book pages, or an outsized book format of any of several dimensions over a foot in height.

Folio is also the title of *The Magazine for Magazine Management*, published at 125 Elm Street, New Canaan CT 06840.

Folk. Music inspired by the traditions, experiences, and emotions of the people of a particular region, country, era, etc. It is usually written in ballad form.

Food/recipe writing. This includes both articles and cookbooks giving recipes tested by the writer. Recipes, which can be either for one category of dishes or a variety of dishes grouped by category, are preceded by a short introduction about food. Articles are succinct and clear. They usually contain visual descriptions but are not so flooded with adjectives as to intimidate a novice cook. Titles, often snappy, are indicative of the content and scope of the pieces they accompany, e.g., "Master Meals with Your Microwave," "Easy Meals for Campers," and "Staying Healthy without Meat." Typical elements of a piece containing recipes are nutritional values, an indication of the ease of preparation, and instructions on when and/or how to serve the dishes described.

Food articles and cookbooks contain recipes presented in any one of at least three ways. The *conventional recipe-writing formula* lists all the ingredients and then in paragraph style explains the procedure. The *conventional-command pattern* differs only in that instead of paragraph format, it enumerates the sequence of steps required to prepare the dish. The *action-step command method* of recipe writing retains the listed ingredients followed by a general procedural explanation (e.g., Mix liquids; stir in batter) that eliminates repeated mention of specific ingredients.

Regardless of the recipe presentation, each culinary formula contains the following basic information: title, yield (in portions or total quantity), ingredients, method of preparation, cooking times and temperatures, and pot or pan and utensil specifications.

Food articles that appear in national cooking and general interest magazines are usually written by staffers. (Some national magazines do accept recipe submissions.) But freelance food writing may be solicited by regional magazines, smaller circulation specialty magazines, and newspapers. In addition to standard articles about food, they may also feature pieces on recipe swapping, eating habits, etc. The "Food and Drink" section of *Writer's Market* and the freelancer's own local newspaper yield specific opportunities for submitting articles and/or tested recipes.

Some publishers specialize in cookbooks of American and foreign cuisine, or books aimed at those who prefer a particular style of food. Besides recipes, cookbooks may also contain articles on cooking trends and the food industry, and selected tips on the art. Writers with cookbook ideas or proposals are advised to contact first the publishers of the cookbooks that they themselves own and use.

Footnotes. A citation of a reference source, or an explanation of text material, that is placed at the bottom of a page. The reader is directed to a footnote by a superior number that is placed (like an asterisk) after the appropriate material in the text and before the footnote itself. Contrary to the style used in scholarly journals, magazine articles and trade books exclude footnotes that cite references. However, editors expect writers to keep records of their sources should a question arise on which the editor might like clarification. (*See: bibliography.*)

Foreign agents. Most American literary agents work with agents abroad in selling authors' material. In cases in which two agents collaborate, the commission paid by the author is 20%, instead of the usual 10% afforded a single agent.

Authors who have no agent are represented in foreign sales by their publishers who are themselves represented by agents. *The International Literary Market Place* lists, country by country, the publishers and literary agents representing authors. Novels, nonfiction books, and occasionally plays are the works most often sold abroad; few agents are interested in marketing shorter work such as articles and short stories.

Foreign markets. Foreign markets are potential buyers of literary works published in this country. Foreign markets include book publishers, book clubs, magazine editors, and radio and TV producers. In some foreign countries, a book club may acquire the translation rights to a book, then sell the actual publication rights to a publisher in its country and language.

Practices surrounding the sale of books, magazine articles, and scripts to foreign countries are not always standardized, and many variables affect the sale of foreign rights. In most cases, book translation costs are paid by the foreign publisher. However, the overall commission paid to agents for rights sold abroad is higher than for those negotiated at home. International book fairs annually bring publishers, editors, translators, and agents together to buy and sell their goods.

It is important that authors' contracts specify who has the authority to contract with foreign publishers. When a domestic publisher handles the sales negotiations overseas, the royalties are usually split, with 75% going to the author, 25% to the publisher. If the author's agent negotiates the sale, he frequently works through a foreign counterpart and each of them receives 10%. If an author owns all foreign rights to his work and sells these foreign rights independently, he earns *all* the royalties.

Royalty scales and advances against royalties vary among countries, with West Germany and England on the high end (an important title may bring 8% on the first 5,000 copies sold, 10% on the next 5,000, and 12% on sales beyond that). Poorer and less literate countries frequently pay much less and may not report book sales figures regularly.

Therefore, the author dealing with overseas markets attempts to secure as much advance as possible from foreign publishers. (Some publishers offer a flat rate.) In the case of specialized textbooks and other titles with limited marketability, an author may settle for an advance of only a few hundred dollars.

In addition to book sales, U.S.-published articles, short stories, plays, and scripts may appear in foreign markets. *Reader's Digest*, for example, acquires world rights to any manuscript it buys, and its foreign editions often re-use the articles. Authors who sell only first U.S. serial rights to an American magazine may sell their manuscripts abroad to publications accepting previously published material. Foreign magazines often have set fees for one-time publication of articles and stories. A list of English-language foreign newspapers appears in *Editor & Publisher Yearbook*, and some English-language foreign magazine and book publishers are listed in *Writers' and Artists' Yearbook*.

Regarding the sales of writing for films, radio, and TV, the Writers Guild of America (East and West) maintains liaisons with some foreign writers' guilds and gives assistance to authors negotiating contractual arrangements with foreign producers. The Guild is listed in this encyclopedia.

Additional information: *International Literary Market Place*.

Foreign rights. Subsidiary rights to publish a work outside its country of origin. Foreign rights include translation rights, the right to publish a work in a particular country, or worldwide rights exclusive of the country of origin; the author/publisher contract specifies which rights a publisher buys and which rights the original author retains. Foreign rights are negotiated by the author's agent, if he has one; by his publisher, if he has no agent.

Foreshadowing. (*See: false plant; plant.*)

Foreword. A brief commentary, included in a book's front matter, in which the author or another person remarks on the book's contents. A foreword is sometimes written by a well-known author or authority to add credibility and sales appeal to the work. Although the publisher often makes arrangements for the foreword to be written, the author's suggestions about experts in the book's particular subject field are usually welcome. (*See: introduction; preface.*)

Formal writing style. Formal writing style is characterized by complex sentence structure and a sophisticated vocabulary. Contractions are rarely used, and punctuation follows standard rules. In addition, formal style avoids slang and trendy phrases. It is used in professional journals, scholarly works, and some textbooks; although a few writers using a formal style (such as Lord Chesterton and Winston Churchill) are widely read and enjoyed.

Formal style in magazine articles is less in demand than the more conversational informal style. Examples of extremely formal writing can be found in legal and business documents; however, such documents are coming more and more under fire as consumers object to their obscurity. (*See: informal writing style; style.*)

Format. This term has four journalistic meanings. It can be a collective word referring to all the physical qualities of a book, magazine, or newspaper, including shape, size, typeface, binding, paper quality, and margin width. Furthermore, *format* can mean the amount of available space, to which the contents of a given page must be adapted (i.e., either reduced or enlarged). Also it can refer to the internal structure of an article. In broadcasting, *format* concerns the makeup of a program for television or radio.

Formula story. This term refers to a genre of fiction writing that uses a familiar theme treated in a predictable way. One of the oldest formula stories is "boy meets girl; boy loses girl; boy gets girl." "Relationship" formulas rely on such universal, emotional appeals. The "loyalty" formula, often used in heroic adventures, emphasizes cooperation and camaraderie in joint survival efforts; the "boy-into-man" formula depicts a young person's growth in responsibility and maturity in a crisis; and the "redemption" formula plots a protagonist struggling to recover his courage.

Formula stories may appear as western novels, commercially successful motion pictures, or short stories in popular magazines. The challenge for writers is to find a fresh approach to these story patterns.

Forthcoming Books. This directory, published every three months and available in most libraries, lists by title and author books scheduled for publication. Its companion publication, *Subject Guide to Forthcoming Books*, is a reference useful to writers with book ideas they want to sell, since it classifies forthcoming books by subject matter, and the writer can see what competition his idea faces from already scheduled titles. (*See: Subject Guide to Forthcoming Books.*)

Foundations. Grants and fellowships from thousands of foundations represent sources of funding for writers in various fields. Funds are available to those engaged in fiction, poetry, journalism, playwriting, and research. Some universities offer "writer-in-residence" fellowships, and writers' colonies such as Yaddo provide food and lodging for artists. The John Simon Guggenheim Fellowships are awarded to individuals engaged in advanced study and research adding to the educational, literary, artistic, and scientific influence of the United States and promoting international understanding in all the arts.

Grant-getting is competitive, and authors who apply for funding often have work in progress or have published successfully in the past. Planning, perseverance, and patience are the mainstays for writers seeking funds for their creative ventures. The publication *Grantsmanship: Money and How To Get It* advises individuals about how to find sources of grants, how to compose application letters, and how to use grant directories. It also lists addresses and telephone numbers where information on grants can be obtained.

The *Foundations Directory*, updated biennially, is available in most libraries. It provides specific information about existing grant opportunities. The directory is arranged geographically and indexes foundations by city, subject matter, and names of donors, trustees, and administrators. Entries covering more than 3,100 foundations in the United States include names, addresses, phone numbers, purposes, activities, and the grant application procedures for each foundation. In addition, the *Foundation Grants Index* summarizes grants over $5,000 made by 400 foundations, and the annual series of *Comsearch Printouts* identifies foundation grants in 66 different subject areas. Both of these references are available from the Foundation Center, 888 Seventh Avenue, New York NY 10106. (*See: National Endowment for the Arts; scholarships, fellowships, internships; writers' colonies.*)

Frankfurt Book Fair. An annual international publishing exhibition, commonly regarded as the largest literary event in the world. The Fair, held each October, is an important bargaining arena for publishers and booksellers both, as every year more than 5,000 exhibitors from ninety-some countries display a total of 280,000 titles. Publishers meet other publishers, packagers, and agents to negotiate foreign rights, translation rights, and reprint rights. (Writers lacking an agent to arrange foreign sales of their work depend on their publishers to sell foreign rights at Frankfurt.) Booksellers look over new titles and buy quantities of books. Librarians, literary agents, and writers also attend the Fair to make contacts, buy or sell manuscripts, and get an overview of the worldwide book market.

Generally the Fair is a forum for exchanging information or discussing terms and granting options by handshake agreement. Formally contracted agreements follow.

Fraternal magazines. As monthly publications of service clubs and fraternal organizations, fraternal magazines publicize the ideals, objectives, products, and activities of the sponsoring association. In addition, their editors seek manuscripts on a variety of general subjects, including case histories of successful members, community concerns, and national/international issues, as well as topics of specific interest to members. To be successful, material must be researched, analyzed, and well-written in the particular magazine's style (generally upbeat).

Fraternal publications usually solicit freelance nonfiction, photos, and fillers, and occasionally solicit humor pieces. Specific requirements of the *Rotarian, Optimist Magazine, VFW Magazine,* and others are listed in the "Association, Club, and Fraternal" section of the annual *Writer's Market.*

Free photos. Freelance writers can often obtain free photographs from companies, associations, and other organizations to accompany articles. When supplying such photographs, the source usually indicates, either on the back of the photographs or in an accompanying letter, the credit line they would like to accompany the illustration. Free photographs are available from various museums, archives, associations, and special interest groups listed in *Writer's Resource Guide.* (*See: photographs accompanying manuscripts.*)

Free press vs. fair trial. A central concern both of jurists and journalists is the conflict between the right of a defendant to a fair trial and the right of the news media to press freedom. While journalists contend that they have the right to report on events and the public has the right to be informed, judges believe that publicity before and during a trial can preclude a fair trial by prejudicing jurors and potential jurors.

A judge who foresees a widely publicized trial has several options at his disposal to insure just treatment of the defendant. A judge may order a *change of venue* (a move to a different locale), or he may postpone the trial. He may restrict the number of media representatives allowed in the courtroom, or impose other courtroom rules regarding press coverage. In addition, those involved in the trial may be prohibited from speaking about the case outside of court, or the jury may be sequestered. Judges also have the right to impose gag orders, which prohibit those involved in a trial from informing the press.

Use of broadcasting and photographic equipment in the courtroom has been a similar source of confrontation between the press and the court. According to the Federal Rules of Criminal Procedure, cameras and broadcasting equipment may not be used in *federal courts*, except in the case of a ceremony. Despite the existence of Canon 3A(7), an American Bar Association guideline prohibiting cameras and other broadcasting equipment in the courtroom, 30 states currently permit cameras and microphones on a permanent or experimental basis.

The free press/fair trial controversy became apparent when the media published either excessive or prejudicial information during the trials or pretrial periods of the following individuals: Bruno Hauptmann, Sam Sheppard, Charles Manson, and David Berkowitz. Coverage of these cases is detailed in books and articles on journalism law and journalism theory. (*See: anonymity of sources; freedom of the press; shield laws.*)

Free verse. (*See: verse.*)

Freedom of information. Laws granting the public access to records and meetings have been passed at federal and state levels. They are rooted in the belief that, since citizens can participate in the government, they have a right to be aware of its activities.

On the federal level, the Freedom of Information Act (FOIA) provides access to records, and the Government in the Sunshine Act requires some federal agencies to announce their meetings in advance and to open them to the public. With passage of the FOIA, the public's right to know was acknowledged, and the burden of justifying availability/secrecy was shifted from citizen to government.

In spite of the FOIA, some kinds of information can still be labeled confidential, including material concerning national security or foreign affairs; trade secrets; personnel or medical data, or other information involving privacy; law enforcement investigatory records (in some circumstances); and information forbidden from disclosure by other laws.

When information is requested from a federal agency, the agency has, under FOIA, ten working days from receipt of the request to respond. If the request is refused, the citizen has recourse by application to the agency's administration, then to the U.S. District Courts. In addition, the agency must inform the requestor of fees involved. A pamphlet that describes how the federal Freedom of Information Act can be used is available for $1 from the Reporters Committee for Freedom of the Press, 1125 15th St. NW, Room 403, Washington DC 20005.

Most states have passed open meetings laws and/or open records laws, which vary regarding regulations and penalties.

Freedom of the press. The U.S. Constitution provides for freedom of the press through the First Amendment, which states: "Congress shall make no law . . . abridging the freedom of speech, or of the press. . . ."

Since the Bill of Rights was adopted, almost 200 years ago, the American press has become increasingly complex. This complexity causes incidents in which conflicts of rights arise. In bringing about compromise in these cases, members of the judicial branch make decisions that sometimes result in qualifications to the First Amendment. The right of the media in courtrooms vs. the right of the defendant to a fair trial, for example, is a continuing legal problem that could not have been foreseen until the advent of electronic mass media.

Interpretations of the First Amendment differ. Some hold to the *absolutist theory*, which states that the amendment grants unconditional freedom (literally interpreting the phrase "Congress shall make no law"). However, since World War I,

court cases have resulted in several formulations that determine the extent of protection granted by the amendment.

Cases that have posed conflicts regarding the First Amendment and that have been debated in the courts involve prior restraint (to prevent dissemination of news or commercials), libel, privacy, freedom of information, fair trial, reporters' privilege, and obscenity. (*See: free press vs. fair trial; libel; right of privacy.*)

Additional information: *Law and the Writer.*

Freelance earnings. For financial reasons, most freelance writers begin their writing careers in the evenings and on weekends while simultaneously working for an employer at another job. Many writers are unsure about the point at which they will be able to support themselves without a steady income from a second full-time or part-time job.

Some freelancers say one should be earning 75%-100% of his regular gross salary as a freelancer before going full-time. Others say that will only wear a person out and that the writer should take the plunge when he feels he has enough sales behind him and enough ideas to move ahead.

Each potential full-time freelancer must examine his own lifestyle and ability to produce salable material and decide accordingly. (*See: full-time freelancing, economics of.*)

Freelance writer, origin of. The term *free lance* was used in the Middle Ages to refer to a knight or soldier who was paid for fighting and offered his services—i.e., his lance—to any available employer.

Today, *free lance* (also spelled as

one word) has evolved into an adjective that describes an editor, writer, or any other fully or part-time self-employed person who works for a number of clients on a temporary or assignment basis.

Freelancer's Newsletter. Produced for the freelance writer, this newsletter reports on new magazines, giving descriptions and freelance article needs; special writing-related services, such as training programs; freelance job opportunities; and writers who are seeking work. The offices of *Freelancer's Newsletter* retain a résumé file, which is open to subscribers. The address of the newsletter is Circle Publications, Inc., 307 Westlake Drive, Austin TX 78746.

Front matter. (*See: book manuscript preparation and submission.*)

Frontispiece. The frontispiece of a book is a page immediately preceding the title page illustrating the book's major theme or subject. Frontispieces were used more frequently in the past than in recent years.

Fulfillment house. A company that fulfills subscription orders for magazines or book orders for a publishing company. The masthead of a magazine frequently shows a different address than that of the editorial offices where subscription orders and changes of address should be sent. That address is usually for a fulfillment house specializing in maintaining magazine subscription lists and producing mailing labels and statistical reports for the circulation director and auditing organizations.

Other fulfillment houses specialize in processing book orders for publishers and book clubs.

Full shot. In motion pictures and television, a camera direction indicating that the audience sees an entire subject or scene, as, for example, a whole person, or a room and all the people in it. It is typed all in caps in a script. (*See: television script terms.*)

Full-time freelancing, economics of. No one knows how many writers make their total income from freelance writing. The most recent readership study of *Writer's Digest* Magazine indicated that 4.5% of its (then) 150,000 circulation were full-time freelance writers, but it is not known whether they also had other sources of income.

A 1981 study by Columbia University, commissioned by the Authors Guild Foundation, surveyed 2,239 book authors and learned that their *average* annual income was $4,775. Most of these authors supplemented their earnings with teaching or other employment.

Persons who want to freelance full time must earn enough to equal a salaried position and an additional 25% to pay their own hospitalization, retirement funds, and other fringe benefits normally provided by an employer.

Most writers who consider full-time freelancing build up experience and bylines over several years before attempting to support themselves entirely by freelancing. They also build a bank balance that they can fall back on in their first year or two as a new "business." After an initial period of writing on any subject that appeals to them and that they can sell to an editor, many writers develop a specialty (or two or three) so that editors will call on them with specific assignments. However, writers still originate the bulk of the ideas they sell. Full-time freelancers also try to obtain steady assignments that can guarantee some consistent income—such as editing a company publication on a monthly basis, or doing public relations or advertising for companies without an advertising or PR agency. The majority of full-time writers are nonfiction writers, not fiction writers, since there are so many more markets for nonfiction. (*See: specializing as a writer.*)

Additional information: *Jobs for Writers.*

Fundraising. Writing for nonprofit organizations in their continuing efforts to rouse interest and solicit money for new projects and ongoing programs can be a temporary source of income for the writer. Though sometimes less obvious than other markets, fundraising projects are accessible to freelance writers who can effectively mix fact and emotion into an appeal message for a diverse audience.

The writer, as a publicity person for a fundraising campaign, works with a campaign director who usually organizes the project and defines its purpose and scope. The writing involves researching the organization or cause, reading reports, interviewing staff and beneficiaries, and getting close to the heart of the operations. The writing is designed to persuade a target audience to care enough to donate money to a particular cause. To this end, the fundraising writer prepares agendas and writes speeches, publicity releases, personal and formal letters, volunteers' manuals, posters, and requests for foundation grants. He writes honestly and sincerely, keeping emotion and sentimentality under control. He writes campaign brochures that contain all the data and themes to be used in the effort, including captioned photographs that tell their own story.

Fundraising writers may work for a variety of philanthropic organizations, including charities, hospitals, museums, colleges, churches, and community groups. Specific organizations are listed in the Yellow Pages of the telephone directory under the heading "Social Service Organizations." Fundraising organizations (listed as such in the Yellow Pages) may provide services to specific groups and offer opportunities for freelancers in search of experience. The United Fund is also a good source of information about local fundraising efforts. In addition, the American Association of Fund-Raising Counsel, listed in the *Encyclopedia of Associations,* provides a list of national fundraising firms and issues a fair-practice code for fundraisers.

Writers usually charge a flat fee for a fundraising campaign package that includes many of the kinds of writing described above. One writer's going rate for a complete campaign brochure taking 20 hours to research and 30 hours to write, have approved, laid out, and printed, is currently around $2,000. For the full-time professional fundraiser who both organizes *and* writes the entire campaign, the fee is usually much higher.

Additional information: *Jobs for Writers.*

Gag order. A rule imposed on the press in certain trials and on other persons involved in the trial to protect the defendant's right to a fair trial. Gag orders vary from case to case, but generally, they serve to prohibit lawyers, judges, law officers, and others connected with a trial from revealing information to the press or the public. In each case, the judge bans that information from becoming public that he deems harmful to the chance for an impartial trial.

Dr. Samuel Sheppard vs. *Maxwell* was tried in the 50s and appealed to the U.S. Supreme Court in 1966. Fraught with sensationalism and adverse publicity, press coverage of this case inspired a rash of gag orders in subsequent cases of the mid- and late 60s.

The Dickinson Rule, established in a Baton Rouge, Louisiana, case in 1972, set a precedent for judges to follow. The case involved two reporters who violated a gag order by writing about a public hearing and were convicted for contempt of court. The judge's rationale for his decision to convict was that even though the gag order was in this case unconstitutional, the reporters were wrong in ignoring the gag order: they could have appealed it instead.

According to a 1976 case, *Nebraska Press Association* vs. *Stuart*, a judge, in order to constitutionally justify issuing a gag order, must be able to prove that: 1) intense and widespread publicity will occur; 2) other measures at his disposal, such as change of venue, will not alleviate the problem of excessive publicity; and 3) the gag order will shield potential jurors from prejudicial information.

In 1968, the American Bar Association adopted the Reardon Report, entitled "Standards Relating to Fair Trial and Free Press." It furnishes guidelines regarding pretrial publicity and is aimed at lawyers, court personnel, and law enforcement officers.

The story of William Farr, a California reporter who achieved notoriety in the mid 70s for violating a gag order and later refusing to reveal his source, exemplifies the contemporary court-press clash on this issue.

140

The gag order is one element of the issue "free press vs. fair trial," which is discussed in this encyclopedia under that heading. (*See: free press vs. fair trial; freedom of the press.*)

Gag submission sample. (See the Appendix to this encyclopedia.)

Gag writing. A gag is usually a short, amusing statement intended to evoke a quick response. Gags supply the captions and ideas for cartoons. They may be casual one-liners, subtle remarks, obvious picture-situations without words, or strung-out multipanel ideas. Techniques common to gag writing include the surprise ending ("He popped the big question all right—who do I think will win the National League Pennant?") and the reverse (a German shepherd walking a person).

Gag writers get their ideas from the themes of other successful cartoons, from newspapers, and from events in their surroundings, as well as from TV and books. They submit gags to an artist whose style they feel best matches the mood and theme of their ideas. A gag writer may submit 10-20 ideas at one time, each single-spaced on 3x5 cards. He assigns a code number to the gag and puts that and his name and address on opposite corners of the front of the card containing the gag, so that all the information can be seen at once by the cartoonist. If the cartoonist accepts an idea, the gag writer shares in the cartoon's earnings.

Writer's Market lists cartoonists in search of gags, as well as greeting card companies that solicit ideas for cartoons. It details likely payment rates—usually between 25% and 40% of the cartoon's sale when working with individual artists, usually a flat rate in the case of greeting card companies. *Writer's Market* also specifies what rights are bought by the potential markets. (*See: comedy writing.*)

Galley proof. This term describes printed copy in its original typeset form. The type size and column width match the book's or article's format, but pages are not cut to size, and so copy appears on long, narrow sheets.

Galley proof was so named when type was composed by hand in a tray called a galley. Today, even though photocomposition is often the typesetting method, both the terms *galley proof* and *galley* refer to the long sheets of typeset copy used for proofreading.

A book editor sends galley proofs to the author for review and corrections. (*See: AA; editorial rewriting.*)

Garden Writers Association of America (GWAA). Newspaper and magazine writers, book authors, and broadcasters make up the international membership of GWAA. This 950-member group publishes the bimonthly *Garden Writers Bulletin* and an annual membership directory. Its Talent Directory referral service furnishes the names of writers and photographers to editors who request them.

Annual awards given by the Association are the Quill and Trowel Communications Awards in eight categories, and a $500 GWAA student scholarship. Meetings include an annual convention and regional symposia.

GWAA can be reached at P.O. Box 10221, Fort Wayne IN 46851, attention GWAA Executive Director Robert E. Sanders. (*See: Council of Writers Organizations.*)

Generalizations. Hasty generalizations in an article, the result of insufficient research on the writer's part, are a beginning writer's hazard. For most subjects, one expert's opinion or one sourcebook is not considered a broad enough basis for an article, since the writer and his readers must draw their conclusions after considering a range of viewpoints.

Genre. This term can refer either to a general classification of writing, such as the novel or the poem, or to the categories within those classifications, such as the problem novel, the *roman à clef*, the ode, or the sonnet. The word *genre* is taken from the French, and means *type* or *kind*.

Genre fiction is a term used in the publishing industry to describe commercial novels, such as mysteries, romances, and science fiction.

Ghostwriting. *Ghostwriting* refers to the task of composing an article, story, report, book, speech, or publication based on the views and insights of another person or organization who is named as or presumed to be the author. Ghosts write life stories for famous people who cannot write or are too busy to take the time; they write confession stories in the name of the narrator; they are the authors behind the pseudonyms on serial westerns and adult gothic romances. Ghostwriters get either no byline or perhaps an as-told-to credit, but generally they receive little public acknowledgment whether they are novice writers or established writers/editors. Nevertheless, they are recognized and respected for their ability to write in the voice of another person. Especially in nonfiction, they are also skilled in writing to the satisfaction of both editor and subject. A good speech or other ghostwritten piece should read exactly as if the other person had written it. The ghostwriter's personality/voice is completely hidden.

Many ghostwriters work in New York or other publishing centers, but freelancers around the country find many ghostwriting opportunities in the public and private sectors of their own states and towns. The domain for ghosted material is limited only by the extent of the writer's imagination. Business reports, in-house publications, grant proposals, trade journal articles, editorials, newspaper columns, and résumés may all be ghostwritten. The writer queries a potential client, demonstrates his proven abilities with written samples, and proposes a writing project designed to give the client favorable exposure. Some ghosts may choose to advertise in local newspapers and professional journals as writers providing "professional editorial assistance." They may offer their expertise as consultants, critiquing the writing of others, offering suggestions, and reworking/refining materials.

Ghostwriters (especially those writing for prominent clients) often earn good incomes for their efforts, as money, not recognition, is usually their chief compensation. Current rates range from $7.50-$25 per hour or $5-$10 per manuscript page. Depending on the assignment, some ghosts establish a flat fee; ghostwriters working as consultants generally charge higher rates, as they are offering distilled information and concentrated advice. They may contact management consultants in the area to get an idea of the going rates. Ghosting a book about a company's history, for example, taking six months to complete, may currently bring its writer $13,000-$25,000; rates for commercially promoted books vary according to the publisher, the subject, the reputation of the ghostwriter, and the book's marketability. (*See: as-told-to article or book; ghostwriting speeches.*)

Ghostwriting speeches. Writers ghost speeches for politicians, business executives, educators, and community leaders who either cannot write well or don't have the time and/or discipline needed to turn out a good speech.

Markets for ghostwriting speeches are as close to home as a writer's own community. Chambers of commerce, large businesses, and community organizations may know people who need speechwriters; local newspapers highlight town leaders, and local business figures. The ghostwriter submits a query (writing samples and evidence of knowledge and interest in a subject), where possible delivering it to a potential client in person, and attempts to establish a need for his writing services. He and the speaker establish a price for the assignment, including at least some percentage of cash in advance. Deadlines are set for a first draft, at which time writer and client smooth over the speech's rough spots. The final draft is delivered to the speaker on time in some agreed-upon form (e.g., a typed manuscript, a 3x5-card outline). In whatever form, the completed speech is the property of the speaker, who may use it however and as often as he wishes.

Payments for speech ghostwriters vary according to the speaker, his needs, and his prominence. National political figures currently pay $1,000 and more for a speech; local large business owners, sometimes $100 for a six-minute talk. *Writer's Market* lists the current rates for other clients in its "How Much Should I Charge?" section.

Gimmick. This term applies to a short, mystery-type story giving clues to help the reader solve a puzzle or uncover a secret before checking the solution, which is found on another page. Gimmick stories, usually running 500-1,000 words, appear in crossword puzzle and some game books, (e.g., the various Dell puzzle publications). They are written in regular short story form up to the point of the climax, when the reader is asked an all-important question. The answer to the question is intrinsic to solving the "mystery."

There are at least three kinds of gimmick stories. The crux of the *fact gimmick* pivots on some verifiable common knowledge that the reader must have to unravel the story, for example, understanding the writ of *habeas corpus*. The *seasonal gimmick* is based on a fact that ties in with a holiday or special occasion. (Seasonal gimmicks should be submitted to editors six to eight months before the tie-in date.) Another popular gimmick is the *detective story*, based on skillfully concealed clues that require no special knowledge to understand.

To succeed, the gimmick story must be carefully constructed and free of contrived clues that strain a reader's credence. The most salable stories, according to one publisher, are those whose content and "gimmicks" are most believable.

Glossary. A glossary is a collection of alphabetically arranged terms in a special discipline, subject, or area of interest and usage, accompanied by definitions. Many scientific and technical works include glossaries as appendices. Most books on specialized types of writing for newspapers, magazines, television, radio, theater, film, etc., contain glossaries. Some glossaries are full-length works in themselves. For example, a work entitled *Language of Journalism: A Glossary of Print Communication Terms* by Ruth Kimball Kent, is a general compilation of terms used in the communications field.

Various professional organizations and interest groups often compose lists of terms related to their occupations. These glossaries often appear in trade magazines aimed at the same readership.

Go-ahead. In the magazine business, when a writer receives a *go-ahead* from an editor, the latter has expressed interest in the writer's story idea and in reading the finished manuscript. However, a go-ahead is not an assignment: the writer receives no guarantee of publication or payment. (*See: assignment, writing on; on spec.*)

Gospel music. Begun as the spirituals sung by Negroes working in the fields of the south; these emotional songs contrasted the hardships and temptations of daily life against the promise of a better afterlife. Eventually gospel became the music of black church services and is recorded today by gospel singers like James Cleveland and Tramaine Hawkins. *Country gospel* music has its roots both in the black gospel music of the south and in the English and American folk hymns of the Appalachians, and is recorded by many popular country artists like Barbara Mandrell and Johnny Cash. Another type of gospel music, *contemporary gospel*, can many times be distinguished from top 40 or easy listening music only by its lyrical content, which must still carry a religious message. Popular contemporary gospel artists include Amy Grant and B.J. Thomas. Black, country, and contemporary gospel music are enjoying more popularity than ever before, with many AM and FM radio stations thriving on a totally-gospel format. For more information, contact the Gospel Music Association, 38 Music Square W., Nashville TN 37203; tel. 615/242-0303.

Gospel Music Association (GMA). This organization is made up of 2,500 songwriters, broadcasters, musicians, merchandisers, promoters, church staff musicians, publishers, gospel music fans, or representatives of performance licensing agencies, talent agencies, or record companies.

The GMA supports a speakers bureau and a hall of fame; it also conducts research programs. The Dove Award, for excellence in the field of gospel music, is presented by the Association.

Publications of the GMA are a monthly newsletter and the annual *Gospel Music Directory*. The GMA convenes annually. The address is 38 Music Square W., Nashville TN 37203.

Gossip column. Gossip columns are probably best remembered from their heyday in the thirties when Louella Parsons and Hedda Hopper wrote syndicated newspaper columns about the Hollywood stars of the day.

Most gossip columns today such as those by Liz Smith and Betty Beale, are about political and entertainment celebrities and are still newspaper syndicated, but some columnists have gone "video" like Rona Barrett on TV news or magazine shows. There are some opportunities to establish local gossip columns with small newspapers; the successful gossip columnist is constantly wary, however, of material that may cause a lawsuit.

Gothic. This type of category fiction dates back to the late eighteenth and early nineteenth centuries. Contemporary gothic novels are characterized by atmospheric, historical settings and feature young, beautiful women who win the favor of handsome, brooding heroes—simultaneously dealing successfully with some life-threatening menace, either natural or supernatural. Gothics rely on mystery, peril, romantic relationships, and a sense of foreboding for their strong, emotional effect on the reader. A classic early gothic novel is Emily Bronte's *Wuthering Heights*.

The gothic writer builds a series of credible, emotional crises for his ultimately triumphant heroine. Sex between the woman and her lover is implied rather than graphically detailed; the writer's descriptive tal-

ents are used instead to paint rich, desolate, gloomy settings in stark mansions and awesome castles. He composes slow-paced, intricate sketches that create a sense of impending evil on every page. Book-length gothics (usually written in first person) are therefore long enough to accommodate lengthy descriptions; many run 65,000-90,000 words long.

A variation of the traditional gothic work is the horror or Satanic tale. It concerns elements of the supernatural or parapsychology, such as witchcraft, the occult, or E.S.P. Since much remains unknown about these subjects, the writer is free to fully use his imagination. In works such as *Rosemary's Baby* or *The Exorcist*, these gothics penetrate the darker side of human existence, including mental disintegration. Interest in the occult and the power of the human mind periodically brings a resurgence in the market for this type of novel.

Though the popularity of the traditional gothic novel has often wavered throughout the years, there are nevertheless many faithful readers and publishers of this vividly escapist fiction. *Fiction Writer's Market* lists book and magazine publishers soliciting gothic material. (*See: romance novel; romantic suspense novel.*)

Government and the writer. As independent businesspersons, freelance writers are subject to certain local, state, and federal regulations, some of which are less obvious than the income tax and Social Security laws. Writers establishing freelance businesses should check with their local city or village government to learn of any taxes, fees, or licenses that may be required of them. For example, a writer who sells a self-published work himself could be required to obtain a vendor's license, charge sales tax on his book, and remit those taxes to the taxing authority on a periodic basis in the community or state in which he is selling. (*See: retirement and the freelance writer; taxes.*)

Government representatives, reaching by phone. Telephone numbers of U.S. legislators are listed in the *U.S. House of Representatives Telephone Directory* and the *U.S. Senate Telephone Directory*. These references are available in many large public libraries, and in all libraries that are regional depositories for government documents.

State legislators' telephone numbers may be obtained from the public information office, the legislative research office, or the clerk of the legislature in the individual state. Telephone numbers for these offices, in turn, are listed in the *Book of the States* and the *State Legislative Leadership Committees and Staff* book available in most libraries.

Members of Congress from larger cities often maintain local offices, which can be found under the member's name in the white pages of the telephone book.

Grammar. Grammar is a series of statements that define the basic structure of a language and how it works. A writer's goal (no matter what his genre or style) is to communicate precisely, logically, directly, and clearly. To succeed, he must understand how to use the basic tool of his craft—language. The issue of grammar and correct usage has been a point of division between scholars and writers for many years.

Traditional grammarians in the eighteenth century relied on the fixed rules of Latin to frame the standards of the English language. They also tried to establish innovations of their own in attempts to improve the language. (For example, the "use of *shall* with the first person" rule.) Their generally strict view of the "right" way to write came from analyzing formal written English. Their influence filtered down to classrooms, where the problem of applying formal rules to everyday English evolved.

In the 1930s, the structural (scientific) linguists began questioning the validity and consistency of some of the rules and definitions established by the traditionalists. They countered with studies of syntax (structure, form) and semantics (meaning) of language and concluded that language is not and cannot be permanently fixed, so long as it is used by individuals in a changing society. They espoused the general theme that a native speaker of the language could not make a mistake, because he was creating language as he spoke. The linguists concerned themselves more with spoken language than written discourse.

Being practitioners of language, most writers find neither school of thought completely satisfactory. But by gleaning both viewpoints they can determine the meaning of "good grammar." They often come to believe that good English is not necessarily "correct" English; rather, it is appropriate English. The language of political discourse in a national affairs magazine is correctly formal; the language of an afternoon radio show may be correctly colloquial and spontaneous. Writers of various genres serve diverse and unique audiences. They use grammar dictated by their purpose, their message, and their readers.

Indeed, some standards of usage in the name of direct, effective communication are necessary. Writers owe their readers and editors an understanding of parallel construction, the use of commas, the difference between *which* and *that*, the function of subject-verb agreement, the rules for forming possessives and plurals, the meaning of homonyms, and the many other "standards" that ensure clear writing. Whether he authors a business report or an advertising filler, the writer is responsible for the clarity and effectiveness of content.

Writers with solid foundations in English grammar and a sense of what is appropriate use reference tools as aids to better communication. Though the choice is a personal one, depending on the writer's needs and purposes, there are a few titles worthy as companions to the essential dictionary. *The Elements of Style*, by William Strunk and E.B. White, is a concise summary of composition and word usage. Some editions of Roget's *Thesaurus* and Theodore Bernstein's *Reverse Dictionary* (a tool for finding words whose definitions are known) are especially valuable. Handbooks of modern English grammar and usage and manuals of style issued by universities and newspapers, can be examined to see which might best serve the writer as a desk reference. (*See: dictionary; language and style, books on; writing, books on.*)

Grants. (*See: foundations; grants, directories of; scholarships, fellowships, internships; state arts councils.*)

Grants, directories of. Grants to writers, for certain projects and under certain terms, are available both from government and private sources. Several directories available in most large public libraries provide data on grants for the prospective applicant.

Grants and Awards Available to American Writers lists primarily those grants of at least $500 in value. The section "Grants and Awards," arranged alphabetically, carries listings that give brief descriptions of and amounts of awards. Also included in each listing are the kind of work that is considered, the eligibility specifications, an address where to apply, and whether or not a nomination is required. This directory is indexed by name of award and name of organization.

The *Annual Register of Grant Support* contains a section called "Literature," which lists information on grants (as well as fellowships, prizes, and awards) available to writers; the section "Languages" lists awards available for translation of literature. Listings give data on prizes such as type, amount, frequency, and eligibility, as well as number of applicants/contestants who previously applied, information on judges (of contests), deadlines, the person to contact, and an address to which inquiries may be sent. The directory's four indexes are categorized by subject, organizations/programs, geographic area, and personnel.

Foundation Grants to Individuals lists awards given to individual applicants (as opposed to organizations). Listings provide descriptions of the awards, including purposes, as well as financial information, application information, and names of officers. The book is arranged in sections according to kinds of prizes, and its indexes are "Index of Grants by Subject," "Index of Grants Restricted by State," "Index of Company-Related Grants," "Index of Grants for Students at Specific Educational Institutions," and "Index of Foundations."

The Foundation Directory contains listings on grants from American nongovernmental sources, in a state-by-state arrangement. Each listing describes the foundation, amount of the grant, availability of scholarships, name of a person to contact, and application information. In addition, the directory includes "Index of Foundations," "Index of Foundations by State and City," "Index of Donors, Trustees, and Administrators," and "Index of Fields of Interest."

In the *Directory of Research Grants*, writers may find the sections "Foreign Languages," "Grants for Canadians," "Humanities," "Media," "Poetry, Writing and Journalism," "Publishing Support," and "Theatre Arts" to be useful. The directory is indexed by name of grant, subject, organization, and type of organization.

Gadney's Guide to 1800 International Contests, Festivals & Grants contains sections on writing and print journalism, film, and broadcasting. In this directory, writers will find descriptions of awards, persons to contact, entry fees, and deadlines. This book contains an "Alphabetical Event/Sponsor/Award Index" and a "Subject/Category Index."

The National Directory of Grants and Aid to Individuals in the Arts, International, provides information on grants and the government, private organizations, and associations that distribute them. Monetary prizes, awards, and competitions are included in addition to grants. Age requirements and other limitations are indicated. Some categories in this directory are film, TV, radio, playwriting, poetry, fiction, and photography.

The Grants Register is published every two years primarily for students at the graduate level or above. In addition to scholarships, fellowships and grants, it also includes exchange opportunities and other kinds of assistance from government agencies, and international, national and private organizations. The subject index to Creative and Applied Arts will be the most useful to writers. (*See: foundations; scholarships, fellowships, internships.*)

Greeting card writing. There are many categories of greeting cards, including studio (contemporary) cards, inspirational cards, mechanical cards that feature pop-up or spring action, risque cards, and softline cards that specialize in expressing personal feelings. Greeting card subject matter ranges from everyday, general wish, and occasion cards (birthday, get well, graduation, wedding) to specialized cards (retirement, home purchase, dieting) to cards aimed at particular readers (boss, friend, grandfather).

Though many card companies have staff writers, opportunities do exist for freelancers.

"Breaking in" rests with knowing what publishers want and need. Greeting card buyers (most of whom are women) usually are more interested in the expression of sentiment than in the artwork that accompanies it. To succeed, each kind of card must have a level of "sendability"; there must be a message appropriate for some occasion and suitable for a particular sender-receiver relationship. Inspirational cards, for example, rely on serious, contemplative verse composed in perfect rhyme and meter and filled with concrete images. Humor, on the other hand, depends heavily on the structure of the message. Puns, implied swearing, gift gags, jokes on age, and slams all have their places. Humor cards often reward the receiver with the unexpected—an unpredictable punchline, a double-entendre, or other surprise. Though verse is still popular in greeting cards, new verse forms and upbeat ways of sending traditional messages are essential elements for success. Personal relationship cards (currently an expanding market) usually rely on succinct prose, figurative imagery, and/or parallel construction outside and inside the card.

Writers discover market needs by studying greeting cards—their style, variety, and format. In addition, they may request tipsheets or market letters outlining specific needs of publishers and requirements for freelance submissions. The National Association of Greeting Card Publishers, 600 Pennsylvania Avenue, S.E., No. 300, Washington DC 20003, issues a list of publishers' specifications for freelance material.

Writers submit greeting card ideas on 3x5 or 4x6 cards in "batches" of ten or fifteen. The verse, prose message, or idea is typed or printed in the center of the card with the author's name and address on the back, along with an identification number for the idea. For humorous and studio card ideas, authors may submit dummies of the size and shape of the proposed card with appropriate attachments and indicated mechanical parts included, or just a typed description of the card idea. Once an author establishes himself in the greeting card industry, some publishers may offer him specific writing assignments for already-designed cards. (See greeting card submission samples in the Appendix to this encyclopedia.)

Payment rates vary: the fee for a card idea may be $25-$75; an artwork and idea package could earn more. Some greeting card publishers also solicit calendar, postcard and plaque ideas, too. The annual *Writer's Market* lists publishers' submission requirements and current needs. It also prints a glossary of the vocabulary of the industry, helpful to potential greeting card writers.

Guarantee. A term that has several different meanings in publishing. It could mean a fee that a magazine publisher agrees to pay for an assigned article, or one that a book club or paperback house agrees to pay the author and publisher as a guaranteed (nonreturnable) advance against royalties for reprint rights. It also appears in book contracts, indicating the author's guarantee that he is the sole author and originator of the material in the book manuscript, and the publisher's agreement that he will publish the book, distribute it, and sell it in certain territories.

Guidebook writing. Cities of adequate size and with significant historical backgrounds usually produce guidebooks for sale in local bookstores. Writers can either obtain assignments for these books from organizations that produce them (such as historical societies, printing companies, and chambers of commerce), or they can write them independently and submit the manuscripts to local printers or publishing companies.

Guidebook writing can be compared to newspaper reporting because the writer finds knowledgeable persons as sources and gathers information from them. Persons who may be able to contribute to guidebooks can be found at chambers of commerce, visitors' bureaus, newspaper offices, libraries, archives, and churches; they may be able to refer the writer to other people whose knowledge he can tap. Guidebook writers sometimes use library resources to obtain background information on subjects they are unfamiliar with.

According to Martin Fischhoff, author of *Detroit Guide*, guidebook writers function as reviewers in that their material is somewhat opinionated, but balanced: they do not omit particular sites or establishments from a guide merely because of their unfavorable impressions.

Since a guidebook is read more often by residents than by tourists, it must report on the out-of-the-way and less prominent establishments in an area, as well as on the best-known ones. Although the extent of coverage varies from book to book (just as each city is individual in character), most guidebooks cover all the following general subject areas: restaurants, shops, bars, sports, the arts, history, annual events, (in calendar form), and places for sightseeing. A good, functional index is an essential component of a guidebook. (*See: restaurant review; travel writing.*)

Haiku. A Japanese verse form in which the first line of a poem contains five syllables; the second, seven syllables; and the third, five syllables. Rhythmic and metrical patterns are not determined by the haiku form, but are left to the poet to include if desired.

Following is an example of the haiku:

> Empty fields of snow.
> Already sparrows nesting
> In the tractor tire
> > M.D. Mastroianni
> > *Modern Haiku*

Characteristics of the haiku's content include allusions, comparisons, and references to nature. Traditionally, poems in this form are left untitled; however, some translators have chosen to attach titles to them. An index entry referring to an untitled haiku usually consists of the first line of the poem, set in quotations marks.

Journals of haiku, such as *Brussels Sprout, A Journal of Haiku; Dragonfly: A Quarterly of Haiku;* and *Modern Haiku,* consider freelance submissions of this verse form, as do general poetry magazines, literary/little magazines, and other types of consumer magazines. *Writer's Market* listings indicate which magazines solicit the haiku. *(See: verse.)*

Half title. The page of a book that includes only the book's title; it excludes the subtitle, the name of the author, and other information. A right-hand page that precedes the full title page, the half title is usually the first of a book's printed pages. Other names for half title are *bastard title* and *pretitle.*

Handwriting. Editors will not accept handwritten material from writers. All submissions must be neatly typed on good bond paper; during the editing process, however, most editors will accept short handwritten interlineations. *(See: author's alteration clause; manuscript preparation and submission; typewriter type styles.)*

Hiatus. A period of time, usually from five to thirteen weeks, in which a program or spot under contract leaves the air; programs on hiatus are given a specific date on which they will recommence broadcasting.

Historical article. (*See: magazine article, types of.*)

Historical research. Both fiction and nonfiction require research for historical accuracy. The inclusion of actual persons, events, backgrounds, and settings adds credibility and realism to historical writing.

Editors expect writers to provide accurate as well as readable manuscripts. If a writer's error is pointed out by the reader of a magazine or book, the writer may lose future assignments with that publisher. (*See: historical writing.*)

Historical writing. This category encompasses an assortment of forms, from profound scholarly articles and books to fillers. *Writer's Market* devotes a section to magazines specializing in history, but by far the larger market for historical nonfiction lies in general interest consumer and trade magazines. While many editors indicate their disinterest in "routine historical pieces," almost any editor will buy a well-written historical piece related to the magazine's content—provided it's slanted right and is fresh and lively in its approach.

In book publishing, over 1,000 titles in nonfiction history are produced each year. Publishers seeking historical fiction indicate their needs in *Fiction Writer's Market*.

Suggestions for researching, writing, and marketing historical pieces are found in *A Guide to Writing History*, by Doris Ricker Marston, and *Researching, Writing, and Publishing Local History* (published by the American Association for State and Local History). (*See: historical research.*)

Hold. In a television or motion picture script, *hold* means the camera should hesitate or "freeze" while focusing on one character to emphasize his reaction to what is happening. The term is typed all in caps in a script. (*See: television script terms.*)

Home office. (*See: taxes; work space.*)

Honorarium. A payment for a manuscript, consisting of a (usually) insignificant amount of money and/or contributor's copies. Honorariums are used almost exclusively by literary/little magazines.

Hook. This term is used in two different media to describe essentially the same technique. In a television script, a *hook* is an event or comment that is placed at the end of an act just before a commercial break, and is intended to hold the audience's attention. *Hook* also refers to an opening scene that piques the viewer's curiosity about the rest of the story. A successful hook ensures that viewers will return to watch the next act. According to screenwriter J. Michael Straczynksi, the hooks in a dramatic program often contain action—a thug blackjacking the hero—while those in comedy programs are usually verbal—a teenager announcing she's been asked to the prom by the class goon.

As used by magazine writers, *hook*

indicates the kind of opening paragraph needed to draw the reader into the article or story that follows. (*See: television writing.*)

Horizontal publication. This term usually applies to a publication for employees in similar jobs within specific trades or professions, i.e., a magazine for salespeople or purchasing agents, regardless of industry. *Sales and Marketing Management* is an example of a horizontal magazine. (*See: vertical publication.*)

Horror. Howard Phillips (H.P.) Lovecraft, generally acknowledged to be the master of the horror tale in the twentieth century and the most important American writer of this genre since Edgar Allan Poe, maintained that ''The oldest and strongest emotion of mankind is fear, and the oldest and strongest kind of fear is fear of the unknown. These facts few psychologists will dispute, and their admitted truth must establish for all time the genuineness and dignity of the weirdly horrible tales as a literary form.''

Lovecraft distinguishes horror literature from fiction based entirely on physical fear and the merely gruesome. ''The true weird tale has something more than secret murder, bloody bones, or a sheeted form clanking chains according to rule. A certain atmosphere of breathless and unexplainable dread of outer, unknown forces must be present; there must be a hint, expressed with a seriousness and portentousness becoming its subject, of that most terrible concept of the human brain—a malign and particular suspension or defeat of the fixed laws of Nature which are our only safeguard against the assaults of chaos and the

daemons of unplumbed space.'' It is that *atmosphere*—the creation of a particular sensation or emotional level—that, according to Lovecraft, is the most important element in the creation of horror literature.

The earliest predecessor of the modern horror genre was the gothic romance novel of the eighteenth century. The nineteenth century produced such classic works of horror fiction as Robert Louis Stevenson's *Dr. Jekyll and Mr. Hyde*, and Guy de Maupassant's *The Horla*.

The nineteenth century also marked the emergence of Edgar Allan Poe, whose work set a new standard of realism in the history of literary horror and had a profound impact on the mainstream of macabre writing.

Early twentieth-century writers of note include Lovecraft, Arthur Machen (*The Great God Pan*); and Algernon Blackwood (*The Willows*). Contemporary writers enjoying considerable success in the horror fiction genre include Stephen King (*Carrie, The Shining, Cujo*), Robert Bloch (*Psycho*), Peter Straub (*Ghost Story, Shadowland*), and Charles L. Grant (*The Hour of the Oxrun Dead, The Sound of Midnight*).

Writers can research current trends in the genre by studying such anthologies as Charles L. Grant's *Shadows*, Kirby McCaulley's *Dark Forces*, and *The Year's Best Horror Stories*, currently edited by Karl Edward Wagner.

Markets for short horror fiction include several men's magazines (*Playboy, Penthouse, Gallery, Cavalier*); *Rod Serling's The Twilight Zone Magazine; The Magazine of Fantasy and Science Fiction; Mike Shayne's Mystery Magazine;* and a number of smaller publications such as *Pulpsmith,*

Skullduggery, Weirdbook, Fantasy Book, Just Pulp, Gothic, Shadows, Black Cat, and *Whispers.* Pay rates range from a very low ¼ cent-½ cent per word among the little magazines to as much as $800-$1,000 per story for the major men's publications. Many major publishing companies have published novels with horror/supernatural themes, including Avon Books, Ballantine Books, Dell Publishing, Leisure Books, Doubleday, and Viking Press. Other magazine and book publishers soliciting horror fiction—a category that includes supernatural horror as well as psychological terror themes—are listed in *Fiction Writer's Market.* (*See: gothic; romance novel.*)

Houghton Mifflin Literary Fellowships. These awards, given for fiction and nonfiction, may be applied for by any writer with a completed or partial manuscript; they are offered on a continual basis. Established in 1935, the fellowships exist to encourage new writers and to support experienced writers in their efforts.

A fellowship consists of $10,000, which includes $2,500 as an outright payment and $7,500 as an advance against royalties.

Past recipients of Houghton Mifflin Literary Fellowships include Philip Roth, for *Goodbye Columbus*; Henry Bromell, for *The Slightest Distance*; Julia Markus, for *Uncle*; and W.P. Kinsella, for *Shoeless Joe.*

To apply, a writer is required to submit an application form, a completed or a partial manuscript (of at least 50 pages), and a description of his proposed (or completed) work. Applications are available from the Houghton Mifflin Company, 2 Park Street, Boston MA 02107.

"How-to" articles and books. The how-to article or book offers the reader a description of how something can be accomplished. It is information plus advice. The writer must be able to convey his knowledge clearly and effectively so the reader will know exactly how to proceed.

Many writers consider the how-to market inexhaustible. Newspaper and magazine editors in nearly every subject area are always interested in how-to articles or fillers that have some element of novelty or immediacy. Many editors require accompanying photographs or illustrations, particularly for craft and hobby how-to pieces for which visual representations of instructions are necessary, such as "How to Build an Electric Car" or "How to Make and Sell Pine Cone Christmas Ornaments."

The increase of how-to books on the market over the past few years has been remarkable, and their popularity is expected to continue. *How to Be Your Own Best Friend* and *How to Prosper During the Coming Bad Years* are just two of many self-help books (which are essentially how-to's) that reached the best-seller lists. Successful how-to book writers are those who are able to spot an impending trend and get their books out at the peak of public interest.

The Huenefeld Report. A newsletter published every other Monday for small book publishing companies (trade, textbook or mail-order and both commercial and not-for-profit types). Its editorial content is aimed at managerial and marketing personnel in book firms. Its publishing address is P.O. Box U, Bedford MA 01730.

Human interest. Human interest refers to emotional appeal in articles. The human interest element is an essential part of all feature writing, adding flavor and depth to the basic information conveyed in the article. A human interest or feature story, as opposed to an objective straight news story, is designed to appeal to readers' emotions. Typical human interest elements include people (a grandmother returning to school for her college degree), animals (a singing dog, a pony that drinks beer), universal desires (love, money, fame), and fears (death, inflation, rumor of war).

Human interest features involving local persons and events can be sold to daily and some weekly newspapers. Human interest elements, such as anecdotes or accounts of personal experiences, can support ideas in magazine articles as firmly as facts or statistics. (*See: feature.*)

Humor. Anything written, spoken, or acted out that causes amusement. Based on incongruity, humor consists primarily of the recognition and expression of peculiarities, oddities, and absurdities in a situation or action. There are two categories of humor: subject-matter humor (something funny of itself) and literary humor (something funny in the phrasing). The former depends on the writer being able to recognize the humorous thing or event and then report it clearly. The latter relies on the means by which the object or event is described, and is often based on the element of surprise.

Humor lies in the angle or point of view from which a writer approaches a subject. The writer may use one or more of the following devices to create humor: irony, exaggeration, parody, understatement, pun, double entendre, malapropism, manufactured words, spoonerism, pairing of unlike elements, and fancy and imagination.

Editors are interested in humor in both fiction and nonfiction. In addition to all-humor pieces, they sometimes look for some humor in articles that treat serious subjects. The spectrum of publications interested in humorous material is broad, but requirements differ greatly. Like any type of article, humorous pieces must be carefully slanted to the publication's readership and editorial needs.

Writers and editors agree that humor is often the most difficult type of writing to do. It is difficult to market, as well, since what is funny to one editor may not amuse another. Humor pieces are sold on the basis of the finished manuscript rather than a query. (*See: irony; parody; satire; spoonerism.*)

Humorous article. (*See: magazine article, types of.*)

Hyperbole. An exaggeration that is so extreme as to render the writer's meaning clearer than it would be in literal form. Hyperbole is used to characterize in the following statement: "Mary changed her mind as often as she inhaled." Other functions hyperbole can serve are to describe someone or something ("His voice was so loud that our relatives on the other side of town called to ask what was going on.") and to establish a mood. (*See: figures of speech; imagery.*)

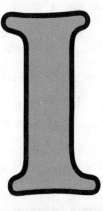

i.e. An abbreviation for *id est*, a Latin term meaning "that is to say" or "namely." The phrase is used to clarify a point, as in this example: The directions read, "Enclose a no. 10 (i.e., business-sized) SASE with your submission."

ibid. An abbreviation for the Latin word *ibidem*, which means "in the same place." It is used in footnotes, with a page number or numbers, to indicate that the same source was cited in the immediately preceding footnote. It replaces all duplicate bibliographic information except page numbers. In a footnote, *ibid* is typed with an initial cap; however, publisher's preferences vary regarding italicizing and use of a comma after this abbreviation. (*See: op. cit./loc. cit.*)

ID/station ID. Identification of a radio or television station, consisting of channel or call letters, or both; the FCC requires it to be broadcast at certain intervals.

Ideas, where to get them. Article and story ideas are in abundant supply everywhere. The writer must train himself to recognize them.

The writer learns to recognize ideas through a number of sources: observation (listening to people's ideas and concerns); experience (the writer's own or someone else's); reading newspapers (news stories, editorials, classified ads, columns, and features); magazines (expanding on a published article or concentrating on just one aspect of it); books, theses, and other printed matter; going to movies; watching television and listening to the radio; traveling.

The successful writer constantly analyzes what is going on around him to determine what interests people and why. He seeks ideas that either directly or indirectly appeal to his reader's self-interest, and focuses on topics directed toward his reader's basic drives: hunger and thirst, sleep, sexual gratification, etc.

A salable article or story idea must be narrow in focus and specific enough to encourage reader identification. The writer must develop an idea with both depth and significance, as he conducts the research and does the writing. Whenever possible the idea should be tied to a news peg or to an impending event or trend. The idea should also be developed with a specific market or audience in mind and slanted toward that market's editorial requirements and readership. (*See: peg; slanting; theme.*)

Idiom. A way of using or constructing language so that the meaning is peculiar to a language or to a singular expression. *Idiom* can also refer to a dialect used by a people, or to the jargon of a trade or profession. An example of an idiom in English is "a horse of a different color," meaning a different matter altogether.

Often, an idiom cannot be translated from one language to another while retaining its original meaning; therefore, an idiom in English may not initially be comprehensible to a foreign person learning English. *Brewer's Dictionary of Phrase & Fable*, the *Dictionary of American Regional English,* and the *Dictionary of American Slang* explain English-language idioms. (*See: dialect;* Dictionary of American Regional English.)

Illustration. Although photographs can be used to illustrate a book or an article, the mass media reserve the term "illustration" for art produced with a pen or brush rather than with a camera. Illustrations include pencil, chalk, or ink drawings; oil, acrylic, designer-color, or water-color paintings; maps, charts, graphs, and tables; and collages.

In printing, illustrations fall into two broad classes: *line* illustrations and *halftones*. A line illustration, the simplest type of illustration and most inexpensive to reproduce, is a drawing composed entirely of solid black areas or lines on a white background. Although it may be printed in a solid color other than black, such a drawing is still considered a line illustration since it may be reproduced simply by being photographed. Any line illustration that is the correct size may be placed directly in pasteup as *camera-ready art.*

Halftones, such as photographs, paintings, and pencil drawings with shading, contain various gradations of tones and require more complex forms of reproduction. Reproduction of a halftone is achieved by photographing it through a ruled or dotted screen; this type of reproduction, sometimes called *continuous tone*, is a more expensive process than the reproduction of line illustrations. Magazine or book publishers must have original photographs to reproduce from. They cannot use clippings of photographs which appeared in newspapers or other magazines since screening an already screened photograph produces a moire pattern.

Magazine editors most often use illustrations for short stories and photographs for articles. Nonfiction pieces sometimes are best served by illustrations, however. A how-to piece may be illustrated with diagrams; a travel article may benefit from a map; an article about new-model cars may be accompanied by a graph comparing prices and options.

Editors generally make their own decisions about and arrangements for illustrations once an article is accepted. If the writer is capable of producing professional quality artwork to accompany the manuscript, he should submit samples with the story or article for the editor's consideration. When black and white photographs are being offered, it is preferable to send contact sheets so that the editor has a range of samples from which to choose. Color should always be submitted in transparency (slide) not color print form. If the writer is not an accomplished artist, he may want to offer *suggestions* for illustrations—an idea for a cartoon, an interesting chart or graph. Such attention to the *visual* appearance of an article or story may improve the chance of a sale.

Illustrations are also an important element in many nonfiction books. From a production standpoint, illustrations are often the primary feature that distinguishes nonfiction books from novels and makes them more costly.

The amount of responsibility a writer must assume for book illustrations varies according to publisher. In some cases—such as children's picture books—the author will have little or nothing to do with the artwork; the publisher submits the manuscript to an in-house art director who engages a freelance artist to do the illustrations. In other cases, depending on the type of book, illustrations are primarily the responsibility of the author, who must either provide the artwork, rough sketches, or recommend sources. In either case, the author's responsibility regarding illustrations should be clearly defined in the book contract.

Imagery. Imagery is description that clarifies for the reader a sensory experience, an action, a thing, a place, or an idea. To create imagery, the writer chooses words so carefully

that the reader feels he is experiencing a situation or a sensation.

Imagery can be literal or figurative. Literal meaning is directly conveyed through the words as they stand; in using figurative imagery, the writer speaks indirectly in order to stir the reader's imagination.

Both fiction and nonfiction writers use this device. The following paragraph, from Walker Percy's novel *The Second Coming*, contains both literal and figurative imagery.

Down, down he crawled, letting himself feet first down a rockslide, first prone then supine because he needed the flashlight. There was no way, he figured, to go wrong going down. He wished for a miner's head lamp and, thinking of it, seemed to catch a whiff of acetylene. The slide leveled gradually and entered a crawl. Dry rock gave way to wet clay. The crawl was longer than he remembered, a good hundred yards. There were places where the ceiling came so close to the floor that he had to turn his head sideways like a baby getting through a pelvis. Progress could only be made by a slow scissors kick and rowing with his elbows. Once he got stuck. The mountain pressed on his back.

The next example, also a combination of literal and figurative imagery, is from a nonfiction piece, "A Sense of Where You Are," by John McPhee:

Then he began another series of expandingly difficult jump shots, and one jumper after another went cleanly through the basket with so few exceptions that the crowd began to murmur. Then he started to perform whirling reverse moves before another cadence of almost steadily accurate jump shots, and the murmur increased. Then he began to sweep hook shots into the air. He moved in a semicircle around the court. First with his right hand, then with his left, he tried seven of these long, graceful shots—the most difficult ones in the orthodoxy of basketball—and ambidextrously made them all.

Figurative imagery is discussed further under separate entries, headed by the respective names of the figures of speech. (*See: figures of speech; hyperbole; irony; metaphor; metonymy; onomatopoeia; paradox; personification; simile.*)

Immediacy. Immediacy—the element of contemporary life—is important in today's magazine articles. Writers who rely only on experiences or events of years ago lose sales, since most modern readers are more interested in present-day events. Despite the fact that some popular television series, some non-fiction books, and many genre novels have been based on historical themes, immediacy is usually necessary in popular magazine article writing.

Imprint. *Imprint* is the term for a publisher's line of books of a particular type; an editor may have an imprint (consisting of his own name) as well. An imprint can appear on a book spine either separately or in combination with the publisher's name. Such labels help categorize books for dealers and educators. *Anchor*, for example, is an imprint of Doubleday & Co., Inc., for books on religion; *Tempo* is the imprint of Grosset & Dunlap, Inc., for books geared to the teenage reader.

Imprints of individual publishers are listed at the back of the titles volumes of *Books In Print*; major imprints are listed in *Literary Market Place*.

In medias res. This Latin term, meaning "in the midst of things," refers to the literary device of beginning a narrative at a dramatic point in a story well along in the sequence of events, in order to immediately capture reader interest.

A traditional convention of epic poetry, this literary technique is also used in novels, short stories, drama, and narrative poetry. When an author begins his story *in medias res*, he usually employs a flashback or series of flashbacks to explain preceding events. (*See: flashback; narrative hook; plot; story.*)

Incident. Applied to the short story, the term "incident" has the same meaning it does in reality: it is a happening of *minor* consequence. In fiction, a *series* of incidents that are logically connected form the plot. The difference between an *incident* and a *story* is that a *single* incident in itself involves no character change, while a story always involves some kind of change in the central character. However, the result of a series of incidents in the story can bring about the change in the central character's thinking. (*See: character change; consequence, a sense of; story.*)

Income of a freelance writer. (*See: full-time freelancing, economics of.*)

Incomes, writing, sources of statistics on. A would-be writer can consult several sources to learn about writers' incomes. Unions such as the Newspaper Guild and the Writers Guild of America are able to provide such information regarding staff writing jobs with newspapers, radio/TV, and films.

The entry "full-time freelancing, economics of" in this encyclopedia cites the average annual income for book authors. As a basis for setting one-time fees for freelance projects, the writer should consult the section "How Much Should I Charge?" in the current edition of *Writer's Market*, and the book *Jobs for Writers*.

Average salaries to be expected in writing-related fields can be located in government publications, e.g., the *Occupational Outlook Handbook*. Similarly, *The Vertical File Index* in most public libraries leads the researcher to pamphlets on specific careers. (*See: book publishing economics [in the Appendix]; full-time freelancing, economics of.*)

Incorporating yourself as a writer. Depending on a full-time freelance writer's level of income, there may be certain advantages to incorporating his freelance business. To see whether it would be worthwhile in a particular case, the writer should consult an accountant/lawyer.

Independent Literary Agents Association, Inc. (ILAA). This national organization is composed of more than 60 literary agencies. All members have met the group's requirements regarding professional expertise. Most agents associated with ILAA deal with trade fiction and nonfiction, but members also represent textbooks, plays, screenplays, television scripts, articles, short stories, and other literary forms.

One goal of this organization is to improve the writer-publisher relationship. Another concern is to better the position of authors *vis à vis* publishers.

ILAA does not perform referral functions and does not furnish specific information about its members. However, a list of ILAA members who are willing to receive query letters (not unsolicited manuscripts) from writers is available from the organization; an SASE must accompany a request for the list.

ILAA's address is c/o Sanford J. Greenburger Associates, 55 Fifth Ave., New York NY 10003. (*See: Society of Authors' Representatives.*)

Independent producer. The motion picture business, which in the past was operated entirely by a handful of studios, is now replete with independent producers. As self-employed entrepreneurs, these producers assemble the script, actors, director, and finances for each of their film concepts.

Many film and television screenwriters work for independent producers. Writers interested in approaching one with a film project usually do so by means of an agent. (*See: screenwriting.*)

Index. An alphabetical listing (with page numbers) of the most important topics in a book, appearing at the end of the volume. An index may also be a directory of published material in periodicals, such as *The New York Times Index* or the *Readers' Guide to Periodical Literature.* (*See: book indexing; periodicals, indexes to.*)

Indexing. Indexing is a skill that requires attention to detail and a penchant for orderliness. An index renders a book more useful to readers and more popular with librarians (who decide what books their institutions should buy).

The basic procedures of indexing consist of reading the book to become acquainted with its contents; rereading the book while making notes of index entries; noting each entry—a key word or phrase and page number(s)—on a card or a slip of paper; sorting, alphabetizing, and editing the cards; and checking the page numbers on the cards against those in the book. To prepare the index for the printer, the indexer either types the entries in alphabetical order on 8½x11-inch paper or numbers the cards in sequential order (in case some are displaced in transit) and submits the edited cards themselves. The indexer is also responsible for proofreading index galleys and page proofs.

Major categories of index entries are personal names, other proper names (e.g., organizations), subjects, and ideas. In preparing entries, research may be necessary, since an index must give the full names of well-known persons (even when the book does not) and must cross-reference words that are synonymous with some entries, when it is suspected that readers might look under one of two different words for the same topic. Also, the indexer may need to consult with the author where "ideas" entries are concerned: he must ascertain that his conception corresponds to the author's.

Indexes are constructed by one of two systems of alphabetization: the word-by-word method and the letter-by-letter (or all through) method. Using word-by-word, the indexer considers only the first word (or the first unit before a space, such as a hyphenated word) as a unit for alphabetization purposes. In the letter-by-letter system, on the other hand, all letters that precede the first punctuation mark, regardless of the number of words, are considered to be one unit. For example, the subjects "bookkeeping" and "book manuscript" would appear in two different alphabetical orders, depending on which system were used. Alphabetizing word-by-word, the indexer would place "book manuscript" first, since *b-o-o-k* makes up the first unit before a space. However, the letter-by-letter system would place "bookkeeping" first of the two words because *b-o-o-k-k* comes before *b-o-o-k-m* (disregarding the space in "book manuscript") in the alphabet.

A person interested in becoming an indexer can instruct himself by reading manuals and stylebooks such as *The Chicago Manual of Style*; but it is unusual to acquire indexing jobs without practical indexing experience. Scholarly organizations and local groups may be outlets for beginners' volunteer indexing work. Local printers may be a source of freelance job opportunities. (*See: American Society of Indexers; book indexing; index.*)

Indirect quote. An indirect quote is information paraphrased by the writer; that is, information quoted in substance rather than verbatim. For example: *Mary Heaton Vorse once said that the art of writing is the art of applying the seat of the pants to the seat of the chair.* Although such remarks are not enclosed in quotation marks, indirect quotes are usually attributed to an identified source. An indirect quote may be rewritten to improve the grammar, shorten it, or make it more precise, but such revision must not distort or misrepresent the original intent of the remarks being paraphrased. (*See: attribution; quotes.*)

Industrial Communication Council (ICC). Members of the ICC work in business and government communication offices, or are educators who teach effective communication within organizations. The association aims to promote effective communication techniques and to evaluate trends in the field. A speakers bureau and placement services are some features of the ICC. It publishes books, an annual "Information-Resources Bank," and a monthly newsletter. A conference is held annually; regional workshops and local meetings are held periodically.

The address of the ICC is P.O. Box 3970, Grand Central Post Office, New York NY 10163.

Informal writing style. Widely accepted in magazine articles and newspaper features or columns today, informal style is a generally relaxed manner of writing that creates an almost conversational rapport between reader and writer. Informal writing style is characterized by colloquialisms, humor, and the occasional use of parenthetical material. To achieve an informal style, writers make use of contractions (*he's* instead of *he is; they're* instead of *they are*), first- and second-person techniques, and occasional sentence fragments.

An informal writing style, while relaxed, does not permit bad grammar, imprecise words and phrases,

or misspellings. In her discussion of style in *Write on Target,* Connie Emerson notes: "One thing is certain. Whatever style you adopt for a particular article, you cannot afford to ignore the elements of good writing. Just because an editor likes fifty-six-word statements doesn't mean your modifiers can dangle or that you're free to disregard punctuation. Singular verbs with plural nouns . . . won't do the job even if your article is loaded with the kind of picturesque writing the editor adores." (*See: formal writing style; style.*)

Information Industry Market Place (IIMP). A directory covering data base publishers, online vendors, information brokers, telecommunication networks, library networks and consortia, terminal manufacturers, and other organizations engaged in providing information. Users can find information in IIMP about personnel, product services, and how to contact an organization. (*See: data bases.*)

Informational article. (*See: magazine article, types of.*)

Infringement of copyright. Violation of a right granted by law to a copyright owner. With some exceptions, the owner of a copyright possesses exclusive rights to reproduce his work; create works derived from the original; sell, rent, or otherwise distribute copies of his creation; and perform or display his work in public.

The law provides for certain kinds of use of copyrighted work by others. (See the entry on *fair use* in this encyclopedia.) For example, under certain circumstances libraries and archives may reproduce copyrighted work, and teachers and students may perform or display copyrighted work. In addition, individuals are permitted to sell or display a single copy of a work. Broadcasters have the right to issue secondary transmissions in some instances and to make one copy of a program (except motion pictures and similar works) that they have been granted the right to broadcast.

When a person has been found guilty of copyright infringement, the plaintiff can recover *actual damages*—which compensate for loss or harm done to himself, his property, or his rights—or *statutory damages*, the amount of which is determined by a judge within the range specified by the law. The court is permitted by law to award recovery of attorney's fees under certain circumstances as well. Where it can be proved that a person has infringed a copyright willfully and for commercial advantage or private financial gain, the infringer is subject to imprisonment in addition to fines and forfeiture of the material. (*See: copyright; fair use.*)

Inner monologue (or inner dialogue). (*See: interior monologue.*)

Inspiration. For a writer, *inspiration* refers to a stimulus compelling creation or expression.

Psychologists Stanley Rosner and Lawrence Abt whose book *The Creative Experience* is the result of interviews they had with creative people in science as well as the arts, reported that:

". . .there is widespread recognition of the significant place occupied by intuition, unconscious promptings and inexplicable insights, and the sudden awareness of relationships. . . .The repeated references in our own interviews to 'I don't know where the idea came from,' and 'It just came to mind,' attest to functions in operation beyond the level of consciousness."

While most writers welcome spurts of inspiration, they don't depend on outside stimuli to accomplish their work. Successful writers realize that the difference between a writer and a would-be writer lies in knowing that inspiration is another word for hard work.

Successful writers work every day whether they feel like writing or not. Clair Rees, author of *Profitable Part-Time/Full-Time Freelancing*, explains: "The one quality dividing real professionals from most would-be writers is discipline. If you can write only when the Muse is smiling you're not likely to get far in the profession. Manuscripts are sold by people who have the grit to sit at the typewriter—and stay there—until an assignment is finished and ready for mailing. Waiting until you're 'in the mood' to write is a luxury the professional freelancer simply can't afford." (*See: ideas, where to get them.*)

Inspirational article. (*See: magazine article, types of.*)

Inspirational writing. Inspirational writing generally incorporates a personal philosophy that the reader might adapt to his own life. Drawing on their own experience or the experience of others, writers of inspirational material strive to create an animating effect on readers, stimulating or impelling them to some action or viewpoint. Writer's Digest School instructor Emalene Shepherd says, "If a writer can make a reader feel healthier, wealthier, or wiser, he has inspired that reader."

Almost any form of writing may be inspirational in tone: articles, books, gospel music, poetry, fillers, curriculum materials, games and puzzles, television and film scripts, and theological and scholarly material. An inspirational article, for example, recounts what an individual, group, or community did to make something better. How the residents of a town worked together to solve a problem or how an individual overcame a narrow-minded prejudice are two examples of inspirational themes. Other inspirational pieces may deal with such attributes as faith, determination, perseverance, and patience.

A logical extension of the inspirational piece is the religious article that offers the reader a guide to developing courage, strength, and fortitude through faith in God. Religious inspirational pieces, sometimes called devotionals, are often first-person stories of how the writer applied religious faith in coping with his day-to-day problems, or biographical-personality sketches of religious figures or admirable individuals.

Religious magazines such as *Guideposts* and *Christian Life* offer the biggest market for inspirational articles, but many general interest and juvenile magazines publish inspirational material with both religious and nonreligious themes. *Reader's Digest* regularly includes articles of an inspirational nature, for example.

Most inspirational articles are based on a narrative structure. The key to writing the inspirational piece lies in describing the facts honestly and well, creating an emotional impact but avoiding preachiness. Although the inspirational article may be written entirely from the writer's own experience, many inspirational pieces can benefit from research before writing. (*See: personal experience; religious writing.*)

Instant book. A book on a topical or newsworthy subject that appeals to a wide audience. Often issued in paperback, this type of book is published and placed on newsstands as soon as possible after the event has occurred, regardless of the publisher's usual production schedules. Among the first was Bantam's book on the Warren Commission Report on the Kennedy assassination.

Other names for the instant book are *extra* and *quickie*.

Insurance, authors' liability. The insurance policies of some publishers extend to provide liability coverage to authors who sign contracts with them. This type of coverage is new in the publishing field, having been introduced by Viking/Penguin; Bantam Books, Warner Books, Little, Brown & Co., Random House and Houghton Mifflin are other companies that have adopted policies covering authors.

Before such insurance was available to authors, book publishers' contracts contained warranty clauses requiring the author to pay all the publisher's expense and legal fees in the case of lawsuits brought about by the book, including those where the publisher won the case.

Amounts of deductibles vary, as do arrangements regarding the party responsible for paying the deductible. With some policies, the deductible is split between the author and the publisher. These aspects of the coverage are stipulated in each individual policy.

Some policies now being purchased by publishers cover copyright infringement, libel, invasion of privacy, and instructions or recipes alleged to be harmful. Employers Reinsurance Corp. and Media/Professional are two companies that currently offer authors' insurance to publishers. (*See: insurance programs.*)

Insurance programs. Since freelance writers lack the fringe benefit of company-sponsored insurance programs, they are responsible for securing personal insurance for themselves. Some professional writers' organizations offer coverage to members at group rates. For example, the American Society of Journalists and Authors, Inc., offers health insurance for individual members or members with families, and The Society of Professional Journalists, Sigma Delta Chi, offers its members insurance plans covering life, health, and accidental death and dismemberment. Other specialized writers' groups may have similar insurance programs. (*See: retirement and the freelance writer.*)

Intercollegiate Broadcasting System (IBS). An association of broadcasting stations at schools, colleges, and universities. Its services to member stations include providing script and transcription libraries; representing the members before government, industrial, and educational institutions; conducting surveys among listeners; and providing information services (predominantly for members).

IBS publishes the *Journal of College Radio*, five times per academic year,

and the *President's Newsletter*, irregularly. In addition, it publishes an annual directory and the *Station Handbook*, a reference source for college and school broadcasting stations.

The annual meeting of this organization is held in March or April. Its address is Box 592, Vails Gate NY 12584.

Interior. In a motion picture or television script, this term indicates an indoor scene; it is followed by more specific information about the location, sometimes describing it in detail. Typed all in caps in a script, *interior* is abbreviated *int.* (*See: television script terms.*)

Interior monologue. This technique is used to add immediacy, naturalness, and simplicity to works of fiction. It also provides added character identification for the reader.

In using this device, the author converts into words the thoughts in the minds of his characters. In this way, the author allows readers to experience vicariously the thoughts and emotions of a character's inner life.

The most effective bits of dialogue are those that most truly represent patterns of speech and thought. To help convey true naturalness, the author can insert interior monologue into an interrupted dialogue, or vice versa. In such instances, the dialogue or interior monologue—whichever interrupts—is enclosed in parentheses and both the interruption and the interrupted part of the work are followed by ellipsis points.

The interior monologue, being a thought represented in words, is either italicized, enclosed in quotation marks or simply started with a capital letter. Here's an example from James Joyce's *A Portrait of the Artist As a Young Man:*

"You know," he said, "you can ask that riddle another way."

"Can you?" said Stephen.

"The same riddle," he said. "Do you know the other way to ask it?"

"No," said Stephen.

"Can you not think of the other way?" he said.

"No," said Stephen.

He looked at Stephen over the bedclothes as he spoke. Then he lay back on the pillow and said: "There is another way but I won't tell you what it is."

Why did he not tell it? His father, who kept the racehorses, must be a magistrate too like Saurin's father and Nasty Roche's father. He thought of his own father, of how he sang songs while his mother played and of how he always gave him a shilling when he asked for sixpence and he felt sorry for him that he was not a magistrate like the other boys' fathers. Then why was he sent to that place with them?

In order to use interior monologue, a writer must first understand it; a method for absorbing the technique is to read examples of it, then practice creating original examples. Interior monologue appears in James Joyce's *Ulysses;* various works of Eugene O'Neill and William Faulkner contain examples of interior monologue. (*See: stream of consciousness.*)

Interlibrary loan. Public and college libraries that do not have a book a writer would like to use for research can sometimes borrow it from an-

other library. The cost to the writer can vary from merely the postage to mail the book to and from the other library to an interlibrary loan fee of perhaps $5-$10. The lending department of the library can advise what kind of fees and waiting time are involved.

International Association of Business Communicators (IABC). This organization has 10,000 members who are writers, editors, audio-visual specialists, and managers of communication and public relations programs for profit and not-for-profit organizations worldwide. IABC is active in education and research; other activities of the organization include an annual international conference, seminars, video teleconferences, an accreditation program, and a placement service hotline open to members. In the accreditation program, members submit portfolios of their work—brochures, publications, speeches, videotapes, or any other forms of business communication, and request an application for an examination—a 4½-hour oral and written test in which candidates are judged by an accreditation board appointed by the IABC president.

IABC convenes annually. Its headquarters are located at 870 Market Street, Suite 940, San Francisco CA 94102.

International Business Writers (IBW). This organization is made up of freelance business writers who produce books, magazine articles, and promotional materials. It exists for the exchange of information and the "improvement of the marketing environment."

IBW conducts research and distributes reports on findings to its members in the monthly *IBW Journal*. The IBW mail address is P.O. Box 753, Times Square Station, New York NY 10108.

International copyright. Refers to copyright protection in all countries that subscribe to various treaties, such as the Universal Copyright Convention (UCC). An American author whose book has been published in the U.S. may obtain international copyright in the more than 50 other countries that are party to the UCC by placing the copyright notice on the title page or the page immediately following it.

In this case, the copyright symbol—©—must be used rather than the word "copyright" or an abbreviation of it, either of which is permitted for protection in the U.S.

A work protected by the UCC must be registered with the U.S. Copyright Office in order for its author to have the right to file an infringement suit in the U.S.

Although the ad interim copyright provision (for books first published in a country other than the U.S. and in the English language) was abolished on January 1, 1978, some works are still subject to import restrictions. Currently, importation of books first published abroad is limited to 2,000 copies.

International copyright convention. According to the Copyright Office of the Library of Congress, there is no such thing as an international copyright that will automatically protect an author's writings throughout the entire world. "Protection against unauthorized use in a particular country depends basically on the laws of that country," the Copyright Office explains. "However, most countries do offer protection to foreign works under certain conditions, and these conditions have been greatly simplified by international copyright treaties and conventions."

There are two major international copyright conventions: the Berne Convention for the Protection of Literary and Artistic Works (commonly called the Berne Union), and the Universal Copyright Convention (UCC), of which the United States is a member. Although these two conventions differ in some respects, the fundamental principle of *national treatment* is common to both. Under this provision, a participating country is required to give the same protection to foreign works that meet Convention requirements as it gives to its own domestic works.

In addition to the two major international copyright conventions, there is also a series of seven Pan-American Conventions—regional agreements that govern to some extent copyright relations in the Western Hemisphere. Moreover, certain countries have adopted bilateral treaties that grant copyright reciprocity between two nations; others have laws granting protection to foreign works under certain conditions without regard to any international conventions or treaties. "In all of these cases," the Library of Congress Copyright Office advises, "the extent of protection and the requirements for securing copyright vary from country to country. An author who wishes to copyright his work in a particular country should first find out the extent of protection for foreign works in that country. If possible, he should do this before his work is published anywhere, since protection may often depend on the facts existing at the time of first publication." (*See: piracy.*)

Additional information: *International Copyright Conventions; The ABC of Copyright.*

International Literary Market Place (ILMP). A directory of book publishers, agents, book clubs, and others in the book industry located in countries besides the U.S. and Canada. ILMP lists approximately 6,900 publishers and 3,500 other organizations; content is categorized by country. (*See:* Literary Market Place.)

International Motor Press Association (IMPA). The 350 members of the IMPA are writers and public relations practitioners whose work concerns automobiles. The Association publishes *Impact*, monthly, and bestows the Ken Purdy Award for automotive writing and the Robert W. Irvin Award for automotive reporting. The IMPA's address is 230 Valley Road, Montclair NJ 07042. (*See: Council of Writers Organizations.*)

International Platform Association. This professional organization is dedicated to public speaking and performing; its membership includes actors, lecturers, business and professional men and women, politicians, musicians, artists, writers, booking agents, and program chairpersons.

The group engages in workshops and annual critique sessions. Activities aim to educate members, improve their skills, and broaden their range of contacts. The organization's publication, *Talent* Magazine, is published quarterly. Awards (named after the association's famous members) are presented at the annual convention held in August in Washington DC. Among these are the Daniel Webster Award, the Winston Churchill Award, the Theodore Roosevelt Award, the Mark Twain Award, and the Lowell Thomas Award.

The association's headquarters are at 2564 Berkshire Road, Cleveland Heights OH 44106.

International Reply Coupons. Material submitted to foreign publications and publishers, including the expanding Canadian market, requires International Reply Coupons to cover the cost of return postage. One of these coupons is exchangeable in any other country for a stamp or stamps representing the international postage on a single-rate, surface-mailed letter. The number of International Reply Coupons required is determined by the weight of the manuscript at the post office, where the coupons may be purchased.

Writers who deal regularly with certain foreign markets find it less expensive to arrange to buy foreign stamps from the country's postal service than to use International Reply Coupons. A country's foreign embassy office in Washington DC, whose address is available at any local library, can provide the writer with information regarding the postal rates for first-class or airmail service from foreign countries to the U.S., and the address to which orders for stamps may be sent.

International research sources. *The Europa Year Book*, an annual two-volume set that furnishes information about international organizations and various countries of the world, is a useful reference for writers needing foreign research sources. It covers approximately 1,500 organizations, giving facts about their activities, financial structures, functions, and organization. A writer/researcher, for example, could find statistics on the Japanese fishing industry, the address of the Swiss National Bank, or the name of the Director General of the British Tourist Authority.

Entries on each country include an introductory survey, and cover such topics as government (including political parties), the judicial system, and religions. In addition, each section describing a country contains a directory section, which provides names, addresses, and other data on media organizations, finance, industry, tourism, universities and colleges, atomic energy, and transport.

The *Year Book* contains an index of international organizations and an index of countries and territories.

International Women's Writing Guild (IWWG). Established in 1976, this organization exists for the personal and professional development of women through writing and writing-related endeavors. Divisions of the guild are the Drama Consortium and the Journal Writers Consortium, which are devoted to special interests. The IWWG directs an annual

week-long conference in July or August at Skidmore College, Saratoga Springs, New York, as well as various regional writing workshops. Information can be obtained by writing Hannelore Hahn, Executive Director, IWWG, Box 810, Gracie Station, New York NY 10028.

Internships. (*See: scholarships, fellowships, internships.*)

Interview. The interview is a research method in which the writer talks with a primary source. The interview may be the foundation on which a personality profile is constructed, or it may be one means of gathering information for an article on a subject the interviewee is familiar with.

The first, and perhaps most difficult, step is to arrange an interview with a subject. John Brady, in his book *The Craft of Interviewing*, says, "Getting an interview with someone is like asking your good-looking cousin to go out with a friend of a friend on a blind date: you must approach the subject Just So. Fortunately, there are *so* many ways of approaching him. You can phone him, write him, telegram him, stalk him, badger him (even if he's a Sonny Liston), plead with him, pay him, or woo his secretary. And you needn't be a celebrity to interview a celebrity—no more than you need be a cab driver to interview a cab driver. What you *do* need for celebrity or cabbie [is] a fetching introduction [and] an interview appointment. . . ." Most people are flattered to be asked about themselves and their jobs.

After gaining an appointment with his subject, a writer must do advance research in two areas: biographical and subject interest. A profile writer should bring to the interview a thorough knowledge of the interviewee's background—date of birth, real name (in the case of actors), home town, education, current job responsibilities, etc.—gleaned from *Who's Who* listings and a review of any published magazine or newspaper articles about the individual. Other sources of background facts are friends, relatives, and professional associates (such as press agents) of the interviewee. In addition, the writer must acquaint himself as thoroughly as possible with the subject area(s) he intends to talk about with the interviewee—politics, nuclear energy, Hollywood, baseball, etc.—by reading and talking with authorities in the field. Based on this knowledge, the writer will be able to prepare incisive questions before the interview, and interpret answers (checking with other sources on new information) and raise additional questions during the interview.

A writer interviewing for the purpose of gathering information need not do exhaustive research, but should have some background knowledge of the topic, know the interviewee's official title, and be aware of the interviewee's status in his field.

A good interview most often depends on *how* the subject is approached. Whether for a personality piece or merely for fact-gathering, the interview is above all a personal situation, an exchange between two or more people. Curiosity, warmth, and intelligence are all valuable assets to an interviewer, and a natural, conversational manner will usually yield good results. Sometimes gentle prodding and a firmer tone may

be necessary to prompt more significant responses from a reluctant interviewee, but badgering him usually results in a defensive, close-mouthed subject and an aborted interview. The writer is advised to save controversial questions until the end of the interview; then, if the subject refuses to respond, the writer still has the bulk of the information he needs.

An interviewer probably should start out with two or three set questions firmly in mind. To avoid routine responses and monosyllabic answers such as "Yes" and "No," the interviewer must ask open-ended questions that give the subject the opportunity to elaborate. And in addition to *listening* to what the subject says, the interviewer must constantly *observe*. Details about the subject—the way he talks, uses his hands, dresses; the setting; the atmosphere—are all important elements in creating a personality profile. As the respondent talks, the interviewer should also listen for possible anecdotes and flush these out as he recognizes them.

Taking notes or recording the interview on tape may be a sensitive issue; many subjects become tense at the sight of a notepad or tape recorder and the result is a stilted, artificial exchange. Professional writers disagree on the ethics of a hidden tape recorder. A solution adopted by many professional journalists is to take notes on or record freely a session with a subject who is accustomed to being interviewed for publication—politicians, civic leaders, entertainers, sports figures, etc.—and to be more discreet with those who are not ordinarily in the public eye—jotting down key words rather than taking full notes, or recording. An interview on a controversial topic or with a controversial individual should always be taped, however, and those tapes kept on file.

Fact-gathering through interviews can be difficult on controversial subjects. In hard news or investigative reporting, the writer can accomplish his task without antagonizing his sources by drawing upon several persons and taking bits of information from each one. This is a technique used by writer George McMillan, who believes that with this method, no single source feels uncomfortable about having revealed the whole story.

One interview with a subject may not be enough to write an article, so the interviewer should make an attempt at the close of the session to keep the door open for follow-up interviews, perhaps saying something like "If I have any additional questions, may I call you?" (*See: attribution; indirect quote; off the record; profile; quotes; tape recorder.*)

Interview article. (*See: magazine article, types of.*)

Introduction. An introduction is the preliminary material leading into the main part of an essay, article, book, etc. The introduction to a book, for example, is a formal preliminary statement or guide to the volume, written by the author or editor to precede the main text. A book introduction may also be a foreword written by someone other than the author to introduce the author and his work to the reader. Here, for example, is the first paragraph of the Introduction by John Buchanan-Brown to the Revised Centenary Edition of *Brewer's Dictionary of*

Phrase and Fable, edited by Ivor H. Evans:

A reference book which has flourished for over a hundred years is clearly something exceptional. Its original compiler needs to hit upon not so much a new area of information of wide and permanent interest as a way of presenting that material and of providing access to it which satisfies and attracts generation after generation of readers. Equally such a compiler needs to place his book with publishers sensitive to changing tastes and aware of the need periodically to give the work that face-lift needed to attract fresh generations of readers to the mass of information within.

The introduction may be part of the front matter or presented as the first part of the text. (*See: lead; manuscript preparation and submission.*)

Inverted pyramid. A style of journalistic writing in which the major points of a news story are related in the first sentence or paragraph and the details elaborated in descending order of importance.

Developed after the Civil War in response to the needs of the growing Associated Press news service, the inverted pyramid replaced the double-ended story form that was based on a chronological order of events. The double-ended story was so called because reporters from the battlefield telegraphed a brief summary of a story before following it with a detailed version. In case the detailed story was delayed through problems with the telegraph service, the newspaper editor still had the summary, which gave the highlights.

Because the Associated Press

served newspapers all over the country, each of which did not always allot the same amount of space to a story, the inverted pyramid structure was designed. It begins with a summary lead giving the who, what, when, where, why, and how details, followed by the most important element of the story regardless of the chronological order in which it occurred. The remaining facts are recorded in order of importance, with the least important details tapering off at the bottom of the pyramid structure.

The inverted pyramid form facilitates editing since it can easily be cut at the end of any paragraph after the summary lead. The most important elements of the story remain, regardless of where the story is cut.

Investigative reporting. Investigative reporting, sometimes called *muckraking* or *exposé writing*, has been part of American journalistic tradition since the early eighteenth century. Investigative reporting is aimed at revealing facts that some person, business, or government agency is trying to keep secret. The investigative reporter goes beyond the official version of an event or circumstance, examining critically every record, statement, or opinion offered by an official source. Investigative reporting is popularly envisioned as involving clandestine meetings with off-record sources and threats from the underworld; in fact, it is most often based on patient, painstaking research and scrutiny of public documents.

Paul N. Williams, author of *Investigative Reporting and Editing* describes investigative reporting as an intellectual process that requires gathering and sorting ideas, building patterns, analyzing options, and making decisions based on logic rather than emotion.

Investigative reporter David Kraslow characterizes investigative reporting as "high-risk" journalism involving a great deal of time, money, pressure, and personal integrity from the investigative journalist.

Newspaper and magazine editors are often reluctant to assign investigative pieces to staff or freelance writers because of the time and financial commitment an investigative piece requires, and because of the potential lawsuit that may result from such an article. (*See: exposé.*)

Additional information: *Investigative Reporting and Editing*.

Iota Beta Sigma. A 3,000-member organization composed of college and high school students and graduates who are currently or have previously participated in academic broadcasting. Iota Beta Sigma bestows awards on members, and holds an annual convention jointly with the Intercollegiate Broadcasting System.

Iota Beta Sigma can be reached at Box 592, Vails Gate NY 12584.

Irony. Irony is a figure of speech in which the intended meaning of a word or statement is the opposite of its literal meaning. For example, Peter De Vries, author of *Let Me Count the Ways* and many other books, once said, "I love being a writer. What I can't stand is the paperwork."

What is stated ironically need not always be precisely the *opposite* of what is suggested, however. Irony may assert somewhat less than it suggests by the use of understatement; for instance, author Fran Lebowitz once remarked, "Having been unpopular in high school is not just cause for book publication." In addition to understatement, irony may be achieved through the use of such devices as hyperbole, sarcasm, and satire.

A particular type of irony, *Socratic irony*, is named for Socrates, the fifth-century-B.C. Athenian philosopher who often feigned ignorance in a discussion with a view toward later defeating his conversational opponent. Socratic irony is a technique that involves adopting another's point of view in order to reveal that person's weakness and eventually to ridicule him. (*See: dramatic irony; hyperbole; satire.*)

Irregular Serials and Annuals. This reference work, in most libraries, provides information on proceedings, yearbooks, handbooks, annual reviews, and other publications that a writer might be seeking for research purposes. The directory is set up alphabetically by subject matter so that if, for example, a writer is working in the area of public health, he can locate publications on the subject, not only from the U.S., but from foreign countries. Entries give the publisher's name and address, indexing or abstracting services in which the periodical is listed, and other details.

ISBN. This acronym stands for International Standard Book Number. ISBN is a tool of the International Standard Book Numbering Agency and is used both for ordering and cataloguing purposes. It consists of the prefix ISBN, followed by a series of ten digits separated by hyphens in this manner: ISBN O-670-38744-4. The first digit is a geographic identifier, the second group of digits is a publisher identifier, the third group is a title identifier, and the fourth a computer code verifying the correctness of the ISBN number.

The ISBN assigned to a book title is never reassigned, even if the title goes out of print. Separate ISBNs are assigned to the various formats in which a title may be published: paper, cloth, multi-media cassette, etc. In addition, revised editions of a book require new ISBNs.

A book's unique identification number is printed on the reverse side of its title page or at the foot of the title page itself. It may also appear at the right foot of the outside book cover and the back of the book jacket. In the case of a paperback, the ISBN also appears on the book's spine.

Books published in foreign countries carry ISBNs with country identifiers necessary for validation.

ISBNs are assigned to book publishers who apply to the International Standard Book Numbering Agency at the R.R. Bowker Co., 1180 Avenue of the Americas, New York NY 10036, for a unique ISBN Publisher Identifier. Upon application and payment of a service fee, publishers receive logbooks containing enough numbers for one hundred, five hundred, or a thousand books. Individuals may purchase single numbers. (*See: ISSN.*)

ISSN. This acronym stands for International Standard Serial Number. ISSN is a tool of the National Serials Data Program of the Library of Congress. It uniquely identifies a periodical title regardless of the language or country in which it is published. It consists of eight digits displayed with the prefix ISSN in this way: ISSN 1432-2981.

Libraries, publishers, and the U.S. Postal Service all use the ISSN system as an aid to ordering, communication, and regulation.

The ISSN is printed on every issue of a serial, preferably at the top corner of the cover or in the area of the publication's masthead. If a serial changes its title, it is assigned a new ISSN.

Assignment of an ISSN is free upon receipt of a completed application form and a suitable representation of the publication at the office of the National Serials Data Program of the Library of Congress, Washington DC 20540. Telephone requests for ISSNs may be made when publication deadlines are a factor. Requests for an ISSN for an already-published serial should include copies of the cover, title page, and masthead. Pre-publication requests should be accompanied by an artist's conception of the same identifying parts of the serial. (*See: ISBN.*)

Italics. *Italics* is any type style in which letters slope to the right. Underlining is a standard way to denote italics in a manuscript in order to emphasize words or parts of words; indicate the titles of periodicals, books, films, plays, and works of art; and to mark foreign words and phrases that have not become part of our language.

Although the use of italics to emphasize words is occasionally necessary, extensive use of the technique can weaken a piece of writing. Emphasis is best expressed by selecting precise words and constructing sentences carefully.

Italic script is not an acceptable typewriter typeface in which to submit an entire manuscript.

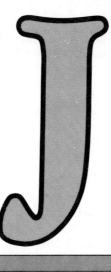

Jargon. A group of words used primarily by members of a particular social, professional, or other group. For example, medical jargon—words that are used to describe anatomy, disorders, and various diagnostic, laboratory, or other procedures—is generally unfamiliar to laypeople. Similarly, writers' jargon includes words and abbreviations like kill fee, on spec, and SASE. Like any dialect, jargon evolves within a subgroup of a larger culture to aid communication about the subgroup's specialized needs; the problem with jargon arises when members of the subgroup, in speaking with (or writing for) the general public, either consciously or unconsciously use jargon to confuse, exclude, or exploit the non-member—as when a doctor, for instance, neglects to explain a painful or risky treatment to a patient in terms he can grasp.

Writers should use jargon judiciously—always defining or making clear from the context what a word or phrase means—to add color and verisimilitude to their writing. By taking pains to translate jargon, writers serve their readers by helping them understand language they otherwise would not, but may have need to. Sometimes a writer's chief duty in covering a story characterized by bureaucratese and obfuscation—the nuclear incident at Three Mile Island, for example—is to cut through the jargon to find out what really happened.

In writing for a specialized market—a highbrow art journal, for instance—a writer will have to use jargon if he is to be taken seriously, but that does not mean that his prose cannot be readable. Clumsy or insecure writers use jargon to obscure the fact that they're not sure what they're talking about, or that they have nothing substantial to say; but jargon is not the primary cause of poor writing.

Additional information: *The Book of Jargon.*

Jazz. A musical style that resulted from the merging of the African music of early slaves with traditional American music forms. It has now evolved into a highly improvisational music form indigenous to America and popular throughout the world.

Jingle. A jingle can be contained in a broadcast advertisement in two ways: a short jingle can alternate with a voice and background music, or the entire commercial can consist of a song whose words provide all the needed information. Most often, a combination of these two approaches is used, with stanzas of musical verse surrounding instrumental interludes that accompany readings of the script.

Music for jingles is unique, ear-catching, and sometimes repetitive. A jingle's melody must have a memorable quality and it must be likeable. In creating lyrics, the writer should avoid crowding many ideas into the message and should consider the facility with which the words can be sung.

The freelance writer who submits jingle material on speculation may send tape-recorded music either to an advertising agency or to a music production house that furnishes agencies with new material. As in other fields of writing, the established jingle writer will find it easier to obtain jobs than the novice, but any writer will find it difficult to market a jingle unless he is very familiar with an agency's philosophy and the workings of a particular ad campaign. Each campaign requires a long period of careful planning, and a jingle presented at the last minute is unlikely to fit the campaign's strategy.

Submissions should contain about six jingles of 30-60 seconds in length, without lead space between each piece; one jingle should fade out and another fade in simultaneously. Individual agencies differ in the form of tape they use: *Songwriter's Market* listings outline preferences as to kinds of tape, as well as other agency requirements. When the writer does get an assignment, it may specify that the agency needs lyrics only, music only, or both lyrics and music for a jingle. Whether working on assignment or on speculation, the jingle writer first submits a tape of his work in a simple form that includes melody and lyrics.

Jingle writers are paid by the job. Most agencies license advertising rights from the jingle composer. Purchasing all rights to a composition, which is sometimes attempted by agencies, is a frowned-upon practice. For a local or regional commercial a writer might be paid $1,000 and up. For a jingle that is part of a national campaign, a writer might be paid $5,000 or more.

Jobs for writers. While the media, book publishing firms, and other businesses provide full-time writing-related positions, many writing and editorial jobs needed by these organizations are adaptable to full- or part-time work at home. Living in the same area as a book publisher who has a rush freelance job is a distinct advantage. In some types of work, however, the freelancer need not even live in the same town as the employer. Copyediting, indexing, proofreading, résumé-writing, column-writing, newspaper stringing, book reviewing, and educational grant proposal writing are jobs that are typically performed by freelancers. The book *Jobs for Writers* guides the freelancer with descriptions and how-to-apply information about writing-related jobs for freelancers. (*See: careers in writing; and other entries* *titled with job names or job titles, e.g., advertising copywriters; book publishing jobs, editorial; book publishing jobs, publicity.*)

Jobs in advertising. (See the Appendix to this encyclopedia.)

Joint contract. A joint contract is a legal agreement between a publisher and two or more authors, establishing provisions for the division of royalties the book generates. For example, if the two authors of *Extra Cash for Women*—Susan Gillenwater and Virginia Dennis—contributed equally to that book, their contract would call for a fifty-fifty split of the royalties. Other books' royalty divisions could be different depending on each author's contribution. (*See: book contract.*)

Journal. A writer's journal is a record of thoughts, impressions, observations, and story ideas. It is a convenient place to store ideas that may often be useful in the future, and that if not written down could be easily forgotten.

Joan Didion, in the essay "On Keeping a Notebook," called the journal " . . . something private, . . . bits of the mind's string too short to use, an indiscriminate and erratic assemblage with meaning only for its maker."

Besides serving as a storehouse of ideas, a journal gives the writer a non-threatening atmosphere in which to experiment with new forms. In addition, it is a means of keeping writing and of disciplining oneself to write every day.

Creating works of literature is not the purpose of a journal. In fact, journal entries are often made without regard to grammar, spelling, logic, or clarity (although the meaning of entries is clear to the writer). Similarly, content can be as mundane as the writer's reaction to a rejection slip, or his subjective observations about a long-term project (such as publishing a novel).

Some books that can be helpful in comprehending the how-to and the reasons for keeping journals are *One to One*, by Christina Baldwin; *At a Journal Workshop*, by Ira Progoff; and *The New Diary*, by Tristine Rainer.

Journal and magazine, difference between. A journal and a magazine, though similar in format, differ in that a journal is usually published by and for a professional group, such as medical doctors or microbiologists, and a magazine is intended for a more general readership. One exception to the nomenclature is a group of magazines called *trade journals* that are published for workers in various industries, such as *American Printer and Lithographer*.

Journal articles are usually contributions by members of the profession that make up its readership; manuscripts are not usually sought from writers outside the profession.

By contrast, magazines appeal to either a general interest audience or to consumers or businesspeople with special interests; most do actively seek manuscripts from freelance writers.

Journalism awards. *Editor & Publisher*, a weekly trade magazine for the newspaper industry, publishes an annual "Journalism Awards" issue the last week of December; a separate pull-out section covers awards for professional journalists such as reporters, columnists, and photographers, and student scholarships and fellowships. (*See:* Editor & Publisher.)

Journalism Educator. This is a professional journal aimed at educators in colleges and universities. Articles deal with research findings and proposals concerning teaching techniques, curriculum, technology, and students. In addition, the journal reports news about faculty members, journalism schools, and professional organizations. *Journalism Educator* is published quarterly by the Association for Education in Journalism. The subscription office is located at the College of Journalism, University of South Carolina, Columbia SC 29208.

Writers who are interested in journalism teaching as a part-time occupation may find it a source of helpful observations as well as a potential market for their own comments.

Journalism Quarterly. This is a professional journal that publishes articles on original research in journalism and mass communication. The journal includes articles on historical research, reports of technological developments, and book reviews. It is published by the Association for Education in Journalism. Writers who are part-time journalism teachers may find each issue's reviews of books and articles on mass communication a helpful resource.

Business and subscription offices are located at the University of South Carolina, 6021 College St., Columbia SC 29208; the editorial office is located at the School of Journalism, Ohio University, Athens OH 45701.

Journalistic ethics. The press has established codes of ethics for journalists to follow in order to maintain itself as a respectable and trustworthy institution in the eyes of the public. However, unlike the medical and legal professions, journalists have not formed a policing body to enforce their codes: conformance must stem from the individual's conscience, and be debated by such related agencies as critical journals, press councils, individual newspapers, and the system of newspaper ombudsmen.

Codes of ethics have been drawn up by journalism organizations, groups of writers in specialties, and newspapers. Two such codes are the Code of Ethics of the Society of Professional Journalists, Sigma Delta Chi; and the Associated Press Managing Editors Code of Ethics. Among newspapers, the Louisville *Courier-Journal* is known for its attention to strict ethical principles; its conflict-of-interest policy was revised in 1982 with provisions that newspersons may not contribute money to political campaigns, but that—on a one-year trial basis beginning in 1982—newspersons may appear on broadcast or cable media regularly and/or for payment.

Reporters, writers, and editors face ethical problems regardless of whether or not codes exist. Such questions arise because journalists must serve the public's right to know while maintaining the privacy of people involved in the news. They must preserve the trust of sources while presenting accurate accounts to their audience. And they cannot allow personal interests—in business or politics, for example—to cloud their unbiased presentation of an issue.

One issue that newspersons deal with is whether to accept press trips or other gifts from a source and risk losing their objectivity. Another ethical question for the media is raised by reporters who pose as persons in other professions in order to obtain information (in exposé stories, for example). Sometimes a newsperson is faced with a conflict of interest when a personal or business interest clashes with his professional obligation to serve the public. (This issue is detailed in the entry "conflict of interest.") And although fabrication of quotes and facts along with plagiarism have not yet been abolished from the profession, they are two practices considered absolutely unethical by virtually all journalists.

A reporter's taking part in a story on which he reports—such as trying to negotiate with a terrorist in a hostage situation—presents another kind of ethical dilemma. In addition, interfering in a person's private life (i.e., the subject of a story) can be unethical when the private facts reported have no bearing on the story in question, or when publishing certain facts does more harm to the subject than it benefits the public.

The press also has the obligation to conform to their local community's norms regarding obscene or shocking words and graphic descriptions of crime or accidents. Being fair is another duty: the reporter should present all sides of a controversy and viewpoints of opposing sides when one person is accused by another.

Revealing the name of a source when anonymity has been requested can lose the reporter future access to that source as well as violate a trust; on the other hand, some newspersons believe that, to preclude instances of fabrication, reporters should be required to reveal sources to their editors.

Often, names of juvenile criminal suspects are withheld from the public out of concern for the future of the accused. Names of victims of some types of crime, especially rape, are also withheld from publication or broadcast.

The freelance writer must confront ethical situations that are peculiar to his field. For example, he must decide whether or not to inform interviewees that he is writing on speculation. Will the articles being done for one magazine help that magazine in its competition with another magazine for which the freelancer also is doing work? The same kind of conflict can arise in book publishing. Publishers' contracts, in fact, specify that authors cannot write books for other publishers that would substantially compete with the works being contracted for. And when holding another job, he faces the problem of whether his freelance work interferes with his full-time work. (*See: conflict of interest; ombudsman, newspaper; plagiarism; press trip; right of privacy; shield laws.*)

Junket. (*See: press trip.*)

Juvenile biography. A narrative account of a person's life, written for young people. Juvenile biographies differ from adult biographies in the writer's approach to the subject. They portray the subject as an understandable human being who is the lead actor in a story. The achievements of the hero are the reason for the biography. For example, *The Value of Determination: The Story of Helen Keller*, by Ann D. Johnson, is a juvenile biography.

Characteristics of successful juvenile biographies for readers aged 6-12 include simple, lucid writing; much dialogue and action; and few descriptive passages. Successful biographies for teens depict both good and bad characteristics of the subject without editorializing, and deal with themes of adult life at a level that can be grasped by adolescents.

The average biography length for readers aged 5-7 years is 1,000 words; 8-12 years, 10,000-25,000 words; and 13 years to adult, over 30,000 words. (*See: biography.*)

Juveniles, writing for. This includes works (both fiction and nonfiction) intended for an audience usually between the ages of two and sixteen. Writing for children is a specialized art which is harder than it looks. The language must be appropriate for the age of the reader, the subject matter must be of interest to the target age group, the opening of the work must be vivid enough to capture the reader's attention, and the writing throughout must be action-oriented to keep it.

The successful writer knows his young audience well. Story ideas begin with a strong character and meaningful, directed action. The use of suspense and the interplay of hu-

man relationships are two features of effective juvenile fiction. Books and stories are told almost exclusively from a single viewpoint (in first or third person), as this technique helps to establish and sustain a sense of reader identity.

Nonfiction for young people takes the form of educational articles, biographies, how-to's, verse, and puzzles. There are very few subjects that cannot be successfully presented to children if the writing is clear, accurate, and tuned into a young person's frame of reference.

Categories of children's books are usually divided in this way: 1) picture and story books (ages 2-9). These are books read to and with children. They have a minimal amount of text (0-1,000 words) and achieve their impact mainly through pictures. 2) easy-to-read books (ages 7-9). These books are read by children themselves. The stories have a definite plot or message and run from 2,000-10,000 words. 3) "middle-age" children's books (ages 8-12). These books are read by the largest cluster of young readers, those interested in just about everything—today, tomorrow, yesterday, people, animals, humor. The texts range from 20,000-40,000 words, and in the case of nonfiction subjects may include pictures/illustrations. 4) young adult books (ages 12-16). These books (50,000-60,000 words) signal a sharp division into those usually read by boys and those usually read by girls. Category novels—adventure and sports, for boys; career and romance, for girls, sexist though these divisions may be—are popular, as are mysteries geared to each sex.

In addition to book publishers, potential markets for juvenile writing include young people's magazines (over 100 in the U.S.), children's story papers, and religious publications. *Writer's Market* and *Fiction Writer's Market* outline details for submitting manuscripts.

Payment for magazine submissions is either by the word or at a flat rate for a certain manuscript length. In the case of books, writers generally get the standard book royalty. Heavily illustrated books, such as picture books, usually call for a royalty split between author and artist. (*See: children's theater; juvenile biography; plays for young actors.*)

K

Kappa Tau Alpha. An honorary fraternity composed of more than 24,000 men and women in all aspects of journalism. The Frank Luther Mott-Kappa Tau Alpha Research in Journalism Award is presented annually by this association, for a book incorporating the best research in journalism or communication.

Kappa Tau Alpha convenes annually at a meeting held jointly with the Association for Education in Journalism. The address of this organization is 107 Sondra Ave., Columbus MO 65202.

Kill. This is a publishing term used to refer to the deletion of part or all of an article or book. (*See: kill fee.*)

Kill fee. A kill fee is paid to a writer who has worked on an assignment which, for some reason, is not published. For example, the editor of a city magazine assigns a writer a 3,500-word article on a local political figure. The next issue of the area's regional magazine carries an in-depth article on the same politician, and the city magazine editor decides his publication's article would be too repetitious. The city magazine editor informs the writer, who has already researched and written the 3,500-word story, that the article will not be published after all. The writer then receives a percentage—from 20%-50%—of the initially agreed-upon price for the manuscript, depending on the publication's policy.

Terms of the kill fee should be established when the assignment is accepted. Clair Rees, author of *Profitable Part-Time/Full-Time Freelancing*, advises the writer to ask for a written agreement or contract defining the terms of the assignment and stipulating the kill fee. If an editor fails to mention a kill fee, the writer should inquire whether such an arrangement is possible. The writer does not ordinarily receive a kill fee unless mention of it is included in the original assignment.

Kill fees are not common. Many magazines do not offer kill fees at all; others offer them only to professional writers with established writing credits. Writer and editor Art Spikol

182

explains: "Look at it from the magazine's point of view: they end up paying . . . for nothing. The writer, at least, can resell the story elsewhere. . . ."

After receiving the kill fee, the writer may submit the article to other markets for a possible sale. Kill fees are offered to writers *on assignment* only; they do not apply to manuscripts submitted on speculation. (*See: assignment, writing on; fees; on spec.*)

Kirkus Reviews. This well-respected biweekly publication furnishes its subscribers with book reviews two months in advance of the books' publication dates; about 4,000 titles are reviewed annually. Novelists, university professors, and experts on various topics who work on the *Kirkus Reviews* staff review both fiction and nonfiction, as well as books for children and young adults. Some self-published books are also reviewed by this service.

Subscribers to *Kirkus Reviews* include librarians, book publishers, producers, magazine and newspaper editors, agents, booksellers, and individuals who want advance evaluations of forthcoming books.

The advantages to the writer of having a favorable review in *Kirkus Reviews* are a possible wider library sale, and promotion material for the dust jacket; the book may also be called to the attention of a producer or other potential subsidiary rights buyer.

The address of this publication is 200 Park Avenue S., New York NY 10003.

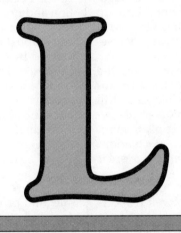

l.c. An abbreviation for *lower case* that is used by proofreaders to indicate that a letter or letters printed as capitals should be lower-case letters. Written in the margin of a galley or page proof, it accompanies the proofreading symbol of a slanted line drawn through the erroneous letter. (See the chart of proofreading symbols in the Appendix to this encyclopedia.)

Lambda Iota Tau. A 4,000-member literary honor society, made up both of men and women. Lambda Iota Tau publishes *LIT*, an annual literary magazine written by members. Released every spring, *LIT* is distributed nationally to libraries. In addition, Lambda Iota Tau's *Newsletter* is issued semiannually in spring and fall.

An honorary president, whose signature appears on membership certificates, is chosen each year on the basis of the literary works he has produced. John Updike is the current honorary president; William Styron is among those chosen in the past.

The organization meets triennially and is represented annually at the meeting of the National Association of College Honor Societies. Lambda Iota Tau can be reached c/o William V. Miller, Department of English, Ball State University, Muncie IN 47306.

Language and style, books on. Two well-known guides to writing and editing style are *The Chicago Manual of Style*, by the University of Chicago Press, and *The Style Manual*, by the U.S. Government Printing Office. The *New York Times*, the *Washington Post*, and the *Los Angeles Times* have all produced guides for newspaper writers, as have both the AP and UPI wire services.

An excellent summary of the elementary rules of word usages, principles of composition, and words and expressions commonly misused is *The Elements of Style*, by William Strunk, Jr., and E.B. White.

American Usage and Style: The Consensus, by Roy Copperud, compares differing opinions on usage in such well-known works as Fowler's *A*

184

Dictionary of Modern English Usage; Evans's *Dictionary of Contemporary American Usage;* and *Webster's Third International,* the *American Heritage,* and *Random House* dictionaries.

Largest College Textbook Publishers. (See the Appendix.)

Latin American writers. Since the early 1960s, a torrent of extraordinary literature has come out of Latin America in a literary renaissance. Much of today's most influential fiction is Latin American, and no writer or student of literature can afford to ignore it.

The two dominant themes of Latin American literature are man against nature, and man against man; stories are often set against a hostile— even dangerous—environment. A recurrent symbol is that of the labyrinth: the labyrinth of rivers, of jungle, of relationships, of crowded towns, of time. The widest-read authors are renowned as stylists; their prose (and their plots) tend to be dense and convoluted. "Magic-realism," a term applied to the work of Gabriel García Márquez and José Donoso, is a style of grotesque (and frequently hilarious) fantasy so richly detailed that it seems real.

The most important fiction writers include Argentinians Jorge Luis Borges, and Julio Cortázar; Colombian Gabriel García Márquez, winner of the 1982 Nobel Prize, whose *One Hundred Years of Solitude* is one of the most important Latin American works; Guatemalan Miguel Ángel Asturias, winner of the 1967 Nobel Prize; Mexican Carlos Fuentes; Peruvian Mario Vargas Llosa; and Brazilians Machado de Assis (1839-1908) and Jorge Amado. Great Latin American poets include Chileans

Pablo Neruda (1904-1973) and Gabriela Mistral (1889-1957), who won Nobel Prizes in 1971 and 1945, respectively; Peruvian Cesar Vallejo (1892-1938), and Mexican Octavio Paz.

Additional information: *The Eye of the Heart* and *Into the Mainstream.*

Law related to writing. (*See: advertising, copyrighted; censorship, literary; copyright; free press vs. fair trial; freedom of the press; lawyers, where to find; libel; model release; shield laws; Volunteer Lawyers for the Arts.*)

Lawyers, where to find. The *Martindale-Hubbell Law Dictionary* is an annual sourcebook published in several volumes and available in most large city public libraries or county law libraries. Information in listings varies according to whether or not the listee subscribes, but every listing includes the lawyer's name, year of birth, college attended, law school attended, and the legal firm he or she is associated with.

Listings in this directory are gathered from the U.S., possessions of the U.S., Canada, and 53 countries abroad. They are arranged alphabetically by geographic areas.

In addition to the above-mentioned listings, the directory contains information on law associations, public-interest law firms, legal aid offices, public defender offices, and American Bar Association committees. The directory also contains a law digest, which summarizes the laws of each state in the U.S., the U.S. federal government, Puerto Rico, the Virgin Islands, and 53 foreign countries. Summaries can be found under specific categories of law, such as garnishment, wills, and divorce; these categories are, in turn, listed under geographic headings. A topical index is included.

The Directory also contains digests of the United States Copyright Law, the United States Patent Law, and the United States Trademark Law.

Writers may watch for possible publication of specialized law directories through The American Bar Association Committee on Specialization. (This idea has been proposed but has not yet materialized.) It would help writers, for example, who want to know which legal firms specialize in publishing or copyright law. Many city bar associations also maintain a lawyer's referral service. Through this service, a writer can obtain (for a limited period of time) consultation for a nominal fee ($10 and up). If the writer wishes to engage the attorney, they then discuss what the attorney's fee would be. Bar associations are usually listed in the white pages of the phone book under the city or county in which they're located.

Lead. This journalistic term applies to a short summary that serves as the introduction to a news story, magazine article, or other copy. Also known as an opening, introduction, or *narrative hook*, the lead is a paragraph or series of paragraphs carefully constructed to capture and hold reader interest.

An effective lead is generally acknowledged to be vital in selling a manuscript—fiction or nonfiction—to an editor. The first few paragraphs of an article or story must impress an editor and encourage him to read on.

The writer should look for lead ideas during the research and preparation phase of the writing project. He cannot assume that the reader is as interested in the subject as he is; rather, the writer must *create* interest by promising that the article or story will deliver something—new information, entertainment, a chance to look behind the scenes of some project or event, or some other "reward" that will encourage the reader to finish the piece. To stimulate reader interest, the lead should appeal to basic human needs and emotions and give the reader a reason to care about the information contained in the article or story.

Depending on the publication he's writing for, an author may choose to open his article with an anecdote, a shocking or startling statement, a quote, a question, a comparison, a generalization, straight narrative, pure information, an enigmatic description or teasing statement, or a summary of the information contained in the entire article. Certain openings work best in particular publications; for example, the pure information paragraph and the summary statement make good leads for articles in professional or trade journals, while the anecdotal lead is common to general interest magazines such as *Reader's Digest*. The narrative lead is perhaps the most popular, certainly in works of fiction and often in articles and features.

While the lead of the traditional news story must be brief and to the point—packing the who, what, when, where, why, and how into the first one or two sentences—the lead of an article or feature may develop more gradually.

Lead sheet. In music publishing, a song's written form. It includes melody, chords, and lyrics, along with the songwriter's name and telephone number. Lead sheets can also be written as chord charts with lyrics. A sample lead sheet appears in the Appendix to this encyclopedia. (*See: lyric sheet; lyrics; musical; songwriting.*)

Lead time. The time at which a manuscript must be on an editor's desk before scheduled publication. In the case of a magazine this could vary from two to six months in connection with seasonal material. In the case of a book, the date by which the manuscript must arrive is indicated in the book contract. Publication usually occurs 9-12 months after the arrival of a satisfactory manuscript.

Leading (pronounced ledding). The amount of white space between lines of type on a typeset page. This type is 10/11 Palatino, which means there is one point of leading (or white space) between each line of 10-point type. The word *leading* comes from the pieces of lead which were inserted on a page of metal type for spacing purposes.

Leading Hardcover Trade Book Publishers. (See the Appendix.)

Leading Mass Market Publishers. (See the Appendix.)

Lecture agencies. These firms secure speaking engagements for their clients, who may be political figures, celebrities, well-known authors, or experts on specialized subjects. Some well-known authors are represented by such firms as American Program Bureau, 850 Boylston Street, Chestnut Hill MA 02167. Other companies, such as Success Leaders Speakers Service, Lenox Square, Box 18737, Atlanta GA 30326, concentrate on lecturers who speak at management conferences, sales seminars, and business conventions.

Lecture agencies seek out some writers as potential speakers; some writers are recommended to them. Some writers send in background data on their books' successes, reviews of or features about their speaking appearances, and solicit lecture engagements. A moderately successful writer could command $1,000-$5,000 in lecture fees.

For their work in promoting their clients as speakers, lecture bureaus receive a commission (usually 30%) on the speaker's fee. (*See: International Platform Association; National Speakers Association; speakers and lecturers.*)

Lecturing techniques. Writers are often called upon to speak before groups on subjects they have written about, or on some aspect of writing. For the freelance writer, lecturing can provide work that varies from, yet relates to, his day-to-day routine and that at the same time brings him extra income both from the lecture itself and increased book sales. Topics writers are frequently asked to speak on include their latest book, contemporary novelists or poets, children's literature, how to freelance for profit, and how to write for film and TV.

A good lecturer is in tune with the audience he plans to address: he takes a different approach speaking to a group of college students than when appearing before the ladies' auxiliary of a conservative fraternal organization. However, the speaker can bring any kind of audience into closer contact with him and his material by involving them—by asking for a show of hands on some aspect of the talk, injecting questions into the speech, or distributing handouts relative to the lecture material. Eye contact with individuals in the audience also adds to a speech's effectiveness.

A speaker must be conscious of the impression projected by his physical appearance: clothing, jewelry, hairstyle, posture, and facial expression all contribute to the audience's response. The speaker's voice is an important tool which, through intonation, can show either enthusiasm and conviction or boredom.

A speaker can rehearse his talk in person (at the location where he plans to speak or elsewhere), in his mind, or on tape. Professionals believe a speech is better spoken from an organized set of ideas in the speaker's mind or from notes, than read from a prepared text. As a courtesy to the audience and the sponsor of the speech, the speaker should limit the length of his presentation to the agreed-upon amount of time.

After the speech, the speaker can give the program's sponsor an evaluation form to receive comments—and names of groups to which he would recommend the speaker. The lecturer can evaluate himself by listening to a tape of the speech. (*See: ghostwriting speeches; speakers and lecturers.*)

Legend. A story handed down from one generation to the next, often of particular importance to a specific culture or nationality. The truth of a legend, as well as its author, is usually unknown; however, legends are frequently accepted as historically true by those in the culture with which the story is concerned.

A legend is distinguished from a myth by its major character, which is a human; a myth's protagonist is a god. (Originally, *legend* referred to a story about a saint.)

Some legends published recently are *Gorman and the Treasure Chest* and *Ruby, the Red Knight* (both published by Bradbury Press), *The Children's Homer: The Adventures of Odysseus and the Tale of Troy* (Macmillan), and *Tales of King Arthur* (Rand McNally). (*See: myth.*)

Legitimate drama. This term refers to plays professionally produced on the stage, as distinguished from drama presented in motion pictures or on radio and television.

The phrase once described the body of plays, Shakespearean and other, characterized by critical acclaim for theatrical or literary merit. The scope of legitimate drama has been broadened in the United States to describe any drama—including farce and melodrama—produced on the stage. (*See: theater.*)

Length of manuscript, average. (See the Appendix.)

Letterhead. (*See: stationery.*)

Letters. These sometimes interesting research documents cannot be used without permission of the author or his heirs, even though they may have been addressed to the person who wants to quote from them. Under copyright law letters are considered the intellectual property of the creator, and while the physical piece of paper may be owned by the receiver, the thoughts and ideas expressed in the letter are the property of the sender.

A writer, for example, who finds a fascinating series of letters addressed to his great-grandmother from his great-grandfather who served in the Civil War, and who wanted to quote from this correspondence in his own book about that war, would be required to clear permission with the heirs of the great-grandfather, if there were others besides himself.

A writer who wanted to publish a book of letters from a famous person to his contemporaries would similarly have to write not only to the persons who received the letters, but to the famous person himself, or his estate if he were deceased.

Unpublished letters, no matter how old, gained copyright protection under the new copyright law on January 1, 1978, as long as there is an heir or someone else capable of owning the copyright in the letters. Anyone who has the right to claim copyright on unpublished letters or other personal manuscripts may register his claim with the Copyright Office if the work has not been registered previously.

Letters column writing. Letters-to-the-editor columns, found in newspapers and magazines, furnish beginning writers with opportunities for exposure. Although there is rarely cash remuneration for the letter writer except in the case of "Op-Ed Page" contributions to newspapers and a few magazines that pay for letters, having his work chosen for publication does give the writer confidence in his skill, and a published sample of his writing. (*See: Op-Ed page.*)

Libel. Libel is a form of defamation, or injury to a person's name or reputation. Written or published defamation is called *libel*; spoken defamation is known as *slander*.

In the United States, each state and the District of Columbia has its own libel law. The Supreme Court made no decisions on this issue until the 1964 *New York Times vs. Sullivan* case, which widened press freedom by devising the actual malice rule. This rule states that, in a libel action begun by a public official, the public official cannot be successful unless he proves actual malice, which can be manifest in the publisher's/writer's knowledge that the material is false or in his "reckless disregard" of whether or not it is false. *New York Times vs. Sullivan*, then, represents the first time that First Amendment principles were applied to libel.

The three prerequisites to a libel suit are defamation, identification, and publication. Defamation (as described previously) is harm done to someone's reputation through the printed or spoken word; it connotes lying. Second, the defamation must be clearly applicable, in the mind of a third party, to the plaintiff, who must prove that the defamation refers to himself; identification can be proven through a nickname, a pseudonym, or circumstances, as well as by the plaintiff's actual name. Finally, in order to be considered libel the defamation must be published. Publication consists of the printing, posting, or circulating of the material, and the subsequent reading of it by someone else.

Defenses against libel include truth, consent, and fair comment. In some cases, the writer may not wish to rely on truth as a defense, even though the alleged libelous statement is true, because to do so would force him to reveal a confidential source. (Truth should not be confused with accuracy, which is not a defense. For example, a statement that has been accurately reported, but that is false, may not be defensible in every case.)

Consent, referring to the consent of the person about whom the alleged libel was committed, is another defense to a libel suit. The rationale of this provision is that anyone who consents to having material about himself published risks the possibility of being defamed by the publication. Consent may be either explicit, implied, or apparent, from the libeled person's actions or words.

Third, fair comment is considered a defense when a reporter or critic has commented on a person, spectacle or performance that has been presented to the public. However, proof of malice can eliminate fair comment as a defense.

A retraction or correction made by a publication, though not a defense to a libel suit, can reduce the amount of damages imposed on a publisher who loses a lawsuit. For example, in some states, the plaintiff may recover only special damages if a retraction has been published.

A person who wins a libel suit may collect damages of one or more of the following types: special damages, compensatory damages, and punitive damages. Special damages relate to material losses, such as that of a job or business, and compensatory damages are paid for intangible losses such as emotional upset or harm to one's reputation. Punitive damages are imposed for malicious or careless behavior on the part of the publisher. Punitive damages are not frequently allowed, but when they are allowed, it is usually in addition to another kind of damage.

One successful libel suit involved the late Paul ("Bear") Bryant and *The Saturday Evening Post*. Bryant accused the magazine of libeling him by reportng that he had attempted to fix a football game. Damages received by Bryant totaled more than three million dollars.

Another suit, dealing with fiction, was brought against novelist Gwen Davis Mitchell and Doubleday & Co., Inc. The plaintiff, Paul Bindrim, contended that Mitchell's novel *Touching* libeled him through the portrayal of a character who was based on him. He was awarded $75,000 in damages.

Through privileges, the law exempts public officials and journalists from libel suits, under certain conditions. Absolute privilege is granted to public officials such as presidents and governors; they are exempted from any libel suit that may result from statements they make when acting in an official capacity. The qualified privilege granted to journalists permits them to report statements that are absolutely privileged (e.g., in a speech by a governor) without being subject to suit. Conditions of the qualified privilege are that the report be fair and accurate and that the writer not be maliciously motivated.

An advertisement can be the basis for a libel suit, but a headline, standing alone, normally cannot. A headline usually must be considered along with the article or broadcast it accompanies. Cartoons are subject to libel suits: an editorial cartoon that was published in the Victoria (British Columbia) *Times* brought $3,500 in damages to William Vander Zalm, cabinet minister. The cartoon, which depicted Vander Zalm pulling out flies' wings, was judged to show him as being cruel and sadistic.

Libel insurance, which can be obtained from large insurance companies, is more easily available to publishers than to freelance writers. However, a writer can sometimes get insurance on a single book for which he has secured a contract, and a few book publishers include their authors in their libel insurance coverage.

Because the law of libel, like other laws, is constantly evolving and changes are sometimes determined by individual cases, the best way to stay abreast of this issue is to read reports of cases and developments in journalism and writing trade journals. (*See: insurance, authors' liability.*)

Libel Defense Resource Center (LDRC). This organization acts as an information source for attorneys and defendants in libel cases and invasion of privacy cases. It continually researches cases taking place at the state and federal levels, and makes information available via a brief, pleading, and information bank; a quarterly bulletin; and statistics concerning the incidence and costs of litigation.

Established in 1980, LDRC is supported by 65 associations, firms, and individuals who represent various areas of the communications industry, including the Authors League of America and the Reporters Committee for Freedom of the Press.

LDRC can assist writers in finding defense attorneys, but it does not maintain a defense fund or a formal referral service.

The address of the Libel Defense Resource Center is 404 Park Ave. S, 16th Floor, New York NY 10016. (*See: lawyers, where to find; Volunteer Lawyers for the Arts.*)

Librarians. A librarian can be a valuable asset to the writer; he is more familiar with the library's collection than the writer is, and is aware of new sources of information the writer-researcher may not have heard about. A writer can often save research time and effort simply by approaching the librarian and asking whether there are any new sources in his field of interest. The librarian can also direct the library user to special collections or departments the latter may be unaware of.

Many libraries now have computerized data bases that can tell the writer where else in the country's libraries a book he wants is, if his own library doesn't have it. Many also have computerized bibliographic services, and if a writer has a specific subject on which he wants to search out newspaper or magazine articles, he can usually obtain ten minutes of free computer search time. If he doesn't find what he's looking for in those ten minutes, he can buy computer time for a nominal fee (such as $1.25 per minute) to pursue the research further, under allied topics. (*See: research aids/techniques; research sources, directories of.*)

Libraries, information on. The *American Library Directory* covers public, college, military, medical, vocational, institutional, law, religious, and special libraries in Canada, the United States, and United States-administered regions. Listings include address, telephone number, number of volumes, income and expenditures, and information on personnel, microforms, and special collections.

Listings of American and Canadian special libraries can be found in the *Directory of Special Libraries and Information Centers*. Volume 1 lists the libraries alphabetically by name, but writers seeking specialized research will find the Subject Index most useful. Volume 2 contains one index of libraries by geographic region, and another of library personnel.

The Bowker Annual of Library & Book Trade Information is an anthology of articles about the field of library science, book publishing, and the information industry. Some of the book's topics of interest to writers are technological developments, library statistics surveys, prices of U.S.- and foreign-published materials, education and salaries of library personnel, and projections on library jobs.

The one-volume *ALA World Encyclopedia of Library and Information Services* contains information on ideas, history, and prominent persons in library science. *The ALA Yearbook: A Review of Library Events* (an illustrated annual published each year since 1976) comprises features, annual alphabetical articles, and biographies and obituaries. *Library Literature* lists library science periodicals, refers readers to publications and films of interest to librarians, and informs the reader about library trends, issues, prominent persons in the field, research, and the history of librarianship. (*See:* Information Industry Market Place.)

Library classification systems. The Dewey Decimal System and the Library of Congress System are used by libraries to aid users in locating volumes.

The Dewey Decimal System, devised in 1876 and still used by most public libraries, was named for its originator, Melvil Dewey, an American librarian. Dewey was also founder of the *Library Journal* and cofounder of the American Library Association.

The Library of Congress System was established in 1897 when the Library decided it needed a more flexible system for its extensive holdings. Many college libraries use the LC system.

Directories showing the many subcategories under each main classification are available in any library (along with a subject cross-reference) so that the writer can look up what call numbers he might like to browse in if the library has open stacks.

See illustration of the major divisions of each system in the Appendix to this encyclopedia.

Library of Congress. Writers outside the Washington DC area can also use the many information and research services offered by the Library of Congress, the world's largest library. Primarily a reference library, the Library of Congress describes the services it makes available to the public in two publications, *Information for Readers* and *Services to the Nation*, both of which are available free of charge from the Library of

Congress, Central Services Division, Washington DC 20540.

Although the primary purpose of the Library of Congress is to provide Congress with the information that that body requires to serve the nation, there are other services offered by its various departments, each of which has a special intent. The one division not directly accessible to the public is the Congressional Research Service (CRS), whose 500 researchers technically work for Congress alone. It is possible, however, for an individual to gain access to the publications prepared by the Congressional Research Service—*Congressional Research Reports, Bill Digests,* and *Current Issue Briefs*—by contacting his congressperson's office and asking the legislative assistant there to request the annual index of the *Reports* and a listing of *Briefs* from the Congressional Research Service. The legislative assistant will then mail these to the constituent seeking the information. If the individual wishes to see a particular report or brief, he must ask the legislative assistant to obtain that publication from the CRS and mail the document to him.

A writer has direct access to the other divisions of the Library of Congress that provide resource information services. One of these divisions, the National Referral Center (NRC), assists persons seeking answers to questions in all subject areas, ranging from science and technology to the arts and humanities, by referring them to knowledgeable organizations or study groups currently working on the subject. The service is based on a computerized, subject-indexed inventory containing descriptions of specialized information resources in all fields (13,000 items).

In response to inquiries, the NRC furnishes suggested contacts, providing name, address, phone number, and a description of the services. Resources include those in government, industry, and the academic and professional communities. The NRC also publishes, on an irregular basis, general and special directories of information resources. A freelancer may write for information (National Referral Center, U.S. Library of Congress, 101 Independence Ave. S.E., Washington DC 20540), call (202)287-5670, or visit—the Center is open to the public.

The Telephone Reference, Correspondence, and Bibliography Section will respond to telephone or mail inquiries by referring questions to the appropriate reference division. In response to written requests, the general reference room will suggest bibliographies. (Bibliographies of scholarly depth must be obtained from the appropriate reference librarian, however.)

The Library's Prints and Photographs Division houses more than eight million pictures, posters, drawings, negatives, and motion pictures, all dealing with some aspect of American history or life. The writer who makes a personal visit to this division will find assistance in locating the pictures he needs, or will receive a recommendation for a picture researcher who will—for a fee—hunt out the required photos. Those pictures selected can be photoduplicated and mailed to the writer; a list of fees and appropriate forms may be obtained from Photoduplicating Services at the Library of Congress. (These fees and forms apply to any other reference materials an individual may want to have duplicated and mailed to him.)

The Science and Technology Division can provide the writer with information about current scientific and technical resources that may not be available in a local library. The reference section of this division also publishes *Tracer Bullets*, a series of guides that provide bibliographies for certain scientific subjects. The freelancer can request a list of those *Tracer Bullets* already published, and then order the ones in which he is interested. There is no charge for this service.

Additional information: *Where to Go for What.*

Library of Congress catalog card number. This number, assigned to a book by the Library of Congress (LC), is used by librarians for classification and ordering purposes. The number is usually printed on the book's copyright page.

A publisher may apply for such a number either before or after a book has been published. For a book that has not yet been published, the publisher first submits an application to the Library's Cataloging in Publication (CIP) Division. Later, he sends an advance complimentary copy of the published book. At this stage, the Library determines whether the book will be kept in its collections, and, if it chooses the book, prepares suitable catalog cards.

To obtain an LC catalog card number for a published book, the publisher submits a copy of the book, along with a letter asking whether the book will be chosen for Library of Congress use and what the assigned LC catalog card number will be.

According to the Library of Congress, the Cataloging in Publication Program "benefits publishers because the cataloging records for CIP titles are entered onto Library of Congress MARC computer tapes, which alert librarians to forthcoming publications and enable them to select and order new publications promptly and accurately." Since CIP data are printed in the books themselves, libraries pay lower cataloging costs and readers have access to the books sooner.

The production or editorial department of a publishing house generally applies for the LC number on the author's behalf, but if an author self-publishes the book he must apply for the number himself by writing Cataloging in Publication Program (CIP), Library of Congress, Washington DC 20540.

Library of Congress Photoduplication Service. A division of the Library of Congress that provides photocopies, photographs, and microfilm reproductions of research material to libraries, organizations, and individuals. According to the Library, this service "will generally make photoduplicates of materials in its collections available for research use . . . . Certain restricted material cannot be copied."

To request photoduplicates, the researcher sends either a purchase requisition or an order form—both available from the Library of Congress—or a letter. Work on an order is sometimes completed in a matter of days, but larger orders may take several months. (Rush service is available for an extra fee.) The Service's "Conditions of Order" statement lists charges for each type of duplication. Sample costs are: 50¢

per electrostatic photocopy of text and line material (subject to a minimum charge per order of $7); a photodirect print from unbound material (up to 17½x17½-inch image size), $7, or from bound volumes, $8.50. Orders of $10 or less carry a packaging and mailing fee of $1.80 for surface mail delivery in the U.S.

All duplicates made by the Library of Congress comply with the copyright law; the recipient of the material is responsible for its fair use. The Library points out: "Written permission from the copyright owner or payment of a royalty fee may be required."

The mailing address of the Library of Congress Photoduplication Service is Photoduplication Service, Library of Congress, Washington DC 20540; the telephone number is (202)287-5640. (*See: copyright; fair use; Library of Congress.*)

Library reprint (scholarly reprint). (*See: reprint.*)

Library use. In addition to using a public library, the freelancer may decide to take advantage of the services of a university library. These libraries are likely to be accessible even to freelance writers who are not students. Most university libraries are open on Sundays and have longer Friday and Saturday night hours than public libraries; a writer who lives near a university can usually take advantage of its research facilities when the local public library is closed.

It is suggested that a writer who wishes to use a university library explain his purpose to the librarian and ask whether he may check out books.

There are also many specialized libraries. Freelance writers researching a certain topic can find sources in the *Directory of Special Libraries and Information Centers*, which has a subject cross-index, as does *Who's Who in Special Libraries*, published by the Special Libraries Association. (*See: librarians; libraries, information on; library classification systems.*)

Lifestyle of the writer—impact on the person. The full-time freelance writing trade can be an exciting, independent business. It may also be fraught with financial and emotional insecurity. Most writers establish themselves only after years of work, which, in the beginning, can yield more disappointment than satisfaction. A novice writer must be prepared to face successive rejection slips over a period of time. His income, unlike a salary, arrives at irregular intervals and in irregular amounts. The new writer faces both the loneliness and the responsibility of working alone. He may meet interesting, stimulating people in the course of research, but the consistent social interaction of a regular job is lacking. Usually, in the beginning, the writer does his own typing, bookkeeping, and correspondence, since he lacks the financial means to hire others.

Writer's block is a potential hazard of freelance writing that each individual manages in his own way. This affliction—as well as other factors— may contribute to long periods without sales and lead the writer to seek temporary employment elsewhere.

The self-employed writer may experience internal conflict between the financial security that another job would afford and the personal drive to create. Such emotional and

195

financial upheaval sometimes causes family divisiveness.

Despite the disadvantages that exist, a successful writing career is enjoyed not only by the authors of best-selling books, but magazine, television, and film writers whose names are not widely recognized. A resilient emotional nature, self-confidence, and a supportive spouse or partner are major factors in launching the new writer on his way. (*See: full-time freelancing, economics of; writer's block; writers, characteristics of; writers' clubs.*)

Light verse. Light verse is intended to entertain, amuse, or please readers. Characterized by brevity (seldom more than ten lines long, four lines being most popular) and conventional rhyme and meter, light verse is usually distinguished by its wit and subtlety and perfection of form rather than by depth or genuine literary significance. It makes use of humor, wit and/or satire, and often contains a "twist" gimmick—a paradoxical or ironic turn to a word, a rhyme, or a common expression.

Subject matter for light verse is virtually unlimited; in many cases, the most ordinary topic—one focusing on a common experience shared by a large number of people—underlies the most salable verse. For example:

Two Fevers

This bright romantic rush of spring
I cannot tolerate,
Especially when flowers and trees
Begin to pollinate.

Though I've spring fever in my heart,
Hay fever's in my head;
And everytime I try to kiss,
I have to sneeze instead.

John Engle, Jr.

Markets for light verse include *Good Housekeeping, McCall's, Rotarian, Golf Digest,* some religious publications, and certain greeting card publishers. Payment may run anywhere from a high $5 per line among the major magazines to 25¢ per line among the smaller publications. The average rate is $1-$2 per line. *Writer's Market* lists editorial requirements and pay rates for light verse markets.

Material should be submitted—one typewritten verse per page—in batches of three or four. An SASE should be included with the submission. (*See: verse.*)

Limerick. A kind of light verse constructed in five lines, the first, second, and fifth of which are in trimeter, and the third and fourth in dimeter. The rhyme scheme of a limerick is usually AABBA, although the following example is a slight variation:

A flea and a fly in a flue
Were imprisoned, so what could they do?
Said the flea, "Let us fly!"
Said the fly, "Let us flee!"
So they flew through a flaw in the flue.

Edward Lear

One school of thought contends that the limerick originated in Ireland, where the people improvised this form at social functions. However, others trace the limerick to the work of Shakespeare, who included it, in imperfect form, in *Othello* and *King Lear.* Limericks became popular after publication of the work of Edward Lear, who wrote the *Book of Nonsense* and *More Nonsense.*

The subject matter of the limerick varies widely, but the limerick is always humorous in tone. (*See: verse.*)

Line of poetry, a. Lines in poetry are measured in vertical, rather than horizontal, space. A line can be one word or a dozen or more. Most magazines pay poets by the line: the same fee is paid for each line, regardless of length. Some, however, pay a flat fee for a poem.

The example below contains 16 lines of poetry, each of which is a different length. The fifth line, even though it contains only a letter and a hyphen, is still regarded as a line of poetry, in this case.

Suggestion

Juggle
the alphabet
of being.
Break
a-
part
the patterned
syllables.
Fling
them
against the dark,
and watch them
write themselves
in stars
on the blackboard
of the night.

by John D. Engle, Jr.
from *Modern Odyssey*
Copyright 1980

The poet must use logic when dividing his work into lines: it is obvious to an editor when a poet has tried to take advantage of the pay-by-the-line policy. The humorous verse below exemplifies such cunning taken to the extreme:

Practical Poet

Dear
Editor,
here's

a
poem
of
mine,
inspired
by
all
that
is
divine.

Will
you
please
pay
me
by
the
line.

From *Laugh Lightly*
by John D. Engle, Jr.
Copyright 1974
The Golden Quill Press
(*See: poetry; verse.*)

Line printer proofs. For editorial functions such as proofreading, some phototypesetting systems can produce inexpensive computer-printed proofs on ordinary computer paper. Line printer type is a plain typewriter type instead of a typeface; the line printer types out the words that have been typeset, indicating variations from the basic text—bold or italic type, bigger or smaller type sizes or spacing—in numbered codes that the computer or an editor familiar with the system can interpret. After proofreaders' and other editorial corrections and the author's alterations are entered into the computer, it can produce *hard type*, which is the actual typeset text, printed photographically on light-sensitive paper, as it will appear in the book or magazine.

A line printer system saves a publisher money in two ways: it is very easy to enter a file and correct and revise text *before* the typeset stage, and it minimizes consumption of expensive photopaper and developing chemicals.

Literary awards. (*See: American Book Awards; Nobel Prize; Pulitzer Prize.*)

Literary critic. This term has two meanings. To the public the phrase refers to the reviewer hired by a newspaper, syndicate, or radio or television network to appraise new books, plays, films, or other literary work and express his opinion of it. To the would-be writer a "literary critic" is a person engaged to analyze or edit a manuscript before it is submitted for possible publication. The functions of literary critics vary, and their services include reading, editing, and providing blue-pencil reports, brief analyses, and rewrites. Some persons who offer their services as literary critics for a fee may also act as agents for the author. Persons who offer literary services are listed in writers' magazines and in the "Editorial Services" chapter of *Literary Market Place*. (*See: criticism of manuscript.*)

Literary executor. A person designated by an author to be an advisor, on the author's death, for his unpublished manuscripts—such as whether to release any of those manuscripts for publication posthumously. The executor of the author's estate insures that his heirs receive the royalties from his already published material.

Literary fiction vs. commercial fiction. To the writer of literary, or serious, fiction, style and technique are often as important as subject matter. Although some literary writers, like Saul Bellow, have become financially successful, mass readership is usually not the primary expectation of authors of serious fiction.

Commercial fiction, on the other hand, is written with the intent of reaching as wide an audience as possible. Some commercial writers take advantage of social trends to which they can connect the subject matter of their work. Similarly, they note the types of fiction that a majority of the public enjoys reading. Commercial fiction is sometimes called *genre fiction* because books of this type often fall into categories, such as western, gothic, romance, historical, mystery, and horror. Western writer Louis L'Amour, with 125 million copies of his 81 frontier novels in print, is an example of a successful commercial fiction writer.

In 1981, approximately 2,325 hardcover and trade paperback novels—both new books and new editions of earlier works—were published. Many of these are mainstream serious fiction, but hardcover young adult "career" novels and other less serious works are also included in the count.

In 1981, approximately 2,782 new and revised editions of mass market paperback novels were also printed. Many of these are popular romances, westerns, mysteries, etc., but the figure also includes paperback reprints of literary works that hit the bestseller list. See the lists of leading hardcover trade book publishers and mass market publishers in the Appendix to this encyclopedia. (*See: avant garde; experimental fiction; mainstream fiction.*)

Literary journal. Writers should note that there is a marked distinction between a little/literary magazine and a literary journal. Literary journals, such as *Kenyon Review* or *Yale Review*, are scholarly magazines most often connected with and financed by a university or foundation. They publish articles on national issues, politics, art, music, international relations, or scholarly research in addition to fiction and poetry. Some literary journals include very little imaginative literature; their strength lies in criticism rather than creativity. While these journals may offer payment, they usually accept little freelance material, relying instead on academic contributors or writers sought out by the editor. Prestige is high, but competition is extremely keen for publication in literary journals. (*See: little/literary magazine.*)

Literary Market Place (LMP). An annual directory covering 73 areas of book publishing. This book is used mainly by those in the book industry, but it can be useful to authors, librarians, broadcast personnel, job-seekers, and academics. A book author, for example, who wants to look up names of publishers to whom his regional book might appeal could use its geographic cross-reference. Or, if he needs to write for permission to quote from a book published by a certain company, he can find in LMP the name of the permissions department head.

The 13 major divisions of LMP are

Book Publishing; Book Clubs; Associations; Book Trade Events; Courses, Conferences & Contests; Agents & Agencies; Services & Suppliers; Direct Mail Promotion; Book Review, Selection & Reference; Radio, Television & Motion Pictures; Wholesale, Export & Import; Book Manufacturing; and Magazine & Newspaper Publishing. Grouped under these 13 divisions are the 73 sections, each of which represents a different aspect of the book industry.

In addition, the directory includes a section called "Names & Numbers," which lists personnel and firms listed in its other sections. This section also serves as an index by listing the section number in which the organization appears in the directory. For instance, writers trying to track down an editor who has moved from one publishing company to another can use the "Names and Numbers" index to find out the editor's current firm.

Listings in LMP include names, addresses, telephone numbers, names of personnel, and other descriptive data on organizations. For example, a publisher's listing in the section "U.S. Book Publishers" contains some or all of the following information: names of editorial, sales, promotion, rights, and permissions personnel; subjects of specialization; its advertising agency; distributors; number of titles published during the previous year; ISBN publisher's prefix, and foreign representatives.

Published by R.R. Bowker Company, this directory is available in most large libraries. (*See: Magazine Industry Market Place.*)

Little theater. These are community theater groups of amateur performers who produce plays for local audiences. They secure the plays they perform from play-leasing companies from whom they buy copies of the script and to whom they pay royalties for the rights to perform it. How much royalty they pay depends on the name and popularity of the author and his work. A percentage of such playscript sales and performance royalties is paid to the playwright by the play-leasing company. Little theater groups are an excellent source of working knowledge about playwriting for the author himself. After he has served his own apprenticeship with a company—perhaps as a stage hand or publicity director, he may wish to approach the group about their producing one of his original plays. Getting such a local production can be an invaluable aid to the new playwright to see what parts of his script do or don't "work" in actual performance.

Little/literary magazine. This term is applied to a noncommercial publication of limited circulation (5,000 or fewer) that is usually literary or political in nature, and often unorthodox and experimental in its approach to prose and poetry. Its audience is composed mainly of other writers, editors, and students of literature.

Little magazines are traditionally the place where quality writers—the men and women who are interested in literary excellence—publish their poetry, fiction, and other creative work. Many fine writers—T.S. Eliot, William Faulkner, Flannery O'Connor, John Gardner, and Joyce Carol Oates among them—made their reputations initially in little magazines.

Little magazines are financed by men and women whose ideal is to present an intelligent and sophisticated writing platform of new and avant-garde forms that may go unpublished in the larger commercial magazines. Editors of little/literary magazines need not compromise their ideals with popular taste because they do not rely on the general public for support.

On the other hand, little magazines are often underfinanced. The editors/publishers of the small literary magazines do not expect to make a profit from their publications; in fact, they seldom break even. For this reason, many literary magazines are short-lived.

Little magazines may develop around a specific theme or describe themselves as "eclectic"—willing to look at any manuscript of quality regardless of subject, theme, or form. Publications may also have a particular regional, cultural, or intellectual focus.

The literaries offer little incentive to the money-oriented writer. Payment is low or non-existent; most authors receive only contributor's copies of the issue in which their work appears, or perhaps a year's subscription to the magazine. Once published in a literary, however, the writer will have the satisfaction of reaching dedicated, interested readers—and occasionally even editors of major magazines and publishing houses who scout small magazines for talent.

Writers are cautioned that many of the little/literary magazines are not copyrighted and that publication in an uncopyrighted magazine places a writer's material in the public domain unless the author's copyright credit line appears with his poem, story, or article. Details on editorial requirements are outlined in *Writer's Market* and *Fiction Writer's Market*. (*See: literary journal.*)

Local color. A term referring to writing in which descriptions of a particular geographic region are prominent. Writers who use local color incorporate speech patterns, descriptions of dress and social customs, as well as characteristic scenery, into their fiction or nonfiction. This element is evident in the work of contemporary writers as diverse as Jimmy Breslin and John Gardner. "Color" is also used to mean any highly descriptive newspaper writing in which the reader's senses are evoked.

Logo. A trademark design, often incorporating the name of the publisher or publication it belongs to. Some well-known examples are the dog appearing on Knopf's Borzoi Books, Bantam Books's rooster, and the flaming torch of Harper and Row's Perennial Library line. (*See: colophon.*)

"Long arm" law. A type of state law that renders persons outside the state who conduct various types of activities in the state subject to the jurisdiction of the state's courts. A writer can in some cases use a long arm law to file suit in his own state for a payment that has been withheld by a publisher in a different state. Not all states have the same long arm statute: the writer can find out from an attorney what type of long arm statute exists in his own state. (*See: complaints against publishers; publishers who default on pay.*)

Long form. A television program of more than one hour in length. (*See: television script terms.*)

Lyric sheet. A song's lyrics typed out on paper, usually single-spaced with double spacing between verses. Lyric sheets should be typed neatly and include the writer's name and telephone number at the bottom. It is submitted by a songwriter with his demo tape to a music publisher or record company. A sample lyric sheet is included in the Appendix to this encyclopedia. (*See: lead sheet; lyrics; songwriting.*)

Lyrics. The words to a song.

Although some lyrics read like a poem—i.e., have a pleasant sound when read without music—this quality is not necessarily essential to a good set of lyrics. Songwriter Doug Thiele comments that "lyrics and poetry are diametrically opposite forms of writing. Poetry is designed to be read and comprehended intellectually. It allows the introduction of complex ideas, which can be alluded to later without calling on the reader's memory. Poetry must be innovative and not clichéd; lyrics require common phrases.

"Lyrics . . . are designed to be felt rather than understood intellectually. They go in your ear in much the same way the moving billboard in Times Square moves, and so only the simplest ideas are allowable in lyrical terms. Lyrics rely on storytelling tools: visual imagery and emotion. Lyrics work when they're emotionally provocative. Honesty is an important ingredient in lyrics, and so, conversational words work best . . . with a little style thrown in.

"In addition, lyrics are designed

to be invisible behind the singer's presentation: they must sound true and honest no matter what the message."

Successful lyrics are those that combine, both in feeling and rhythmic pattern, with the music they accompany—for example, normally stressed syllables should not be changed to fit the stressed musical beats. In the same vein, it is better to end a line with a vowel sound than a consonant, because a vowel ending is not as abrupt and can be sustained by the singer if he desires.

The length of a typical song does not allow for wordiness; every word should contribute to the meaning. The lyrics should state their point as soon as possible. Similarly, the title of a song—which should be repeated often throughout the set of lyrics—should reflect its main idea. A line of lyric is best when it can stand alone as a complete thought and is void of conjunctions such as *and*, *but*, and *so*. Positive ideas are more effective than negative ones. The names given to persons in a song are more likely to contribute to successful lyrics when they are not out of the ordinary; however, a lyricist should feel free to use an unusual name to convey a particular image.

Some lyricists compose their own music to fit their words; others collaborate with another person. A beginning lyricist should not expect the music industry to locate a composer to write music for the words he submits; the only acceptable procedures are for the songwriter either to write his own music or to work with a collaborator before the piece is submitted to a music publisher.

Lyrics, like other forms of writing, are subject to lawsuits when they defame a person. Therefore, when basing his lyrics on a real event, the lyricist should be careful to change the names of the persons involved. (*See: songwriting.*)

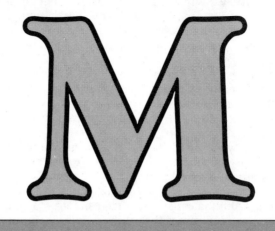

Magazine, alternative. A publication directed toward individuals whose lifestyles and/or cultural, political, or literary values differ from current "establishment" values. Alternative magazines cover a wide range of special interests, and provide a forum for expressing unconventional or minority ideas and views that wouldn't necessarily be published in the commercial or popular press.

Many alternative publications are "little" magazines that do not pay except in contributor's copies. According to the editors of *Writer's Market*, writers should be aware that some of the alternative magazines deal with freelancers in a less-than-professional manner; they may remain at one address for a limited time, or prove unbusinesslike in their reporting on and returning of submissions.

The writer will also find, however, a number of well-established, well-paying markets among the alternative magazines, such as *Mother Jones*, *Harrowsmith Magazine*, and *The Mother Earth News*. Editorial requirements for alternative magazines are listed annually in *Writer's Market*. (*See: little/literary magazine; newsweekly*.)

Magazine article, types of. Articles fall into many categories, some of which have been established by repeated use and others that defy labeling. A writer need not be ruled by classifications each time he begins a new piece: achieving the effect he desires outweighs constructing the article to fit a certain category.

Designated types of articles can be useful, however, in communication between writer and editor. Following are brief descriptions of some of the article types consistently bought by editors.

The *informational article* is meant to familiarize the reader with a topic of interest to him. It primarily contains facts, such as the article "The Eighth

Annual Salary Survey" which appeared in *Student Lawyer*.

The *how-to article* is a demonstration or explanation of how to accomplish something, e.g., "Sew Halloween Costumes for Pennies" published in the "Pins and Needles" section of *Ladies Circle*. A subcategory of the how-to is the self-improvement article, which is sometimes called a "you" article because of the likely use of *you* in its title. Illustrations are an integral part of many how-to articles.

A *service article* is about a consumer product or service; it outlines the characteristics of several of the same type of commodity. Articles advising the consumer of points to consider and problems to avoid in a purchase are also called service articles. Samples of such articles might be a round-up on the types of paint to use on lawn furniture or a guide to selecting and buying a used car. One typical *Changing Times* service article was entitled "Buying a New Car: How to Drive Home a Bargain."

A piece in which the writer recounts an ordeal, process, or event he has undergone is a *personal experience article*. It inspires, educates, or entertains the reader. "How (and Why) I Became Involved in My Son's Education," published in *Redbook*, is an article of this type.

Another kind of article, the *interview article*, is based primarily on an interview with one person. Interview articles take one of three forms: the *question-and-answer format*; the *success article*, which outlines a person's rise to success; or the *profile*, which sometimes contains subjective observations by the writer as well as direct quotes from the interviewee. This third type can be biographical, professional, or

ideological in emphasis. "Red Smith in the Final Innings," published in *Writer's Digest*, is an interview article; "Jesse Helms," published in the *New Yorker*'s "Reporter at Large" section, is a profile.

The *think article* involves an analysis of facts, events, or trends as the writer perceives them. The writer must present informed opinion and draw conclusions that are intended to persuade the reader. Think articles commonly appear in quality magazines and on newspaper op-ed pages. *Harper's* published "Gilding the News," a think article that analyzes the journalistic methods and practices of the media and the audience response they provoke.

In the *historical article*, different aspects of historical events can be covered in a light manner for popular magazines, or through in-depth research for scholarly publications. "Evolution of the Delta/Mississippi River Levee System," which was published in *Delta Scene* is a historical article.

The *travel article* can pertain to any place in the world, but—like other kinds of articles—it must have a specific focus. "Add Another Country to Your Stops," an article about Iceland printed in *Atlantica*, falls into this category.

Published in both consumer and trade magazines, the *product article* is intended to serve readers. Since editors are wary of publishing articles that seem to be free advertising, they impose rigid guidelines on the product article; one such article is "Gun Journal Test: Remington's Model Four & Model Six," published in *Gun Journal*.

In those infrequent circumstances in which a freelance writer is at the scene of an event and newspaper reporters are absent, the result could be a newspaper *spot-news article*. This kind of story can also be written in an in-depth form as a background article for a magazine or a Sunday supplement. The spot-news article "He Was Dead," about the trial of convict-writer Jack Abbott, ran in the "Nation" section of *Time*.

The *exposé article* is the result of the writer's intensive research and investigation. It often includes an element of shock that is substantiated with fact, and its subject is often corruption in business or government, or a similar issue. The most famous exposé in recent years was the series of articles concerning the Watergate scandal, written by two reporters for the Washington *Post*, Bob Woodward and Carl Bernstein, in the early 70s.

A *seasonal article* is written about a holiday, season of the year, or timely observance. This kind of article must be submitted months in advance of the anticipated publication date. "Suddenly It's Spring!," which appeared in *National Wildlife*, detailed the events of the short-lived spring of northern New England.

The *inspirational article* often concerns the successful efforts of an individual or group to improve a situation that affected them. Through it, the writer passes along a philosophy that the reader (ideally) is able to adopt. This kind of article sometimes has a religious theme. "Getting Along with Aging Parents," which appeared in *Home Life*, is an example of the inspirational article.

The *humorous article*, one of the most difficult kinds to write, can be a source of generous financial reward for the writer. Most successful humorists have attained their status only after years of experience. In a humorous article entitled "Motormouth," which appeared in *Parents*, the writer described the incessant talking of her 10-year-old son.

Being aware of the article categories helps the writer structure his work and accommodate the needs of editors. (*See: exposé; historical writing; "how-to" articles and books; humor; inspirational writing; interview; round-up article; seasonal material; travel writing.*)

Magazine editorial contract. Freelance writer Mike Major has devised a contract, called a "Speedy Reply/Agreement Form," that he sends in duplicate with each query letter. (One copy is to be returned to the writer; the other is for the editor's files.) His contract provides space for the editor to reply regarding need for the piece; Major's own terms—such as amount of payment, type of rights being sold, assurance of a byline, the fact that the work will be produced on assignment, etc.; a space for the editor's signature; and a guarantee for the author's work. (This contract, which has been reproduced in the Appendix, may be copied word-for-word or adapted to suit a writer's purposes—without requesting permission from Major or from Writer's Digest Books.)

Major says that individual writers may construct contracts appropriate to their needs. He points out that a beginning writer may have to soften the language and approach. But for established professionals, sending a printed contract with each query letter contributes to the writer's image as a serious businessperson. A contract can also bring a writer power to negotiate, since documenting his terms shows an editor that he is aware of the various aspects of an article sale and is knowledgeable enough to establish those terms. Another advantage to a printed contract is that it is convenient for the recipient: an editor need only check a response on the form and in some cases sign it. And whether the query is accepted or rejected, the writer will stay abreast of the needs of various markets by receiving replies on the contracts.

A copy of "PEN Standards for Magazine and Periodical Assignments" is available free, for a stamped, self-addressed envelope, from PEN American Center, 47 Fifth Avenue, New York NY 10003. Also see the Code of Ethics of the American Society of Journalists and Authors in the Appendix to this encyclopedia. (*See: negotiating with editors.*)

Magazine Index. (*See: periodicals, indexes to.*)

Magazine Industry Market Place (MIMP). A directory of magazines and organizations related to the magazine industry. It includes information on magazine personnel, circulation, advertising rates, and subject matter; reference books; syndicates; editorial services; stock photo agencies; direct mail services; trade organizations; contests; and other types of magazine-related services. Listings are similar to those in MIMP's sister publication, *Literary Market Place*, and include brief descriptions of firms' services. Authors of self-published books who wanted to contact the book review editor at a specialized magazine, or a writer who wanted to contact a magazine's permissions editor for reprint permission, would find these names listed.

The book also contains a section called "Names & Numbers," which provides names, addresses, and telephone numbers of personnel and organizations listed in the other sections.

Published by R.R. Bowker Company, this directory is available in most large libraries. (*See:* Literary Market Place.)

Magazine Industry Newsletter. (*See:* Media Industry Newsletter [MIN].)

Magazine personnel. A magazine staff consists of editorial, advertising, production, circulation, and administrative departments. The magazine's revenue from circulation and advertising determines the number of employees.

Although most magazine jobs that involve writing are found in editorial departments, being employed in another department occasionally leads to an editorial position. News-oriented magazines hire persons for staff writing; but many magazines depend on freelance writers for most articles.

Positions on magazines' editorial

staffs vary, as do the duties and titles associated with each one. The top-ranking person, usually called the editor, editor-in-chief, or editorial director, is responsible for generating ideas, advance planning, offering final criticism of each issue's content, and supervising the publication. Positions next in line may be called executive editor or managing editor. Junior editors are responsible for reviewing unsolicited manuscripts for possible publication, senior editors for rewriting submitted material, and copy editors (or copyreaders) for polishing spelling, style, syntax, and punctuation. A researcher gathers information and checks facts in completed manuscripts; some magazines hire reporter-researchers, who interview, gather facts, and present their material to staff writers to be turned into articles. Assisting editors with correspondence, proofreading, typing, and other miscellaneous tasks are duties involved in the entry-level position of editorial assistant.

A contributing editor is a freelance writer whose material is used so frequently that he is listed on the masthead and/or given space to work at the magazine's offices.

A significant number of staff-written articles are published in magazines; the authors of these may be listed on the masthead as staff writers, or be among the various editors on the magazine staff.

Departments other than editorial sometimes use the services of writers. Promotion managers hire writers to turn out advertising copy for the magazine, circulation directors need assistance in writing direct-mail packages for potential or renewing subscribers, and public relations practitioners hire writers to compose press releases and do other PR-related writing.

A sample organizational chart for a magazine appears in the Appendix to this encyclopedia. (*See: contributing editor; copyeditor; masthead, how to read one.*)

Magazine Publishers Association (MPA). An organization of approximately 200 magazine publishers who produce more than 900 magazines. Members' magazines may be of categories other than consumer, but they must be published at least four times per year.

MPA maintains an office in Washington that stays abreast of legislation and Postal Service affairs. The Association's Circulation Marketing Department informs members on magazine circulation marketing matters. Also, MPA operates a library of materials on the magazine business. The Association holds an annual management conference in the fall.

Awards presented by this organization are the Henry Johnson Fisher Award, to a magazine executive who has made a significant contribution to magazine publishing; and the Stephen E. Kelly Award (of $25,000), to the advertising agency that has produced the best magazine print advertisement of a given year.

MPA's committees include Advertising Marketing, Circulation Marketing, Education, Government Affairs, Postal and Alternative Delivery, Publishing Management, and Transportation. The MPA can be reached at 575 Lexington Avenue, New York NY 10022.

Magazine publishers, multiple. The term *multiple (or chain) magazine* *publishers* is often applied to companies that publish several magazines. They may all be allied in subject matter, such as the MacFadden Womens Group (confessions) or East-West Network (in-flight magazines); or they may be a variety of publications in different trade or technical areas, such as those owned by the Chilton Company (automotive, electronics, instruments, etc.).

Writers who submit manuscripts to a multiple publisher should not assume that a rejection from one confession magazine editor, for example, is a rejection from other editors at magazines owned by the same company; the manuscript can be resubmitted to another confession magazine editor at the same company.

Writer's Market listings give individual editors' names as well as publications' company affiliations.

A list of the multiple holdings of various magazine publishers appears in *Standard Rate and Data Service* directories of consumer, farm, and business publications, available in most libraries.

Magazine publishing economics. According to a survey of its members conducted by the Magazine Publishers Association and tabulated by Price Waterhouse, 51.08% of the member magazines' revenue came from advertising; 48.92% from circulation. (Generally, however, smaller, specialized magazines depend more heavily on circulation income than on advertising revenue,

since the number of advertisers they can attract is limited—usually advertisers whose products relate directly to the magazines' editorial content.) A total of 170 magazines, representing over 2.8 billion printed copies in 1981, participated in the survey.

Breaking down the circulation income by source, the survey reported that subscription income contributed 33.3% of the magazines' revenue, and single copy sales accounted for 15.62%.

As for expenses (expressed as a percent of total revenues), advertising expenses accounted for 8.21% of revenues; circulation expenses, 24.58%; editorial, 7.75%; manufacturing and production (paper, printing, and binding costs), 32.45%; distribution (primarily second-class postage costs), 8.62%; other operational costs, 3.55%; and administrative costs, 5.87%.

The average pre-tax operating profit as a percent of revenue for the industry in 1981 was 8.97%; assuming corporate taxes of 46%, net income for the 170 magazines responding was 4.8%. (A more detailed breakdown of magazine publishing economics appears in the Appendix to this encyclopedia.)

Magazine, starting a new. When starting a new magazine, a publisher's first consideration is to ascertain that an audience for his ideas exists; then he must locate that audience. Costs for printing and delivering the product are other factors that must be considered. In addition, the publisher must determine whether income to cover his costs and profit will be generated solely from subscribers and newsstand sales or from a combination of circulation and advertising revenue.

In figuring the economics of a new magazine, a publisher can consult a printer for bids, a postmaster about postage, and an advertising letter shop regarding costs of reaching prospective customers by direct mail.

A magazine publisher budgets on a yearly basis, first estimating his total income (with the aid of the circulation manager and the advertising manager), then setting aside a percentage of that estimated amount for federal taxes and net profit. Third, he allocates the remainder of the estimated income to each of the five departments, which typically are production, editorial, advertising, circulation, and administration, for further development of the magazine.

A new major magazine requires the investment of millions and several years' effort before turning a profit. If the magazine publisher is a lone person performing all the functions of a "little" magazine's staff, then his estimates of revenue and expenses are even more crucial to the success of the publication.

The publisher of a magazine whose business is also a corporation computes his annual income tax with Schedule J of the federal income tax form. The publisher of a small magazine, such as a poetry magazine, uses Schedule C of his personal income tax form for this purpose. (*See: book publishing economics [in the Appendix].*)

Magazines, classes of. Magazines can be divided into three major groups according to content and audience. *Consumer magazines*, read by the general public, include both slick mass circulation publications such as *Reader's Digest* and secondary magazines geared toward smaller, specialized groups of readers, such as *The Kiwanis Magazine* or the literary magazines.

Trade journals are specialized publications aimed at people employed in a particular profession or trade. *Advertising Age, Nation's Business, Billboard,* and *Progressive Grocer* are examples in this category. Some trade journals are published for persons in a certain occupation, regardless of the industry—such as *Sales Manager's Bulletin*—while others seek readership among all persons in various occupations within a single industry—such as *Ceramic Industry.*

Company publications, also called house organs, are issued by corporations and institutions. The audience of a company publication can be internal (employees and dealers), or external (stockholders and the public), or both these groups. Two such publications are *Caterpillar World* and *Corvette News.* Each class of magazine is discussed further under a separate heading in this encyclopedia. (*See: company publication; little/literary magazine; major magazine; secondary magazine; trade journal.*)

Magazines, deceased. When a magazine goes out of business, the manuscripts it has bought rights to are still the literary property of the magazine, and as such can be transferred to someone who buys and/or renames the magazine.

When a writer has sold material to a magazine that dies before the piece is published, the writer must be certain that the publication rights he sold to the magazine revert to him before attempting to resell the work to another market. If the writer has sold all rights to the material, he may not resell it without arranging with the purchaser (if he can be located) to reacquire rights. (*See: paid for but not published; rights to manuscripts.*)

Magazines, reviews of. While writers' magazines and *Writer's Market* describe the editorial requirements of magazines from the freelance writer's point of view, other publications like *The Whole Earth Catalog* and *Coevolutionary Quarterly* periodically carry mini-reviews of new and/or outstanding publications that give the writer insight into current editorial content. Some newspaper syndicates also publish columns that highlight (panning or praising) selected articles from current magazines. The directory *Magazines for Libraries*, edited by Bill Katz, contains descriptions and evaluations of most of the major magazines carried by public, school, and college libraries, and Katz's column "Magazines" appears in every issue of *Library Journal*.

Mail/delivery services. A writer has the option of shipping a manuscript either through the U.S. Postal Service or by private carrier.

Via the Postal Service, manuscripts can be sent either first class or fourth class; fourth class features a special low book or manuscript rate. First-class mail is guaranteed faster delivery than fourth-class mail, but it is, of course, more costly; in addition, first class does not apply to parcels weighing more than 12 ounces. (Anyone who wishes a piece of mail weighing more than that to receive first-class handling should send it *Priority Mail*, same as first class mail handling.) Any package, whether first or fourth class, can be insured against loss or damage for a small

fee. (Some writers and photojournalists insure their manuscripts/photos for the amount of money it would cost to have them retyped or reprinted.)

Another service the Postal Service offers is *Express Mail*, which can, in some instances, deliver letters and packages in less than a day. Express Mail service is offered in some foreign countries as well as in many large cities in the U.S.; the cost of sending an Express Mail item includes insurance.

When it is necessary to send a letter with a manuscript, it may either be packed inside the box or attached to the outside of the package. When a writer wants a record of receipt of his letter or manuscript, he can send it *Registered Mail* or *Certified Mail* and a signed receipt will be returned to him; Registered Mail, however, receives more careful handling en route, and is, therefore, sometimes slower in delivery. Both Registered Mail and Certified Mail are hand-delivered—i.e., they must be signed for, not dropped into a mailbox.

Mail sent *Special Delivery* receives better treatment and faster delivery than first-class mail; any class of mail, except Express Mail, is eligible for this option. Special Delivery items are delivered every day, including Sundays and holidays, but are not required to be hand-delivered.

Besides the address and return address, there are certain instructions that should be indicated on the outside of a piece of mail. Special Delivery mail should be labeled with a sticker available from a post office; Priority Mail must be marked as such on all sides of a piece. The phrase "return postage guaranteed" printed below the return address ensures that the writer will recover his manuscript in the event that the letter or package is undeliverable. (If special-fourth-class manuscript mail does not carry this marking, it probably will *not* be returned to the sender if for some reason the addressee cannot be located.) A final technicality decrees that a package may not be marked "do not bend" unless it contains stiffeners.

An alternative to the Postal Service for heavier manuscript packages is United Parcel Service (UPS); in some cases, UPS is cheaper than the government service. The sender is charged according to the weight of his package and the distance it will be transported; insurance is included in this cost. A fuel surcharge is added to the bill—as is a fee for the optional service of having the package picked up. UPS parcels must be signed for, so there is a record of delivery.

Federal Express is another nationwide delivery company; using this service, it is possible to have a package reach its destination the day after it is sent. Other national delivery services, such as the Greyhound Bus Line Package Express, are listed in the Yellow Pages, as are local firms.

Additional information: *National ZIP Code and Post Office Directory*.

Mail-order materials for writers. Writing supplies such as paper, envelopes, typewriter ribbons, mailers, and file folders can be obtained from mail-order companies, some of which advertise in writers' magazines. While the writer who does not live in an area where appropriate retail stationers are available may sometimes pay a higher cost for supplies purchased by mail than for those purchased in retail stores, he benefits from the convenience of having the items delivered to his home or office.

Mail-order publishing. A method of marketing books direct to the consumer through the mail. In this type of publishing, the projected sales and number of interested consumers are greater than those in conventional publishing.

Mail-order publishing is a relatively new concept initiated about 20 years ago. Publishers reach a considerably larger number of potential buyers with this approach than by distributing books only to bookstores, since not all the consumers who receive direct-mail packages are persons who would seek out books for themselves. Mailing lists for these sales efforts are obtained through various means—the publisher's own mail-order customer list, and lists rented from publishers of similar books or from organizations whose members have a known interest in the type of book being offered.

Typical categories of books marketed by mail are self-help, self-education, and literary classics. Unlike book club arrangements, mail-order purchases do not commit the buyer to purchasing a certain number of books.

A writer whose book is sold by mail order receives a different royalty from that of traditionally marketed books—in some cases only half the rate as for the same type of book sold through conventional outlets.

Mainstream fiction. Fiction that transcends popular novel categories such as mystery, romance, or science fiction is called mainstream fiction. Using conventional methods, this kind of fiction tells stories about people and their conflicts but with greater depth of characterization, background, etc., than the more narrowly focused genre novels. It is not, however, experimental in style as are more avant-garde works. Some examples of contemporary mainstream fiction would be the work of James Michener, John Updike, and Joyce Carol Oates. The term is sometimes used interchangeably with *serious* or *contemporary fiction*.

Major magazine. This type of mass circulation consumer magazine is characterized by slick paper stock, a healthy advertising/editorial ratio, and good pay rates for writers.

A writer who markets work to a major magazine such as *Woman's Day* or *Playboy* faces steep competition, mainly from established professionals; however, some beginning writers break into this field every year.

Sale of an article or short story to a major magazine currently brings the writer from $300-$3,500. (*See: magazines, classes of; secondary magazine.*)

Make-good. Compensation that a station pays to a sponsor when a commercial has been canceled or broadcast with errors. More often, it refers to a rescheduled spot that was missed by the station at its scheduled time.

Manuscript length, average. (See the Appendix to this encyclopedia.)

Manuscript preparation and submission. Manuscript drafts submitted to publishers should be typed as neatly as possible, double-spaced, on 8½x11-inch white bond paper—and only on one side of the page.

(The writer should be sure to keep a carbon copy for his files.) Margins, including those at the top and bottom, should measure at least 1¼ inches. In addition to these general rules, certain manuscripts—such as plays or film scripts—are prepared according to specific guidelines. (See entries on those topics in this encyclopedia.)

The first page of an article or short story manuscript contains the author's legal name and address in the upper left-hand corner. In the upper right-hand corner are listed the approximate number of words (e.g., 2,500—*not* 2,463) in the manuscript, the rights offered for sale, and the author's copyright line—consisting of the Copyright word or symbol, year, and author's name (e.g., Copyright 1983, John Doe). About one-third of the way down the page the work's title and author's byline (either a pen name or legal name) are double-spaced and centered right and left. The text begins a double space after the byline. Succeeding pages carry only the author's last name and the page number.

Articles, stories, and poems of fewer than five pages may be folded and mailed in number ten envelopes, while longer pieces require 9x12- or 10x13-inch envelopes and are left unfolded.

Scripts for television, motion pictures, and plays must be submitted in binders, while greeting card verses and cartoon gag lines should be typed on 3x5-inch sheets of white paper or card stock. Writers submitting poetry should type only one poem per page. Editors specify in *Writer's Market* the maximum number of poems that may be submitted at one time to their magazines.

With any submission, the author

should enclose a self-addressed, stamped envelope or postage and mailing label for the return of his work. An example of a sample manuscript page appears in the Appendix to this encyclopedia. (*See: book manuscript preparation and submission; reporting time on manuscripts; SASE.*)

Market research. Writers can earn extra income and improve their interviewing skills by working in market research. Many private companies, as well as the government, conduct polls and surveys for which they hire outgoing, diplomatic, patient, and intelligent persons. These interviewers work either as employees or as independent contractors. The latter arrangement leaves the interviewer responsible for deducting his own income tax (and self-employment tax, if he earns more than $400 per year).

Market researchers may conduct interviews on the street, in shopping centers, at home or at an office (by telephone), or throughout an entire state or region. They solicit persons' views on social issues, politics, or consumer products. Depending on length and type of report, the researcher may be paid a flat fee—such as $10 per report—or by the hour, averaging $8-$30 per hour.

The writer who becomes involved in market research must avoid using his subjects or their answers as material for his own writing, respecting their privacy. In addition, a private company is likely to dismiss him, and the government to fine him, for doing so.

Names and addresses of market research companies are listed in the *International Directory of Marketing Research Houses and Services.* (*See: magazine publishing economics [in the Appendix]; self-publishing.*)

Market, studying the. The successful freelancer spends a considerable amount of time determining not only the exact editorial needs of various magazines, but which magazines are directed at which audiences—since a magazine's content directly reflects its readers' tastes.

Every page of a magazine can tell an alert freelancer something about the kinds of articles the editors are looking for—and what his own chances are for making a sale to them. The articles themselves clue the writer in to a publication's style and tone; the ads tell about the readers' lifestyles; the masthead and contents pages reveal whether a magazine is primarily staff- or freelance-written.

Here's what freelancer Connie Emerson, in *Write on Target*, her book about magazine market analysis, has to say about magazine cover blurbs:

The cover lines shout loud and clear which articles are the ones the magazine's editor believes will attract the most readers. Chances are good that article ideas *along the same general lines* on *related or parallel themes* are the ones that the editor will receive most favorably in the future. They will also tell you in no uncertain terms about the publication's slant—the conception a magazine has of its readers' interests and values and the role it wants to fill in their reading. This conception evolves from the editors' knowledge of the probable educational level of its readers, the magazine's own taboos, sacred principles and style, along with a variety of other editorial preconceptions. It's up to you, the writer, to detect a magazine's self-concept. Discerning the difference an editor sees between his or her publication and its competitors will result in sales.

Sample copies of some magazines are available from their publishers free or for a small fee. The writer may also be able to borrow copies of trade journals from companies that subscribe to them; the library and the newsstand are other places to obtain copies of periodicals to study. In addition, the directory *Writer's Market* can help a writer study the market; it summarizes publications' various editorial requirements and taboos, including whether a publication has a set of writer's guidelines a freelancer can send for to tailor his work to a magazine's needs.

As valuable as actual market analysis, however, is simple awareness of popular interests and trends; it can keep a writer's thoughts synchronized with readers' (and therefore magazines') needs. (*See: Writer's Market.*)

Mass market paperbacks vs. trade books. These two categories of books differ in sales outlets, audience, and press run. Mass-market paperbacks are sold by supermarkets, drugstores, airports, newsstands, and chain bookstores. They are directed toward an extremely large audience, so their subject matter tends to be nonspecialized or of wide appeal. A typical press run for this category is at least 200,000. Mass market fiction accounts for about half of all the fiction that is published.

Trade books, on the other hand, are sold at chain bookstores, college bookstores, and department stores. Subject matter of this kind of book frequently concerns a special interest, such as jobs in the arts or holistic health care; the format can be either hardcover or paperback. Trade books are directed toward the layperson rather than the professional. A printing of 10,000 is common for a trade book except for fiction where 4,500 would be the median print order. A chart of the leading mass market paperback publishers appears in the Appendix to this encyclopedia.

Masthead, how to read one. The masthead of a magazine, usually located on the editorial page, lists members of the magazine's staff, editorial and advertising office locations, company officers, subscription rates, and related publishing information.

A freelancer pays particular attention to a magazine's masthead in analyzing that publication as a potential market for his work, since the masthead indicates the name of the magazine's current editor and, in some cases, the editor to whom freelance submissions should be sent. Whenever possible, the writer should avoid addressing a manuscript merely to "The Editor"; the masthead of a recent issue will provide the writer with the correct spelling of a specific editor's name and title.

The masthead also reveals something about the staff structure of the publication. If there are many layers of associate editors, department editors, assistant editors, writers, researchers, or editorial assistants, chances are the magazine is written almost entirely by staff members. If very few staff members are listed, however, the publication probably depends on freelancers for at least some of its material. Comparing the names of staff members with article bylines on the contents page gives the writer an idea of how many and what types of articles are staff-written, and how many pieces are apparently the work of freelancers. (Many magazine editors and staff writers may pen several pieces for the same issue, writing under assumed names; the writer can't assume that all non-staff bylines are freelance pieces.)

A magazine's masthead often includes the names of contributing editors—freelancers who write regularly for that publication. This information helps in determining a certain article idea's chances for acceptance by that publication: if one of the contributing editors is a specialist in a particular field—fashion, for instance—a writer's chances of selling a fashion article to that magazine may be considerably less than to a magazine that doesn't have a fashion expert on call.

The masthead will sometimes list the magazine's editorial requirements and offer special instructions to writers concerning freelance submissions.

Media Alliance (MA). This 2,000-member organization, made up of writers, editors, and broadcast workers, both staff persons and freelancers, assists members in honing professional skills and protecting professional rights. Its social network enables members to overcome the isolation that is characteristic of much media work. Underlying all activity is the recognition that media workers play a pivotal role in shaping society; consequently, the Alliance is active in defense of the First Amendment, developing media access for groups traditionally deprived of such access, and building awareness of the responsibilities of media workers. Media Alliance services include a job file, a network/referral service, continuing education classes, and a monthly newspaper, *MediaFile*. Membership committees include: Editors Guild, Photographers Group, Rights and Grievance, Art Writers Guild, MA Program Committee. Headquarters are at Fort Mason, Building D, San Francisco CA 94123. (*See: Council of Writers Organizations.*)

Media Industry Newsletter (MIN). An 8-page weekly newsletter that reports on topics of interest to top advertising management in such communications media as newspapers, magazines, TV, radio, and cable. Its content includes material on magazine start-ups, ad selling, advertising rates, and media personalities.

This publication was formerly called *Magazine Industry Newsletter.* More information can be obtained from the offices of the *Media Industry Newsletter*, which are located at 18 E. 53rd Street, New York NY 10022.

Media ownership. The takeover of some publishers by other media organizations or other businesses has brought both criticism and favorable responses.

Some newspaper theorists point to lack of competition, which can result from "one newspaper" cities as well as cross-media ownership of newspapers and broadcasting stations. Both threaten the principle of providing for the public a variety of ideas and viewpoints from which to form their own opinions. Another peril of media concentration, according to critics, is the potential for news management. Conglomerates also have been criticized because they present the possibility for conflict of interest between the parent company and the media organizations. Results of various studies have upheld both sides of the media ownership issue.

Two major advantages of book publishing conglomerates, according to Dean R. Koontz, are the advanced marketing techniques and the additional capital with which businesses have furnished the publishing world. Koontz's book *How to Write Best-Selling Fiction* contains his rebuttals to ten criticisms of conglomerate ownership in the book industry. (*See: conglomerates—book publishers; magazine publishers, multiple.*)

Additional information: *How to Write Best-Selling Fiction; Who Owns the Media?*

Media personnel directories. (*See: directories.*)

Media reviewers. In addition to those publications (both national, such as the *Columbia Journalism Review*, and regional, such as the *St. Louis Journalism Review*) that critique media institutions, personalities, or trends, the National News Council (1 Lincoln Plaza, New York NY 10023) meets four times a year to discuss formal complaints that have been leveled against national media and could not be resolved by the parties involved. The results of their findings are published every three months in *Quill*, the magazine of the Society of Professional Journalists. Media coverage is also assessed on programs such as the Public Broadcasting System series, *Inside Story*. (*See: ombudsman, newspaper; Ombudsman, Office of, U.S. Department of Commerce.*)

Medical writing. A writer working in this field is immersed in two fields at once: writing and medicine. He must stay abreast of the continuous developments of medical science by reading the journals and other publications read by health practitioners. In preparing the material, the writer must pay scrupulous attention to detail, since inaccuracies could mislead the public or perhaps even cause serious harm to a patient. Since stories can be delayed because of drawn-out research processes, the medical writer must also have patience. Because of the technical nature of the field, preparation for interviews about medicine often requires much time and concentration. Some universities now offer courses specifically for the science and medical writer; however, a writer can enter this specialty with a good background in the natural sciences and an understanding of medical jargon.

The freelance writer finds abundant opportunities in the medical field. Jobs include work on clinical papers, scientific exhibit brochures, physician's brochures, special report reviews, clinical abstracts, manuals/guides, medical movie scripts, and medical textbooks. In addition, medical products companies seek freelancers to write speeches, package inserts, and pharmaceutical advertisements. Individual researchers employ freelancers to help write/edit books and articles. Their needs are sometimes announced in the classified sections of professional journals; writers may advertise their availability for this work in the same manner. Medical writers seeking staff positions may find openings on large daily newspapers.

The writer can take precautions to ensure that his finished piece is as accurate as possible: these include taping the interview, verifying quotes with the interviewee, and mailing (or reading over the phone) a copy of the finished manuscript to the interviewee for deletions or changes.

Professional organizations of interest to medical writers are the American Medical Writers Association, 5272 River Road, Suite 370, Bethesda MD 20015; and the National Association of Science Writers, Box 294, Greenlawn NY 11740. (*See: science writing.*)

Memoir. A memoir is an author's commentary on his life, his experiences, and the times. It usually focuses attention on personalities and events that the author feels have significantly influenced his life. A memoir often details one phase of the writer's life rather than the whole of it. (For example, the memoirs of a President during his term of office.) (*See: biography.*)

Metaphor. A figurative comparison that usually uses some forms of the word *is* although a verb is not absolutely essential to a metaphor. It is generally considered a strengthened simile. "He's nothing but a bag of wind" or "She's a doll" exemplify this technique.

The mixed metaphor, which is an inconsistent image, should be avoided as in "Publicity is a two-edged sword, somebody said once, and it can get you into hot water."

Metaphors must be used with caution. Too many, too close together, can obscure rather than clarify meaning. (*See: figures of speech; imagery; simile.*)

Meter. (*See: verse.*)

Metonymy. The figure of speech that substitutes the name of one thing for the name of another. With this technique, the substituted name is associated with the original by a common quality or function, as when "Pollyanna" refers to a person who is excessively optimistic, or "the White House" refers to the President. Metonymy can be used for quick characterization. (*See: figures of speech; irony.*)

Microform. Any of several forms used to store greatly reduced photographic images of legal documents, books, newspapers, or other periodicals in a stable, convenient-to-handle medium. A microform can only be read by using a special device to project the images on a reading screen; each microform requires a different device to light and magnify the images it holds.

The primary kinds of microforms used in libraries include: *Microfilm,* a long strip of photographic film wound on a reel, is most often used to store newspapers and magazines.

A *microfiche* is a 4x6- or 3x5-inch sheet of film. A *microcard* is a 4x6- or 3x5-inch opaque card onto which a sheet of photographic film holding images is laminated; it is somewhat more difficult to read than the other forms.

Mid-list books. Mid-list books are those titles on a publisher's list that are neither highly promotable books the publisher thinks will hit the bestseller lists, nor scholarly or literary works that the publisher feels deserve publication but which he expects will have limited sales. A mid-list novel, for example, is usually mainstream fiction by a new or unknown writer that is not expected to be a blockbuster and is not a category novel—such as a mystery or science fiction—for which there is a well-defined market. Whether fiction or nonfiction, mid-list books' promotion budgets are usually small. Nevertheless, they offer the freelance writer an entrée to the reading public and an opportunity to build a following.

Model release. A model release is a form signed by a model or other subject of a photograph (or the subject's legal guardian if the subject is a minor). It authorizes the photographer's use of the photograph for business ("trade") as well as editorial purposes.

Legally, without the subject's consent, a photographer may not display or publish a photo featuring a person for any purpose other than to educate or inform. If a photograph is to be used for any advertising or display purposes, a model release is often necessary for objects (buildings, signs, etc.), as well as for persons who appear in it. Writers should remember that a book jacket is considered advertising.

In the majority of cases in which the photographer has obtained a signed model release, he is legally protected. However, if the photograph is not used in the manner contemplated by the release—for example, if the subject appears in an altered form, or if the subject is presented in an embarrassing light and has not given legal consent for such a variation—the photographer would have little protection if a lawsuit should occur. The release is not valid if it is obtained by coercion or fraud.

Suggested contents of a model release are a generalized description of all the ways the photograph may be used (e.g., in advertising and editorial media, both print and electronic), and the date the release is signed. Some model releases mention compensation. It is preferable to pay some consideration for a model release, but compensation is not necessary for the release to be valid—only *consent* is. Model releases can be composed by the photographer and printed or typed, or forms can be purchased from firms advertising in photography journals. A sample model release form appears in the Appendix to this encyclopedia. (*See: illustration.*)

Money, illustration of. The federal government places restrictions on the practice of printing illustrations of money in newspapers, magazines, books, etc. An illustration may not represent a bill at its actual size: it must be either reduced to less than three-fourths or enlarged to more than 1½ times the piece of currency's actual size. Reproducing color pictures of paper money is also prohibited; illustrations of money must be in black-and-white.

The government also specifies the kinds of written material with which illustrations of money can be used. According to the Treasury Department, "To be permissible an illustration must be accompanied by numismatic, educational, historical, or newsworthy information relating directly to the item that is illustrated. Illustrations used primarily for decorative or eye-catching purposes are not permissible." Time, Inc. won a recent lawsuit challenging these various restrictions, but the Treasury Department is expected to appeal the case.

While editors more than writers need be aware of these restrictions, writers' illustration ideas for their articles might be affected by these regulations.

There are similar restrictions on the illustration of U.S. and foreign postage stamps, government securities, White House press passes, etc.

Monologue. (*See: comedy writing; soliloquy.*)

Motif. An idea or theme that recurs throughout a work, closely allied to the main theme. For example, the recent Broadway hit *Mass Appeal*, a play about the friendship between a middle-aged parish priest and a young seminarian, has an underlying motif of priest as actor—an idea not directly stated in the dialogue, but made obvious through staging. Many motifs appear in a single complex work.

Motion picture script. A motion picture script, or *screenplay*, is often written from an outline and a treatment, as is a television script. The screenwriter commonly divides his story into three acts (although the number can vary—television movies, for instance, consist of six acts of equal length), of which the first and third usually consume one-fourth of the film's total time, and the second occupies one-half the time. The first act presents a conflict and the action's rise to crisis; the second act complicates the problem, leaving the protagonist in a quandary that is resolved in the third act. Each act is divided into *scenes*, each of which must be numbered in the writer's final draft.

Screenplays can range from 100-150 pages in length, although 120 is the preferred length; one page of script is generally equal to one minute of time on film.

Structurally, screenplays can be written in a *shot-by-shot sequence*, or in *master shots*. When writing shot-by-shot, the writer begins each scene with a scene indication, then proceeds to divide that scene into individual camera shots and angles; but the master scene script is less complicated and usually preferred. Here, as before, the scene begins with a scene indication, followed by a narrative description of the action, without specifications about how that action is to be photographed. Either format contains description of the action, dialogue, or a combination of both, depending upon what's happening in that scene. (Since the basic motion picture script format is virtually identical to the script format used for television drama, see the Television Script Sample in the Appendix to this encyclopedia.)

Although screenplays can vary considerably in the degree of their complexity and readability, (as opposed to the readability of the pre-screenplay treatment), it might be wise to bear in mind the caution of scriptwriter John Gregory Dunne, who reminds writers that because it is a form in which words are secondary to potential images, a screenplay is usually difficult to read; the better a script reads, the better it is to be suspicious of the script. (*See: screenwriting; television script; treatment.*)

Additional information: *The Complete Book of Scriptwriting.*

Motion picture script terms. (*See: television script terms.*)

Motivation. Every believable character in fiction is motivated by a desire to satisfy a basic human need—such as for food, shelter, or love. Planning motivation for characters aids the writer both in plot construction and characterization.

Experiences in a character's past, for example, can be the factors that drive him to fulfill his need, thus motivating the action in a story. Physical or psychological characteristics (or a combination of the two), can also be the catalyst for a character's motivations. A physical handicap to be overcome is an obvious example of such motivation, but other physical traits can influence motivation as well.

Character traits can also motivate a character. Distasteful qualities such as greed and vengefulness are usually given only to villains, since a central character with an offensive trait loses reader sympathy. On the other hand, the major character is usually motivated by a sympathetic or positive trait or emotion such as love, altruism, or physical or spiritu-

al survival. (However, even a character motivated by an admirable cause cannot be presented as perfect: as a human being, he must possess flaws of personality or character.)

In order to be believable, any action taken by a character—regardless of motivation—must be both rational and in keeping with the situation. For example, a medical student might decide to go into research in order to find a cure for the disease that killed his father (the motivation being the desire to save other families pain and grief). If, on the other hand, this character's decision were based on his reading an article about an epidemic, his motivation would be too weak, and therefore unbelievable.

Taking a psychology course that covers different theories of human needs can heighten the writer's understanding of motivation. (*See: characterization.*)

Movies from books. (*See: tie-in.*)

ms. The abbreviation for *manuscript*—as well as *mss*, for *manuscripts*—used widely by writers and editors.

Multiple contract. A kind of book contract by which the publisher agrees to publish, and the author agrees to have published, two or more consecutive books by the author. (*See: book contract; option clause.*)

Multiple sales. By offering a magazine "one-time rights only" to his material, a freelance writer can often generate additional revenue by selling the same article or story to a number of non-competing publications. Newspapers in different geographical locations are particularly likely markets for multiple sales (but the author should be sure his copyright credit line appears with the piece, since many newspapers are not copyrighted—and his work falls into the public domain if published there without a copyright notice).

Magazines with different readerships—including many regional magazines, house organs, trade journals, religious publications and Sunday supplements—also buy one-time rights to material. (*Writer's Market* lists editors' requirements on rights.)

Most of the top-paying slick magazines prefer to buy First North American Serial Rights, which prohibits the writer from selling the same article or story elsewhere simultaneously. Even if the nonfiction writer must sell all rights to an article, however, he is free to create "spin-offs" from the finished piece; that is, he can rework his original material—including information he wasn't able to use in the final draft of the article—into a second or third completely rewritten article slanted to any number of non-competing publications.

In the same way, a fiction writer may offer one-time rights to a short story; once that story is published, he may re-submit the piece to a non-competing magazine with the offer of second rights. Religious magazines, in particular, often buy second rights to short stories.

The writer may also be able to get more mileage out of his work by selling reprints to specialized magazines on occasion. *Reader's Digest*, for example, buys previously published material, as do some religious and secondary publications. Occasionally, a publication will sell to the public a large number of reprints of a published article; in this case, the writer receives additional payment.

In pursuing multiple sales, the writer must exercise care in retaining second rights to his article. "One-time rights only" should be clearly indicated in the upper right-hand corner of the first page of the manuscript. In purchasing one-time rights, the magazine or newspaper agrees to publish the material once; after publication, rights to the piece revert to the author. When the writer does make subsequent sales, he should inform the editors of where the same article previously appeared. (*See: rights to manuscripts; simultaneous submission.*)

Multiple submissions. (*See: simultaneous submission.*)

The Music Business. (See chart in the Appendix to this encyclopedia.)

Music Royalties. (See chart in the Appendix to this encyclopedia.)

Music types. Categories of music are described in this encyclopedia under headings: A/C (adult contemporary), classical music, disco, folk, gospel music, jazz, reggae, rhythm and blues (R&B), and rock.

Musical. A stage production in which songs are used to reinforce the major points of the story being acted out. The three major elements of a musical usually are song, dance, and dialogue.

Though a writer working in this form cooperates with a variety of theater personnel during production, the writing phase of the project is done in close collaboration with a composer and a lyricist. The writer, or *librettist*, who in most cases is also a playwright, creates dialogue in collaboration with the composer and the lyricist, who compose the songs (where someone multitalented is involved, it takes only two people, or perhaps just one person, to write a musical). The librettist's product is the musical's *libretto*, or *book*, which contains action, character, situation, setting, dance, dialogue, and plot. Often, the book has been completed before the songs are inserted.

Compromise is essential in the working relationship entailed in musical writing. For example, a section of dialogue may have to be deleted if it can be better stated with music, or an otherwise fine song may be cut if it does not enhance the plot.

A musical's songs, known as *show songs*, are of the popular rather than the classical variety. The types of songs used in musicals are named for their functions: the *establishing song*, the *opening song*, the *reprise*, the *relief song*, and the *comment song*.

To copyright their work, authors of musicals should request Form PA (for a work of the performing arts) from the Register of Copyrights, Library of Congress, Washington, DC 20559.

Broadway music royalties are usually 6% of the weekly gross split between bookwriter, lyricist, and composer. (*See: comment song;* Dramatist's Sourcebook; *establishing song; opening song; relief song; reprise.*)

Additional information: *Writing the Broadway Musical.*

Mystery story. A form of narration in which one or more elements remain unknown or unexplained until the end of the story. The modern mystery story contains elements of the serious novel: a convincing account of a character's struggle with various physical and psychological obstacles in an effort to achieve his or her goal, good characterization, and sound motivation. The general term *mystery story* is often applied to three other types of fiction.

In the *detective story* a detective or detective-substitute is presented with a puzzle that he or she must solve; the emphasis here is intellectual rather than emotional. This type of story is known commonly as the "whodunit."

The *horror story* is a gothic tale of frightening events and bizarre occurrences in which the hero or heroine is pursued by some evil force, natural or supernatural. The emphasis is emotional rather than intellectual: it appeals to readers who derive a certain thrill from fear, apprehension, and terror.

The *adventure story* type of mystery combines some of the intellectual and aggressive elements of the detective story with the personal danger technique of the horror story: the main character, pursued or threatened in some way, must accomplish a death-defying task or mission. The spy novel is the most common form of the adventure story published today.

Mystery Writers of America, Inc. This organization of 1,500 members is "dedicated to the proposition that the detective story is the noblest sport of man." The membership includes published writers, novice writers, and persons in writing-related fields, such as publishers, editors, and agents. Its motto is "Crime Does Not Pay—Enough!"

Annual activities include a convention, presentation of the Edgar

Allan Poe and Raven Awards, and publication of an anthology of members' work. A newsletter, *The Third Degree*, is issued monthly. In addition, the Mystery Writers of America operates a reference library of materials concerning crime and police procedures.

The headquarters of this organization is at 150 Fifth Avenue, New York NY 10011.

Myth. A traditional story, usually involving gods or other supernatural beings, that attempts to explain the workings of the natural or spiritual world or to rationalize the perils of human existence. Myths are common to all cultures and sometimes parallel each other—for instance, all cultures have a series of creation myths, many of which involve a great flood.

Over thousands of years, myths evolve from a simple way of bringing order to a mysterious universe into (in literate societies) a highly de-

veloped literature that no longer carries the force of belief, but that does carry the weight of a civilization's intellectual and artistic development. Philosophers, writers, artists—even scientists—use the familiar figures and events of mythology as symbols to express their ideas in a vivid way. Anyone familiar with Greek mythology, for example, will not have to read too extensively into Freud to be able to grasp the basic concept of what he termed the "Oedipus complex."

Until the nineteenth century, Western readers studied only Greek, Roman, and—to a lesser degree—Norse myths; scholars next began working through ancient Oriental and Middle Eastern mythic literatures; today there is scarcely a culture anywhere that has not had its myths transcribed and analyzed. (*See: legend.*)

Additional information: *Before Philosophy: The Intellectual Adventure of Ancient Man; The Golden Bough; The Sacred and the Profane.*

n. Following a page number in an index, this abbreviation indicates that that page includes a footnote on the indexed item.

N.B. (Nota bene). Latin for "note well." A writer may use the abbreviation N.B. to advise the reader to take note of a particular point or reference in his material, as in this example: "The market listing read: 'We are particularly interested in stories and articles with Christmas themes. (N.B. Submit seasonal material three to six months in advance.)' "

Names, using real. A writer who wishes to use the real name of a person in a fictional piece, with or without a quotation from that person, must obtain permission from that person, regardless of whether the material is favorable or unfavorable. Permission is a defense in an invasion-of-privacy suit as long as the material is within the scope of the permission. If the person is a public figure, of course, and what the person has said is a matter of public record, no permission is necessary; nor is permission necessary in most states if the person is dead and the manuscript does not invade the privacy of living descendants.

Trade names and brand names may be used in a story without permission *if* they are not mentioned in a derogatory context and should be capitalized unless they are not capitalized as used. (*See: trade name; trademark.*)

Narration. Narration is a manner of writing in which the author tells what happened. Fiction may be narrated either from the viewpoint of the author's persona or another character. In connecting the series of events in a story, narration can incorporate other fictional elements, such as description, exposition, and dialogue. (*See: magazine article, types of; magazines, classes of.*)

Narrative hook. A literary device used at the beginning of a story or a novel for the purpose of arousing a reader's curiosity and encouraging him to read further. A narrative hook may take any number of forms—a startling quotation, a mention of murder or disaster, a vivid description of a fascinating character.

Anything that stimulates a reader's curiosity and promises action to come makes an effective hook; but it should be accomplished in approximately the first 200 words. Other than that, there are no rules.

Compare the narrative hooks of two classic novels: *Moby Dick*'s "Call me Ishmael." and the opening paragraph of *A Tale of Two Cities*.

It was the best of times, it was the worst of times, it was the age of wisdom, it was the age of foolishness, it was the epoch of belief, it was the epoch of incredulity, it was the season of Light, it was the season of Darkness, it was the spring of hope, it was the winter of despair, we had everything before us, we had nothing before us, we were all going direct to Heaven, we were all going direct the other way—in short, the period was so far like the present period, that some of its noisiest authorities insisted on its being received, for good or for evil, in the superlative degree of comparison only.

The two hooks have nothing in common except that each is a single sentence—yet no one who has read either one can forget it.

Narrator. The one who tells a story. In fiction, the narrator of a story is most often referred to as the *viewpoint character*; that is, one who carries the emotional focus of the story. The narrator may either be someone involved in the action of the story, or the author himself. Generally, however, the narrator is not the author's own voice, but the voice of a character created by the author to tell the story.

Narrators are sometimes found in dramatic works and films, usually as characters within the play or motion picture. In Tennessee Williams's drama *The Glass Menagerie*, for example, one of the characters, Tom Wingfield, narrates the introduction and the conclusion of the play, and some of Woody Allen's motion pictures use the technique of narrator-turned-character. (*See: viewpoint.*)

National Association of Recording Merchandisers (NARM). A professional organization of 600 members involved in the manufacturing, distribution, and retailing of records. (It was formerly known as the National Association of Record Merchandisers.) Annual awards are presented by NARM for bestselling material on a recorded medium, and for bestselling artists. Scholarships are available to members' families through the NARM Scholarship Foundation. NARM publications include the monthly *Sounding Board* and the quarterly *Anti-Piracy News Digest*.

The Association is affiliated with the Video Software Dealers Association.

NARM headquarters are located at 1060 Kings Highway N., Suite 200, Cherry Hill NJ 08034.

National Association of Science Writers (NASW). Members of this professional organization are writers and editors who prepare scientific information for the layperson.

Activities of NASW include competitions and an annual joint meeting with the Council for the

Advancement of Science Writing. NASW gives annual awards and publishes a newsletter, plus a *Guide to Careers in Science Writing* (single copies free for enclosed SASE, # 10 size) and a *Handbook for Press Arrangements at Scientific Meetings*. The address of the organization is P.O. Box 294, Greenlawn NY 11740.

National Association of State Textbook Administrators. The objectives of this association are to foster a spirit of mutual helpfulness among textbook administrators; to arrange for continuing study and review of textbooks in order to develop stronger, more serviceable texts; to authorize surveys, tests, and studies to benefit text adoption committees; and to find the best component products for textbook production.

The Association meets semiannually with the Association of American Publishers and the Book Manufacturers Institute to discuss and approve (or disapprove) textbook specifications. Its headquarters are located at 201 E. 11th Street, Austin TX 78701. A list of state textbook administrators' names and addresses appears in the Appendix to this encyclopedia. (*See: textbook selection process.*)

National Audio-Visual Association (NAVA). The 1,800 members of NAVA work in the audiovisual industry as dealers, manufacturers, producers, and suppliers of products related to audiovisual media and microcomputers. Within the organization are a number of Councils, including those covering industry and business, materials, non-theatrical film distributors, and AV equipment manufacturers.

NAVA holds the COMMTEX (Communications Technology Expositions) International each January, in addition to the annual Audio-Visual America, an exhibit and seminar. It publishes the bi-weekly *News* and the annual *Audio-Visual Equipment Directory*. NAVA presents the Audio-Visual Award of Excellence (for innovative use of audiovisual media), the Media Educator of the Year Award, and the Distinguished Service Award.

The address of the Association is 3150 Spring Street, Fairfax VA 22031.

National Book Awards. (*See: American Book Awards.*)

National Book Critics Circle (NBCC). This organization, made up of book critics and book review editors, exists to raise the standards of book reviewing and book criticism and to foster public appreciation of literature and book criticism. It meets annually, presents awards annually, and publishes the *NBCC Journal* irregularly. The NBCC can be reached c/o Nine Iroquois Rd., Ossining NY 10562.

National Endowment for the Arts (NEA). The National Endowment for the Arts is an independent agency of the federal government, created in 1965 to encourage and assist the nation's cultural resources. The major goals of the NEA are to promote the creative development of the nation's finest talent, to strengthen and support cultural organizations, to further the availability of the arts to Americans, and to preserve the cultural heritage of the U.S.

The NEA allocates grants to eligible arts and cultural organizations; awards fellowships to qualified individuals in the arts; sponsors the National Endowment Fellowship Program for arts administrators; produces films; and publishes a number of newsletters, pamphlets, and directories on the arts. Additional information about the goals and services of this organization as well as the specific grants and fellowships of interest to writers, may be obtained from the Public Affairs Office, National Endowment for the Arts (NEA), 2401 E Street N.W., Washington DC 20506.

National Federation of Press Women, Inc. (NFPW). This association is made up of almost 5,000 women and men who work in all communications fields, either full-time or as freelancers. Its activities include an annual communications contest, educational workshops, and youth projects. The NFPW operates a speakers bureau, grants journalism scholarships, and annually presents an award to a woman of accomplishment. The *Leader Letter* and *Press Woman* are published monthly, and a directory is published annually; a convention is held each June. The National Federation of Press Women can be reached at Box 99, Blue Springs MO 64015.

National League of American Pen Women (NLAPW). This association of 6,300 professional women comprises three divisions: Art, Letters, and Music. Proof of professional work (i.e., in the case of writers, proof of sale of three original works—or one in the case of a book-length manuscript—within the last five years) is required for membership. Its activities include art exhibits, contests in the arts, seminars, and a biennial convention. The NLAPW operates biographical archives and a 3,000-volume library, and grants scholarships. It publishes a newsletter, a roster, and *The Pen Woman* magazine. The NLAPW is located at 1300 17th Street N.W., Washington DC 20036.

National Magazine Awards. This annual program for editorial excellence is sponsored by the American Society of Magazine Editors (ASME) with a grant from the Magazine Publishers Association, and administered by the Columbia University Graduate School of Journalism. Entrants, which are nominated by magazines published in the U.S., are magazines rather than individual writers.

The contest is divided into the following eight categories of editorial content and presentation: public service, design, fiction, reporting, essays and criticism, single-topic issue, service to the individual, and general excellence. In some categories, an entry may be a single article or a series, while in others—fiction, for example—contest guidelines specify the number of pieces required in an entry.

Each magazine that wins a National Magazine Award receives a plaque, a reproduction of the stabile "Elephant" by Alexander Calder, and an inscription of its name on a tablet on display at the Columbia University School of Journalism. Also, editors whose magazines win awards, writers whose articles win awards, and magazines that are chosen as finalists all receive certificates.

More information on the National Magazine Awards may be obtained from the American Society of Magazine Editors, 575 Lexington Avenue, New York NY 10022.

The National News Council. (*See: media reviewers.*)

National Panhellenic Editors' Conference (NPEC). An organization made up of 26 editors of magazines of the National Panhellenic Conference, an association of "women's fraternities." NPEC stages workshops at its biennial conventions.

Headquarters of this group are located at 6750 Merwin Pl., Worthington OH 43085.

National Press Club (NPC). This is a private social club of reporters, writers, and others employed in news-editorial capacities by media organizations. It publishes the *Record* 48 times per year, presents awards, and sponsors a speakers bureau. The headquarters of NPC is located at the National Press Building, 529 14th Street N.W., Washington DC 20045.

National Speakers Association (NSA). Composed of approximately 1,700 professional speakers, semiprofessional speakers, and persons interested in the field, this organization strives to make the speaking profession more visible to the public. It also serves as a learning and communication medium for speakers and those who'd like to speak—such as writers who are also lecturers. NSA sponsors a Mentor/Mentee Program through which less experienced speakers can meet with experienced professionals. Although its annual membership directory is used by organizations seeking speakers, the NSA does not perform referral or booking functions.

Activities of NSA include an annual convention, awards presentations, and workshops. In addition to the membership directory, the association publishes *Speak Out*, a monthly newsletter.

NSA's headquarters are located at 5201 North 7th Street, Phoenix AZ 85014. (*See: International Platform Association; lecturing techniques.*)

National Union Catalog. This index represents the works catalogued by the libraries contributing to its cooperative cataloguing program; it refers the user to published materials, such as books, pamphlets, atlases, and periodicals, catalogued by the Library of Congress and about 1,100 other libraries participating in the National Union Catalog reporting program.

The *Catalog* is arranged by author or, in cases of title entry, by title. Each entry includes all available cataloguing data. All titles represented by Library of Congress printed cards without mention of a contributing library are held by the Library of Congress. Entries supplied by participating libraries indicate the first library to report holding an item; additional location reports are published in the *National Union Catalog Register of Additional Locations*. By using these two catalogues the user can identify at least one location for all materials reported in the *Catalog*.

The *National Union Catalog* is regularly printed in nine monthly issues, three quarterly cumulations, and in annual and quinquennial (5-year) cumulations. The *National Union Catalog Pre-1956 Imprints* (754 volumes), makes available in book form the total *National Union Catalog* maintained on cards by the Library of Congress since 1901. (*See: interlibrary loan.*)

National Writers Club (NWC). The National Writers Club has two categories of members: professional members, who have either been published in national magazines, had a book published on a royalty basis, or had a stageplay, screenplay, or teleplay produced; and associate members, who have a serious interest in writing. The NWC operates a 2,000-volume library, and sponsors contests as well as a home study magazine writing course. It distributes to its members research reports on various aspects of writing, copyright, etc. Its publications include *Authorship, Flash Market News, NWC Newsletter*, and *Freelancer's Market*. Conventions are held periodically. The address of the National Writers Club is 1450 S. Havana, Suite 620, Aurora CO 80012.

National Writing Project. This association of more than 96 writing programs for teachers comprises writing centers patterned after the Bay Area Writing Project of the University of California, Berkeley. The programs are collectively referred to as the National Writing Project Network.

Individual programs were instituted primarily by universities and are located throughout the U.S., in Canada, and in Europe. More information on the National Writing Project may be obtained from the National Writing Project, 5635 Tolman Hall, University of California, Berkeley CA 94720. (*See: Bay Area Writing Project.*)

NBC. (*See: broadcast networks.*)

Nebula Awards. These are annual awards presented to science fiction writers by the Science Fiction Writers of America (SFWA), in each of four categories: best novel (40,000 words or more), best novella (17,500-40,000 words), best novelette, (7,500 to 17,500 words), and best short story (under 7,500 words). Winners are chosen by members of SFWA, but are not required to be members themselves to enter the competition. Works of science fiction or fantasy are eligible as long as they have been published by a trade book publisher or in a nationally circulated magazine. Each recipient is presented a trophy.

Members of the annual World Science Fiction Convention also vote for winners of Hugo Awards (named after Hugo Gernsback). (*See: Science Fiction Writers of America.*)

Negotiating with editors. A freelance writer who has sold to the same publication over a period of time may rightfully negotiate with the editor for higher pay rates. Budgets at most magazines are limited, but many editors are willing to recognize loyal, talented writers by paying them fees higher than their base.

A book author also has the opportunity to negotiate, but only before he signs the contract. (*See: book contract.*)

Additional information: *Profitable Part-Time/Full-Time Freelancing.*

Net receipts. The amount of money a book publisher receives on the sale of a book after bookseller's discounts, special sales discounts, and returned copies. Some authors' book royalties are figured on a percentage of net receipts rather than retail price of the book.

Neustadt International Prize for Literature. Established in 1969, the Neustadt International Prize for Literature was endowed by, and named for, a family of Oklahoma industrialists. It is presented to a poet, fiction writer, or dramatist for outstanding achievement. Candidates for the prize do not apply, but must be nominated by members of an international jury, which changes for each award. The judging is based solely on literary merit; any writer in any language is eligible, but a representative sample of his work must be available in either English or French.

The prize, which consists of $25,000 and an eagle feather cast in silver, is awarded biennially at the University of Oklahoma.

Inquiries should be addressed to Editor, *World Literature Today*, 630 Parrington Oval, Room 110, Norman OK 73019.

New journalism. A style of writing that emerged in the 1960s. Also known as "interior" or "personal journalism," "documentary narrative," and "parajournalism," the term "new journalism" is attached to the work of a group of writers that includes Tom Wolfe, Truman Capote, Jimmy Breslin, Gay Talese, Gloria Steinem, Hunter Thompson, Norman Mailer, and a host of others with equally divergent writing styles. *In Cold Blood*, Truman Capote's 1966 book described by its author as a "nonfiction novel," is generally considered to be the forerunner of the new journalism movement.

Tom Wolfe, one of the most successful of the new journalists, defines the style this way: "I think the New Journalism is the use by people writing nonfiction of techniques which heretofore had been thought of as confined to the novel or short story, to create in one form both the kind of objective reality of journalism and the subjective reality that people have always gone to the novel for." Wolfe describes these techniques as scenic construction, full use of dialogue, interior monologue, and the recording of such details as gestures, habits, manners, style of clothing, eating, and traveling—everything, Wolfe explains, generally symbolic of people's everyday lives.

It is the use of interior monologue—describing a subject's inner thoughts and feelings in a nonfiction piece—that has become one of the most controversial devices employed by the new journalist; a journalist, it is argued, cannot possibly observe or listen to the inner thoughts of another person. Yet Wolfe, Talese, and other new journalists have effectively written about what they thought an article's subject was thinking at a certain time.

A second criticism of the new journalism is that it is too personal, too subjective; the writer becomes more important than the person or event he is writing about. At the hands of less talented writers, the intrusion of the personal results in rambling, unedited, "off-the-top-of-the-head" pieces that fail to capture reader interest or identification. For the skilled new journalist who is able to manage it effectively, however, the personal imprint is what appeals most to some readers.

Many writers mistakenly believe that the new journalism demands less discipline than articles written in a conventional style. The most successful new journalists, however, are those who are using the techniques of basic news and feature writing as well as experimenting with innovative forms. Gay Talese says of the new journalism: "This form cannot succeed, I do not believe, unless the old style of reporting precedes it . . . the constant interviewing of your subject or subjects, getting to know everything you can about this person."

Because of its emphasis on subjectivity, using the new journalism style in writing news stories is more loudly criticized than using a personal journalism approach in creating magazine articles and newspaper features. The magazine and feature story writer has never been tied to the strict formula and premium on objectivity required of a straight news story; the devices that characterize new journalism have, according to many journalists, been long used in various forms by writers throughout the years, Ernest Hemingway, Lillian Ross, Daniel Defoe, and H.L. Mencken among them. (*See: objective writing.*)

New product release. A freelance writer may have the opportunity to write such releases for a small company or for an individual who does not regularly engage an advertising agency, and who wants to publicize a new product in appropriate trade journals or consumer magazines. This represents a source of freelance work that can often be found in the writer's own community.

A new product release consists of a brief descriptive text sometimes accompanied by a 5x7 glossy photograph. This kind of writing calls for an informal style: contractions, colloquialisms, and humor are used. Since brevity is necessary, each word is important. The textual part of a new product release package informs the reader of the name, the potential uses and users, the function, the advantages, and the cost of the product, as well as where consumers may obtain it. At the end of the product information, the writer gives a name for the editor to contact for more information regarding the product, and the time required by the manufacturer for delivery.

The new product release mailing list typically contains names of 200 periodicals. (The writer should try to obtain the name of an editor of a specific department of the magazine as well.) *Writer's Market* lists trade journals and consumer magazines that may be candidates for new product releases. With each release, the writer inserts a return post card or envelope—in case the editor wants more information or will indicate when he'll run the release—and cardboard to protect the photo in the mail.

Reading ads for small companies' products and advertising in newspaper classifieds are means for the new product release newcomer to find clients. A writer who has done this kind of work previously may be able to depend on referrals to obtain new clients. A sample new product release appears in the Appendix to this encyclopedia.

The New York Public Library Photographic Service. Freelance writers in towns without extensive library facilities who would like to secure a photocopy of something that is probably in the New York Public Library can, for $3 per title, have a search and cost estimate made of the fee to secure the photocopy they want. Further details are available from the Photographic Service, The New York Public Library, Fifth Avenue at 42nd Street, New York NY 10018. Information about photocopies from newspapers can be sent to the Newspaper Annex of the New York Public Library, 521 West 43rd Street, New York NY 10036. (*See: Library of Congress Photoduplicating Service.*)

The New York Times, back copies of. Since the *Times* is our national newspaper "of record," freelance writers sometimes wish to secure for reference back copies of particular news stories they have located in the *New York Times Index* in their local libraries. If the writer's public library has microfilmed copies of the *Times*, the library's microfilm reader may also be equipped with a printer to provide an inexpensive photocopy of a portion of a page the writer wishes to copy. If the writer's public library does not carry microfilmed copies of the *Times*, the writer may wish to order a back copy from the *Times* (if the issue is within the last six months), or contact the Newspaper Annex of the New York Public Library, which accepts prepaid mail orders for reprints. The *New York Times* cannot provide a research service for the writer but if the writer knows the specific date of the issue he's looking for, he can send an inquiry about back copy costs to the *Times* Back Copy Department, 229 W. 43rd Street, New York NY 10036. (*See: The New York Public Library Photographic Service.*)

John Newbery Medal. Established in 1922, this award is presented annually for the best book written for American children. The award, a bronze medal, was named for John Newbery, an eighteenth-century British bookseller, who originated the idea of publishing books for children. The award almost invariably increases sales for the award-winning book—especially among schools and libraries.

News release. (*See: publicity writing.*)

Newsbreak. A newsworthy event or item as described in a newspaper or news broadcast. Magazine editors also use the term to refer to a news item as it affects their particular readership. For example, a clipping about the opening of a new shoe store might be a newsbreak filler item of interest to a trade journal in the shoe industry. Some editors also use the word *newsbreak* to mean funny typographical errors.

Newsletters. Newsletter production for local clients furnishes the freelance writer-editor with a dependable income source and leaves time to spare for other writing pursuits.

Newsletters, which vary in size, shape and complexity, are circulated by businesses, and nonprofit organizations, and other groups of people sharing a common interest—a suburban community, for instance, or a softball league. A freelancer can enter the specialty of newsletter production either by replacing the editor of an existing newsletter or by proposing that a newsletter be published where none exists.

A newsletter writer gets story ideas from local newspapers, and from officers, employees, and volunteers at the organization. A notice placed in the newsletter itself may also result in story leads.

Duties involved in the newsletter production process are research (including interviews), writing, rewriting, meetings with the client, taking or obtaining photographs or other artwork, preparing material to be typeset, delivering material to and picking it up from the typesetter and proofreading (the galleys and blueprint). The freelancer who produces a newsletter must schedule time for each of these steps, recognizing that some of them require cooperation with the client or the printer. In addition, the first issue that the freelancer works on requires *start-up time*, or time for him to become acquainted with the organization and his contacts within it.

Margaret Wills Ward, newsletter publisher for a small condo community, advises the independent small newsletter publisher to have samples printed both by photostatic and offset processes in order to compare the value of each for the cost. Another consideration of the publisher is paper weight; it must be heavy enough to prevent ink from bleeding onto the other side of the page and interfering with the print there. An advertising cutoff date should be scheduled so that advertisers are aware of when they must commit themselves, thereby making them less likely to ask the publisher to call back later, Ward says.

Not all freelancers take on the responsibility of the entire production process: some—engaged by the organization or its printer—only write copy, for example.

Most fees for newsletter work are charged on a flat rate per number of pages, with an hourly fee used as a base. Work for a nonprofit organization brings a slightly lower fee than that done for a business.

When proposing a newsletter to a potential client, the writer should take samples of newsletters produced by other organizations, as well as tearsheets and other credentials of his own. Producing a trial newsletter is a way that writer and client can work together on a let's-see basis before committing themselves.

Some current how-to books on newsletter editing are listed in the *Subject Guide to Books In Print* under the heading "News-Letters."

Newspaper ads for small businesses, writing. Small businesses that can't afford to contract with an advertising agency are likely prospects for freelancers who can write advertisements to appear in local daily and weekly newspapers. Freelancer Fred Drewes, for instance, hit upon a particular type of ad that sold well, was easily produced, and for which he faced little competition: single-column "article/ads" that various businesses could place in appropriate sections of the paper. A feature titled "Calling All Homemakers," for example, paid for by a furniture outlet, would appear on the lifestyle page and contain interesting facts related to furniture—along with a brief sales message that concluded with the store's address, phone number, and business hours. A small photo of the proprietor and his byline usually appeared in the ad/article. Drewes ghosted for ten such clients over a period of eight months,—"The Home Front," "Your Car Needs Our Care," etc.— charged $10 per weekly insertion of the ad, and cleared $100 per week.

Drewes believed that locale had something to do with his success selling his article/ads, that small towns and cities ranging from 8,000 to 25,000 population provided little in the way of advertising or writing facilities, and so businesspeople were eager to take advantage of his services. He recommended beginning with neighborhood and home town businesses and gradually moving further afield as clippings accumulated.

Drewes's success demonstrates the fertility of the small-town market, where the number of potential accounts and low-key way of doing business make up for lower rates of pay. Writers who live in small towns or rural areas can earn a respectable income serving local businesses. (*See: business writing.*)

Additional information: *How You Can Make $20,000 a Year Writing (No Matter Where You Live).*

The Newspaper Guild, AFL-CIO. This union, primarily composed of newspaper employees in news and business departments, bargains contracts with publishing companies that establish working conditions and minimum rates of pay. Following is a sample of minimum weekly rates provided for starting reporters under Newspaper Guild contracts in effect August 1, 1985: $856.00, New York *Times*; $411.14, Detroit *Free Press*; $400.18, Sacramento *Bee*; $397.00, Denver *Post* and *Rocky Mountain News*; $370.63, Cleveland *Plain Dealer*; $352.35, Washington *Post*.

Newspaper indexes. (*See: periodicals, indexes to.*)

Newspaper Organization Chart. (See the Appendix to this encyclopedia.)

Newspaper readability. Although neither The Newspaper Fund nor the American Newspaper Publishers Association (ANPA) has any national statistics on the reading levels for which newspaper copy is written, one paper, the Worcester (Massachusetts) *Evening Gazette,* commissioned a readability study of its news and feature pages. As reported in the newspaper trade magazine, *Editor & Publisher,* the paper discovered that article readability varied from the fourth and fifth grade levels to that of college sophomore. By departments, some scores ranged as follows: local news, 11.1; business news, 10.3; arts and entertainment, 9.7; family today features, 8.3; sports news, 6.6. (The numbers represent the school grade reading level needed to understand the text.) The average score for the entire newspaper was 9.2. (*See: Fog Index; readability formulas.*)

Newspaper reporting. A staff reporter on a newspaper works either as a beat reporter, who regularly gathers news from the same sources—such as police court or city council—or a general assignment reporter, who is given an individual assignment for each event or story he is to cover. On large papers, reporters may develop specialties covering developments in business, education, medicine, or science.

To be successful as a reporter, a person must be curious, observant, and able to adapt to different persons and situations. Good reporters have a "nose for news" as well; i.e., they are able to discover subjects suitable for news stories, then research them. A good reporter must be a "go getter," competitive, persistent, willing to dig for details, able to produce under pressure.

In a 1981 survey of American newspaper reporters and editors, reporters named variety, autonomy, creativity, and learning as advantages to their work. Favorable aspects of their jobs noted by reporters include ego satisfaction, the opportunity to work outside an office, having the status of an "insider," feeling that they accomplished something every day, and working as a detached observer.

The same respondents pointed to lack of time, too little communication with and direction from editors, low pay, and bad hours as frustrating aspects of their work.

Some newspaper editors prefer to hire reporters with liberal arts degrees; others prefer journalism degrees. The increasing numbers of journalism school graduates in relation to available jobs has made the market highly competitive for newcomers.

It is common for reporters to begin their careers on small newspapers, where there are more opportunities, then move to larger ones. (*See: newspapers, daily—writers on; newspapers, weekly—writers for.*)

Newspapers, back issues. Some small as well as most large newspapers usually keep clips of back issues in a *morgue*, or library, in which material is arranged by subject. Writers can usually gain access to these references by contacting the newspaper's librarian. In addition, some large public libraries house back issues of major national newspapers on microform.

Newspapers, daily—writers on. Though most of the well-known daily newspapers are published in large cities, some smaller cities publish them as well, and offer staff and freelance opportunities to writers and editors. Whether or not a small city paper comes out daily is determined by its own budget and the population of the surrounding area. A daily is issued each morning or afternoon or both; some papers do not publish on Sundays.

Perhaps the most evident advantage that a daily newspaperperson has over a weekly newspaperperson is a higher income, often thanks to newspaper unions, whose power is strongest in large cities. (Median starting salary on a daily is about $200 per week; less on weeklies.) Another advantage to the large-staffed dailies is that employees can usually depend on more regular hours, although any newspaper worker should be prepared for unexpected assignments, since his work depends on happenings in his surroundings.

The opportunity to specialize in politics or education or other subjects is more readily available to daily newspaper workers, since dailies' staffs are larger than those of small-town and suburban papers. The editorial budgets of major newspapers afford the reporter on a large-city daily more opportunities for investigative work; weekly newspaper reporters seldom receive investigative assignments. But by the same token, a writer or editor who takes his first job on a daily may miss out on the comprehensive learning opportunity available to his weekly newspaper counterpart, who is likely to be assigned to tasks in various departments.

In recent years, many American dailies have been bought by newspaper chains; this phenomenon has both beneficial and harmful effects. While it strengthens the newspaper financially, some experts believe that the predominance of chains weakens and eventually destroys independent papers, thus repressing the traditional spirit of editorial competition. (*See: conflict of interest; newspapers, weekly—writers for.*)

Additional information: *Opportunities in Journalism.*

Newspapers, directories of. Two directories, set up geographically, are the *Editor & Publisher International Year Book* and the *Ayer Directory of Publications*. *E&P Year Book* lists foreign as well as U.S. newspapers; Ayer's does not include foreign papers but *does* list U.S. and Canadian magazines. Writers seeking the names and addresses of publications and their editors in a specific locale will find both these directories in most public libraries, or in the editor's office at their local newspaper. (*See: periodicals, directories of; periodicals, indexes to.*)

Newspapers, weekly—writers for. The more than 8,000 newspapers in this country that are published in rural areas, small towns, and suburbs, are referred to by the collective term "weekly," even though some of them (a minority) are actually published at larger or smaller intervals than a week. Most weeklies are the size of a standard newspaper, while others use tabloid format or an irregular paper size. Similarly, generalizations regarding page count cannot be made: some weeklies comprise eight pages, and others run more than one hundred. The most common days of issuance are Thursday and Friday.

Because a journalist hired to work on a weekly is expected to perform a mélange of duties, this type of work is excellent training for those who aspire to staff positions at large-city dailies. Specifically, a reporter is likely to find himself editing, rewriting, proofreading, writing editorials and headlines, designing pages, and taking photographs. Some editorial staff members even function periodically in the paper's advertising department.

This variety of duties is rarely performed in a 40-hour work week: a staff member typically works as many as 70 hours per week. In addition, he is paid less than a large-city journalist of comparable background. The absence of unions in most small-town newspaper operations is a contributing factor to this situation.

Advantages of small-town newspaper work include the opportunity for bylined features to build a portfolio. Although salaries are lower in rural areas than in cities, so is the cost of living. Some reporters use weeklies as stepping stones to more sophisticated jobs in journalism, while others discover that the advantages of small-town life and newspaper work are satisfying in themselves. (*See: conflict of interest; newsweekly.*)

Additional information: *Opportunities in Journalism.*

Newsweekly. More commonly (but less correctly) known as an *alternative weekly* or a *metropolitan weekly*. A weekly paper, usually a tabloid, that is distinguished from a suburban or small-town weekly by its urban readership, concern with urban issues, and political liberalism. Newsweeklies are the offspring of the underground papers of the 1960s; most of their readership is aged from the late teens to the early forties; live in an urban central core of downtown and inlying suburbs; are college-educated; and maintain alternative or "postcountercultural" lifestyles to some degree.

Newsweeklies are published in major cities, particularly cities on either coast and cities with a revitalized inner city; they are characterized by in-depth coverage and analysis of news and controversial topics not covered or barely covered by the daily newspapers. A great advantage to newsweeklies is that, since they are not the local newspaper of record, they can pick and choose the stories to cover. Newsweeklies also report on the particular arts their readers follow, in greater depth than most dailies can.

The quality of writing in a newsweekly is generally high; the pay, generally low. Newsweeklies can be either easy or difficult markets to break into, depending on the individual paper's reputation, but they are an excellent training ground for young writers.

Some of the most successful and respected newsweeklies are Boston's *Phoenix*, the Chicago *Reader*, and the San Francisco *Bay Guardian*.

Nobel Prize for Literature. Endowed by Alfred Bernhard Nobel, this award is one of the most highly valued and respected of literary prizes. It is presented annually to an author, on the basis of all his work, by the Swedish Academy of Literature in Stockholm. The recipient, according to Nobel's will, is the person "who shall have produced in the field of literature the most distinguished work of an idealistic tendency." Authors do not apply for this award; a winner is chosen by the Swedish Academy of Literature from nominations provided by the Swedish Academy and other academies, previous winners, professors of languages and of the history of literature, and presidents of authors' organizations.

American writers who have won the Nobel Prize include: Sinclair Lewis, 1930; Eugene O'Neill, 1936; Pearl S. Buck, 1938; William Faulkner, 1949; Ernest Hemingway, 1954; John Steinbeck, 1962; Saul Bellow, 1976; and Isaac Bashevis Singer, 1978.

The prize itself consists of a gold medal and a substantial sum of money. Nobel also endowed prizes for physics, chemistry, medicine, and peace.

Nom de plume. A French phrase that means "pen name." (*See: pen name.*)

Non sequitur. Latin for "it does not follow." A *non sequitur* is a false argument or conclusion, an illogical inference that does not follow from the previous statements. The phrase is often used as a noun in English, as in this example: "To presume that your story is no good because the *Atlantic Monthly* rejected it is a *non sequitur*."

Nonfiction books, marketing. The key to effective book marketing is research; research into the competition, research into finding the right publisher, and just enough research into the book's subject itself to put together a compelling proposal. Like a magazine article, a nonfiction book is usually sold before it's written; the advantage to the author of book over magazine writing, however, is that a successful book query yields the author an *advance*—a percentage upon signing the contract, the rest upon delivering portions of the manuscript. In effect, a book writer is paid as he's writing the book—rarely, however, enough to support him completely during that period.

The first marketing step for the writer with a book idea is to identify the book's audience; this will not only help the writer choose appropriate publishers to query (and bolster his sales argument), but also later make the actual writing easier as he keeps his audience in mind. Research in the *Subject Guide to Books In Print* (at the library) and in bookstores will help him determine how much competition his book will have; he may find it advisable to find a new slant on the subject or even drop the project altogether.

After firming up the book's subject and slant, the writer should research the topic itself until he feels he knows enough to assemble a detailed chapter-by-chapter outline—generally, a paragraph summarizing the information contained in each chapter.

The writer then selects a publisher. *Literary Market Place* lists U.S. publishers alphabetically, with cross-indexes; by field of activity, e.g., mail-order or textbooks; by subject matter; and by geographic area. *Writer's Market* contains more detailed information on the editorial requirements of U.S. and Canadian publishers. The writer should also look at publishers' imprints on books they see on library shelves and in bookstores; check recent issues of *Publishers Weekly* and bestseller lists to see which publishers are producing which kinds of books. Once the writer selects a publisher (or publishers), he writes a query letter briefly describing the book, identifying its audience, discussing the competition, and stating his credentials to write the book—including practical, professional, and/or academic experience in the field. The writer must be able to tell the prospective editor/publisher how the proposed book differs from others that have been written on the same topic; what is new in the book; or how this interpretation improves upon those of the past. He then puts together a *book proposal*—the letter, outline, and a sample chapter—packages it neatly (*always* enclosing an SASE), and mails the bundle to the proper editor at the prospective publishing house.

A busy publisher can take weeks or even months to reply, so the writer may wish to send proposals to several publishers at once. This practice is called *multiple submission* and is perfectly acceptable as long as 1) that publisher's *Writer's Market* entry okays it and 2) the author advises each editor that the book is being considered elsewhere. Multiple submission decreases total waiting time dramatically, increases the chances of a timely book being accepted and published while the topic is hot, and sometimes permits the author to choose the best deal from among competing publishers. (*See: book manuscript preparation and submission; synopsis.*)

Nonfiction novel. A work in which real events and persons are written in novel form, but are not camouflaged, as they are in the *roman à clef*. In the nonfiction novel, reality is presented imaginatively; the writer imposes a novelistic structure on the actual events, keying sections of narrative around moments that are seen (in retrospect) as symbolic. In this way, he creates a coherence that the actual story might not have had.

The Executioner's Song, by Norman Mailer, and *In Cold Blood*, by Truman Capote, are the most notable examples of the nonfiction novel. (*See: faction; new journalism; roman à clef.*)

Nonfiction sales to movies. Books and articles based on actual events can be the foundations for sales to television (for movies, docudramas, miniseries, and specials) or the motion picture industry. For example, the TV movie *Guardian Angels* appeared originally as an article in the *New York Daily News*; the Broadway and Hollywood musical *The Best Little Whorehouse in Texas* was based on an article in *Playboy*. Ted Schwarz, an author of nonfiction books who has sold material to television documents at least one case in which a writer sold material to television on the basis of a "strong title and a brief description of plot and characters," but the usual procedure, he says, is to submit a title, a brief description of the story, and an outline. Notes and other research materials used by the writer in covering the story can also encourage sales, as they can point out other aspects of the story that might have been left out of the article or book, but that might be suitable for a motion picture.

According to Schwarz, the television industry abides by the "*TV Guide* rule," which states that a major criterion for a successful movie idea is that it be able to attract a large audience by means of its title and a three-line description such as those appearing in *TV Guide*.

Selling material to the motion picture or television industry must be accomplished through an agent. If a freelance writer or a staff writer thinks he has a possible film subject, an agreement between the writer and the major subject or subjects of the story (assuming they're not in the public domain) is also essential, since it prevents a movie production company or another writer from undertaking the same project at the same time. Such an agreement stipulates the ratio of the split of income between the writer, the subject, and the agent, as well as the length of time that the writer has exclusive access to the subject as source and any documents relating to the story. The agreement should be either written or examined by an attorney. It is signed by all parties involved, in the presence of witnesses. It is suggested that scripts, treatments, and outlines be registered with the Writers Guild of America West.

The freelance writer who intends to sell nonfiction material to Hollywood must ascertain that he still owns the appropriate rights, and has not sold them to a publication. In the case of a staff writer, the television and film rights usually belong to the publisher from the beginning, but the writer is sometimes awarded all or part of the income from the movie sale that results from his article or series. (*See: agents, television; screenwriting; television markets; television writing.*)

Nostalgia. Derived from the Greek words meaning "return home" and "pain," *nostalgia* refers to a longing to return in thought or in fact to one's home, to a former time in one's life, or to one's family and friends. Nostalgia writing is a wistful examination of people, customs, items, or incidents from the past; it is personal and emotional in contrast to historical writing, which is objective and factual.

As a category of writing, nostalgia describes a type of personal experience article intended to evoke from the reader an emotional response approximating the feeling the writer recalls. The most effective nostalgia pieces are written about subjects that have universal appeal; they focus on commonly shared experiences that transcend geographical location, age, sex, and economic and social background.

Some types of nostalgia pieces described by Connie Emerson in her book *Write on Target*, include *personal reminiscence articles, whatever-happened-to* or *do-you-remember-when* pieces; *celebrity reminiscence roundups*, consisting of personal recollections centered on one theme (e.g., "My first job" or "My most embarrassing moment"); and *historical nostalgia* (e.g., a music magazine may feature a piece on rock-and-roll stars of the 1950s).

Another type of nostalgia piece is the *quiz*, which is usually introduced with a paragraph of prose and continues with a series of questions related to nostalgic aspects of days gone by. Questions usually deal with personalities, literature, sports, television shows, etc., of a certain decade; other nostalgia quizzes may be of the psychological variety (e.g., "Did You Have a Happy Childhood?").

The last type of nostalgia piece Emerson outlines is the anti-nostalgia article, which satirizes the nostalgia craze and offers proof that "the good old days" were not actually all that good.

More than 150 markets for nostalgia are listed annually in *Writer's Market*. Many religious publications use reminiscences. General interest magazines such as *The Atlantic Monthly, Capper's Weekly, Ford Times, Good Housekeeping*, and *Reader's Digest* publish nostalgia, as do automotive, retirement, and city and regional publications. Several of the food-and-drink, sports, antiques, and music magazines carry an occasional nostalgia piece. Moreover, many of the magazines that don't buy nostalgia as a distinct article type do accept articles and short stories that include nostalgic elements or themes. As with any type of article, the writer must carefully study the editorial requirements of the market to which he is submitting a nostalgic piece.

Notable Books. "Notable Books" is a list published annually by the American Library Association. The roster of fifty books represents those works deemed significant by virtue of the knowledge and pleasure they afford to adult readers. The list is compiled by a panel of library professionals and without the influence of publishing companies.

Note-taking. Writers use three basic methods to accomplish the rapid note-taking that is necessary during interviews.

Shorthand is a fast and convenient means of taking notes, especially when a tape recorder is unavailable;

however, it is a skill that requires training and practice. Through experience, some writers have devised their own systems of shorthand or abbreviation. The tape recorder can be an invaluable aid to note-taking in interviews; it is discussed under the entry "tape recorders" in this encyclopedia. (*See: tape recorder.*)

Novel writing. The structure of a novel resembles that of a short story in that it consists of a series of conflicts and temporary victories, then reaches a climax wherein the major conflict is either resolved or accepted as unsolvable. A dénouement is sometimes added at the end.

The novelist uses four devices in creating his work. *Scenes of movement*, the counterpart of the narrative used in nonfiction, present word pictures that show characters in action. *Characterization* involves lending believability to characters; it can be accomplished through description (physical and/or psychological), dialogue or thoughts of the character being described, dialogue of other characters, and scenes of movement. A *plot* consists of a problem, subsequent actions of characters relative to the problem, and the outcome of the situation that the original problem created. Finally, *dialogue* between characters should be believable, but it cannot be so detailed as to bore the reader; it should be condensed into the most important and most interesting lines of a seemingly real-life conversation. In order to seem real, a character's speech must be suitable for his personality, occupation, education, and other characteristics.

The novel allows the writer more time for characterization and plot development than the short story

does. The novelist also has the liberty of changing point of view by switching the story's narrators, a technique that the short story writer can rarely employ successfully.

In conceiving novels, different writers use different starting points: some begin with a character; others begin with a theme; still others invent a plot twist to begin their work.

Designing an idea outline is the first step in writing a novel. Such an outline includes general conceptions of plot, theme, characters, point of view, and the emotions to be conveyed to the reader. Most idea outlines are about 3-6 pages long. Detailed plot synopses could run 10-30 pages. Research, which can consume from one-tenth to one-third the total time spent creating the novel, is undertaken next to add credibility to the book and to cultivate the writer's imagination. After completing the bulk of the research, the novelist begins writing a first draft. Methods for this stage of novel-writing vary with the individual. (*See: characterization; climax; conflict; dénouement; first draft, revising and rewriting; plot.*)

Novelette. This is a short novel averaging between 7,000 and 25,000 words. Also called novellas, they are sometimes published as separate units by small press publishers. *Billy Budd* and *The Old Man and the Sea* are examples of this genre. (*See: novel writing.*)

Novelization. Creating novels from popular movies is a specialty of some writers. The novels they write— referred to as movie "tie-ins"—are produced by paperback book publishers that have bought the adaptation rights from the original screenwriter or copyright holder. (*See: tie-in.*)

Novella. A relatively short work of prose fiction comparable in length to a long short story or novelette, approximately 7,500-40,000 words. *Novella* is an Italian term that means "a story." (*See: novel writing; novelette; short story.*)

Novels for young people. Books written for children (excluding picture books) are divided into two groups according to the ages of the readers: novels written for children under twelve years of age and those written for children over twelve years of age. The main character in a children's novel should be no younger than the age group of the book's intended audience; however, the character *can* be a year or two older than the novel's oldest reader.

Novels for teenagers revolve around characters aged fourteen to seventeen, who are involved in more complex plots and show more depth than those characters in novels for the under-twelve group. Also, novels for the older group employ a more sophisticated writing style, vocabulary, subject matter, and general treatment.

In writing a novel for children over twelve, the author should remember that his work will be read predominantly by young teenagers, since older teenagers are likely to read fiction written for an adult audience. Therefore, the plot and the situations of the characters should be identifiable to the child of junior high school age.

Reading children's novels is an important step toward understanding their audiences. A public librarian or school librarian can be an invaluable guide to an author's study. (*See: juveniles, writing for.*)

Novels, marketing. An important marketing tool is knowledge of which types of books are published by which houses. A publisher of mainstream fiction, for example, would reject a category novel simply because it would be incongruous with the rest of his line of books. Book publishers' listings in *Fiction Writer's Market* indicate the kinds of novels sought by each company. Reading catalogues of publishers' releases is another way to become familiar with their products. Many publishers send their catalogues free to writers on request. Or the author can refer to the *Publisher's Trade List Annual*—a collection of most publishers' current catalogs available at public libraries. Writers can also make note of novels in bookstores and libraries, jotting down the names of publishers whose works seem most compatible with their own.

Advances from some publishers to best-selling authors may amount to five or six figures, but advances to first-time authors may be only a few thousand dollars or even non-existent. Similarly, royalties vary, but the usual rate is 10% of the retail price on the first 5,000 copies, 12½% on the next 5,000 copies, and 15% thereafter.

As the first contact from new authors, most publishing houses prefer to receive either a query letter or an outline and three sample chapters of the book; however, some request that a complete manuscript be submitted at this stage.

Fiction Writer's Market listings provide details on the procedures of individual book publishers. (*See: book contract; book manuscript preparation and submission.*)

NPR. (*See: broadcast networks.*)

Number of writers, statistics on. The number of freelance writers has not been accurately determined by any survey, probably because of the difficulty in doing so. A study conducted in 1975 by the National Research Center of the Arts, Inc., concluded that 13% of Americans wrote stories or poems in their leisure time. Figures compiled on writers by the Census Bureau represent mostly full-time staff writers (such as newspaper reporters) and only those full-time freelance writers who have so declared themselves.

Professional organizations for writers are another source of statistics, but their figures are limited to their own membership.

Numbers, how to show in manuscripts. Most style manuals state the preference that numbers from one to ten be represented as words, and numbers higher than ten be represented as numerals. However, when producing books containing money figures, statistics, or scientific data, some editors forgo these style rules and use numerals throughout the text to promote readability.

O&O station. A radio or television station that a network *owns* and *operates*; e.g., Chicago's WBBM, owned by CBS.

Objective writing. Writing that reveals little or nothing of the personality, thoughts, or feelings of the writer. Objective writing focuses on external things and events, presenting reality as it is—or as it appears to be—unaffected by the personal reflections, sentiments, or emotions of the writer. Newswriting is an example of nonfiction objective writing.

Henry Fielding, Anthony Trollope, and Ernest Hemingway strove for objectivity in much of their work. Saul Bellow is considered by some critics to be an objective fiction writer. The objective viewpoint is not as popular in fiction however, since readers tend to want to identify emotionally with the characters and material in stories. (*See: new journalism; objectivity; subjective writing.*)

Objectivity. A journalistic ethic requiring a reporter to present a complete, accurate, and undistorted account of any news event he covers, and to keep his newswriting free from personal opinion or prejudice.

The ethic of objectivity was developed during the first half of the twentieth century, largely because of the growing influence of the wire services. Until then, news had been deliberately slanted according to the biases of the newspaper that carried it, but the Associated Press and other wire services found it impossible to prepare a news story to fit the slant of each of their clients. This, coupled with the public's growing dissatisfaction with biased news, led to the development of the "straight news" story, and the separation of fact and opinion.

By the beginning of the first World War, the straight news story had become the standard form of reporting. When it was discovered that the American people had little understanding about the causes of war, however, a glaring deficiency of the facts-only form was made apparent. During the next two decades, as American life became more complex with the coming of the New Deal

244

and the advent of the cold war, the larger newspapers realized that it was necessary to *interpret* news as well as report it.

The growth of interpretive reporting was slow, however. Journalists were afraid to jeopardize the separation of fact and opinion, and saw interpretive reporting as being subjective rather than objective. Interpretive reporting, which is prevalent today, *is* considered to be objective reporting: interpretive reporting *explains* the facts; it does not judge or advocate as does editorial opinion.

The ethic of objectivity has been criticized in recent years as an unattainable ideal. Journalist Bill Moyers was quoted in *Newsweek* as saying, ". . .of all the myths of journalism, objectivity is the greatest." Every account is somehow influenced by the reporter's personal judgment, his own powers of observation and consciousness: merely deciding which facts to include in a story and which facts to leave out prohibits complete objectivity.

Many individuals in the newsgathering and reporting field contend nonetheless that, if journalists strive for an objective presentation of the news, the result should approach the ideal. Daniel R. Williamson, in his book *Newsgathering*, outlines the five basic precepts journalists observe in attempting to present an objective account:

(1) *impartiality*. A news story must contain all viewpoints—presented with reasonably equal balance—if it involves controversy.

(2) *absence of conflict of interest*. A reporter involved with causes or organizations may be vulnerable to suspicion of partiality.

(3) *opportunity of denial*. A reporter is required to give an individual about whom he is making a damaging allegation a chance to deny or refute that allegation.

(4) *absence of cronyism*. This breach of ethics occurs when personal relationships—such as those between a reporter and his news sources—influence news coverage.

(5) *avoidance of vengeance*. A reporter should not use his access to the media to report unfairly on individuals he personally does not like.

While these observances are not required of the freelance nonfiction writer as they are of newspaper or broadcast journalists, the ethic of objectivity nevertheless provides an effective guideline in all nonfiction writing. (*See: conflict of interest; new journalism; press trip; subjective writing.*)

Obscenity. (*See: censorship, literary; freedom of the press; pornography.*)

Occult. *Occult* refers to supernatural phenomena. Occult subjects include ghosts, ESP, astrology, demoniac possession, and witchcraft. Typical markets for occult writing are astrological and psychic publications, and some confession magazines. Non-occult publications as well may be interested in a documented supernatural story slanted to their readership. For example, a theater magazine may accept a piece on theatrical ghosts; an animal magazine may be interested in an article about a ghostly cat. The supernatural often plays a part in gothic romance novels.

Certain book publishers listed in *Writer's Market* express interest in the occult as a subject for a longer work of either fiction or nonfiction. (*See: gothic.*)

Off the record. When information is said by an interviewee to be "off the record," he expects the writer to keep it confidential and exclude it from his story.

If the writer does incorporate off-the-record material into his story, he risks losing future opportunities to interview the same source; however, the reporter's responsibility to accurately inform his readers must also be taken into consideration. The decision he makes is more often an ethical than a legal one.

Some reporters attribute off-the-record information to "informed sources" rather than to a specific person. Other writers have alleviated the off-the-record problem by setting guidelines with the source at the outset of the interview: for example, both may decide that the interviewee will indicate, during the course of the interview, which comments are off the record. Or the writer may grant the interviewee the right to turn off the tape recorder before making an off-the-record remark.

One writer, using a direct approach, informs his subject at the start of the interview that no information he receives will be considered off the record. His intention is to have the subject refrain from revealing any information he doesn't want to see in print; or to avoid having his hands tied by a source who tells him something off the record (perhaps something he already knows) with the idea that this manner of disclosing the information to the reporter will prevent him from printing it.

If a source is crucial to the story but is reluctant to consent to an interview for attribution, the writer may decide on a "background" discussion—similar to White House briefings without attribution. The goal is to get a better understanding of the topic from an authoritative source who feels the subject is too sensitive to permit the use of his name, or who wants to send up a trial balloon on a controversial subject.

For example, writer John Behrens believes a number of sources fear political, social, and financial backlash if they comment on contemporary issues. It's especially true among middle management business and government officers, he believes. Behrens describes an instance of backgrounding as follows:

I may do a major business story on taxes and tax shelters and I want a comment from a regional IRS official. The source knows he has the knowledge and the right to comment but he fears repercussions. He is willing to discuss the questions and offer examples as well as his interpretations. These may vary from official positions. I can always get the departmental stance but his unofficial explanations give me a better idea of how I can use materials I've already acquired. Furthermore, I've got examples to better illustrate parts of the story thanks to his background session.

The problem both for beginning and professional writers these days is the caution of knowledgeable people—doctors, lawyers, engineers, and others—about being interviewed for attribution. Quasi-investigative techniques are sometimes necessary. To prepare a piece on Camp David, a publicly funded recreation area for U.S. presidents, Behrens had to undertake a letter-writing campaign to members of Congress to persuade Carter Administration officials to provide basic information. Finally, several government officers offered "leads" and background as long as he promised not to use their names.

Investigative reporters use methods that can be applied in some freelance writing assignments, Behrens contends in his book, *Typewriter Guerrillas,* in which prize-winning reporters describe their techniques.

Offprint. (*See: reprint.*)

Off-screen. A term used in television and motion picture scripts to indicate a sound or voice heard, but not seen, by the audience. (*See: television script terms.*)

Ombudsman, newspaper. A newspaper ombudsman, usually a veteran reporter or editor, serves as an external spokesperson for the public and an internal critic for the newspaper. According to guidelines adopted in 1982 by the Organization of Newspaper Ombudsmen (ONO), the ombudsman's duties are to: 1) represent the reader who has complaints, suggestions, questions, or compliments; 2) investigate all complaints and recommend corrective action when warranted; 3) alert the newspaper to all complaints; 4) serve as an in-house critic; 5) make speeches or write to the public about the newspaper's policies, attitudes, and operations; and 6) defend the newspaper publicly or privately when warranted.

In order to perform those functions, ombudsmen write newspaper columns, give speeches, circulate memoranda within the staff, and distribute questionnaires to persons mentioned in news stories.

The editorial independence of the ombudsman is a subject of debate in the newspaper field. Some believe that the person in this position should be exempt from contributing editorially to the newspaper for which he works, in order to preserve his neutrality in serving the interests of both the newspaper and the public; others point to the prohibitive expense of hiring an ombudsman full-time.

Use of the ombudsman in the United States came into existence only recently, the first newspaper ombudsman program having been established in 1967. Currently, 35 ombudsmen serve newspapers in the U.S.

Ombudsman, Office of, U.S. Department of Commerce. As part of the U.S. Department of Commerce, the Office of the Ombudsman can refer the researching writer to authorities in most areas of business, industry, and trade. The Office can be reached by writing Office of the Ombudsman, Bureau of Domestic Business Development, Industry and Trade Administration, U.S. Department of Commerce, Washington DC 20230, or calling (202) 377-3176. (*See: Census Bureau, Department of Commerce.*)

On spec. An editor may respond to a writer's query letter by offering to look at the proposed article "on speculation"; that is, the editor expresses interest in the article idea and agrees to consider the finished piece for publication. In his response, the editor will usually indicate desired word count and terms of payment if the article is accepted. However, he is under no obligation to buy the finished manuscript.

For this reason, many full-time

freelancers write only on assignment, with a firm commitment from an editor to purchase the article. However, the writer who is not well-established enough to write only on assignment will find that an invitation to submit an article on spec generally means that the editor is interested in the idea and will buy the finished manuscript—if it is submitted within a reasonable length of time and meets editorial specifications. (*See: assignment, writing on; query.*)

On the air. Refers to the period of time that a program or commercial is broadcast.

One-act play. This form of drama, also called a *one-act* or *one-acter*, takes from 25-60 minutes to perform. Its time limitation restricts the content of the play: the plot must be kept simple, extraneous elements must be excluded, and no more than one set should be staged. However, a one-act play must include a complete story and theme and solid characterization.

One-act plays are published more often for high school, college, and amateur use than for commercial production, although such theaters as the Actors Theatre of Louisville sometimes stage them. *Writer's Market* lists play publishers and play producers, and *Dramatists Sourcebook* lists competitions that consider one-act plays. (*See: dinner theater; dramatic convention; dramatis personae; plays for young actors; playwriting.*)

Onomatopoeia. A word whose sound represents a physical sound. Deliberate use of such words is most frequent in poetry, but occurs in prose—and in common speech—as well. *Plop, click,* and *sizzle* are onomatopoeic words. (*See: figures of speech; imagery.*)

op. cit./loc. cit. These two Latin abbreviations are used in footnotes to indicate that a source has been previously documented in that list of notes. *Op. cit.* stands for *opere citato,* meaning "in the work cited," and *loc. cit.* stands for *loco citato,* which means "in the place cited."

These abbreviations are preceded by the author's name and sometimes followed by a page number. However, when footnotes contain references to more than one book by the same author, *op. cit.* and *loc. cit.* may not be used to refer to that author's work. (*See: ibid.*)

Op-Ed page. Harrison E. Salisbury of the *New York Times,* who created the Op-Ed page, points out in his introduction to *The Indignant Years:*

The Seventies ushered in an age of scepticism. Not one institution of American society escaped reexamination . . . Nothing in society was too profound or too trivial to be put under the magnifying glass of critical analysis. It was into this era that the Op-Ed page of *The New York Times* was born, a child of its times, a calculated effort to meet what was perceived as one of the great needs of our times, a place where men and women could express themselves on what was closest to their hearts, strongest in their passions, most fiercely in their principles. The criteria for Op-Ed could not have been more simple: to have something challenging to say and to say it with eloquence.

Salisbury goes on to explain:

That was and is the cornerstone of Op-Ed. It gave more emphasis to the right since one of my precepts was not to repeat or reinforce the liberal views already expressed by *Times* columnists and *Times* editorials. We sought out the Walt and Eugene Rostows, the Bundys, the right-wing Republicans. We gave everyone a platform, the more diverse the better. We never published a 'cartoonist.' We invented an entirely new form of art and brought in a whole new group of artists, mostly Europeans. They did not illustrate. They spiritually reinforced what we were talking about. Often people demanded to know what the drawings 'meant.' We never would tell them.

We solicited contributions all over the world from high and low and read every contribution submitted—soon they came in by the hundreds. They run thousands a year now. Every one used was paid for—not much, usually about $150 for 750 words—but paid. The innovation caught on like wildfire. *The Washington Post* was so eager to imitate us they started theirs three days before ours, having learned our start-up date. And there is not a paper in the country of any consequence which does not have an Op-Ed these days. And of course it brought in Op opinions to *Time* and *Newsweek*, to the networks and elsewhere.

Not all newspapers publish opinion essays from freelancers, and many do not pay for the material they do publish. Those that do solicit opinion pieces are listed in *Writer's Market*. To these newspapers the freelancer submits a titled, well-written essay, unfolded in a manila envelope and accompanied by an SASE, to the "Op-Ed Editor" or "Viewpoint Editor" of the paper. (*See: opinion essay.*)

Open-end transcription. A syndicated radio program in which time has been left at both beginning and end for the station to insert local commercials.

Opening song. In a musical, the song that usually begins an act. It has an establishing function, but also serves to incite the audience's interest. "Tradition," from *Fiddler on the Roof*, falls into this category. (*See: musical.*)

Operetta. (*See: musical.*)

Opinion essay. A short article—usually fewer than 1,000 words—in which the author offers his personal commentary on some event, condition, or situation about which he has a special knowledge or interest. Newspapers publish this kind of article on their Op-Ed (opposite editorial) pages. Alternative, child care, general interest, health, and women's magazines use it as well. Publications that seek opinion essays from writers are listed in *Writer's Market*. (*See: essay; Op-Ed page.*)

Opinion poll interviewing. (*See: market research.*)

Option clause. A clause often found in author-publisher book contracts that grants the publisher the right to publish the author's next book. The option clause is sometimes called the *right of first refusal* because it allows the publisher first crack at the author's next book, which the publisher may or may not decide to take on. In other words, this type of clause ordinarily binds the author rather than the publisher.

For this reason, the option clause might be better deleted from many contracts. As agent Georges Borchardt notes in *Law and the Writer*, if a publisher does a terrible job publishing an author's first book, why should the author subject his second book to the same fate? Borchardt explains the dangers of the option clause:

Some option clauses state that the publisher may acquire your next book on the same terms as your first; some state that the publisher need not make up his mind until several months after he has published book number one. Both of these stipulations should be avoided. The option to contract for your next book should be on terms to be agreed upon within a stated period of time, and if it is a work of nonfiction the option should be exercised on the basis of a synopsis, within a month of submission . . . If the publisher and author cannot agree within the stated period of time, the option should expire.

Borchardt's counsel is important. When a specific time period within which a publisher must make a decision is not defined in the clause, the publisher may wait to determine how well the first book sells before making a decision. While the publisher prolongs the moment of decision, the author is not free to submit his book proposal elsewhere.

The Authors Guild says, "The best way to deal with an option clause is to delete it from the publisher's contract form." (*See: book contract.*)

Additional information: *Law and the Writer; A Writer's Guide to Book Publishing.*

Organizing article/book material. The way in which a writer organizes research material for an article or book is as individual as the way in which he writes the actual manuscript. Different writers approach the organization process in different ways, and their systems range from complex arrangements of systematically classified index cards to casual groupings of related notes. One professional writer uses a coding system of colored pencils for related research materials. Another writes short segments of the article he's working on immediately following each interview. Many professional writers favor the cut-and-paste method to reorganize their first draft for smoother transitions. In many cases, the way a writer organizes his research material depends entirely on the type of article or book he's writing; organizational methods may change from one project to the next.

That they *do* organize their research material before beginning to write is the one thing good writers have in common. No matter what method a writer uses, organization of research is essential. Editors will often reject a well-researched manuscript because a writer did not take the time to organize the information collected.

As vital as the organization process is, however, overemphasizing its importance may be dangerous.

As writer Dickson Hartwell explains in *A Treasury of Tips for Writers*, "Just as the tendency to over-research is a sign of a lack of confidence in one's own ability to get started with the actual writing, so is a predilection to over-organize."

During the organization process, the writer should select the essential information that relates to the theme or peg of the piece and file away any tangential information that, while not necessary to this particular project, might be useful for other books or articles. The writer should spend enough time organizing this essential material to be thoroughly familiar with the information, notes, anecdotes, etc., that he intends to use, and then determine some type of order or outline in which to present that material. When the first draft is completed, the writer can refer back to this outline to make sure the manuscript covers all the intended points. (*See: first draft, revising and rewriting; outline; research aids/techniques.*)

Additional information: *A Treasury of Tips for Writers*.

Originality. The quality of being creative, inventive, or out of the ordinary. This characteristic is difficult to define precisely in relation to writing. As one editor remarked in a *Writer's Digest* article, "If you could pinpoint the exact nature of originality, it wouldn't be original any more." As elusive as it may be to define, however, originality in articles, stories, and books is precisely the quality editors are constantly searching for.

Given that there are virtually no new ideas under the sun, originality in writing becomes largely a matter of clothing a worn subject in a new approach. There are few article topics and story themes that have not been done before, but the creative writer faces—and meets—the challenge of expressing those topics and themes in an individual way, giving fresh insight to an idea in order to make it *seem* as if the subject hadn't been done before.

In respect to copyright law, the term *originality* does not refer to literary skill, artistic value, or uniqueness; rather, it means that the work is created by the author and not originated by someone else. (*See: creativity; plagiarism.*)

Oscar Awards. The Oscar Awards are presented annually by the Academy of Motion Picture Arts and Sciences. The 15 categories of awards represent various skills involved in film production; additional awards for general contributions to the motion picture industry exist, but are not necessarily presented yearly.

Writing for film is recognized by two awards: Best Screenplay Written Directly for the Screen, and Best Screenplay Based on Material from Another Medium.

Music for film is judged in three categories: Best Original Score, Best Original Song Score and Its Adaptation or Best Adaptation Score, and Best Original Song.

Outcue. The last words in the copy for a radio ad. Often, all spots for the same account employ the same outcue, e.g., the address or slogan of the sponsor. Air talent listens for the outcue as a signal to come on-air with whatever is scheduled to follow.

Outdoor Writers Association of America, Inc. (OWAA). Established in 1927, the Outdoor Writers Association of America is a nonprofit professional and educational organization comprising newspaper and magazine writers, editors, photographers, broadcasters, artists, cinematographers, and lecturers engaged in the dissemination of information on outdoor sports—hunting, boating, fishing, camping, etc.— and on the conservation of natural resources. In addition to conducting an annual conference, the organization publishes a monthly bulletin containing market coverage, writers' opinions, news of writers in the field, and craft improvement articles. Members are required to publish a specified quantity of paid material annually. Membership applicants must be sponsored by an active OWAA member. The address of the OWAA is 3101 W. Peoria Avenue, Phoenix AZ 85029.

Additional information: *Successful Outdoor Writing.*

Outline. An outline is a general description indicating only the main features of an article, story, book, speech, or other project. It is a means of organizing material in which the order and general relationship of ideas are expressed so as to reveal a work's intention.

For a nonfiction writer, an outline serves as a plan or guide that provides a solid basis for the development of his article. Depending on a writer's preference and ability to organize, the outline may take various forms: it may be written out, or merely a mental arrangement of facts; it may be a formal, detailed organization of ideas, or a brief collection of key words or statements indicating the progression of a piece. Whatever form the outline takes, its primary purpose is to enable writers to organize their material and focus their attention on the subject of the article. Although important in providing a framework for an article, an outline should always be flexible enough to accommodate new ideas that develop from a writer's research and actual writing.

The nonfiction book author also uses an outline in preparing a book proposal. This more in-depth outline features chapter-by-chapter highlights in the order in which they'll appear in the book. This outline, together with one or two sample chapters and a specialized cover letter introducing the book's subject and explaining its salability, make up the book proposal an author submits to a publisher. (*See: nonfiction books, marketing.*)

Out-of-print books, how to find. The Manhattan Yellow Pages, available in libraries, lists bookstores that handle out-of-print books in the section "Book Dealers—Used & Rare." In addition, the annual *American Book Trade Directory*, in the section "Retailers & Antiquarians in the United States & Canada," lists this type of bookstore by state and city. Some book search services advertise in the back pages of the *New York Times Book Review.*

The section "Micropublishers" in

Literary Market Place lists publishers of microfilm and similar materials, some of which contain out-of-print books and papers. Specific microforms are listed in *Guide to Microforms in Print* and *Micropublishers' Trade List Annual*.

Overseas Press Club of America (OPC). The 1,600 members of the OPC are correspondents, reporters, editors, photographers, freelance writers, and book authors. They work overseas, have worked overseas in the past, or have worked in the news media for at least three consecutive years.

The organization presents several annual awards for reporting and photography concerning events overseas or foreign affairs. OPC members have access to various press clubs around the world.

Some of the organization's committees are Archives and Research, Book Publishing, Foreign Journalists Liaison, and Freedom of the Press. OPC publishes the semimonthly *Overseas Press Club Bulletin;* the annual *Dateline,* which contains articles by outstanding journalists; and a membership directory. The OPC's address is 52 E. 41st Street, New York NY 10017.

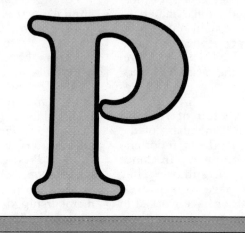

Pace. Tempo, or rate of progression. This term, which applies to both fiction and nonfiction works, refers to a written work's effect on the reader through the text's rate of movement.

A writer creates a slow pace by using substantial amounts of narration, description, and digression. Action, dialogue, and a series of incidents following in rapid succession quicken the pace. A writer varies pace to accommodate different moods and action in his writing, alternating between a rapid tempo and a more relaxed one, depending on the material and the effect the writer wishes to produce.

Pace is a feature of filmed or staged as well as printed material: the swift pace of an action-packed detective drama, for instance, contrasts with the leisurely exploration of a nature subject in a television documentary.

Pad. To lengthen an article or book by adding text or detailed material related in a peripheral way, such as appendixes, tables, and lists. The latter may be desired by some book publishers to add reference material to a book, especially the type that in revised editions could be changed without affecting the pagination of the rest of the text; however, magazine editors generally reject articles padded with superfluous information that adds no significant value to a specifically focused manuscript.

Page proof. A reproduction copy of typeset matter after division into page form and before actual printing. On a page proof, galley corrections have been made and line art illustrations, footnotes, and display type (chapter heads, ornaments, and occasionally subheads) will usually appear in their proper positions.

Page proofs are carefully examined and read by the publishing house's proofreader as a final check. Depending on the nature of the book and the production schedule that has been set for it, an author may or may not see page proofs of his book.

Since editorial and design changes at the page proof stage are costly, time-consuming, and likely to delay production of the book, trade book authors generally must have a specific provision to see page proofs written into their contracts, and must pay for any author's alterations required at this stage. (*See: author's alteration clause; galley proof.*)

Page rate. The method by which some magazines pay writers, as opposed to a word rate or a flat fee. In this sense, a *page* refers to a printed page rather than a manuscript page.

Paid for but not published. A magazine may sometimes accept and pay for an article that for one reason or another never reaches print. In many cases, a paid-for piece is never published because editorial policy changes; in other cases, a magazine's editor moves to another publication and the editor who replaces him doesn't like the piece.

A writer anxious to know if and when his purchased story or article will appear in print may send a polite inquiry to the editor who bought the piece. If this action does not prove satisfactory, the writer may follow up with a letter advising the publication of the guidelines for reclaiming rights to an unpublished manuscript established by the American Society of Journalists & Authors, Inc., and requesting the editor's consideration of same. According to these guidelines, if after one year (12 months) the article or story has not appeared in print, all rights to the manuscript should re-

turn to the author, who may submit it elsewhere for publication. The author should be permitted to retain the original fee paid for the manuscript. (*See: kill fee; magazines, deceased; rights to manuscripts.*)

Pamphlets. (*See:* Vertical File Index, The.)

Pan. To swing a motion picture camera from left to right or from right to left, without moving the camera base, in order to show a broad view of a location or scene. The direction is given as PAN RIGHT or PAN LEFT. "WHIP" indicates a rapid pan. (*See: television script terms.*)

Paperback originals. (*See: mass market paperbacks vs. trade books; paperbacks, history of; trade paperback.*)

Paperbacks, history of. The first paperback novel, *Malaeska: The Indian Wife of The White Hunter*, was published in June, 1860. The 128-page book, written by Ann Sophia Winterbotham Stephens, a widely respected hardcover novelist of her day, was published by Irwin P. Beadle and Company and sold for ten cents.

The first "dime novel," as it came to be called, was an immediate success; a print order of 60,000 for *Malaeska* sold out within two months. Other publishers followed suit with paperbacks of their own. Dime novels came to enjoy tremendous popularity, creating a reading habit among those who previously could not afford to buy books.

As the competition increased, however, the literary level fell. Dime novels eventually gave way to the larger "pulp" magazine format.

Paperbound originals attempted a

comeback in the 1930s, but failed to capture reader interest; the failure did, however, encourage Robert de Graff to initiate in 1939 his Pocket Book line of twenty-five-cent reprints of popular hardcover books, thus establishing the foundation for the entire modern paperback book industry.

In the next several decades, the success of paperback reprints stimulated keen competition among publishing houses. Pocket, Bantam, Signet, and other publishers vied for the best books in every category—mystery, western, suspense, romance, etc. The shortage of good books by well-known authors created an economic suicide situation: to get the book he wanted, a publisher was forced to pay more than he would earn. The reprint line quickly became saturated with "loss leaders"—books offered at a loss by publishers in order to get rack space and attract customers to their entire line of books.

Although it was obvious that paperbound publishers would have to change their source of supply, it was magazine publisher Roscoe Fawcett who made the first move. When his line of original paperbacks—Gold Medal Books—debuted in 1950, they paved the way for the paperback originals industry that is still growing today.

In *A Writer's Guide to Book Publishing*, Richard Balkin discusses current trends in the paperback book industry. Today, says Balkin, most of the mass-market houses are either owned by conglomerates or are subdivisions of hardcover houses. Many hardcover houses have trade paperback lines, as do most of the mass-market publishers. All nine major mass-market publishers have established their own hardcover imprints, or are affiliated in one way or another with a hardcover house (Avon's parent company, for example, also owns Hearst Books and William Morrow).

Balkin reports that in the last ten years or so, mass-market publishers such as Avon, Dell, Warner, and Ballantine have increased their output of paperback originals, which ranges from 40%-50% of their lists. There are several reasons to account for the increase of original titles, Balkin says: the increasing price of hardcover books and subsequent consumer reluctance to buy them; a decreasing reluctance on the part of critics to review paperbacks; a greater consumption of paperbacks as high school and college texts; and the frequently high prices and occasionally extravagant auctions for paperback reprint rights. (Balkin cites *Princess Daisy*, for example, for which Bantam paid author Judith Krantz $3.2 million.)

Other factors that have influenced the increasing number of original paperbacks include the need for more titles than hardcover houses can supply, and the fact that it is cheaper to commission a book for, say, $5,000 and control all rights, than to lease paperback rights only, for, say, $7,500 for only seven years.

The ongoing trend toward paperback originals is good news for novelists, particularly writers of "category" fiction, which is a growing area for the industry. The same is true, however, of nonfiction books with wide readership appeal. Trade (quality) paperback publishers are also increasing the number of originals in their paperback lines. (*See: category fiction; mass market paperbacks vs. trade books; trade paperback.*)

Parable. A short narrative designed to teach some religious principle, moral lesson, or universal truth. A parable is often an allegory in which each character in the story represents an abstract concept, such as obedience or honesty, that is illustrated through comparison with real-life events. Perhaps the most widely recognized parables are those told by Christ in the New Testament—the stories of the prodigal son and the good Samaritan are two examples. Parables often provide an excellent source of universal themes for all types of stories. (*See: fable; proverb.*)

Paradox. An apparently self-contradictory statement that actually contains truth. For example, Oscar Wilde said, "Life is far too important a thing ever to talk seriously about." George Bernard Shaw once remarked, "The truth is the only thing that no one will believe."

Like wise sayings and quotable quotes, paradoxes come to an individual in a flash of inspiration. A writer ordinarily cannot sit down at his typewriter with the intention of creating a paradox; for this reason, paradoxes are found infrequently in most writing. (*See: irony; satire.*)

Parallelism. A principle of grammatical construction requiring elements or ideas similar in content and function, and of equal importance, to be expressed in similar form. This structural principle—known also as *parallel construction*—applies to all parts and units of speech, from words, phrases, and clauses to sentences, paragraphs, and whole units of composition.

Faulty parallel structure is a common problem for beginning writers, but even skillful writers occasionally have trouble with parallelism. Attention to parallel structure is essential to the construction of clear, effective sentences; it enables the reader to recognize immediately the coordinating elements and ideas in a composition.

The key to parallelism lies in using consistent verb tense, person, voice, and grammatical structure to express coordinating elements and ideas. For instance, the writer should avoid shifting verb tenses, as in this example: "The ball *rolled* down the stairs and *bounces* on the landing." Since the verb in the first clause is past tense—*rolled*—the verb in the second clause should also be past tense. *Bounced*, not *bounces*, is correct.

Similarly, the writer should avoid shifting from second to third person or from active to passive voice within a sentence. Grammatical units such as clauses, infinitives, and phrases should be kept parallel; an infinitive, for instance, should be followed by an infinitive of similar form and function. For example, "She liked *to read* books and *seeing* movies, " is not parallel. The correct construction is, "She liked *to read* books and *to see* movies."

Parallelism also requires that a writer use articles and prepositions consistently. For example, "This project can be done in one, two, or in three steps," should, according to the principles of parallel structure, be expressed as either "This project can be done in one, two, or three steps," or "This project can be done in one, in two, or in three steps."

Similarly, a writer should maintain consistent grammatical construction when using correlative expressions such as *both, and; not, but; not only, but also; either, or;* and similar phrases. "He is both a bore and dense," is an example of this type of faulty parallel construction. The sentence should read, "He is both boring and dense."

Absolute parallel structure is not always necessary. The primary concern is that the grammatical *functions* are parallel, even though the grammatical *forms* may not be. For instance, in the sentence, "He drove *recklessly* and *without regard for traffic signals*" both *recklessly* and *without regard for traffic signals* modify the verb *drove;* their grammatical functions are the same, and so the construction is parallel.

Parallel construction applies only to elements of *equal importance* in a sentence. The writer should avoid a series of words or phrases that seem to modify the same element but in fact do not. For instance, "Delia left, and she had a friend" is parallel in construction. The two clauses are not of equal importance, however, and the sentence should be expressed in this way: "Delia left with a friend."

Paraphrase. A paraphrase is a restatement of a passage or text in other words so as to make it clear. Paraphrasing must not be used carelessly. In researching information for a book or article, for example, a writer may come across some interesting ideas that he would like to incorporate into his own material; in order to avoid plagiarizing the information, however, the writer must be certain to credit paraphrased words and ideas to their proper source.

Spoken remarks—made during an interview, for example—may also be paraphrased and attributed to the source as an indirect quote. When-

ever paraphrasing, a writer must take care that his restatement of another's words and ideas—whether written or spoken—is accurate and true to the meaning of the original material. (*See: attribution; indirect quote; plagiarism; quotes.*)

Parody. A humorous, satirical imitation of a person, event, novel, story, poem, play, film, or other subject. By following the style and substance of the original work, a parody may seek to ridicule, criticize, or merely amuse without devaluing the original.

Since it involves by its very nature a certain amount of imitation of the original, parody often poses a special problem in the area of copyright law. The writer or other artist who attempts to parody some literary composition, film, or other work risks copyright infringement in too closely imitating the copyrighted work of another. Protection from copyright infringement in regard to the creation of parodies is based on the concept of "fair use"; that is, permissible use of copyrighted material, which does not constitute infringement. (This subject is discussed in more detail under the entry "fair use" in this encyclopedia.)

There are no clearly defined boundaries regarding how much a parodist may appropriate from an original copyrighted work. Recent court cases support the following basic guidelines: 1) a parodist may use only enough of the original material sufficient to cause a reader or viewer to "recall and conjure up" the original work on which the parody is based; 2) copying that is virtually complete or almost verbatim—even though it may contain grotesque, burlesque, or parodic elements—is not protected under the "fair use" defense; 3) the copyrighted material itself must be the object of parody—and not merely used *within* a parody—in order to be protected under the fair use concept; 4) the use of copyrighted material should in no way confuse the public into believing the parody has any association with the original work; 5) the resulting work imitating the copyrighted material should not be in economic competition with the original.

Guideline two, above, came about as a result of a 1958 case in which Jack Benny was sued regarding the film *Autolight*, a parody on the film *Gaslight*. The court denied Benny the fair use defense on the grounds that a substantial amount of material (in this case, dialogue) had been copied. Guideline three was reflected in the 1975 case *Walt Disney Productions vs. Mature Pictures Corp.*, in which the latter used the "Mickey Mouse March" as background music for an erotic scene depicting sexual deviation. The court decided that copyright infringement had occurred and that parody was not a defense, because the "Mickey Mouse March," although used in the film, was not the subject of the parody.

These criteria apply also to the infringement of trademark registration. An individual is not protected under the fair use concept in parodying a trademark if the parodist's satire of the registered trademark 1) confuses the public, misrepresents a product, or damages the value of the trademark; 2) attempts to cash in on the good name and trade of the trademark owner; or 3) is so similar to the original that it leads the public to believe that a distinctive product or service is being offered by the parodist.

Fair use and copyright infringement in regard to parody are often complicated legal areas. The writer who intends to imitate the copyrighted work of another for the purpose of creating parody should have a thorough understanding of the law of copyright and concept of fair use in order to avoid potential legal conflicts. The market for parody seems limited today to a few publications such as the more literary men's magazines, the *New Yorker*, and *Mad*, which wants not prose submissions but descriptions of visuals that can illustrate them. Brief passages of parody also appear in drama, film, and television reviews. Some non-books—such as the cat-hating books—might also be considered parodies. (*See: copyright; fair use; trademark.*)

Participation. The sharing of commercial time and costs for the same broadcast program by more than one sponsor.

Pay on publication. Many publications, particularly among the smaller markets, pay the freelancer for a manuscript only after the story or article has been published. The editor of a pay-on-publication magazine may accept a freelance submission and hold it indefinitely without ever printing it. The passage of time or a change in editors may make the manuscript otherwise unusable or, because the pay-on-publication policy is characteristic of smaller markets that operate on tight month-to-month budgets, the magazine may go out of business. Even if the piece is eventually published, it may be many months before the freelancer receives any money.

The pay-on-publication policy is

strongly criticized by professional writers. Writer and editor Art Spikol comments: "Selling an article to a market that pays on publication is like selling a bed to somebody and not requiring payment until they actually sleep in it."

Although most books on writing caution freelancers to avoid pay-on-publication markets, they also acknowledge that these smaller magazines are often the easiest for beginners to break into. Writers are warned to protect themselves when dealing with pay-on-publication markets. "If you do place a manuscript with one of them," says Lois Duncan, author of *How to Write and Sell Your Personal Experiences*, "ask for a written guarantee that if publication and payment do not occur within a set time (six months seems appropriate to me), you will be allowed to withdraw the manuscript and submit it elsewhere." (*See: full-time freelancing, economics of.*)

PBS. (*See: broadcast networks.*)

PE (printer's error). A typesetting error; also called a *typo*. When an editor or proofreader goes through galleys clearing up typos, making last-minute revisions, incorporating the author's alterations, etc., he marks the typos PE to distinguish them from editorial changes. This is an accounting procedure: if copy is set by a firm independent of the publisher, the publisher will be charged only for editorial revisions and not for mistakes the typesetter has made. Another reason for keeping track of typos and revisions is that if an author has made more than the percentage of alterations his contract allows for, the typesetting cost will come out of his royalties.

Peg. The one angle of a subject on which a nonfiction writer develops his article. Most good article subjects suggest several pegs, and each of them can be developed into a separate, salable article slanted toward a different type of market. For example, a writer who planned to write about vegetable gardening could use three different pegs for three different articles: how to use vegetable plants in a landscaping/decorative scheme; how to convert to the French intensive method of gardening for economy and self-sufficiency; and how to grow an easy-to-care-for vegetable garden indoors. The first article could be slanted toward a landscaping trade journal; the second, toward an alternative magazine; and the third, toward an apartment dweller's magazine.

PEN American Center. Established in 1921, PEN is a world association of poets, playwrights, essayists, editors, and novelists. The organization defines as its purpose "to promote and maintain friendship and intellectual cooperation among men and women of letters in all countries, in the interests of literature, the exchange of ideas, freedom of expression, and good will." PEN has more than 80 centers in Europe, Asia, Africa, Australia, and the Americas. Membership is open to "all qualified writers, translators and editors who subscribe to the aims of International PEN." Membership is by invitation of the Admission Committee after nomination by a PEN member. To qualify for membership, an applicant must have "acknowledged achievement in the literary field, which is generally interpreted as the publication by a recognized publisher of two books of literary merit." The address of this organization is 47 Fifth Avenue, New York NY 10003.

Pen name. Also known as a *pseudonym* or a *nom de plume*, a pen name is used by an author instead of his real name. Mark Twain was the pen name of Samuel L. Clemens; Theodore Geisel writes under the name Dr. Seuss.

Whether or not a writer uses his own or a pen name depends on a number of factors. The pen name might represent co-authors writing under one name. An author's own name may be unsuitable, either because it is too similar to that of an established writer, is difficult to pronounce, or is somehow ridiculous-sounding. In other cases, an author writing different types of material—children's picture books and romance novels, for example—may wish to maintain different literary identities for different literary pursuits. Very prolific writers often employ pen names if they produce several books a year or find themselves with duplicate bylines in the same issue of a magazine. Finally, a writer may choose to publish under a pen name merely to avoid recognition.

The freelancer writing under a pen name generally types his real name and address in the upper left-hand corner of the first page of his manuscript. (His real name should also appear in the upper left-hand corner of succeeding manuscript pages.) The title of his article or story is followed by his pen name. This indicates that the writer wishes his pen name to byline the article; the editor will, however, pay the writer with a check made out to the author's real name.

If for some reason the writer wishes to conceal his identity from the editor to whom he submits his manuscript, he types his pen name in the upper left-hand corner of the first page as well as in the byline position; his real name does not appear at all on the manuscript.

The writer using only a pen name and not his real name should notify his bank and local post office, advising them that he may be receiving checks and mail in that business name. He would also file his income tax return showing his pen name on Schedule C, for example, "John Smith doing business as (or dba) William Jones." (*See: byline.*)

PEN Prison Writing Program. A division of PEN, the writers' organization. It sponsors an annual writing competition for writers in prison and provides sources of information on writing to prisoners. This information ranges from answers to commonly asked questions and referrals to other programs for prisoners to listings of magazines that accept prisoners' writing. The Center distributes some free publications and sometimes receives books and magazines that it also gives to prisons. (Writers who wish to donate used books to prisoners as a tax-deductible gift should contact PEN for further information.)

The Center's competition, the Writing Awards for Prisoners, offers nine awards annually: first-, second-, and third-place prizes in fiction, nonfiction, and poetry categories. Entries are accepted from September 1 to March 1; awards are presented in late spring. Winning pieces are published in *The Fortune News*. Contest requirements and other information on the Center's services may be obtained from PEN American Center, 47 Fifth Avenue, New York NY 10003.

Performing right. One of the rights granted to a copyright owner under the copyright law. It stipulates that the person who owns the copyright to a work has the sole right to publicly perform, or to authorize public performance of, that work. According to the law, performing includes reciting, rendering, playing, dancing, and acting. This can be accomplished, "either directly or by means of any device or process or, in the case of a motion picture or other audiovisual work, . . . (by showing) its images in any sequence or . . . (making) the sounds accompanying it audible."

To *perform publicly* a work is "to perform or display it at a place open to the public or at any place where a substantial number of persons outside of a normal circle of a family and its social acquaintances is gathered" or "to transmit or otherwise communicate a performance or display of the work . . . (publicly, as defined above) whether the members of the public capable of receiving the performance or display receive it in the same place or separate places and at the same time or at different times." The latter part of this definition refers to programs aired on closed-circuit television, programs recorded for delayed broadcasting, and similar electronically produced programs.

Exceptions to the performing right include performance of a copyrighted work by students and teachers in nonprofit schools and in governmental agencies, by persons conducting/participating in religious services, and by those who perform

works for the handicapped. All others must get permission from the copyright owner. (*See: copyright.*)

Performing rights organizations. These organizations collect royalties on behalf of songwriters and publishers for work that is performed in clubs, on television (including cable television), on radio, and on jukebox records. The three major American performing rights organizations are American Society of Composers, Authors and Publishers (ASCAP); Broadcast Music, Inc. (BMI); and SESAC, Inc. (SESAC formerly stood for Society of European Stage, Authors and Composers but the title is no longer applicable.)

Performing rights organizations license broadcasters and other establishments where music is performed (such as nightclubs) by charging each licensee a fee. In the case of broadcasting stations, the fee is normally determined by a percentage of the adjusted gross income of the station. In the case of non-broadcast licensees, the fee may be fixed in the terms of the capacity of the establishment, its entertainment budget, and other factors. Methods of establishing how often music is performed—which differ from organization to organization—include surveying network or station music logs, and as SESAC does, examining charts in trade magazines.

In order to collect performance royalties, the songwriter must be affiliated with the same organization his publisher belongs to. Since music publishers commonly divide their various corporate affiliates among the different organizations, it is possible for an already affiliated writer to work with the publisher he desires without changing organizations.

Both ASCAP and BMI divide performance royalties between publisher and writer, after having extracted a small percentage for overhead. On the other hand, SESAC divides 50% of its income between publisher and writer and retains the other half for its own purposes.

Addresses of the three major American performing rights groups are as follows: American Society of Composers, Authors and Publishers, 1 Lincoln Plaza, New York NY 10023; Broadcast Music, Inc., 320 W. 57th Street, New York NY 10019; and SESAC, Inc., 10 Columbus Circle, New York NY 10019. (*See: subsidiary rights.*)

Periodic sentence. A sentence that cannot be fully understood until it has been read completely. Also called a *suspended sentence*, the periodic sentence draws the reader along by withholding an essential element or idea until the end. For example: "Once the story action is outlined and the character description completed, I can begin to write the novel."

A writer uses periodic sentences to break up the monotony of the standard subject/verb/complement sentence pattern and add variety to his writing. Since the reader must keep in mind the subordinate ele-

ments as he progresses toward the main idea, periodic sentences often require greater concentration to be understood and should be used sparingly.

Periodical. A publication issued at regularly recurring intervals of more than one day, but less than a year, is classified as a *periodical*. The term is applied primarily to magazines and journals; it does not ordinarily refer to newspapers. (*See: periodicals, directories of; periodicals, indexes to.*)

Periodicals, directories of. *Ulrich's International Periodicals Directory* and the *Standard Periodical Directory* are two references that categorize periodicals by subject matter. Two monthly directories, *Consumer Magazine and Farm Publication Rates and Data* and *Business Publication Rates and Data*, are also arranged by subject matter. They contain information such as advertising rates, and production and circulation details, as well as a profile of usual editorial content of import primarily to persons interested in advertising in magazines and journals.

Those periodicals that consistently buy freelance material from writers are detailed in *Writer's Market*, which gives information on the publication's editorial focus, the types of material published, rates of pay, the length of time in which the editor will report on manuscripts, rights purchased, and other details. Both consumer magazines and trade journals are categorized by subject.

Periodicals, indexes to. These directories and microfilms help writers do research, by cataloging information published in magazine, newspaper, or journal articles by title, subject,

263

and author. Most are available at large public libraries or college libraries. Some general indexes to magazines are *Readers' Guide to Periodical Literature*, *The Magazine Index*, *Access: The Supplementary Index to Periodicals*, *Popular Periodical Index*, and *Abstracts of Popular Culture*. Some indexes to newspapers are *Facts on File*, the *New York Times Index* and the *Christian Science Monitor Index*. *Ulrich's International Periodicals Directory* tells the reader if a magazine publishes its own index and which periodical indexes also carry it.

Indexes to publications for specialized fields include *Education Index*, *Business Periodicals Index*, *Psychological Abstracts*, *Art Index*, *Periodical Indexes in the Social Sciences and Humanities*, *Abstracts and Indexes in Science and Technology: A Descriptive Guide*, and *Index Medicus*. (*See: periodicals, directories of*; Readers' Guide to Periodical Literature.)

Permissions. Permissions involve granting either an author or a publisher the right to excerpt copyrighted material—a passage, page, chapter, short story, or poem—for use within another work. For example, if a writer plans to copy an illustration or quote more than a few lines from a copyrighted work, he must get written permission to do so. Obtaining permission to quote or copy material is the responsibility of the author, not his publisher; many publishers do, however, have their own printed forms for authors to use. Since some copyright holders specify the exact form an author must use in giving credit, all permissions should be obtained before the manuscript is typeset.

Obtaining permission to excerpt material does not ordinarily involve a fee if the intended use is incidental—for example, if a novelist wishes to introduce a chapter with a passage from another writer's work, or the author of a nonfiction book quotes a paragraph from a reference volume written by an authority in the field. Although many requests of this type are considered "fair use," written permission is nevertheless solicited in many cases, just to be on the safe side.

In selecting material for an anthology or collection of critical essays, however, an author may be required to pay permission fees to various copyright holders; the same may be true of a translation, a book containing artwork, or a reprint of a book no longer in print, if the material for these does not fall into the public domain.

"Many anthologies have extremely high permission costs," notes Richard Balkin, author of *A Writer's Guide to Book Publishing*. "An anthology of contemporary poetry or drama could cost upward to $15,000 in permissions alone. Every editor will consider these costs before making a decision, and they will definitely influence the final verdict on whether or not to sign up the book."

A publisher, says Balkin, usually allocates a permissions budget, pays the fees, and then deducts the costs from the anthology editor's future royalties. "It is very important for the anthologist to make sure that the house is going to lay out the permissions costs and that this is stated clearly in the contract," Balkin advises.

Balkin reports that permission fees for magazine and journal articles generally run about $10 per page. Fees for other material vary considerably, depending on the particular publisher or copyright holder, as well as the current reputation or prestige of the author of the selection. (*See: anthology; fair use; public domain; quotes.*)

Personal experience. A writer's personal experience can provide the information for any number of articles, including personality profiles, opinion pieces, and how-to articles. A wide variety of magazines also solicit the pure personal experience article—the true adventure or experience written as an article in the first person.

The effectiveness and marketability of the personal experience or "intimate" article depends primarily on the universality of its subject. What the author is writing about must be relevant or interesting to other people besides himself; the story must be one with which his audience can identify. For this reason, successful personal experience articles often appeal directly to the reader's feelings and emotion.

An engaging style is also vital to the personal experience piece. The author must express honest feeling without sentimentality, and avoid sermonizing or taking too didactic a tone.

Like any type of article, the personal experience piece must be well-organized. Insignificant details and tangential information must be edited out, and illustrative anecdotes woven into a tightly knit structure. The personal experience piece must have a clearly defined focus: the story must be shaped so as to make a definite point and result in a satisfying conclusion. And although the article may be based on the writer's own experience or opinion, supporting quotes from recognized authorities or significant statistics and other factual information can add strength and credibility to the piece.

A personal experience piece may take many forms: confession, nostalgia, opinion or controversy, humor, self-help and inspiration, or commentary on current trends and lifestyles. It appears in general magazines such as *Reader's Digest* and the *New York Times Magazine* as well as in hundreds of other consumer and trade publications.

The primary element of a good personal experience piece is that it has something worthwhile to say. According to one writer, "unless your experience, your advice, your opinion is to some extent original, you'll have little to offer editors or readers." (*See: first person short story.*)

Additional information: *How to Write and Sell Your Personal Experiences.*

Personification. Personification is a figure of speech in which inanimate objects, abstractions, animals, and ideas are attributed human form, characteristics, or sensibilities. "The wind shrieked through the windows," and "The sauce bubbled over onto the burner, hissing for attention," are examples of personification—giving human qualities and characteristics to inhuman things.

Personification is frequently used as a literary device in poetry. The prose writer—both of fiction and nonfiction—also uses personification to strengthen the imagery of his article or story. (*See: figures of speech; imagery.*)

Persuasive writing. Sometimes called *argument*, this kind of writing tries to incite the reader to an action, such as buying, contributing, or adopting a particular point of view. In a larger sense, almost all writing has to be persuasive, but advertising, publicity, and propaganda exemplify persuasive writing in its more intense form.

The persuasive writer can achieve his purpose either through emotional appeal or logical appeal. For example, the magazine ad with the headline "The Advantages of Renting Office Furniture" appeals to the reader's logic, while the one headed "The Colorful Fall Getaway" appeals to his emotions.

Fundraisers for animal protection organizations, environmental causes, and cultural institutions all rely on persuasive writing to meet their goals. Writers may find some helpful books on the subject under the categories of "Persuasion (Psychology)" and "Persuasion (Rhetoric)" in the *Subject Guide to Books In Print*.

Photo processing labs. If the writer who takes his own photographs is unable—because of lack of knowledge, equipment, or time—to develop and print his own film, he must rely on a commercial photo processing lab.

Martin Hershenson, Contributing Editor of *Modern Photography* magazine, believes that because the proper processing and print of film—particularly color film—is so critical, a photographer will probably have to try several firms before finding one that produces quality prints or transparencies at a reasonable price.

The *Directory of Professional Photography*, published annually by Professional Photographers of America, Inc., and available in most libraries, lists commercial photo processing labs and services. Professional photo developing labs also advertise regularly in photography magazines such as *Modern Photography*, *Petersen's Photographic Magazine*, and *Popular Photography*. The writer/photographer will find photo processing labs located in his own community in the Yellow Pages under "Photo Finishing—Retail."

Photo release. (*See: model release; sample in the Appendix to this encyclopedia.*)

Photocopied manuscripts. In sympathy over increasing costs of typing services, paper, and postage, and in response to improvements in photocopying quality, many editors who once insisted on seeing the original, good-bond copy of a manuscript now accept photocopied submissions from writers.

Photocopying a manuscript is primarily a convenience for an author, as well as a precautionary measure; if a manuscript is lost or damaged in the mail or misplaced at an editor's office, the writer has the original copy on file and need not take the time and expense of retyping the manuscript.

In submitting a photocopied manuscript, however, the writer should advise the editor that the manuscript is not a simultaneous submission being considered by several editors at the same time (unless, of course, it *is* a simultaneous submission). The photocopied manuscript should also be of excellent quality, as clean, neat, and legible as the original. (*See: multiple submissions.*)

Photograph/picture sources. In addition to the information under the headings "free photos," "photographer-writer relationship," and "photographs accompanying manuscripts," in this encyclopedia, writers may find leads for other illustration materials in directories such as *Picture Sources,* published by the Special Libraries Association and available in most libraries, and the *Writer's Resource Guide.*

Also, *Photographer's Market* contains a section on stock photo agencies—companies that sell photos on a variety of subjects. (*See: free photos; photographer-writer relationship; photographs accompanying manuscripts.*)

Photographer-writer relationship. In some situations a writer chooses a photographer to take pictures to accompany the text of a book or article he is writing. Photographers who work with freelance writers play an important part in determining the salability of a manuscript.

Writers try to choose photographer-partners especially suited to their particular kind of writing and the specific markets that buy their work. Local camera clubs and classified ads in local newspapers are sources for finding available photographers, as are college art departments (if they teach photography). The selection process involves the writer's examining the photographer's portfolio. He evaluates the subject matter, the quality and style of the work, and how it relates to the type of writing he does.

The writer supplies his photographer-partner with a draft of the manuscript, or at least an outline of the main points, and works with him to determine ways to enhance the writing with visuals. Actual photographs are chosen from the contact sheets the photographer makes. Prints picked for publication are accompanied by photographer's model releases in those cases where the photographs may be used for other than editorial purposes. The writer should also get a brief statement signed by the photographer granting the use of a photograph(s) in conjunction with a specified manuscript to appear in a particular publication.

The photographer may be paid in one of three ways: 1) the writer and photographer can agree in advance on a flat fee for the shooting and prints, or a percentage of the total article price for the photographs; 2) if the photographer is a member of the American Society of Magazine Photographers or some other professional photography association, the photographer might have a fixed fee that the writer has to agree to; or 3) the writer can suggest (in advance) to the editor a qualified local professional photographer, with the editor making the photo selections from the contact sheet and paying the photographer directly. (*See: American Society of Magazine Photographers; photographs accompanying manuscripts; photojournalism.*)

Photographs accompanying manuscripts. Many professional writers maintain that, for certain markets, a freelance article manuscript has a much better chance of selling when accompanied by a selection of high-quality photographs and presented to an editor as a complete package. In fact, some editors *require* pictures to accompany article submissions.

Ideally, a writer should be able to take his own pictures, and if he intends to illustrate his own article he must study the photo requirements of the market as thoroughly as he studies the editorial requirements—noting whether the magazine uses color, black and white, or a combination of the two; determining the ratio of posed to unposed shots and horizontal to vertical pictures; and identifying the types of people, amount of action, and related elements characteristic of the magazine's photographs. Some magazine editors supply editorial guidelines for photographers as well as for freelance writer contributors.

If the writer is unwilling or unable to take his own photographs, he may either team up with a photographer (the photographer-writer relationship is discussed in this encyclopedia), or search for free or inexpensive photos. Government agencies, chambers of commerce, trade associations, travel bureaus, and large businesses often maintain public information departments that supply writers and editors with photographs as well as facts in exchange for photo credit acknowledgment. Private picture agencies may have thousands of good photos in stock, but one-time use may cost the writer anywhere from $25 to several hundred dollars and involve additional research and security deposit fees. Generally it is editors rather than writers who deal with private photo agencies. The photo credits of published pictures will give the writer additional ideas for picture sources for the editor to contact.

Photographs should be fully captioned and protected by sheets of cardboard or fiberboard, with rubber bands binding the package together. It is important not to write on the backs of photos or attach paper clips, since both damage prints.

Editors generally buy the manuscript and accompanying photos for a flat package rate, but some magazines pay extra for pictures. *Photographer's Market* and *Writer's Market* detail the specific photo policies of individual publications. (See: *captions [cutline]; illustration; photographer-writer relationship; photograph/picture sources.*)

Photographs, marketing. Freelance magazine writers have discovered that photographic skills can increase the size of their article checks. That often leads writer/photographers to seek primary markets for their photographs as well. Book publishers, calendar companies, ad agencies, trade journals, and newspapers indicate the diversity of potential markets. Success rests in knowing the unique needs of the journal or company and being able to meet those needs with quality photographs. The annual *Photographer's Market* details where and how to sell photographs nationwide. It summarizes the business of photojournalism, including specific information on payment, copyrights, model releases, and work-for-hire agreements.

Photography, legal and ethical aspects. (See: *model release; privacy, invasion of.*)

Photojournalism. The art of relating news or communicating the significant details of an event through photographs. The substance of photojournalism is the carefully composed or uniquely captured picture.

The newspaper photojournalist usually works with a reporter in covering an event. His job is to record on film some of the significant action of an event, so that the newspaper reader can tell a great deal about the story from one (or a few) pictures.

In the *photo essay* or *photo story*, the photographer is alloted more space in which to communicate; the photojournalist presents an event, a personality, a situation, or a geographic area, predominantly through photographs. A photo essay may contain captions and/or a copy block, but the photos are the element that attracts the reader and holds his attention. The photographer sometimes writes the copy, sometimes collaborates with a writer. In the layout process, the photographer works with a design editor in order to convey the right tone, using only photos that reflect his chosen theme.

Life magazine and the now defunct *Look* magazine contain excellent examples of photo essays.

The term *photo essay* is used interchangeably with *photo story* and *picture story*, although the latter term can be used to describe an event recorded in photographs but lacking the photo essay's unity of mood. (*See: model release; photograph/picture sources; photographs accompanying manuscripts.*)

Picaresque. This term, derived from the Spanish word *pícaro* (rogue, knave), applies to novels or tales that relate, in a series of humorous or satiric episodes, the adventures of a rogue.

A typical picaresque novel tells the life story of a rascally but engaging hero or heroine who triumphs in one situation after another by his or her own wit and cunning; the hero's scampish but good-hearted ways are contrasted against a realistic background of middle-class life.

The picaresque novel form originated in Spain in the sixteenth century with the anonymous work *La vida de Lazarillo de Tormes* (*The Life of Larry Tormes*). Well-known picaresque novels include DeFoe's *Moll Flanders*, Twain's *Adventures of Huckleberry Finn*, Cervantes's *Don Quixote*, and Fielding's *Tom Jones*. A more recent work of fiction that may be considered picaresque is Erica Jong's *Fanny: Being the True History of the Adventures of Fanny Hackabout-Jones*.

Picture book. Written for children to read or have read to them, a picture book usually contains from 500-2,500 words and from 32-48 pages. (They can also have no words at all, or very few in a shorter book, even though a writer created the concept to be illustrated.)

The text of a picture book is well organized and carefully constructed, since its audience has little experience with literature. Because picture books are often read aloud and children have an instinctual fondness for rhythm, poetic techniques (e.g., alliteration, consonance, assonance, and onomatopoeia) can enhance a picture book's story. Other techniques attractive to children are the repeated anecdote, used in *The Three Little Pigs*, and the refrain, used in *The Gingerbread Man*.

Vocabulary in this category of writing is simple, since the books are intended for children even if read by adults. Sentence construction is likewise uncomplicated; it often uses the active voice and mimics speech patterns. In general, the narrative of a picture book sounds appealing when read aloud.

As publishers usually choose the artist to illustrate a picture book, the author who has an artist in mind should secure approval from the publisher before asking the artist to proceed. To approach the publisher with the idea of collaboration, the author should submit one or two samples of art with the manuscript. (*See: juveniles, writing for; picture book submission techniques.*)

Additional information: *The Children's Picture Book: How to Write It, How to Sell It.*

Picture book submission techniques. As for any book, the children's picture book author should first research likely markets for his work by checking *Writer's Market*, and publishers' catalogues, if possible, before submitting a manuscript. In the picture book field, it's usually not necessary to query unless, in the course of research, the writer discovers that a particular publisher prefers that; instead, the writer should pay special attention to his proposal package. A picture book manuscript, although brief, is somewhat complex; it usually may be typed any of several ways according to what the manuscript seems most suited to and what the author is comfortable with.

The manuscript may be typed as any other manuscript would be, with illustration suggestions made separately at the end, or included in the cover letter; or typed page for page as the writer envisions the book, with the illustration suggestions keyed onto a page following each manuscript page, or keyed onto the manuscript page itself. Or, if the writer feels confident doing so, he can make up a dummy of the book to accompany the plain typed manuscript, either sketching in the art ideas himself or just typing the descriptions separately from the text.

The picture book proposal cover letter probably should reflect even more care than a cover letter normally does. Ellen E.M. Roberts, author of *The Children's Picture Book: How to Write It, How to Sell It,* suggests discussing why the author wrote the book as well as his qualifications to do so, and including (favorable) sample comments from any young readers he may have tested the book with.

One mistake many novice picture book authors make is assuming that art must accompany a manuscript. Art is not at all necessary; picture book editors are skilled at visualization, and may well have an artist in mind whose style fits the manuscript. Art might in fact be a hindrance to selling the book: some publishers do not even want suggestions about art from the author, reasoning that art is the province of the artist.

What matters most in submitting a picture book manuscript is the originality of the idea and its appropriateness for the publisher: a publisher geared toward pre-schoolers will probably not accept a book for older children, no matter how wonderful it may be. Similarly, the exact length of a manuscript and the complexity of its vocabulary are secondary to the ideas; editor and writer can adjust those after discussion.

The only real taboo in picture book publishing is submitting finished artwork with the proposal: this is the unmistakable mark of an amateur—

worse, an amateur who has not researched the field. The size, color, and method of printing the art can only be determined after a book is budgeted and designed.

Piracy. The term *piracy* describes the unauthorized use of copyrighted materials, such as books, recordings, and films; copyrighted material reproduced or manufactured without permission of the copyright owner is pirated material. The term is currently applied primarily to the unauthorized reproduction of records, tapes, and video cassettes, while the unauthorized use of literary material is called a pirated edition. (See the "pirated edition" entry in this encyclopedia.)

Because it is a violation of the exclusive right of copyright, the act of piracy is illegal in the United States and in the many other countries that subscribe to one of the international copyright conventions. (It may, however, be considered within the limits of the law in countries that are not members of such a convention.)

Despite its illegality, record, tape, and film piracy is a practice widespread throughout the world. As a consequence, record, tape, and film manufacturers have called for stiffer penalties and more serious legal sanctions for those found guilty of trafficking in pirated recordings and movies. In response, the United States Congress recently passed a law making piracy and counterfeiting a felony carrying penalties as high as $25,000 and five years in jail. (*See: copyright; international copyright convention; pirated edition; plagiarism.*)

Pirated edition. This term refers to an unauthorized edition of a literary work, usually republished in another country without permission of the copyright owner.

Since the establishment of international copyright conventions during the late nineteenth and early twentieth centuries, pirated editions have become less common. However, pirated editions may still be found in those countries that do not subscribe to one of the international copyright conventions. (*See: international copyright convention; piracy.*)

Plagiarism. Using or closely imitating another person's material without permission, acknowledgment, or compensation, representing it as one's own work. Plagiarism is illegal when it involves infringement of copyright. Under the new copyright law, an individual found guilty of infringement of copyright is liable for either (1) actual damages suffered by the copyright owner as a result of the infringement, and any profits of the infringer that are attributable to the infringement; or instead of actual damages and profits, (2) statutory damages of a sum of not less than $250 nor more than $10,000, as the court considers just. Additional remedies for infringement are detailed in the new copyright law.

Plagiarism may also occur legally—that is, without copyright infringement—when material in the public domain, noncopyrighted works, or works in which the copyright has expired are reprinted under claimed authorship of the plagiarist. While this type of plagiarism is not illegal, it is nevertheless unethical. A writer discovered to be a plagiarist of uncopyrighted works, while not liable under the law, will nonetheless establish an exceedingly bad reputation for himself as an author.

To avoid plagiarism, a writer should give full credit to his sources of information, and obtain written permission from copyright owners to use their copyrighted material in his own work. (See: *copyright; fair use; paraphrase; piracy; public domain; quotes.*)

Additional information: *Law and the Writer*.

Plant. Information woven into a work of fiction for the purpose of making incidents that occur later in the story consistent and believable is known as a *plant*. Any object, fact, person, or condition a writer plans to use in the course of a short story or novel must be *planted* in order to make subsequent events related to the plant convincing.

In the second paragraph of *The Open Window*, for example, author Saki (H.H. Munro) plants the information that the main character, Framton Nuttel, has retired to the country to recuperate from a nervous disorder and knows no one in the village; as a result, the young woman in the story is able to frighten him out of his wits with a completely fabricated tale of ghosts tramping through the open window in the room.

The movie *Jaws* contains another example of effective planting. At the beginning of the film, the audience learns that the oceanfront town in which the action takes place depends almost entirely on the summer resort trade for its livelihood. That information becomes significant when, as the film progresses, the town's officials at first refuse to acknowledge the danger of a shark in the waters, and later refuse to close the beaches for fear the tourist trade will suffer.

In mystery stories, clues are said to be "planted." A plant in this sense can be the *absence* of information, as in Dorothy L. Sayers's *Five Red Herrings* in which the contents of an artist's case are listed and it later develops that one color—white—is missing. The absence of white is the plant.

Plants are vital to story credibility; they rid a story of coincidence. Plants must, however, be introduced subtly rather than overtly. In *How to Write Best-Selling Fiction*, Dean R. Koontz discusses the dangers of heavy-handed planting. Although he is speaking primarily of novel writing here, his remarks apply to short stories as well:

Events in a story should never be foreshadowed by having the author speak directly to the reader. For example, *never* write a sentence like this one: "If only Becky could have known that Ralph would betray her on Wednesday, she would not have told him her priceless secret at dinner on Tuesday evening." And here's a sentence that's even worse than that: "As she danced and laughed and drank champagne on New Year's Eve, little did Polly know that her life would be in ruins by the end of January." During the early stages of the novel's growth as an art form, authors thought it permissible to directly address their readers in the middle of a story, either to emphasize a thematic point or to crudely foreshadow upcoming plot developments. The modern reader is sophisticated and simply will not tolerate intrusions of that sort because they shatter the fragile illusion of reality that makes a story enjoyable.

The writer should also take care to

plant only information that is necessary to the story action: plants left dangling are annoying both to editors and readers; a principle perhaps best illustrated by Anton Chekhov's counsel to beginning playwrights: "If a gun is hanging on the wall in the first act, it must fire in the last." All plants introduced in a story should be brought to a conclusion that satisfies and convinces the reader. (*See: false plant; plot.*)

Play publishing and production. There are two ways to earn money with a play. The first way is to sell it to a play publisher, who has the organization for printing and selling playscripts, and for selling performing rights to drama groups. The publisher thoroughly knows his market—the many thousand small drama groups in schools, churches, clubs, community centers, etc., all across the country—and he wants plays that will have wide, long-lasting appeal. He does not want material of narrow, local interest; he does not want topical subjects and references that will quickly make a play out-of-date.

The typical amateur drama group wants a play to have a catchy, comprehensible title, to be a comedy rather than a tragedy (though tragedy is not completely taboo), and have more female than male roles. It does *not* want excessively large casts; over-elaborate, costly costumes; complicated, expensive sets; or controversial themes or language.

Publishers usually don't read untested scripts. Writers should get the play produced and send proof of production—photos, programs, reviews, etc.—with the script. Terms of payment vary somewhat from publisher to publisher. There is usually no advance on purchase; typical offers are 25%-50% of the performance royalties collected by the publisher, and 5%-10% of playbook sales receipts.

Payments may be higher for playwrights whose previous work has already succeeded in publication, but the beginner is not in a strong position to bargain. A published play that proves itself popular with audiences and drama groups may yield a flow of royalties for many years.

The other way for a dramatist to make money is by direct sale of performing rights to a theater company or play producer. Chances for such sales are better if the author can write about assigned subjects and make his script precisely fit the casting and financial resources of the customer. For such commissioned work, terms are negotiable—usually some advance payment and, if the play succeeds, royalties on performances.

After the customer company has finished with the play, it can perhaps be sold—with some adaptation if necessary—to a publisher for general distribution. Play publishers and professional theaters that accept freelance material are listed in the "Scriptwriting; Playwriting" section of *Writer's Market*.

Other publishing opportunities and information about playwriting contests and awards can be found in *The Dramatists Sourcebook*, published by the Theatre Communications Group (TCG), 355 Lexington Avenue, New York NY 10017. This reference guide also lists membership and service organizations, artists' colonies, fellowships and grants, and submission guidelines for more than 100 professional theater companies nationwide, plus much additional information of interest to playwrights. (*See: dinner theater; Dramatists Guild; one-act play; play royalties; theater.*)

Play royalties. If a "first-class" theater contracts to produce a playwright's script, and that playwright is an active member of the Dramatists Guild, the playwright is eligible to use the Guild's Minimum Basic Production Contract, which stipulates that, on a first-class production, the author will receive 5% of the first $5,000 gross weekly box-office receipts, 7½% of the next $2,000, and 10% of anything over $7,000.

"First class" is a technical business designation that generally applies to a production presented in a large city, in a large theater, for an indefinite run. Stock, amateur, Equity-waiver, regional or LORT (League of Resident Theatres), or Off-Broadway theaters interested in producing a playwright's script usually negotiate royalty fees on an individual basis. These agreements may offer the playwright anywhere from a flat fee per performance to 5%-20% of the gross box-office receipts from the show's run. (*See: Dramatists Guild; playwriting.*)

Plays for young actors. Dramas written to be performed by children to entertain other children and/or adults. This kind of drama differs from children's theater in that the latter is intended to be performed by adults, for children.

The key to writing successful plays for young actors is simplicity.

Because the director and actors of these dramas are not usually experienced in the complexities of the theater, elements such as play concepts, staging, setting, and costuming are flexible. Plays for children use the techniques of fiction writing and begin with an immediate drama. They are printed in play-script form with simple, appropriate stage directions, setting descriptions, etc.

Plays for young actors have children's interests and capabilities in mind. Elementary-age children, for example, usually perform for an audience of their peers. Children sometimes are given the opportunity to invent the play's dialogue and action for play outlines that are published in some trade publications for educators.

Dramas for very young children (ages 4-6) usually take less than 15 minutes to perform. Elementary and junior high school plays often run 15-25 minutes. Their subject matter may be curriculum-related (historical events or literature being studied) or connected with the celebration of a holiday or special occasion. Scripts generally call for five to seven main characters, with parts divided equally between the two sexes, and a flexible number of minor characters, so as to involve as many young actors as possible.

Plays written for high school students are usually one- or three-act dramas performed for mixed audiences and running 25-50 minutes. Light comedies currently make up 90% of the plays published for high-school-age people; light romances, family living, and maturing experiences are other subjects successfully handled by these actors. Girls at this age are often less self-conscious about acting than their male peers, so plays frequently contain more female than male parts. One-act plays may call for casts of six or nine; three-act plays, casts of ten to fifteen.

Formats for amateur plays vary; specification sheets are sometimes available from the editorial offices of play publishers. Other markets for children's plays include the professional education magazines and juvenile magazines that sometimes publish plays or play outlines in their issues. The drama outlines suggest a bare framework for a play; children themselves fill in the specifics and then act out the play they had a hand in writing.

Amateur plays for young actors may sometimes be bought outright, rather than on a royalty basis. (Payment ranges on the average from $50 to $500.) Specific markets are detailed in *Writer's Market*; buyers of musicals are listed in *Songwriter's Market*. (*See: children's theater.*)

Playwriting. A play has the same basic requirements as a work of fiction: it must contain interesting characters presented in convincing conflict that is logically resolved by the end of the piece. A play must offer emotionally important dramatic action, expressed in effective dialogue. The dramatist's goal is to establish a link between the spectator and the stage, to involve the audience in the play's action and thus evoke an empathetic response from the playgoer.

Although there are many innovative ways to structure drama—one-actor shows, "choreopoems," plays consisting of one long act or of a series of interwoven vignettes—the majority of plays tend to fall into one of two formats: the one-act play,

which is relatively uncomplicated in order to be satisfactorily resolved in half an hour to an hour's time; or the full-length play, which contains two or more acts (which may be further broken down into scenes) and runs up to 2½ hours. (See the Play Format Notes in the Appendix to this encyclopedia.)

The playwright's primary tool is dialogue: it is all-important, since theater is a spoken medium. The dramatist cannot rely on visuals to help make a point, as the screenwriter can (although clever staging can emphasize or counterpoint particular lines). Good stage dialogue is extremely difficult to write. It cannot exactly reproduce the rambling, disjointed sentences and phrases in which real-life people speak, yet it must sound realistic. Without seeming stilted, chatty, or contrived, it must give the audience all the background information they need to understand the characters' motivation. It must also be interesting; a playwright cannot afford to let his audience's attention lag.

Because drama is a live medium, the playwright should do all he can to make his work performable. The best way to learn about performing is to perform: in addition to attending plays and reading plays and theater criticism, the dramatist not already active in theater should join an amateur dramatics group and work in every possible aspect of it—acting, directing, constructing sets, collecting props, running lights, etc. Through a combination of play analysis and practical dramatic experience, the beginning playwright learns how to write dialogue that is easy to memorize and deliver, how to structure effective scenes, how to develop character through dialogue.

(He also learns what *not* to do.) He will learn, too, about the business end of the theater, and make contacts within the local theater community. In this way he can either find a group to produce his plays or at least a number of actors willing to do readings that will help him revise and polish his work. (*See: dinner theater; Dramatists Guild; one-act play; play publishing and production; play royalties; theater.*)

Plot. The sequence in which an author arranges a series of carefully devised and interrelated incidents so as to form a logical pattern and achieve an intended effect. A *plot* can also be called the structure, backbone, or framework of fiction. Essentially, it is a causal sequence of action that progresses through conflict to a climax and ends with a resolution.

The difference between a plot and a story has been explained by English novelist E.M. Forster: "We have defined a story as a narrative of events arranged in their time sequence. A plot is also a narrative of events, the emphasis falling on a causality. 'The King died and then the queen died' is a story. 'The King died, and then the queen died of grief' is a plot."

A sound, believable plot is essential to a salable story, although it may not be the strongest or most evident element. How much emphasis a writer puts on plot depends on his conception of the story and what he has to say. Writer and creative writing teacher R.V. Cassill has commented, "In some cases—and this is often true of first-rate contemporary work—the plot is so elaborately interwoven with the other threads of fiction that its presence is only detectable under a determined scrutiny. . . . When plot is properly integrated with the over-all scrutiny, it can be first among those elements that give the illusion of life to fiction." Plot is generally more important in genre fiction (romance, western, science fiction, etc.) than in serious literary fiction. (*See: plant; story.*)

Plug. An advertisement for a product, program, or service; sometimes provided free by a radio station as a public service announcement (PSA).

Poetic license. *Poetic license* refers to the privilege claimed by a writer (poet, novelist, dramatist, essayist, etc.) to deviate from conventional form, established rules, and perhaps even fact and logic in order to achieve a desired effect.

Writers, particularly poets, have claimed the "license" to invert word order, introduce archaisms, use—or overuse—figurative language, employ contractions such as *e'er* and *o'er*, and otherwise depart from standards of ordinary speech. But such breaches of grammar, misuse of idiom, mispronunciation for the sake of rhyme, or similar devices are no longer excused in serious verse.

Poetry. The oldest form of literature and the first to be put into written form. An extremely complex and subjective concept, poetry cannot be completely or precisely defined. It is generally agreed, however, that poetry as a literary form expresses, through extraordinary use of language and a highly developed artistic form, a unique and imaginative interpretation of a subject. Good poetry creates an emotional impact and aesthetic effect by appealing primarily to a reader's senses and emotions.

Poetry is often used as a synonym for *verse*. Although all poetry may be considered verse—speech or writing in metrical form—not all verse may be thought of as poetry. The distinction between the two lies in the profundity of thought and emotion. For example, "Mary had a little lamb, its fleece was white as snow," is both lyrical and metrical; it does not, however, represent the depth of thought, imagination, and emotion that characterizes poetry.

Poetry is further distinguished as a literary form from *prose*—spoken or written expression that is not metrical. Poetry makes greater use of such literary devices as metaphor, simile, allusion, alliteration, and onomatopoeia than does prose. The emphasis in poetry is on economy of language—as the poet compresses as much meaning as possible into the fewest possible words, the language is elevated to a unique artistic expression.

A more fundamental distinction between poetry and prose is that a writer may use prose to communicate information and ideas that, when expressed by a different arrangement of words, still convey the same basic message. In a poetic composition, however, the purpose of which is to create an emotional impact, words and ideas cannot be separated from form; the two are inextricably linked. Poet Judson Jerome explains in *The Poet's Handbook*: "Great poetry may contain great wisdom, but that is never the reason it is great poetry. It is not enough. It is the form, the shaping of the language, which makes poetry endure. It is not what it meant to the poet that is important; rather, it is the effect it has on an audience."

Although there are many kinds of poems—classified in part according to style, subject matter, form, intended effect or purpose, metrical pattern, and point of view—there are three acknowledged major divisions in Western literature: narrative, dramatic, and lyric. (*See: poetry book publishing; poetry, dramatic; poetry, lyric; poetry, marketing; poetry, narrative; verse.*)

Additional information: *The Poet's Handbook*; *The Writer's Manual*.

Poetry book publishing. Once a poet has had several poems published in quality magazines (those respected by the literary community), he usually considers publishing a collection of his poems. One of the most important factors in getting a first book accepted will be the list of credit lines from those magazines in which the poet's work was first published. Since the market for poetry is neither large nor profitable, even the poet with an impressive list of credits will have a difficult time finding a publisher, however. Publishers most receptive to a book of poetry are the small presses listed in *Writer's Market* and *The International Directory of Little Magazines and Small Presses*.

Another option is self-publishing, wherein the poet hires a printer to produce the book for him. The poet might get bids from several local typesetters and/or "instant" printers or contact some of the small poetry book printers that advertise in writers' magazines. Prices for such books could vary considerably depending on whether they were printed from camera-ready typewritten copy, or from typeset copy; the type of paper and binding; the page size; number of copies printed, etc.

A third route may be an arrangement with a cooperative publisher, in which the poet assumes part of the cost of publication. (Cooperative publishing is not to be confused with subsidy publishing. See the entry for "subsidy publishing" in this encyclopedia.) (*See: poetry; poetry, marketing; subsidy publishing; verse.*)

Additional information: *The Poet's Handbook.*

Poetry, dramatic. One of the three divisions of poetry in Western literature, dramatic poetry is the most immediate of the forms. A dramatic poem presents a story through dialogue and action rather than through exposition. Plays, dramatic monologues, and dramatic lyrics written in verse—such as Shakespeare's plays in blank verse—are classified as dramatic poetry.

The dramatic monologue is perhaps the only popular form of dramatic poetry used by contemporary poets. T.S. Eliot's *The Love Song of J. Alfred Prufrock* is an example of dramatic monologue. (*See: poetry; poetry, lyric; poetry, narrative; verse.*)

Poetry, lyric. Lyric poetry is the most inclusive of the three major poetry divisions in Western literature. *Lyric* describes any relatively short poem that expresses the personal thoughts and feelings either of the poet himself or of the narrator-voice of the poem.

Most of the poetry published today is lyric. The term includes hymns, sonnets, songs, odes, and elegies among its many forms. (*See: poetry; poetry, dramatic; poetry, narrative; verse.*)

Poetry, marketing. Generally speaking, poets do not make a living from their poetry. The few commercially successful poets—Rod McKuen and Ogden Nash, for example—are not usually taken seriously by the literary community. A poet must, however, find the audience and media appropriate to his talent and recognize that some verse is simply better suited than other verse for commercial markets: greeting card and poster publishers, church magazines, and some women's publications, for example. And, as noted in *Writer's Market*, some commercially successful poets have syndicated newspaper columns or contracts with popular magazines; others combine their writing with singing or other performance.

The poet to whom literary esteem is more important than commercial success will probably get his start in the little/literary magazines. These publications are listed in *Writer's Market* and *The International Directory of Little Magazines and Small Presses.* Other good resources are university libraries, and quality bookstores that devote a rack to poetry magazines. There are hundreds of different literary and little magazines being published, some given exclusively to poetry, and others that publish both poetry and prose. A poet must obtain sample copies (sample copies of literary and little magazines are rarely available free of charge) and study them carefully to determine which magazines are publishing the type of poetry he is writing.

In addition to studying the different publications carefully, the editors of many poetry magazines advise poets to solicit opinions on their work from other poets before submitting poems for publication. The poet should not expect to receive criticism on his work from the editors of poetry magazines to which he submits material; nor should he send his poems to professional poets, requesting their opinions.

The most likely environment for a writer to find knowledgeable criticism and support is in a writers' group or workshop. The National Federation of State Poetry Societies (1121 Major Avenue, N.W., Albuquerque NM 87107) may be able to advise a poet whether a chapter of his state poetry society meets in his area. A poet may also check his local library or nearby college or university for information about other writers' groups in the area.

Unless a specific magazine indicates otherwise, the general rules for submission of poetry are these: poems should be typed (usually double-spaced) on 8½x11-inch white paper, one poem to a page. The author's name and address should appear in the upper right-hand corner of each page. The poet should keep a carbon or photocopy of each poem, and a careful record of where the material is submitted. Three to five pages of poetry should be included in the submission packet, along with an SASE. Covering letters are not necessary, nor is an indication of line count. As Judson Jerome cautions in *The Poet's Handbook,* "Proofread carefully—and if you are weak in spelling, grammar, or usage, get help. . . . The poem as submitted should be exactly as you would like to see it appear, down to the last comma and capital. Editors tend to be very impatient with careless or illiterate manuscripts, especially of poetry." Poets are advised to keep a minimum of 50 poems in circulation at all times.

A poet seeking publication must act on his own behalf. Reputable literary agents do not handle poetry because there is so little money in it. Poets should, therefore, be wary of so-called "agents" who, for a fee, agree to read their work and place it. Likewise, poets should learn to recognize the hundreds of "vanity" gimmicks and schemes designed to exploit beginning poets—the contests that require competitors to purchase the book in which the winning entries will be published in order to enter. For regular announcements of reputable contests and publishing opportunities in general, poets can subscribe to *CODA: Poets & Writers Newsletter,* published by Poets & Writers, Inc. (201 W. 54th Street, New York NY 10019). (*See: poetry; poetry book publishing.*)

Additional information: *The Poet's Handbook.*

Poetry, narrative. One of the three major divisions of poetry in Western literature, narrative is probably the oldest type, with a long tradition in epic and ballad forms. The narrative poem tells a story, primarily through exposition or through a combination of narration and dialogue, as in the narratives of Robert Frost or Robert Browning. Book-length narrative poems called epics are tales of heroic events set against vast and exotic backgrounds. Well-known epics include the *Iliad,* the *Odyssey,* and *Beowulf.* The form is not popular today. (*See: poetry; poetry, dramatic; poetry, lyric; verse writing.*)

Poetry Society of America. Founded in 1910, the Poetry Society of America is the oldest and largest group of its kind working for appreciation of poetry and for wider recognition of the work of living American poets. Its membership of 1,400 professional poets comprises both traditionalists and experimentalists. Associate members include critics, lecturers, librarians, educators, and patrons. The Society awards numerous monthly and annual prizes for poetry. The organization is located at 15 Grammercy Park, New York NY 10003.

Poets & Writers, Inc. This organization defines its purpose as, "to serve as an information clearinghouse and service organization for the nation's literary community." In addition to maintaining biographical archives on poets and fiction writers, Poets & Writers, Inc., provides a telephone information service to people seeking either answers to questions of a general literary nature or the current address of a poet or writer listed in its publication, *A Directory of American Poets and Fiction Writers.* The organization also publishes *CODA: Poets & Writers Newsletter,* as well as booklets on literary agents, copyright, literary bookstores, and sponsors.

In addition to living poets and fiction writers whose work has been published in the United States, *A Directory of American Poets and Fiction Writers* also lists writers who perform their work and who are available for lectures and readings. Writers who wish to be listed in the directory should contact the organi-

zation at 201 W. 54th Street, New York NY 10019, for publication requirements.

Poets laureate. In England, the court poet appointed for life by the prime minister to write poems celebrating official occasions. Ben Jonson was the first such, appointed in 1619. The current poet laureate is John Betjeman.

In the U.S., poets laureate are chosen by individual states; however, not every state names one. A poet laureate may not necessarily be well known.

Among the states that do choose poets laureate, selection procedures vary. In Kentucky, for example, a member of the legislature drafts a resolution proposing that a particular poet be chosen; if the resolution is passed, that person becomes poet laureate, a position he holds for life. More than one person may hold this position at once. At present, Kentucky has two poets laureate: Agnes O'Rear and Lilli Chaffin.

Point of view (POV). In television and motion pictures, a camera direction indicating that the audience sees the scene as if they were looking through the eyes of the actor in that scene. In a script, whether abbreviated or spelled out, this term is typed all in caps. (*See: television script terms.*)

Political campaign writing. A freelancer may find a part-time job or full-time career as a political campaign writer. Depending on the nature and extent of a candidate's campaign, a campaign writer's duties may include ghosting speeches, writing press releases, answering correspondence, and perhaps even shaking hands and tacking up posters. In general, the larger the campaign, the greater the chances of two, three, or several campaign writers being employed by a candidate. A writer will usually have more responsibility and more varied duties working for a candidate running for local than for national office.

The primary function of a political campaign writer is to provide his candidate with a steady supply of facts, figures, ideas, words, and phrases. Consequently, the job requires good research and writing skills. A newspaper background, particularly one with a focus on politics or public affairs, may be helpful.

A campaign writer's first task is to acquaint himself thoroughly with his candidate's background, personality, physical habits, speech characteristics, and thinking processes in order to write speeches and prepare biographical and informational literature that effectively projects the candidate's image. The writer must also familiarize himself with the audience the candidate hopes to reach, and target his material to that audience.

There are several routes a freelancer might take to land an assignment as a political campaign writer. One is to contact his home state's Democratic or Republican Party headquarters. Another is to send a brief letter to the executive director of local party headquarters (listed in the white pages of the phone book), outlining his qualifications and inquiring whether any candidates are in need of a freelance writer. A freelancer may personally seek out local elected officials and indicate his availability. He may also contact advertising agencies handling campaign publicity for political candidates, since these agencies often take on extra help during a campaign.

Financial terms are negotiated between the writer and candidate or the campaign manager. For the average freelancer, a fair rate in most locales will run a bit higher than the salary paid topscale newspaper reporters. (According to Newspaper Guild figures, the current reporter salary ranges from $272-$721 per week, depending on the city.) Freelancers negotiating for payment for their services are advised to avoid promises of future rewards in lieu of adequate salary; freelance campaign writing may, however, lead to an offer of a full-time position with the candidate. (*See: ghostwriting speeches; political writing.*)

Political writing. There is a variety of markets for articles containing political themes. *Writer's Market* lists several publications in the "Politics and World Affairs" section that emphasize politics for the general reader interested in current events. These publications include *American Opinion Magazine, Foreign Affairs, The Libertarian Review, The Nation,* and *The New Republic.* Many general interest magazines solicit political material, as do business and financial publications, regional magazines, and weekly newspaper magazine sections. The op-ed page of the daily newspaper is another outlet for the political writer. *Writer's Market* also lists under "Trade Journals/Government and Public Service" those publications geared toward the professional involved in government.

Many of the book publishers listed in *Writer's Market* indicate that they are looking for books on political and current affairs subjects. (*See: political campaign writing.*)

Pony. An informal word for materials used in place of the original work being studied in a literature course. Used especially to refer to literal translations of literary works in foreign languages, this term can also denote a synopsis, a set of notes, and other supplements used in conjunction with a work of literature. Writers—especially those with teaching backgrounds—can obtain assignments from publishers of these study guides. (*See: abridgment.*)

Popular fiction. Generally, a synonym for category or genre fiction; that is, fiction intended to appeal to audiences for certain kinds of novels.

In *Writing Popular Fiction*, author Dean R. Koontz describes popular fiction as "those stories we can easily apply labels to—science fiction, fantasy, mystery, suspense, gothic, western, erotica." Popular, or category, fiction is defined as such primarily for the convenience of publishers, editors, reviewers, and booksellers who must identify novels of different areas of interest for potential readers.

Popular fiction is distinguished from *mainstream fiction*, fiction that does not comfortably fit into the categories described above. Because mainstream fiction is generally written for a narrower, more intellectual audience, it has traditionally been regarded by educators and critics as being superior to popular fiction. As Koontz observes, however, many writers whose literary efforts have gained immortality—including Mark Twain and Edgar Allan Poe—

have been category writers. In recent years, popular fiction writers such as Raymond Chandler, John D. MacDonald, and Alistair MacLean have attained not only financial success but also considerable critical acclaim for their work. Koontz offers this advice for the writer who may not have considered the economic realities that govern the publishing industry: "Since genre fiction is more widely read than mainstream, the writer's market for category work is larger than for mainstream. Publishers, like any businessmen, operate within the law of supply and demand."

Koontz lists five elements required of genre novels, elements that don't always appear in mainstream fiction: 1) a strong plot; 2) a hero or heroine; 3) clear, believable motivation; 4) a great deal of action; and 5) a colorful background. (*See: fiction; mainstream fiction.*)

Additional information: *How to Write Best-Selling Fiction.*

Pornography. Literature, art, photographs, or films characterized by substantial sexual content are sometimes classified as pornography. Generally used as a synonym for obscenity, the term is now coming more to mean material, such as explicit pictures, drawings, and descriptions of sexual activity, "which lacks serious literary, artistic, political or scientific value." Of particular interest to writers is the fact that published works may be legally proscribed on the basis of alleged obscenity; First Amendment protection of expression does not extend to works deemed obscene by a court. Since obscenity is a complex legal issue, the writer who fears that an obscenity charge may arise from the publication of his work should consult a lawyer.

Freelancers interested in writing erotic short fiction may find a market in the men's magazines listed in *Writer's Market*. Editorial requirements in terms of degree of sexual explicitness and theme vary widely among these magazines, so writers are advised to study the publications carefully before submitting material. Pay rates range from $100-$2,000 (*Playboy*, *Penthouse*, and *Hustler* are at the high end of the scale), with the average being about $250-$300 for a story.

Certain book publishers solicit manuscripts of approximately 40,000 words for pornographic novels. Publishers seeking "erotica" and "adult erotic fiction" are listed in the book publishers section of *Writer's Market*. The best market directory, according to one writer of erotica, is the local adult bookstore, where a writer can check books for the names and addresses of publishers. (*See: censorship, literary.*)

Postage rates for writers. (*See: International Reply Coupons; mail/delivery services.*)

Postal Service. (*See: mail/delivery services.*)

Potboiler. Something written expressly for the purpose of making money quickly. The term refers to writing projects a freelancer does to keep the pot boiling—in other words, to *eat*—while he works on major articles, stories, or books.

Depending on the writer's facility and knowledge of the marketplace, a potboiler may run anywhere from a six-line how-to, to a 1,500-word short story, to a 65,000-word novel—any writing project, in other words, designed to bring in a quick check with a minimum outlay of time and trouble. A practice that can be slanted to nearly any market the writer knows well, the secret of successful potboiling lies in quantity and quick production: a project that eats up more time than it's worth isn't a practical potboiler.

Because they are usually penned in a hurry, few potboilers can boast of superior literary quality. Nevertheless, potboilers should be submitted as cleanly and professionally as any other material. (*See: filler.*)

PR Aids Party Line. A weekly newsletter that announces opportunities for publicists. All media are covered in the publication, which consists of one sheet (two pages).

Freelance writers seeking specialized research materials, photographs, etc., from companies and organizations can sometimes obtain a free listing of their needs in this newsletter. *Party Line* is published by Public Relations Aids, Inc., which is located at 330 W. 34th Street, New York NY 10001.

Practice of writing, the. Writing is a skill acquired through education but developed largely through practice. Like the Olympic swimmer, the well-trained writer achieves success through consistent effort exerted over a period of time. While a good liberal arts education is almost a given, the writer must continue to analyze his writing, compare it to the work of talented contemporaries, and strive to improve his style.

The key to developing writing skills is discipline, which is shown by daily writing: the practicing writer composes something each day, even if one day's writing consists only of an entry in a journal.

Observation skills are also necessary to good writing: the writer must be adept at extracting ideas for articles and books from his everyday experiences and surroundings.

Many writers find time for their art while holding full-time jobs. (*See: journal; note-taking.*)

Preface. This term is applied to preliminary remarks written as an introduction to a book by its author or editor. A preface usually explains a book's subject, purpose, and plan; it often contains acknowledgments of assistance in creating and publishing the book. Occasionally, a preface, as well as the foreword, will be written by another authority in the same field to lend extra credibility to the book. (*See: foreword; introduction.*)

Preferred time/prime time. Time of day when a large audience listens, or when the audience for a specific product is likely to listen to a broadcast. In radio, these are usually *morning drive* (5:30 to 9 a.m.) and *afternoon drive* (3 to 6 p.m.), when most drivers are on the road.

Preliminary edition. A prepublication—often paperbound—edition of a book, usually prepared from photocopies of the final galley proofs; also known as "bound proofs." Designed for promotional purposes, preliminary editions serve as the first set of review copies to be mailed out. Many consumer review media such as the *New York Times Book Review* section, *Publishers Weekly*, and others have a long lead time and require copies well in advance of publication in order to synchronize the review with the book's arrival in stores.

Occasionally, preliminary editions are distributed to sales representatives and wholesale or chain store book buyers; these are sometimes called *special reader editions*. A few preliminary editions may also be sent to experts in the book's subject field, or to well-known individuals whose endorsements may help sell a book, in order to solicit testimonials or dust jacket blurbs for second and third editions of the book. (*See: page proof; prepublication review; review copy; testimonial.*)

Premise. A statement that an author makes through the events and outcome of a story. A premise is not necessarily a truth that is generally accepted; it is, however, true in relation to the story. For example, the premise of a short story may be "arrogance leads to loneliness," "arrogance leads to power," or any other statement that pairs a personality trait with a resulting situation. Though the reader might not agree with the premise of a story, he cannot deny that it is true within the boundaries of the specific story character's experience.

Every premise implies a character, a conflict, and a resolution. The writer usually establishes a premise before writing a story, so that he can easily stay with one story line. For other writers, the premise grows out of the development of the characters in the writer's pre-story planning. All aspects of a story should contribute to the author's original premise.

In television, the writer seeking a scriptwriting assignment must "pitch" a story—present a premise orally—before he can obtain a contract to work up a treatment and/or final script. (*See: television writing.*)

Prepublication review. Certain publications review forthcoming books well in advance of their official publication dates, using preliminary editions prepared from photocopies of final galley proofs. Such an advance notice is called a *prepublication review*.

Prepublication reviews appear primarily in three trade publications: *Publishers Weekly, Library Journal,* and *Kirkus Reviews*. These publications, which are read by librarians, reviewers, bookstore and wholesale book buyers, and mass market and book club editors, can influence the success of a book by inducing potential subsidiary rights sales, as well as increasing library sales and bookstore orders.

Conversely, a poor review can dampen the enthusiasm and sales efforts of the publishing house. (*See: Kirkus Reviews; preliminary edition; review copy.*)

Presentation. A description of a proposed television series an author gives to a producer. (*See: television script terms.*)

Press card. Also known as a *press pass*, a press card is an identifying card carried by journalists that enables them to gain access to events, people, or locations to cover a story for the newspaper or magazine with which they are affiliated.

Freelance writers, most of whom are not affiliated with a magazine or newspaper, do not have the credentials necessary to admit them to "for press only" events or places. In order to obtain a press pass, and thus gain entry to otherwise restricted areas, a freelance writer usually must ally himself with some specific newspaper, magazine, or syndicate market. In some cases, presenting a letter of assignment from a magazine or book publisher indicating that he is working on a story may admit a freelancer to a "for press only" area or event. (*See: business cards.*)

Press Encyclopedia, The World. A two-volume reference work that describes the print and electronic media establishments in approximately 180 countries. The entries are written so that the press can be understood in relationship to other elements of the individual societies, such as political systems, philosophies, and economic systems.

The encyclopedia is arranged by country, and it contains a Classification System by which the following subjects (further broken down into more than 70 topics) are covered: basic data (such as number of daily newspapers and literacy rate), size of the newspaper industry, economic framework, censorship and limitations on access to news sources, state-press relations, news agencies, and attitudes toward foreign media.

Press galleries. Galleries that overlook the House and Senate chambers where accredited members of the media may observe floor debate on legislation in Congress. Within the rooms entering into the galleries, reporters have the help of several staff members, who answer telephones, manage news conferences for members of Congress, issue press releases from committee hearings, and in general act as liaison between Congress and the press.

There is a gallery for members of the daily press; another for representatives from magazines; a radio and television gallery; and a press photographer's gallery. Rules for eligibility are published in the Congressional Directory and are concerned mainly with the fact that the applicant earns more than 50% of his income from a news gathering organization and lives in the Washington DC area.

Press release. (*See: publicity writing.*)

Press trip. A press trip (sometimes referred to as a *junket*) is a trip furnished to a writer by a business that has an interest in a proposed article topic. For example, the public relations firm handling a new hotel may provide a newspaper travel editor with a free trip and accommodations in anticipation of receiving favorable mention in an article. While the greatest number of press trips are offered to travel writers and business writers, any journalist may receive this type of invitation.

A practice related to press trips is offering a writer gifts, such as meals or tickets to a cultural event.

A press trip can present the writer with an ethical dilemma in that his loyalty may be divided between his readers and the sponsor of his trip. Whether or not to accept an invitation is the writer's personal decision that may be made on the basis of what—if anything—he is expected to write regarding the sponsoring business; what percentage of the expenses are paid by the business; and the degree of objectivity the writer is able to retain.

A discussion of press trips appears in the Society of American Travel Writers Ethics Code in the Appendix to this encyclopedia.

Prestige copy. A broadcasting term for copy that lacks a selling element, but presents a favorable image of a company or product.

Pricing/selling. (*See: negotiating with editors.*)

Primary listening area. The geographic area in which listeners receive consistently good reception from a radio station.

Primary source. A primary source is one that provides the writer with original, firsthand information. Primary research is based on the writer's own experience and observation, direct contact with other people (usually in an interview), or information gleaned from personal papers, correspondence, diaries, or manuscripts written at the time or on the scene of the person or subject being studied. Because it is closest to the source, primary research is preferred over secondary research, which is based entirely on already published material such as books, newspapers, magazines, and information available through computerized abstracting services. (*See: secondary sources.*)

Privacy Act. In 1974, the U.S. Congress passed the Privacy Act, which gives individuals some control over the personal information the government compiles about them. Under the Privacy Act, an individual has the right to request his personal files, the right to sue the government for letting other individuals see his files, and the right either to have information in his file corrected or to enclose a personal statement regarding information the government refuses to change.

The Privacy Act is by no means all-inclusive. It applies only to files held by an agency under the executive branch of the federal government, and even then only to files that are primarily about the person who requests them and that are organized in a retrieval system. In other words, the Privacy Act does not apply to files held by the legislative or judicial branches, by state or local governments, or by private organizations; to information about an individual contained in a file about some other person, event, or organization; or to information not organized for easy retrieval.

A writer can, of course, use the Privacy Act to see *his* confidential files. But the writer may also run up against the Privacy Act when he is doing research and not be permitted access to government files containing confidential information about another person. (*See: Freedom of Information.*)

Privacy, invasion of. An individual's privacy is protected by various statutory and common laws from invasion by newspapers, television, radio, magazines, books, pictures and motion pictures, advertising, creditors, and wiretapping. "Public figures' " rights tend to be defined by law somewhat differently from private citizens'.

Generally, a person's right to privacy can be invaded in one of four ways:

1. *intrusion.* Bruce W. Sanford in *Synopsis of the Law of Libel and the Right of Privacy* notes, ". . . this type of invasion of privacy . . . usually involves the wrongful use of tape recorders, microphones, cameras, and/or other electronic recording or eavesdropping devices to record a person's private activities." Privacy is invaded when the intrusion occurs; actual publication of information obtained is irrelevant to the claim of "intrusion." Reporters were found to have intrusively invaded the privacy of a physician when they posed as patients in order to enter his office and secretly take photographs and make recordings.

2. *misappropriation.* The majority of states, either by common law or by statute, recognize as an invasion of privacy the use of a person's name, likeness, or personality for advertising, trade, or commercial purposes or for one's own use or benefit without that person's written consent. Harry M. Johnston III in *Law and the Writer* points out, however, that exceptions are "news" and "material or subjects of general interest to the public." An individual won a case on the grounds of misappropriation when a Georgia court, in the case *Pavesich* vs. *New England Life Insurance Co.*, ruled that the insurance company used the individual's name without consent in an endorsement. In contrast, a suit filed by Joe Namath, *Namath* vs. *Time, Inc.* (1976) was declared not to invade his privacy. Namath's photograph and name were used by *Sports Illustrated*

in an advertisement for the magazine. The athlete did not have a case for invasion of privacy because, according to the court, the photo had previously been published editorially by the magazine, it was newsworthy, and it was used merely to convey the "nature, quality, and content" of the magazine, not to endorse the magazine.

3. *publicizing in a false light*. The publication of nondefamatory but untrue information about an individual, information which places him in a "false light" before the public and would be considered offensive or highly offensive to the average person, is considered an invasion of privacy. As established in the case of *Time, Inc.* vs. *Hill* (1967), material, in order to be considered as presenting someone in a false light, must be published "with knowledge of falsity or reckless disregard for the truth." The Hill case involved *Life's* report on a Broadway play, *The Desperate Hours*, which is based on the James Hill family's encounter as hostages. In the final decision (in this case, that of the U.S. Supreme Court), *Life* was considered to be within the law because no actual malice was shown.

4. *public disclosure of private and embarrassing facts*. The publication of facts concerning an individual which, while they may be truthful, are private and embarrassing, constitutes an invasion of privacy. A news report or photograph of an event that takes place in *public*, however, is not an invasion of privacy. A well-known case in this area is *Cox Broadcasting* vs. *Cohn* (1975), which concerned broadcasting the name of a rape victim. Although the victim was deceased, her father sued the television station that had reported her name. He lost the case, however, because the victim's name was included in judicial records, which were open to the public. (*See: libel; right of privacy; right of publicity.*)

Additional information: *Law and the Writer; Synopsis of the Law of Libel and the Right of Privacy.*

Privileged communication. Confidential communication that the law may not require the parties involved to disclose. Depending on the jurisdiction, privileged communication may apply to that between a husband and wife, lawyer and client, doctor and patient, religious counselor and believer, and, in some cases, journalist and news source. The right of journalists to protect their news sources has been sharply limited in a number of significant court cases, however, and some journalists have gone to jail for refusing to reveal their sources of information. The press continues to strive for legislation to protect news sources from disclosure.

The term also has a second meaning: it refers to the press's right to publish or broadcast a full, fair, impartial, and accurate report of legal or legislative proceedings, even though statements made in those proceedings are defamatory or libelous. For example, if a reporter reports statements made by witnesses during a trial which later turn out to be false and libelous, he may be permitted to defend such statements on the ground that they are conditionally privileged.

The defense of conditional privilege is lost, however, when it is "abused"; that is, when it can be shown that a statement was published or broadcast by the media even though the newspaper or broadcaster knew the statement to be false or had serious doubts as to its truth. (*See: libel; shield laws.*)

Prizes, writing. The directory *Literary and Library Prizes* lists many book awards, and the annual *Literary Market Place* lists prize contests for writers of poetry, short stories, scholarly articles, etc. Prizes for journalists, fiction and nonfiction writers, and film, video, and audio writers are detailed in some books described in the entry "contests, writing" in this encyclopedia; some other contests and prizes are described in the entries "Nobel Prize," "Pulitzer Prizes," and other entries headed by prize names.

Product article. (*See: magazine article, types of.*)

Professional versus amateur. There is a widespread belief that the professional writer is wealthy and famous, lunches with New York editors, and jets about the country interviewing celebrities and sports personalities and government officials. An amateur writer, it is likewise assumed, pecks out stories on a rusty old Remington at the kitchen table after the kids have gone to bed, has never met or spoken with an editor, and has no access to the exciting and stimulating subjects about which the professional writer writes.

In reality, the difference between a professional writer and an amateur lies not in the writing profession's external trappings but in the writer's own attitude toward his work. Flaws in grammar and word choice, lackluster style, sloppy plotting or research, poor organization, and absence of point in a manuscript are all marks of the amateur rather than the professional. The amateur writer takes a very subjective view toward his work. He is too easily satisfied with a project once it is finished, and unwilling to change a single word. He fails to study the market to which he submits his work, and then attributes the inevitable rejection either to the market's blindness to the merits of his masterpiece or to his own failure as a writer.

A professional writer, on the other hand, recognizes that writing is a profession rather than a hobby. He is able, says Lois Duncan in *How to Write and Sell Your Personal Experiences*, to be objective. "He regards writing as a business," Duncan continues, "and his stories and articles and books as products he is offering for sale. If his commodity is rejected he does not consider it an insult. He realizes that he has probably offered the wrong thing to the wrong person at the wrong time, chalks it up as a learning experience, and sends his material somewhere else. At the same time, he tries to figure out what *would* be right for that market that rejected him, so that next time he can offer something more in keeping with its needs."

It doesn't matter whether a writer lives in New York City or Newark or Newtonsville. It makes no difference how many New York editors he knows. The writer who works hard at his writing, studies the market, and—specifically for that market—produces a polished manuscript that skillfully treats its subject is a professional writer. The writer who is not willing to work hard at his writing will remain an amateur.

Profile. The profile, or personality sketch, is an article—not a question-

and-answer interview—whose main subject is a person who is for some reason noteworthy. Profile subjects may be entertainment or sports celebrities, people in the public eye, or figures of notoriety; they may also be individuals who have interesting jobs, unusual hobbies, or inspirational philosophies. Almost all magazines, both consumer and trade publications, carry personality profiles; some daily newspapers also buy profiles from freelancers.

When the profile writer chooses his subject he must determine 1) *why* that individual is noteworthy and 2) *to whom* he would be interesting (i.e., potential markets). The second step requires research: the writer reads previously published material about the subject; checks appropriate records (depending on the subject) such as Dun and Bradstreet reports, and college transcripts; and conducts interviews with people who know the subject and can round out the information offered by the subject himself.

The profile writer then interviews the subject—usually more than once—to get a fuller view of him. The profile's success is often in proportion to the interviewer's skill: the writer should recognize effective anecdotes and provocative quotes; his questions should provoke responses that reveal the subject's opinions, aspirations, passions, and peeves— responses with emotional content.

During the interview the writer should also be aware of how the subject talks, what he is wearing, what the surroundings are like—everything the writer observes that helps illuminate the subject, enhances the profile.

The finished piece should not glorify the subject; rather, it attempts to create on paper a comprehensive picture of the individual's personality—warts and all. Although the profile may—depending on length—contain a certain amount of personal background information— home town, early life, schools, marriage(s)—the focus of the article should be *current*—the individual is interesting because of what he does or is *today*.

The profile is built upon anecdotes, "appearance words" (that help the reader form a mental picture), and revealing quotes from the subject and the people who know him.

The term *profile* usually refers to a personality piece; however, some magazines "profile" places and events using the techniques described above. (*See: interview.*)

Program log. A catalogue of data (such as length, sponsor, and time of day to be broadcast) on announcements, commercials, newscasts, and most other material (other than music) that is broadcast. The Federal Communications Commission requires all radio stations to keep a program log.

Programmed instruction (PI). A kind of teaching that involves a stimulus, a response, and a reward. It is modeled on the theories of behavioral psychologists, who invented it. Other names for programmed instruction include *self-paced instruction, individualized instruction,* and *computer-assisted instruction (CAI).*

Programmed instruction can be taught through textbooks or computers. A small piece of information, called a frame, serves as a stimulus by requiring a response from the student. The student is then rewarded by being allowed to move on in the program, or told to review the material if he responded incorrectly. A series of frames and responses, which can be structured in different ways, makes up a PI text.

When the writer has completed a PI text, he tests it on persons who represent his intended audience. A 90/90 ratio, occurring when 90% of the students learn 90% of the material, is satisfactory: if the writer has not achieved it, he must rewrite the text until he does.

Textbook publishers and local businesses are markets for PI texts. However, this field is specialized, and some markets accept only writers with established reputations or with teaching experience. Publishers require sample frames and an outline of the program; businesses need to see samples of the writer's work. A textbook of 60-200 frames and 32-64 pages can earn the writer a flat fee of $1,000-$2,500. For a more complex text, the writer can earn considerably more—and sometimes obtain a royalty as well. Rights purchased by the publisher vary and are outlined in the individual contract. On specific assignments for industry, the writer usually turns over all rights to the company.

A successful PI writer possesses several diverse attributes. He needs a strong sense of logic; he must also be a creative thinker—and a deft writer—since he faces the challenge of accommodating students of all levels of intelligence (though not necessarily of different grades) with

one program. Similarly, he must know his audience and appeal to them accordingly: PI can be geared either to schoolchildren, assembly-line workers, or highly educated persons. A PI writer must also be a skillful researcher and interviewer in order to give himself the proper background he needs to write different texts.

Promo. A radio or television announcement that promotes one or more of the station's programs.

Promotion by author. An author who has the necessary knowledge of potential buyers, the desire, and the financial resources may consider promoting his book alone or in conjunction with his publisher. Bookstores are generally hesitant to buy the books of new authors, and publishers limit their promotion budgets to a percentage (averaging 10%) of sales income.

Promotion can take the form of classified ads, letters, lectures, television and radio broadcasts, queries to newspaper editors about reviews or features, or sales pitches—either direct or indirect—at bookstores. When approaching newspaper editors and other publicity contacts, it is advantageous to apply the desired publicity to their needs; this can be accomplished by giving the newspaper editor a local angle for his feature, or pointing out the book's market slant to a bookstore manager. In any case, the author must consult with the publisher's publicists regarding promotion strategies to avoid duplication of effort.

The author should remember that, even though the publisher's marketing staff may promote the book, the author must personally finance the travel and other expenses of his independent promotional ventures. However, it is sometimes possible, through negotiation, for an author to obtain part of the total promotion cost from the publisher. (*See: self-publishing.*)

Proofreader's symbols/marks. Many of the changes on manuscripts indicated by proofreaders are denoted by a standard set of symbols that are understood by typesetters and printers as well. A chart of these proofreader's symbols appears in the Appendix to this encyclopedia.

Proofreading. This term usually applies to the process of reading composed copy (printer's proofs) in order to identify and correct errors in that copy. In *Jobs for Writers*, Elizabeth L. Dugger describes proofreading as "the painstaking, word-for-word, character-for-character comparison of typeset galley proofs against the original manuscript to see that nothing was omitted, added, or changed by the compositor, that words have been divided correctly at the ends of lines, and that the type specifications (specs) regarding typeface, style, and margins were followed." In some jobs, the proofreader may also be responsible (prior to typesetting) for checking the copy for spelling, grammar, and style, as well as for doing the comparison work after copy is typeset.

In identifying and correcting errors in composed copy, the proofreader uses a fairly standard set of correction marks. A chart of these standard proofreading symbols appears in the Appendix to this encyclopedia. (*See: editing, freelance.*)

Proofreading as a specialty. (*See: editing, freelance.*)

Propaganda. The deliberate dissemination of information or ideas intended to persuade people toward or away from a belief, action, individual, movement, nation, institution, or organization. Propaganda may consist of opinions, facts, arguments, allegations, or rumors presented by word of mouth or through printed and visual material, music, drama, or any of the mass media. Certain acts such as demonstrations, assassinations, and hijackings may also be perpetrated for propaganda purposes.

The term is derived from the Congregation for the Propagation of the Faith, a committee founded in the seventeenth century by Pope Gregory XV to propagate—that is, to spread—Christianity to foreign lands. It took on a negative connotation during World War II when falsified reports and opinion-influencing discussion came to be labeled propaganda.

Although propaganda can be used to promote both good and bad causes, it is generally disclaimed as being unfairly slanted. It is distinguished from education, which seeks to inform through reason. Often appealing to desires, fears, and prejudices, propaganda is criticized because it does not give fair and impartial consideration to opposing views.

In a free society such as the United States, the propaganda of political organizations, special-interest groups, and individuals such as writers, filmmakers, and publishers is not often restricted or censored. Individuals and organizations are, however, protected by law from libel, slander, fraudulent claims for commercial products and services, and other situations that may result from malicious propaganda. (*See: censorship, literary; persuasive writing.*)

Proposal/prospectus. A detailed plan of a proposed new enterprise, such as a new publication or a new company, that is used as selling material for that project. A prospectus usually involves a description of the contents and projected market for the proposal. It is often used in relation to textbook proposals and in proposals for foundation grants. (*See: outline; textbook publishing.*)

Prose. All spoken and written language that is not expressed in a regular rhythmic pattern. *Prose*, as distinguished from *poetry*, is the ordinary form of communication in words. The distinction between prose and poetry cannot always be clearly defined, however; there are often poetic elements in prose compositions, as well as prosaic poetry. (*See: poetry.*)

Prose poem. A style of writing constructed in prose form (sentences and paragraphs rather than lines), but possessing the dramatic language of poetry—imagery, rhythm, cadence, assonance, alliteration, etc. Karl Shapiro's *The Bourgeois Poet* is a volume of prose poems. Here is an excerpt:

Poems, flowers of language, if that's what you are, grow up in the air where books come true. And you, thin packet, let your seed fly, if you have any.

Protagonist. A protagonist is the central character of a story or play. Plot is created when this character faces a conflict, and if another character is the cause of the conflict, that character is called the *antagonist.*

Protagonist is often incorrectly used as a synonym for *hero*; similarly, *antagonist* is incorrectly used for *villain.* Actually, a hero is an admirable character, and a villain is one who embodies evil; regardless of the characters' personal qualities, the character who demands the most attention of readers is the protagonist, and the character who opposes him is the antagonist.

Proverb. A short familiar saying, usually of unknown or ancient origin, that expresses a useful thought, supposed truth, or moral lesson, *proverb* is synonymous with *adage, aphorism, apothegm, maxim, saying,* and *saw.* Writers searching for ideas or universal themes for their work may develop an article, story, or novel from a well-known proverb.

PSA. (*See: public service announcement.*)

Pseudonym. A pseudonym is a fictitious name used to conceal the identity of an author. More generally, *pseudonym* is a term for any alias. (*See: pen name.*)

Psychological novel. A narrative that emphasizes the mental and emotional aspects of its characters, focusing on motivations and mental activity rather than on exterior events. The psychological novelist is less concerned about relating *what* happened than about exploring *why* it happened. Although a drama such as *Hamlet*, James Joyce's novel *Ulysses*, or much of the work of Henry James may be considered psychological, the term is most often used to describe twentieth-century works that employ such techniques as interior monologue and stream of consciousness. Two psychological novels among those published in recent years are Judith Guest's *Ordinary People* and Mary Gordon's *The Company of Women*.

The label "psychological novel" is not necessarily an exclusive one. A work of science fiction, for example, may also be psychological. Contemporary mystery novels in particular are becoming more psychologically oriented. Unlike the straight crime puzzlers of the past, present-day mystery and crime fiction emphasizes character motivation and analyzes action—particularly criminal action—in terms of a character's psycho-history. The novels of Lawrence Sanders (*The First Deadly Sin*, *The Third Deadly Sin*) allow the reader to explore the inner mind of the main character—usually a murderer—and to tune in to his motivations, emotions, and the forces affecting his decisions and actions. (*See: interior monologue; stream of consciousness.*)

Public domain. Material not protected by copyright, patent, or trademark, and therefore available to the general public for use without fee, is said to be in the public domain.

Certain types of material cannot be copyrighted, and so fall immediately into the public domain. News stories and feature articles that ap-

pear in uncopyrighted newspapers become part of the public domain once they are published. (Many features and columns appearing in the newspaper *are* copyrighted, however—as shown by the copyright symbol, year, and copyright owner's name—and a writer must obtain permission from the author, newspaper, or syndicate in order to use this material.) Most government publications are uncopyrighted and, therefore, in the public domain. Facts—well-established information—cannot be copyrighted. Jokes cannot be copyrighted. Ideas, titles, and transcripts from public hearings cannot be copyrighted. All of these are in the public domain.

Material immediately becomes part of the public domain when it is published in an uncopyrighted publication unless the author's own copyright symbol, year, and name appears with his piece; or unless a reasonable effort is made to add the notice to copies distributed without it and if registration is made for the work within five years after the publication without notice.

The author cannot secure a copyright for material once it is published without a copyright notice, except under certain conditions. (He may, however, revise the material and copyright the new version of the work.) Writers should be aware that most newspapers, many literary and little magazines, and some other publications that accept freelance submissions are not copyrighted. Once material is published there, it falls into the public domain, and anyone may make whatever use of it he wishes, including reprinting it without notifying or obtaining permission from the author. That's why it's important for an author to request that the editor of an uncopyrighted publication publish the author's own copyright notice with his poem, story, or article in an uncopyrighted publication.

A work once copyrighted may also fall into the public domain once its copyright period runs out. Before January 1, 1978, copyright protection under the old law was for 28 years and could be renewed just once for another 28 years. Any copyrighted material over 56 years old (except for material whose copyright expired from 1962 to 1977 and was renewed each year for one more year by Congress while it considered a new copyright bill) would now be in the public domain. Under the new law, copyright is for the author's life, plus 50 years.

An author may use as he pleases, without obtaining permission, any material he finds in the public domain. (*See: copyright.*)

Public relations (PR) representative. This person is responsible for presenting and maintaining a favorable image of his company or institution before the public. Persons work in this capacity for hospitals, universities, and other institutions, as well as for private corporations. In business the title of the PR representative may be Director of Corporate Communications, rather than Public Relations.

One important function the PR representative performs is working with top management in forming the company's public relations policies. He also is up to date on trends in the field in which he works, and with the activities of competing companies and organizations, as well as of his own.

Community relations is a major

concern of a PR person whose company/institution is active in a small region, while a PR representative who works for a national or international company/institution seeks favorable national exposure (through magazines and broadcast networks) as well as through local media. In addition, presiding over employee relations is a responsibility sometimes delegated to the PR representative.

A public relations office communicates through newspaper features, press releases, brochures, open house gatherings, exhibits, speeches, commercials, and public service announcements, and seeks opportunities to send company or institution representatives to radio and television talk shows, especially if they are nationally known and respected spokespersons.

Because the PR representative either writes or approves of every communication that his company dispatches to the public, he must possess a command of language. He must also be well versed in photography, since the photos he sets up (either alone or with a photographer) must be striking enough to capture an editor's attention.

The Publicity Club of Chicago offers *Public Relations People: Who They Are and What They Do*, a free booklet on careers in public relations. It can be obtained from the Publicity Club of Chicago, 1441 Shermer Road, Northbrook IL 60062. (*See: public service announcement; publicity writing.*)

Additional information: *Professional's Guide to Publicity.*

Public service announcement (PSA). A public service announcement is a period of broadcast time given by a station to a community group, in accordance with the Federal Communications Commission stipulation requiring television and radio stations to operate in the public interest. The publicist who seeks broadcast time for his organization must assess the needs of—and therefore the audiences of—available stations to find the ones most likely to comply with his request.

A public interest announcement can take several forms. Straightforward announcements that inform the audience of an event are heard in station breaks, spot announcements, and community calendars. News releases, telephone call-in talk show programs ("two-way radio"), editorials, features, panel discussions, and interviews are longer broadcast items of which the PSA may be only a part; whatever form of PSA is written, economy of words and emphasis on facts are essential to good copy.

A public service announcement must be typed, double-spaced—no more than one on a page—with 2-inch side margins on 8½x11-inch bond paper. Words should not be hyphenated at the ends of lines; the copy should contain no abbreviations. A paragraph should not end at the bottom of a page: continuing it on to the next page keeps broadcasters from mistaking the end of a paragraph for the end of the PSA. The publicist also inserts phonetic spellings of unfamiliar names and words.

While the actual announcement begins one-third of the way down the page, other information belongs at the top: the name, address, and phone number of the organization, along with the publicist's name, should be typed in the upper left corner. The dates to broadcast the announcement go in the upper right corner; it is best to submit copy 15 days before the first day it is intended to be broadcast.

One kind of PSA, the spot announcement, is programmed by time at radio and television stations. The following word counts for radio serve as a guide to the PSA writer: 25 words can be read in 10 seconds, 50 words in 20 seconds, and 150 words in 60 seconds. In television copy, which is read at a slower pace, 20 words can be read in 10 seconds, 40 words in 20 seconds, and 125 words in 60 seconds. PSAs for television, of course, should be accompanied by an appropriate visual in the slide or tape format preferred by the individual station. The longer the PSA, the more slides required, since a single slide makes for a dull, static spot; it's important to keep the TV station's needs in mind when assembling a PSA. (See the sample PSA appearing in the Appendix to this encyclopedia.)

Public TV. Some broadcast licenses are allocated by the Federal Communications Commission to provide educational programming to schools and the general public. The licenses are assigned to colleges and universities, state and local municipalities, or community groups. Funding comes from government appropriations, foundation and corporate support, and viewer contributions.

There are currently 299 public television stations. They broadcast material that reinforces and enriches conventional classroom study, promotes public awareness of local, regional, and national issues, and fosters cultural and artistic expression. Writers may find the programs featuring interviews with authors especially helpful.

The major source of programming is the Public Broadcasting Corporation, through five major affiliates: WNET, New York; WTTW, Chicago; WGBH, Boston; KQED, San Francisco; WQED, Pittsburgh; and WETA, Washington, DC . In addition, there are smaller stations and independent production groups—such as Children's TV Workshop and the Agency for Instructional TV—that produce and distribute programming to stations. Although the agency for Instructional Television does not solicit freelance scripts, it gives freelance assignments to scriptwriters. Freelancers interested in educational programming may contact the Director of Production, Agency for Instructional TV, Box A, Bloomington IN 47402, with a cover letter and samples of their work.

Depending on their size and budget, local educational television stations may or may not produce original programming and/or only distribute programs originating elsewhere. Inquiries from qualified professional scriptwriters should be directed to the program director at the local station.

Publication Consent Agreement. (See the Appendix.)

Publicity writing. Publicists, who are either self-employed or members of the PR staffs of advertising agencies, are engaged by companies, non-profit organizations, politicians, celebrities, and others to send press releases (and sometimes photographs) to the appropriate media about some newsworthy product or event. A publicity writer combines the creativity of a magazine writer with the fact-finding ability of a newspaper reporter. Publicity aims to emphasize the benefit of something or the good qualities of someone by affecting the reader emotionally.

For a writer who intends to enter the publicity field, experience as a newspaper reporter can be helpful, since a knowledge of what is truly newsworthy— as opposed to puffery—can increase the success the publicist has in placing material in the media. Volunteer work with non-profit organizations can help a writer enter this field by giving him experience and contacts. Also, photography skills can be an asset to this type of career.

Simplicity is the key to writing the news release: its style is direct and the message is concise; elaboration with adjectives is rare. According to publicist Thomas J. Rizzo, the who, what, when, where, and why should be stated at the outset. He advises constructing the copy so that deleting the name of the client or cause would render the press release difficult to understand. At the same time, the release should be so constructed that it will be easy for an editor to run it as is, without any changes.

A news release is typed on $8\frac{1}{2}$x11-inch white bond paper. Copy for the print media is double-spaced; that for the broadcast media is triple-spaced. Side margins are $1\frac{1}{2}$ inches each. In the upper left corner, the writer types his name, address, and phone number, and the name of the sponsoring organization two spaces below.

The final item to be placed in the upper left corner is the phrase "for immediate release," typed in all caps. (A specific date can substitute for the phrase, but it should be used only if the release must wait.) The writer indicates the city of origin and the date, either at the beginning or the end of the copy, and places either "-30-" or "### " at the end of the release. Ideally, an entire press release consists of only one page. (See the news release and new product release samples in the Appendix to this encyclopedia.)

Some experts advise creating a catchy or appropriate headline for a press release for a print medium, in case it happens to be suitable for the editor's needs. However, editors do accept press releases that lack headlines. (*See: political writing; public service announcement.*)

Public's right to know. (*See: freedom of information.*)

Publisher's catalogue. A promotional booklet sent by a book publisher to bookstores, libraries, and individuals. Such catalogues are commonly issued by hardcover publishers twice a year, in spring and fall; by paperback publishers more frequently. They inform consumers about the newest releases and other current titles, providing short summaries of the books' contents, authors, and intended audiences.

A publisher's catalogue is one means of researching a company's editorial emphasis before submitting a manuscript to an editor there. In many cases, publishers send catalogues free for a request and an SASE; *Writer's Market* listings furnish details on obtaining publishers' catalogues.

Publishers, music. (*See:* Songwriter's Market.)

Publisher's rep. A representative of the publisher who calls on bookstores, wholesalers, etc., to sell the new and backlist titles of the publisher. He may be either employed by the publisher (sometimes called "house reps") or be an independent entrepreneur representing several publishers and paid on a commission basis for books sold.

The term also refers to the representative of a magazine publisher who calls on magazine wholesalers to monitor the distribution of the magazine to appropriate outlets in the wholesalers' retail trading area.

Publisher's Trade List Annual. A multivolume set of directories available in most libraries containing publishers' current catalogues. Catalogues are listed alphabetically by publisher and show both the current and backlist titles of the company. It is most useful to writers researching book ideas to see what subjects have been treated most recently by publishers the author has in mind as prospective markets for his own book ideas.

Publishers Weekly (PW). A trade magazine covering current events in the publishing industry. Each issue contains an interview-profile of an author or other person influential in publishing, announcements of personnel changes, and PW's own lists of paperback and hardcover bestsellers. The department "PW Forecasts" features brief reviews of soon to be published fiction, nonfiction, how-to, paperback, and children's books.

News in other categories is regularly reported under "Rights and Permissions," "Bookselling & Marketing," and "Calendar" (announcements of workshops, conferences, seminars, and courses).

The two largest special issues of *Publishers Weekly* announcing forthcoming books are the fall announcement number in August and the spring announcement issue in January. A religious books issue is published twice a year (usually in February and September); a children's books issue, in February and July; the International/Frankfurt Book Fair issue, in September; and the ABA convention issue, in May. The annual summary, published in March, briefly reports on important events—such as prizes, awards, and bestsellers—of the previous year.

Writers find PW useful in learning what books are planned for publication by which publishers. They can then evaluate their own ideas in relation to potential publishers. Most libraries subscribe to *Publishers Weekly*. PW's address is 205 E. 42nd St., New York NY 10017.

Publishers who default on pay. When a writer receives no payment for accepted material from a publisher, and that publisher is listed in *Writer's Market*, the writer can consult Writer's Digest Books for assistance in contacting the publisher on the writer's behalf.

If the publisher in question is not listed in *Writer's Market*, there are other possible options. He 1) may be able to file a claim in small claims court; 2) can consult an attorney about the existence of a long arm law in his state by which to sue the publisher in the writer's state; or 3) can notify the U.S. Postmaster in the city where the publisher is located about possible mail fraud. Sending a copy of such a letter to the publisher sometimes encourages the publisher to come forth with the payment. (*See: complaints against publishers; "long arm" law.*)

Publishing, courses in. For the college student or other adult seeking a career in publishing, or the individual already employed in the publishing industry and interested in professional advancement or enrichment, a number of courses—both academic and professional—are offered by colleges and universities, publishing houses, industrial firms, and professional organizations.

Several academic institutions offer credit and non-credit courses for both undergraduate and graduate students in various aspects of publishing: manuscript editing; printing, layout, and design; graphics techniques; book promotion; copyrights and contracts; textbook publishing; publishing finance and accounting; and related subject areas. Two of the best known are the Radcliffe Publishing Procedures Course at Harvard, and the Diploma Program in Book Publishing at New York University. Professional programs, such as the one offered by Folio Magazine Publishing Corporation, include workshops, seminars, and conferences in all areas of publishing. These programs are designed primarily for professionals in the field.

Literary Market Place lists courses for the book trade in its "Courses, Conferences, and Contests" chapter. *Guide to Book Publishing Courses: Academic and Professional Programs* is another directory available in most public or college libraries that may be useful to writers seeking staff jobs with publishing companies. (*See: continuing education.*)

Publishing house. This term originated with the early publishing companies, many of which were family-operated enterprises. Today, *publishing house* is synonymous with *publishing company.*

Publishing party. This is an essentially social function given occasionally by a publishing house in honor of a recently published author. At a publication day party, the author, the author's agent, some of the publisher's employees, reviewers, trade journalists, representatives of radio and television, and a few relatives of the author gather for the primary purpose of celebrating the accomplished book. In addition, persons interested in buying paperback rights or other subsidiary rights that have not already been sold are invited by the publisher.

The job of organizing a publishing party belongs to the publisher's publicist, who sometimes chooses a location connected in some way to the book. For example, a party in celebration of *Scruples* was held at a San Francisco store similar to the store in the novel. (*See: autographing party.*)

Puff. A publicity release that praises an individual, product, service, or organization. Because it does not involve objective presentation of information and generally has little or no news value, newspaper and magazine editors are not receptive to articles based solely on puff. One-sided, poorly researched pieces built only on information supplied by somebody's publicity department and that describe their subjects only in the most positive terms are not, according to many editors listed in *Writer's Market*, seriously considered for publication.

Book publishers, on the other hand, welcome puff as a tool for promoting book sales. Testimonials by well-known individuals that appear on the dust jacket of the book and attest to its quality are, in essence, puff. (*See: blurb; book promotion.*)

Pulitzer Prizes. The Pulitzer Prizes in Journalism, Letters, Drama, and Music are a group of annual awards established in 1917 under the terms of the will of Joseph Pulitzer (1847-1911), a Hungarian-born newspaper owner and editor (the New York *World*) who is also remembered for endowing the Columbia University School of Journalism.

Designed for the "encouragement of public service, public morals, American literature, and the advancement of education," awards of $1,000 ($500 before 1942) have been presented annually since 1917 for distinguished work in United States newspapers, as well as for distinguished achievement in literature, drama, and music by Americans. Included in the letters awards are those for fiction, biography, history, poetry, and general nonfiction. In addition to the 12 awards in journalism, there are also three traveling fellowships for graduates of Columbia's Graduate School of Journalism.

Eligibility requirements and competition deadline information may be obtained by writing Secretary,

The Pulitzer Prize Board, 702 Journalism, Columbia University, New York NY 10027.

Pull back. An indication in a motion picture or television script that the camera should move back from a particular scene for a wider view. In a script, the term is typed all in caps. (*See: television script terms.*)

Pulp magazine. A popular magazine printed on coarse, low-quality paper stock and usually containing lurid or sensational articles and stories. Although the term historically connotes low standards of taste and literary quality, a great deal of good writing has been published in pulp magazines. The term is seldom used today.

Pulp magazines, or *pulps*, enjoyed success and popularity in the 1920s and 1930s. They were inexpensive for publishers to produce (being printed on cheap paper, displaying little decoration, and representing a low-paying market for writers) as well as inexpensive for consumers to buy.

The first pulp magazine, *Argosy*, was introduced as such in 1896; it had existed since 1882 as a children's magazine, and when the publisher, Frank Munsey, changed its target audience to adults and its content to adventure stories, he began printing it on lower-quality pulp paper. Adventure was the only category offered by the earliest pulps, but later it was joined by love, detective, western, and science fiction magazines with such titles as *Love Story*, *Detective Story*, *Western Story*, and *Amazing Stories*.

Just after World War II, the pulp magazine business began to suffer noticeably when competition from paperback books and comic books became a serious threat. In addition, publishers had escalating production costs to contend with. During this period, some publishers ceased publication, others intensified their use of market research and national advertising, and another group of publishers converted their pulps to slicks—thus establishing the men's general interest magazine. A company specializing in reprints of the early twentieth century pulp magazines for collectors is Odyssey Publications, P.O. Box G 148, Greenwood MA 01880. (*See: pulp writer; women's slick magazine.*)

Additional information: *Magazines in the Twentieth Century.*

Pulp writer. Someone who writes for pulp magazines. The term traditionally referred to those who wrote for confession, western, and other "pulp" (paper) magazines, but is seldom used today. Well-known writers whose work appeared early in pulp magazines include Edgar Rice Burroughs, A. Conan Doyle, Theodore Dreiser, Dashiell Hammett, Rudyard Kipling, Booth Tarkington, and Edith Wharton.

Punch. In radio, emphasis placed on a particular line or on a commercial.

Puzzle writing. Writers interested in constructing and selling puzzles may choose from a variety of puzzle categories: straight crossword puzzles, topical crosswords, wordsearch puzzles (also called word find and seek-a-word), fill-ins (known also as Kriss Krosses), anacrostics, acrostics, cryptograms, mazes, brain teasers, and word games. Requirements vary considerably from magazine to magazine, so the puzzle writer is advised to request editorial specifications on puzzle submissions from the magazine to which he intends to send his material. One requirement that applies to all categories of puzzles and that is common to nearly all puzzle publishers is extreme accuracy: the puzzle writer must take special care to make certain the drawings, numberings, spellings, and definitions are all correct before submitting the puzzle. Puzzle publishers ordinarily require that a list of the sources for each word in the puzzle accompany the submission.

There are a number of magazines that publish nothing but puzzles. The best-known are those in the Dell Puzzle Publications group: *Dell Crossword Puzzles*, *Dell Word Search Puzzles*, *Official Crossword Puzzles*, and others. Publishers who publish puzzles exclusively are listed in the "Puzzle" section of *Writer's Market*.

Puzzles are often considered to be filler material, and are accepted as such by a wide variety of consumer, trade, and company publications. Religious, juvenile, teen and young adult, and general interest magazines in particular solicit puzzles of all types. Their requirements and typical rates of pay are listed in *Writer's Market*.

Puzzle writers who concentrate on crossword puzzles should be aware that published crossword diagrams—the arrangement of open squares and black spaces—are used over and over again, and are, in effect, in the public domain. Only the arrangement of words within the diagram can be copyrighted.

q.v. Quod vide; which see. This term most often appears in footnotes, encyclopedia entries, and book reviews; it follows a reference to another work or entry that can be looked up. For instance, an encyclopedia article on airplanes might read, " . . . invented by Wilbur and Orville Wright, q.v.," meaning that the reader should then look up the encyclopedia entry for the Wrights if he wishes to know more about them.

Query. A query is a sales letter to an editor that is designed to interest him or her in an article or book idea. A query usually refers to nonfiction only, but could be a requirement for novel-length fiction as well, especially when a particular market is swamped with fiction submissions. The purpose of a query letter is twofold: it attempts to convince an editor that a proposed idea is good for his readership, and it tries to make him believe that the writer can turn out a well-written piece.

Though queries are as individual as the submissions they accompany, there are general guidelines writers may use to structure their proposals. Knowing what to include and what to omit in a query may mean the difference between a sale and the slushpile. No query alone will sell a manuscript, but a bad one may prevent an editor from even considering an idea.

The lead paragraph of the article query letter, for example, may include an alluring but concise summary of the article's central idea and the style and point of view in which it will be written. Subsequent paragraphs may support the article's premise with facts, anecdotes, and observations. The writer may also share some of his sources of information and describe briefly his qualifications (if they are relevant) for developing the idea. The query closing may be a straightforward request to do the article, and may specify a proposed length for the piece and a delivery date.

Another form of query, the outline query, begins with a lead in double-spaced type that might not be the exact wording to be used in the article, but which favorably represents the author's writing style. The balance of the outline query (typed single-spaced) provides the same information, examples, and credentials as those described in the basic query.

Specific items to omit from a query letter include discussion of fees, the writer's opinion of the article idea's worth, and requests for advice. Editors read well-written, up-front queries that make their point succinctly.

In addition to content, there are technical aspects to submitting a successful query: keeping the letter to one single-spaced typed page, if possible; addressing the current editor by name; referring to the writer in the first person; enclosing an SASE; and ensuring accuracy in spelling, grammar, and writing mechanics. Samples of the writer's work and a list of credits may accompany a query letter. In addition, if the writer has tantalizing photographs that illustrate his story idea, he may enclose three or four of them with the letter.

Listings in *Writer's Market* often indicate whether an editor prefers a query letter or a complete manuscript. A sample query letter appears in the Appendix to this encyclopedia.

Quill and Scroll Society (QSS). An international organization of high school students involved in journalism and creative writing. In a school that has established a Quill and Scroll Society chapter, the newspaper, the yearbook, and the literary magazine are all eligible to induct members. Individual students, in order to become members, must be recommended by their schools.

The Society publishes a chapter manual, a stylebook, and the quarterly magazine, *Quill & Scroll*. In addition, it publishes materials for students, teachers, and school administrators, including booklets on effective editorial writing and managing publications, as well as a principal's guide.

QSS conducts research, presents scholarships, and sponsors the National Writing Contest and the Current Events Quiz. Its headquarters are at the School of Journalism and Mass Communications, The University of Iowa, Iowa City IA 52242.

Quotations, books of. Quotations can be helpful to a writer or lecturer who needs a succinct introduction to his material. They also can be used to lend authority to points made within a piece.

Books of quotations include *Bartlett's Familiar Quotations* (considered the classic work in this field), *The Book of Quotes*, *The Dictionary of Biographical Quotation*, *The Great Quotations*, *The International Thesaurus of Quotations*, *The Quotable Woman*, *Quotation Dictionary*, *A Treasury of Humorous Quotations*, and *The Writer's Quotation Book*.

Quotations references are subdivided either by subject or by speaker/writer. Other current titles can be found listed under "Quotations" in the *Subject Guide to Books In Print*.

Quotes. This term can be used to refer either to the words enclosed in quotation marks or to the quotation marks themselves.

When quoting published material, the writer should be aware of the restrictions imposed by copyright law. Material in the public domain (e.g., government records or publications, works on which the copyright has expired) may be quoted without the publisher's permission, provided the source is given, but quoting of copyrighted material is subject to the copyright owner's approval. (The writer quoting from government publications, though, must be careful about whether or not the material originated with the government, since federal publications are exempt from copyright restrictions but sometimes incorporate copyrighted material.) The "fair use" provision of the copyright law, however, allows for the direct quotation of short passages for criticism, teaching, or research purposes.

There is no set number of words or sentences an author may quote from another's copyrighted work without permission. Traditionally, however, writers using only a few sentences from a long work have simply attributed the source of the material in their own manuscripts. (Since poems and songs are so short, permission must be requested before excerpting from them.)

When writing a publisher for permission to quote, it is courteous, as well as expedient, to include an SASE for his reply.

Quotes from printed material must be reproduced exactly as they appear on the page. Words may be omitted with the use of an ellipsis— as long as the context is not changed—and incorrect spelling or usage may be acknowledged by placing "(sic)" after the word or phrase in question.

When quoting material from a live interview or speech, the writer faces the decision of whether or not to correct faulty grammar or insert words for the sake of logic. To avoid the risk of misquoting, the writer can either paraphrase the person's quote (leaving out quotation marks) or tape the entire interview to ensure an accurate record of it. When using only some of the interview, he must be careful to avoid quoting out of context and misrepresenting the speaker's idea.

Quotations can add authority to an article, but the writer must learn to decide when a quote would enhance his work and when too many would detract from it. (*See: attribution; copyright; fair use; libel; plagiarism.*)

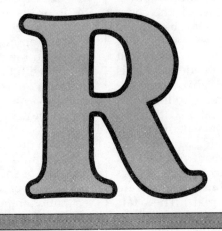

Radio commercials. Advertising copywriting for radio is concise and colorful. Using short phrases, it appeals to the senses of the listener through well-chosen adjectives. Repetition, a conversational tone, and a central theme are fundamental to successful copy.

Finished copy must meet certain format specifications. It must be typed all in capital letters, double-spaced, on a continuity form. This form also includes the references to music or sound effects to be used, the name of the client, the length of the commercial, and the first and last dates the commercial will be broadcast. The copywriter makes liberal use of punctuation: dashes and commas indicate pauses; exclamation points and underlining, emphasis. Copy for the air never includes abbreviations. (See sample radio commercial script in the Appendix to this encyclopedia.)

Before a spot is taped or read on the air, the writer times his work by reading it aloud. At this stage, he includes phonetic spellings—or any spellings that are more logical—for words that are difficult to pronounce. Commercials most often last either 60 seconds (which can accommodate 120-160 words) or 30 seconds (60-80 words).

Most of the necessary information is supplied by the client's account executive, but a writer may wish to consult the client's print ads, other printed information on the product, or the client himself. Dictionaries or handbooks of pronunciation are also helpful, especially with foreign words and proper names. (*See: radio drama; television commercials.*)

Radio copywriting. The key characteristics of a successful copywriter are organization and the ability to work quickly without losing creativity or imagination. Because of unpredictable clients and schedules, a day-by-day engagement calendar is a necessity.

Copywriters work either full-time or part-time. Some begin working while still in college, although larger radio stations usually require a college degree and two years' experience in the radio field as prerequisites for filling the position. Smaller stations that do not require the full-time services of a copywriter will sometimes hire a person to perform a combination of tasks, e.g., copywriter-traffic (getting ads written, scheduled, delivered on time) and copywriter-producer.

An aspiring copywriter should take a résumé and copy samples to an interview. During the interview, it is not uncommon for the interviewer to ask the writer to create radio copy on the spot. (A sample radio commercial script is included in the Appendix to this encyclopedia.)

Currently, a freelance copywriter can earn from $10-$50 per script or $100-$250 per week at part-time copywriting. (*See: advertising, copywriters; broadcasting; drama.*)

Radio drama. Virtually moribund in the United States since the advent of television, radio drama is making something of a comeback, largely due to funding from arts councils, private foundations, and interest in public broadcast circles. The leading domestic exponents currently are the CBS Mystery Theatre, the National Radio Theatre, and NPR (National Public Radio) Playhouse. In addition, religious broadcasters rely extensively on inspirational radio plays: the country's oldest continuing series are *Unshackled*, produced by the Pacific Garden Mission, and *Heartbeat Theatre*, produced by the Salvation Army.

While radio drama of the so-called Golden Age was almost exclusively commercial, the current burst of activity is virtually unlimited in subject matter, approach, tone, atmosphere, and audience. It is particularly well suited to humor and expressionist fantasy. The medium itself offers both opportunities and limitations for a writer: because the length of a production is usually only 15 or 30 minutes, complexity of plot and depth of characters are limited; but within seconds, the radio dramatist can transport his characters to a distant area or a time in the future or past.

Radio is the most evocative of dramatic forms and arguably the most involving—hence the phrase "theater of the mind" so frequently applied to it. In a nonvisual form almost all key action must be relayed through the dialogue. Still, advanced electronics have enabled "sound texturing," that is, the blend of dialogue, sound, and music, to convey the total impression. Some writers see radio as an opportunity to pen uninterrupted discussions, but sophisticated novel-like plotting and rapid scene shifting have been tried successfully.

Because of the comparatively low expense of radio productions, producers have more leeway to experiment with new writers. Authors who have written for radio include Arthur Miller, Edward Albee, John Gardner, Arthur Kopit, David Mamet, Harold Pinter, Tom Stoppard, Samuel Beckett, Max Frisch, Bertholt Brecht, Friedrich Duerrenmatt, and Eugene Ionesco. Seminal figures in the U.S. radio drama writing are Norman Corwin, Arch Oboler, humorist Stan Freberg, and Lucille Fletcher, whose *Sorry Wrong Number* is to radio drama what *The Necklace* is to the short story.

Pay for dramatic radio scripts varies from as little as $75 to $2,000, depending on length and buyer. A sample radio drama script page appears in the Appendix to this encyclopedia. (*See: religious broadcasting; soap opera, writing for; unities.*)

Radio terms. (*See individual entries under the headings: across the board; ad-lib; affiliate; announcement; availability list; cart; continuity; co-op copy; day-book; disc jockey; donut; double spotting; down and under; dub; fact sheet; Federal Communications Commission; hiatus; ID/station ID; make-good; O&O station; on the air; open-end transcription; out-cue; participation; plug; preferred time/ prime time; prestige copy; primary listening area; program log; promo; public service announcement; punch; remote pickup/remote; ROS; saturation; script; service; signature; simulcast; sound effects (SFX); spec; sponsor; spot; stand by; start date/stop date; station rep.; sustaining program; tag; TFN; time signal; traffic; TWX; up and out; up full.*)

Radio, writing for. (*See: radio commercials; radio copywriting; radio drama.*)

Raison d'être. French for "reason for existing" or "justification for existence." A dedicated writer, for example, may cry, "Creating literature is my raison d' être!"

The phrase may be used to describe the motivation, purpose, or primary goal of literary characters. For instance, pursuing and killing the great white whale is Captain Ahab's raison d' être in *Moby Dick*. (*See: motivation.*)

Readability formulas. Readability formulas indicate the difficulty of written material according to the skill (by school grade level) needed to understand it. They are necessary because of the inconsistency between the percentage of persons who have completed a given grade level and the reading ability of those same persons. For example, even though 75% of adults in the U.S. have graduated from high school, not all of them can read at twelfth-grade level. (It is estimated, in fact, that more than half cannot.) Further, a reader is apt to misunderstand—or even ignore—material that is too difficult. Popular magazines must maintain fairly low readability levels because their business depends on sales—which in turn depend on readability.

One readability standard, the Flesch formula, determines a passage's level of difficulty by the number of syllables per 100 words and the average number of words per sentence. The Dale-Chall formula, which also considers the average number of words per sentence, incorporates a list of 3,000 familiar words into the calculations. The percentage of words that do not appear on the list determines word familiarity. Factors used in the Farr-Jenkins-Paterson formula are the number, per 100 words, of one-syllable words, and the average number of words per sentence. The Danielson-Bryon formula determines readability by counting spaces between words as well as characters per sentence.

The Cloze test is a standard that involves a reader in the actual testing process. For the test, every fifth word of a passage is deleted, and the reader is instructed to fill in the blanks left by those words. The writing is judged readable to the extent that the substituted words are accurate.

The Fog Index is another formula that uses word length and sentence length as variables, as described by its creator, Robert Gunning, in his book, *The Technique of Clear Writing.* Author Gunning advised writers: "Use the (formula) as a guide after you have written, but not as a pattern before you write. Good writing must be alive; don't kill it with system." (*See: Easy Listening Formula; Fog Index.*)

Reader identification. This term is used primarily to describe the process by which a reader projects himself into a work of fiction, associating himself with the adventures, conflicts, desires, feelings, and responses of the characters in the story. Damon Knight explains in *Creating Short Fiction*: "Identification with the central character is strongly desired by readers of commercial fiction. A woman reading a gothic romance wants to imagine herself as the heroine and live through the latter's perils vicariously. A man reading a western story wants to imagine himself tall in the saddle." Strong reader identification in fiction is achieved by providing the reader with strong, believable characters involved in a significant conflict in pursuit of a goal. Many commercial magazines that publish short fiction actually *require* that the protagonist and setting of a short story are such that the magazine's readers can easily identify with them.

Reader identification—through choice of subject matter—is important in nonfiction writing as well. Peggy Teeters, author of *How to Get Started in Writing*, says, "Keep reader identification in mind when you are writing; it will help you sell your manuscripts. Whenever the reader can nod his head and say, 'That's the way it was' or 'Hey, that's what happened to me!' you're on your way to a sale."

Reader (or first reader). (*See: book publishing jobs, editorial.*)

Readers' Guide to Periodical Literature. An index to general interest magazines, in which magazine contents are categorized by subject and author. The number of magazines indexed in this publication varies; currently it is 181.

The *Readers' Guide* is published semimonthly nine months of the year, and monthly three months of the year. Large libraries subscribe to it; small libraries, children's departments of libraries, and school libraries may instead have the abridged version of this index available.

The *Readers' Guide* has been published since 1901. Another subject-author index to recent general interest periodicals, *The Magazine Index*, has been produced in microfilm form since 1977. It indexes 370 publications. (*See:* Abridged Readers' Guide to Periodical Literature; *periodicals, directories of.*)

Ream. From the Arabic word for bundle—*rizmah*—a ream is a quantity of paper, usually considered to be 500 sheets. (Some paper manufacturers and printers designate 480 sheets as a ream.) The writer may find it more convenient and economical to buy paper by the ream from a stationery store rather than purchasing it in smaller quantities in college bookstores or variety stores.

Record album liner notes. The copy by a staff or freelance writer describing the song and the artist performing on a record. Freelancers with special knowledge of, or contacts with, a recording artist may secure a freelance album liner assignment from the record company producing the album. Pay rates in 1982 for such copy ranged from $100-$250.

Recordkeeping. Because a writer must attend to the business side as well as the artistic aspects of his work, business records are important. They prepare him for annual income tax filing (as well as possible audit), and keep for future reference such data as market information and the status of manuscripts. With this information documented, the writer can keep accurate track of sales, expenses, marketing efforts, and other data the IRS may require the writer to produce, if it challenges him. Records are also important for learning how long it takes to do certain kinds of jobs, what kinds of freelance work are most profitable, etc.

A filing system used by many article writers, for example, contains the following categories: *in process, current manuscripts out,* and *business record.* The *in process* file comprises articles currently being written or queried on, and file folders containing notes to be used in writing the pieces.

Current manuscripts out lists the markets submitted to, postage spent, the article's title, date sent, and the date the article was either returned or sold.

An annual *business record* is kept on purchases of paper and supplies, postage, equipment upkeep, depreciation, illustrations and other costs, rent, phone, electricity, and trans-

portation. Of course, receipts must be kept on all tax-deductible expenses.

Fiction writers keep similar files on work-in-progress.

To supplement a filing system, a writer can use a wall or desk calendar with space for noting appointments, deadlines, phone calls, and work schedules. Some examples of writers' records appear in the Appendix to this encyclopedia. (*See: query; taxes.*)

Additional information: *The Complete Handbook for Freelance Writers; A Treasury of Tips for Writers; Writer's Market;* and the *Guide to Record Retention Requirements.*

Recto page. A page appearing on the right-hand side of a book. All numbered recto pages have odd numbers. (*See: verso page.*)

Redundancy. The use of more words or phrases than are necessary to communicate an idea; needless repetition.

Redundancy is a common problem in the work of beginning writers who believe such reiteration will produce greater emphasis. In other cases, writers express an idea in both positive and negative terms when only one statement is ordinarily needed to convey the message.

Stating an idea once, clearly and concisely, should suffice. In a long piece of writing, however, it is advisable to provide the reader with a summary at the end, highlighting the major points of the piece. (*See: readability formulas; tautology.*)

Reference books for writers. (*See: background information, books of; directories; periodicals, directories of; periodicals, indexes to; research sources, directories of.*)

Additional information: *Writer's Resource Guide.*

Reggae. A music form combining Jamaican calypso music with rock influences in a distinctive 4/4 repeating rhythm pattern. Lyrics in reggae are linked to social, economic, and religious influences of the Jamaican and other black peoples.

Regional book publishing. Some book publishers market to a portion of the U.S. instead of to the entire country or world. Finding a regional publisher is an advantage for an author whose book idea appeals only to readers in a limited geographic area. *Literary Market Place* contains a section of book publishers arranged by geographic location.

Regional English Expressions. (See the Appendix to this encyclopedia.)

Regional magazine. A regional publication is a category of magazine that covers a specific geographic region, such as an area of a country, a city, or a state. There are numerous regional magazines in existence, and their editorial requirements vary.

Brian Vachon, author of *Writing*

for Regional Publications, has categorized regionals into five groups. *Large city magazines* are concerned with either a city or a city's events and issues; they sometimes cover the surrounding area as well. Included are arts and restaurant reviews and accounts of muckraking and controversial articles. *Positive publications*, which can be either privately or government-owned, emphasize the favorable aspects of a region. The *newspaper insert*, or Sunday magazine, is able to offer the reader the most timely information. *Environmental magazines*, many of which are sponsored by government agencies or nature organizations, devote themselves to conservation and other natural-resource issues. *Guide and tour books* are the regional publications that reflect an evident sense of pride in an area. Their audiences are made up of tourists and visitors unfamiliar with the region a given book covers.

A regional magazine can confirm the positive emotions a reader has for his home, console a reader with nostalgic feelings for a former home, or inspire a person who hopes some day to live in the magazine's locale. Not all subscribers to a given regional publication live in the area the magazine covers; for example, many people in the "lower 48" read *Alaska* magazine.

A beginning writer can acquire valuable experience working for a regional, and the successful freelancer is one who researches a magazine and shows an awareness of its needs in his query letter.

Some examples of regional magazines are *Yankee, New Hampshire Profiles, Los Angeles Magazine,* and *Michigan Environs.*

Pay rates for writers are usually

low; privately owned magazines with large circulations pay best. Individual listings in *Writer's Market* indicate specific dollar amounts. (*See: city magazine.*)

Rejection slip. The written communication from an editor informing the writer that his submitted work has not been accepted. The rejection slip can take any of several forms, including a printed form on a 3x5-inch card or a personal letter. It is accompanied by the returned manuscript.

Manuscripts are rejected for any number of reasons and they may have nothing to do with the value of the manuscript itself. The editor may have just bought something similar; he may have just assigned the idea to another writer; he may have published another story on or related to the topic too recently to take it on again. Few editors have the time to include these reasons— or detailed criticism if the article or story *is* faulty—so the writer should not expect more than a short printed note of rejection. If the editor does take the time to offer some comment, the writer can take note of the reason and apply it to his future writing or marketing efforts. And if the editor does add a hand-written note at the bottom of the rejection slip indicating a willingness to look at other ideas, the writer should take that encouragement literally.

A good reminder to beginning writers is to have more than one idea or manuscript in progress at a time, so that individual rejection slips are not so debilitating. And if the writer has faith in the idea, he already has a list of other markets to which he can slant subsequent resubmissions. (As the writer gains more experience and accumulates comments from editors, he may decide to revise parts of a manuscript before resubmitting it.)

A writer need not give up after five, ten, or even fifty rejections, as the story "I Can Climb Higher Than You," by Jesse Stuart, shows. It was rejected 47 times before being accepted by, then winning the title "Best Story of the Year" from one of the same magazines that had previously rejected it. (*See: reporting time on manuscripts.*)

Relief song. A song in a musical that provides a tone that contrasts with that of the previous scene. A *respite*, one category of relief song, gives the audience a sense of relief from the tension caused by the story's events—"Gee, Officer Krupke!" in *West Side Story* interjects a comical tone into the tragic story. In contrast, a *novelty number* shoots energy into a placid series of events. "Once in Love with Amy" is a novelty number in *Where's Charley?*. A third kind of relief song, the *interlude song*, is inserted between events, such as "Poor Professor Higgins" in *My Fair Lady*. (*See: musical.*)

Religious broadcasting. Radio and television programs, stations, and networks that specialize in religious material offer opportunities for writers to use their skills in various capacities. In this field, staff positions are more abundant than freelance jobs. The writer who becomes involved in writing for the religious electronic media will most likely be paid less than one who writes for secular radio and television, since many religious stations depend on listener contributions rather than commercial advertising for their operating funds. Staffs of religious stations are generally small; consequently, staff writers are sometimes called upon to perform various duties.

Staff positions at religious broadcast stations include reporter, script editor, announcer, assignment editor, newswriter, cameraperson, programming planner, continuity writer, and advertising (or public service announcement) writer. Writers are hired for these jobs either on a full-time or part-time basis. At small Christian commercial stations, the norm is to employ no more than one full-time writer.

Freelance writers are most often used in religious broadcasting to create dramatic scripts for radio. Radio drama for this market is religious in theme and conforms to the goals and needs of the particular station that it is written for. Before submitting a script, the writer should become familiar with the nature of the program and should know what geographic area(s) it reaches.

The Christian Broadcasting Network, located in Virginia Beach, Virginia, produces religious drama in soap opera style. Other religious broadcasters include Moody Radio Network, National Catholic Telecommunications Network, National Religious Broadcasters, Protestant Radio and TV Center, Inc., and PTL Television Network, whose addresses are given in *Broadcasting/ Cablecasting Yearbook* under "Producers, Distributors." (*See: religious writing; soap opera, writing for.*)

Additional information: *The Religious Writers Marketplace; Writing to Inspire.*

Religious writing. The field of religion offers writers many opportunities to publish through periodicals, books, and instructional materials.

There are more than 300 major magazines in the U.S. that emphasize religion. They can be grouped into the following categories: denominational, nondenominational, family, journals of opinion, magazines for church leaders, inspirational, official publications of national organizations, and Christian comic and picture books. Examples of major religious magazines are *Catholic Digest, Christianity Today, Guideposts, Hadassah, Moody Monthly,* and *The Upper Room Daily Devotional Guide.*

The current trend in this field is toward a human interest tone. Today's editors look for articles of a practical nature that are less dogmatic than those of the past, and generally eschew articles that are preachy or saccharine. Controversial topics are now accepted in fiction and given in-depth treatment in articles. In spite of these changes, however, religious overtones are still present in the magazines.

A religion writer must know his readers thoroughly, because each market is specialized and holds sacred a common set of beliefs, values, and taboos. It is important to become familiar with the publication as well; some small religious magazines have formats to be followed by the writer (e.g., number of typed characters per line) because they are limited in staff, time, and money for manuscript preparation. Writers should be aware that not all the religious magazines are published solely for nationwide audiences. Some—especially publications for organization members—are published regionally as well.

Although an article may sell for as much as $400, fees paid to writers by religious magazines are generally lower than those paid by other types of consumer magazines.

Trends in religious book publishing are reflected by the categories of books published, which in turn are influenced by such factors as Sunday school lessons. The semiannual religious book issues of *Publishers Weekly*—usually in February and September—are indicators of trends. Similarly, *Subject Guide to Books In Print* lists books in the religious field, under "Bible—Appreciation," "Christian Life," "Christianity—Psychology," "Faith," "God," "Jewish Religious Education," and "Jewish Theology." Some libraries may also have the directory *Religious Books In Print*.

Royalties in the religious publishing field may vary from the standard trade royalty of 5%-15% of list price to 5%-10% of the net receipts; and advances may be limited to a few hundred dollars at some smaller houses.

Publications used in Sunday schools and parochial schools make up an important segment of materials used for religious instruction. Although teacher's books, study books, workbooks, games, and time lines all require writers, the freelance writer finds the most frequent opportunities in the church school take-home paper. This type of publication is a magazine or leaflet intended to reinforce a student's spiritual values during the week, between class meetings.

Materials for Jewish religious instruction include mini-courses, games, songbooks, plays, teacher's manuals, and task cards; freelancers may tailor their material to one of several age groups, from preschoolers to high school students. Educa-tors in Catholic schools use religion-centered filmstrips, films, textbooks, duplicating books, pamphlets, and trade journals. (*See: audiovisual communication; juveniles, writing for; religious broadcasting.*)

Additional information: *Religious Publishing and Communications*; *The Religious Writers Marketplace*; *Writing to Inspire*.

Remainder. In book publishing, remainders are copies of a book that are slow to sell. A remainder book company sometimes purchases leftover stock from the publisher at a considerably reduced price. In this situation, the author receives either a reduced royalty, or—if the publisher has sold the remainder stock at below manufacturing cost—no royalty. These arrangements are detailed in the author's book contract.

Remote pickup/remote. A program or commercial broadcast live from a site other than the studio.

Reporters, writers, and editors, how many. Figures on file with the Bureau of Labor Statistics in 1982 showed that 59,371 persons listed their occupations as "reporters or correspondents" and 115,377 as "writers and/or editors."

Of the reporters, 35,574 worked for newspapers, 5,960 in radio and television, 1,232 for news syndicates, and the balance for miscellaneous firms.

Of the writers and/or editors, 23,792 worked for newspapers, 9,551 for magazines, 6,136 for book publishers, 4,920 for radio and television stations, 7,704 in advertising, 7,440 for the federal government, 4,261 for religious organizations,

1,950 for computer and data processing services, and the balance for a wide variety of business, industry, labor, and specialized organizations.

Reporting time on manuscripts. Reporting time on manuscripts is commonly acknowledged to be six weeks to two months for magazines and two to three months for book publishers, but the writer should check *Writer's Market* or *Fiction Writer's Market* for specifics on individual publishers. For a reply from a literary agent, a writer should allow three weeks to two months; from a literary critic, three weeks for short pieces and two months for a book. If the usual reporting period passes with no reply, the writer should send the publisher a letter inquiring about the status of the manuscript; an SASE should accompany the letter. The writer who receives no response at this stage should write the publisher, advising that the manuscript submission has been withdrawn from consideration by that firm and that another original copy is being submitted elsewhere. (*See: rejection slip.*)

Reprint. A reprint is a part of a publication, such as an article or chapter, that has been reproduced for use as a separate publication. Publishers offer reprints to their readers free or at minimal cost. Another term for reprint, which is used in literary and scholarly publications, is "offprint." Scholarly reprint publishers may reprint entire books of narrow appeal (usually from university presses) in small, expensive editions. Book publishers also sell reprint rights to other publishers, book clubs, etc. (*See: transcripts of broadcasts.*)

Reprint rights. This refers to the right granted by the copyright owner/author to a magazine to reprint an article, poem, or story after it has already appeared in another publication. Reprint rights are also called second serial rights, especially when they refer to a portion of a book that is being sold to a magazine or newspaper for printing after the book is published. If the magazine rights were exercised before publication of the book they would be first serial rights.

A magazine or newspaper editor would pay less for reprint rights to a piece than for rights to first-time use of original copy in his publication. Markets that will buy reprint rights indicate so in their listings in *Writer's Market*. (*See: multiple sales; rights to manuscripts.*)

Reprint, writer's fee for. When a writer is approached by a magazine publisher who is interested in reprinting one of his published articles, the publisher may make a specific offer or ask the writer to set his own fee. In the latter case, the author usually sets a word rate or article flat fee, which equals a percentage (say, 25%-50%) of the new publisher's pay rate for an original article as shown in *Writer's Market*. (*See: self-syndication.*)

Reprise. In a musical, the recurrence of a song that has already been performed. In later uses of a song, the title and the melody remain unchanged, but the lyrics are sometimes altered.

A reprise is a scene in itself. It can advance the plot or explicate character in a short time. In either case, it enhances the story, and its recognition value is a major part of its effect on the audience. "Tonight," from *West Side Story*, is used as a reprise. (*See: musical.*)

Research aids/techniques. In researching a subject, writers use a wide range of techniques in addition to approaching librarians and consulting traditional reference books. Books in the children's room of a public library, for example, can be helpful in that they present material in simplified terms; thus, reading them can enlighten the writer/researcher on topics that are very technical or foreign to him. A special library, which houses material on one subject or a group of related subjects, is conducive to in-depth research, as it offers specialized books and librarians expert in the field.

A writer may find information resources outside the library as well. The public relations office of a business, university, or museum, for example, yields the most up-to-date and/or historical information on a topic, while a professional organization leads the researcher to well-respected practitioners for opinions. Similarly, bibliographic items, prefaces, and introductions in books can provide the writer with names of persons who may be helpful. (Their addresses, if not given in the books, may be listed in directories of specific professions or associations, or in telephone books.) Embassies in Washington are helpful when gathering information about foreign countries. When the writer has located a primary source, he arranges to interview that person, either in person or by telephone.

A newspaper, in either the writer's home town or another city, is another valuable research source; a researcher can write the newspa-per's librarian, a department editor, or a specialty reporter, either of whom may be able to supply the telephone number of an expert on a subject the paper has written about. The mail survey, a questionnaire that serves as a simultaneous interview of several persons, can be another means of requesting information. Chambers of commerce provide a great deal of printed material, as does the federal government.

Radio and television talk shows can also furnish information for the writer. Some programs make transcripts or cassettes available, which the writer may need in order to validate his source with an editor.

Sometimes a writer can draw on his own experience for information: he may have traveled to the place with which his article is concerned, for example, or have played the sport he is writing about.

As another research tactic, the writer can simply advertise that he is researching a certain topic, choosing either a newspaper or a specialized magazine to reach possible sources. (*See: data bases; directories; interview; libraries, information on; periodicals, indexes to; primary source; research services, freelance; research sources, directories of; secondary sources; telephone usage, tactics on; transcripts of broadcasts.*) Additional information: *Writer's Resource Guide.*

Research by correspondence. Two kinds of letters are used in a writer's research. The writer may send a *request for information* to an authority in a field related to his article. This type of letter, which is specific and brief, is addressed to one person by name. The writer either encloses an SASE

316

or offers to reimburse the addressee for postage and photocopying costs. (Government agencies, however, absorb the cost of postage.) A short *thank-you letter* to those experts who reply to these letters is a professional courtesy that may aid the writer on future projects, should he need to call upon the same source. To those sources who provided assistance or information, writers sometimes send copies of the finished article after it is published. (*See: research aids/techniques; researching article material.*)

Research note-taking. When gathering material from printed sources, writers take time to digest what they read and then note key ideas in their own words. This method gives them an understanding of the material that facilitates their work at the writing stage. (Any ideas that are exceptionally well phrased may, of course, be quoted verbatim, as long as the writer gives credit either in a footnote or in the text itself.)

During the note-taking process, it is essential that the writer take down page numbers, magazine issue numbers, titles of books, the name of the library he is using, and other data, so that he can later supply an editor with his sources without a time-consuming search. Some writers prefer using 3x5 cards for these notes; others simply note the sources alongside their references in a notebook on each writing project. If the writer is doing a book, a more detailed bibliography on sources (book title, author, publisher, city of publication, copyright date, etc.) should be compiled as the research is being done. (*See: interview; tape recorder.*)

Research services, freelance. Various research jobs are available to freelancers interested in working for others, while writers who need help with their own research can seek out a freelancer for hire.

Freelancers interested in doing research work for others can query universities, public libraries, and marketing research firms. University professors sometimes hire researchers from outside the university, while freelance authors can find university graduate students to aid *them* in research. Researchers can sometimes find announcements of freelance research job openings posted on a public library's employee bulletin board.

Places to list freelance research services are *Literary Market Place* (the sections "Research & Information Services" and "Editorial Services") and the classified section of *Publishers Weekly*. Rates of pay, which vary with experience, geographic area, and nature of the work, range from $5-$20 per hour; some fees for special jobs are higher.

To find work in genealogy, researchers place ads in the *Genealogical Helper* or inquire at a local library. The genealogical researcher currently earns from $6-$10 per hour if he is certified, from $3-$5 per hour if uncertified. Genealogists become certified by both the Board of Certification of Genealogists, 1307 New Hampshire Avenue, N.W., Washington DC 20036; and the Genealogical Society of the Church of Jesus Christ of Latter-day Saints, 50 East North Temple, Salt Lake City UT 84150. (*See: directories.*)

Additional information: *Writer's Resource Guide.*

Research sources, directories of. Through libraries, writers have access to bibliographies of reference books and other kinds of research sources.

Three sources used regularly by reference librarians, for example, are Sheehy's *Guide to Reference Books*, Walford's *Guide to Reference Material*, and the *American Reference Books Annual*.

Two books that can lead the writer to other sources are the *Directory of Directories* and the *Guide to American Directories*, which are either arranged by subject matter or have subject cross-indexes.

Writers who want to see what books are currently in print on certain subjects can refer to the *Subject Guide to Books In Print*. If they want to locate the publisher of a specific book whose title or author's name they know, they can refer to *Books In Print*.

If the writer is seeking specialized research material, he may want to refer to the *Research Centers Directory* or the *Directory of Special Libraries and Information Centers*.

For research materials that may be in specialized forms, the writer can consult the *Subject Guide to Microforms in Print* and the *Encyclopedia of Information Systems and Services*. (*See: celebrity addresses; data bases; periodicals, indexes to.*)

Additional information: *Writer's Resource Guide*.

Researching article material. The research aspect of writing can seem overwhelming, but a methodical approach can simplify the task by giving the writer a path to follow.

An article can be researched efficiently if the writer has chosen a *peg*, or *slant*. A peg, by concentrating on one aspect of a topic, gives the article a focus and enables the writer to

market it to a specific magazine. For example, two possible pegs of the topic "bubble gum" are "How is it manufactured?" and "How have marketing techniques for it changed over the years?"

Research begins at a library, where the writer checks *Readers' Guide to Periodical Literature*, other indexes, and the card catalogue for previously published articles and books on his chosen topic. Reading published material gives him background information as well as further sources in the form of experts' names. (If the writer uncovers a recent article on the same topic with the same slant as his projected one, he begins researching a different peg, since chances of selling a new peg will be better.)

The next step is addressing the experts mentioned in the published material. The writer may do this by telephone, personal interview, or mail. Firsthand information from, or opinions of, experts lends authority to an article.

These three steps form the basis of article research. Follow-up letters or telephone calls are sometimes necessary, however, to clarify or augment points made during an interview. (*See: organizing article/book material; research aids/techniques.*)

Residual rights. Rights that the copyright owner has retained; or rights that he has sold but may expect to re-own in the future, such as rights that have been transferred and may be returned to him under the copyright law after 35 years.

The term *residual rights* also refers to a particular kind of rights owned by performers. These rights provide for performers to be paid for use or sale of their recorded, taped, or filmed work; the amount of payment is determined in the performer's contract or the union contract under which he works. For example, a television producer contracts to use a commercial for a given number of weeks. After the first period has ended, he is given the option to use the commercial for another designated period, but from that point on, he must pay fees, called *residuals*, to the performers.

Resolution and reversal. (*See: falling action.*)

Restarting your writing. There are several methods of restarting a writing project too lengthy to be completed in one session. Following are three standard practices; individual writers can, of course, invent other methods more personally suitable.

One technique is to stop in the middle of writing an idea or a sentence. At the start of the next writing session, the writer, having this idea in his mind, knows exactly how and where to pick up.

As another way to begin, some writers retype the last page typed in the previous session; this helps remind the writer of the mood and style of his piece.

A third method consists of destroying the last page typed in the previous session, then reconstructing and retyping it from memory. This technique sets the writer's mind, as well as his fingers, in motion.

Restaurant review. A critical account of the writer's experience at a restaurant, written for a newspaper or magazine. The restaurant review usually includes comments on food, service, atmosphere (including other patrons), and menu.

To qualify for restaurant reviewing, a person must have an appreciation for food and its preparation, have dined out frequently, and have an ability to write about food. Knowledge of food may come from professional experience in the food industry, experience preparing fine cuisine at home, or study of books in the field. The unpublished reviewer should approach an editor with sample reviews and a letter explaining his interest in restaurant reviewing. (For this first impression, he might review a restaurant that is out of the way and that is not often reviewed.)

A general guide for payment is that the reviewer receives enough to double his dining expenses. Once the freelance reviewer is getting regular assignments from one publication, he is likely to be paid monthly, the payments being based on the average cost per month of his meals.

One way to minimize expenses, and at the same time get the opportunity to sample several dishes from the menu, is to visit a restaurant with a group of friends or of associates in the food industry. (The latter could add another dimension to the reviewer's own critical sense.)

An ideal situation for the reviewer is being seated where he will not be observed by the head waiter and where he has a comprehensive view of the room. No matter where his table is located, the reviewer should make it a point to sit with his back to the wall.

A strategy used by one reviewer is to make certain that his photograph is not included in his column. Omitting the photograph lessens his chances of being recognized by restaurateurs, who sometimes provide atypically choice service to critics' tables. Another way to avoid being found out as a critic is to use a different, fictional name each time reservations are made.

In addition, when taking a tape recorder to a restaurant, discretion is necessary: one reviewer advises that it is best to keep this tool concealed until after the entrée has arrived; another never takes a tape recorder, and has learned to take notes on index cards on his knee, under the table. To be fair to the restaurant, the critic should visit it at least twice before writing a review. Similarly, good judgment and a keen sense of taste are needed during the meal, so the critic should not overindulge in alcohol.

Because restaurateurs in some cases threaten or take legal action when faced with unfavorable reviews, the reviewer should keep his notes so that he can later prove that his comments were based on the actual situation he encountered.

Writers interested in acquiring more background in the food field and restaurant reviewing should read the works of food writers James Beard, Julia Child, and M.F. Fisher; major food magazines such as *Gourmet* and *Bon Appetit*; and leading newspaper reviewers such as Mimi Sheraton in the *New York Times*. (*See: arts review*.)

Résumé writing, business of. A writer who creates résumés for others can establish a full- or part-time business at home. Earnings, which depend on the writer's geographic location, range from $35-$85 per résumé.

Résumé writers obtain new clients through newspaper classified advertisements and referrals from clients. The client schedules an appointment with the writer, at which time he is interviewed and/or asked to fill out a questionnaire. During the interview, the writer gathers such information as what field the client is in, what type of work he is interested in doing in the future, what jobs he has held in the past (and at present), how much education he has, what his military background is (if any), and what his personal history entails (i.e., family, hobbies, memberships, health, height, weight, age, address, and telephone number). Based on the information gathered from the interview and/or questionnaire, the writer drafts the résumé, then proofreads the finished product and presents it to the client for a second lookover. Some writers deliver the finished résumés to the client. Writer Jan A. Noble, Sr., suggests charging a flat fee for all services involved in preparing a résumé.

Regarding the client's initial inquiry, Noble advises: "Tell (the client) that if he is dissatisfied with the résumé, you will refund his money in full. But don't promise anything but a professional résumé prepared confidentially. You can't guarantee that it will get him a job or that it will get him an interview with a particular employer."

A freelance résumé writer can sometimes associate with an employment agency by paying the agency a commission of 5%-10% for every referral he obtains from them, and/or by making his business card available in the agency's office. Writers interested in working for another person can seek full- or part-time work at commercial résumé services, which advertise in the Yellow Pages. (*See: résumés.*)

Résumés. Though all résumés contain the same basic information, they can be divided into categories on the basis of purpose. The *sequential résumé* lists all an employee's previous jobs, and the duties performed in each, accompanied by the dates he began and left each with the most recent job listed first. The *functional résumé*, especially beneficial to employees with little experience or with periods of unemployment, omits dates and details an employee's jobs in terms of accomplishment.

In the *skills résumé*, sections headed by names of skills, such as editing, proofreading, and pasteup, that the applicant has used, follow the applicant's name and address, which are placed first among the items. Following these two sections are "Education," "Experience," "Personal Background," and "Job Objective." The "Experience" section is where the applicant denotes specific companies or organizations for which he has worked.

The *creative résumé* breaks the rules of standard résumé form and appearance. For example, it could contain artwork, be printed on colored paper, or be designed in the form of an advertisement. This type of résumé succeeds only in certain fields. Before using it, the writer should consider whether creativity is appropriate to the field in which he is seeking work.

Finally, the *curriculum vitae* is a kind of résumé that contains, along with the applicant's qualifications for a job, more details about his professional memberships, publications, etc., than does the con-

ventional résumé used in business. It is used to apply for jobs in academe. (*Curriculum vitae* is a Latin term meaning "the course of one's life or career.")

All résumés should begin with the employee's name, address, and telephone number. (Including an alternate telephone number where a message can be taken gives the applicant the advantage of ensuring that the employers will be able to reach him.) Sometimes personal data, such as family situation, health status, height, and weight, are included as well, if such information strengthens the job-seeker's candidacy.

Stating salary requirements on a résumé is detrimental, since it can decrease negotiating power at the interview stage. Similarly, names and addresses of references are better replaced by a strong letter of recommendation sent along with the résumé, or a statement that they are available on request.

Indicating a career or job objective is a practice that, though instituted recently, is becoming accepted as standard. The applicant includes this information (usually in a short phrase, such as "reference librarian") below the heading "objective" or "employment objective." This heading is placed after the applicant's personal data and before information on his work experience, which is followed by a description of his educational background. If the applicant would accept employment in any of several jobs, he may list all the jobs, in order of preference, under one of these two headings.

The applicant who is qualified to work in more than one field may wish to prepare a separate résumé for each field, according to "Merchandising Your Job Talents," a U.S. Department of Labor publication. This tactic can also be helpful when the applicant will approach different kinds of institutions that seek different kinds of credentials. ("Merchandising Your Job Talents" is available in those public libraries which are depositories for U.S. Government publications.

Samples of functional and simplified résumés appear in the Appendix to this encyclopedia. (*See: résumé writing, business of.*)

Additional information: *Resume Writing: A Comprehensive, How-to-Do-It Guide; What Color Is Your Parachute?; Who's Hiring Who;* and *Martin's Magic Formula for Getting the Right Job.*

Retainer. A retainer is a working arrangement by which a writer is paid a fee at regular intervals but works for the client irregularly, on an as-needed basis. The client could be a business, a non-profit organization, a politician, a professional association, or the sponsor of a special event.

With the guaranteed income of a retainer, the freelance writer can be discriminating in accepting writing assignments from other sources. (On the other hand, the writer on retainer is at the client's beck and call.) Retainers give the writer firsthand knowledge of certain businesses or organizations, which can sometimes be applied to freelance articles. The writer should, of course, be concerned about potential conflicts of interest in his other writing jobs.

Pay from a retainer client is usually received in monthly or semi-monthly installments, having been originally established as a flat fee for a set period of time, as outlined in a letter of agreement. Rates depend on the writer's ability and experience, and the field the client is in.

Retirement and the freelance writer. Unlike the employee, who is compensated by his employer, the full-time freelance writer must anticipate retirement and take the initiative in providing for it. The federal government has devised two plans for setting aside retirement funds for self-employed persons.

Under the Keogh Act (the Self-Employed Individuals Tax Retirement Act) of 1962, a self-employed person is entitled to establish a retirement fund that is tax free until he withdraws it—presumably at retirement when his tax bracket is lower. Specifically, this law allows for a writer to set aside as much as 15% of his net annual income, the maximum allowed being $30,000 per year, in an Internal-Revenue-Service-approved account. This savings is tax deductible for that year. Funds must remain in the account until the owner reaches age 59½; the owner must begin to draw on them when he reaches age 70½. In addition, he is not obligated to deposit money every year. Penalties for early withdrawal are the discontinuance of tax-free accumulation of interest and a tax penalty.

The Individual Retirement Account (IRA) is another version of the retirement fund established by an individual. Under the new tax law of 1982, any worker may establish an IRA account of up to $2,000 per year for single persons, $2,250 for married persons, whether or not the employee's company also has a retirement program.

For persons wishing to invest,

there are various plans available through banks, savings and loan associations, and other financial institutions. (*See: social security.*)

Additional information: *Law and the Writer.*

Returns. A term that refers to books that a bookstore was unable to sell and has sent back to the publisher. One type of arrangement between publisher and bookstore is that a bookstore may receive full credit on books that are returned during the first year after they were bought.

When returning paperback books, the wholesale distributor keeps the books' pages, which it sometimes sells as paper pulp, returning only the covers. When dealing with hardcover books, the bookstore returns the complete product. Many publishers also offer a "self-remaindering" program whereby the bookstores clip a designated portion of the dust jacket or an inside page and mark the book down for sale in their stores. The clipped portions are then returned to the publisher in exchange for a small amount of credit.

The "reserve against returns" clause of an author's contract denotes that the publisher can estimate the amount of returns he expects on sales to bookstores and pay the author's royalties based on that estimate. Returns on a first novel, for example, could run as high as 50%. If more sales (fewer returns) are actually made, the publisher later pays the remaining royalties owed.

Reversion of rights. The writer should make certain that this clause (also called the *out-of-print, termination,* or *discontinuance of manufacture* clause) is included in his book contract with a publisher. The reversion of rights clause should provide that, when the publisher allows the original hardback edition of a book to go out of print and declines to reprint the book within a reasonable time period, *all* rights—not just publication rights—revert to the author.

Conventional clauses require that the author, upon discovering the book to be out of print, write to the publisher, requesting that the book be reprinted. According to the suggested contract established by Poets & Writers, Inc., the publisher must then notify the author within 60 days of receipt of this request, indicating his intention to comply or not. This suggested contract states that the publisher will reprint the book within six months of this correspondence, "unless prevented from doing so by circumstances beyond his control." If the publisher does not respond at all to the author's request, or if he fails to reprint the book within the six months, all rights revert to the author, with the exception of those licenses (rights) previously granted by the publisher to another party. Other contracts may give the publisher longer than six months to reprint the book. It is important, however, to establish a deadline—whether it be six months, two years, or whatever the author feels is reasonable.

It is often the author's responsibility to determine whether or not his book has gone out of print, since some publishers do not advise authors of the fact. Failure to receive a royalty statement may be the author's first clue that the book is no longer in print. The author should then write the editor or the president of the company asking if the book has gone out of print, and if so, to cancel the contract and revert the rights to him. If the reply is that the book is "Temporarily Out of Stock," then a printing date should be expected from the publisher almost immediately. If the reply is that the book will not be reprinted, the author may wish to notify the publisher of an interest in buying either the negatives, plates, or remaining copies of the book at the cost of manufacture or the remainder cost, since the reversion of rights or discontinuance of manufacture clause also normally offers the author the right to buy the negatives or plates of the book, as well as remaining copies of the bound book, at a discount.

An author should make certain to include a precise reversion of rights clause in his contract, since a reprinter may be interested in publishing the book at some point in the future. This would mean another advance and royalty for the author. There is also the possibility that an out-of-print book will be "rediscovered," as was the case with *The Awakening*, an 1889 novel that was revived in the late 1960s and early 1970s during the period of intensely renewed interest in women's literature. *The Awakening*, once out of print, has been reprinted in several editions since 1972. (*See: author's copies; book contract; Poets & Writers, Inc.; reprint; rights to manuscripts.*)

Review copy. A free copy of a bound book, sent to newspapers, magazines, journals, and syndicates that carry book reviews, and often to radio and television programs that discuss books or interview authors. A publisher distributes review copies in the hope of securing the "free" publicity that good reviews stimulate.

Of course, this type of publicity is not really free; review copies subtract from the publisher's profit and they do not earn any royalties for the author. The number of review copies distributed is, therefore, usually limited to approximately 100-150 books. A smaller publisher may send out only 25 books to reviewers, particularly if the book has a very specialized interest; a major publisher, on the other hand, may distribute as many as 500 review copies of an anticipated bestseller.

Publishers have their own lists of reviewing media to whom they regularly send review copies. They may supplement a general list with an individually selected roster of specialist newspapers, magazines, journals, etc., slanted toward the subject matter of the book. A publisher will often make use of an author's expertise, inviting him to suggest publications likely to review the book, as well as contacts in the book's subject field who may be willing to promote it.

Although an effective means of securing "free" publicity, getting a book reviewed is by no means an easy method of promotion. While there are a number of consumer review media, none but the *New York Times Book Review*—a Sunday supplement to the *New York Times*—and the *New York Review of Books* are devoted almost exclusively to reviewing new titles; even these media can review only a few thousand new books each year. Combining the number of book reviews that appear in major newspapers such as the

Chicago Tribune and national magazines such as *Time, Harper's, Newsweek,* and *The New Yorker,* as well as the many smaller newspapers, regional publications, and journals that regularly review books, does not even come close to the total of more than 40,000 new books published each year. Consequently, competition among publishing houses is keen for the little media space that is available for book reviews.

Of course, a review in a national publication may not always work to a book's advantage. A less-than-enthusiastic discussion of the book can hurt sales rather than help them. (*See: prepublication review; promotion by author.*)

Revising and rewriting. (*See: first draft, revising and rewriting.*)

Rhyme. (*See: verse.*)

Rhythm and blues (R&B). A popular music form stemming from the rhythms and emotional intensity of black music, rhythm and blues is also identified as *soul* music. It currently combines aspects of modern rock music for popular sounds.

Right of privacy. The right of privacy is a legal right protecting a living individual's peace of mind, spirit, sensibilities and feelings, and allowing that person to live as he sees fit without his name, visage, or activities becoming public property, unless he waives or relinquishes that right.

As a general rule, "public figures," corporations, and public institutions have no right of privacy, nor can relatives of deceased persons suffer invasion of their right of privacy from any grief or embarrassment caused by publicity concerning the deceased. (*See: libel; privacy, invasion of; right of publicity.*)

Additional information: *Law and the Writer; Synopsis of the Law of Libel and the Right of Privacy.*

Right of publicity. Many people in the public eye—entertainers, sports figures, and other celebrities—object to the exploitation or *misappropriation* of their name, likeness, or performance for pure advertising and commercial purposes without their consent, and the law supports their "right of publicity."

As a general rule, this right dies with the person, although some courts have enforced the rights of heirs of such celebrities as Elvis Presley and Humphrey Bogart to control the commercial exploitation of their celebrity relatives. (*See: libel; privacy, invasion of; right of privacy.*)

Additional information: *Law and the Writer; Synopsis of the Law of Libel and the Right of Privacy.*

Rights For Sale. (See the Appendix to this encyclopedia.)

Rights license period. This term refers to the amount of time that a publisher owns the publishing rights to a particular book. In most cases, when an author signs a contract regarding a hardcover book, the publisher retains the publishing rights to the book for as long as the book stays in print. However, when the book goes out of print, the author may usually reobtain the rights by terminating the contract a certain number of months after the book goes out of print.

To publish a paperback version of a book, the paperback publisher licenses rights from a hardcover publisher. The *rights license period* for such a book is usually five years.

Rights to class assignments. Freelance writers who have been students in college classes where an assignment involves, for example, creating hypothetical advertising copy for a local company sometimes complain that their ideas and/or portions of their manuscripts have been appropriated by the instructor and proper credit and/or remuneration have been denied the student. Ideas, of course, are uncopyrightable, but there is an ethical as well as a legal question regarding misappropriation of another's literary property for one's own advantage.

One college faculty handbook addresses this question this way: "The right to assign work to students that may contribute to their own or to general knowledge, is accompanied by the obligation not to exploit them or to infringe upon their academic freedom, and to give full credit for work done by them." The American Association of University Professors' Statement on Professional Ethics reads in part: ". . . a teacher . . . . avoids any exploitation of his students for his private advantage and acknowledges significant assistance from them."

One way freelance writers might forestall any intentional or unintentional misappropriation of their work is to use a copyright credit line (i.e., copyright/year/name) in the upper right-hand corner of manuscripts where they think the problem might occur.

Rights to manuscripts. Rights are sold to editors and publishers in varying forms and degrees. An established writer usually has more power to negotiate than a novice does; nevertheless, any writer should try to avoid, in most instances, selling all rights to a piece of work. The kinds of rights most commonly sold to magazine editors are outlined below. Rights granted to book publishers are discussed in the entry on subsidiary rights in this encyclopedia.

First serial rights are sold to periodicals (serials). Included in these rights is the agreement that the periodical will be the first publisher of the material. First serial rights can be restricted to include a particular area; for example, modified versions are first North American serial rights and first U.S. serial rights.

Second serial (reprint) rights are rights sold to a newspaper or magazine with an article, story, or poem that has previously been published in another periodical. An excerpt from a published book, regardless of whether it was previously published in a periodical, will also customarily be sold to a periodical with second serial (reprint) rights.

Foreign serial rights, rights sold to a market abroad, can be sold by a writer—provided he still has the rights. For example, if a writer has sold first U.S. serial rights to an American magazine, he is free to market the same piece in Europe; if, however, a U.S. publisher has purchased "first serial rights," without any limiting phrase, the publisher may have foreign editions and be assuming he has ensured that he will be the first to publish it in any country in the world.

The term *syndication rights* refers to rights sold to a syndicate under the term "serial rights." A book published in installments in several newspapers, for example, would be placed under this category. If the newspaper installments appeared before the book's publication, the author would be syndicating first serial rights to the book; if the installments appeared after publication, he would be syndicating second serial rights.

Simultaneous rights are rights sold to two different publishers (whose circulations do not compete) at the same time. The publisher who owns several magazines might also buy simultaneous rights to use the same piece in two or three of his publications. When a piece is being submitted to more than one publication simultaneously, it is best to advise the editors accordingly.

When an editor buys *all rights* to a piece, the writer loses his right to sell it to another publisher. A work-made-for-hire agreement is one that includes the writer's selling of all rights in addition to the copyright.

A writer can also sell rights to his work to other media, namely theater, television, and film. *Dramatic rights, television rights,* and *motion picture rights* are often offered at a percentage of the total price as an option to buy for a specific period of time. The property is then brought to the attention of people in the industry—actors, directors, studios, or television networks—for possible production.

The copyright law that took effect January 1, 1978, provides the creator of a piece of writing with all rights as soon as the work is complete. He may sell all or part of those rights, but the power to decide which, belongs to him. A chart showing the various rights available for sale in a manuscript appears in the Appendix to this encyclopedia. (*See: check con-tract; copyright; dramatic rights; magazine editorial contract; simultaneous submission; subsidiary rights; work made for hire.*)

Rising action. Although most often used relative to the plot structure of a play, the term *rising action* can also be useful in describing the plot structure of some works of fiction.

Rising action refers to the first stage of the plot that begins with the presentation of essential information through narration and dialogue (particularly information about what events have occurred before the action begins), rises through a complication (the protagonist encounters some conflict or opposing force), and peaks at the crisis or climax (the moment of highest intensity, when a decision must be made or an action taken to resolve the conflict). The events that occur from the moment of crisis until the end of the play or story are described as *falling action.* (*See: climax; crisis; falling action; plot.*)

Rock. Music form that originated in the 1950s as *rock-and-roll* and had evolved from a meshing of blues, gospel, jazz, folk, and ragtime sounds. It was characterized by strong, driving rhythms played by small groups rather than the big bands of the previous era. The music was made popular by black entertainers such as Chuck Berry and Little Richard but soon was picked up by white performers such as Elvis Presley and Jerry Lee Lewis, among others. In the 60s, rock was strongly influenced by British groups such as the Beatles and the Rolling Stones. In the 70s, some rock music was typified by an emphasis on electrified instruments and became known as *heavy metal rock* or *acid rock* (because of its identification with the hallucinogen LSD or "acid"). In the late 70s, punk rock originated in Britain with its high-energy sound and with lyrics and performers' attire and routines aimed at making social statements about today's lifestyles.

Rock music is continually evolving. To keep up with the changes in rock music, songwriters should listen to local radio stations that program currently popular rock singles and albums, and read trade/consumer magazines such as *Billboard*, *Cashbox*, and *Rolling Stone*, as well as record and concert reviews in other magazines and in newspapers.

Roman à clef. The French term for "novel with a key." This type of novel incorporates real persons and events into the story under the guise of fiction. Robert Penn Warren's *All the King's Men*, in which the character Willie Stark represents Huey Long, is a novel in this genre. (*See: faction.*)

Romance novel. Also known as the *category romance*, the romance novel is a type of category fiction in which the love relationship between a man and a woman pervades the plot. The story is told from the point of view of the heroine, who meets a man (the hero), falls in love with him, encounters a conflict that hinders their relationship, then resolves the conflict. As opposed to many gothic romances, settings in these stories are always contemporary; the characters are modern. Though marriage is not necessarily the outcome of the story, the ending is always happy.

Romance is the overriding element in this kind of story: the couple's relationship determines the plot and tone of the book. The theme of the novel is the woman's sexual awakening. Although she may not be a virgin, she has never before been so emotionally aroused. Despite all this emotion, however, characters and plot both must be well-developed and realistic: contrived situations and flat characters are unacceptable.

Throughout a romance novel, the reader senses the sexual and emotional attraction between the heroine and hero. Lovemaking scenes, though sometimes detailed, are not generally too graphic, because more emphasis is placed on the sensual element than on physical action.

Romance novels fall into three distinct formats. The *sensual romance*, which is currently the bestselling type, is illustrated by the Candlelight Ecstasy, Silhouette Desire, and NAL Rapture lines. The emphasis in these plots is on the sensual tension between the hero and heroine, as well as the sizzling sexual scenes. The *spicy romance*, which includes Harlequin SuperRomances, Harlequin Presents, Silhouette Special Editions, and Jove's Second Chance at Love, is exemplified in stories in which married characters resolve (to a happy end) their problems; books in these lines consist of less sex and more story, compared to some other lines of romances. The *sweet romance*, which is on the wane at the moment, is published in the Mills & Boon/Harlequin Romances, Silhouette Romances, Bantam's Circle of Love, and NAL's Adventures in Love. Many of the heroines in sweet romances are virgins, and the stories contain little if any sex.

The appeal of the romance recently reached the teenaged market, and Scholastic Books, Silhouette, NAL, and Bantam are approaching this age group with romances highlighting relationships of 16-year-old contemporary heroines and their 17- to 18-year-old beaux. The stories concern the problems of growing up and the difficulties of romantic encounters in youth. Explicit sex and highly controversial issues such as abortion and unmarried pregnancy are not considered by editors of teenage romance novels.

Today's romance novel differs from its counterpart of the past in that it reflects society's increasing respect for women. "Bodice-rippers" and "rape sagas," though still being published in the historical romance field, are becoming less popular than category romances, as authors and readers increasingly subscribe to the values fostered by the women's movement. Some publishers now recommend in their guidelines that the heroine have a career; others are loosening the restrictions on the status of women deemed acceptable heroines. Heroines in Ballantine Books's "Love and Life" romance line, for example, may be divorced, widowed, or married, as well as single women.

Each publisher of romances has detailed, specific guidelines regarding his line. The publisher will stipulate, for example, whether the setting may be a foreign country or within the U.S., whether the heroine may engage in sex outside of marriage, whether marriage will oc-

cur at novel's end, and whether the heroine is in her 20s, 30s, or another age group. In addition, publishers specify lengths for romances, which usually are from 50,000-60,000 words; books in some lines, however, are longer, such as Harlequin's Worldwide SuperRomances, which run about 95,000 words.

The romance writer's submission to a publisher includes a query letter, a synopsis and the first 50 pages of the novel, and an SASE. It is advantageous for the writer to provide in the letter not only a summary of his experience, but also an indication of his familiarity with romance novels, i.e., how many of which publishers' romances he has read.

Yearly sales of romance novels currently represent one-fourth of mass-market softcover volumes. Most romance writers are women, but some male authors have broken into the market by using female pseudonyms. Many novels in this genre are written by first-time novelists. *Fiction Writer's Market* lists publishers who solicit romance novels. Advances vary, but $3,000 could be an average for a new author, and royalty could be 6% and up on retail price.

A Romantic Book Lovers' Conference is held every April in New York City. Writing workshops, publishers' hospitality suites, and an opportunity to meet agents are features of this three-day event.

The Romance Writers of America is an organization dedicated to spreading the legitimacy of the romance novel and giving it recognition as a popular genre of adult fiction. Its members attend national and regional conferences for publishers, editors, readers, writers, and agents.

Three publications for and about romance readers/writers and the industry are: *Romantic Times*, 163 Joralemon Street, Suite 1234, Brooklyn Heights NY 11201; *Boy Meets Girl*, Rainy Day Books, 2812 W. 53rd Street, Fairway KS 66205; and *Affaire de Coeur*, 5660 Roosevelt Place, Fremont CA 94538. (*See: gothic; Romance Writers of America; romantic suspense novel.*)

Romance Writers of America (RWA). This is a new organization, established in 1979. Writers need not be published to join RWA, whose more than 1,500 members include individuals in 10 foreign countries and more than 60 local chapters.

RWA strives to make romantic fiction a recognized genre to increase interest in it, to support and encourage writers in their careers, and to provide market information. The Golden Heart Award, presented annually, recognizes an RWA member who is an unpublished writer of romantic fiction. The Golden Medallion Award, presented annually, recognizes the best in published romantic fiction. RWA publishes a bimonthly newspaper, *Romance Writers Report*. It holds an annual conference and regional conferences. RWA's president is Bobbie R. Jolly; executive secretary, Patricia Hudgins. Headquarters of the organization are at 5206 F.M. 1960 West, Suite 207, Houston TX 77069.

Romantic suspense novel. The romantic suspense novel is a modern emergence of early gothic writing. This genre evolved in the 1950s with such writers as Mary Stewart and Victoria Holt; around 1960, romantic suspense novels began appearing in paperback.

Though the genre resembles the traditional gothic in that it pits an admirable heroine against some force of evil, it has distinctive characteristics of its own. Romantic suspense novels differ from the usual gothic form in tone, setting, and character. Whereas gothic novels do not include sexually explicit scenes, romantic suspense novelists may choose to incorporate either sexually vivid passages or nonexplicit episodes. In addition, recent novels have not bound their heroines to bleak estates and gloomy mansions; rather, they have freed them to roam the world in either a historical or contemporary setting. Romantic suspense novels are not confined to a mystery angle in their plots; instead, they may emphasize the mounting anxiety of the heroine's confrontations with evil.

The genre is recognizable when contrasted with other writing. It is not a detective mystery story because the law (police) rarely gets involved in the action. It also differs from traditional "male" suspense novels because it moves more slowly and has more character interplay and psychological conflict than the fast-paced violence of suspense thrillers. Though romantic suspense novels have a small male readership, they are written mostly by women, for women.

The market for this escapist fiction is a potentially lucrative one for writers: the skillfully written work may sell 100,000 copies and more in softcover. Authors' advances and royalties may range from $1,500 for a short paperback to five figures for a novel by a well-established writer. Book publishers and magazines soliciting romantic suspense novels are listed in *Fiction Writer's Market*. (*See: gothic; romance novel.*)

330

ROS. Run of schedule. Refers to a commercial whose broadcast time is scheduled by the station rather than the sponsor.

Ross Reports Television. This monthly New York Television Talent Report is used by actors, writers, technicians, and other TV personnel to keep abreast of producers of television commercials, dramatic serials, and other New York and West Coast television script markets. Subscription information is available from Television Index, Inc., 150 Fifth Avenue, New York NY 10011.

Round character. A round character is a fictional person so specifically portrayed and described as to be recognizable and individually different from any other character in a novel, play, or film. The protagonist and other main participants of a work are usually round characters: their development is complicated and tends to focus on their inner person (motivations, human traits, flaws, conflicts, distinctive qualities). Hamlet, for example, is a round character.

Minor characters are generally flat, less fully developed characters. (*See: character; flat character.*)

Round-up. In journalism, a news story or broadcast compiled from a number of sources or geographic areas. The term also refers to a short broadcast of the latest news.

Round-up article. A kind of article containing direct quotes on a subject from various notable persons. The writer chooses a topic that is likely to bring opinionated or subjective responses during interviews, then rounds up the responses for the article. Examples of round-up articles

are "The Nation's Five Top Football Coaches Pick the All-Time Greats" and "Three Up-and-Coming Starlets Talk About Beauty." Round-ups can be sold to a wide variety of magazines whenever a writer finds a topic of interest to a magazine's readership and a group of interviewees whose opinions that audience respects or is curious about.

Royalties. (*See: book contract.*)

Royalty auditing services. If his contract includes the right, an author may hire an auditing service to check a publisher's records when he believes that he is not being paid the agreed-upon amount in royalties. Underpayment of royalties by publishers has three major causes: clerical error, disputable interpretations of contractual clauses by publishers, and overly high projections by publishers of the number of returns. (Most publishers' contracts contain a provision allowing the withholding of a percentage of royalties to cover the subsequent return of books previously ordered.)

An accountant engaged in such a situation reviews the publisher's records, which include billings, discount schedules, ledgers, and inventory; interprets contracts; composes reports; and serves as a negotiator. Fees for these services range from $50-$70 per hour. However, since royalty examinations in general have been known to cost from

$2,500 to $25,000, only an author with sales sufficient to warrant such an audit usually engages an accounting firm. A publication, "Author's access to information from book publishers," is available free, for an SASE, from PEN American Center, 47 Fifth Avenue, New York NY 10003. (*See: book contract; book publishing economics [in the Appendix]*.)

Royalty publishing. The method of publishing a book in which a publisher purchases a manuscript it thinks has a reasonable chance of selling enough copies to pay for its publication and turn a profit. As payment, the author receives a *royalty*—a percentage of the book's income—for every copy the publisher sells. (Royalties on textbooks and professional books are based on net receipts rather than the retail price.) The standard royalty rate for clothbound books is 10% of the retail price on the first 5,000 copies, 12½% on the next 5,000, and 15% on everything thereafter. Original mass market paperback royalties are 6% and up of net sales.

In most cases, the publisher gives the author an *advance* against royalties, which may be paid as a lump sum or in two or three separate payments upon delivery of various portions of the manuscript. Depending on the book, the author's reputation, and the book's projected sales, the advance can range from as little as a few hundred to many thousands of dollars; once the accumulated royalties exceed the amount of the advance, the author receives royalty payments quarterly or semiannually on additional sales of the book. A sample royalty statement and a chart of book publishing eco-

nomics appear in the Appendix to this encyclopedia.

Some authors who find it difficult to place their books with commercial publishers are exploring alternative methods of publication. (*See: co-publishing; self-publishing; small press; subsidy publishing; trade paperbacks.*)

Running gag. A running gag is a situation or punch line repeated at intervals in a comic routine. Some famous comedians repeat a running gag throughout their careers—Jack Benny's radio routine, for example, in which Rochester would need a small amount of money for something and pinch-penny Benny would go to the basement (unlocking noisily chained doors, etc., in the process) to get the money from his vault. (Because of his skillful and frequent use of the running gag, Benny has been called the master of this technique.)

A stand-up comic sometimes takes advantage of a joke that fails in front of an audience. During the same routine, each time a joke fails to elicit laughter, the comedian, as a running gag, explains the first unsuccessful joke. This variation is used by Bob Hope and Johnny Carson.

The classic example of the running gag was in the Broadway show, *Hellzapoppin*: a delivery boy appears from time to time with a plant, announcing, "Flower delivery for Mr. Abercrombie." Each time he tries to deliver the plant, it is larger and more awkward, until, at the end of the play, it is a tree in which the delivery boy sits in the lobby. As the theatergoers depart, they hear him announce, "Flower delivery for Mr. Abercrombie." (*See: comedy writing.*)

Said, substitutes for, in dialogue. In their attempt to use verbs of attribution that are interesting and varied, some writers choose inappropriate verbs to substitute for *said*. The resulting sentence can contain a verb that is awkward or simply illogical (when an unsuitable verb is chosen).

The key to using colorful verbs of attribution lies in refraining from overusing them. Although such words as *muttered, prompted, pleaded,* and *warned* can be used judiciously to clarify the emotional overtones of a scene, overuse of substitutes is often unnecessary; in a section of effective dialogue, the word *said* doesn't register in the mind of the reader. A fiction writer, through what his character says and does, has much better means of establishing character; in fact, unusual verbs of attribution tend to draw attention to the mechanics, and not the meaning, of a piece of dialogue.

Other pitfalls of dialogue writing are redundancy, as in "he asked, questioningly," and use of a verb when a modifier is needed, as in " 'Please come in,' he smiled," instead of " 'Please come in,' he said, smiling."

When a substitute for *said* interrupts the flow of reading or reasoning, it should be changed. *Said,* being the simplest word, is often the most effective. When the speaker of each statement is clear to the reader and the section of dialogue is fairly short, neither the word *said* nor a substitute is necessary.

St. Louis Journalism Review. (*See: media reviewers.*)

Salvaging a manuscript. A manuscript that has been returned to an author wrinkled or crumpled may be salvaged from the time and expense of retyping by ironing the pages. A touch-up with the iron will also remove paper clip marks impressed on manuscript pages.

Freelance writer/teacher Elizabeth Allen offers the following directions for restoring wrinkled pages: "Get out your iron. If it is a steam iron, do not use water. Set it on Wash-and-Wear. Then iron each page of your manuscript. It will look as though you had just gotten it ready for its first flight." Sometimes only the first page needs freshening this way. Other writers who have experimented with the ironing trick recommend that the page be ironed on the back rather than the front, so as not to smear the ink.

There may come a time when a manuscript is so rumpled that pressing the pages will not restore respectability. If a writer feels the material in a worn manuscript still has a chance, he must retype it before submitting to another market. (*See: manuscript preparation and submission; photocopied manuscripts.*)

Sarcasm. This term applies to taunting, bitter remarks spoken or written with the intention of hurting another's feelings. Sarcasm involves a deliberate personal attack, and is usually expressed in a contemptuous, sneering manner. Sarcasm may make use of irony; that is, saying one thing but meaning the opposite. Unlike true irony, however, sarcasm makes no attempt to disguise the real meaning beneath the apparent one. Sarcasm is always bitter and derisive, whereas irony need not be cruel. (*See: humor; irony; satire.*)

SASE. This acronym stands for "self-addressed, stamped envelope." An SASE is a necessary part of every submitted manuscript or query letter. Some editors will not reply without it.

Satire. A literary technique that mocks a powerful or influential personality, institution, moral code, or social trend, often using exaggeration and irony to point out the flaws and shortcomings of its target. While anger and contempt frequent-

ly underlie a work of satire, the satirist's most powerful tools are wit and humor, which pique the reader's or listener's sense of the ridiculous and thus undermine the subject—hence Mark Twain's statement that "against the assault of laughter nothing can stand." No matter how strongly the satirist feels about his subject, if he wishes to be effective he must remember to entertain his audience, not preach to them.

Satirists of ancient times include the Greek playwright Aristophanes and the Romans Juvenal and Horace. (Some experts classify all satire either as Juvenalian—meaning that it incorporates bitterness— or Horatian, which is more lighthearted mockery.) The seventeenth and eighteenth centuries produced the English satirists Pope, Dryden, and Swift, and the French satirists Molière and Voltaire.

Among the best-known American satirists are Robert Benchley, James Thurber, and S.J. Perelman. Cartoonist Garry Trudeau and newspaper columnist Art Buchwald are highly regarded contemporary political satirists; popular satirists of a more general nature are essayist Fran Lebowitz and *New York Times* columnist Russell Baker. Satiric essays appear in the *New Yorker*, *Esquire*, and other comparatively "literary" magazines, while the *National Lampoon* and *Mad* Magazine are wholly devoted to satire. (*See: humor.*)

"Satisfactory" clause. A clause found in every publisher/author contract; it allows the publisher to reject a completed manuscript if it is not found to be "satisfactory." What constitutes "satisfactory" may be specified in detail, in general, or not at all; since a writer who cannot deliver a satisfactory manuscript may be obligated to repay the publisher any advance he has received, the satisfactory clause is a topic of some concern to book authors.

Sometimes a contract allows the publisher to reject a manuscript based on the condition of the market. For instance, if an author has contracted to write a book about Alpine wildflowers, but three other works on Alpine wildflowers are published between the time the author contracts for the book and the time he delivers the completed manuscript, the publisher can legally reject the manuscript, even if it is a superb work—*if* the market clause is present in the contract.

The Author's Guild has revised the satisfactory clause in its standard contract so as to shift the burden of proof of unacceptability to the publisher. The contract states objective criteria a manuscript must satisfy, rather than allowing a publisher's subjective judgment to determine acceptance or rejection ("The Author shall deliver a manuscript which, in style and content, is professionally competent and fit for publication"). This enables the author to sue a publisher he feels has unjustly rejected a contracted manuscript. Under the previous contract, an author's only legal recourse was to prove the publisher acted in "bad faith."

Saturation. Frequent, short-term use of broadcast advertising.

Scene. This term has several meanings. In its most comprehensive sense, *scene* means the place where some action or event occurs.

In drama, *scene* refers to a division within an act of a play, indicated by a change of locale, abrupt shift in time, or the entrance or exit of a major character.

Similarly, a scene in a screenplay begins with a change in either time or place. Each scene serves to pass along essential information to the audience, and is therefore an integral part of the story. *Dialogue scenes* are those that consist primarily of dialogue, and *action scenes* contain mostly action; however, all scenes usually incorporate both elements.

The term *scene* is also used by fiction writers to describe a unit of dramatic action in which a single point is made or a specific effect is achieved. A series of scenes arranged in a logical, dramatic sequence form a story.

In her book *How to Write Short Stories That Sell*, author Louise Boggess defines the essential elements of an effective scene. Each scene of a story, she says, should have a purpose: it should advance the story action by assisting or hindering the protagonist in the solution of his conflict. Second, each scene should take place within a definite time period and locale. The third essential element is character: the viewpoint character appears in all scenes, along with one or more minor characters who produce the conflict action. Action—mental, physical, or emotional—is another essential ingredient of a scene. Finally, the scene ends, according to Boggess, when the viewpoint character summarizes (in thoughts or dialogue) his choices for action and decides on one as a possible solution to his problem or conflict.

Blocking out the scenes before you write the story provides the means of combining your plot summary and your character development. (*See: story.*)

Scholarships, fellowships, internships. Financial assistance is available to writers through scholarships and fellowships sponsored by governments, corporations, and private foundations. These awards can be used for study, travel, or a combination of the two; usually the purpose of the award is predetermined. By contrast, an internship is a temporary position, sometimes paid, that is offered by a corporation or nonprofit organization. It is designed to afford the intern experience in and exposure to the career field of his choice, without a permanent commitment on the part of either employer or employee.

The National Endowment for the Arts, 2401 E Street, Washington DC 20506, offers fellowships and residencies to published writers and organizations. Categories applicable to writers are the Literature Program, the Media Arts Program, the Music Program, and the Theater Program.

In addition, information on scholarships, fellowships, and grants, along with addresses of application offices, can be found in a number of directories, such as *The Grants Register*, a biennial book reporting on awards offered in the U.S. and abroad by governments and private organizations. *Study Abroad* provides information on fellowships and grants; listed are government programs, privately sponsored awards, teacher exchange programs, and awards for women. Data on scholarships, fellowships, internships, and grants are furnished in *Foundation Grants to Individuals. The*

Student Guide to Fellowships and Internships contains descriptions of and facts about fellowships, as well as an introductory section on the how-to of applying.

Another source for persons seeking internship opportunities is *Internships*, an annual directory listing primarily American internships and providing articles related to the practical aspects of interning.

The *Subject Guide to Books In Print* lists other recently published sources on these topics. (*See: foundations; grants, directories of.*)

Schools for writers. (*See: Associated Writing Programs; correspondence courses for writers.*)

Schools, supplementary books for. Books (both fiction and nonfiction) for school library use that are not textbooks are chosen by committees made up of school supervisors, librarians, and teachers. Eligibility is based on the recommendations of teachers, principals, supervisors, and publishers. Criteria used in adopting supplementary books include literary quality, appeal to children, validity of content, and the reading levels of students. Publishers' sales representatives call on schools and colleges to sell such supplementary books as well as regular textbooks related to curricula. Writers who want to write such books can review the kinds of books bought by schools—and the publishers that produce them—by reading the announcements and reviews of new books in *School Library Journal* and the Children's Book Issues of *Publishers Weekly*—usually in February and July each year.

Science fiction. Science fiction can be defined as literature involving elements of science and technology as a basis for conflict, or as the setting for a story. The science and technology are generally extrapolations of existing scientific fact, and most (though not all) science fiction stories take place in the future. There are other definitions of science fiction, and much disagreement in academic circles as to just what constitutes science fiction and what constitutes fantasy. This is because in some cases the line between science fiction and fantasy is virtually non-existent. Despite the controversy, it is generally accepted that, to be science fiction, a story must have elements of science. Fantasy, on the other hand, rarely utilizes science, relying instead on magic, mythological and neo-mythological beings and devices, and outright invention for conflict and setting.

Some of the basic elements of science fiction have been in existence for thousands of years. There have always been fortune tellers, prophets, clairvoyants, and other extraordinary people who sought to foretell the future. The grand adventure in an exotic setting—a recurring story structure in science fiction—has been a literary theme almost as long as the desire to know the future. Tales of mythological gods and their involvement with humans are echoed by modern-day science fiction stories of encounters with alien beings. The heroic quest, occurring so often in all mythologies, is paral-

leled by stories of pioneering space explorers.

There is some disagreement about when the first true science fiction story was written, but most scholars feel that *True History*, written by a Greek, Lucian of Somosata, about 175 A.D., was the first real science fiction story. This tale dealt with a trip to the Moon in a ship borne aloft by a great whirlwind.

The direct ancestor of modern science fiction is generally considered to be Mary Shelley's *Frankenstein: or, The Modern Prometheus* (1818). Over the next few decades, authors such as Poe, Stevenson, and Verne expanded the field, developing what was known as the "scientific romance." H.G. Wells capped the development of the scientific romance and, in 1926, science fiction emerged as a distinct *genre* (under the name "scientifiction") with the publication of the first all-science fiction magazine, *Amazing Stories*.

The pulp magazine era was just beginning at this time, and the explosion of markets for short stories in magazines helped science fiction gain a firm foothold in the American literary scene. The market for original paperback novels opened up in the 1950s. Such major talents as Robert A. Heinlein, Isaac Asimov, and Arthur C. Clarke emerged during this period, and brought the field to maturity. Under the influence of scores of writers and editors—as well as of films—science fiction has reached its current state of development.

Contemporary science fiction, while maintaining its focus on science and technology, is more concerned with the effects of science and technology on *people*. Since science is such an important factor in writing science fiction, accuracy with reference to scientific fact is important. Most of the science in science fiction is hypothesized from known facts, so, in addition to being firmly based in fact, the extrapolations must be consistent. Science fiction writers make their own rules for future settings, but the field requires consistency. For example, if a future is established in which mass transit is the *only* form of personal transportation, a character cannot be shown driving a personal vehicle just because it is convenient to the plot. In the same manner, in a setting derived from our own world, it would be inconsistent to introduce a human being who has reached the stage of evolution in which it reproduces asexually.

Whatever the background, science fiction, as other forms of fiction, is dependent upon the "standard" elements of storytelling—plot, characterization, theme, motivation, etc.—for success. Many would-be science fiction writers miss this fact, and attempt to dazzle readers with gimmicks and gadgets, to no effect.

Beyond inconsistency and an overabundance of gadgetry in place of a good story, there are few taboos in science fiction. Anyone wishing to write science fiction should spend time reading both current and past work to gain insight into its distinct characteristics.

There are several subcategories of science fiction, including science fantasy, sword and science, and time travel, each having its own peculiarities. Extensive reading in the field can aid the neophyte in identifying these subcategories, and is recommended for anyone wishing to write science fiction. (Beginners should also note that editors and writers prefer the abbreviation *SF* to *SciFi* for their specialty genre.)

Among the better-known science fiction authors today are Poul Anderson, Isaac Asimov, Ray Bradbury, Arthur C. Clarke, Harlan Ellison, Robert A. Heinlein, Frank Herbert, Damon Knight, Ursula K. Le Guin, Barry Longyear, Larry Niven, Frederik Pohl, Robert Silverberg, and Roger Zelazny. (*See: fantasy in children's literature; myth.*)

Additional information: *Understanding Science Fiction, Writing and Selling Science Fiction*, and other titles listed in the Bibliography to this encyclopedia.

Science Fiction Research Association (SFRA). This organization, which was established in 1970, exists "to improve classroom teaching; to encourage and assist scholarship; and to evaluate and publicize new books, new teaching methods and materials, and allied media performances."

Twelve countries are represented in SFRA's membership, which is composed of students, teachers, professors, librarians, futurologists, readers, authors, booksellers, editors, publishers, and scholars. Academic affiliation is not a requirement for membership.

Members receive SFRA's publications *Science Fiction & Fantasy Book Review* (ten times per year), *SFRA Newsletter* (ten times per year), and the annual membership directory, as well as Kent State University Press's quarterly *Extrapolation*, and the Canadian publication *Science-Fiction Studies* (published three times per year).

The Association's annual national meeting features authors of science fiction and fantasy, papers written by members, discussions, and the presentation of the Pilgrim Award for "outstanding contributions to science fiction and fantasy scholarship." Current president of the SFRA is Dr. James Gunn, who can be reached c/o English Department, University of Kansas, Lawrence KS 66045.

Science Fiction Writers of America (SFWA). Composed of writers of all forms of science fiction—stories, novels, radio plays, teleplays, and screenplays—this professional organization exists to foster an interest in the genre, both among students and the general public. It sponsors conferences, discussions, lectures, seminars, and a competition for the Nebula Awards. In addition, it publishes the bimonthly *SFWA Forum*, a quarterly *Bulletin*, an annual directory, and a model contract.

The SFWA's annual awards banquet is held each April; locations alternate between New York City and the West Coast. The SFWA mail address is 68 Countryside Apartments, Hackettstown NJ 07840. (*See: Nebula Awards*.)

Science writing. Specialization in publishing and increasing development of technology are two factors leading to expanding opportunities in science writing, both for freelancers and staff writers.

Opportunities exist for staff members on consumer magazines, trade and professional journals, newspapers, wire services, and broadcast networks. Freelance science writers produce magazine and newspaper articles; books; press releases; and educational, industrial, and public relations audiovisual materials.

Technical journals like the *Journal of the American Medical Association* are written by researchers, but journalists are sometimes hired as editors on their staffs. Topics in the areas of family health, psychiatry, and sexuality are generally sought by magazines read by women; editors tend to prefer women writers to cover these topics.

A college education may give a science writer an advantage in that he has been exposed to science as a field; he can thus decide whether or not to pursue it as a specialty. Some universities offer specialized courses in science writing that teach individuals the analytical skills demanded of today's science writers.

A writer who is unestablished in the scientific community or who lacks a specialty in science should be aware that many editors prefer articles written by scientists with writing skills rather than those written by general freelancers without scientific backgrounds.

Trends in the field of science take the form of an abundance of research being carried out on certain topics. A freelancer, using his marketing instincts, keeps abreast of such trends by scanning indexes to find subjects most written about in recent journals and magazines.

The Scientists' Institute for Public Information (SIPI) (355 Lexington Avenue, New York NY 10017) operates the Media Resource Service, which can refer writers to scientists in various fields. These experts can furnish technical information and opinions on scientific issues. The toll-free number of SIPI is (800)223-1730, or (212)661-9110 in New York State. The Media Resource Service operates from 8:30 a.m. to 8:00 p.m. Eastern Standard Time, and an answering service is available outside those hours.

The National Association of Science Writers (P.O. Box 294, Greenlawn NY 11740) considers applications of persons who have been directly involved in the dissemination of scientific information for a minimum of two years.

A science writer's pay is usually higher than that of a general writer. A temporary job currently yields from $8-$18 per hour, while full-time work can net the science writer from $20,000-$40,000 per year. (*See: medical writing.*)

Screenplay. (*See: motion picture script.*)

Screenwriting. The writer who aspires to be a scriptwriter for movies or television should live in Southern California, where most American movies and programs are produced, if he expects to make a steady living at it. Also—unlike writers for other media—he should consider a literary agent necessary: producers often will not accept manuscripts otherwise, although in some cases they will look at scripts that have been preceded by a query and are accompanied by a standard release form. (See sample in the Appendix to this encyclopedia.) Besides providing access to studios and producers, the screenwriter's agent serves him by interpreting contracts and negotiating deals. Agents who are willing to work with previously unproduced screenwriters are listed in *Writer's Market, The Complete Book of Scriptwriting*, and in a brochure available through the Writers Guild of America, West.

The script market is not as clearcut as the market for other kinds of writing. Not every script that's sold or optioned actually becomes a film—generally, of twenty to thirty purchased or optioned screenplays, only one is produced. To increase the chance of production, would-be screenwriters should read and study scripts in order to learn this specialzed craft, in which prose is subordinate to the visual element.

Prominent producers caution novice screenwriters to avoid practices that mark them as amateurs. These include script covers that contain garish or poorly executed artwork (largely considered optional in the first place), a list of characters, ideas for casting (unless the script was written with a specific star in mind), submitting a story synopsis *with* the screenplay, an over-abundance of camera directions not necessary to the telling of the story, the inclusion of apologetic notes, and putting the Writers Guild of America registration number on the cover page in an obvious way.

Legal protection for a script is crucial. It can be secured through registration with the Copyright Office and the Writers Guild of America, West, 8955 Beverly Boulevard, Los Angeles CA 90048. (*See: rights to manuscripts; television writing.*)

Script. A group of pages that contain the written-out elements of a film, play, radio, or television program.

Script samples. Examples of single pages from audiovisual and television scripts are reprinted in the Appendix to this encyclopedia; copies of scripts of already produced movies and television shows are sold by California companies. According to one company, average cost, postpaid, for the script of a television segment (one program from a series) is $12.50, and for the script of a movie, $25. These firms usually advertise in the classified advertising pages of *Writer's Digest*.

Seasonal article. (*See: magazine article, types of.*)

Seasonal jobs for writers. Freelance writers can find temporary or seasonal work for extra income. Such work is determined by overloads at corporations or by the temporary nature of certain projects.

Local, state, and national political campaigns begin their activity as much as a year in advance, which is the same time writers should seek employment as speechwriters or as writers for printed promotional materials. A speechwriter's fee depends on the level of candidate he works for. A speech for a local political candidate may yield $250; for a statewide candidate, $375-$500; and for a national candidate, $1,000 or more. For other campaign public relations work, a writer can earn up to 10% of the campaign's budget.

Another area that uses seasonal writers for publicity material is fundraising for nonprofit organizations such as social service agencies. A freelance writer working for this type of campaign would be likely to produce a campaign brochure, agendas for meetings, speeches, publicity releases, personal letters, and form letters. A sample flat fee for work on a fundraising brochure, which might represent 50 hours of work including research, writing, layout, and printing supervision, is $2,000.

Corporations in all fields encounter a yearly surplus workload in the form of an annual report, a printed disclosure of financial activity. Work on an annual report is sometimes assigned to a freelancer, e.g., when the company's in-house staff is too small to handle the project. The production of these reports involves writing, layout, editing, and proofreading skills. Graphic arts are also a part of annual reports, and the writer skilled in that area who can deliver a text-illustration package is more in demand as a freelancer. Hourly rates range from $20-$50; writers working on a flat-fee basis earn $1,500-$7,500, depending on the complexity of the report.

Freelance writers may also find seasonal work at publishing houses, which often hire extra help during the busier phases of their production cycles. Seasonal proofreading can be a steady source of income for a number of consecutive weeks. A proofreader currently earns $7-$10 per hour. Research for publishers pays $10-$30 per hour or more; it is sometimes done for a flat fee. Copy for a book dust jacket, while generally written in-house, can be assigned to a freelance writer; it would currently bring him $60-$75 per jacket for a job that includes writing copy for the front, back, and inside covers. (*See: seasonal material.*)

Additional information: *Jobs for Writers.*

Seasonal material. Holidays, anniversaries of historical events, national week-long observances, and seasons of the year supply topics for freelance magazine and newspaper articles. *Seasonal material* is the term used to describe an article, story, poem, greeting card, or book that has a holiday or another timely observance as its theme.

Writers who produce seasonal material need to plan their work around editors' schedules, which usually require seasonal articles from three to eight months in advance of the publication date. *Writer's Market* listings indicate individual editors' requirements for seasonal submissions. Another way to become familiar with editors' preferences is to record dates of acceptance—and dates of rejection for articles returned because they were submitted too late.

A writer who is more comfortable coordinating his work schedule with holidays instead of publishing schedules could write, for example, a Christmas story in December and file it until June, when he would retrieve it to revise and submit to a publication. Because rejected holiday stories and articles can be submitted the following year, it is best to avoid including timely elements like current events.

For the writer who plans to do seasonal writing, a file of articles and pictures, categorized by month, can be a source of inspiration. Photos or other illustrations are equally as important to seasonal articles as they are to other magazine submissions.

Some references that indicate holidays and other special observances include the *World Almanac*; a compilation called *Chase's Calendar of Annual Events*, published by Best Publications, 180 N. Michigan Ave., Chicago IL 60601; and brochures produced by state governments and the U.S. Government Printing Office, Washington DC 20402. In addition, each issue of the *Standard Rate and Data Service Business Publications Directory* carries a page listing "Promotional Dates" (National Baby Week, Law Day, etc.) for the coming months.

Secondary magazine. A secondary magazine is one with relatively low circulation that is intended for an audience with a specialized interest. *Indiana Business* and *The Old Bottle Magazine* are examples of secondary magazines.

Secondary magazines are considerably more receptive to the work of new writers than are the major magazines. It is possible for an energetic freelancer to live entirely by his income from full-time writing for secondary magazines if he can publish sufficient articles per month.

Knowledge of, interest in, or curiosity about a particular subject is a prerequisite for writing for secondary magazines. Hobbies and personal experiences are sometimes prime ideas for articles, while many other sources can provide background information for writers who lack knowledge of, but are interested in, a topic. Since many readers of secondary publications are extremely well-versed in the subjects they cover, the writer who does not have a solid grounding in the subject he's writing about had better do thorough research.

As in all freelance writing, work for secondary magazines requires previous market study. (*See: major magazine.*)

Secondary sales. Under the new copyright law, a writer is obligated to sell only one-time rights for his work to a publication unless he agrees otherwise in writing. Therefore, after selling first rights only to a publication, the writer may be able to locate additional magazines or newspapers with noncompeting circulations in order to make secondary sales and receive additional profit from the same manuscript.

An accepted means of informing an editor which rights are for sale is to indicate such rights in the upper right corner of the manuscript—for example, "First North American Serial Rights Only."

When a previously published piece is submitted to a second publisher, the writer should inform the publisher of the publication history of his submission. (*See: multiple sales; rights to manuscripts; simultaneous submission.*)

Secondary sources. In using only secondary sources, the writer runs the risk of his research being inaccurate, since he is depending on the work of other writers, whose work may contain misquotations, misinterpretation, printing and typographical errors, etc. However, secondary sources should not be ignored, because they can provide useful supporting information for an article, as long as they are verified for accuracy.

Primary sources, e.g., persons interviewed in the research process, are necessary to write most articles, because a writer cannot usually construct an effective article solely from secondary sources. The writer also needs to check one person against another as well as the written record. (*See: primary source.*)

Second-level story. Every work of fiction should contain a second level in addition to the surface level of action and dialogue. The *second-level story* deals with the inner lives of the characters—their psychological growth (and periods of regression), attainment of insights, realizations of universal truth. Psychologically speaking, the second-level story is where the *real* action takes place; in some fiction, in fact—the work of Henry James, for instance—there's next to no surface-level action at all.

The second-level story strengthens a piece by lending purpose to the series of incidents and credibility to the characters. It's what makes a story or novel more than just a good read; it makes the characters stick with the reader long after he's finished with it. The more skillfully the surface level and the second level are interwoven, the more valuable the work of fiction that results. (*See: fiction.*)

Selection (or main selection). In book club offerings, a book given primary importance among all the books offered during one period. (*See: alternate; book clubs; book club selection.*)

Self-criticism. Although necessary to the work of all writers, self-criticism can become a pitfall if it is overcome by perfectionism. When that happens, a writer tends not to write anything because he is afraid his work will be inadequate.

Self-criticism is frequently the basis for a writer's hypersensitivity to all criticism. In *The Writer's Survival Guide*, authors Jean and Veryl Rosenbaum explain: "Writers spend inordinate amounts of time deprecating their talent, questioning their abilities, and worrying about acceptance. One side effect of this perpetual self-criticism is that writers tend to bristle when others—critics or readers—comment unfavorably about their work, since it confirms their worst fears."

Writers who overindulge in self-criticism should remember: 1) though their work should be of quality, every piece of writing will not be a masterpiece; and 2) there is a point at which the writer must deliver responsibility for judgment to the editor. (*See: first draft, revising and rewriting.*)

Self-mailer. A commonly used type of direct-mail promotional piece containing all its parts on a single printed sheet. An envelope is not used with a self-mailer; instead, the sheet is folded and the address is placed on the outside. Sometimes a self-mailer contains a built-in reply form, with instructions to the consumer to clip, fold, and staple it before returning.

Expenses for this form of direct mail are relatively low because only one form is printed; stuffing, sealing, and/or clasping of envelopes is not necessary; and the cost of postage is usually less than for a more elaborate mailing piece.

Retailers, in particular, use the self-mailer heavily.

Self-publishing. Authors who do not sell their manuscripts to commercial publishers will generally follow one of two routes. *Subsidy publishing* (the author's paying a publisher to produce a book for him) is an investment with the prospect of little or no return. In a *self-publishing* arrangement, the author keeps all income derived from the book, but he pays for its manufacturing, production, and marketing, the latter of which can be very expensive. The

most important factor for an author to consider before self-publishing a book is whether or not he can earn enough from his own efforts in book sales to pay back his investment.

Self-published books are usually successful when there is a specific, easy-to-reach audience with the need for that particular book and when the author has a cost-efficient way to reach them. For example, an author who is regularly called upon to speak at regional and national conventions because he is knowledgeable about a certain topic has access to large groups of potential buyers of his book, without having to depend on costly direct-mail promotions or personal visits to innumerable bookstores to sell it. Self-publishing a book can sometimes lead to further distribution by a regular publishing company, if sales are encouraging.

Although a single proprietorship is often the most effective arrangement for the self-publisher, prospective associates who may be able to contribute financial support or publicity contacts should not be overlooked. Another option is to become part of a writers' cooperative, an organization composed of writers who contribute to the publication of other members' work as well as their own. Cooperatives are funded by grants, members' contributions, and product sales. (*See: sponsored books; subsidy publishing.*)

Additional information: *The Book Market; The Encyclopedia of Self-Publishing: How to Successfully Write, Publish, Promote and Sell Your Own Work; The Publish-It-Yourself Handbook; Publish It Yourself: The Complete Guide To Self-Publishing Your Own Book; The Self-Publishing Manual: How to Write, Print & Sell Your Own Book.*

Self-syndication. Self-syndication is the marketing of one's own columns or articles to newspapers and/or magazines. Self-syndication involves submitting completed pieces to editors and publishers (usually local to begin with), promoting and selling the column idea, establishing payment rates, billing the publications, securing a copyright (usually on an advance collection of columns), and earning 100% of the proceeds. Self-promoted newspaper columns are sometimes offered gratis to an editor to gain initial acceptance, after which publication the writer earns as little as $2 for weeklies and $5-$25 per week for dailies, depending on circulation. Even though fees from any one newspaper may be small, when columns or features are sold to others in noncompeting circulation areas, proceeds build.

One device used by new column writers to build readership is to encourage questions or comments from readers; the editor can gauge reader interest in the topic by the amount of mail it generates at the paper. Another device is to offer some free booklet on a related topic (which the author has either prepared himself or obtained from an appropriate source) to encourage reader response.

Besides being one way "to get into print," self-syndication may be a route to eventually being acquired by an established national syndicate. (*See: contributing editor; syndicated column.*)

Additional information: *The Road to Syndication.*

Sell copy. Copy written primarily to persuade the consumer to buy or do something. In book publishing, sell copy takes the form of subtitles and material on dust jacket flaps, such as blurbs and testimonials. In magazines, it is the cover copy enticing the newsstand buyer. In television, it can be commercials for a product, promotion for an upcoming program, or a public service announcement for a social service agency.

In many fields of business, forms of sell copy include that used in advertising, promotion, speeches, radio continuity, public relations, sales letters, publicity releases, and brochures.

In his book *Sell Copy*, Webster Kuswa describes the opportunities for writers to produce sell copy for businesses. According to Kuswa, it is possible for a freelancer who works full-time in this field to earn $25,000-$45,000 per year. He advises the person intending to freelance to calculate the hourly rate that his salary currently brings, and double that amount; then in the future to raise his fees in proportion to the experience he gains. (*See: advertising copywriters; blurb; business writing; direct-mail advertising; newspaper ads for small businesses, writing; political campaign writing; publicity writing; radio copywriting; speechwriting; television commercials.*)

Semimonthly. Issued or occurring twice a month (i.e., every half-month). A *semimonthly* magazine, for example, is published twice a month. (*See: bimonthly.*)

Semiweekly. Issued or occurring twice a week (i.e., every half-week). A *semiweekly* newspaper, for example, is published twice each week. (*See: biweekly.*)

Sequel. A story connected with a previously written one by means of plot and/or characters. The sequel can continue the plot of the previous story (which is complete in itself, as well), or place the same characters in a different situation or adventure.

The writer of the original story owns exclusive rights to his characters, even when they are used in a later work by another. When a writer intends to write a sequel using the characters of another writer, he must secure permission from the original creator. In the case of a deceased writer, depending on the copyright date of the original work, permission should be sought from his estate.

Serial comma/Harvard comma. A serial comma, also known as the Harvard comma, is one that is placed before the conjunction in a series of items in a sentence. The sentence "The design is bold, bright, and colorful" uses a serial comma, although it would also be correct without a comma after the word *bright*.

Whether a serial comma is used is a matter of the style preference of each individual publication. *The Associated Press Stylebook* advises omitting the serial comma except when one of the elements of the series includes a conjunction, or when the elements of the series are complex, i.e., long phrases. The first exception can be seen in the following sentence: They sat down to a meal of fruit, potatoes, peas, bread, and tur-

key and dressing. (If *dressing* were not included, the comma after *bread* would not be used, according to *The Associated Press Stylebook*.) The exception regarding long phrases is shown in the following sentence: He acquired the writing assignment because he was willing to work quickly to meet the short deadline, he had written a convincing query letter, and he had published related material within the last two years.

The *Chicago Manual of Style*, the *U.S. Government Printing Office Style Manual*, and *The Elements of Style* recommend using a comma before the conjunction in a series that contains three or more items. The punctuation in the following sentence is correct, according to their styles: Olympic training requires skill, talent, and persistence.

Serial rights. (*See: rights to manuscripts.*)

Series. A group of related articles or books covering the same subject or theme. Series for newspapers and for radio and television news broadcasts—run in daily, weekly, or even monthly installments—are written by staff writers or freelancers well-known to the publication or station; magazine series are often written by contributing editors. Nonfiction books are sometimes serialized in periodicals—*The New Yorker*, for instance, publishes several each year—and novels are occasionally serialized in magazines like *Family Circle*.

Newspaper and magazine series tend to be investigative or analytical pieces on controversial (even dangerous) subjects requiring much legwork from reporters: a 1982 Pulitzer-Prize-winning series, written by Sydney P. Freeberg and David Ashenfelter and published in the *Detroit News*, dealt with abuse of Navy personnel. Editors prefer to assign such large projects to staff people, often to a staff team as a built-in check and balance. Newspaper and magazine series thus are not a big freelance market—although when a freelancer having the right background, interests, and contacts lands a series, it usually pays well.

Series fiction can be very lucrative, however—particularly series paperback novels. (*See: series books.*)

Series books. A series of novels is a group of books in which the same character appears in different adventures or situations. Don Pendleton has created a series of more than 30 books about the character Mack Bolan and his attempts to avenge the murder of his family; the series' novels include *Arizona Ambush* and *War Against the Mafia*. John D. MacDonald's series character, Travis McGee, is a detective who appears in the books *The Deep Blue Good-by* and *Bright Orange for the Shroud* (among others). A contemporary American suburbanite, Rabbit Angstrom, is the central character in John Updike's series, which includes *Rabbit Run*, *Rabbit Redux*, and *Rabbit is Rich*.

Service. The practice of regularly contacting or calling on an advertiser in order to maintain his account.

Service article. (*See: magazine article, types of.*)

Service mark. Similar conceptually to the term *trademark*, a service mark is a word, symbol, name, or device used to identify the services (as op-

posed to a product) and advertising of an individual, corporation, or other entity, and to distinguish those services or advertising from that of others. The slogans used by a dry-cleaning establishment to describe the services it provides for customers (e.g., "One-Hour Martinizing") are examples of service marks. Freelance writers may sometimes work with a client to develop the idea for a service mark. (*See: trademark.*)

SESAC. (*See: performing rights organizations.*)

Setting. The time and location in which a story takes place. The term is used in connection with short stories, novels, plays, motion pictures, and television programs.

Although a particular setting can be the inspiration for or a powerful presence in a story, it cannot be the essence of it. Other elements, such as plot and characterization, are also necessary to a meaningful story.

Sexism in writing. The women's movement has made publishers aware that many women pursue careers outside their traditional roles. Sexism in publishing is manifest in two forms: stereotyped roles and male-oriented words.

Stereotyped females, formerly prevalent in textbooks, are gradually being abolished from American book publishing. According to McGraw-Hill's *Guidelines for Equal Treatment of the Sexes in McGraw-Hill Book Company Publications*, "Women and girls should be shown as having the same abilities, interests, and ambitions as men and boys."

Nouns and pronouns that disregard females are being replaced with more inclusive words or combinations of words. The terms "he or she," "person," and others are gradually coming to replace other, sexist words. Because using two pronouns can be awkward, though, sexism can often be avoided by recasting passages in the plural and using the pronouns "they," "them," and "their."

One means by which both sexism and stereotyping are avoided is to use nonsexist descriptions of occupations, e.g., "newspaper men and women," "police," "fire fighters," "flight attendants." (See the Preface to this encyclopedia regarding the use of *he* in this book.)

SFX. (*See: sound effects [SFX].*)

Shelf life. How long a hardcover or paperback book remains on the bookstore shelf or newsstand rack depends entirely on its salability. An original hardcover novel might last three months; a bestseller, two years or longer. A paperback original might have only five or ten days to reach its potential buyer, whereas a reprint of a bestseller might be available for several years. The competition from newly published books for shelf and rack space continually forces off books that have not been promoted, either formally or by word of mouth from satisfied buyers, and therefore don't sell.

Shield laws. Enacted to grant confidentiality in court proceedings between newspersons and their sources, shield laws have been adopted by more than half the states. Depending on the individual law, a reporter may be protected from revealing information only, or the information and the source;

some shield laws permit confidentiality under certain circumstances only. Shield laws usually protect only newspersons, not freelance writers; however, several states now include freelancers among those who are protected.

There is no federal shield law, but many journalists believe they are exempt from the obligation to reveal their sources on the basis of the First Amendment. Besides, they fear that revealing a source's name would break future contact with that source, thus infringing on the public's right to know. The court, on the other hand, holds that granting reporters immunity from revealing information when subpoenaed obstructs due process of the law and gives reporters special privileges as citizens.

Reporters who have been jailed for refusing to reveal sources and whose cases received wide-ranging publicity include Myron Farber and William Farr.

Short stories for young people. Though the structure of a short story remains the same regardless of audience, the writer of stories for juvenile markets must consider features of particular appeal to the age group of his intended audience.

The needs of kindergarten-age readers require a simple plot and a story length of no more than 500 words. Older children, who read stories of from 800-1,000 words, need drama, action, a quick pace, and a definite plot. Writers of short stories for teenagers must include plot, characterization, conflict, suspense, and a satisfying solution; the story's situation should be in keeping with teenagers' interests and lifestyles, e.g., school, part-time work, and interpersonal relationships.

In any children's short story, the main character is the same age as or older than the reader; he is never younger than the reader and is seldom an adult. The story's time span should be confined to two days or less. Anthropomorphism (attributing human qualities to a nonhuman being or an inanimate object), a device some writers of stories for young children fall back on, is unacceptable to most editors.

Opportunities for marketing children's short stories exist at both secular and religious publications. *Writer's Market* and *Fiction Writer's Market* direct the writer to magazines seeking short stories for children. (*See: juveniles, writing for; short story.*)

Short story. A piece of fiction that revolves around a character with a specific problem to solve. The method the author uses to help him solve his problem is the *plot*; the point the author wants to make (or to prove) in the story is the *theme*. An essential ingredient of a short story is the recognizable change—for better or worse—that occurs in the main character or in his situation as a result of having solved his problem (or having recognized his failure or inability to do so).

The short story usually ranges from 2,000-7,500 words—eight to thirty double-spaced, typewritten pages—in length. It contains only the number of characters and scenes necessary to its plot. (A common flaw in beginning writers' stories is including superfluous characters and scenes.) Similarly, the time span of the story is usually limited: one day or one week for the main action is common.

The short story has existed for thousands of years; one of the earliest known short story collections is *Tales of the Magicians*, which originated in Egypt between 4,000 and 6,000 years ago. In the Middle Ages, the short story took the forms of the beast fable and the *exemplum*, which contained morals, and the *fabliau*, which was a bawdy tale written in verse.

Edgar Allan Poe was the first to establish rules for the short story: his concept values unities of mood, time, space, and action, and stipulates that a story reach for only one effect—an effect determined in advance by the author, and reflected in all events of the story and every word of the composition.

Annual collections of contemporary short stories include: *Prize Stories, the O. Henry Awards (1983); The Best American Short Stories (1983);* and *The Pushcart Prize: The Best of the Little Presses.*

Magazine markets for short stories include those in the literary/little, women's, men's, children's, religious, regional, and science fiction categories, which are detailed both in *Writer's Market* and *Fiction Writer's Market.* (*See: confession; short stories for young people; short story; vignette.*)

Short-short story. A miniature story of 2,000 words or less. While, as in a regular short story, the main character gains insight by responding to and learning from a situation, the short-short story is built on a theme rather than a complex plot. Its author conveys a bit of philosophy through his character's change of attitude, which results from his response to a situation. Though a change in attitude is evident at the end of every short-short story, it need not necessarily result in a brighter outlook on the part of the character. But the reader must infer, at the end of the story, that the character's new attitude—whether brighter or more gloomy—will be integrated into the character's philosophy.

The short-short story covers a brief period of time and has as few characters and scenes as possible; it must be effective without background, description, or extra words, relying totally on characterization, conflict, and resolution.

The axiom "don't tell the reader, show him" is especially appropriate to the short-short story, where it makes for economy of words as well as literary effect. Markets for short-short stories are listed both in *Writer's Market* and *Fiction Writer's Market*. (*See: confession; short story; vignette.*)

Show don't tell. A common admonition from editors to beginning fiction writers who fail to use dialogue and action to reveal a character's emotions, relying instead solely on narration. It is the difference between actors acting out an event, and the lone playwright standing on a bare stage recounting the event to the audience. (*See: emotion in writing.*)

sic. Latin for *thus* or *so.* Usually enclosed in brackets or parentheses, *sic* is inserted after a word, phrase, or expression in a quoted passage to in-

dicate that the word or phrase has been quoted exactly as it was written, even though it may seem strange or incorrect. Writers use *sic* to disclaim responsibility for errors in grammar, spelling, etc., that may appear in the material they are quoting verbatim.

For example, if a writer were to use the following statement as a quotation from the newspaper in which it appeared, he would insert *sic* after the word *pants*: "Playboy Enterprises estimates that removing ornamental pants [sic] from its offices would save $27,000 a year." (*See: quotes.*)

Sidebar. A short feature that accompanies a news story or magazine article. It elaborates on human interest aspects of the story, explains one important facet of the story in more depth, or provides additional factual information, such as a list of names and addresses, that would read awkwardly in the body of the article.

A sidebar is often given distinctive graphic treatment by being screened or boxed or bordered, or set in a different typeface from the main article. It is usually given a title separate from that of the main article.

Sigma Tau Delta. An honor society of 46,000 men and women studying English. This group presents writing awards and a graduate-school fellowship. It publishes the *Rectangle*, the minutes of the board of directors, and a newsletter, all semiannually. It convenes biennially. The headquarters of Sigma Tau Delta are located at Northern Illinois University, DeKalb IL 60115.

Signature. A sound or piece of music used consistently with a particular radio program; very often synonymous with "theme." Signature is also used in magazine and book publishing to refer to a group of pages printed at one time and folded into a unit—such as a 16-page signature.

Simile. A figure of speech based on comparison. In a simile, two things are compared to each other, generally using either the word *like* or the phrase "as . . . as." The two things or person and thing being compared must be dissimilar in more ways than they are similar, since one purpose of the simile is to make the unfamiliar (e.g., a new character) immediately familiar to the reader. For example, the writer might use comparison to describe a new character in a story as Maugham did in *Of Human Bondage*: "She had large black eyes and her nose was slightly aquiline; in profile she had somewhat the look of a bird of prey. . . ." In his description of a student's rented room, John Irving used this simile: "It was a cheerless place, as dry and as crowded as a dictionary. . . ." (*See: figures of speech; imagery; metaphor.*)

Simulcast. A program that appears on both radio and television at the same time or on AM and FM radio at the same time.

Simultaneous submission. A manuscript submitted for consideration to more than one publishing company at the same time is known as a *simultaneous submission* or *multiple submission*. Once taboo, multiple submission has become a moderately common practice in publishing today for certain kinds of articles, for some book proposals, and for fin-

ished book manuscripts. Although many magazine editors listed in *Writer's Market* indicate that they will accept photocopied, previously published, or simultaneous submissions, some editors still prefer to see the original typed copy of a manuscript and to know that other magazines are not considering the same material at the same time. Major magazine markets that pay top prices expect to get an exclusive look at the ideas presented to them; simultaneous submissions should not be made there. Smaller magazines such as religious publications, company magazines, etc., which pay lower rates, and whose readerships are unlikely to overlap with other magazines in the same field, are usually more willing to look at simultaneous submissions. A writer, therefore, may be able to sell one-time rights to the same story or article a dozen times.

It is usually more acceptable for the freelance magazine writer to submit multiple *queries*—particularly if the subject of the article is a timely one—than to ask the editor to read an entire article that the writer may end up withdrawing from consideration because he has sold it elsewhere.

The practice of submitting the outline and sample chapters of a book proposal to more than one publishing house at the same time has become more common in the past decade. An original cover letter, carefully typed and addressed to the appropriate editor, should accompany the photocopied outline and sample chapters for each submission.

Opinions vary among writers as to whether the editor should be apprised in the cover letter that the manuscript is being considered by other publishers. Approximately half the book publishers listed in *Writer's Market* indicate that they will accept simultaneous submissions; many of them do, however, insist that the author advise them that the manuscript is a multiple submission, and some require that the author indicate the names of other publishers considering the material. (*See: ethics for writers; multiple sales; photocopied manuscripts; spin-off.*)

Sine qua non. Latin for "without which not." The phrase is used to describe an absolutely indispensable condition or something essential. *The Dictionary of Literary Terms*, by Harry Shaw, offers this example: "Conflict is the *sine qua non* of every work of genuine fiction."

Slang. Words that are used colloquially but that have not been recognized as standard English. Although in most cases inappropriate for use in books because of its tendency to become outdated vis à vis the longevity of a book's use, slang can be used justifiably in a story to set the scene or to establish the dialect of a character. But even for these two effects, slang becomes intrusive if used too frequently.

Slang words are usually acceptable for use in newspapers, magazines, and other timely publications, and writers may use such media to stay abreast of changes in usage, new slang words, and new idioms. (*See: idiom; language and style, books on.*)

Additional information: *Dictionary of American Slang*.

Slanting. Slanting refers to the writer's skill in aiming his articles (or stories) at a particular market.

Successful writers spend as much time creatively researching the markets as they do writing.

The object of market study, of which slanting is part, is to be able to sell a piece most directly and expediently. It is a simple process, involving five steps: 1) conceiving an idea; 2) checking the *Reader's Guide* to see what's already been published and by whom; 3) selecting from *Writer's Market* those magazines whose needs seem most suitable; 4) obtaining and studying three or four copies of each prospective market (magazine); and 5) writing the article or story with the editor's needs in mind.

Appropriate slanting can be achieved when the writer has learned, through studying magazines, such factors as the interests, occupations, socioeconomic status, and psychological makeup of his prospective readers.

A writer can sometimes revise and partially rewrite an already published article to give it a different slant, thereby adjusting it to suit the needs of a second magazine. For example, as *Writer's Digest* nonfiction columnist Art Spikol points out, an article on stress tests could be sold to a wide variety of publications, depending on the approach. "Why Top Execs Get Stress Tests" might be the title of a piece sold to an in-flight magazine, while the same research material slanted toward sports magazines could be an article called "How a Stress Test Can Help Improve Your Game." (*See: market, studying the.*)

Slice of life. A type of short story, novel, play, or film that takes a strongly thematic approach, depending less on plot than on vivid detail in describing the setting and/or environment, and the environment's effect on characters involved in it. The slice of life emphasizes mood and atmosphere rather than action, and builds to an emotional peak through carefully selected detail, skillful characterization, and naturalistic dialogue. Unlike a traditional work that has a beginning, middle, and end, the slice of life is a seemingly unselective presentation of life as it is; a brief, illuminating look at a realistic rather than a constructed situation, revealed to the reader without comment or interpretation by the author.

A slice-of-life work is not without structure, however. It has some plot or plan to it, and, as in a conventional work, the viewpoint character undergoes a change, however slight it might be. The story makes a definite thematic point, but comes to no conclusion. The reader does not know what came before the events of the story, nor does he know what lies ahead for characters. As one writer notes, "The story ends and life goes on."

Writer and critic Vera Henry believes that many slice-of-life short stories, for instance, are actually parts of novels, written or unwritten. Slice-of-life stories require exceptional mastery of technique. They are difficult to write and even more difficult to sell. *The New Yorker*, Atlantic, *Esquire*, and *Paris Review* often publish such stories, but these markets demand literary excellence and the competition is extraordinarily keen.

Literary and little magazines are more interested in slice-of-life material than are commercial markets, most of which require strongly plotted stories, and it is in such maga-zines that the slice-of-life writer has the best chance of publishing. Literary magazines are listed in *Fiction Writer's Market* and *The International Directory of Little Magazines and Small Presses*.

Some examples of well-known slice-of-life works are the Alan Sillitoe novel *Saturday Night and Sunday Morning* (later made into an important film); the Elmer Rice play *Street Scene* (later adapted into an opera scored by Kurt Weill); and *Small Change*, a film by François Truffaut.

Slick. (*See: major magazine.*)

Slugline. A newspaper reporter or wire editor places a slugline at the top of each section of copy on a story; it explains in a word or short phrase the story's subject. Also known as a slug, catchline, guide, or guideline, a slugline serves to keep all copy on the same story together throughout production and printing.

Slushpile. This is a collective term for unsolicited material received by book publishers or magazine editors. Editor Elaine Stanton describes the term in this way: "What is slush, after all, but what is left after the snow has started to melt? And it is only natural that editors will choose first to read the 'snow' that is the substance known to them, authors they regularly work with, staff material, and material submitted by agents."

In recent years, some book and magazine publishers have discontinued the departments that handled unsolicited manuscripts and announced in their *Writer's Market* listings that they would only accept submissions from agents. Some writers without agents have managed to circumvent this policy by directing an advance query to a specific editor's name and, when the idea has sufficient appeal, getting a go-ahead to submit the manuscript to the editor's personal attention.

Small press. A category of publishing, sometimes called the *alternative press,* in which firms generally operate on low budgets. Small press houses are independent organizations whose budgets depend on the publishers' personal funds, donations from authors, and grants.

Small press works of fiction and poetry, which make up more than half the products turned out in this field, are of serious literary quality: experimental fiction and ethnic fiction are characteristic of books published by the small press. Small press nonfiction tends to be concerned with social issues, political thought, and ideas not yet current among the general public.

Many small presses distribute review copies of their books to newspapers, special-interest magazines, and little magazines and send annual catalogues to bookstores, libraries, and individuals. Small press houses also place a small amount of advertising in the print media.

In working with a small press publisher, the writer plays a larger role in the publishing process than he does with a larger publishing house. He may take part in some or all of the editing, layout, graphic design, binding, printing, promotion, and advertising.

The writer is not guaranteed an advance from a small press publisher, because the publisher's financial status often is precarious, and depends largely on outside sources.

Since this industry has not adopted a standard royalty as the commercial presses have, the writer should ascertain that terms for royalties and/or other forms of payment are spelled out in his contract. *Fiction Writer's Market,* in its "Small Press" section, contains advice on dealing with the small press.

Small press publishers can help self-publishing authors by offering advice through personal correspondence and publications, and by reviewing self-published books in small press magazines. *Small Press Review* is one such magazine; a monthly, it is devoted to reviews of small press works as well as other information about the field.

The Committee of Small Magazine Editors and Publishers (COSMEP) and the Coordinating Council of Literary Magazines (CCLM) are two major organizations in the small press field. Members of COSMEP include self-publishers as well as those involved in the small press. Another organization involved in promoting the works of small press writers is the Small Press Book Club, which is operated by Dustbooks, Box 100, Paradise CA 95969.

The International Directory of Little Magazines and Small Presses assists the writer in locating small press publishers. Along with names and addresses, the listings in the Directory furnish information on content, payment, and reporting times. (*See: Committee of Small Magazine Editors & Publishers [COSMEP]; Coordinating Council of Literary Magazines; little/literary magazine; magazine, alternative; self-publishing.*)

Soap opera, writing for. Soap opera has its roots in radio drama (originally sponsored by soap companies), in which dialogue is a fundamental factor. Even though television is now the primary medium for "the soaps," skill in writing dialogue is still as important as the ability to construct plots and invent scenes with a prevailing emotional element.

Included in the staff of a soap opera are one or two head writers, who construct the show's *long-term projection* (also called the *book* or the *bible*), which is a narrative containing the story's plot and character development for shows to be produced during the following six months. A soap opera's two to four dialogue writers are hired by the head writers; they write the scenes from the head writer's week-by-week outline of the long-term projection. (Head writers earn six-figure incomes, out of which they pay their dialogue writers.)

Unlike a freelance writer, a soap opera staff writer works on a contractual basis. A 13-week period is the typical range of a contract. In addition, all writers for soap opera must belong to the Writers Guild of America.

The responsibilities of a soap opera writer are varied. Besides writing, he is expected to take part in casting characters; ascertain that each actor works the required number of days; stay abreast of the competition; and be available for last-minute script changes.

Some head writers in soap opera have put forth this advice for the aspiring soap opera writer: perfect your dialogue-writing skills; study television writing or screenwriting, either formally or informally; and critically view the soap operas on television. Those in the business point out that breaking in is much more difficult for a writer who lives outside New York and Hollywood, since many writers with industry connections live in those cities.

When actually writing to a producer, the writer should include a résumé, short tear sheets, and a letter mentioning previously published dialogue. Unsolicited manuscripts are not accepted. (*See: radio drama; religious broadcasting.*)

Social security. Social security refers to the U.S. government's tax-and-insurance system through which salaried and self-employed persons can build a base for retirement income. A self-employed writer qualifies to make social security payments if he earns $400 or more per year and if he writes on a continuous basis. For every $390 earned annually, the writer gains a quarter of coverage—four quarters if he earns $1,560 or more in 1984. No one can earn more than four quarters in a year.

A writer may work both as an employee and as self-employed. He computes the tax on the employee earnings first and then figures the self-employed tax on the balance. But he does not pay a tax on more than earnings of $37,800, the social security taxable ceiling as of 1984. (Ceiling in 1985 is $39,600 and expected to be $41,700 for 1986.)

A writer must reach insured status before he becomes eligible to receive social security benefits. The number of quarters of coverage based on his income determines his status.

A writer attains *currently insured* status when he has accumulated six quarters of coverage during the thirteen-quarter period immediately preceding the time of receiving benefits, i.e., retirement or disability, or death. His survivor or survivors may receive death benefits.

A writer reaches status of *fully insured for life* when he has earned either 40 quarters of coverage or a total ten-year income equivalent to the amount that would earn him four quarters coverage per year. He may earn these quarters consecutively or nonconsecutively.

The writer may draw full monthly retirement benefits at age 65, or he may retire at 62 and receive smaller payments. The social security office computes an individual's monthly payment from his average earnings during his career.

Medicare, disability insurance, and survivor's insurance are other social security benefits available to the self-employed writer. In order to be eligible for any type of social security benefits, the writer himself must register with the social security office if he does not already have a social security number. (*See: retirement and the freelance writer.*)

Society columns. Only a few newspapers today carry these columns, which report the social activities of the community's leading figures. In earlier days, newspapers restricted such coverage to those families who were in the local equivalent of the Social Register. Now such columns, usually part of the lifestyle sections of daily newspapers, report the social life of any well-known members of the community, especially in connection with fundraising activities for local charities. They are usually written by staff reporters, not freelancers. (*See: gossip column.*)

Society for Collegiate Journalists (SCJ). A 31,000-member association of college students. It sponsors national contests for members, and awards the Medal of Merit, the Edward E. McDonald Award, the Distinguished Service in Journalism Award, and the Outstanding Chapter Award.

The Society publishes *The Collegiate Journalist* semiannually; it holds a convention biennially. The SCJ can be reached c/o John David Reed, Journalism Department, Eastern Illinois University, Charleston IL 61920.

Society for Technical Communication (STC). This is an international association of persons who are professionally or personally interested in technical communications; members include publishers, artists, scientists, engineers, and educators. Technical communication refers to the conveyance of information on any subject—not just the obvious scientific or engineering topics—for which the user needs an explanation. Technical communication can be as simple as an instruction sheet for assembling a toy and as complicated as a computer program for a space shuttle. Awards are presented to members for audiovisuals and publications. The STC presents scholarships and sponsors writing contests for high school students. Its annual conference is held in May. Headquarters of the STC are at 815 15th Street, N.W., Suite 506, Washington DC 20005.

Society of American Travel Writers (SATW). This organization is concerned with conservation, historic preservation, and quality travel reporting. Members include writers, editors, photographers, broadcasters, travel film lecturers, and public relations representatives. Annual awards are based on contributions to conservation, preservation, and beautification. The *Annual Directory of Members* and *Travel Writer* are published by the SATW, which meets annually. The address of the organization is 1120 Connecticut Avenue, N.W., No. 940, Washington DC 20036. The Ethics Code of the Society appears in the Appendix to this encyclopedia.

Society of Authors' Representatives (SAR). This 55-member organization consists of New York City-based agents who handle various forms of literature and drama. The SAR convenes annually; its publications include *The Literary Agent*, a brochure describing what the literary agency can and cannot do for his client. A copy of this will be sent on request to writers enclosing a self-addressed stamped # 10 envelope. Sample U.S. and foreign contracts are also available, for 75¢ and 50¢, respectively, plus a # 10 SASE. The Society's mailing address is P.O. Box 650, Old Chelsea Station, New York NY 10113. (*See: Independent Literary Agents Association, Inc.*)

Society of Children's Book Writers (SCBW). The SCBW is an association of children's book writers, editors, publishers, illustrators, and agents that serves to exchange information and improve conditions in the children's book field. The organization convenes annually in August and sponsors meetings at the regional level. It publishes the *Bulletin* bimonthly. Annual awards include the Golden Kite Award and two grants. The Society of Children's Book Writers can be reached at P.O. Box 296, Los Angeles CA 90066.

Society of Magazine Writers. (*See: American Society of Journalists and Authors.*)

Society of Professional Journalists, Sigma Delta Chi (SPJ-SDX). This national organization has 30,000 members and 314 active chapters. To become a professional member, an applicant must, at the time of application, be principally engaged in journalism (more than 50% of his working hours) and have been engaged in journalism for at least one year.

The society annually awards the Wells Memorial Key, the Distinguished Teaching in Journalism Award, Distinguished Service Awards in Journalism, and Outstanding Graduate Citations. The Mark of Excellence Contest is another annual activity. SPJ-SDX publishes *The Quill*, a monthly magazine, as well as materials for the public. An annual meeting is held in November, and regional conferences take place every spring. The address of the organization is 840 N. Lake Shore Drive, Suite 801 W, Chicago IL 60611.

Society of Technical Writers and Publishers. (*See: Society for Technical Communication.*)

Soliloquy. A speech in which a character, either while alone, unaware of, or unconcerned with the presence of others, expresses his thoughts aloud. This convention, most often found in drama, is used to reveal a character's innermost thoughts and feelings, or to provide the audience with necessary information. An important convention in Elizabethan drama, some of the best-known soliloquies are found in Shakespearean tragedies such as *Hamlet*, *MacBeth*, and *Othello*. During the nineteenth century, when theater artists were determined to create the illusion of reality on stage, soliloquies were virtually eliminated from plays; the convention has been revived in the twentieth century, however, by such dramatists as Eugene O'Neill, Thornton Wilder, Tennessee Williams, Edward Albee, and Samuel Beckett.

A soliloquy differs from an *aside*, an artificial device rarely used today, that describes words spoken aloud by a character that are audible to the audience but presumably not to the other characters onstage. The soliloquy may be considered a *monologue*, although the latter term is usually reserved for an extended speech—in a narrative as well as a drama—delivered by one character and heard but not interrupted by others present. (*See: monologue.*)

Song Lead Sheet. (See the Appendix.)

Song Lyric Sheet. (See the Appendix.)

Songwriter's Market. An annual directory describing commercial outlets for songwriters' compositions. Its sections dealing with markets for songwriters are "Music Publishers," "Record Companies," "Record Pro-

ducers," "Advertising Agencies," "Audiovisual Firms," and "Play Producers & Publishers." Listings in these sections include names, addresses, and telephone numbers of the companies; name of a person to contact; types of music the companies deal in; and information on how to submit material.

Other listings in the directory are included in the sections "Managers & Booking Agents," "Contests & Awards," "Organizations and Clubs," "Publications of Interest," and "Workshops." "Close-up" articles, which appear throughout the book, are profiles of noted songwriters and others in the music business.

The appendix to *Songwriter's Market* introduces the songwriter to the practical aspects of the music industry, describing such fundamentals as payment, copyright, and record-keeping; furnishing advice on how to submit material; and providing words of caution about the unethical side of the music business.

Songwriting. New York City, Nashville, and Los Angeles are the three music publishing and recording centers in the U.S. To approach a music producer or publisher in any of these cities, a songwriter must have both a typewritten lyric sheet and a professionally produced demo tape; sometimes a lead sheet is required as well.

If a writer is presenting to a publisher, a good general rule is: when making a demo of a ballad, a piano/voice or piano/guitar version is sufficient. When making a demo of a rock or rhythm-and-blues tune, the writer should always indicate the rhythm when it is an intrinsic part of the song.

It is also helpful to the writer if, before this stage, his music has been played locally—for example, on radio or by a local group. Such exposure helps prove that the music is marketable.

AGAC/The Songwriters Guild has devised a songwriter's contract that is used by some AGAC members; it includes a fair-deal royalty and the return of the material to the writer if the publisher fails to achieve commercial release within the designated period. Some publishers use different contracts, but the AGAC reviews other contracts free for its members. Some music publishers who do work under the AGAC contract indicate that fact in their *Songwriter's Market* listings.

The Copyright Law of 1909 provided for the payment of royalties on sheet music and records as well as for public performance rights, but it was only with the Copyright Law of 1976 (effective 1978) that jukebox performance royalties were established.

Mechanical royalties in 1983 for the sale of records and tapes were 4¢ per song, maximum, split between songwriter and publisher less reasonable publisher's expenses. Royalties on sheet music range from 3%-8%; performance royalties vary widely depending on the vehicle and frequency of performance, etc. (*See: A&R [artists' and repertoire] representative; AGAC/The Songwriters Guild; lead sheet; lyric sheet; lyrics; musical; performing rights organizations; record album liner notes.*)

Sonnet. A poem of fixed form that originated during the Renaissance and is still widely used. The word *sonnet* is derived from the Latin word for "song" and, ultimately, "sound."

Most sonnets contain 14 lines of pentameter (usually iambic). Most are rhymed according to one of various "schemes" or patterns, though there is wide variation in modern usage. The "Italian" form, developed by Petrarch and Dante, introduces an idea in an *octave*, or eight-line section made up of two *quatrains*, or four-line units, and concludes with a *sestet*, or six-line section made up of two *tercets*, or three-line units. The "scheme," in which repeated letters indicate the line endings that rhyme with one another, is *abba abba* in the octave. There are many patterns for the sestet, such as *cde cde* or *cdc ede*. The "English" form, developed especially by Shakespeare (hence sometimes called the "Shakespearean sonnet") rhymes *abab cdcd efef gg*.

Sonnets tend to be unified in thought, the whole poem developing a single idea—but this, in practice, is no more true of the sonnet than of other short poems. A series of related sonnets is sometimes called a "sonnet sequence." Petrarch and Dante wrote sonnet sequences in Italian, and Sir Philip Sidney's sonnet sequence, *Astrophel and Stella*, introduced the practice in English. Most of the great poets in English have written sonnets; some of the major practitioners, besides those mentioned above, are Milton, Wordsworth, Yeats, Frost, and Cummings. (*See: verse.*)

Sound effects (SFX). Sounds to be broadcast; produced by either taping the actual sounds or creating sounds with other materials, e.g., crumpling paper close to the microphone to simulate the crackling of fire.

Space advertising. Units of *space*—such as one column, two columns, one page, or a double-page spread—are purchased by advertisers from newspapers and magazines. In contrast, advertising placed on television or radio is purchased in units of *time*, such as 30 seconds or one minute. (*See: advertising copywriters; radio commercials; television commercials.*)

Spacing of manuscripts. Editors at magazines and newspapers expect manuscripts submitted by freelancers to be double-spaced. Exceptions are made for poetry, which is sometimes single-spaced, with double spacing between stanzas.

Speakers and lecturers. Writers should not overlook the numerous opportunities to speak on their area of expertise: writing. Such appearances bring both direct lecture income and indirect income through increased sales of the author's books. Freelance writers can secure speaking engagements through local schools and colleges, as well as through various agencies. The directory *Speakers and Lecturers: How to Find Them* lists data on such agencies—commercial booking agencies, college and university speakers bureaus, companies, government agencies, professional societies, and trade associations. Included are approximately 4,200 speakers and lecturers and their topics; the directory indicates whether or not a fee is in-

volved. Freelance writers who are also lecturers might write the publisher of *Speakers and Lecturers*, about being included in the directory. The address is Gale Research Company, Book Tower, Detroit MI 48226.

The *Directory of Personal Image Consultants* catalogues speechwriters; listings in the biennial directory include specialty, credentials, number of staff members, teaching methods, fees, and principal clients. Individuals and corporations throughout the U.S. are represented. The directory also lists consultants in speech, dress, personal public relations, and motivation; information can be obtained from Editorial Services Company, 1140 Avenue of the Americas, New York NY 10036. (*See: International Platform Association; lecture agencies; National Speakers Association.*)

Spec. Shortened form of *speculative*. Refers to a radio spot written in an attempt to obtain a particular client's account. (*See: on spec.*)

Special sales. Any sale made by a publisher to a type of outlet that he usually does not deal with. The term *special sales* is a relative one, having a different meaning for each publisher. A premium book, or a book sold to an organization that distributes or sells it, is one kind of a special sale, as is a book sold to a convention on a topic of interest to the attendees.

Depending on quantity, books sold as special sales may yield higher-than-usual discounts for the organizations that buy them, as well as lower-than-usual royalties for their authors. (*See: sponsored books.*)

Specializing as a writer. The beginning writer usually writes on a variety of topics until he becomes known to editors. His early writing experience gives him the opportunity to find a topic that interests him enough to specialize in.

The specialist, after having written many articles and/or books, will find that both editors and the public have begun to associate his name with his subject. Because of this, he sometimes finds assignments easier to obtain and manuscripts easier to sell. In addition, the specialist writer discovers that, as he accumulates knowledge on the same subject, research becomes easier. Similarly, he has an opportunity to establish rapport with his interview contacts.

Even an established specialist writer must generate most of his own assignments in order to earn a steady income, however, and his writing usually includes both his specialty topic and new subjects he finds interesting.

Speechwriting. This involves the same kind of research as writing an article, with one valuable addition. Much of the work in writing a successful speech rests in getting to know the speaker himself. By talking with a client, the writer learns his opinions, biases, frames of reference, sense of humor, personality, and natural style of speaking. This information is bolstered by seeking out written verifications of the client's opinion (as in the voting records and position papers of politicians) and tracking down hard facts (as in the annual reports and records of companies). In his search for background information, the speechwriter uses available resources in government offices and agencies, libraries, universities, and communities. In the case of prominent political figures, the League of Women Voters, the Library of Congress, and the various arms of political parties are valuable contacts.

After knowing the speaker and understanding his unique needs for a speech, the writer tailors his words to a specific audience in a unique setting. The speech may be given formally or informally; it may be presented to the speaker's colleagues or his constituents; it may be designed to inform or persuade; it may be heard by a crowd of 500 or a gathering of 50. As does a magazine article, a speech projects a definite message (theme) with an appropriate beginning, middle, and end. It is written in a style appropriate to its audience. A businessperson's speech is generally filled with elements of reason, logic, and the language of business; it often deals with the speaker's business, commercial ventures in general, or a mixture of civic and business interests. A politician's speech, on the other hand, might cover any one of a spectrum of topics presented with verve and emotion.

Whatever the speech topic and purpose, whoever the speaker, the speechwriter composes a message mainly for an audience's ear. The writing is clear, concrete, simple, precise; the theme must be easily recognizable. Prose for speakers differs from prose for readers in several ways: speech sentences are shorter and contain more imperative, interrogative and exclamatory phrases; they may include slang, sentence fragments, and contractions; they are concerned with the sounds of words and the rhythms and repetitions of the language. (*See: ghostwriting speeches.*)

Spin-off. The recycling of a book or article, part of a book or article, or research material compiled for a book or article. The shrewd writer is always looking for spin-offs to increase his income in return for minimal additional work. Spin-offs include multiple sales to noncompeting markets, squeezing a second (or third) article out of research conducted for a different piece, or even selling reprints of a published article to a company or organization having a special interest in its subject.

Writers go about spinning off their work in many ways. Magazine writers may make a point of doing copious research instead of just enough, or may specialize in articles appealing to a wide audience in order to sell to regional publications around the country. Book authors learn to shape chapters for easy condensation, query large-type or foreign publishers, or pursue lecturing or teaching careers on the side.

A full-time freelance writer soon finds that he cannot afford to forgo spin-off profits. Whatever his field, the active freelancer will discover ways and means to make his work go further.

Spitballing. A procedure through which a writer may present a script. He relates the story in an oral presentation (also known as *pitching*) that is concise, yet captivating. (*See: television script terms.*)

Sponsor. An advertiser who finances a program in exchange for having his commercials broadcast during the program.

Sponsored books. Books that are financed by a company, association, institution, foundation, or other group to serve its interests in some direct or indirect way, written by either a freelance writer, an expert in a particular field, or a company employee. For example, a state arts or humanities council (or both) might finance a book dealing with some aspect of state history; a large glassware manufacturer might underwrite a book about art glass; some other firm might wish to commemorate a business anniversary or offer consumer information on a selected topic. The firm or organization would use the book as part of a public relations or marketing campaign. Sponsored books distributed at no cost or at a discount cost are known as *premium books.*

A writer might conceive of a book idea after reading about an event involving a company, association, or region. He would then approach a trade publisher or a publisher specializing in sponsored books, such as the Benjamin Company, with an outline and a prospective company or organization that might benefit from the book. (It is difficult to have a book idea accepted by approaching a company directly—unless the author knows a company executive or has inside information about its operations.)

Sponsored publishing can sometimes present problems to the writer if the underwriter wishes to exercise editorial control. For instance, a state council may wish to have historic exploitation of Native Americans or other minorities downplayed; a corporation may wish its founder's unsavory business practices overlooked. Generally, an underwriter who commissions or funds the actual writing of a book, in addition to its publication expenses, will expect more control over the content than one who funds an already written book.

The writer's fee for a sponsored book varies widely, and is not necessarily proportionate to the amount of writing produced. In general, however, this field of writing pays well. The book sponsor usually offers the writer a flat fee for the entire project; sometimes a royalty is included, especially if the book is likely to have a long life. (Royalties vary, and are different from those paid by trade book publishers. A minimum royalty might be 5% of the book's cost, in bulk, to the sponsor.) The writer's fee must be negotiated on the basis of the individual project; variables include the writer's name and reputation, and the amount of time allotted for the book.

Writing a sponsored book is one way for a writer—especially one proficient in nonfiction writing—to break into print. Sponsored books of wide circulation make the author's name known to great numbers of people. Still, some writers of sponsored books elect to have their bylines omitted.

Some sponsored books may also be produced by regular trade publishers; the sponsoring organization agrees to pay part of the production costs, or simply contracts to purchase a certain number at an agreed-upon price from the initial press run. The attempt here is to have the book reviewed and distributed as though it were a normal trade book. (*See: co-publishing; self-publishing; small press; subsidy publishing.*)

Additional information: *How You Can Make $20,000 a Year Writing.*

Spoonerism. Named for W.A. Spooner, an English clergyman and warden of New College, Oxford, who frequently made such slips, *spoonerism* describes a transposition of the initial or some other sounds of two or more words. "Let me sew you to a sheet" (for "Let me show you to a seat") and "a well-boiled icicle" (for "a well-oiled bicycle") are examples of spoonerisms. A spoonerism may be a witty turn of phrase or an accidental slip of the tongue.

Sports writing. Today's sports writing covers more sports, more categories within each sport, and a wider range of sports-related subjects than that of previous eras. Women's, high school, and college sports are given newspaper space; participant sports such as hunting and fishing have separate columns; and sports that are considered minor by some, such as swimming and track, are attracting more attention from editors. For this reason, the aspiring sports writer benefits by learning about as many sports as possible.

A good sports writer has enthusiasm for sports in general, as well as the journalistic ability to avoid the clichés that tend to become rampant in this field in the work of its less skilled writers. (Current clichés include "the pitcher's best friend" meaning a double play in baseball, and "acrobat," referring to a wide receiver on a football team.) Good writing is essential to a sports writer's work, since his product must have entertainment value. In addition, accuracy is crucial in a sports write-up, since its audience pays close attention to facts.

In covering competitions, the sports writer will find athletic directors and publicity directors helpful contacts. Similarly, fanatical fans can be valuable assistants in that their records on high school and college sports are often more extensive than those kept by the schools themselves.

Specializing in sports enables the aspiring writer to begin accumulating publishing credits as early as high school. Sports reporting done during a writer's high school and college years can be added to his résumé when he seeks employment at a daily or weekly newspaper.

Beginning sports reporters who work on small newspapers are often assigned other duties and non-sports stories as well. On large newspapers, sports writing is unique among specialties in that the beginning reporter motivated toward it can often cover sports without previous general-assignment experience. However, a novice's assignments consist of high school and community group games, while coverage of college and professional events is usually reserved for more experienced sports writers.

Spot. A radio or television commercial; sometimes refers to advertising time sold separately, without regard to programming. A spot may also be a public service announcement.

Spot-news article. (*See: magazine article, types of.*)

Stable. A collective term used to describe those authors whose work is regularly produced or run by one publishing house or publication. The editor of a business journal, for example, may refer to the freelancers who often write for that magazine as his "stable" of writers. Or a book editor may refer to the authors he works with as his "stable."

The designation was more widely used some years ago when many authors were tied by contract to one publishing house. Now, because writers frequently publish through several houses, the word is seldom used.

Staff writer. Positions for writers exist both in print and broadcast media organizations.

Most writers on the staffs of large magazines have obtained their positions as the result of previous experience, either as freelance writers for magazines or in the newspaper field. Sometimes, however, a writer is offered a position in an organization upon completion of an internship there. At smaller magazines, which rely on freelancers for most of the articles, the editor doubles as the staff writer. A magazine staff writer's duties can include writing original articles based on extensive personal interviews, mail and phone research that the magazine preferred to do itself rather than assign to a freelancer; and/or writing headlines, captions for illustrations, editorials, contents page copy, and sometimes promotional material for the circulation manager.

Staff writing positions in broadcasting are also obtained through previous journalistic experience, in the case of radio and television news departments; or after successful freelance assignments, for television sitcoms and comedy/variety shows. (*See: stringer.*)

Stage directions. In *Playwriting: The Structure of Action*, playwright and academic professor Sam Smiley describes the purpose and principles of stage directions:

"The major, overall function of stage directions is to provide essential information to the production people about how they should present the play visually and vocally. Stage directions include *all* words other than the dialogue. It is crucial for the dramatist to compose directions for the theatre artist rather than for a reading public. Poor directions usually result from an author's ignorance of what they should be or his confusion about to whom they should be directed. The guiding principles for stage directions are: (1) Only necessary stage directions should be admitted. (2) They describe physical actions that take the place of dialogue. (3) They indicate the proper reading of a word or a speech when the dialogue does not suffice. (4) They suggest pauses and other considerations of timing. (5) They explain specific matters about visual elements of production, such as scenery, properties, and lighting. A playwright should strive, however, to avoid stage directions and work the necessary bits of information into the dialogue."

In addition to the principles of necessity and clarity, Smiley notes that stage directions should not tell the director, designers, and actors how to do their jobs by imposing interpretations and limitations that have not been woven into the dialogue.

Smiley describes three main types of directions: introductory, environmental, and character. Introductory directions such as the character list, indication of time and place, and a description of the setting precede the beginning of the dialogue. Environmental directions, which include specifications about time, space, light, temperature, and physical objects, may appear in the introductory material or throughout the play. Character references state or qualify what the characters do and say.

Stage directions should be simply stated, Smiley says. Brief, declarative sentences, or sentence fragments, are most functional. It is better, according to Smiley, to indicate an action such as laughing as a stage direction—(He laughs.)—rather than use the words "ha ha" in the dialogue. All character entrances and exits should be noted in the stage directions.

Stage directions in the script are enclosed in parentheses. Instructions are typed in upper- and lower-case letters, with the exception of character names, which are always in caps. For example: (HANK moves to the bar and pours a drink. He hands it to EMILY.)

"Adroit stage directions are vital," Smiley explains, "and a playwright should exercise artistry in their composition." Some additional guidance on Play Format appears in the Appendix to this encyclopedia. (*See: playwriting.*)

Stamps, illustrations of. Illustrations of postage stamps may be used for philatelic, educational, historical, and newsworthy purposes, according to the U.S. Department of The Treasury. However, the government places restrictions on printing some types of illustrations of stamps.

Black-and-white illustrations of U.S. or foreign stamps, whether or not the stamp is shown as having been canceled, may be printed at any size, as may color illustrations of canceled U.S. or foreign stamps. On the other hand, color illustrations of uncanceled U.S. or foreign stamps must be printed at a size smaller than ¾ of, or larger than 1½ times the stamp's actual size. This restriction applies also to illustrations of stamps used in philatelic advertising; stamps may not be illustrated at all in other types of advertising.

Illustrations of revenue stamps are subject to the same restrictions as illustrations for postage stamps, except that, according to the U.S. Department of The Treasury, "colored illustrations of United States revenue stamps are not permitted." (*See: coins, illustrations of; money, illustrations of.*)

Stand by. In broadcasting, refers to backup copy to be used in an emergency. As a verb, *stand by* is a signal to radio personnel that they are about to go on the air.

Standard Directory of Advertisers. An annual directory of 17,000 corporations that advertise nationally or regionally. The classified edition, in which listings are arranged by the companies' products, is published in April; the geographic edition, in which listings are arranged by state and city, is published in May. Each edition contains a tradename list, an alphabetical index, and a classifica-

tions index.

The following data are included in the listings: name, address, and telephone number of the company; names of personnel; products of the company; advertising agency engaged by the company; advertising budget; month of the year in which annual advertising budget is devised; amount of sales; media through which the company advertises; scope of product distribution (such as national or regional); and number of employees.

The *Standard Directory of Advertisers* is supplemented by nine monthly publications along with weekly bulletins. The directory is also called the Advertiser Red Book. (*See:* Standard Directory of Advertising Agencies.)

Standard Directory of Advertising Agencies. This directory, also known as the Agency Red Book, lists more than 4,000 U.S and foreign advertising agencies. Included in the listings are the names, addresses, and telephone numbers of the main and branch offices; names of managers and account executives; clients; number of employees; year of the company's establishment; memberships; and annual billing broken down by medium—magazines, newspapers, radio, television, direct mail.

The directory is published in February, June, and October, and is supplemented nine times per year. It contains a geographical index, and a special market index that lists agencies specializing in advertising directed toward specific groups, such as blacks, Hispanics, the medical field, and the resort industry. (*See:* Standard Directory of Advertisers.)

Standard Rate and Data Service. This publishing company issues directories that contain advertising-related data on various media. One volume covers consumer and farm magazines; another, business magazines. Other directories are for newspapers, direct mail, television and radio. In the magazine and business directories, each listing contains a summary of the editorial content that writers may find a useful adjunct to *Writer's Market*. Listings in the newspaper directory point out special sections of newspapers, which may offer freelance opportunities; the radio directory lists information on audience and programming, which may be of use to the freelance advertising copywriter; the direct-mail directory catalogues various mailing lists that might assist writers in research.

Standard Time Zones of the U.S. (See the Appendix.)

Stanza. (*See: verse.*)

Start date/stop date. In radio advertising, the first and last dates a commercial should be run; usually indicated on both the copy and the cart.

State arts councils. Operated by state governments, state arts councils distribute grants to writers and artists. In most cases, however, grants are made to organizations rather than to individuals, so a writer interested in applying for state grants should make his initial overtures to a school, college, or other potential sponsor. Poets and fiction writers, for example, are eligible for both short- and long-term residencies in the "artists in the schools and community" programs sponsored by some state arts councils. They teach writing and read their work in the sponsoring schools, which are usually expected to provide matching funds to the amount granted by the arts council.

An arts council is usually located in each state capital. Addresses of state arts councils are available through the arts departments of public libraries.

State government publications. State travel offices and economic development offices can provide writers with material that can be useful in research. Travel writers, for example, can obtain free glossy black-and-white photographs and descriptive information on tourist attractions in each state; business writers can obtain statistics and forecast information about the state's leading industries from the economic development offices. Most of these offices are located in state capitals; their phone numbers, and sometimes their addresses, can be found in the white pages of the capital city's telephone book.

Some world almanacs include the addresses of the State Chambers of Commerce, along with general information about each state, in their annual editions. *The Directory of State Chamber of Commerce and Association of Commerce and Industry Executives,* available from the Chamber of Commerce of the United States, 1615 H

Street, N.W., Washington DC 20062, lists all the state chambers. (*See: U.S. government publications.*)

Station rep. A person or company that sells radio or television advertising time to potential sponsors, usually national, sometimes regional in scope.

Stationery. A supply of stationery that includes printed letterhead and business cards is an integral part of the freelance writing business, especially for the nonfiction writer. Printed stationery conveys the image of a writer who is serious and responsible. It is especially valuable to a writer whose name is yet unfamiliar to editors.

A letterhead need not be expensively designed—a college-level art student or commercial artist willing to freelance for a reasonable fee can save a writer the expense of engaging a professional graphic design studio to design the letterhead or create a distinctive logo. A faculty member in the art department of a local college or university can probably recommend a competent student to do the job, or may be able to direct a writer to freelance artists in the local area.

Professional typesetting is recommended. Many printing operations (including "quick printers") offer typesetting services; other professional firms are listed under "Typesetting" in the Yellow Pages.

The writer may want to get cost estimates from several printers before ordering business stationery. Paper will probably be the biggest expense, but a good 25% rag bond is necessary for quality, professional-looking letterheads.

Once a writer has had letterhead printed, he can often avoid the expense of additional typesetting fees by using that imprinted stationery to create other business materials. For example, he may cut the imprinted name and address from his letterhead and paste it to the top of a page on which he has typed his résumé or invoice form. Most professional printers can make a master of this original pasted-up copy; there is no need to have the name and address typeset again. A writer's stationery can be produced by most commercial print shops listed in the Yellow Pages under "Printers—Commercial."

Business cards also enhance the writer's professional image; they may be handed to interviewees or posted on bulletin boards at locations where a writer's services could be advertised.

Statistics. Statistics are facts or numerical data tabulated in a way to give information about a specific subject in condensed form. Statistical information is used in articles to emphasize a point or to support an argument on an issue. A reference containing statistics on various American institutions is the annual *Statistical Abstract of the United States.* Published by the U.S. Department of Commerce, the book is a compilation of tables and graphs reflecting social, economic, and political activity in the United States. A bibliography of state statistical abstracts is also contained in this publication.

Other sources of statistics are one-volume almanacs such as the *Information Please Almanac.* (*See: background information, books of; data bases.*)

Additional information: *How to Lie with Statistics.*

Status quo. Latin for "state in which." The expression is used in English to mean "the existing condition," "the existing state of affairs," or "things as they are."

Steal my idea? One of the questions most frequently asked by beginning writers expresses concern about having a manuscript rejected while its idea is stolen by the same editor, who supposedly assigns it to another writer. Actually, editorial piracy—conscious or unconscious—is so rare among reputable publishers that it need not worry writers.

The question of piracy often arises when a writer sees his idea published in a magazine shortly after his submission was rejected by the same publication. However, the assumption that an idea has been stolen is usually incorrect: the published article was, in most cases, assigned and/or bought months earlier than the rejected one was submitted.

An idea in itself is not copyrightable; only the writer's particular presentation and structuring of information is. For example, a writer who, after having read several magazine articles on federal funding of abortion, decides to write an article on the same subject and submit it for publication, may legally do so. But if the writer uses actual sentences or word-for-word paragraphs from the previously published stories for his own article, he is infringing on the original authors' copyrights. (*See: copyright; editorial ethics.*)

Stereotype. Stereotypical characters—simple stock types that are instantly recognizable—are a major flaw in many beginning writers' work (and, critics say, in the work of many established authors as well). The brainless, buxom blonde; the black kid who's a whiz on the basketball court and the dance floor; the bloodless, myopic, absent-minded professor have all been written about over and over again. It's not that people possessing these characteristics don't exist; they do. But that doesn't mean those are the only, or even the most important, traits those characters have.

Stereotypical characters arise from laziness, condescension, or a lack of imagination on the writer's part. Some writers simply aren't very perceptive; others can't understand people who aren't like them. Sometimes a writer puts so much effort into a fully realized hero or heroine that all the supporting characters receive short shrift.

As Damon Knight writes in *Creating Short Fiction*:

Resist the impulse to stereotype your characters according to their occupations or their media images. The reader can do that himself; why should he pay you to do it? Let's say your character is a police sergeant with almost twenty years' experience. He need not be a wrestling fan, a beer drinker, or a Republican. He may be a Marxist and a Transcendental Meditation student who breeds dahlias and has a child bride. Give your characters credit for being as complex and interesting as you are, and give them a little slack. Listen to what your unconscious has to say about them; find out what *they* want to do. (*See: stock character.*)

stet. This word of Latin derivation is used on manuscripts to mean "let it stand." Editors and proofreaders place the word *stet*, encircled, in the margin to indicate that a marked change or deletion should be ignored, and the copy typeset in its original form. Sometimes the word is used in conjunction with a row of dots placed under the material to be left unchanged. These dots are called *stet marks*. (See the "Proofreaders' Marks" in the Appendix to this encyclopedia.)

Stock character. This familiar figure-type traditionally appears in certain kinds of writing. For example, such stock characters as villains and heroes are regularly on hand in melodramas and category fiction. Other stock characters include the rich socialite, the confidante, and the evil authority figure.

The use of too many stock characters leads to their becoming merely cliché figures who contribute little to the strength of a work. It can also reinforce the bad habit of lazy characterization in the writer. (*See: character; cliché; foil; round character.*)

Stock response. Certain stimuli in works of art and literature may produce stereotyped or predictable reactions from readers and spectators. Traditionally, authors and filmmakers have relied heavily on the stock response; audiences have been conditioned to applaud heroes, jeer at villains, and thrill at the bad guys' getting shot.

Since a stock response may interfere with or prevent a more appropriate and less conditioned response from an audience, conventional exploitation of the stock response has fallen out of favor in recent decades. Genuine literary artists now attempt to avert stock responses by shaping their material carefully so as to produce more individual responses. Filmmaker Arthur Penn, for instance, in *The Left-Handed Gun, Bonnie and Clyde*, and *Little Big Man*, pioneered the use of graphically detailed violence to show the pain and horror of death, thus preventing audiences from easily dismissing onscreen events.

Stock situation. A conventional pattern, incident, or situation common in fiction and literature. For example, "boy meets girl, boy loses girl, boy gets girl" is a stock situation. Mistaken identity, the love triangle, and quest for revenge are all recurring patterns in literature. Stock situations sometimes fail to rise above the level of stereotype because they lack fresh, original treatment; others become contemporary classics when the author makes the situation plausible through believable characters, convincing motivation, and a suspenseful plot. The film *Breaking Away*, for instance, is a fairly typical story of initiation, but because of the freshness and fullness of its characters it charmed critics and moviegoers alike. (*See: formula story; stock character.*)

Stories in textbooks. Most stories are reprinted from books or magazines, but some textbook publishers buy individual stories for reading texts directly from freelance writers. It is important to query a publisher before submitting a manuscript because some publishers use no freelance work, and there is usually a seven-year interval between revisions of existing textbooks when new material *is* needed; if the writer has not queried first, his chances of submitting unneeded—and ignored—material are great.

Reading textbooks are planned in series, each of which is divided into grade levels. In some series, upper grades develop material introduced in earlier grades; in others, each grade level is given a separate study unit.

Peculiarities of textbook writing include vocabulary limitations in material for young children, and space limitations that can cause a story to be drastically cut during the publishing process. Nor will a writer necessarily receive a byline accompanying his work: some publishers list all writers' names at the beginning of a textbook instead of giving individual bylines.

Most writers cannot rely for guidance on memories of the textbooks they were exposed to in school, because texts have changed dramatically since the late 60s. Today's school readers try to present believable situations and realistic human behavior, as well as nonprejudicial treatment of women and minorities. Writers can sometimes examine textbooks currently in use by contacting the professional librarian at their local board of education, or by contacting school librarians in their area.

Story. A story is a narrative told orally or written, either in prose or verse. It is designed to interest, amuse, entertain, or inform an audience of readers or listeners. It involves its audience emotionally, encouraging them to care what happens to the characters.

A problem common to beginning writers is the inability to distinguish between a story and an incident. A story differs from an incident in that it possesses a quality of completeness: a character moves through a conflict to a conclusion, never completely the same at the end of the action as he was at the beginning. It is this change, for better or worse, that makes a story.

A further distinction exists between story and plot. A story is the sequence in which events occur as part of a happening; a plot is the sequence in which the author arranges or dramatizes those events. A murder mystery, for example, may be based on the following events: a man and woman engaged in an adulterous affair scheme to murder the man's wife; they drug her with a lethal dose of sleeping pills one evening and rig up a fake suicide note; an astute detective uncovers the crime and eventually brings them to justice. That is the story—the chronological sequence in which the events occurred. The author may decide the story would be told more effectively, however, if it began with the wife's death and ended with the uncovering of the affair and the murder. This sequence of events is the *plot*.

Robert Louis Stevenson, noted storyteller and novelist, had this to say about creating a story:

There are only three ways of writing a story: you may take a plot and fit characters to it; or you may take a character and choose incidents and situations to develop it, or you may take a certain atmosphere and get action and persons to express and realize it. (*See: plot.*)

Story analysts. Full- or part-time readers employed by film studios to read scripts submitted by agents, producers, stars, and freelancers. They report to the studio's story editor.

Story rejection terms. Some editors explain their reasons for rejecting manuscripts when they send rejection slips to writers, although they are not obligated to. Following are editors' elaborations on common reasons given for rejecting short stories.

When a story is *too sentimental*, it exaggerates the emotional appeal with which the author tries to capture the reader. Sometimes, too, characters are portrayed as being overwhelmingly good; the author neglects to present at least some undesirable traits to make the characters seem human, not superficial.

The story that *lacks a theme* will usually be rejected. The plot of a story must tie in with a theme or—as in most confession stories—a lesson.

A story that contains a *melodramatic plot* is replete with magnification of events and emotions. When a plot is *contrived*, it depends on circumstance or coincidence for its resolution, and is therefore not believable.

An editor may remark that a story contains *wooden characters*. In that case, he means that the characters seem unnatural. Woodenness is often created through dialogue, so a fiction writer needs an awareness of natural speech patterns and of the peculiarities and skill levels in speech of persons at various ages. The term *characterless characters* refers to characters that have no unique qualities and so elicit no empathy from readers. They are essentially stock characters.

An editor's comment that the writer is *telling, not showing*, points to his overuse of narration and insufficient use of scenes and dialogue that would bring the story to life. On the other hand, a story that is rejected on the basis of its *purple prose* contains overstated, flowery language.

When rejecting a confession story, an editor might comment on a *passive narrator*, ruled more by outside circumstances than by his own will. An *unsympathetic narrator* is also a basis for rejecting a confession. This type of character embodies a prominent undesirable quality, so the reader is repelled by, rather than drawn to him. (*See: article rejection terms; description; dialogue; narration; show don't tell; stock character.*)

Storyboard. The layout for a television commercial. Sometimes called a *board*, it is made up of pairs of frames that show both the video and audio parts of the broadcast. The upper frame—usually in the shape of a television screen—displays a scene, while the smaller lower frame supplies a verbal description of the scene and indicates the announcer's and actors' spoken parts.

A storyboard is produced in more than one stage, since it is subject to approval by agency executives and the client. Its final form may be a flat, paper-and-cardboard sheet, a cardboard accordion shape, a book, a filmstrip, or a little movie.

In a good storyboard, the visual element outweighs the verbal (copy), and both elements are related, i.e., what is shown corresponds to what the announcer says, as when words are superimposed on the image. (Superimpositions are effective in commercials because of their power to reinforce an oral message.) A variety of camera distances and angles—the majority of shots being close-ups—and a minimum of characters and scenes also contribute to a successful television ad.

Advertising executive Maxine Paetro advises the job-hunting copywriter not to include too many storyboards in a portfolio, because of the difficulty in reading them as compared with the ease of reading a printed ad. "If you load up your book [portfolio] too heavily with boards, you may find half your book will go unseen," she cautions, in *How to Put Your Book Together and Get a Job in Advertising*. (*See: television commercials.*)

Stream of consciousness. The writing technique in which prose is intended to imitate real-life thought processes, i.e., it presents a character's thoughts and sensations exactly as they pass through his mind; the author does not distinguish between levels of consciousness, but runs complex and apparently random (but actually carefully plotted) patterns of memories, images, and fantasies one after another. Works of James Joyce, Virginia Woolf, Dorothy Richardson, and William Faulkner contain stream-of-consciousness writing.

Stream of consciousness is a difficult technique to master; it's challenging even to read. The prudent writer severely restricts the length of stream-of-consciousness passages until he is sure of his skill. (*See: interior monologue.*)

Stress and the writer. Certain aspects of the writing profession, such as deadlines, rejections—even acceptances—can bring about stressful situations that are peculiar to writers.

Writer Tom Mach, in a *Writer's Digest* article, "How to Cope With the Stress of Writing," points out that although writers need some stress in order to be creative, an excess of it can lead to physical or psychological harm. As researchers have found, when the body is continuously compelled to react to stress, it eventually (after a period of years) fails to return to its normal, relaxed state. The result of this perpetual tension can be a physical disorder such as high blood pressure, kidney damage, diabetes, heart attack, or weakened resistance to disease. In one's emotional existence, stress can cause discord in personal relationships, lack of self-confidence, or depression.

According to Mach, beginners and established writers alike experience stress, but each stage of writing brings a different set of stressful situations. For example, a tyro may be anxious while waiting for a reply from an editor, but his more experienced cohort may feel tension that results from publicity tours or slow book sales.

In his *Writer's Digest* article, Mach cites the following seven causes of stress that are common among writers: physical strain, deadlines, writer's block, self-doubt, rejection, outside interference, and financial woes. (See the "Stress Test" and "Type A Writers" in the Appendix to this encyclopedia.)

The books listed below provide insight into the causes and methods for the management of stress. (*See: drugs and writers; lifestyle of the writ-*

er—impact on the person.)
Additional information: *The Relaxation Response; The Writer's Survival Guide; Stress Without Distress;* and *The Stress of Life.*

Stress (poetry). (*See: verse.*)

Stringer. A writer who submits material to a magazine, newspaper, wire service, or television station from a specific geographical location. He is distinguished from a staffer because he works away from the home office. Some magazines call such writers stringers, others call them correspondents. They are part-time contributors, not full-time employees. They may be paid by the assignment or at an hourly rate.

Stringers function as reporters with assignments to be researched, written, and sent in to the publication. Spot news is usually telephoned to the home office and "written up" there. Occasionally the stringer is assigned to do initial research and set up local interviews for a staffer who writes the actual story. In addition to their assigned obligations, stringers are on the alert to advise editors of local developments that might deserve wider coverage. They may submit feature articles as well. A stringer has deadlines to keep and may or may not have a by-line. Some have gone on to write columns for their publications.

Stringers apply for work on local weeklies and broadcast media, city dailies and nationally news-oriented trade publications. Trade magazines that are produced by small staffs rely heavily on the input of qualified writers nationwide who have a working knowledge of a particular technical specialty. Some consumer magazines also use stringers, however, sometimes listing them on the masthead by city or region. Independent stringers may work for more than one non-competing newspaper or magazine. Payment is usually by the column-inch in newspapers, by flat fee for magazines.

Stringers are also used by television and radio stations; they film or tape as well as write stories. Most of the opportunities are in the feature story area; most of the work can be found in medium-sized cities. Work is submitted on speculation to either the news director or the assignment editor.

The term *stringer* originated from the practice of measuring a stringer's typeset copy in a galley tray in the days when newspapers were set in hot metal, and the lines of type were tied together with string.

Strophe. (*See: verse.*)

Style. Style is an elusive concept, one that defies precise definition. E.B. White had this to say on the subject: "There is no satisfactory explanation of style, no infallible guide to good writing, no assurance that a person who thinks clearly will be able to write clearly, no key that unlocks the door, no inflexible rules by which the young writer may shape his course."

Every writer, whether he creates fiction or nonfiction, poetry or drama, catalogues or textbooks, displays an individual style that involves not only his method of presentation, but also his very expression of ideas. Style is to some extent inherent. Every writer possesses a style, good or bad. Writing style may nevertheless be developed, through the practice of writing and the comprehension and mastery of grammatical techniques.

Three criteria can determine the effectiveness of writing style. They are naturalness from the writer's point of view, acceptability from the reader's point of view, and appropriateness to the content of the piece.

Good writing style is rarely characterized by complex constructions and polysyllabic words. Rather, it is a quality that evolves, refining itself with practice. (*See: formal writing style; informal writing style; language and style, books on; slang.*)

Style sheet. Many book publishing houses issue a set of guidelines on style to help authors prepare their manuscripts according to the particular preferences of the individual publishing house. Style sheets usually refer to physical style—e.g., handling of numbers, hyphenation, references to gender—rather than literary style, although there are exceptions. Some publishers of paperback romances, for instance, issue very specific guidelines to plot, setting, and so on—down to the heroine's age and appearance.

Subhead. This publishing term is used two different ways. *Subheads* are brief explanatory headlines that appear periodically in the main body of the text. They are used both in magazine articles and within book chapters.

Another kind of subhead—usually called a subtitle—is a secondary explanation of a book's or article's main title; it is placed below the title.

Subject Guide to Books In Print. An annual directory listing books in print according to subject categories corresponding to those of the Library of Congress. Listings, which are alphabetized under each category according to author's last name, also provide such information as title, name of publisher or distributor, publication date, price, indication of illustrations, Library of Congress number, and ISBN.

Individual works of fiction, poetry, and drama are not listed in this compilation, but anthologies are. Translated works are listed in categories such as "French Fiction—Translations into English."

Subject Guide to Books In Print is printed in more than one volume; the last volume of each annual series contains an alphabetical listing of abbreviations of publishers and distributors, with addresses. (*See: Forthcoming Books; Subject Guide to Forthcoming Books.*)

Subject Guide to Forthcoming Books. Published bimonthly, this series supplements *Forthcoming Books* and lists books planned for the subsequent five months. It is arranged by subject categories, in alphabetical order, most of which categories are those used by the Library of Congress. An additional section is devoted to juvenile books. Individual listings appear in alphabetical order by author's last name and contain such information as title, publisher, publication date, price, and publisher's order number. Writers of nonfiction books use this publication, in addition to the *Subject Guide to Books In Print*, to check the competition for their own nonfiction book ideas.

The indexes in *Subject Guide to*

Forthcoming Books are by subject, juvenile books, new publishers and distributors, and a key to publishers' & distributors' abbreviations. (*See:* Forthcoming Books.)

Subjective writing. Writing characterized by the personal, reflective involvement of the author. Based on the writer's own experiences or on his reactions to the experiences of others, subjective writing centers on the expression of personal thoughts, impulses, and feelings. A subjective writer asserts his own personality in his writing and reveals something of his life or his views to the reader. (The objective writer avoids any such intrusion of his own background or opinions in his writing.)

Almost any type of writing can be subjective. Autobiographies are, naturally, almost entirely subjective; much contemporary poetry, such as the work of Dylan Thomas and Robert Lowell, is subjective; Virginia Woolf's novels and essays and John Dos Passos's poems, plays, and novels are particularly subjective.

An author's material is described as subjective only if the ideas and emotions expressed by him or his characters are his own ideas and emotions, representative of his own personality. Seldom is the "I" narrator of a first-person novel the voice of the author; more often than not, that "I" is a character created by the author to tell the story. Someone reading a contemporary women's novel, for example, should not assume that, because the "I" narrator of the story has an abortion, the author of the book is revealing that she herself has had an abortion and takes a positive stand on the subject. All writing is to a certain extent inevitably subjective, but a reader should not assume that the events of a novel or the emotions revealed in a poem are necessarily autobiographical.

One danger in subjective writing is that the author becomes so self-reflective that much of what he has to say is of little importance to the reader. Even the subjective writer must write about matters that interest many people, not just himself—topics with which his reader can identify. As is true of all material written to be read, the purpose of subjective writing is to communicate. Personal introspection and unfocused rambling that cannot be generalized to a larger population than the author himself will not usually result in readable writing or effective communication. (*See: objective writing; personal experience.*)

Submission of manuscripts. (*See: manuscript preparation and submission.*)

Subplot. A minor or secondary plot in a play or work of fiction that may highlight or contrast the principal plot. In Lawrence Sander's novel *The First Deadly Sin*, for example, the main plot involves a police detective's pursuit of a mass murderer; a subplot running throughout the narrative deals with the illness and hospitalization of the police detective's wife, and its effect on his personal and professional life.

Novels, plays, films, and teleplays all can have subplots, but the short story is too concise a form to include them. (*See: plot.*)

Subscription books. A type of book that is marketed as a group, usually by direct mail or by door-to-door salesmen, but sometimes in retail stores. Most subscription books are encyclopedias, but general reference books, atlases, dictionaries, and literary classics can fall under this category as well. The various Time-Life series, sold by direct mail, are examples.

Different publishers make different arrangements with the consumer regarding the purchase of a set of subscription books. Sometimes the entire series is paid for at once; sometimes each book is paid for as it is received. The consumer is not always required to purchase all books in a set.

Subsidiary rights. A term that usually refers to rights to a book other than book publication rights. Subsidiary rights include dramatic, radio, television, motion picture, foreign, and serial rights.

Profits from subsidiary rights are divided between author and publisher. The actual terms of those divisions—i.e., which party has the right to sell them and who receives what percentage of the earnings—is spelled out in the contract for the sale of the manuscript. The Authors Guild has established guidelines for negotiating division of subsidiary rights. It advises that the author receive at least 80% of the earnings on a British edition, 75% on foreign editions, 50% on paperback and book club sales, and 90% on movie and television sales.

Even though terms are agreed on in the contract, the author's income depends on the success of the publisher or agent in selling the various subsidiary rights. A chart of the possible "Rights for Sale" appears in the Appendix to this encyclopedia. (*See: book contract; rights to manuscripts.*)

Additional information: *Law and the Writer.*

Subsidy publishing. *Subsidy publishing* refers to a publishing venture that is financed entirely by the author. The subsidy publisher profits on every book he produces, while the author takes the financial risk. Reviews are hard to obtain on subsidy-published books, and for most books published by this method, it is estimated that only one of ten authors recoups his investment. On the other hand, persons who can afford the cost of production have the satisfaction of seeing their ideas, opinions, or information set forth in a permanent form to share with others.

A major factor that distinguishes subsidy publishing from self-publishing is that in the subsidy business, ownership and distribution of the book belong to the publisher, while in self-publishing, they belong to the author.

Before entering into a subsidy publishing agreement, an author should determine the policies of the publisher. The *Writer's Digest* reprint "Does it pay to pay to have it published?" (available for an SASE, from Writer's Digest Books, 9933 Alliance Road, Cincinnati OH 45242) enumerates basic questions that should be addressed to a subsidy publisher.

Although a subsidy publisher usually pays the author's copyright fee, the book should be copyrighted in the author's name. Similarly, the author should retain all rights to his work. The agreement should provide for a royalty greater than that paid by a trade publisher, the latter of which is currently 10%-15% of the retail price.

Some advantages of subsidy publishing are short production time, little chance of rejection, and royalties that are tax free until the author recovers his original investment.

Subsidy publishers advertise in newspapers and magazines, and will discuss details during in-person interviews with authors in various cities their salespersons visit. (*See: self-publishing.*)

Sunday magazine. Formerly known as a Sunday supplement, this is a category of magazine that is inserted in a Sunday newspaper. Material published in a Sunday magazine is timely and of regional focus. It often deals with news-related subjects, although its longer production lead time—sometimes six weeks before publication—makes it unsuitable for fast-breaking news.

One purpose of the Sunday magazine is to provide in-depth material that usually cannot be accommodated by the newspaper itself. What was recently a hard news story, for example, is sometimes recapitulated with additional information, interviews, and interpretive analysis and written as a feature for publication in a Sunday magazine.

Features published in Sunday magazines usually require more research than those published in the newspaper. Investigative articles, articles of opinion, how-to articles, round-up articles, and personality profiles are other categories sought by many Sunday magazine editors. Although there are exceptions, the writer submitting material to these magazines generally should avoid history and fiction.

Since editors depend on freelance writers for most Sunday magazine articles, the category represents a market with numerous opportunities; the frequency of publication indicates the quantity of material required. In addition, these publications are generally receptive to the work of new writers.

Earnings in the Sunday magazine category are relatively low; very few local publications pay as much as $150 minimum per article. Nationally distributed magazines, however, like *Parade*, pay $1,000 for 800-1,500 words.

Sunday supplement. (*See: Sunday magazine.*)

Super. Abbreviation for *superimpose*. In television and motion pictures, titles are often superimposed over scenes. Sometimes one picture is superimposed over another. In television advertising, a slogan or other message is sometimes superimposed over a shot. (*See: storyboard; television script terms.*)

Surprise ending. A sudden and unexpected twist in the action at the end of a narrative—usually a short story. A surprise ending differs from a *trick ending* in that information making the surprise ending logical and satisfying to the reader is planted early in the story. Editors do not like surprise endings in which, for example, the main character turns out to be a dog. O. Henry (William Sidney Porter) and Saki (H.H. Munro) are noted for their mastery of the surprise ending. Stories featuring the surprise or twist ending are often found in *Alfred Hitchcock's Mystery Magazine*. (*See: plant; trick ending.*)

Suspense. Suspense is the element of both fiction and some nonfiction that makes the reader uncertain about the outcome. While most obvious in mystery stories such as those published in *Ellery Queen's Mystery Magazine* or *Alfred Hitchcock's Mystery Magazine,* suspense is present in all good fiction.

Suspense can be created through almost any element of a story, including the title, characters, plot, time restrictions, and word choice. For example, if the plot involves the hero trying to reach an intended victim before a bomb is set to explode, the author has used *time restriction* as a suspense device.

Another means for creating suspense is to use the *objective viewpoint* in which the story is told, not through the mind and feelings of a major character, but only by what he says and does. That character may have some secret that affects the outcome of the story, but since the author never tells us what he's thinking—or remembering—but only what he says and does in the present, the viewpoint adds to suspense.

The reader may also be tantalized as an *impending event* is gradually unfolded.

Just as readers will remain loyal to a writer who offers well-constructed, suspenseful plots, they are likely, as are editors, to reject one who resorts to trickery. A trick ending, for example, introduces a solution in the form of a character or a piece of information that has not been alluded to before.

Suspension of disbelief. The mind of the reader, viewer, or listener willingly effects a *suspension of disbelief* when the author's successful rendition of a fictional character or event seems "real" to the reader. This process allows the reader or audience member to accept the imaginative aspects in a work of fiction, poetry, or drama.

Ben Jonson made the first allusion to this concept, when he wrote, in *Discoveries:* "To many things a man should owe but a temporary belief, and suspension of his own judgment." Coleridge, in *Biographica Literaria,* described this idea as "that willing suspension of disbelief for the moment, which constitutes poetic faith."

Sustaining program. In broadcasting, a program that is not sponsored by a commercial advertiser.

Symbolic quote. A statement in an article that is put in quotation marks, but is not a specific quote from one single person; instead, a symbolic quote is a composite of ideas expressed by several persons in different interviews. For example, a quote that is a composite of several different quotes from middle management executives of Midwestern companies may be attributed to a single middle management executive with a Midwestern company.

Symbolic quotes are used to avoid repetitive quotes from similar persons, and to let one symbolic representative of similar sources be the spokesperson; however, some writers and editors consider use of the symbolic quote to be somewhat unethical. When a writer submits an article containing symbolic quotes, the editor must be notified, since he may have a policy of using quotes only from specific individuals.

A symbolic quote is distinguished from a *paraphrased quote* in that the latter is the idea expressed by only one person, in many of that person's exact words. (*See: composite character; paraphrase.*)

Sympathy. The act of or capacity for understanding or sharing the feelings of others; the expression of pity or compassion. Sympathy—a "feeling with"—is often confused with *empathy*, the ability to project one's personality *into* someone else and feel with that other person on a personal and deeply involved basis.

Sympathy is an important element in writing. It is that feeling that a writer strives, through skillful characterization, to evoke from readers. A reader who doesn't care what happens to the characters in a story will most likely put down the book or turn to another piece in a magazine. In order to engage the reader's capacities for identification and sympathy, then, a writer must create characters the reader can care about. (Developing in-depth profiles of a story's characters before they start to write is one way some writers achieve this.) When the reader experiences concern, admiration, sorrow, approval, pity, or compassion for a character, the writer has succeeded in creating a sympathetic character.

In order to create engaging characters, an author must himself be sympathetic and understanding, both toward his characters and toward the human condition in general. In *Writing the Novel*, Lawrence Block explains, "A first principle of characterization may seem fairly obvious, but I think it's worth stating. Characters are most effective when they are so drawn that the author can identify with them, sympathize with them, care about them, and enjoy their company." Hallie and Whit Burnett concur with Block in their *The Fiction Writer's Handbook:* "A writer without sympathy or understanding for his characters or for the

human condition would have difficulty arousing emotional response in any reader." (*See: characterization; reader identification.*)

Syndicated column. A syndicated column is a piece of writing sold simultaneously to different newspapers or magazines by a business concern (syndicate), usually for a commission on the sale price. (Some syndicates pay writers a salary or buy material outright.) Syndicated columns are promoted and sold to publications that pay for them according to the size of their circulation. The syndicate's commission is usually 40%-60% of the net proceeds of the column (gross receipts less the cost of salespeople, promotion, mailing, etc.). Writers of nationally syndicated columns currently may earn $50,000 or more a year; most syndicated columnists earn much less.

Because syndicates' primary customers are newspapers, material submitted for syndication must be clearly and succinctly written. Currently popular syndicate material includes how-to articles and personality pieces about entertainers and sportspeople.

In addition to columns, national syndicates may also handle features, puzzles, news, cartoons, and photographs. Some syndicates are interested only in certain specialties, e.g., education features, financial analyses, articles of interest to women. *Writer's Market* lists topics, submission requirements, and syndicate outlets for more than 50 syndicates around the country. The *Syndicate Directory* of *Editor & Publisher* magazine (11 W. 19th St., New York NY 10011) tells which syndicates handle current syndicated columns and classifies all syndicated columns by subject matter, so a writer can see what the existing competition for a new column idea is. (*See: self-syndication.*)

Additional information: *The Road to Syndication.*

Syndicates. (*See: syndicated column.*)

Synonym. A word having the same or nearly the same meaning as another word in the same language. For example, *gratitude* is a synonym for *thankfulness; cranky* is a synonym for *ornery.* A word or expression recognized as another name for something—such as *Ma Bell* for the Bell Telephone System—can also be described as a synonym.

Using synonyms to express the same ideas or subjects in a more effective, interesting way is one device a writer employs to add variety to his work. Since two words are seldom identical in meaning, however, a writer must choose synonyms carefully. Although the denotative meaning—that is, the dictionary definitions—of two words may be similar, the connotative meanings—those implied or associated—may be entirely different. Some individuals may say a man who lifts weights for four hours every day is a physical fitness *fanatic;* the man may huffily reply that he is a physical fitness *enthusiast.* In other words, two words may mean basically the same thing, and yet have very different implications.

There are many directories of synonyms available, but perhaps the best known is *Roget's International Thesaurus.* This reference book, which lists words by topic, includes not only synonyms and antonyms (words opposite in meaning to other words), but also slang, regional, colloquial, and foreign terms. *Roget's International Thesaurus* does not define words, and a writer mustn't choose synonyms randomly from the book without regard to precise shades of meaning and connotation, which could be confirmed by consulting a dictionary. The thesaurus is, however, an aid to the writer seeking exactly the right word to express a thought, or a less predictable way of communicating an idea. Writers who prefer an alphabetical arrangement of synonyms to arrangement by topic use books like *The Synonym Finder.* Whichever source the writer uses, a caution against *overuse* is in order. (*See: thesaurus.*)

Synonym finder. (*See: thesaurus.*)

Synopsis. A statement giving a brief, general review or condensation of a topic or subject. It is most frequently used to describe the plot summary of a story, novel, or play.

A synopsis also forms part of a book proposal that an author submits to a publisher. A proposal generally consists of a comprehensive summary of the contents of the proposed book (the synopsis), along with two or three sample chapters and an outline detailing chapter-by-chapter highlights of the work. (*See: book manuscript preparation and submission.*)

Syntax. *Syntax* refers to sentence structure, the arrangement and grammatical relations of words, phrases, and clauses in a sentence. Although the word is often used as a synonym for *grammar,* syntax is actually a branch of the science of grammar. (*See: grammar.*)

Table of contents. A listing at the beginning of a book or magazine, indicating chapter, article, or story titles and their corresponding page numbers. A table of contents can also include brief descriptions of each article, or titles of the sections, as well as the chapters, of a book.

An integral part of the front matter of any published book, a table of contents is also a necessary accompaniment to an author's query letter to a potential publisher on a nonfiction book idea. The writer should submit to the publisher a proposed table of contents that contains at least a one-paragraph description of each chapter. This provides the publisher with a concise and convenient way to evaluate the book's contents.

Tabloid. A weekly newspaper printed on paper that is half the size of a standard newspaper, and characterized by its emphasis on emotional impact. In addition to regular newsstand sales, they are also sold at the checkout counters of some supermarkets.

In general, stories printed in tabloids concentrate on unusual angles of more popular news stories. Their lively tone is evidenced by the inviting leads and upbeat, sometimes surprise endings.

Subject matter covered in most tabloids includes celebrities, consumer issues, unusual human interest, self-help, strange phenomena, handicapped persons, and developments in medicine. In addition, *news features*—articles elaborating on one phase of a recent news event—are prominent in tabloids.

A freelance writer who sells to a tabloid will earn varying rates, depending on the size of the publication. Fees range from less than $50 to more than $1,000.

Taboos. Writers may wonder whether or not there are still taboos, or subjects undesirable to editors, in the magazine world. Such restrictions do indeed exist: one example is shown by the field of religious magazines, whose taboos correspond to those in the religious groups they represent. Writers and photographers should be aware of areas of religious restriction, such as smoking, drinking, dancing, card playing, gambling, caffeine consumption, and certain styles of dress. In addition, any given juvenile magazine is almost certainly a market in which taboos exist. In general, magazines in this category reject subject matter that is too mature for their readers. Other types of magazines have limitations as to acceptable material, which may or may not be associated with societal taboos. Generally, such taboos are derived out of the political and economic interests of a publication's readers. For example, a strongly environmentalist magazine would never accept an article arguing that economic need warrants draining and building on the nation's remaining coastal marshlands—nor would a construction publication publish an article advocating legislation to freeze coastal development. A feminist magazine would never welcome a friendly portrait of Phyllis Schlafly or Hugh Hefner, nor would a right-wing women's magazine be delighted to publish a sympathetic portrait of either Gloria Steinem or Madalyn Murray O'Hair.

Even though taboos exist in some markets, writers of many years of experience should remember that as standards change with time, so do taboos. Some religious magazines, for example, now publish material dealing with homosexuality, theological questions, and challenges of hierarchy: in the past, such topics would have been unacceptable.

The easiest way for writers to avoid violating editors' restrictions is to check the listings in *Writer's Market* and write for sample copies and editorial guidelines. (*See: confession; juveniles, writing for; religious writing; short stories for young people.*)

Tag. A bit of information the announcer adds to the end of a previously taped radio commercial; it consists of such information as the sponsor's name, address, and business hours.

Tag (character tag). A descriptive technique that helps to quickly identify a character throughout a story. Tags are not character traits but project the specific outer person with unique gestures, speech patterns, or other background details. These vivid identification labels are effective when used consistently in the characterization of a subject; they can even make flat characters appear round. They often project a character as positive or negative: a negative tag may blind the major character to another character's trait, or a positive tag can hide the negative traits of supporting characters. Tags can make readers either sympathize with or dislike a character. Tags are most successful when they are neither too obvious nor too disguised.

Writers have many kinds of tags with which to build character identification. A *name tag* depends on the connotation of a name, e.g., Bobby Jo as a Southerner. An *action tag* refers to the peculiar body movements of a character—a limp, a way of frowning when thinking. A *speech tag* consists of a character's unique voice quality, word choice, inflection, or delivery. *Background tags* identify a character by age, education, social status, or religion, e.g., a Harvard scholar, an orthodox Hindu. *Sensory tags* are used to create images in the reader's mind, e.g., a highly-perfumed woman. *Mental tags* show how a character thinks, such as calmly or bizarrely.

Writers can also tag characters by using figures of speech to describe them, e.g., a voice as soothing as nails across a blackboard. (*See: characterization.*)

Talent. Although superior talent is perceived by most critics and editors to be an inborn quality, there are other personal factors that play a role in determining a successful writing career. Many published writers are proof that persons with limited talent can develop the writing skills needed to please readers. On the other hand, a talented writer who lacks energy and/or persistence may not publish as much material as a writer with less talent whose ambition effects his success.

Thomas Wolfe wrote of talent in *The Web and the Rock*: "If a man has a talent and cannot use it, he has failed. If he has a talent and uses only half of it, he has partly failed. If he has a talent and learns somehow to use the whole of it, he has gloriously succeeded, and won a satisfaction and a triumph few men ever know."

Talk shows. A television or radio talk show appearance presents the writer with an opportunity to reach large audiences in his marketing efforts. However, appearing on a broadcast medium can be an overwhelming experience for the initiate. Author Raymond Hull has outlined some strategies for making broadcast interviews run smoothly. Before the program, the writer can prepare himself in several ways. Watching/listening to the program can teach him about the interviewer's techniques and the program's format—e.g., whether there is a group of guests or only one. For an interview in another city, proper scheduling is crucial. The writer should be sure that he arrives in town with ample time to spare and that he arrives at the station one-half hour before the program begins. (Staying in the city for a day after the interview can result in other promotion opportunities.) It is also important that the writer learn about the program's audience, so that he is prepared to discuss his book in a way most interesting to that particular group.

Personal preparation involves dress, voice, and self-confidence. For television, a white shirt or blouse is inappropriate for best camera effect; a blue one is most suitable. A low-pitched voice—which can be acquired through practice with a tape recorder—is the most pleasing to the ear. A course in public speaking may help give the writer the self-confidence necessary for a television appearance.

It is advisable to take a copy of the book being promoted to the interview: the copy sent by the publisher (in the case where the publisher has arranged the interview) could have been lost. During the interview, the writer may also mention the book's title a few times, in suitable contexts.

The writer should be aware that he may be on camera whether or not he is speaking. Similarly, at the end of the program, the show may remain on the air for some seconds even after the conversation has stopped. In radio interviews, the writer must remember to verbalize all his responses: a shake or nod of the head communicates nothing in this medium!

After the program, the staff and crew should receive the courtesy of a thank-you. (*See: promotion by author.*)

Talking book. (*See: blind writers' resources; books, tapes of.*)

Tape recorder. This tool is useful to the writer during interviews, since it accurately and completely records the subject's responses, enabling the interviewer to concentrate on his subject, his surroundings and new questions he may want to ask.

Tape recorders can be purchased in a range of sizes and in many different degrees of quality. The pocket-sized ones are preferred by many writers because they are inconspicuous: they tend not to intimidate the interviewee. Using a high-quality tape recorder reduces the risk of malfunction—and thus of distractions—during interviews. The interviewer should always test both batteries and recorder in advance of any interview.

Some optional features of tape recorders can facilitate the interviewing and writing processes. Some models are equipped with sound devices that signal the end of a tape. Also available is the tape counter, which allows the writer to note, during the interview, the point on the tape at which significant comments are made. A similar device, the cue button, increases the tape speed; it can be used during the writing process to locate a particular statement. The review button also helps the writer locate particular places on the tape. It quickly winds the tape in reverse, while the recorder emits sound.

The microphone is another tape recorder feature available in various forms. Some are plugged into the tape recorder and may be detached at will; others are built into the machine. An accessory to the microphone, the wind screen, minimizes wind sounds and so is useful for outdoor taping.

An inexpensive accessory to the tape recorder, the telephone jack, is used to tape telephone interviews. (*See: tape recordings, reference file of.*)

Tape recordings, reference file of. Interview tapes containing material on controversial subjects should be retained in case of a lawsuit arising from the article. Subject to rules of admissibility, a tape recording can come to the writer's defense since it may prove what was said during the interview.

When the possibility of a lawsuit exists, the writer should check the state's statute of limitations, which might apply to his article (depending on where it is published, the type of claim against the article, etc.). (*See: interview; recordkeeping.*)

Target audience. The group of readers toward which a magazine or book is directed. It is characterized by similarities in age, education, income, values, interests, needs, and other such characteristics.

The salability of a piece of writing can be determined by the needs or wants of its intended audience and the skill with which the writer fulfills those needs or wants.

In the magazine field, the audience's needs are assessed by the editor, and the writer's chances of finding an audience here are greater, since there are thousands of established magazines with clearly defined target readerships. If a writer were planning an article on single-parent families, for example, he would decide on an audience to which it should be directed, then study magazines to find one aimed at his target audience. In this case, a women's magazine, a magazine on parenting, or a religious magazine would likely be suitable. Finally, the writer would submit a query to the editor of the publication he chooses.

Similarly, before a book is written, the professional writer has researched the existence of a need and the size of his proposed audience and uses that information when approaching a publisher.

Writer's Market listings provide descriptions of publications' audiences. (*See: writer's guidelines.*)

Taste. The ability to perceive and appreciate that which is harmonious, appropriate, or beautiful, particularly in literature, art, or decorum. Although certain standards of good and bad taste are established in any society, what is considered appropriate is often a subjective matter, subject to frequent change. Some critics believe that taste can be improved by studying and analyzing excellent examples of art and literature; many artists and writers, however, contend that taste is a limiting concept that stifles imagination and self-expression. Pablo Picasso once declared, "Taste is the enemy of creativeness." Antoine de Saint-Exupéry, author of *The Little Prince,* wrote, "Good taste is a virtue of the keepers of museums. If you scorn bad taste, you will have neither painting nor dancing, neither palaces nor gardens."

Although taste may well be a matter of subjectivity, the writer who in-

tends to sell his work to consumer and trade magazines, or to most publishing houses, is obliged to stay within the realm of what is generally considered "good taste." For example, some satirical magazines' idea of humor would not be considered good taste by most other magazine editors. In general, magazine editors consider bathroom humor, cartoons ridiculing religion, ethnic jokes, jokes that demean women, and humor about handicapped persons in poor taste.

Writers who feel confined by society's standards of appropriateness may have more success submitting their work to alternative publications such as the ones listed in *Writer's Market* and *The International Directory of Little Magazines and Small Presses.*

Tautology. Unnecessary repetition of the same idea in different words, without the addition of meaning or clarity. Tautologies such as "free giveaway" and "advance reservation" are frequently found in spoken and written expression. The careful, concise writer ruthlessly edits redundancy from his work.

Taxes. All writers who earn a profit, i.e., whose earnings are greater than their expenses, must pay federal income tax. Those with incomes of $400 or more after deductions are required to pay social security tax and to submit a self-employment form, Schedule SE, in addition to the Form 1040 and Schedule C tax forms.

A part-time freelance writer cannot claim losses as deductions unless he has earned a profit in two of five consecutive years. A writer earning less profit is considered to be a hobbyist rather than in business.

The writer should be aware of all aspects of his business that are tax-deductible and should keep detailed records, especially receipts, to prove his claims. Some deductible items are classes, including those taken as research or as refreshers in technique (but not as preparation for writing), mileage for travel, and dues of professional organizations. Writing supplies and expenses such as paper and postage are also deductible, as are the purchase, repair, maintenance, and depreciation of such writing or writing-related equipment as typewriters, tape recorders and cameras.

A writer may deduct expenses for the room in his house in which he works, but only if he writes regularly and uses the room solely for freelance writing. The section "The Business of Writing" in *Writer's Market* elaborates on how to calculate deductions and depreciation.

Depending on where the writer lives, he may be required to pay state or city business taxes as well as income tax. Information on local taxes is available from individual state or city tax offices. Since tax laws are subject to frequent amendment, it is best to obtain instructions each year from a local tax office. (*See: recordkeeping; retirement and the freelance writer; social security; travel.*)

Additional information: *Law and the Writer.*

Teachers & Writers Collaborative, Inc. This nonprofit organization sponsors a program of creative arts education through which writers, painters, dancers, filmmakers, and musicians are brought into class-rooms. The Collaborative's original emphasis was on language arts, and it has established three assumptions concerning the teaching of language. They are as follows: 1) "Children who are allowed to develop their own language naturally, without the imposition of artificial standards of grading, usage, and without arbitrary limits on subject matter, are encouraged to expand the boundaries of their own language"; 2) "Grammar and spelling develop as a result of an attachment to language and literature, not vice versa. Teaching these skills before children feel they are relevant stifles their interest in language"; and 3) "Children who write their own literature and read other children's are more likely to view all literature as an effort to deal with experiences in creative ways, whatever that experience may be."

The Teachers & Writers Collaborative publishes *Teachers & Writers Magazine*, as well as books and other publications on the teaching of the creative arts. Its address is 5 Union Square, New York NY 10003. (*See: Teachers & Writers Magazine.*)

Teachers & Writers Magazine. This publication is issued five times per academic year by Teachers & Writers Collaborative, Inc., an agency through which writers and artists in other fields are brought into the classroom to work with teachers and children. The magazine's content consists of teaching ideas, news digests, interviews, book reviews, letters, editorials, features, and excerpts from the diaries kept by artists who participate in the program. Student work and contributions from others are also published.

The Teachers & Writers Collaborative, Inc., is located at 5 Union Square, New York NY 10003.

Teaching writing. Teaching, which offers a supplementary income to the freelance writer, can involve the writer with various age groups and with all types of writing. In preparing for classes, he often learns new material; and in teaching others, *his* analytical, organizational, and communicative skills are expanded.

One way to become involved in teaching is to apply for a position with a creative writing program sponsored by some elementary and secondary schools. Teaching certification may be required, especially if students receive academic credit for the course. Some schools, however, offer enrichment courses for which no credit is given. Generally, teachers of enrichment courses do not need certification. Payment for a teaching writer is approximately $25-$35 per hour, although the exact rate is determined by the aspects of the particular program.

A variation of these programs are writer-in-residence programs, which are known by different titles in each state. Funds are provided by state arts councils, individual schools, and/or the National Endowment for the Arts; information is available from state arts councils, whose addresses can be obtained from the local public library.

High schools offer writers work teaching journalism. A part-time job pays from $4,000-$6,000 per year. Teaching certification is required for teaching high school journalism; a writer with a college degree may be eligible for a provisional certificate or for enrollment in additional courses leading to a teaching certificate.

Independent teaching is another option for writers. Students of the independent teacher are most often a mixture of adults and teenagers. A newspaper photo and press release, along with signs posted in the community, make up one kind of self-promotion campaign. A conference room rented from a business can serve as a classroom, and student fees can be based on comparable course fees at a local college (those fees are published in the course catalogue). Many courses founded by an independent writer are sponsored by educational institutions, such as the adult education departments of high schools or school districts. In such cases, the instructor's sponsor furnishes facilities, publicity, and a salary.

Tearsheet. A tearsheet is a sample of writing in its published form, cut from the newspaper or magazine in which it appeared.

Teaser. The opening scene of a teleplay. Its action is designed to intrigue the audience so that it will watch the following scenes. Other words for *teaser* are *hook* and *prologue*. (*See: television script terms.*)

Technical writing. Though the term *technical writing* refers to instructions or descriptions on any subject matter, it is currently being used to mean writing for the fields of engineering, government, industry, and science. Increasing development in these areas in the past decades, as well as the scarcity of writers who are scientifically oriented, have made technical writing a career of abundant opportunity.

Various types of organizations hire technical writers: corporations, university researchers, advertising agencies, newspapers, and government and private organizations that carry on research in the physical and social sciences.

Private companies, particularly those that conduct research and manufacture parts and equipment for specific customers, represent the largest market for jobs in technical writing. The private company engages a technical writer who, working closely with engineers, first produces a technical proposal that aims to sell the product, and then provides periodic progress reports detailing the work for the customer. Finally, the writer produces a handbook and an instruction manual to accompany the finished product. A writer may specialize in one of these phases of the job, or he may participate in all three.

At present, a technical writer can earn from $18,000-$25,000 per year at a full-time job, and from $10-$18 per hour in temporary work. The Yellow Pages, under the headings "Employment Contractors—Temporary Help" and "Technical Manual Preparation Service," lists sources of temporary employment in this field. (*See: Society for Technical Communication.*)

Telephone usage, tactics on. The telephone can aid a writer both in effectively conducting present business and in acquiring new projects.

When planning telephone interviews, it is helpful to be cognizant of long-distance rates, which vary according to time of day and day of the week. An interviewer in California, for example, may initiate a call at 7 a.m. to New York, where the time would be 10 a.m. In doing so, he would be taking advantage of low rates without inconveniencing the interviewee.

The writer who spends a great deal of time doing long-distance telephone interviews may benefit from installing a WATS line (Wide Area Telecommunications Service) or contracting with a private long-distance discount service such as MCI or Sprint. In addition, telephone tape-recording attachments are available so that a writer can tape a telephone interview. Taping a telephone call is not illegal so long as it is not being taped for an illegal purpose. The writer should ask the interviewee when the conversation begins if he may record for factual accuracy, then they proceed; the subject's agreement on the tape is his backup.

Another business technique related to the telephone is the use of an electronic answering service. This device allows an associate to reach the writer on his first attempt. Without such a tool, the writer faces the risk of losing assignments, since an editor is usually more likely to approach another writer than to make repeated attempts to telephone the same one.

As an alternative, the writer opposed to electronic answering devices can contract with a live answering service—which is expensive—or consider adding such custom-calling services as call waiting or call forwarding to his private or office line. Call waiting also prevents the writer from losing calls from prospective clients that may come in when he is conducting a lengthy telephone interview.

In querying editors about possible assignments, the writer should use the telephone judiciously. Most editors prefer query letters to telephone calls, except in cases of urgent timeliness. A map showing the area codes for the U.S. appears in the Appendix to this encyclopedia. (*See: time zones.*)

Teleplay. The script for a television program or a made-for-television movie. (*See: television script terms.*)

Teletext. (*See: electronic text.*)

Television commercials. The work of the television copywriter involves a group of duties besides writing, because jobs in this field often overlap among departments. Sometimes one person plays the combination role of writer-producer. The writer may be called upon to work along with the account executive, assessing the client's needs and studying the intended consumers of the product, who will make up the commercial's audience. With the producer, the writer may help choose the technical crew and actors for the commercial, and supervise wardrobe selection.

The copywriter spends several hours each week—along with other agency personnel—meeting with clients to discuss their needs, their past successes and failures, and their marketing problems. Working at a large advertising agency, the copywriter may spend only 15 minutes per week in actual writing.

Though this type of work differs from that of most writers, the television copywriter possesses certain specialized skills for which he is rewarded financially. He must be able to think in visual terms and to create a theme that will both entertain the audience and sell a product in a very short time. If he works for a small agency, the copywriter may also have a low budget to challenge him.

One advertising director suggests that the writer ask himself three questions about any television commercial he produces: 1) "Does the commercial make clear what the product or service is?" 2) "Does it show how the product or service is different or better than others?" and 3) "Is the tone of the commercial compatible with where the consumer is, in relation to the need for the product?"

Generally, a copywriter is expected to have a liberal arts background and knowledge of television production. The majority of opportunities are in staff positions at advertising agencies, and freelance work is rare. However, copywriters who work for large agencies sometimes do outside work; when accepting outside assignments, writers must avoid working on competing accounts, as this is unethical.

A writer interested in working in this field should write to an agency, submitting a résumé and requesting an appointment to show his writing samples, and discuss his commercial ideas for the agency's clients. (*See: Standard Directory of Advertising Agencies.*)

Television Information Office (TIO). An information service whose goal is to serve as a liaison between the television industry and the press, the educational system, and the general public. It is sponsored by the National Association of Broadcasters, the three national commercial television networks, individual television stations, and station groups.

TIO maintains a press list that is made up of publications and established writers. Writers and editors on the list receive research results and press releases on trends in the television industry.

Writers may use the TIO Research Center and Library, which houses books, magazines, articles, theses, dissertations, government reports, and transcripts of speeches, debates, and panel discussions. This service is available by appointment only.

Also accessible to all writers are publications that are sold inexpensively. Some publications currently available are "The ABCs of Radio and Television," "TV Mini File," "TV Sets-in-Use," "Television and the Child," "Commercial Television as a Teaching Tool," and the Roper study of public attitudes toward media. A list of all publications distributed by TIO can be obtained for an SASE by writing TIO Publications List, 745 Fifth Avenue, New York NY 10022.

Television, jobs in. Staff positions in television are numerous and varied. Most are in four major areas: production, news, engineering, and public relations. Production jobs include floor directing, camera operation, lighting, switching, directing, and set construction. Newswriting, reporting, editing, and photography are duties performed by persons in a television station's news department. Engineering work comprises electronics maintenance, mechanical maintenance, and master control

operation. Public relations practitioners are responsible for such duties as writing press releases and producing public service announcements.

Freelance television opportunities are outlined in *Jobs For Writers*. A Television Station Organization Chart appears in the Appendix to this encyclopedia.

Television Licensing Center (TLC). This office acts as an intermediary between television producers and educators who use television programs in the classroom. Through TLC, educators obtain rights to use tapes of programs, either for one year or for the life of the tape; from the fee paid by the educator, TLC distributes payments to copyright holders.

TLC members are colleges, universities, schools, school districts, and libraries; an institution becomes a member after one of its teachers has signed the TLC Master Licensing Agreement. There is currently no membership fee.

Programs that have been approved by television producers for educational use are listed, along with users' fees, in the *TLC Guide*, a bulletin sent to members. Before licensing a program listed in the *Guide*, a member may preview it— i.e., borrow the videotape from TLC and/or make a copy from it—for 45 calendar days. If he decides not to license the tape he has previewed, he erases any copies he has made (since use of unlicensed tapes is in violation of the copyright law). If, on the other hand, he decides to obtain rights to a tape, he sends the Supplementary Licensing Form to TLC, who then bills him. Fees vary among the programs and series offered, and the member pays a higher amount to obtain rights for the life of the tape than for one year.

TLC is a division of Films Incorporated, a film distribution company. Its address is 5547 N. Ravenswood, Chicago IL 60640. (*See: Copyright Clearance Center; fair use of broadcast materials.*)

Television markets. Freelance writers find markets for their work in the television series, the made-for-television movie, the documentary, the soap opera, etc. There are also a limited number of freelance jobs available for television advertising copywriters.

Selling material to television is difficult for the writer who lives outside the two centers of the industry, New York and Los Angeles. Another complicating factor is that a writer usually needs an agent to be able to sell his work to a television market. A list of television agents to whom writers may submit teleplay scripts appears in the *Writer's Market*.

Once he has made a sale, the writer can join the Writers Guild of America, which negotiates contract terms with producers. (See sample contract rates in the Appendix to this encyclopedia.) (*See: documentary; screenwriting; soap opera, writing for; Writers Guild of America.*)

Television Program Material Release Form. (See the Appendix.)

Television script. The television writer usually delivers a script to a producer one step at a time, developing it from premise to outline to script.

The *premise* is the idea for a story. It contains the basic plot, i.e., a beginning, a middle, and an end, but does not describe the story's elements in detail. It is often delivered verbally to the producer.

The outline, also called the *treatment* or the *story*, represents a great amount of effort on the writer's part. At the outline stage, he writes a narrative of the story, filling in details of plot, characterization, and emotional impact, but usually omitting dialogue. (The character's statements are written in, however, in narrative form, e.g., "John tells Jane to get out.") The outline may include camera directions.

A *format* for a series of one-hour television programs may range from one to eighty pages, containing a narrative description of what the series will be about, the leading characters, and several typical plots.

The *script*, or *teleplay* for the individual show consists of dialogue, camera directions, and stage directions. The plot of a teleplay is structured much like that of a novel or short story, except that it necessarily emphasizes action rather than reflection on the part of characters, and it usually ends at the climax. Other elements peculiar to the teleplay are the *prologue* (also called the *teaser* or *hook*), which is the first scene of the drama; and the *tag*, an epilogue in the form of a brief scene sometimes appended to the end of the drama to tie together loose story ends.

Television script terms. Definitions of these terms are listed at their alphabetical locations in this encyclopedia: angle; beat; backstory; close shot; close-up; cut to; dissolve; establishing shot; exterior; fade in; fade out; full shot; hold; interior; long form; off-screen; pan; point of view; presentation; pull back; scene;

spitballing; super; teaser; teleplay; treatment; two shot; voice-over; wide angle.

Television writing. Like screenwriters, television writers should live in Southern California or New York City, since it is difficult to keep abreast of changes in television series without living in the area where they are produced. Writers attempting to break into television, however, face considerable financial risk by moving to New York or Los Angeles without a sale, an agent, or a contact in the industry.

Writers Guild rules prohibit a member writer's actually writing a script without a contract guaranteeing compensation, but novice (i.e., non-Guild) writers who aspire to breaking into the field must usually do so by writing entire scripts on speculation—without an assignment or guarantee of production. The unknown freelancer presents prospective agents with a completed script, rather than a mere idea, a plot synopsis, or a treatment because he must demonstrate that he can write a produceable script.

Before a would-be writer heads to Hollywood—or even *writes* to Hollywood—he should be thoroughly familiar with the peculiarities of television scriptwriting. He must be able to neatly structure a script around commercial breaks, and write convincing characters for series that have been created by other writers. He should understand production limitations and confine an episode's action to a series' standard sets; he must also be able to figure out what subject matter is taboo for a particular series.

Most teleplays are bought in the early spring of each year, although the introduction of the two-season year has created a year-round need for television scripts. To sell his work, a television writer should have an agent. Experts advise the aspiring scriptwriter to proceed by writing a teleplay on speculation and mailing it to an agent. (Listings of agents can be found in *Writer's Market*.)

A booklet containing television writers' minimum rates, which are established by the Writers Guild of America, is available for a small fee from Writers Guild of America West, 8955 Beverly Boulevard, Los Angeles CA 90048.

Protection for a television script can be secured either through Writers Guild of America registration (registrants need not be members) or Copyright Office registration. (*See: audiovisual communication; screenwriting; soap opera, writing for; television commercials; television script; Writers Guild of America.*)

Additional information: *The TV Scriptwriter's Handbook.*

Tempo. (*See: pace.*)

Testimonial. An endorsement of a product intended to induce others to buy that product. Testimonials often appear on the dust jackets of books, recommending those works to potential buyers. These endorsements may be from celebrities, recognized authorities in the subject field, other well-known authors, or sometimes individuals who are not well known at all, but who represent satisfied readers of the book.

Testimonials can be an effective means of promotion, since market research indicates that people are more likely to buy a product that other people have recommended. Other research tests show, however, that the testimonial is effective only when the endorser is an actual expert or someone with whom the potential buyer can identify.

A publisher's publicity department generally takes care of soliciting testimonials from individuals—including other authors—whose names and/or remarks they feel will stimulate sales of the book. An author may suggest to his publisher the names of celebrities or authorities he believes will respond favorably to his book. The writer who intends to publish his own book may attempt to gather endorsements for his book while it is still in the manuscript stage; these testimonials can then be incorporated into the dust jacket copy (or cover, if the book is paperback) when the book is printed. (*See: blurb.*)

Textbook publishing. A writer who intends to write a textbook has the best chance of having it published if he has teaching experience in the field he proposes to cover in the book, knowledge of his research field, and the ability to write clearly.

Before beginning a textbook manuscript, the writer must determine what other books have been written on the topic. Such research involves analysis of the topic coverage, organization, problems and examples (if a science book), and style of existing books.

After the writer has determined the audience for his text and completed his basic outline and objectives, the writer must test the book's teaching capacity. A publisher needs to know whether a book is ef-fective in practice when considering it for publication. If the writer is a teacher, he tests his book by using it (or the completed sections) in a classroom, and giving it to other teachers to use as well.

Next, the author chooses a publisher. Most textbook publishers specialize in a particular learning level, so the author must determine the appropriate publisher for his type of textbook. (*Writer's Market* describes some textbook publishers and their needs.)

The package that a writer submits to a textbook publisher is known as a prospectus. It consists of the writer's résumé, as well as data on the manuscript itself, including title, synopsis of the contents, a description of the competition, and an indication of the proposed audience and market for the book. Also included in a prospectus are the estimated length of the book; a description of the number and kinds of illustrations, if any, to be used; an indication of whether copyrighted material will be used; and a statement of how much of the manuscript has been written, along with an estimate of time needed to complete the manuscript. The prospectus also includes an outline of the manuscript and the parts of the actual text that have been tested. With the prospectus, a writer should send a short letter informing the publisher of the subject matter and grade level of his book, and an SASE. The letter and prospectus should be typed (the prospectus double-spaced) on 8½x11-inch paper; they are mailed flat to the publisher.

A textbook publisher's response, which is usually received in four to six weeks, can be in the form of a phone call, a visit from an editor, a contract, or a letter—which can ask for more material, suggest revisions, or reject the manuscript.

Textbook publishers sometimes research the market themselves, by questionnaires, visits to teachers, market reports, and attending teachers' conferences, for example. In such a case, an editor devises a plan for a textbook and chooses an author, who then writes the book.

An author who plans to write a textbook must be aware that each state has established criteria by which it chooses books to be used in its schools. Also, textbooks written for elementary school use are often part of a series, so the writer in this field should be prepared to work on books for several grade levels.

Royalties for elementary school and secondary school textbooks range from 3%-5% of the publisher's net receipts; those for college-level texts range from 10%-15%.

A press run of printed and bound textbooks is usually 5,000-10,000 copies. In some cases, more books are printed but are left unbound until needed.

A list of state textbook administrators and their addresses appears in the Appendix to this encyclopedia. (*See: schools, supplementary books for; stories in textbooks; textbook selection process.*)

Textbook selection process. In some states, a book selected for use as a textbook in schools is adopted on a statewide basis; in others, a book can be adopted by an individual school district. To find out if a state has statewide adoption (and might give favorable preference to a particular author as a native or resident), the writer should contact the director of the state department of education at his state capital. (*See: National Association of State Textbook Administrators.*)

TFN. " 'Til further notice"; sometimes used on commercial copy instead of a final broadcast date.

Theater. Beginning playwrights dream of selling their first works to Broadway producers. This goal is virtually impossible without a good agent, who will seldom agree to handle the work of a newcomer; the fact that Broadway rarely sees new plays these days increases the odds against the novice's breaking in. Play producers are most receptive to plays that have been performed, since such plays are likely to have had their rough spots smoothed out and have proven audience appeal.

There are other markets, however, more open-minded about the work of new playwrights—and closer to home. Local groups and clubs perform children's plays and church-related plays. Most high schools and colleges stage dramatic productions at least once a year; schools with flourishing drama departments may produce a dozen. Some communities have drama groups, made up of talented amateurs and/or former professionals, that may be receptive to new material. The dinner theater, another locally based market, is an outlet for playwrights who produce light entertainment. No matter which local market, however, getting produced is often easier for the playwright who has been involved with the group in another capacity, e.g., as a stagehand or actor.

The more ambitious new playwright, however, can approach a regional professional equity theater, such as Actors Theatre of Louisville or Chicago's Goodman Theatre, that solicits new plays and whose productions often reach Broadway; an off-Broadway theater such as the Manhattan Theatre Club, or a play publisher. The "Scriptwriting/Playwriting" section of *Writer's Market* details the guidelines for different theaters and publishers around the country.

Plays that are produced on Broadway earn the playwright royalties, which are based on weekly box office receipts. The Dramatists Guild and the League of New York Theatres and Producers, Inc. have established the following royalty system for the playwright's earnings: 5% of the first $5,000 gross weekly box office receipts, 7½% of the next $2,000, and 10% of amounts of more than $7,000. (*See: children's theater; playwriting.*)

Theme. The theme of a story is the point a writer wishes to make. It poses a question, a human problem. The plot is the series of events that proves or disproves that point. The plot is like the trunk and branches of a story; the theme is the carefully hidden roots. The theme should never be obvious, but without it, a story is trivial.

A theme may be as simple as "Honesty is the best policy" or as complex as the violence in the work of Joyce Carol Oates. Oates says, "I have been aware for many years of the precariousness of our life in America." This precariousness is her theme.

In the religious writing field, the theme is often the power of prayer. In stories for children and young adults it frequently deals with character development. In the mystery field, it says that crime does not pay.

The theme may be concerned with social issues: Charles Dickens wrote of child exploitation in *Oliver Twist* and *David Copperfield*; *All Quiet on the Western Front* and *The Deer Hunter* tell of the ugliness and tragedy of war. The theme of Thomas Wolfe's *You Can't Go Home Again* is implicit in the title. The theme of the TV series *Dallas* is the destruction caused by greed and ruthless ambition.

A theme is a natural, unobtrusive part of a story. The writer starts with an idea; as his story develops, it is influenced by his own philosophy or his observation of the human condition. This is his theme, the quality that brings with it a sense of values and drama.

Thesaurus. A thesaurus is a reference book listing synonyms and antonyms. Some thesauri arrange words alphabetically, while others group them according to subject.

Peter Mark Roget first published, in 1852, his *Thesaurus of English Words and Phrases Classified and Arranged so as to Facilitate the Expression of Ideas and Assist in Literary Composition*—and many subsequent editions and variations have followed. A current edition reminds writers that "In a dictionary you start with a word and look for its meaning. In *Roget's International Thesaurus*, you start with your idea and find the words to express it."

Using a thesaurus helps the writer find the exact words he needs to convey a meaning or image. This kind of reference also helps him avoid being repetitive, since it enables him to choose different words having the same meaning.

Writers must avoid the tendency, however, to use too many unfamiliar words when simpler ones would serve as well.

Think article. (*See: magazine article, types of.*)

Third person major character viewpoint. In this angle of narration, the author centers everything on the life of the main character. By following *only* what the main character sees, hears, feels, and thinks, the writer, and therefore, the reader, inevitably begins to identify with the character, and care what happens to him. While dialogue is in the first person, the narration by the author is told in the third person. Here is the opening of a story by Sean McMartin from *Ellery Queen's Mystery Magazine:*

John Laverty sprawled on the sofa like a carelessly tossed suit. Alongside him, her posture more dignified, his wife skimmed a newspaper. The Nine O'Clock Newsbreak was on TV. John barely noticed the orange-and-black swirl of the daily fire. TV news stories were chosen strictly for color values, by cameramen.

Their daughter, Mary Kate, was by now giggling and shrieking at a pajama party for ten-year-olds two houses down and they had one of their rare evenings alone. A homicide dick in one of the most murderous cities in the world had little enough of the simple pleasures and John welcomed the opportunity to wind down, think as little as possible, and just plain enjoy.

His wife suddenly gasped and dropped the paper. "John, that's *our* house!"

He caught the tail-end of the reporter's overvoice "—Park Avenue and One Hundred Seventy-eighth Street."

The tenement on the right of the driveway to what had been O'Day's Garage was ribboned with flames, smoke, and a snakepit of streaming fire hoses. The picture shifted to the top floor rear where a fire-escape stood out like the skeleton of a prehistoric monster. There was a gnawing pain in John's chest.

They had lived for years now in a split-level on Long Island and The Bronx had been left behind forever. But it *had* been their house. God! The mind was a con artist, fragmenting and hiding memories in a thousand scattered pockets, making you believe they would die in peace. Then a word, an odor, a picture . . .

30. This symbol is typed at the end of a newspaper story to denote the end of that piece of copy. The origin of this practice is unknown, although several stories attempt to explain it.

The most popular story places the origin of "30" in the Civil War period when news was transmitted by telegraph. The first message sent to a press association in the U.S. contained 30 words, and so its sender, as was the practice, indicated this with the number "30" at the end. The "30" was retained for all telegraphed news, and eventually, for news stories in general.

Other theories reported in William Metz's *Newswriting: From Lead to "30,"* maintain that "30" evolved from the symbol "XXX," which was placed at the end of the very early, handwritten news items. The symbol, interpreted as a Roman numeral, became, naturally, "30."

Still others have related the origin

of "30" to an early typesetting practice that used the symbol to indicate the end of a line; the original Associated Press quota of 30 items per newspaper per day; and a reporter who added his name, Thirtee, to the end of a telegraphed message, which was changed by the telegrapher to 30. Some magazine writers use the symbol "30" to indicate the end of an article; others use three number marks (such as # # #); still others simply type "The End."

Thomas' Register of American Manufacturers. This multi-volume reference lists addresses of manufacturers, producers, importers, and other suppliers to American industry. Volumes I-IX of *Thomas' Register* are set up alphabetically by product, with manufacturers listed geographically under each product. Volumes X and XI are alphabetical manufacturer lists. Subsequent volumes reproduce the manufacturers' catalogues.

These directories, available in most public libraries, can be useful to writers who want to track down companies that make products on which they're seeking resource material.

Thor Power Tool Ruling. An Internal Revenue Service rule that resulted from the 1979 case *IRS vs. Thor Power Tool Co.* This rule limits the extent to which businesses can reduce the value of their inventoried goods to lessen the amount of tax they pay on profits. In book publishing, the only inventoried goods permitted to be counted as losses are books that have been remaindered or destroyed.

The major consequences of Thor for the writer are that: 1) books are re-maindered sooner so their exposure to the public is more limited; and 2) publishers are less willing to take chances on books that seem risky.

Publishers have responded to the ruling by producing smaller first printings. This is more costly to them, and so the consumer faces a higher price for the book.

Reference, professional and textbook publishers perhaps are affected more strongly by Thor, because their press runs are generally larger than those of trade book houses. One printing of a reference or scholarly book is intended to be sold over a period of years, so books are more likely to be in stock during more than one taxable year.

Thriller. A film, novel, or play intended to arouse feelings of excitement or suspense. Works in this genre are highly sensational, usually focusing on illegal activities, international espionage, sex, and violence. A thriller is often a detective story in which the forces of good are pitted against the forces of evil in a kill-or-be-killed situation. Ken Follett (*Eye of the Needle*, *The Key to Rebecca*) and Frederick Forsyth (*The Day of the Jackal*, *The Odessa File*) have written a number of successful novels in this genre. Alfred Hitchcock directed countless film thrillers, including the classic *Psycho*. (*See: suspense.*)

Tie-in. This term refers to a work issued in two or more media—for example, a motion picture and a paperback or hardcover book based on that motion picture, or a television mini-series and a book based on that mini-series. This merchandising venture is designed to stimulate sales of the work in both media by strategic timing of issuance and joint promotion. A paperback based on a motion picture may, for example, be released two or three months before the motion picture is scheduled to open; the paperback sales are not only profitable in themselves, but also serve to promote the forthcoming movie. Or a bestselling novel, made into a movie, is reissued with a new cover touting the movie and its stars. Once the movie is released, it in turn promotes the book.

For a few years at the end of the 1970s, tie-ins were becoming more and more important as money-making enterprises as the relationship between the motion picture industry and the publishing business grew increasingly stronger. Traditionally, the movie rights to books published by hardcover publishing houses have been sold to movie companies, but gradually, instead of just buying rights, Hollywood studios began working with hardcover publishing houses, arranging joint ventures in which the publication of a mass-market paperback was tied in with the release of a movie bearing the same title. Soon the film producers themselves began to hire freelance writers and prepare their own book versions of certain movies, licensing the book publication rights to these "novelizations" to paperback and sometimes hardcover publishers as part of a package deal.

Novelizations, a term that describes the movie-to-book process, were not immediately recognized as profitable in themselves. Movie producers originally thought of them primarily as "mini-posters" that would help promote a movie. It wasn't until the novelization of The Omen sold more than 3½ million copies in 1976 that the value of novelizations became apparent.

From then on, tie-ins became the focus of complicated, big-money deals, but the bottom soon dropped out of the tie-in market as novelizations proved to be disappointing literarily and financially.

Publishers who lost hundreds of thousands of dollars on movie tie-ins soon realized that the correlation between a movie's success and its tie-in sales isn't a simple one. The kind of movie seems to be more important than its box-office receipts: comedies and love stories do not sell, but horror, fantasy, and science fiction do. Well-written novelizations of "content" films such as *Brubaker* and *The Elephant Man* also sell well.

Currently, publishers approach novelizations cautiously. One symptom of caution is that the writer's payment has dropped; remuneration for a novelization—usually a flat fee, with no royalties involved—averages $3,500-$15,000, sometimes more, depending on the writer's reputation and the amount of work he must do. (*See: novelization.*)

Time advertising. (*See: radio commercials; space advertising.*)

Time signal. In radio, the combination of a ten-second commercial from a sponsor or the station's call letters with an announcement of the time of day.

Time zones. The U.S. comprises seven time zones within the Standard Time System: Eastern Time, Central Time, Mountain Time, Pacific Time, Yukon Time, Alaska-Hawaii Time, and Bering Time. (A map showing these time zones appears in the Appendix to this encyclopedia.)

Being aware of the time difference between zones can aid the writer in plans for travel or long-distance telephone interviews—and in the latter case, sometimes save him money. A California writer, for example, can use the lower-rate morning hours to call an Eastern contact where the time is three hours later.

Most states in the U.S. participate in Daylight Saving Time, which begins each year on the last Sunday of April and ends on the last Sunday of October. Under this system, clocks are moved forward one hour in the spring and moved back one hour in the fall. Arizona, Hawaii, and part of Indiana do not convert to Daylight Saving Time. Freelancers traveling between time zones should keep these time differences in mind when making appointments and allowing for travel time.

Timeliness. In article writing, the timeliness of a story can make it necessary for the writer to bypass the customary query letter and telephone an editor about his piece. For example, a writer who gains access to a celebrity who will only be visiting his town for one day will need a no or a yes, I'd-like-to-see-the-story from his editor right away.

Seasonal articles, though they have an element of timeliness, cannot be sold in the same season their subjects (e.g., holidays) take place. Editors require that seasonal articles be submitted months ahead of their intended publication date; their preferences in lead time generally range from three to six months.

These lead times refer to magazines, of course; newspaper editors work on shorter seasonal deadlines. (*See: lead time; seasonal material.*)

Title page. A page at the beginning of a book that carries the work's full title (including subtitle), the author's or editor's name, the publisher's name, and any other publishing information required by the author-publisher contract or desired by the publisher. There may also be various credits such as the name of a translator, photographer, or illustrator on the title page. Sometimes a quotation or illustration appears on this page.

The title page is often the second printed page of a book, following the *half-title* page in the front matter. The title page may also be the first printed page in some works that do not have a half-title page. (*See: half title.*)

Titles. Although every title is the result of creative effort, inventing one is not necessarily purely inspiration. There are patterns to follow (usually based on successful titles) and literary devices to incorporate; both of these approaches can help the writer express a title effectively.

Suggested devices to use in creating effective titles are alliteration, superlatives, mysticism, negativism, interrogative words, prepositional phrases, and quotations, either from another literary work or from the work being titled.

The important elements of good titles are clarity and suspense. The title should give the reader a direct indication of the work's content or plot, but should not, in the case of fiction, reveal too much of the story. Other functions of a title are to entice potential readers, to instill curiosity, to give an indication of what type of book or story a work is, to set the tone for the piece, and to clarify a theme. Book titles, especially, are chosen for *sales appeal* as well as clarity. Book titles are often short so they can be printed in larger type, making them visible from farther away in a bookstore and making them easier to read when the jacket is reproduced in small scale in ads or shown on television.

The writer should remember that a title usually influences an editor, either consciously or unconsciously; in that sense, creating an effective title is part of the writer's sales effort. However, an editor who buys a manuscript has the right to change a title; the writer may or may not be informed of a change.

Worn-out titles and phrases are unwelcome at publishing houses. To avoid submitting an already used title, a writer can compare his completed title with those listed in book indexes and periodical indexes.

Tone. The tone of a piece of writing is set by the author's attitude toward his characters or subjects; he chooses words and literary techniques to create the atmosphere he wants. For example, is the effect to be achieved sombre, playful, ironic, intimate, or some other attitude? Whereas a speaker can partly indicate tone by changes in voice or manner, the writer must rely on language and literary devices alone.

"Tony" Awards. These awards for accomplishment in the Broadway theater are presented annually by the League of New York Theatres and Producers, Inc., under the official name the Antoinette Perry Awards. Each winner receives an embossed silver medallion. Various categories of theater work are recognized; awards applicable to writers are Best Play and Best Musical. The address of the League of New York Theatres and Producers, Inc., is 226 W. 47th Street, New York NY 10036.

Tools, writing. Writing is a business requiring very little initial monetary investment. Although some equipment is necessary for both the published writer and the would-be published writer, the major tools of the trade are energy and imagination.

Every beginning writer should own a typewriter, a bookcase, and a file cabinet. Nonfiction writers should have a tape recorder and a camera. Established writers who can afford the expense of a photocopying machine may find it a convenience to their home offices. Another useful, though not essential, piece of writing equipment is the word processor.

There are opportunities for increasing sophistication in a freelance writer's equipment. However, the writer need not dispense substantial amounts in the beginning: his investments can correspond to his actual or projected earnings. (*See: camera; tape recorder; typewriters; word processor.*)

Topical. This adjective is applied to subjects and concerns of current interest. In writing and publishing, topical subjects are often called "hot" topics. A few years ago, for example, "disco" was a hot topic. The book market was flooded with "How to Disco" books. Magazines were filled with articles on "What to Wear to the Disco" and "How to Meet Men/Women at a Disco." As public interests wax and wane, so do related hot topics. Writers try to stay abreast of topical subjects by keeping their reading materials as catholic as possible.

The subjects a writer chooses for nonfiction books and articles should always be timely—that is, of contemporary interest. There is a danger in a too-topical idea, however, both in book proposals and article ideas. In *A Writer's Guide to Book Publishing*, Richard Balkin says that while there is always room for the serious, carefully researched, well-written book that has permanent value, many writers make the mistake of submitting proposals for books whose subjects are one to three years out of date. He explains:

Certain subjects of topical interest become popular for a year or two. Then they either become permanent features, such as ecology, maintaining a long life; or they abruptly fade into obscurity. The publisher, during the period of intense interest, receives scores of proposals from authors who attempt to jump on this bandwagon, though many of these are hastily conceived proposals (often for anthologies and reprints) that arrive too late to be of real interest. In the past few years back-to-the-land, the occult, women's studies, pollution, and counter-culture have been subject areas heading the fad list. While such topics may deserve the consumer and publishing attention they get, the average publisher can be overcontracted in those fields by the time the topic is nationally popular, or feel that the wave has crested.

Book authors also need to remember that there is usually a 6- to 12-month production period between delivery of the manuscript and the published book.

Art Spikol, author of *Magazine Writing: The Inside Angle*, warns against the too-timely article idea. In the event such an article is rejected, "there's no time to sell it elsewhere since its only significance was its timeliness."

A subject need not be contemporary to be topical. It does, however, need to be of contemporary *interest*. The Festival of Dionysus held in ancient Athens may not appear to hold any current interest for readers. However, if a fraternity at a local college holds an annual Festival of Dionysus, a writer has found a topical angle to the subject. In other words, contemporary treatment and reference can make the oldest subject topical. (*See: ideas, where to get them; timeliness.*)

Tour de force. French for "feat of strength, skill, or virtuosity." The phrase is sometimes used to describe an exceptional achievement by an author. The phrase also applies to an artful technique in dealing with a difficult situation in writing. John Updike's *Centaur* is a tour de force for its use of classical myth in a contemporary setting; Thomas Pynchon's *Gravity's Rainbow*, for the way it combines science with fiction.

Trade books. Trade books are so called because they are distributed principally through retail trade bookstores and libraries, as distinguished from books sold through subscription series, and other means of reaching consumers directly. Trade books include novels, nonfiction and children's books. (*See: trade paperback.*)

Trade discount. A discount in the sale of trade books granted to a bookseller by a publisher. The range of American trade discounts on quantity orders is considered 40%-50%, but each publisher has an individual discount schedule—a chart showing the percentage of discount per number of books ordered.

Trade journal. A magazine or tabloid published for persons in a certain business or profession. Roundup articles on opinions or products, information on new developments, ideas, tips, how-to articles, and convention reports are the kinds of material usually found in trade journals.

The beginning freelance writer will find a good starting point in the trade journals, since they represent a field with less competition than the consumer magazines. Also, since some editors have fewer writers to work with, they usually offer help and advice to the writers to whom they assign articles. Although trade journals pay less than consumer publications, they furnish the novice with experience and exposure while he develops his skill.

Trade journals, also called trade publications, can be categorized in different ways according to different functions. A vertical trade journal is published for all ranks and departments of the same industry (e.g., the apparel industry), while a horizontal trade journal is aimed at persons in

the same job who may or may not be employed in the same industry (e.g., salesmen). Some trade journals are company publications, read by employees and/or stockholders; others are independently published, and financed by advertising. In addition, these periodicals can be classified according to the fields they cover. Industrial publications include articles on manufacturing; merchandising publications, retailing; and professional journals, new developments in medicine, education, and other professions.

Depending on the amount and the quality of work he produces, an article writer working for a trade journal will usually have one of the following titles: freelancer, stringer, correspondent, contributing editor, or field editor. Photographs are especially important to a trade journal article, since they usually tie in closely with the article or help to convey its message.

Consistent buyers of material for trade journals are listed in *Writer's Market*.

Trade list. A catalog listing all one publisher's books in print; one means of advertising for a publisher. Besides titles, a trade list includes content descriptions of the newest books, plus prices and details on ordering both new and backlist titles. Trade lists are produced either annually or semiannually; many appear in the *Publisher's Trade List Annual*. (*See:* Publisher's Trade List Annual.)

Trade name. A name by which a person, corporation, or business entity is known. A legal question frequently asked by writers is whether a pen name or pseudonym can be considered a trade name. Usage is the key factor in this situation. As use is made of the name and the name begins to take on meaning and gain recognition value among the general public, the writer acquires a "property interest" in the name. The greater and more extensive the use made by the writer publishing under the name, the greater and more easily available the protection is by state and federal laws preventing unfair competition. One writer may not, for example, pass off his own work as the work of a well-known and successful writer by using that famous writer's name, or even a name very similar to it that may confuse the general public or lead them to believe that it is the work of the famous author. Nor may a writer use as a major character in his own work a character that has, over time, become identified in the public mind with another author who created the character.

Trade paperback. Published either as an original or as a reprint of a hardcover book, a trade paperback is distributed through book stores—as opposed to the mass-market paperback, which is smaller sized and is distributed through newsstand racks in drugstores, airports, supermarkets, etc., in addition to bookstore outlets.

As the cost of hardcover book production increases, some publishers are turning to the trade paperback as a way to reach the book-buying public at less cost. Authors' royalties on trade paperbacks vary by publisher but may range from 6%-8%: the 6% based on the retail price of the first 10,000-20,000 copies; 7% on the next 10,000-20,000; and 8% thereafter.

Trade publisher. (*See: trade books.*)

Trademark. The Lanham Act of 1946 defines a trademark as "any word, name, symbol, or device or any combination thereof, adopted and used by a manufacturer or merchant to identify his goods and distinguish them from those manufactured or sold by others." A trademark is distinguished from a *service mark*, which identifies *services* provided by a merchant, and from a *trade name*, which, in a general sense, is a name, title, or designation under which a person, corporation, or other entity operates or does business. All three terms—trademark, service mark, and trade name—apply to symbols protected by law in order to prevent unfair competition practices.

Registration of a trademark, service mark, or trade name is a means by which certain words, symbols, devices, etc., are recorded in state or federal registration systems, thereby giving constructive notice to all others in the state or country of the registrant's appropriation of the particular mark or name as his own. This registration is merely evidence of prior appropriation, however; in order to acquire any real "rights" to a trademark or name, the individual or manufacturer must use the term: in other words, merely registering a mark or name does not guarantee exclusive rights to that symbol under the law; usage is the determining factor. In fact, another party who has made extensive use of the name or mark prior to the registrant's attempt at appropriation will be protected in its use despite the registrant's claim to it.

Federal registration of trademarks and service marks is accomplished through the U.S. Patent and Trademark Office, Washington DC 20231, which will provide an application and information on request. The duration of trademark registration is 20 years, as is the renewal period.

The notice of trademark registration is either the symbol ®, the phrase "Registered in U.S. Patent and Trademark Office," or the abbreviation of the same, "Reg. U.S. Pat. and Tm. Off." It is preferred that a form of the notice follow the trademark word or symbol each time it is used.

Each state has its own trademark laws, which usually include a provision for registration and periodic renewal of trademarks, trade names, and service marks. The registration procedure varies widely from state to state, although it usually involves an official form that must be filled out in strict compliance with the Secretary of State's instructions. This form, together with the registration fee (usually $10), is filed with the Secretary of State. If the mark has not been previously appropriated and is one that qualifies for registration, the applicant will receive a certificate that is generally considered to be evidence of registration in any subsequent legal action or proceeding involving the particular mark. The main benefit of state registration is that it gives constructive notice of appropriation throughout the state.

There are several advantages to federal registration of trademark provided under the Lanham Act of 1946. These include the right to subsequently register the trademark in many foreign countries; the right to sue for infringement of the mark in the federal courts; constructive notice of appropriation to the entire country; the right to stop importation of foreign goods carrying infringing marks; a broader scope of what is registerable than is found in many state courts; and a broader and more meaningful range of remedies than is found in many state registration systems. But there is an important limitation of federal registration under the Lanham Act: trade names are not registerable as they are under most state statutes.

It should be noted that failure to police its usage can result in a trademark's becoming a generic word—the name of some product or service totally lacking in distinctive character, and therefore not eligible to be registered as a trademark. The terms "aspirin" and "cellophane," for example, were once valid trademarks that have lost their distinctive character and thus their claim to trademark rights.

For this reason, many manufacturers insist that trademarks used in the media—newspapers, books, magazines, etc.—be capitalized. If a short story writer says of a character, "Jack ordered a Coke from the waitress," "Coke," which is a trademark, should be capitalized. The same with Merit cigarettes, Dexter shoes, and the like. The term "Xerox," often used as a generic term for "photocopy," is actually a valid trademark and should be capitalized in written work.

The whole area of trademark, trade name, and service mark legislation is clouded by confusion and inconsistency in application and definition of terms. Influence of common law is great in trademark legislation cases. A writer involved in or anticipating a trademark-infringement problem should consult with an attorney familiar with the law of the jurisdiction involved. (*See: copyright; service mark; trade name.*)

Traffic. The department of a radio station that is responsible for programming and scheduling.

Transcripts of broadcasts. A television or radio program can be a research source for the writer, and a transcript is a permanent record he can refer to as many times as necessary. Both private and public broadcasting networks offer transcripts of programs, primarily those of a news or documentary nature. Sometimes a fee is charged. (Addresses of major networks can be found in the entry "broadcast networks" in this encyclopedia.)

ABC offers transcripts of its programs "Nightline," "This Week," "Viewpoint," and "20/20"; the cost per transcript is currently $2. Documentaries broadcast on NBC are transcribed and may be obtained free from the network; transcripts of other NBC programs may be used in the network's offices.

CBS television network transcribes documentary programs, morning news, and evening news. Writers who need a transcript for article research may write or call the network's Press Information office, explaining the project and requesting a free transcript.

Similarly, Public Broadcasting Service (PBS) transcribes "Nova," "The McNeil-Lehrer Report," "Wall Street Week," and "Washington Week in Review," among other programs. The cost as well as the format of the transcripts varies. (Some are summaries, others are printed verbatim from the program's text.) In addition, programs broadcast on National Public Radio are available on cassette or reel-to-reel tape. All tapes from NPR contain an hour's programming.

Writers should remember that transcripts for copyrighted programs are subject to copyright laws; therefore, quoting substantial amounts from a transcript requires written permission from the original copyright owner or the network, as the case may be. (*See: broadcast networks.*)

Transition. A passage in a work of literature or a film that leads from one section to another.

In nonfiction, a transition serves to give the article cohesiveness and logic. It can link either sentences, paragraphs, or sections, and is often accomplished by inserting words or phrases into a sentence or paragraph to connect it smoothly to the preceding one. Sometimes, an effective transition is achieved by merely adding one word, such as "however."

The key to a good nonfiction transition is unobtrusiveness, i.e., inserting the transition in such a mechanical and contextual way that it does not distract the reader. Notice the following transition, from an article on billiards: " . . . there is still the time-honored bugaboo: a talent at pool is the sign of a misspent youth.

"Actually, the game has a tradition, if not respectability, behind it."

The word "actually" implies a contradiction to the idea of a "misspent youth" expressed in the first sentence. The statement that the game has a "respectability" further supports the counter-argument. The second sentence serves as a logical transition to a discussion of the history of the game.

Transitions in fiction lead the reader from character to character, from place to place, or from present to future (or past). The writer can mention a possible action in one paragraph and begin describing its actuality in the next. Another means of bridging gaps of time is to connect time's passage with a character's corresponding emotions. With this method, however, the transition, i.e., the emotional response, must be related to a significant element of the story. By the same token, the mere passage of time does not justify the author's outlining of all "events" in a character's life; only those relevant to the plot should be mentioned. Here, for example, is a brief transition describing a lapse of five months and the character's emotional relationship to the time gap. "She was heartbroken the first month, furious the second, elaborately indifferent the third; and she was in her second month of determination to forget him, when he walked into her office and said 'Hi' as if he'd never been away."

To move from character to character, the writer need only instill thoughts about one character into the mind of another, then move on to the subject of the thoughts. For transitions from scene to scene, the double-jump (the use of four spaces rather than the usual double space) is often an effective technique. To maintain reader interest, though, the writer must allude to forthcoming action before the break.

Transitions are also used in the audio and visual media, where they take on different forms. Television, theater, and films use sound effects, lighting, music, and camera techniques as linking devices, while radio drama typically includes transitions of music, sound effects, and periods of silence.

Translating of languages. Writers with proficiency in a foreign language can profit from translation work, in either commercial or literary form. Full-time translation jobs do exist, but they are rare; however, freelance work abounds. Although the East Coast presents the most freelance opportunities, jobs can be secured in any area of the country.

Markets for commercial translation include scientific researchers, patent attorneys, international corporations, publishing companies, and government.

In translating literature, a writer must secure permission from the copyright owner, usually through his publisher. Short works may be completed before submission to a potential publisher, while book inquiries should include two translated chapters, a synopsis, a résumé, and a letter informing the publisher that the translator has permission from the original author to complete the project.

A new translator who is not yet established may want to work through an agent. Experienced translators, on the other hand, advertise their services through such means as the Yellow Pages and direct mail. Current rates average $40 per thousand words. Professional organizations, both local and national, can provide association with other translators. A national organization is the American Translators Association, 109 Croton Ave., Ossining NY 10562. Information on their Translator's Model Contract is available for a self-addressed, stamped envelope from

PEN American Center, 47 Fifth Avenue, New York NY 10003.

Translation rights. One of the subsidiary rights of the owner of a copyright, such as a book author. Sales of these rights to foreign publishers are made either by the author's agent or his publisher on the author's behalf. Contacts are made either with foreign agents or the foreign publishers themselves, frequently at international gatherings such as the Frankfurt Book Fair. Industry standard royalty percentages are 7% of the retail hardcover price on the first 10,000 copies, 8% on the next 10,000, and 10% thereafter. The Authors Guild recommends that the author's share of these royalties be 75% (of the 7%, 8%, or 10%) on foreign editions, and 80% on British editions, but some publishers split 50/50 with the author. Paperback royalties are usually lower.

A publisher that decides to produce its own translated edition for a foreign language market pays the translation fee and splits the royalties between original author and translator at an agreed-upon rate. The translator's royalty is a percentage (usually 15%-20%) of the original author's royalties.

Travel. Travel expenses related to the writing business may be deducted from federal income tax. It is necessary to save receipts that verify transactions, and to keep records of expenditures throughout the year.

Tax-deductible items include trips for research and for conferences and courses. However, a writer may deduct costs of only those educational functions of a refresher-course kind; the cost of a course taken in order to become a writer is not tax-deductible.

Transportation cost may be figured either in terms of mileage or operating expenses of the writer's car. The IRS allows a deduction of twenty cents per mile for the first 15,000 miles traveled and eleven cents for each additional mile. Automobile operating expenses include costs for gasoline, oil, tires, maintenance, and depreciation. (The total yearly cost of these needs may be deducted if the writer uses his car solely for business; otherwise it is prorated according to the percentage of the car's use for business.)

Other tax-deductible expenses of travel are those for food and lodging. Such expenses may be deducted in their entirety if the writer's entire trip is devoted to business. If he takes a trip that is partly for business and partly for pleasure, deductible expenses must be prorated according to the amount of time spent on business. (*See: recordkeeping; taxes.*)

Travel article. (*See: magazine article, types of.*)

Travel Journalists Guild (TJG). This organization is made up of 55 professional freelance travel writers, photographers, and filmmakers. It was established in 1980, with Bern Keating as founding president. To be eligible for membership, a writer must submit samples of published or produced work.

The TJG meets once or twice a year, in different locations around the world. It is a member of the Council of Writers Organizations.

Information about the TJG can be obtained by writing Executive Secretary, Travel Journalists Guild, P.O. Box 2498, Grand Central Station, New York NY 10163. (*See: Council of Writers Organizations.*)

Travel writing. The travel article has two basic objectives: to inform the reader by way of facts and to enlighten him by way of impressions. The travel writer must be perceptive enough to look beyond landmarks and scenery (although both are important) to the less conspicuous elements of his trip, such as people, customs, and atmosphere. Therefore, travel writing requires the personal qualities of energy, enthusiasm, curiosity, insight, and imagination, as well as the skill of observation.

Although the travel writer makes a considerable amount of notes during his actual travels, there is often preliminary research to be done before he leaves. Information can be obtained from travel bureaus, chambers of commerce, books, magazines, other travelers, and newspapers in the town of destination. In addition, querying editors and informing them of the travel destination can help the writer in focusing his research, since it is possible that editors will make suggestions when making assignments.

The travel writer should be prepared either to take photographs or to collaborate with a photographer, because photographs are an essential part of most travel pieces.

A travel article can be written in any of a variety of styles; here are four basic ones. The *quality* article displays a sophisticated writing style that includes imagery. The *spe-cial-interest* article relates the trip to another of the readers' interest, e.g., sports. The *Me-and-Joe* piece is written in narrative form and includes dialogue and other fictive techniques, while the *mile-by-mile* article resembles a log and mentions each activity along the route and at the destination.

Markets for travel articles include magazines for women, men, families, sports enthusiasts, outdoorsmen, and organization members. Often one trip results in a group of articles, each of which is given a different peg, for non-competing magazines. *Writer's Market* lists many categories of potential markets; payment is denoted in the individual listings.

An organization that promotes travel writing is the Society of American Travel Writers, 1120 Connecticut Avenue, Suite 940, Washington DC 20036. A Code of Ethics for the Society of American Travel writers appears in the Appendix to this encyclopedia. (*See: Travel Journalists Guild.*)

Travelwriter Marketletter. A monthly newsletter for writers who specialize in travel writing. It includes the following sections: "Trips" (descriptions of trips and tours sponsored by cities, states, regions, and airlines for writers); "Marketwatch" (data on publications, including editorial needs); "Books" (brief reviews of books on travel writing and writing in general); and "Freelancers Achievements" (news of publication and other travel writers' accomplishments).

Travelwriter Marketletter is available both as a 10-page printed publication and through NewsNet, a computer data base. Its publication address is The Plaza Hotel, Room 1723, Fifth Avenue and 59th Street, New York NY 10019.

Treatment. The narrative, sometimes containing key dialogue, that the scriptwriter writes as a preliminary to the script. The treatment is also called the *outline* or the *story*. (*See: television script terms.*)

Trick ending. Although many editors use this term synonymously with "surprise ending" or "twist ending," other editors consider a trick ending to be one that is illogical and unsatisfying, or that brings about a story's resolution by means of incredible coincidence. (*See: deus ex machina; endings, story; surprise ending.*)

Trilogy. This term, from the Greek *trilogía*, originally referred to a series of three tragedies performed at the festival of Dionysus in ancient Greece. Now any group of three dramatic or literary works, individually complete but related in subject or theme, is called a trilogy.

A classic dramatic trilogy is Sophocles' *Oedipus Rex*, in which the tragedy of Oedipus is dramatized in *Oedipus Tyrannus, Oedipus at Colonus*, and *Antigone*. A contemporary example is Preston Jones's *A Texas Trilogy*, made up of *The Last Meeting of the Knights of the White Magnolia, Lu Ann Hampton Laverty Oberlander*, and *The Oldest Living Graduate*.

Perhaps the best-known contemporary literary trilogy is Tolkien's *Lord of the Rings* series: *Fellowship of the Ring, The Two Towers*, and *Return of the King*. (*See: sequel.*)

Triteness. Words or phrases that have lost freshness, originality, and effectiveness because of continual overuse are characterized by triteness. *Cliché* and *hackneyed language* are two other terms used to describe trite expressions in writing or speech. Triteness need not apply exclusively to words and phrases, however; overdone article and story themes—for instance, "My First Trip To Europe"—are also described as trite. Learning what is trite and what is not comes from wide reading habits and comparing the work of quality writers with mediocre ones.

The careful writer avoids trite expressions and edits clichés from his work. Tiresome phrases such as "nipped in the bud" and "do your own thing" mark the writer as lazy, unimaginative, and amateurish. A manuscript cluttered with clichés is almost invariably rejected by editors.

Sometimes, however, a cliché or well-known slogan can be twisted to produce a fresh, original thought. For example, someone once remarked, "He who laughs last has no sense of humor." Another well-worn phrase was rejuvenated with this ironic twist: "It's not whether you win or lose, it's how you place the blame."

Successful writers continually strive to express themselves in fresh, imaginative ways, and to rid their writing of triteness. (*See: cliché.*)

Truth as a defense against libel. (*See: libel.*)

Twist ending. (*See: surprise ending.*)

Two shot. A television or motion picture scene in which the camera shows two characters. A *three shot* would show three characters. These terms are typed all in caps when used in a script. (*See: television script terms.*)

TWX. A teletype machine or a message from a teletype machine.

Type "A" Writers. (See the Appendix.)

Typewriter, emergency. Many universities and community colleges rent typewriters in their libraries or student centers. Such rental services can come to the aid of a writer on deadline whose typewriter breaks down on a weekend or evening, when typewriter repair shops are closed. In addition, "Secretarial Services" listed in the Yellow Pages indicate which firms have 24-hour answering services and may also be available for emergency manuscript typing.

Typewriter type styles. Editors prefer manuscripts typed in classic, easy-to-read type, *not* the newer faces available with some machines, particularly not the script faces. Editors generally prefer pica type, because it's bigger than elite, and easier on the eyes.

In determining the average word count of a manuscript, the writer should remember that a page of elite type contains more words than a page of pica type.

Typewriters. There is no one brand or style of typewriter that is suitable for every writer; rather, each individual should make a choice based on his personal preferences, and perhaps on his physical surroundings. Well-known writers use typewriters of all sorts: manuals, electrics, and word processors. Their choices are determined by typing skill, the kind of writing they do, and whether or not they have access to electricity. (Writing while traveling often restricts the writer to using a portable manual typewriter.)

Typewriters vary in sophistication, and therefore in cost. Features included, as well as the brand name, determine how much the consumer pays for this tool. For example, a typewriter may be equipped with special symbols or functional keys in a different color from the letter keys. It may have a self-correcting mechanism or a keyboard that locks during return. Some typewriters use only carbon ribbons, while others can use either carbon or the less expensive cloth and nylon.

Mathematical symbols, unusual typefaces, and foreign-language letter accents can be added to a typewriter's capacity by ordering specific elements (for those typewriters with a type ball) or specific keys from the manufacturer.

A writer whose work requires a considerable amount of revision or a large volume of repetitive correspondence may benefit from a word processor. However, a writer should have a profitable business in order to justify the expense of such a machine. Most often, for freelance writing purposes, a neat manuscript typed on a manual typewriter is equally as salable as the product of a fancy machine. (*See: typing; typing services; word processors.*)

Typing. The range of typing abilities among professional writers is broad: some use the hunt-and-peck method, while others are masters of fast, accurate typing. Regardless of a writer's typing skills, the manuscripts he submits to editors must be free of errors, strikeovers, corrections, and smudges.

Community colleges and vocational schools are likely to offer typing courses directed toward adults. Self-instruction books can be helpful; the *Subject Guide to Books In Print* lists books on typing under the headings "Typewriting" and "Typewriting—programmed instruction."

Typing services. Some writers have their final-draft manuscripts typed by professional typists, for one of several reasons: 1) to get a neater, more professional-looking manuscript; 2) to avoid yet another urge to rewrite; and 3) to save their own time for more creative work than typing.

A writer can learn of available typists (and current charges) through classified advertisements in writer's magazines such as *Writer's Digest* and from bulletin boards at local colleges. Also, writers sometimes place their own classifieds in local newspapers, seeking typing services.

Before typing of a manuscript is begun, the writer and typist should agree on the type of paper to be used; the format, including spacing and widths of margins; the style of type; the typist's preference as to typewritten or longhand first draft; and the amount of editing, if any, to be performed by the typist. Editing work can impose an additional fee, or it and its fees can be stipulated in the typist's part of the agreement.

Some writers prefer to have their work picked up and delivered by the typist, for which they pay an extra fee; others transport it by mail. If the U.S. Postal Service is used, the writer should enclose a self-addressed, stamped envelope with three times the amount of postage that was needed to send the material to the typist. This amount will cover the typist's mailing of the original copy, the new copy, and one carbon copy of the typed manuscript.

Costs of typing are tax-deductible expenses of a writer's business. For tax purposes, the writer should request itemized bills and receipts for all transactions from the typist. (*See: recordkeeping; taxes; word processor.*)

412

U

Unabridged. Not shortened or condensed. *Unabridged* is a label often applied to a dictionary that represents the most comprehensive, definitive edition in a series by the same publisher. Unabridged dictionaries are large, usually containing more than 250,000 entries. Given its cumbersome size and the fact that it often includes words that are either obsolete or used only in isolated contexts, an unabridged dictionary may not be a practical expense for some writers.

The writer should bear in mind that an unabridged dictionary is complete only in the sense that words and definitions have not been deliberately omitted in order to condense the book. Because a dictionary is unabridged does not mean that it contains the definition of every word in the language—but rather a very broad sample of it. (*See: dictionary.*)

Unauthorized biography. An account of a person's life written without his cooperation or, in the case of a deceased person, without the co-operation of his estate or heirs. Depending on public whim, subjects of unauthorized biographies have ranged from movie and TV personalities to rock stars, sports heroes, and political figures. Timing and immediacy are important factors in marketing such a work.

Average advances range from $2,000-$5,000 from leading publishers, but can go much higher depending on the topic, the times, and the writer's track record.

Some celebrities have claimed that they alone have the right to write their own biographies. While the courts have not upheld that opinion, James Cagney did recently succeed in having the acknowledgment page of a biography about him show that the book was an unauthorized biography. (*See: biography.*)

Unconscious. Those mental processes existing or operating just outside conscious awareness. The unconscious can influence a writer's life and work in a number of ways.

In their book, *The Writer's Survival Guide*, therapists Jean and Veryl Rosenbaum describe the unconscious part of the mind as an invisible tape recorder imprinted with all the emotions and events of childhood. "The unconscious retains the forgotten, profoundly affecting conscious decisions, feelings, and choices," say the Rosenbaums. "The positive facet of the unconscious stimulates creative thought and works silently on problem solving."

Unconscious activity exerts control over conscious behavior in the adult, the Rosenbaums explain. That is why it is so important for adults, particularly writers, to uncover unconscious attitudes that may be inhibiting the creative process:

Writers depend dramatically on memory to recall and record idiosyncrasies in people's characters, to describe moments from long ago with clarity, and to capture moods from the past. A writer's personal psychological history is a hidden treasure because the creative imagination can take any experience and develop it into a unique story. Inside every memory rests the spark of a story, play, poem, lyric, screenplay, novel, or article, waiting for the bellows of imagination to fan it.

Damon Knight, author of *Creating Short Fiction*, echoes the Rosenbaums' conviction about the influence of the unconscious on the writer. Knight encourages writers to "collaborate" with their unconscious minds:

Now writing, like any art (and also very much like creative science and invention), is a thing you can't do without the close collaboration of the two parts of the mind. When you think about a creative problem, or even when you think something as simple as 'I wish I had an idea for a story,' you are sending a message to the unconscious. The return message may be in the form of a sudden realization, or an image, or some tantalizing ghost of an idea. It may come weeks or months later, even years.

The Rosenbaums believe that a writer's block or other inability to successfully create can be traced to an unconscious source. In *The Writer's Survival Guide*, they outline a method of unlocking the subconscious by preparing a psychological history—or *psychogram*—through which a writer can identify and then learn to eliminate or control self-defeating influences (such as guilt or inferiority) from his unconscious.

Knight takes a different view of a writer's block or slump. He believes such a creative stall can be interpreted as a significant signal: the unconscious mind is attempting to communicate a message to the writer. Take the case of a writer who cannot complete an important scene in a short story, for example. According to Knight, the writer has not adequately consulted with his unconscious about the scene; consequently, his unconscious is now signaling that the conception of the scene is wrong, or that the writer does not understand his characters completely. By allowing his unconscious enough time to work on the problem, the writer should be able to overcome the block. (*See: interior monologue; stream of consciousness;*

writer's block.)

Additional information: *The Writer's Survival Guide; Creating Short Fiction.*

Uncopyrighted publications. Some magazines and newspapers are not copyrighted as publications. The writer who submits material to such periodicals should be sure his article, story, or poem carries his own copyright credit line. Otherwise, the material would be placed in the public domain on publication and thus could legally be copied by another writer. In order to publish in an uncopyrighted magazine without subjecting the piece to nonpayment by others who reprint from it, the writer should request that the editor publish his personal copyright notice (consisting of his name, the year, and the copyright symbol) with his work. (*See: copyright.*)

Understatement. A device in which a writer uses deliberate restraint in expressing his idea. In understating, a writer phrases his remark less strongly than would be expected, or communicates the idea in negative terms. A critic for a Hearst newspaper, for example, who was assigned to write a review of Hearst friend Marion Davies's latest film, is reported to have closed his review this way: "Marion Davies was never better."

As with other humor techniques, the writer must take care in using understatement that his reader understands the effect he is trying to achieve. Context is important in making sure the reader realizes an idea is being understated. (*See: humor.*)

Unfinished manuscripts, how to resume work on. (*See: restarting your writing.*)

United Press International (UPI). One of the two major wire services in the United States, United Press International (UPI) is a privately owned commercial news agency established in 1958 in a merger of United Press and International News Service. From its 40 foreign bureaus and more than 100 domestic bureaus located throughout the United States, UPI gathers, prepares, and distributes local, national, and international news and photographs to newspapers and radio stations that pay for the service. It rarely buys spot news items or freelance features from non-staff members.

The headquarters of UPI are located at 220 E. 42nd Street, New York NY 10017. (*See: Associated Press; wire services, jobs in.*)

U.S. government as a resource. The United States government can be a valuable information source on almost any conceivable subject. The U.S. Government Printing Office issues thousands of publications covering a legion of topics; in addition, there are a number of government bureaus and agencies that can provide the freelancer with, or refer him to, sources of facts and data, experts in a subject field, bibliographic material, and answers to specific questions. For the phone number of a specific agency call (202) 655-4000. (*See: Census Bureau, data bases, Department of Commerce; Federal Information Center Program, General Services Administration; Library of Congress; Ombudsman, Office of, U.S. Department of Commerce; United States Government Manual; U.S. government* *publications.*)

United States Government Manual.
An annual directory published by
the U.S. National Archives and
Records Service, the *United States
Government Manual* provides
comprehensive information on the
agencies, divisions, and members of
the legislative, judicial, and executive branches of the U.S. government. It includes all departments,
agencies, and boards, and is indexed
by name, subject, and agency. A
valuable reference volume for writers seeking government experts in
specific subject areas, the *Manual* is
available for purchase from the Superintendent of Documents at the
U.S. Printing Office, Washington
DC 20402. (*See: U.S. government publications.*)

U.S. government publications. A
writer has various means of access to
these publications, which can be
valuable sources for article and book
research. Until 1982, a writer could
receive a free monthly announcement of government publications as
they became available. Budget cuts,
however, have forced the discontinuance of that practice.

Now the writer's source of information is the *Catalog of United States
Government Publications,* issued quarterly and incorporating approximately 1,000 new and popular
backlist publications listed by author, title, and subject. Some public
and college libraries serve as depositories from which the actual publications may be borrowed. A "List of
Depository Libraries" may be obtained by writing the Superintendent of Documents, U.S.
Government Printing Office, Wash-

ington DC 20402.

In addition, the Government
Printing Office has several bookstores throughout the country from
which publications may be purchased. Writers can also write for a
free copy of the *Consumer Information
Catalog,* a list of pamphlets and
booklets available from the Documents Distribution Center, U.S.
Government Printing Office, Pueblo
CO 81009. (*See: data bases; U.S. government as a resource;* United States
Government Manual.)

U.S. government, writing for. The
Office of Personnel Management,
1900 E Street NW, Washington DC
20415, is the agency of the federal
government responsible for the re-
cruiting, examining, training, and
promoting of federal workers. In
that respect, it absorbed many of the
same functions of the U.S. Civil
Service Commission under which
many of the 7,440 writers and editors currently employed by federal
agencies were hired.

Entry-level positions of Editorial
Clerk or Editorial Assistant are required to edit for basic grammar and
structural clarity, verify references,
prepare publication formats, and
proofread. Applicants for these positions must have some experience
and may be required to take appropriate tests. Positions as writers and
editors at higher levels are evaluated
on their education, experience, and
training in relation to the specific duties of the position.

The Office of Personnel Management has ten regional offices around
the U.S. where applicants may inquire about writing-related positions. The writer should call the
Federal Information Center in his
state to find out whether there is an

OPM regional office in his area. (See the list of these Centers in the Appendix to this encyclopedia.)

In addition to writing-related job opportunities with the federal government in Washington, the OPM regional offices may also be able to advise about regional opportunities.

United States Ski Writers Association (USSWA). This Association comprises 350 ski writers who work in the newspaper, magazine, television, and radio fields. Its purpose is to encourage the improvement of ski journalism and assist ski journalists in their work. Annual awards presented by USSWA include Skier of the Year and the Golden Quill Award, presented to the person who has best served and assisted ski journalists in performing their work. Publications include *U.S. Ski Writers Roster* and *Ski Writers Bulletin.* An annual convention is held.

The USSWA, based in Glens Falls, New York, has seven regional divisions: Eastern, Midwest, Northern California, Northwest, Rocky Mountain, and Southern California. The Association can be reached at Seven Kensington Road, Glens Falls NY 12801. (*See: Council of Writers Organizations.*)

Unities. In establishing principles of dramatic composition, Renaissance critics drew on Aristotle's observations of the three unities that were incorporated into dramatic works: unity of time, unity of place, and unity of action. The unity of time limited a play's fictional time span to one day; the unity of place limited its physical setting to one place. Similarly, only one plot per drama was permitted by the principle of unity of action.

The unities are rarely followed by today's writers of plays in English. However, the time limitations imposed by radio drama render the use of the unity of action desirable in that genre. (*See: radio drama.*)

Universality. This is an important element for writers to consider, since articles and stories intended for sale to magazines must have wide appeal. Some beginning writers have experiences that are intensely interesting to themselves and their families, but that, when written up as magazine articles, for example, lack the universal human interest quality required of saleable material. The same consideration must be given by beginning nonfiction book authors and first novelists to their highly personalized books which must contain universal themes and elements as well as their subjective responses.

Magazine article writers aiming at *specialized* magazines, of course, must focus on that particular subject matter.

University press. A publisher directly or indirectly associated with a university. University presses traditionally have specialized in scholarly works of no interest to the commercial press, but many such presses now regularly publish quality books of wider appeal. State university presses, in particular, now publish books about the state or geographic area in which the institution is located.

In recent years, some university presses have begun to publish fiction and poetry of high literary merit, especially by regional writers, that probably could not be published commercially. Some of these books, however, have achieved respectable sales, and the practice is somewhat controversial, with one faction arguing that profits can be plowed back into utterly noncommercial work, and the other maintaining that a university press is no place for fiction at all—particularly fiction that might have found a mainstream publisher.

Unsolicited manuscript. An unsolicited manuscript is a book, article, story, or poem submitted by a writer without the publisher's having requested it. Publishers are under no legal obligation to be responsible for unsolicited manuscripts, so the writer should always consult the listings in *Writer's Market* to make sure a publisher is willing to look at unsolicited manuscripts and then be sure to include an SASE when submitting one. (*See: slushpile.*)

Up and out. In radio advertising, a direction to increase the volume of music or sound effects, then fade it out.

Up full. In radio advertising, a direction to increase the volume of music or sound effects to the maximum.

USA Today. A national newspaper established by the Gannett Company in September 1982. Although *USA Today* has its own staff, and draws on the resources of the many newspapers in the Gannett chain, the publication uses freelance material to some extent. The individual sections of the paper to whose managing editors queries should be sent are: Managing Editor, News; Managing Editor, Money; Managing Editor, Sports; and Managing Editor, Life. *USA Today's* address is P.O. Box 500, Washington DC 20044.

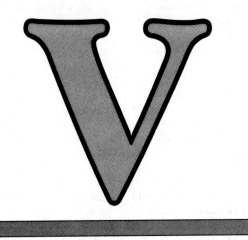

Vacations, writers'. Since a freelance writer works for himself, he is responsible for scheduling both his work hours and his leisure time. An ambitious person tends to find himself overworked, and possibly unaware that he needs the refreshment of periodic vacations in order to work effectively.

Some writers, on the other hand, find that the travel they do for research provides not only a welcome change from the restrictions of their offices, but a refreshment of spirit that brings them eagerly back to the assignment. (*See: travel writing.*)

Variety. This is a weekly newspaper that reports on entertainment industries; its coverage is international. *Variety* publishes news about television, cable television, motion pictures, radio, records, night clubs, auditoriums, theater, and notable individuals in entertainment.

A comedy writer who wants to reach a performer (and potential client) can sometimes find in *Variety* the address of the club or resort at which that person will be appearing.

Variety has bureaus in ten cities; it is published by Variety, Inc., 154 W. 46th Street, New York NY 10036.

Verbal, oral. These words are often confused, and tend incorrectly to be considered synonymous. *Verbal*—the more inclusive of the two terms—applies to *all* words, spoken or written, in which thought or feeling is expressed. *Oral*, which means uttered by mouth, describes only that which is *spoken*.

The confusion regarding correct use of these two terms is complicated in part by the seemingly contradictory case of *verbal agreement*, a term that means oral agreement—agreement expressed only in speech and not in writing.

The writer achieves clarity by using the word *oral* rather than *verbal* to mean spoken language.

Verbatim. A term that means "in exactly the same words," or "corresponding word for word to the original source or text."

The term is often used in relation to direct quotations, those that record another person's remarks verbatim—that is, word for word, exactly as the remarks were spoken or written. (*See: plagiarism; quotes.*)

Verbiage. Wordiness; an overabundance of words in written or spoken expression. The word has a negative connotation, often implying communication that is meaningless and insincere. Editors tend to reject manuscripts marked by verbiage, preferring carefully edited writing characterized by economy of words and a tight style to manuscripts cluttered with superfluous detail, excessive abstractions, and circumlocution. (*See: pad.*)

Verification of quotes, facts. This is important to a writer's credibility—and to other aspects of his reputation, since misquoting in some instances leads to libel suits; in others, to a loss of confidence in the reporter on the part of a source or an editor.

Many novice writers erroneously accept unquestioningly all material they read in their article sources, e.g., newspapers and magazines. Instead of relying on another writer who may be in error—in this case, the author of the research source—the writer should verify quoted statements with the persons who made them, and facts with additional sources. In investigative research, of course, verification of facts is essential; after information is learned firsthand, other persons or sources should be consulted.

This kind of checking and cross-checking helps the reporter or researcher learn important information, clarify contradictory statements, and discover errors that have crept into already published material. (*See: interview; libel.*)

Verisimilitude. Having the appearance or semblance of truth or fact; likelihood; probability. A writer attempts to achieve the quality of verisimilitude in his work through such skillful selection of narration and dialogue that the reader will be caught up in the work as representative of "real life."

Vernacular. Language native to the people of a particular country or locality. *Vernacular* applies to the natural pattern of speech used daily by persons in a certain geographical area, and is distinguished from more formal language used primarily in schools and in literature. For example, the sentence structure of a "Pennsylvania Dutchman" speaking English—"Throw the horse over the fence some hay"—is an example of vernacular.

A work written in the native language of a particular country or locality is described as "in the vernacular." Editors prefer just enough use of such language to give the flavor without being hard to read when overused. The word is also applied to vocabulary peculiar to a particular trade or profession. (*See: dialect;* Dictionary of American Regional English.)

Vers libre. (*See: verse.*)

Verse. Judson Jerome, author of *The Poet's Handbook*, analyzes the various forms of verse as follows:

Verse is writing that uses lines. Any writing, good or bad, poetic or prosaic, that is broken into consciously determined line units is verse.

Free verse, also called *vers libre*, is that in which the length of the lines is not measured by a specific number of units.

Thus any piece
of writing that is broken into lines of irregular length may be
called free verse, whether
it advertises nylons, records Samson's celebration of light,
or explains prosody drily
as this.

Before this century most verse, free or otherwise, began each line with a capital letter. Most of the line breaks in free verse occur at the end of grammatical phrases, so the line break constitutes a kind of punctuation. Free verse can be analyzed into metrical units (explained below), though there is no set number of such units per line. Some free verse poets use line breaks to divide individual words, sometimes putting single letters or groups of letters on a line for special effects:

is that you &
i are more than you
& i(be
ca
us
e It's we)

e.e. cummings

Metered verse is that in which the length of the lines is measured by an arbitrary number of units. The language is made to fit some predetermined design of the poet. Some poets, for example, have written on adding-machine tape to impose an arbitrary limit on the number of spaces and characters in a line. Any such measure can be used to meter poetry, as:

This writin
g has ten let
ters per lin
e but varies
in the numbe
r of spaces.

Syllabic verse is the simplest, common type of metered verse. Line length is determined by the number of syllables, as:

Each of these lines has
five syllables. Some-
times that requires di-
viding the end words.

Accentual verse is that in which line length is determined by the number of stresses, regardless of the number of syllables, as:

Anglo Saxons *sang* their *mead* songs
in *lines* of *four* em*phat*ic *feet*
with no *fixed pat*tern im*pos*ed on the *number*
of *light syl*lables, nor *set* positions—
but the *first* or second *stress* in the *line*
had to al*lit*erate with the *heavy beat*
in the *third* position, *start*ing the *sec*ond half.

As in this example, there is some unavoidable ambiguity about which syllables should receive stresses; in the last line, *half* might as readily be stressed as *second*. Writers of accentual verse have to work at keeping the rhythm strong so as not to lose control of stress placement.

Accentual syllabic verse is the most common—and most complex—form of metered verse in English. Certain fixed combinations of number of syllables and placement of accent are called *feet*. Line length is then determined by the number of feet in a line. For example, the combination of one unaccented syllable and a following accented syllable is called an *iamb*. A line with five feet, most of them iambs, is called a line of *iambic pentameter*, as:

a LA de DAH ap PROACH to
    verse   will DRIVE
the COM   mon READ   er
   SCREAM ing UP   the WALL

Such a rigid pattern of alternating stresses is almost impossible—and quite tedious—to maintain. In practice, almost every "iambic" line has one or more variations.

Feet common in English and American poetry are the following: (U =unaccented syllable; slash =accented syllable)

iamb (u/)
the HILL   is GREEN   and STEEP

trochee (/u)
STEEP and   GREEN is   YONder
   HILL side

spondee (//)
STEEP GREEN   YON HILL

anapest (uu/)
o ver THERE   is a HILL   that is
SHIM   mer ing GREEN

dactyl (/uu)
GREEN is the   SHIM mer of
   HILLS at this   AL ti tude

Another foot, the *pyrrhic*, consists of two unaccented syllables—and cannot be used except as a substitute for other kinds of feet, usually iambs:

i SIGH   in the   en CHANT
   ment of   her EYES;
one SYLL a ble   is ALL   she SAID
   to me.

Rising meter refers to iambs, anapests and spondees—which end with accents. *Falling meter* refers to trochees and dactyls. If a line of rising meter ends with an unaccented syllable (or sometimes two) after the final foot, those syllables are called *hypermetrical*. Endings with unaccented syllables are called *feminine*; those are *masculine* which end with stress.

Verse paragraphs function much as paragraphs function in prose; they are indicated on the page simply by spaces between groups of lines or initial indentation. A long poem such as *Paradise Lost* is broken into verse paragraphs, and a short poem such as *Mending Wall* may be a single verse paragraph.

Strophe is another word for *verse paragraph*, particularly for those units that seem to turn away from the subject matter to introduce a new mood or new dimension of thought.

Stanza is a group of lines more formally determined than verse paragraphs or strophes. (The stanza is to the verse paragraph or strophe as metered verse is to free verse.) Stanzas usually have a fairly fixed pattern, or formula, in which lines of the same length are repeated in the same sequence, often reinforced by rhyme patterns.

A poem is a group or groups of lines. In addition, however, there are some traditional formulae for whole poems, such as the sonnet, a fourteen-line poem in iambic pentameter, usually with one of several traditional rhyme schemes.

Fixed forms, thus, are traditional designs for whole poems. The most common fixed forms in English poetry are *sonnets, sestinas, villanelles, haiku* and *limericks*, but there are many other fixed forms deriving from other languages.

Verso page. A page appearing on the left-hand side of a book. All numbered verso pages have even numbers. (*See: recto page.*)

Vertical File Index, The. The Vertical File Index provides information on pamphlets, including title, author, address, and cost. It is published monthly, except August, by the H.W. Wilson Company. Listings are categorized by both title and subject.

This reference is usually available in the reference departments of medium-sized or large libraries, and often provides writers/researchers with additional sources of information not available in a card catalog or periodical index.

Vertical publication. This term refers to a publication directed at the entire spectrum of a specific industry, such as *Apparel Industry Magazine*, which may be read by design, manufacturing, sales, finance, management, or training personnel within the garment industry. (*See: horizontal publication; trade journal.*)

Vet. A term used by editors when referring to the procedure of submitting a book manuscript to an outside expert for review before publication. A manuscript is usually vetted at the publisher's expense, although some authors may use the same procedure themselves before submitting their final draft to the publisher. What the author pays to have a manuscript vetted depends on the relationship of the vetter to the author, the vetter's interest in the book (whether he may possibly contribute a foreword to it), and other factors. Costs to the author could vary from fifty to several hundred dollars. The term is believed to have originated from the

verb used by veterinarians to mean subjecting an animal to a physical examination; adapted by others to mean investigating or evaluating in a thorough manner.

Videlicet. (*See: viz.*)

Video display terminal. A computer/word processor terminal containing a screen on which text typed on the keyboard appears. (A computer *terminal* consists of a keyboard and a screen.) The screen, similar to a television screen, is a cathode ray tube (CRT), a term sometimes used interchangeably with VDT.

Other names for the VDT are *editing terminal, layout terminal, word processing terminal, video-editing terminal, video-layout terminal,* and *videotext terminal.* (*See: word processor.*)

Videotape. Magnetic tape on which both picture and sound are recorded electronically. Unlike film photography—the alternate means of storing moving pictorial information—videotape recording does not depend on chemical development: it is capable of immediate replay.

Videotape is a medium through which lucrative opportunities are available to persons with appropriate skills. A writer who can operate a video camera or who can collaborate with a videotape artist can produce materials for education, training, entertainment, business, and advertising.

The Association of Independent Video and Filmmakers, Inc. (AIVF) is a nonprofit trade association open to such producers, directors, and technicians. Its headquarters are at 625 Broadway, New York NY 10012. *How to Enter and Win Video Contests*, edited by Allan Gadney, informs the writer of available grants, fellowships, and cash prizes in the video field. *Writer's Market, Photographer's Market,* and *Artist's Market* list details on videotape markets for freelancers. (*See: audiovisual communication.*)

Videotext. (*See: electronic text.*)

Viewpoint. This term refers to the mind of the character through which the reader is told a story. There are several kinds of viewpoint, labeled according to the characteristics of the viewpoint itself and the storyteller with whom the viewpoint originates.

Objective viewpoint is used when the narrator relates facts but avoids emotion. *Subjective viewpoint,* the type most used in fiction, incorporates a character's thoughts and emotions into the storytelling. The reader thus shares in the character's emotional life.

A short story can be told in the first person through the mind of either a major or a minor character; the latter viewpoint is useful as a technique if there is a minor character—but no major character—who is present in every scene. It can also be used if the major character is difficult for the reader to identify with. Most short stories, however, use the technique of single-major-character viewpoint.

Longer works of fiction, such as novelettes and novels, are able to use forms of viewpoint that can reveal the thoughts of more than one character to the reader. Using the

omniscient viewpoint, an author can relate the perceptions of any of his characters or detach himself from them to serve as narrator. The *detached viewpoint,* on the other hand, lets the reader sense that he is watching the story as it unfolds; the author gives decriptions and impressions, but never through the perception of a character.

The *multiple-character viewpoint* is used to tell a story from the perspectives of different characters, one at a time. Unlike works using the omniscient viewpoint, this viewpoint stays with one character for a considerable length—for example, a chapter in a novel. This technique is useful when the story must, but the characters are unable to, make an extreme change of scene. (*See: first person viewpoint; third person major character viewpoint.*)

Vignette. A short piece of writing intended to convey an image of, or cast illumination on, a scene, a character, or a situation. Characteristics of the vignette are exactness of phrase construction and an emotional tone.

In television, a vignette is a brief (5 seconds to 30 seconds) incident shown to illustrate a point or principle. Television commercials such as those by AT&T on the "Reach Out and Touch Someone" theme are examples. (*See: slice of life.*)

vis-à-vis. French for "face to face." This term may be used as an adjective to describe persons facing each other, as on opposite sides of a dining table. It can also be used as a noun to mean "one who is opposite or opposing" (e.g., a person of equal rank, position, etc.).

The term is most often used as a preposition, however, meaning "in relation to," "compared with," or "in regard to." For example: The Senator's position vis-à-vis the nuclear energy bill was indefinite.

viz. An abbreviation of *videlicet*, a Latin word meaning "that is to say." *Viz.* is an expression used primarily in formal English to mean "namely." Although common in eighteenth- and nineteenth-century prose, *viz.* is seldom used in contemporary writing. (*See: i.e.*)

Voice-over. A television/motion picture term referring to the use of a person's voice when that person or character does not appear in the scene being shown. Documentaries often use voice-overs. When used in a script, this term is typed all in caps, or abbreviated as VO. (*See: television script terms.*)

Volunteer Lawyers for the Arts. This nationwide organization of lawyers offers free legal services to persons in the creative arts, including writers, on matters related to practicing art. Eligibility for these services is determined by the writer's income; in some cases, even though writers qualify for free legal services, they are responsible for paying court costs.

For information on free legal aid, or to locate branches in other cities, writers should contact one of the following: Bay Area Lawyers for the Arts, Fort Mason Center Building C, San Francisco CA 94123, (415)775-7200; Lawyers for the Creative Arts, 623 S. Wabash, Suite 300 N., Chicago IL 60605, (312)427-1800; or Volunteer Lawyers for the Arts, 1560 Broadway, Suite 711, New York NY 10036, (212)575-1150.

Washington Independent Writers (WIW). A 1,000-member organization of freelance writers in the Washington DC area. It acts as a medium for the exchange of information, ideas, and knowledge, and the encouragement of professionalism and fairness.

WIW publishes a newsletter, a membership directory, and other publications. It belongs to the Council of Writers Organizations. Headquarters address of WIW is 205 Colorado Bldg., 1341 "G" St. NW, Washington DC 20005. (*See: Council of Writers Organizations.*)

Western Writers of America (WWA). The WWA is made up of freelance writers who specialize in western fiction or nonfiction of many forms, including books, short pieces, scripts, and juvenile material. The Golden Saddleman Awards and the Spur Awards are granted by this organization. The WWA publishes a monthly, *Roundup*, and convenes annually. Its headquarters are located at 1052 Meridian Rd., Victor MT 59875.

Wide angle. In television and motion pictures, a term that refers to a scene shot from a distance or with a wide-angle lens in order to show the audience an all-encompassing view. *Wide angle* is typed all in caps in a script. (*See: television script terms.*)

Widow. A typeset line considerably short of the standard copy width, standing by itself at the top of a column or page. Unsightly widows—those less than two-thirds or half the standard line measure—should be eliminated. This can be done either in layout or by editing and resetting some copy; the method depends on the type of publication, the design/layout/typesetting budget, and imminence of deadline. The pasteup artist can cheat on page length to move the widow to the bottom of the previous page or column, or move an additional line or two of copy to the page or column the widow begins; the editor can edit in or edit out a few words in the paragraph and have it reset, thereby increasing the widow to an acceptable width or eliminating it altogether.

Writers should take care to avoid widows in their typed copy as well.

Wills. Authors have special, professionally related considerations to make when drawing up their wills. Under the copyright law effective in 1978, a literary work is protected for the duration of the author's life plus the succeeding 50 years. An author's will can specify who owns the copyright and who is to receive the royalties earned by his work subsequent to his death.

Another point that may be made in an author's will is a requirement that a particular unpublished work or works not be published posthumously. (*See: lawyers, where to find.*)

Wire services, jobs in. Jobs available at the wire services are primarily those in news reporting and photography. The major wire services have branches throughout the world. (*See: Associated Press; United Press International.*)

Women in Communications, Inc. (WICI). Women in Communications, Inc., is a professional organization for women and men in all fields of communications. Its 12,000 members work in advertising, communications education, film, magazines, newspapers, photojournalism, public relations, publishing, radio, technical writing, and television. There are 86 campus chapters and 80 professional chapters in addition to members-at-large.

WICI's purposes are to unite members for the purpose of promoting the advancement of women in all fields of communications; to work for the First Amendment rights and responsibilities of communicators; to recognize distinguished professional achievements; and to promote high professional standards throughout the communications industry. The Clarion Awards competition is sponsored annually to recognize excellence in all areas of communications.

The organization publishes a national magapaper, *PRO/COMM, The Professional Communicator*, ten times per year; and a national directory of professional members biennially. A national professional conference is held annually.

The national headquarters address is P.O. Box 9561, Austin TX 78766.

Women in writing. While there is little discrimination against women writers today, this has not always been the case; women's parity with men in the profession is a relatively recent development. The rediscovery and study of women writers of the past is a booming scholarly field today.

The major problem women writers (and would-be women writers) have suffered throughout history is lack of opportunity to write. Women traditionally have not been allowed—either by custom or necessity—to be educated and while it is not essential to be highly educated in order to write, it is essential to be literate. There have always been exceptions—the Greek lyric poet Sappho, the mystical essayist Teresa of Ávila, the seventeenth-century American poet Anne Bradstreet—but for the most part, writing was not considered seemly activity for wives and mothers; the most literate women were usually courtesans, nuns, aristocrats, or daughters of aberrant intellectuals who believed women should be educated. Nor have women—with childbearing and rearing, housekeeping, and economic duties—had leisure time in which to write.

It was only with the growing popularity of the novel in the nineteenth century (as general literacy increased) that women achieved significant influence in any literary genre; even then, however, the novel was considered a disreputable and inferior form, beneath those practiced by men of letters, who wrote essays and poetry. But Mary Shelley, Charlotte and Emily Bronte (who first published under male pseudonyms), George Sand (born Amandine Aurore Lucie Dupin), and George Eliot (Mary Ann Evans)—an assortment of spinsters, intellectuals, and political radicals—are some of the most important literary figures of the century.

In studying women writers, it is necessary to remember the distinction between writing and being published: many women who wrote are lost to history. Emily Dickinson, for instance, published a comparative few poems during her lifetime, but took pains to ensure that her poems would all survive and be published. It is very likely that many fine women writers did not take such pains. Today academicians pore through nineteenth-century periodicals, diaries, and letters for evidence of literary endeavor, but materials older than that are seldom available.

Additional information: *The Madwoman in the Attic: The Woman Writer and the Nineteenth-Century Literary Imagination; Silences.*

Women's National Book Association (WNBA). The WNBA includes men as well as women. Its members, who work in all occupations allied to the publishing industry, include publishers, authors, editors, librarians, booksellers, literary agents, designers, educators, critics, administrative personnel, and individuals engaged in book production, marketing, finance, and subsidiary rights.

The Association maintains its archives at Columbia University. It publishes *The Bookwoman*, a magazine, three times per year. A WNBA board meeting is held annually.

The WNBA presents the biennial Women's National Book Association Award (formerly called the Constance Lindsay Skinner Award) to "a distinguished bookwoman for her extraordinary contribution to the world of books and through books, to the society in which we live." Its Lucile Micheels Pannell Award is for "the most effective program bringing books and children together."

WNBA chapters are located in Binghamton, New York; Boston; Cleveland; Detroit; Los Angeles; Nashville; New York City; San Francisco; and Washington DC-Baltimore. The Women's National Book Association can be reached c/o Sylvia Cross, 19824 Septo Street, Chatsworth CA 91311.

Women's slick magazine. This type of magazine is characterized by quality paper, color illustrations, national advertising, and well-known writers. The nonfiction editorial content deals with various topics related to women's interests: homemaking, marriage, family, sex, psychology, personal care, and interpersonal relationships; plus topics of interest to the working woman: careers, investments, time management, and hiring and firing household and child care employees.

A substantial number of women's slick magazines publish fiction as well as nonfiction. Generally, editors seek fiction aimed at readers 21-34, and avoid stories set in the past, stories told from the viewpoint of a child or an elderly person, slice-of-life pieces, and plots concerned with topics such as crime.

The women's slick differs from the confession magazine primarily in its audience, which determines its slant. The reader of the women's slick generally is better educated, has wider interests, and is of higher socioeconomic status than the reader of the confession magazine, who is usually a blue-collar worker or wife and comparatively tradition-bound. The subject matter in confessions is much more restrictive, concentrating as it does on personal and family relationships and problems and avoiding topics that can't be treated from the first person emotional viewpoint.

At present, the women's slicks pay from $200-$5,000 for articles and $1,500 average for short stories. (*See: confession.*)

Word count. Magazine writers usually indicate on page 1 of manuscripts the approximate number of words contained in the piece. Total number of words can be estimated with the procedure outlined here. First, every word (including *a, an,* and *the*) on the first full three pages of the manuscript is counted, and the average number of words on those pages is calculated. Then, the average, representing the estimated number of words per page, is multiplied by the total number of pages in the manuscript. Finally, the total word count is rounded to the nearest hundred (e.g., 3,500, not 3,463 words) and typed in the upper right corner of page 1.

Word processor. A word processor is a specialized kind of computer designed for writing, editing, proofreading, and sometimes, spelling. The three basic components of a word processor that the writer makes contact with are the keyboard, the display, and the printer. (The combination of the keyboard and display is sometimes referred to as the *terminal.*) The *keyboard* of a word procesor is composed of letter keys arranged like those on a typewriter and other, special, keys, which give the word processor its operating instructions (e.g., the "print" button commands the printer to produce material on paper). The *display* is a screen that shows the user what he has just typed on the keyboard of, or retrieved from the memory of, the word processor. Displays range in capacity from one line to approximately 55 lines, which is comparable to a typewritten page. (Some of the newest displays allow for the number of characters per line to be changed.) The *printer* reproduces on paper material that has been typed into the computer via the keyboard or recorded on a disk. Speed and quality of print are factors that vary from printer to printer.

Like all computers, a word processor contains the following parts: the central processing unit, the internal memory or random access memory (RAM), input/output devices, and memory devices. The *central process-*

ing unit serves as the computer's brain; for example, it can compare a correct spelling with an incorrect one, or indent a block quotation. The *random access memory* temporarily stores information that has been entered into the computer. Its size, or capacity, varies from one computer to the next. The *byte* is the unit of measurement that labels a memory's—or a disk's—capacity. To a word processor, a byte is a letter, an exclamation point, or a space. Information in the internal memory is erased when the computer is turned off, unless it has been recorded, for storage, onto an external memory device—a disk or a tape. Input/output devices are parts of the computer where information is either entered or obtained by the user. They include the keyboard, disk or tape drives, the screen, and the printer. Finally, external memory devices are materials on which information can be permanently stored, such as disks and tapes.

Some word processors, called *stand-alones*, have all these elements in one unit, and others, the *modulars*, have separate units for the keyboard, the display, and the printer.

Word processors store information on magnetic disks, which can be duplicated, erased, or removed from the computer and filed. The computer's disk drive(s) allow the stored material to be displayed on the screen. A word processor with multiple disk drives is preferable to a machine with only one, since it offers advantages such as ease of duplicating disks and more available storage space.

Other kinds of data processors, such as home computers, can do word processing through use of word processing programs (for spelling, grammar, other purposes). However, the writer should acquaint himself with certain features of a home computer before purchase, since, on some computers, word processing is not facilitated: for example, home computers that use ordinary television sets as their display screen may not have adequate sharpness in the character images.

A major advantage of a word processor to the writer's work is that revisions can be made faster and more easily. Additions, deletions, correction of typos, and changes in content can be made when the copy is still on the screen, so the printed copy can represent the final, polished draft instead of the first, unrevised one. Also, retyping an entire piece merely to add a word, a sentence, or a paragraph is unnecessary.

Form letters, such as queries, follow-ups on no replies, and requests for payment, can be recorded in the word processor's memory, so that the writer can print a letter from the disk, adding only the address of the recipient, the salutation, and his own signature.

Costs of word processors vary widely with the features and capabilities of the machines. Stand-alones cost from $4,000-$10,000, and modular word processors are sold at prices ranging from $7,500-$22,500. Similarly, word processing programs for home computers are sold in a range of prices; currently, name-brand programs cost from $100-$500. The Business-to-Business Yellow Pages lists manufacturers and dealers of word processors and word processing supplies.

Word processor programs offer a new opportunity for freelance writers who can create this "software" for computer manufacturers. See the "Data Processing" chapter of *Writer's Market* for buyers of such programs.

Additional information: *The Word Processing Book*.

Work made for hire. This term, often called simply "work for hire," designates work prepared either by an employee as part of his ordinary full-time job responsibilities, or by an individual specifically contracted to produce a particular work under written agreement with an employer. A work made for hire—as it concerns writers—is defined under the copyright law as "a work specially ordered or commissioned for use as a contribution to a collective work, as part of a motion picture or other audiovisual work, as a translation, as a supplementary work, as a compilation, as an instructional text, or as an atlas, if the parties expressly agree in a written instrument signed by them that the work shall be considered a work made for hire."

Of importance to writers is the question of who owns a work made for hire. If a writer is an employee, any work he prepares for his employer in the course of his employment normally belongs to the employer, not to the writer. For example, a staff writer on a city magazine who has been assigned by the magazine's editor to do an article on a local celebrity holds no claim to that article and cannot attempt to sell it elsewhere; the magazine that employs the writer is deemed to be the author and owns all the rights comprised in the copyright. Of course, an employee might be able to negotiate a written agreement with his employer, specifying that the employee

owns all or part of the copyright. In the absence of such a written agreement, however, all rights to the work belong to the employer.

In the case of a work specially commissioned—a freelance article assignment, for example—the writer owns the copyright unless the author and the purchaser expressly agree in a document signed by both of them that the work shall be considered a work for hire. Where no such agreement exists, the writer is considered to be the legal author, and retains all rights unless transferred in writing.

A commissioned work is not automatically a work made for hire, although many publishers may attempt to pressure a writer into signing an agreement making it so. Obviously, wherever possible, the writer would attempt to negotiate a contract calling for different terms, thus preserving his right to other rights in his work.

When a piece is considered a work made for hire, the person who assigns the work owns the rights to it permanently. This should not be confused with an agreement that stipulates that "all rights" will be purchased, with no mention of the term "work made for hire." In the case of a sale of "all rights," the writer or his heirs may regain the rights after 35 years by following the termination procedure delineated in the copyright law.

Even the duration of the copyright in a work made for hire is different from other works. It lasts for 75 years from the year of its first publication, or 100 years from its creation. On all other works, the copyright is good for life of the last surviving author plus 50 years.

Peter C. Gould and Stephen H.

Gross note in *Legal & Business Aspects of the Magazine Industry* that the term "work made for hire" is inflammatory when applied to freelance writing. They quote from the American Society of Journalists and Authors:

A "work made for hire" agreement specifically relegates the independent writer, so far as the article under consideration is concerned, to the status of employee and creates a mythical—but nonetheless presumably legally binding—relationship in which the author agrees to function as a hired hand, while the publisher assumes the mantle of "creator" of the work, with all the rights of ownership vested in the creator under the law. . . . This effort, subverting the intent of the law and contrary to ethical publishing trade practices, is condemned by the American Society of Journalists and Authors.

Gould and Gross discuss the aspects of the work-made-for-hire agreement that rile the American Society of Journalists and Authors. A publication that establishes a work-made-for-hire agreement with a writer has the following rights to the article: "Any subsidiary or derivative use may be made of the work without further permission. The copyright notice need not be in the author's name and there is no need of re-assignment. There is no problem of revision and editing of the work. . . . A work made for hire is not subject to termination."

The most important thing for a freelance writer to remember is that unless there is an express written agreement, signed by both parties, that the work is "made for hire," the work does not fall into that category. Even where the entire copyright is assigned by the author, he can get it back eventually. But once a work is legally designated a work made for hire, an employment relationship is deemed to exist, and the employer is considered the author for all time, no matter who wrote the piece.

Work space. Most writers would probably agree that the home office, a complete room used only for writing, is the ideal arrangement; however, it is impractical or impossible for many. Perhaps more important than having one's own office is having a particular place, which is used consistently and regularly, reserved for writing. This place can be a desk, a garage, a portion of a room, or merely a portion of a table.

Just as a work space need not be expensive, writers with limited financial means have put together practical, functional equipment built from unconventional materials. For example, a desk can be built by laying a door over two low filing cabinets; bookshelves can be built of planks and bricks; cork board hung on a wall is an inexpensive bulletin board and space-saver. (*See: camera; tape recorder; taxes; tools, writing; typewriters; word processor.*)

Working Press of the Nation. This is a five-volume set of annual directories published by the National Research Bureau, Inc. It lists organizations and personnel in various media, providing such information as names, titles, addresses, and telephone numbers of personnel in the industry. Directory titles are as follows: Volume 1, *Newspaper and Allied Services Directory*; Volume 2, *Magazine and Editorial Directory*; Volume 3, *TV and Radio Directory*; Volume 4, *Feature Writer, Photographer and Syndicate Directory*; and Volume

Writers, biographical directories of

5, *Internal Publications Directory.*
Volume 4 of this series can be of
special interest, since it is the directory that lists freelance writers. Included in each listing are the writer's
name, his home address, areas in
which he specializes, and magazines
in which he has had material
published. The possibility of assignments resulting from editors' referring to the directory is one
advantage of being included.

Freelance feature writers interested in being listed in *Working Press of
the Nation* should write to the National Research Bureau, 310 South
Michigan Avenue, Chicago IL 60601.
At present, listings are free of
charge.

Working Press of the Nation is available in most large libraries. (*See: directories.*)

**World Intellectual Property Organi-
zation (WIPO).** This is an agency of
the United Nations that is devoted to
the protection of intellectual property, which comprises industrial property such as rights in inventions, and
copyright in creations in the arts.

WIPO is especially active in providing technical assistance requested by developing countries. Writers
seeking information about the copyright laws in a particular foreign
country may be able to get advice on
their question from the Public Information Officer of WIPO, whose address is 34 chemin des Colombettes,
1211 Geneva 20, Switzerland.

The Writer. This monthly magazine,
established in 1887, has an audience
of freelance writers. Its content,
largely instructional, relates to the
work of the writer of traditional literary forms—short story, poem, article, novel, etc.

The Writer covers certain markets
regularly each month of the year.
"Special Market Lists" are usually
published as follows: sports and recreation and outdoors, January; trade
journals and house magazines, February; poetry, March; juvenile and
young adult magazines and city and
regional, April; men's and adult
magazines, the popular market, detective and mystery, western, science fiction and fantasy, confession
and romance, travel magazines,
May; lifestyle, women's and garden
publications, fillers and short humor, greeting cards, June; book publishers, July; general articles, August; articles (technical and scientific, health, education, agriculture,
fine arts, hobbies), September; fiction (general magazines) and fiction
and nonfiction (literary magazines),
October; television and drama, November; and religious magazines
and syndicates, December.

The Writer's editorial and subscription offices are at 120 Boylston
Street, Boston MA 02116. (*See:* Writer's Digest.)

Writers, biographical directories of.
Directories that furnish biographical
material on authors can be useful to
a writer in researching nonfiction or
in gathering lecture material.

Contemporary Authors is a series of
105 volumes, begun in 1962, of nontechnical book authors published by
commercial publishers or university
presses.

The biennial *Writers Directory* contains more than 15,000 descriptions
of fiction and nonfiction writers
from various countries, all of whom
have published at least one book in
English. The *Directory's* "Index to
Writing Categories," a cross-reference section, groups the writers list-

ed according to kind of writing (e.g., children's nonfiction) or subject matter (e.g., medicine/health).

Among directories dealing with authors of childrens' books are *Twentieth Century Children's Writers* and *Something About the Author*. Other directories of specialized writers include the *Contemporary Writers Series: Contemporary Poets* (Vol. I), *Contemporary Novelists* (Vol. II), *Contemporary Dramatists* (Vol. III), and *Contemporary Literary Critics* (Vol. IV). Revised every five years, the series lists living writers who write in English. The *National Playwrights Directory* contains approximately 500 entries of living American playwrights—arranged alphabetically by author's last name—and an index of plays.

Creative Canada is a series of references to visual artists, musicians, and performing artists, as well as writers, not all of whom are living. Another Canadian directory is *The Writers' Union of Canada: A Directory of Members*. Its 300 members write in such categories as literary fiction, political commentary, bestsellers, travel, humor, cookbooks, memoirs, and children's books. (*See: biographical references; directories, writer-related;* Working Press of the Nation.)

Writer's block. Every writer, no matter how successful, is susceptible to this syndrome, which may be manifested by a dearth of ideas, a state of self-dissatisfaction, or an inability to organize.

One step toward conquering writ-er's block is to acknowledge the fact that it comes from within the self and is not determined by outside circumstances or persons. Performing work-related tasks, such as reading, tidying one's desk, corresponding with other writers, or speaking before a local organization can help the writer during a period of block. Also, buying a new piece of equipment or a reference book may raise the writer's spirits.

Causes of writer's block vary with the individual. For many writers, block results from sheer gut fear that their writing isn't any good, and that once it's in print *other* people will see it and realize it's no good. In other writers, the disorder results from fear of disapproval or offending another person. (The writer's fear is based on his own *projections* of how others will react.) For example, if the writer gives an Irish name to the villain of a story, he may dread hearing the reaction of his Irish friends. Similarly, if he injects religiously controversial material that contradicts his family's beliefs, he may fear his parents' disapproval. Finally, the writer may feel that by including in a story the same unfortunate experience that actually happened to someone he knows, he would be exposing a confidence.

Another fear caused by projection is the writer's feeling that others will interpret unseemly events in his fiction, such as illicit drugs or adultery, as autobiography.

A third cause of writer's block is attempting to write against one's own values in order to suit the needs of a particular publication or audience.

Some writers have discovered through psychotherapy that their cases of writer's block were caused by psychological problems unrelated to their work.

Additional information: *The Writer's Survival Guide.*

Writers, characteristics of. All writers have certain skills in common, but personal characteristics also seem to play a role in whether or not job satisfaction and/or financial success is reached in this field.

Personal qualities necessary in one who intends to become a freelance writer are energy, persistence, independence, curiosity, and discipline. A writer must have enough energy to work by a schedule that is determined by deadlines and therefore can involve extra or irregular hours. Persistence and a thick-skinned personality help the writer through periods of receiving rejection slips or unfavorable reviews. Only the person who is independent enough to tolerate working alone for long periods will be happy as a freelance writer. Curiosity, which supplies ideas and impels him to learn, is the catalyst for a writer's work; while strong personal discipline enables him to produce finished manuscripts.

Persons interested in writing jobs in business and industry can also take steps to ensure future job satisfaction. The U.S. Department of Labor produces the *Occupational Outlook Quarterly*, which is available in public libraries. It describes job requirements, working conditions, education, and other characteristics needed to fill various job descriptions. Another publication, "Toward Matching Personal and Job Characteristics" is also available from the U.S. Superintendent of Documents. (*See: careers in writing; talent.*)

Writers' clubs. A writers' club is an informal group established for mutual guidance and encouragement among writers. Activities of club meetings include reporting sessions, which compel each member to recount his accomplishments, and manuscript critiques, which are designed to provide the writers with honest evaluation and advice. These planned discussions often digress to other writing-related ones, such as discussions on how or where to sell a particular piece or how to overcome a case of writer's block. Sometimes a club invites a prominent local writer to speak to the group.

One of the major aims of writers' clubs is to instill motivation and enthusiasm in members through interaction with other professionals.

Although current editions no longer carry them because of space limitations, earlier editions of *Writer's Market* listed local and regional writers' clubs, indexed geographically. Copies of these editions are in most public libraries. (Club officers may have changed but the persons listed may still be located through local telephone books for more information about the club.) Beginning in 1982, the National Writers Club, 1450 S. Havana, Aurora CO 80012, began publication of a *Directory of Local Writers' Organizations*. Latest publication date and price can be obtained by writing the National Writers Club. (*See: writers' organizations.*)

Writers' colonies. Writers' colonies are retreats for writers. There are a handful of colonies scattered around the United States offering writers and other artists (painters, sculptors, composers) a place to work and think. Each colony presents its residents a unique writing environment—from the stateliness of a mansion surrounded by gardens to the informality of a community-type arrangement that invites writers' families, too. Writers' colonies may encourage interaction among their residents, or they may represent a sanctuary for the creative process. Two of the oldest colonies are the MacDowell Colony in Peterborough, New Hampshire, and Yaddo in Saratoga Springs, New York.

Some of the colonies offer free room and board; others request their residents to prepare meals and buy their own groceries. Voluntary contributions are often encouraged. Lengths of stay vary. Some colonies take beginners; others do not.

Applications for admission to most writers' colonies include submitting writing samples and recommendations from former residents or other appropriate persons. Addresses and other information about specific writers' colonies are sometimes available from Poets and Writers, Inc., 201 W. 54th Street, New York NY 10019 and from the Center for Arts Information, 625 Broadway, New York NY 10012. (*See: scholarships, fellowships, internships.*)

Writers' conferences. Organized learning/writing experiences. Writers' conferences around the country offer varied settings, purposes, and formats to meet the specific needs of writers. They may range from one-day seminars to month-long assemblies. Some are highly focused both in theme and enrollment, e.g., Writing Workshop for People over 57; Experimental Writers' Workshop. Others are broad in extent and renowned by reputation, e.g., Bread Loaf Writers' Conference.

Some writers' conferences hold contests or offer private critiques of manuscripts submitted prior to the conference opening. Some may be lecture oriented; others offer numerous question-answer opportunities. Some provide writers with the option of consulting privately with a staff member during the conference.

A list of conferences held nationwide appears in the May issue of *Writer's Digest* and in the annual *Literary Market Place*.

Writer's Digest. Established in 1920, this is the largest circulation national American monthly magazine aimed toward freelance writers. The magazine emphasizes guidance in three major areas: the kinds of manuscripts bought; how to write them; where to sell them. Articles cover a wide spectrum of writing-related subjects: techniques for writing stories, articles, novels, nonfiction books, audiovisual materials, speeches—any writing for which a freelancer is used. Regular columns in the magazine cover fiction, nonfiction, poetry, scriptwriting, New York and West Coast markets, and monthly updates to the market information contained in the annual directory *Writer's Market*. The publication carries interviews with well-known writers, information on subjects involving legal matters, and material on the business of writing. *Writer's Digest* is located at 9933 Alliance Rd., Cincinnati OH 45242. (*See: The Writer.*)

Writer's guidelines. This is a printed reference sheet supplied to writers by editors. It describes a magazine's purpose and audience, and outlines specifications for submitting material. In a writer's guidelines sheet, the editor indicates specific word lengths for material; categories and topics needed; need for, and policy on, photographs; and, sometimes, rates of pay. Some book publishers—such as those with romance novel imprints—also have writer's guidelines pointing up the specific restrictions of heroine's age, plot structure, etc. The object of writer's guidelines is to provide for smooth dealings between writer and editor, and to guide the writer in selling his material by detailing the publisher's needs and requirements. (*See: style sheet.*)

Writers Guild of America. A labor union representing professional writers in motion pictures, television, and radio. Like any other labor union, its chief purpose is to insure the protection and well-being of its members through the processes of collective bargaining under the National Labor Relations Act of the United States. The Guild was founded in 1954 as the result of an amalgamation of the Screenwriters Guild, the Radio Writers Guild, and the Television Writers Group.

For administrative purposes only, the union is divided by the Mississippi River into the Writers Guild of America, East, and the Writers Guild of America, West. In all other respects it is a single union, jointly holding national agreements with producing organizations. A National Council, made up of members of East and West, meets semiannually

in New York and Los Angeles. Annual meetings of the membership are held simultaneously in New York and Los Angeles each September.

The Guild presents annual awards for outstanding achievement in writing in the areas of its jurisdiction. Each Guild publishes its own monthly newsletter; jointly they publish a directory of members. Each also has a registration service for manuscripts.

Membership in the Guild can be acquired only by the sale of literary material to or employment for, writing services in motion pictures, television, and radio. At WGA West there is an initiation fee of $1,500, with basic dues of $25 per quarter, and an assessment of 1% of a writer's gross earnings in any of the fields of jurisdiction, also payable quarterly. Fees for WGA East are $1,000 initiation, and annual dues of $50 plus 1½% of gross earnings.

A booklet listing the Guild's minimum rates for scripts of various lengths is available from either Guild for $4, which includes postage, plus applicable sales tax for residents of New York and California. Some sample script rates for screenplay and teleplay from this booklet appear in the Appendix to this encyclopedia. The Guild, East, also publishes a booklet, "Professional Writer's Teleplay/Screenplay Format," for $2.90, which includes postage, plus applicable sales tax. A certified check, or a money order made out to "Writers Guild of America" should accompany any order.

Writers Guild of America, West, is located at 8955 Beverly Boulevard, Los Angeles CA 90048. Writers Guild of America, East, is located at

555 West 57th Street, New York NY 10019. (*See: Writers Guild Script Registration Service.*)

Writers Guild Script Registration Service. Since a writer's rights under the law begin when a work is completed, the Writers Guild of America has formed a registration service to verify the completion date and identity of formats, outlines, synopses, storylines, or scripts for theatrical films, television, and radio. (Book manuscripts, plays, music, lyrics, illustrations, and legal documents are not eligible for registration with the Guild.) Some agents and producers will not accept a script unless it has been registered with the Guild; this minimizes the charges of story theft that are bound to be made in industries so barraged with material that ideas often overlap. (If a *Writer's Market* entry doesn't mention registration, it's generally safe to assume that that agent or producer will accept unregistered work.)

A writer does not have to belong to the Guild to register his work. To do so, he must send an 8½x11-inch unbound copy of the manuscript to the registration service, along with his registration fee ($5 for Guild members, $10 for nonmembers). The manuscript is sealed, dated, given a registration number, and filed; a receipt is sent back to the author, who then is responsible for inscribing the registration number on his copies of the manuscript. The Guild keeps the manuscript on file for ten years, at which time the work will be destroyed, unless the author renews the registration by repaying the registration fee.

The mailing address of the registration service is Writers Guild of America, West, 8955 Beverly Boulevard, Los Angeles CA 90048. (*See: copyright.*)

Writers—made or born? (*See: talent.*)

Writer's Market. This annual directory currently lists 4,000 freelance writing markets in the U.S. and Canada, including book publishers; company, trade, and consumer magazines; syndicates; film, television, theatrical, and audiovisual producers; advertising agencies; and greeting card publishers. *Writer's Market* also lists services a freelance writer might want to know about—author's agents, contests and awards, and writers' organizations. Individual entries are revised yearly (although the editors advise supplementing *Writer's Market* with the market information published monthly in *Writer's Digest*, or checking the latest issue of a publication before querying an editor who might have moved on since *Writer's Market* copy deadline).

Writer's Market listings give as complete a picture of a market as possible, providing a market's address(es); phone number; names of editorial personnel; circulation, distribution, format; readership (or audience) profile; pay rates, manuscript lengths, and seasonal deadlines; rights purchased; kill fees; types of work the editors are looking for; and tips from the editors on how to break in. In addition to the listings, front and back chapters deal briefly but thoroughly with the business of freelancing, including manuscript preparation, recordkeeping, and what rights to sell. A regular feature is "How Much Should I Charge?," which lists rates of pay for different kinds of writing and writing-related work. Other pages show current postal rates, and reproduce a standard author's contract.

Writers' organizations. Writers' organizations exist for two reasons: professional advancement and sociability. Large organizations (Writers Guild, Authors League, American Society of Journalists and Authors) are concerned mainly with the economic advancement of the writer. National and local clubs offer writers the camaraderie of other writers, by mail or in person. Many of the leading professional writers' groups are described in individual entries in this encyclopedia.

Writers' organizations and associations are also described in the *Encyclopedia of Associations*, available in most libraries. Specific entries are located by consulting the alphabetical title listing and *keyword* index in the back of the volume, such as *Dramatists* Guild, Associated *Business* Writers of America, etc. (*See: writers' clubs.*)

Writers' unions. Trade organizations that, through negotiations, enhance the writer's power in dealing with publishers or producers.

Countries in which writers have formed unions include England, Canada, Sweden, Denmark, Norway, and West Germany. These foreign unions have sometimes succeeded in obtaining fairer treatment from publishers by collectively refusing to submit work to them; compelling publishers to deliver payment of advances or royalties; raising royalty payments; instituting fair payment procedures, such as paying for rewrites; and establishing a means of payment for use of books in libraries.

In the U.S., The Newspaper Guild has successfully negotiated salary rates for reporters and copy editors, and the Writers Guild of America negotiates with producers for film and television fees. Currently, the U.S. has no union for writers of books and articles; however, the proposal for a union, called the National Writers Union, was adopted at the American Writers Congress in October 1981. (*See: American Writers Congress.*)

Writer's Yearbook. An annual magazine published by Writer's Digest and distributed through bookstores and newsstands January through March Issues average 128 pages and contain the editorial requirements of the top 100 magazine markets, the top 30 book publishers, and other specialized markets. Interviews with best-selling authors and articles of instruction in fiction and nonfiction technique are also included. The publication is also available by mail from Writer's Digest, 9933 Alliance Road, Cincinnati OH 45242.

Writing, books on. Books for freelance writers fall into several broad categories. They may be general works designed to help improve writing style, or biographies of well-known writers intended to inspire. How-to books offer information, for example, on the techniques of writing magazine articles, interviewing, or getting credible motivations for story characters. Specialized works explain how to write and sell children's picture books, television scripts, or greeting cards.

Most nonfiction books on writing are listed in the *Subject Guide to Books In Print*, under the following general categories: "Authorship—Handbooks, Manuals, etc.," "Authors and Publishers," Journalism—Handbooks, Manuals, etc.," "Reporters and Reporting" and "Writing," and under specific headings such as "Advertising Copy," "Fiction—Authorship," "Medical Writing," "Authorship—Juvenile Literature," "Moving Picture Authorship" and "Playwriting." The *Subject Guide* is in any library.

The two most prolific publishers of books for writers are Writer's Digest Books, Cincinnati, Ohio; and *The Writer*, Boston, Massachusetts.

Writing—business versus hobby. Whether a writer writes for love or for money, it's the profits he makes—or doesn't make—that determine his legal status for tax purposes. A writer who earns a profit from his writing is considered by the government to be in business and is required to report his earnings to the Internal Revenue Service, even if the writer considers himself a hobbyist and does not deduct writing-related expenses; indeed, he will then pay *more* tax than if he took what deductions he could.

Conversely, a writer who wishes to deduct his writing losses cannot do so unless he shows some yearly profit two years out of every five: if he does not show profit—even $1 a year—his writing is legally considered to be a hobby and so his expenses cannot be deducted. (*See: taxes.*)

Writing courses. Courses of organized study are available to freelance writers, poets, playwrights, novelists, and others wishing to further their expertise in a particular field of writing. The ideal writing courses are taught by instructors who are also professional writers. Instructors may teach literary skills and reader consciousness; perhaps more importantly, they may function as editors who critique the publishability of student writing.

Writing courses are offered by many colleges and universities around the country. They are available both through degree programs on campus and home study. Some proprietary schools also offer home study courses in writing. For addresses for further information, see entries in this encyclopedia on Associated Writing Programs and correspondence courses for writers.

Writing instruction on film, tape, cassette, record. The films and recordings departments of many public libraries have collections of well-known authors reading their works and/or discussing the techniques of their writing, which freelancers, students, and teachers may find helpful. Some publishers of curriculum materials for schools also sell home study tapes for adults on grammar, interviewing, speed reading, memory development, etc. The professional librarian of the local board of education may have such companies' catalogues available for examination.

Writing schools, home study. (*See: correspondence courses for writers.*)

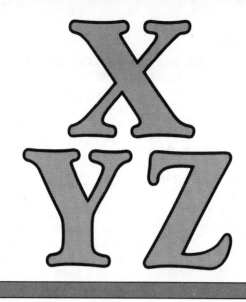

Xenophobia. The fear of, or hatred toward, foreigners or strangers. Since an unwillingness to appreciate or to become familiar with cultures other than his own only narrows a writer's viewpoint, xenophobic authors tend to be quickly relegated to literary obscurity.

Xenophobia as a theme does occur in various literatures; it is important, for instance, in American ethnic fiction, since ethnic Americans tend to be objects of xenophobia.

Yearbooks, encyclopedia. These references, which report both on general news and highlights of a given year, can be useful in researching articles summarizing the events of a previous year; nostalgia writers and fiction writers use older editions for reference. Yearbooks are usually published in February or March of the year following the one being covered.

For more immediately available information, newspaper indexes and *Facts on File* can be consulted. (*See: background information, books of.*)

Yellow journalism. A newspaper style that emerged in the late 1800s. It is characterized by sensational accounts of crime and scandalous events, and by stories about crusades undertaken by "average" people. Newspapers of this genre introduced the banner head (a large, bold headline that occupies the entire width of the page); the Sunday supplement, and liberal use of photographs and illustrations.

The best-known practitioners of yellow journalism were New York *World* owner Joseph Pulitzer and New York *Journal* owner William Randolph Hearst, who during the late 1890s battled for the largest newspaper readership. One tactic in this circulation war was each publisher's luring of staff members from the competing paper to his own. The comic strip the *Yellow Kid* and its creator, Richard Outcault, were part of this ongoing bargaining. Outcault's comic strip character was the basis for the label *yellow papers*, applied to Hearst's and Pulitzer's newspapers; this tag evolved into the term *yellow journalism*.

During the prime of yellow journalism, its characteristic techniques were practiced across the country—in Cincinnati, St. Louis, San Francisco, Denver, and Boston, as well as in New York, but widespread use of such techniques had disappeared by 1910.

The banner headline and the Sunday magazine, which are now professionally accepted practices, are two surviving characteristics of yellow journalism. The term *yellow journalism*, as used today, refers to sensational reporting or photographs.

Young adult. A term used by librarians, book publishers, and booksellers to refer to the books published for young people between the ages of 12 and 17. Some publishers and librarians have lowered the minimum age level to 10 recognizing the interest of some of today's younger people in more adult themes. As Clarion Books' editor and publisher James Cross Giblin pointed out in a *Writer's Digest* article:

Fifteen years ago, the taboo barriers in this field, which had stood for generations, broke down right and left.

Authors rushed into the breach with realistic novels that treated such hitherto "forbidden" subjects as premarital sex, child abuse, homosexuality, drug use, alcoholism, madness, and incest. . . . Judy Blume, Paul Zindel, S.E. Hinton, and many other authors successfully rode this wave of 'new realism,' establishing their reputations. . . . .

Meanwhile, opponents of realism in young adult fiction, reflecting the new conservatism in the country, are mounting campaigns to have books they find offensive removed from the shelves of school and public libraries.

Recently a different kind of novel has come to the fore—the romance novel aimed at the young adult market. (*See: censorship, literary; novels for young people; romance novels.*)

"Z" pattern. A pattern of descriptive prose writing through which the reader is exposed to both the depth and breadth of a scene. A paragraph written in this pattern first details the most distant elements of that scene, then gives a general description of the intermediate area, and lastly paints a word picture of the foreground and its elements.

The "Z" pattern has been adapted to writing from its use in advertising. In an ad design pattern, the reader's eye is attracted to the headline from the upper left corner to the upper right corner, then down the page diagonally to the lower left corner, and finally to the lower right corner, where the name of the advertiser is often placed.

ZIP Code information. The ZIP Code for a particular city or town can be determined by using one of two sources. The United States Postal Service publishes an annual directory of ZIP Codes, called the *National ZIP Code & Post Office Directory*, which is available for public use at post office branches. This book is also sold at post offices, though it may not be available at small branches.

In addition, local telephone directories list the number of the government's 24-hour ZIP Code information service. The telephone number is given in the white pages under "United States Government" in the listing for the "U.S. Postal Service."

APPENDIX

One of the joys of a good reference book is coming to what you think is the end, and then discovering a rich new vein to be mined. No matter how well a topic is explained in the text it is dramatically clearer when it is illustrated with an actual example, or codified into a chart or table. But trying to include such samples and lists in the main body of our encyclopedia seems a little like trying to stuff an octopus into a box! Those of us who like books to be well ordered find an Appendix the perfect place to provide such illustrative examples.

The Appendices which follow are in alphabetical sequence, and they are also listed by page number on the contents page.

Like those happy childhood gifts of boxes within boxes, at the end of these Appendices, you'll find another helpful tool: a bibliography leading you to further exploration of the writer's world.

Advertising Agencies' Costs and Profits

The following figures represent percentages of gross* income unless otherwise stated, based on a survey of 272 advertising agencies in 1980.

Rent, light and depreciation, 7.95%

Taxes (other than U.S. income), 4.30%

Other operating expenses, 17.13%

Total payroll, 61.27%

Payments into retirement plans, 2.23%

Insurance for employee benefit, 1.89%

Total expenses, 94.77%

Profit before U.S. income tax for all agencies, 5.23%

U.S. income taxes, 1.17%

Net profit, 4.06%

Profit before U.S. income tax for incorporated agencies, 5.20%

U.S. income tax for incorporated agencies, 1.25%

Net profit for incorporated agencies, 3.95%

Net profit for incorporated agencies (as percentage of sales—i.e., billing), .92%

---

*Gross income comprises commissions, agencies' service charges, and fees. Source: Annual studies of advertising agencies' costs and profits conducted by American Association of Advertising Agencies. Figures are averages for agencies of all sizes.

Area Codes

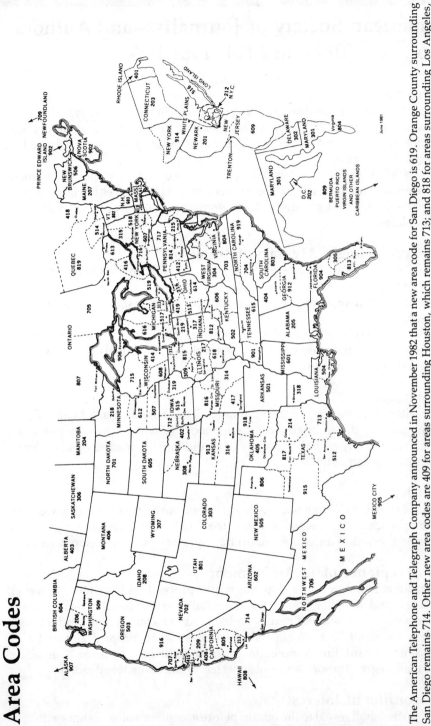

The American Telephone and Telegraph Company announced in November 1982 that a new area code for San Diego is 619. Orange County surrounding San Diego remains 714. Other new area codes are 409 for areas surrounding Houston, which remains 713; and 818 for areas surrounding Los Angeles, which remains 213. Although the rest of New York City remains area code 212, Brooklyn and Queens are now area code 718.

445

American Society of Journalists and Authors Code of Ethics and Fair Practices

Preamble

Over the years, an unwritten code governing editor-writer relationships has arisen. The American Society of Journalists and Authors has compiled the major principles and practices of that code that are generally recognized as fair and equitable.

The ASJA has also established a Committee on Editor-Writer Relations to investigate and mediate disagreements brought before it, either by members or by editors. In its activity this committee shall rely on the following guidelines.

1. Truthfulness, Accuracy, Editing

The writer shall at all times perform professionally and to the best of his or her ability, assuming primary responsibility for truth and accuracy. No writer shall deliberately write into an article a dishonest, distorted or inaccurate statement.

Editors may correct or delete copy for purposes of style, grammar, conciseness or arrangement, but may not change the intent or sense without the writer's permission.

2. Sources

A writer shall be prepared to support all statements made in his or her manuscripts, if requested. It is understood, however, that the publisher shall respect any and all promises of confidentiality made by the writer in obtaining information.

3. Ideas

An idea shall be defined not as a subject alone but as a subject combined with an approach. A writer shall be considered to have a proprietary right to an idea suggested to an editor and to have priority in the development of it.

4. Acceptance of an Assignment

A request from an editor that the writer proceed with an idea, however worded and whether oral or written, shall be considered an assignment. (The word "assignment" here is understood to mean a definite order for an article.) It shall be the obligation of the writer to proceed as rapidly as possible toward the completion of an assignment, to meet a deadline mutually agreed upon, and not to agree to unreasonable deadlines.

5. Conflict of Interest

The writer shall reveal to the editor, before acceptance of an assignment, any actual or potential conflict of interest, including but not limited to any financial interest in any product, firm, or commercial venture relating to the subject of the article.

6. Report on Assignment

If in the course of research or during the writing of the article, the writer concludes that the assignment will not result in a satisfactory article, he or she shall be obliged to so inform the editor.

7. Withdrawal

Should a disagreement arise between the editor and writer as to the merit or handling of an assignment, the editor may remove the writer on payment of mutually satisfactory compensation for the effort already expended, or the writer may withdraw without compensation and, if the idea for the assignment originated with the writer, may take the idea elsewhere without penalty.

8. Agreements

The practice of written confirmation of all agreements between editors and writers is strongly recommended, and such confirmation may originate with the editor, the writer, or an agent. Such a memorandum of confirmation should list all aspects of the assignment including subject, approach, length, special instructions, payments, deadline, and guarantee (if any). Failing prompt contradictory response to such a memorandum, both parties are entitled to assume that the terms set forth therein are binding.

9. Rewriting

No writer's work shall be rewritten without his or her advance consent. If an editor requests a writer to rewrite a manuscript, the writer shall be obliged to do so but shall alternatively be entitled to withdraw the manuscript and offer it elsewhere.

10. Bylines

Lacking any stipulation to the contrary, a byline is the author's un-questioned right. All advertisements of the article should also carry the author's name. If an author's byline is omitted from a published article, no matter what the cause or reason, the publisher shall be liable to compensate the author financially for the omission.

11. Updating

If delay in publication necessitates extensive updating of an article, such updating shall be done by the author, to whom additional compensation shall be paid.

12. Reversion of Rights

A writer is not paid by money alone. Part of the writer's compensation is the intangible value of timely publication. Consequently, if after six months the publisher has not scheduled an article for publication, or within twelve months has not published an article, the manuscript and all rights therein should revert to the author without penalty or cost to the author.

13. Payment for Assignments

An assignment presumes an obligation upon the publisher to pay for the writer's work upon satisfactory completion of the assignment, according to the agreed terms. Should a manuscript that has been accepted, orally or in writing, by a publisher or any representative or employee of the publisher, later be deemed unacceptable, the publisher shall nevertheless be obliged to pay the writer in full according to the agreed terms.

If an editor withdraws or terminates an assignment, due to no fault of the writer, after work has begun but prior to completion of the manuscript, the writer is entitled to compensation for work already put in; such compensation shall be negotiated between editor and author and shall be commensurate with the amount of work already completed. If a completed assignment is not acceptable, due to no fault of the writer, the writer is nevertheless entitled to payment; such payment, in common practice, has varied from half the agreed-upon price to the full amount of that price.

14. Time of Payments

The writer is entitled to payment for an accepted article within ten days of delivery. No article payment should ever be subject to publication.

15. Expenses

Unless otherwise stipulated by the editor at the time of an assignment, a writer shall assume that normal, out-of-pocket expenses will be reimbursed by the publisher. Any extraordinary expenses anticipated by the writer shall be discussed with the editor prior to incurring them.

16. Insurance

A magazine that gives a writer an assignment involving any extraordinary hazard shall insure the writer against death or disability during the course of travel or the hazard, or, failing that, shall honor the cost of such temporary insurance as an expense account item.

17. Loss of Personal Belongings

If, as a result of circumstances or events directly connected with a perilous assignment and due to no fault of the writer, a writer suffers loss of personal belongings or professional equipment or incurs bodily injury, the publisher shall compensate the writer in full.

18. Copyright, Additional Rights

It shall be understood, unless otherwise stipulated in writing, that sale of an article manuscript entitles the purchaser to first North American publication rights only, and that all other rights are retained by the author. Under no circumstances shall an independent writer be required to sign a so-called "all rights transferred" or "work made for hire" agreement as a condition of assignment, of payment, or of publication.

19. Reprints

All revenues from reprints shall revert to the author exclusively, and it is incumbent upon a publication to refer all requests for reprint to the author. The author has a right to charge for such reprints and must request that the original publication be credited.

20. Agents

According to the Society of Authors' Representatives, the accepted fee for an agent's services has long been ten percent of the writer's receipts, except for foreign rights representation. An agent may not represent editors or publishers. In the absence of any agreement to the contrary, a writer shall not be obliged to pay an agent a fee on work negotiated, accomplished and paid for without the assistance of the agent.

21. TV and Radio Promotion

The writer is entitled to be paid for personal participation in TV or radio programs promoting periodicals in which the writer's work appears.

22. Indemnity

No writer should be obliged to indemnify any magazine or book publisher against any claim, actions, or proceedings arising from an article or book.

23. Proofs

The editor shall submit edited proofs of the author's work to the author for approval, sufficiently in advance of publication that any errors may be brought to the editor's attention. If for any reason a publication is unable to so deliver or transmit proofs to the author, the author is entitled to review the proofs in the publication's office.

ASJA Suggested Letter of Agreement

originating with the writer (to be used when publication does not issue written confirmation of assignment)

DATE

EDITOR'S NAME & TITLE
PUBLICATION
ADDRESS

Dear EDITOR'S NAME:
This will confirm our agreement that I will research and write an article of approximately NUMBER words on the subject of BRIEF DESCRIPTION, in accord with our discussion of DATE.

The deadline for delivery of this article to you is DATE.

It is understood that my fee for this article shall be $ AMOUNT, payable on acceptance, for which sum PUBLICATION shall be entitled to first North American publication rights in the article.[1] If this assignment does not work out after I have submitted a completed manuscript, a guarantee of $ AMOUNT shall be paid to me.

It is further understood that you shall reimburse me for routine expenses incurred in the researching and writing of the article, including long-distance telephone calls, and that extraordinary expenses, should any such be anticipated, will be discussed with you before they are incurred.[2]

It is also agreed that you will submit proofs of the article for my examination, sufficiently in advance of publication to permit correction of errors.

I hereby warrant that the article will be original and, to the best of my abilities, accurate in all particulars.

This letter is intended to cover the main points of our agreement. Should any disagreement arise on these or other matters, we agree to rely upon the guidelines set forth in the Code of Ethics and Fair Practices of the American Society of Journalists and Authors. Should any controversy persist, such controversy shall be submitted to arbitration before the American Arbitration Association in accordance with its rules, and judgment confirming the arbitrator's award may be entered in any court of competent jurisdiction.

Please confirm our mutual understanding by signing the copy of this agreement and returning it to me.

Sincerely,

(signed)

WRITER'S NAME

PUBLICATION

by _____
              NAME AND TITLE

Date _____

Notes

[1] If discussion included sale of other rights, this clause should specify basic fee for first North American rights, additional fees and express rights each covers, and total amount.
[2] Any other conditions agreed upon, such as inclusion of travel expenses or a maximum dollar amount for which the writer will be compensated, should also be specified.

AMERICAN SOCIETY OF JOURNALISTS AND AUTHORS, INC.
1501 BROADWAY, SUITE 1907, New York NY 10036 • (212)997-0947
Copyright © 1982, American Society of Journalists and Authors, Inc.

On "Work Made for Hire": A Statement of Position

Announced April 28, 1978
American Society of Journalists and Authors

It has long been the established practice for responsible periodicals, in commissioning articles by free-lance writers, to purchase only one-time publication rights—commonly known as "first North American rights"—to such articles, the author retaining all other rights exclusively and all revenues received from the subsequent sale of other rights reverting to the author.

This practice is affirmed by the Code of Ethics and Fair Practices of the American Society of Journalists and Authors (ASJA), the national organization of independent nonfiction writers. The philosophy underlying this tradition has been further reaffirmed by the Copyright Law of 1976, which took effect in January of 1978 and states explicitly that copyright is vested in the author of a work and commences at the moment of creation of that work. "Copyright" is, literally, the "right to copy"—i.e., to publish in any form; that right is the author's, transferable only by written agreement and only to the degree, and under the terms, specified by such agreement.

It has come to the attention of the ASJA that certain periodical publishers have recently sought to circumvent the clear intent of the law by requiring independent writers, as a condition of article assignment, to sign so-called "all rights transferred" or "work made for hire" agreements. "All rights transferred" signifies that the author, the recognized copyright owner, transfers that ownership—and the right to all future revenues that may accrue therefrom—to the publisher. A "work made for hire" agreement specifically relegates the independent writer, so far as the article under consideration is concerned, to the status of an employee and creates a mythical—but nonetheless presumably legally binding—relationship in which the author agrees to function as a hired hand, while the publisher assumes the mantle of "creator" of the work, with all the rights of ownership vested in the creator under the law.

Both types of agreement clearly presume that the work being produced has an inherent value beyond one-time publication. Both the law and the ASJA Code of Ethics recognize that presumption, and it is the intent of both documents that the transfer of any rights beyond one-time publication take place only as the result of negotiation that assigns a monetary value to each such specific right a publisher seeks to acquire. Both types of agreement described above deny the author's

452

basic role as owner and creator and seek to wrest from the writer, even before the work has been produced, all future interest in revenues that may derive from that work.

This effort, subverting the intent of the law and contrary to ethical publishing trade practices, is condemned by the American Society of Journalists and Authors. The demand for blanket assignment of all future right and interest in an article or other creative work simply *will not be met* by responsible independent writers. Publishers who persist in issuing such inequitable agreements in connection with commissioned works will find that they have done so at the certain risk of losing a healthy flow of superior professional material. The result, for those periodicals, is likely to be a sharp and inevitable decline in editorial quality—an erosion and debasement of the standards on which periodicals must rely in order to attract readers and maintain their own reputations.

Audiovisual Script Sample

AMERICA'S RAILROADS
How the Iron Horse Shaped Our Nation

Pictures	Sound
1. LONG LAP DISSOLVES. MONTAGE OF BUSY AIRPORT, PLANES TAXIING, OR A TAKEOFF. HIGHWAY INTERCHANGE, VERY BUSY, TRUCKS, SEMIS. FREIGHT AND PASSENGER TRAINS. BUSY FREIGHT TERMINAL. BUSES. DISSOLVE TO	MUSIC--GUITAR OR BANJO, IMPROVISATION THAT INCLUDES BITS FROM FAMILIAR RAILROAD TUNES. NARRATOR (voice over): America today is crisscrossed and tied together by transportation networks. It's hard to believe that lack of transportation was ever the nation's number one domestic problem.
2. SEVERAL LONG, SPACIOUS SHOTS OF LANDSCAPES TYPICAL OF LOUISIANA PURCHASE STATES, AS LAND WOULD HAVE APPEARED THEN: FLAT, FERTILE (BUT UNCULTIVATED) PLAINS, VIRGIN FOREST, SMALL FARM WITH LOG CABIN, MAYBE RAIL FENCE. FARMER AT WORK WITH HORSE AND PLOW.	Yet less than 175 years ago, when our government paid 15 million dollars for the great midsection of our continent, many thought the purchase foolish. There would never be a way for people to reach most of these vast land areas, they said, and no way to get their products out. (PAUSE)
3. DISSOLVES--TRAINS RUNNING ON FLATLANDS, WINDING THROUGH MOUNTAINS, CROSSING TRESTLE, MAYBE BRIDGE ACROSS GREAT SALT LAKE, ON FERRY BOAT. EMPHASIS IS ON VARIETY OF SETTINGS, RATHER THAN CARGO, PEOPLE, KINDS OF TRAINS, ETC.	Nothing in our country's history molded its growth more than its railroads. How it happened is a fascinating story. Copyright 1979 Cypress Films

Book Contract Terms

A beginner negotiating his first book contract may not be able to get his publisher to agree to all of the following terms, but *Writer's Digest* recommends them as a standard to shoot for.

The Grant Clause: Author's basic grant to the publisher should cover only English language book publication rights in the United States, Canada and the Philippines. Should not grant "all rights" nor "the work."

Royalties: Should be based on the retail list price, not the publisher's net price. For hardcover trade books, should not be lower than 10% on the first 5,000 copies; 12½% on the next 5,000; and 15% thereafter. (The writer may have to split his 10% with the illustrator in juvenile picture books; textbooks and juveniles may pay a lower rate.) Trade paperback royalties should be no less than 6% of list price on the first 20,000 copies and 7½% thereafter. Original mass market paperback royalties should be no less than 6% on net copies sold (distribution less returns).

The Advance: Should be non-returnable, with the final payment due on submission of manuscript rather than publication of book.

Subsidiary Rights: Author's share should be no less than 80% on British edition, 75% on foreign editions, 50% on paperback reprint and book club sales; 90% on movie and TV sales; 90% on first serial (pre-publication) rights and no less than 50% on second serial sales.

Payments: Statements of accounting and payments (if any) should be made semi-annually.

Warranty Clauses: Author should only be liable if judgment is recovered in a suit against the publisher. (Author will be called upon to provide documentation for defense purposes, however.)

Copyright: Should be in the author's name.

Option Clause: If one is given, should only grant the publisher an option to publish the next book on terms to be negotiated by the parties (not on the same terms provided in the current contract). The option clause should be keyed to submission of a *proposal* for the next work, not on submission of the next work itself. The publisher should be required to say yea or nay to the new proposal within 30-60 days.

Termination: Author should be entitled to recover his rights if the book is no longer available for sale through regular trade channels or listed in the publisher's catalogue, and is not reprinted within six months after notice from him.

Publication Date: Should be within one year from delivery of manuscript.

Editor's Note: Sample U.S. and foreign contracts are available for 75¢ and 50¢ respectively, plus a No. 10 self-addressed, stamped envelope from the Society of Authors' Representatives, P. O. Box 650, Old Chelsea Station, New York NY 10113. A helpful guide for the use of authors negotiating contracts with book publishers is available to members of the Author's Guild. See Author's Guild entry in this encyclopedia.

Book Publisher: Organizational Chart

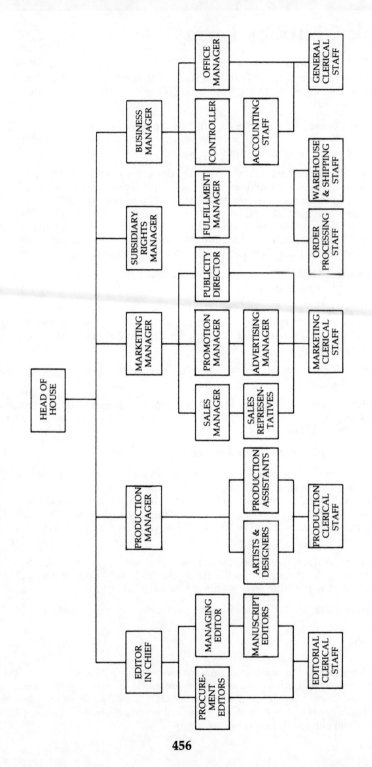

456

Reprinted from *Book Publishing: What It Is, What It Does* with permission of R.R. Bowker Company. Copyright © 1981 by Xerox Corporation.

Book Publisher Reader's Report

Here is an example of the kind of report which would be prepared on a submission by an editor at a book publishing house. Some such reports would suggest rejecting a manuscript. Others, like this, are enthusiastic recommendations for publication. This book report was prepared by editor Sandra McCormack at St. Martin's Press. The book's title was changed and published as *The House on Prague Street*. It was a Book of the Month Club selection, and the Bantam Books paperback edition was published in February, 1983.

THE OLD HOUSE
by Hana Demetz

I think this is an extraordinary book. Quite beautiful! It is a Holocaust testimony, but one that is bearable to read and still extremely moving.

These are the memories of the woman, Helenka, born in Czechoslovakia of a German father and a Jewish mother, who came from an extremely privileged background--of Jews that were practically assimilated. Very wealthy, patriotic and good people. All caught up in the terrible prison camps, because the proud, patriarchal grandfather decreed the family should stay around in case their country needed them. Only Helenka's mother stays outside, and she sort of starves herself to death in order to use her food stamps to send packages to her family in the camps. There is death all around, but it is still outside the horror of what could have been for this half-Jewish family, and Helenka is still a teenager going to school and filled with some very ordinary girlish preoccupations. She falls in love with a young German soldier, actually a very nice young man, and it is a relief to know that there really were some nice young Germans even in their army. And even though Helenka's mother has wanted her to see everything that was happening so that Helenka could bear witness in the future--"Just let her see everything. Someone will have to know about it later on."--the mother still tries to capture some semblance of a normal schoolgirl growing time for her daughter. When Jews are forbidden the regular schools, the mother finds a private school at great hardship and self-deprivation. And when that one is closed, she finds another school, a special vocational one.

First the boyfriend dies. Helenka's mother dies. Then her best friend. And everyone's relatives and best friends. But still, oddly enough, there is not despair. It rather seems that it is all in a dream world. Helenka is put to work in a munitions factory; there they can hope that the Allies will bomb it--preferably when they are safe. And Helenka and the other survivors still notice when spring comes. Then when the war is over

Helenka's father is killed by a revolutionary mob, for the Allies have allowed the Russians to get to Czechoslovakia. Helenka makes an actual trip even further into the dream world of her childhood and returns to her grandfather's home. It is occupied by six skeletal survivors of Auschwitz, who show her the numbers tattooed on their bone arms. And in Yiddish one of them tells her, "Go away, child, and don't come back. Don't disturb us. You don't know, you haven't seen. You haven't suffered. You haven't endured. We are the last. Don't disturb us."

The book has a very quiet tone, but it is still very powerful. And perhaps because the really dreadful Holocaust scenes are never confronted, the horror of it is more possible to come to grips with. There is one brief moment when a freight train is seen with its doors open to show the skeletal mass of prisoners in striped suits and it is stunning in impact. This will probably be very well received critically and it might even have some kind of real impact. Under any circumstance though--even a small one--it has to be done.

Book Publisher's Royalty Statement

Joe Bloome
100 Sunshine St.
Anywhere, CA 92601

Title: How To Write Novels That Sell   Retail Price: $15.95
Royalty earnings for period of July 1 to December 31, 1982.

Type of Sale	Units Sold	Royalty rate	Amount earned
Regular edition	1,650	10% of retail price	$2,631.75
Book Club rights		50% of advance of $3,187.50	1,593.75
Second serial		50% of $1,000.00	500.00
Japanese translation		50% of advance of $2,000	1,000.00
L.A. Times Syndicate		50%	300.00
		Total earnings	$6,025.50

Adjustments

Advances	(4,000.00)
Permission fees paid	(152.73)
Books purchased	(85.93)
Net Amount Due—Check Enclosed	$1,786.84

Editor's Note: This is an example of what a royalty statement on a mythical nonfiction book might look like. Many books, of course, do not have subsidiary sales such as those shown here; others might have more.

Book Publishing Economics

Freelance authors should be aware of the expenses that publishers face in producing their books and which influence the royalties publishers pay. After the writing of a book is completed, there are editorial costs and expenses for production, promotion, and distribution that must be financed.

Following is a chart detailing the hypothetical expenditures of a publisher. It outlines figures for a hardcover nonfiction book written by a previously unpublished author.

Nonfiction Book by New Author

Print order: 15,000 copies (Hardcover, 6"x9", 272 pages)
Retail list price: $15.00
Cost to bookstore (47% average bookstore discount): $7.95

	Publisher's Expenses	Publisher's Income	Author's Income
12,000 books sold over lifespan of book at publisher's income of $7.95 each, less 5% bad debt: $7.55		$90,600	
2,000 returned bookstore copies sold at remainder prices		3,200	
1,000 unsold (review, author, and office copies; damaged; otherwise unsaleable)		0	
Author's advance against royalties	$ 3,000		$ 3,000
Royalties (10%, 12½%, 15% of retail price* on first, second, and third 5,000 copies; less advance)			
for first 5,000 copies: 5,000 x 10% of $15.00 = $7,500			
for second 5,000 copies: 5,000 x 12½% of $15.00 = $9,375			
for additional 2,000 copies: 2,000 x 15% of $15.00 = $4,500			
total royalties $21,375			
less $3,000 advance 3,000			
royalties paid to author $18,375	18,375		18,375
Publishing expenses:			
a. editorial costs (editor's work with author on this book plus a pro-rata share of cost of reading all the other manuscripts that were not publishable)	15,000		
b. production costs (personnel, design, typesetting, paper, paste-up, printing and binding)	26,800		

460

	Publisher's Expenses	Publisher's Income	Author's Income
c. cost of carrying inventory	2,800		
d. advertising, publicity and promotion plus overhead pro-rata share of these departments—marketing, order processing, shipping labor.	15,000		
Salesmen's commissions (based on varying commissions to wholesalers, sales reps calling on bookstores, the publisher's own "house" accounts and direct consumer sales) averaging 7% of publisher's net income	6,342		
Pro-rata share of other administrative costs (bookkeeping, clerical, comptroller, employee benefits, rent, taxes, general overhead pro-rated among all the titles published that year)	5,000		
Publisher's net profit $1,483 (1.6% profit before taxes)	$92,317	$93,800	$21,375

*Some publishers pay royalties based on net receipts, not retail prices.

The preceding chart represents the finances of the publishing of a trade hardcover nonfiction book. (Print order on a novel could be as low as 3,000-5,000 copies.) As you can see, the publisher could have invested his $92,317 in something other than a book and gotten a greater percentage of return on his money. Why does he do it? In hopes of finding books on which he can earn subsidiary rights income from paperback reprinters, book clubs, foreign translations. Those subsidiary sales and reprint editions of his own on some books help the publisher make up for the loss and minimal profit on other books. Trade book publishers average about 7% profit before taxes.

Textbooks, trade paperbacks, and books sold only by direct mail would have different economics. In mass paperback book publishing, a typical print order would call for 150,000-1,000,000 copies, and up to 50 percent of books could be returned unsold. The author's royalties for an original paperback are generally from 6%-10% of the retail price; a paperback reprint of a hardcover book could split royalties 50-50 between author and original publisher.

Books Published by Subject/Format
A Comparison 1971 vs. 1981

Classifications with Dewey Decimal Numbers	All hardbound and paperbound					
	1971			1981		
	New Books	New Editions	Totals	New Books	New Editions	Totals
Agriculture (630-639; 712-719)	241	83	324	398	76	474
Art (700-711; 720-779)	932	314	1,246	1,458	235	1,693
Biography (920-929)	853	944	1,797	1,481	379	1,860
Business (650-659)	550	150	700	1,040	302	1,342
Education (370-379)	1,020	230	1,250	1,020	152	1,172
Fiction	2,066	1,364	3,430	5,003	652	5,655
General Works (000-099)	715	297	1,012	1,514	229	1,743
History (900-909; 930-999)	949	1,029	1,978	1,856	465	2,321
Home Economics (640-649)	381	96	477	957	151	1,108
Juveniles	1,991	232	2,223	2,901	201	3,102
Language (400-499)	400	136	536	649	112	761
Law (340-349)	415	246	661	1,132	316	1,448
Literature (800-810; 813-820; 823-899)	1,383	1,603	2,986	1,521	256	1,777
Medicine (610-619)	1,252	403	1,655	3,163	625	3,788
Music (780-789)	214	188	402	297	101	398
Philosophy, Psychology (100-199)	947	407	1,354	1,221	244	1,465
Poetry, Drama (811; 812; 821; 822)	932	562	1,494	1,063	120	1,183
Religion (200-299)	1,140	427	1,567	1,931	347	2,278
Science (500-599)	2,225	472	2,697	2,798	577	3,375
Sociology, Economics (300-339; 350-369; 380-399)	4,268	1,827	6,095	6,679	1,122	7,801
Sports, Recreation (790-799)	645	245	890	1,099	165	1,264
Technology (600-609; 620-629; 660-699)	1,057	252	1,309	1,877	436	2,313
Travel (910-919)	950	659	1,609	376	96	472
Totals	**25,526**	**12,166**	**37,692**	**41,434**	**7,359**	**48,793**
Mass Market Paperbacks						
Fiction			1,970			3,097
Non-Fiction			1,015			1,078
Totals			**2,985**			**4,175**
Paperbacks Other Than Mass Market						
Fiction			93			399
Non-Fiction			7,198			12,011
Totals			**7,291**			**12,410**

Reprinted from the February 5, 1973 and the October 1, 1972 issues of *Publishers Weekly*, published by R.R. Bowker Company, a Xerox company. Copyright 1973 and 1982 by Xerox Corporation.

Complaints Against Publishers/Agents

The types of complaints received most often by the editors of *Writer's Market* about publisher or agent listings in that publication or the market columns of *Writer's Digest* are these:

No report on manuscript....................................... 55%
    Magazine 37%
    Book Publisher........... 14%
    Agent 4%

No report on book manuscript to fee-charging agent........... 5%

Nonpayment for magazine article/story........................ 19%
    Published 8%
    Accepted.................. 8%
    Assigned.................. 3%

Nonpayment royalty (including no royalty report) 1%

Dissatisfaction with subsidy publishing: lack of communication, product, promotion, sales, etc. 8%

Accepted manuscript not yet published after lengthy wait...... 3%

Mail returned from post office (mss, follow-up letters) addressee unknown/no forwarding address 8%
    Magazines 5%
    Book Publishers........... 2%
    Agents.................... 1%

Miscellaneous (Market needs not those reflected in WM/WD listings, incorrect addresses, other) 1%

                                             100%

Copyright Circulars, Free on Request

The following circulars, which give detailed information on topics of interest to writers and educators, may be obtained free on request by writing the Information and Publications Section, Copyright Office, Library of Congress, Washington DC 20559.

The circular number to request is listed at the end of each entry.

Copyright Form

When to Use This Form: Use Form TX for registration of published or unpublished non-dramatic literary works, excluding periodicals or serial issues. This class includes a wide variety of works: fiction, non-fiction, poetry, textbooks, reference works, directories, catalogs, advertising copy, compilations of information, and computer programs. For periodicals and serials, use Form SE.

FORM TX
UNITED STATES COPYRIGHT OFFICE

REGISTRATION NUMBER

TX _____ TXU

EFFECTIVE DATE OF REGISTRATION

Month ___ Day ___ Year ___

DO NOT WRITE ABOVE THIS LINE. IF YOU NEED MORE SPACE, USE A SEPARATE CONTINUATION SHEET.

1

TITLE OF THIS WORK ▼

PREVIOUS OR ALTERNATIVE TITLES ▼

PUBLICATION AS A CONTRIBUTION If this work was published as a contribution to a periodical, serial, or collection, give information about the collective work in which the contribution appeared.   Title of Collective Work ▼

If published in a periodical or serial give: Volume ▼   Number ▼   Issue Date ▼   On Pages ▼

2

NOTE

Under the law, the "author" of a "work made for hire" is generally the employer, not the employee (see instructions). For any part of this work that was "made for hire" check "Yes" in the space provided, give the employer (or other person for whom the work was prepared) as "Author" of that part, and leave the space for dates of birth and death blank.

a

NAME OF AUTHOR ▼

DATES OF BIRTH AND DEATH
Year Born ▼   Year Died ▼

Was this contribution to the work a "work made for hire"?
☐ Yes
☐ No

AUTHOR'S NATIONALITY OR DOMICILE
Name of Country
OR { Citizen of ▶ _____
Domiciled in ▶ _____

WAS THIS AUTHOR'S CONTRIBUTION TO THE WORK
Anonymous?   ☐ Yes ☐ No
Pseudonymous?   ☐ Yes ☐ No
If the answer to either of these questions is "Yes," see detailed instructions.

NATURE OF AUTHORSHIP Briefly describe nature of the material created by this author in which copyright is claimed. ▼

b

NAME OF AUTHOR ▼

DATES OF BIRTH AND DEATH
Year Born ▼   Year Died ▼

Was this contribution to the work a "work made for hire"?
☐ Yes
☐ No

AUTHOR'S NATIONALITY OR DOMICILE
Name of Country
OR { Citizen of ▶ _____
Domiciled in ▶ _____

WAS THIS AUTHOR'S CONTRIBUTION TO THE WORK
Anonymous?   ☐ Yes ☐ No
Pseudonymous?   ☐ Yes ☐ No
If the answer to either of these questions is "Yes," see detailed instructions

NATURE OF AUTHORSHIP Briefly describe nature of the material created by this author in which copyright is claimed. ▼

c

NAME OF AUTHOR ▼

DATES OF BIRTH AND DEATH
Year Born ▼   Year Died ▼

Was this contribution to the work a "work made for hire"?
☐ Yes
☐ No

AUTHOR'S NATIONALITY OR DOMICILE
Name of Country
OR { Citizen of ▶ _____
Domiciled in ▶ _____

WAS THIS AUTHOR'S CONTRIBUTION TO THE WORK
Anonymous?   ☐ Yes ☐ No
Pseudonymous?   ☐ Yes ☐ No
If the answer to either of these questions is "Yes," see detailed instructions

NATURE OF AUTHORSHIP Briefly describe nature of the material created by this author in which copyright is claimed. ▼

3

YEAR IN WHICH CREATION OF THIS WORK WAS COMPLETED This information must be given ◀ Year in all cases.

DATE AND NATION OF FIRST PUBLICATION OF THIS PARTICULAR WORK
Complete this information Month ▶ _____ Day ▶ _____ Year ▶ _____
ONLY if this work has been published.   ◀ Nation

4

See instructions before completing this space

COPYRIGHT CLAIMANT(S) Name and address must be given even if the claimant is the same as the author given in space 2.▼

TRANSFER If the claimant(s) named here in space 4 are different from the author(s) named in space 2, give a brief statement of how the claimant(s) obtained ownership of the copyright.▼

APPLICATION RECEIVED

ONE DEPOSIT RECEIVED

TWO DEPOSITS RECEIVED

REMITTANCE NUMBER AND DATE

DO NOT WRITE HERE
OFFICE USE ONLY

MORE ON BACK ▶ • Complete all applicable spaces (numbers 5-11) on the reverse side of this page.
• See detailed instructions.   • Sign the form at line 10.

DO NOT WRITE HERE

Page 1 of _____ pages

DO NOT WRITE ABOVE THIS LINE. IF YOU NEED MORE SPACE, USE A SEPARATE CONTINUATION SHEET.

PREVIOUS REGISTRATION Has registration for this work, or for an earlier version of this work, already been made in the Copyright Office?
☐ Yes ☐ No If your answer is "Yes," why is another registration being sought? (Check appropriate box) ▼
☐ This is the first published edition of a work previously registered in unpublished form.
☐ This is the first application submitted by this author as copyright claimant.
☐ This is a changed version of the work, as shown by space 6 on this application.

If your answer is "Yes," give: **Previous Registration Number** ▼   **Year of Registration** ▼

5

DERIVATIVE WORK OR COMPILATION Complete both space 6a & 6b for a derivative work; complete only 6b for a compilation.
a. Preexisting Material Identify any preexisting work or works that this work is based on or incorporates. ▼

b. Material Added to This Work Give a brief, general statement of the material that has been added to this work and in which copyright is claimed. ▼

See instructions before completing this space

6

MANUFACTURERS AND LOCATIONS If this is a published work consisting preponderantly of nondramatic literary material in English, the law may require that the copies be manufactured in the United States or Canada for full protection. If so, the names of the manufacturers who performed certain processes, and the places where these processes were performed must be given. See instructions for details.
Names of Manufacturers ▼   **Places of Manufacture** ▼

7

REPRODUCTION FOR USE OF BLIND OR PHYSICALLY HANDICAPPED INDIVIDUALS A signature on this form at space 10, and a check in one of the boxes here in space 8, constitutes a non-exclusive grant of permission to the Library of Congress to reproduce and distribute solely for the blind and physically handicapped and under the conditions and limitations prescribed by the regulations of the Copyright Office: (1) copies of the work identified in space 1 of this application in Braille (or similar tactile symbols); or (2) phonorecords embodying a fixation of a reading of that work; or (3) both.

a ☐ Copies and Phonorecords   b ☐ Copies Only   c ☐ Phonorecords Only   See instructions

8

DEPOSIT ACCOUNT If the registration fee is to be charged to a Deposit Account established in the Copyright Office, give name and number of Account.
Name ▼   **Account Number** ▼

CORRESPONDENCE Give name and address to which correspondence about this application should be sent. Name/Address Apt/City/State/Zip ▼

Area Code & Telephone Number ▶

Be sure to give your daytime phone number

9

CERTIFICATION* I, the undersigned, hereby certify that I am the
Check one ▶
☐ author
☐ other copyright claimant
☐ owner of exclusive right(s)
☐ authorized agent of _____
Name of author or other copyright claimant, or owner of exclusive right(s) ▲
of the work identified in this application and that the statements made by me in this application are correct to the best of my knowledge.

Typed or printed name and date ▼ If this is a published work, this date must be the same as or later than the date of publication given in space 3.

date ▶

✍ Handwritten signature (X) ▼

10

MAIL CERTIFICATE TO	Name ▼	Have you: • Completed all necessary spaces? • Signed your application in space 10? • Enclosed check or money order for $10 payable to Register of Copyrights? • Enclosed your deposit material with the application and fee? **MAIL TO:** Register of Copyrights Library of Congress, Washington D.C. 20559
Certificate will be mailed in window envelope	Number/Street/Apartment Number ▼	
	City/State/ZIP ▼	

11

For further information about copyright registration, notice, or special questions relating to copyright problems, write:

Information and Publications Section, LM-455
Copyright Office
Library of Congress
Washington, D.C. 20559

Do not submit photocopies of these pages for registration of works. The Copyright Office will only accept original applications supplied by the office for registration purposes.

466

Federal Information Centers

ALABAMA
Birmingham (205)322-8591. Toll-free tieline to Atlanta, GA
Mobile (205)438-1421. Toll-free tieline to New Orleans, LA
ALASKA
Anchorage (907)271-3650. Federal Building and U.S. Courthouse, 701 C Street, 99513
ARIZONA
Phoenix (602)261-3313. Federal Building, 230 North First Avenue, 85025
ARKANSAS
Little Rock (501)378-6177. Toll-free tieline to Fort Worth, TX
CALIFORNIA
Los Angeles (213)688-3800. Federal Building, 300 North Los Angeles Street, 90012
Sacramento (916)440-3344. Federal Building and U.S. Courthouse, 650 Capitol Mall, 95814
San Diego (619)293-6030. Federal Building, 880 Front Street, 92188
San Francisco (415)556-6600. TTY Number: (415)556-3323. Federal Building and U.S. Courthouse, 450 Golden Gate Avenue, P.O. Box 36082, 94102
Santa Ana (714)836-2386. Toll-free tieline to Los Angeles
COLORADO
Colorado Springs (303)471-9491. Toll-free tieline to Denver
Denver (303)234-7181. Bldg. 41, Box 25006, Federal Center, 80225
Pueblo (303)544-9523. Toll-free tieline to Denver
CONNECTICUT
Hartford (203)527-2617. Toll-free tieline to New York, NY
New Haven (203)624-4720. Toll-free tieline to New York, NY
FLORIDA
St. Petersburg (813)893-3495. William C. Cramer Federal Building, 144 First Avenue, South, 33701
Tampa (813)229-7911. Toll-free tieline to St. Petersburg
Other Florida locations (800)282-8556. Toll-free line to St. Petersburg
GEORGIA
Atlanta (404)221-6891. Federal Building and U.S. Courthouse, 75 Spring Street, SW, 30303
HAWAII
Honolulu (808)546-8620. Federal Building, 300 Ala Moana Boulevard, P.O. Box 50091, 96850
ILLINOIS
Chicago (312)353-4242. Everett McKinley Dirksen Building, 230 South Dearborn Street, 33rd Floor, 60604
INDIANA
Gary/Hammond (219)883-4110. Toll-free tieline to Indianapolis
Indianapolis (317)269-7373. Federal Building, 575 North Pennsylvania, 46204
IOWA
Des Moines (515)284-4448. Federal Building, 210 Walnut Street, 50309
Other Iowa locations (800)532-1556. Toll-free line to Des Moines
KANSAS
Topeka (913)295-2866. Federal Building and U.S. Courthouse, 444 SE Quincy, 66683
Other Kansas locations (800)432-2934. Toll-free line to Topeka
KENTUCKY
Louisville (502)582-6261. Toll-free tieline to Cincinnati, OH

LOUISIANA
New Orleans (504)589-6696. U.S. Custom House, 423 Canal Street, Room 100, 70130

MARYLAND
Baltimore (301)962-4980. Federal Building, 31 Hopkins Plaza, 21201

MASSACHUSETTS
Boston (617)223-7121. J.W. McCormack Post Office and Courthouse, Room 812, 02109

MICHIGAN
Detroit (313)226-7016. McNamara Federal Building, 477 Michigan Avenue, Room M-25, 48226
Grand Rapids (616)451-2628. Toll-free tieline to Detroit

MINNESOTA
Minneapolis (612)349-5333. Federal Building and U.S. Courthouse, 110 S. 4th Street, 55401

MISSOURI
St. Louis (314)425-4106. Federal Building, 1520 Market Street, 63103
Other Missouri locations (800)392-7711. Toll-free line to St. Louis

NEBRASKA
Omaha (402)221-3353. U.S. Post Office and Courthouse, 215 North 17th Street, 68102
Other Nebraska locations (800)642-8383. Toll-free line to Omaha

NEW JERSEY
Newark (201)645-3600. Federal Building, 970 Broad Street, 07102
Trenton (609)396-4400. Toll-free tieline to Newark

NEW MEXICO
Albuquerque (505)766-3091. Federal Building and U.S. Courthouse, 517 Gold Avenue SW, 87102

NEW YORK
Albany (518)463-4421. Toll-free tieline to New York City
Buffalo (716)846-4010. Federal Building, 111 West Huron, 14202
New York (212)264-4464. Federal Building, 26 Federal Plaza, Room 2-110, 10278
Rochester (716)546-5075. Toll-free tieline to Buffalo
Syracuse (315)476-8545. Toll-free tieline to Buffalo

NORTH CAROLINA
Charlotte (704)376-3600. Toll-free tieline to Atlanta, GA

OHIO
Akron (216)375-5638. Toll-free tieline to Cleveland
Cincinnati (513)684-2801. Federal Building, 550 Main Street, 45202
Cleveland (216)522-4040. Federal Building, 1240 East Ninth Street, 44199
Columbus (614)221-1014. Toll-free tieline to Cincinnati
Dayton (513)223-7377. Toll-free tieline to Cincinnati
Toledo (419)241-3223. Toll-free tieline to Cleveland

OKLAHOMA
Oklahoma City (405)231-4868. U.S. Post Office and Courthouse, 201 Northwest 3rd Street, 73102
Tulsa (918)584-4193. Toll-free tieline to Oklahoma City

OREGON
Portland (503)221-2222. Federal Building, 1220 Southwest Third Avenue, Room 318, 97204

PENNSYLVANIA
Philadelphia (215)597-7042. Federal Building, 600 Arch Street, 19106
Pittsburgh (412)644-3456. Federal Building, 1000 Liberty Avenue, 15222

RHODE ISLAND
Providence (401)331-5565. Toll-free tieline to Boston, MA

TENNESSEE
Chattanooga (615)265-8231. Toll-free tieline to Atlanta, GA

TEXAS
  Austin (512)472-5494. Toll-free tieline to Houston
  Dallas (214)767-8585. Toll-free tieline to Fort Worth
  Fort Worth (817)334-3624. Lanham Federal Building, 819 Taylor Street, 76102
  Houston (713)229-2552. Federal Building and U.S. Courthouse, 515 Rusk Avenue, 77002
  San Antonio (512)224-4471. Toll-free tieline to Houston
UTAH
  Salt Lake City (801)524-5353. Federal Building, 125 South State Street, 84138
VIRGINIA
  Norfolk (804)441-3101. Federal Building, 200 Granby Mall, Room 120, 23510
  Richmond (804)643-4928. Toll-free tieline to Norfolk
  Roanoke (703)982-8591. Toll-free tieline to Norfolk
WASHINGTON
  Seattle (206)442-0570. Federal Building, 915 Second Avenue, 98174
  Tacoma (206)383-5230. Toll-free tieline to Seattle
WISCONSIN
  Milwaukee (414)271-2273. Toll-free tieline to Chicago, IL

50
Common Errors in Writing

The Associated Press's Writing and Editing Committee prepared the following list primarily for newspaper writers but magazine article writers will find some good reminders here too. Most are examples of word usage. Some are spelling problems. Some are grammatical rules. The committee, headed by Wallace Allen, *Minneapolis Tribune*, published this list in 1974, but the bulk of it was assembled and written over several years by Dick Reid, an assistant managing editor of the *Minneapolis Tribune*, in *Tribune* staff memos as Common Flaws, Ltd.

1. Affect, effect. Generally, *affect* is the verb; *effect* is the noun. "The letter did not *affect* the outcome." "The letter had a significant *effect*." BUT *effect* is also a verb meaning to bring about. Thus: "It is almost impossible to *effect* change."

2. Afterward, afterwards. Use *afterward*. The dictionary allows use of *afterwards* only as a second form.
    The same thinking applies to *toward* and *towards*. Use *toward*.

3. All right. That's the way to spell it. The dictionary may list *alright* as a legitimate word but it is not acceptable in standard usage, says Random House.

4. Allude, elude. You *allude* to (or mention) a book. You *elude* (or escape) a pursuer.

5. Annual. Don't use *first* with it. If it's the first time, it can't be annual.

6. Averse, adverse. If you don't like something, you are *averse* (or opposed) to it. *Adverse* is an adjective: *adverse* (bad) weather, *adverse* conditions.

7. Block, bloc. A *bloc* is a coalition of persons or a group with the same purpose or goal. Don't call it a *block*, which has some 40 dictionary definitions.

8. Compose, comprise. Remember that the parts *compose* the whole and the whole *comprises* the parts. You *compose* things by putting them together. Once the parts are put together, the object *comprises* the parts.

9. Couple of. You need the *of*. It's never "a couple tomatoes."

10. Demolish, destroy. They mean to do away with *completely*. You can't partially demolish or destroy something, nor is there any need to say *totally* destroyed.

11. Different from. Things and people are different *from* each other. Don't write that they are different *than* each other.

12. Drown. Don't say someone *was drowned* unless an assailant held the victim's head under water. Just say the victim *drowned*.

13. Due to, owing to, because of. We prefer the last.
    Wrong: The game was canceled *due to* rain.
    Stilted: *Owing to* rain, the game was canceled.
    Right: The game was canceled *because of* rain.

Ecology, environment. They are not synonymous. *Ecology* is the study of the relationship between organisms and their *environment*.
Right: The laboratory is studying the *ecology* of man and the desert.
Right: There is much interest in animal *ecology* these days.
Wrong: Even so simple an undertaking as maintaining a lawn affects *ecology*.
Right: Even so simple an undertaking as maintaining a lawn affects our *environment*.

15. Either. It means one or the other, not both.
Wrong: There were lions on *either* side of the door.
Right: There were lions on *each* side of the door.

16. Fliers, flyers. Airmen are *fliers*. Handbills are *flyers*.

17. Flout, flaunt. They aren't the same words; they mean completely different things and they're very commonly confused. *Flout* means to mock, to scoff or to show disdain for. *Flaunt* means to display ostentatiously.

18. Funeral service. A redundant expression. A funeral *is* a service.

19. Head up. People don't *head up* committees. They *head* them.

20. Hopefully. One of the most commonly misused words, in spite of what the dictionary may say. *Hopefully* should describe the way the subject *feels*.
For instance:
Hopefully, I shall present the plan to the president. (This means I will be hopeful when I do it.)
But it is something else again when you attribute hope to a non-person.

You may write: Hopefully, the war will end soon. This means you hope the war will end soon, but it is not what you are writing. What you mean is: I hope the war will end soon.

21. Imply and infer. The speaker *implies*. The hearer *infers*.

22. In advance of, prior to. Use *before;* it sounds more natural.

23. It's, its. *Its* is the possessive; *it's* is the contraction of *it is*.
Wrong: What is *it's* name?
Right: What is *its* name? *Its* name is Fido.
Right: *It's* the first time he's scored tonight.
Right: *It's* my coat.

24. Lay, lie. *Lay* is the action word; *lie* is the state of being.
Wrong: The body will *lay* in state until Wednesday.
Right: The body will *lie* in state until Wednesday.
Right: The prosecutor tried to *lay* the blame on him.
However, the past tense of *lie* is *lay*.
Right: The body *lay* in state from Tuesday until Wednesday.
Wrong: The body *laid* in state from Tuesday until Wednesday.
The past participle and the plain past tense of *lay* is *laid*.
Right: He *laid* the pencil on the pad.
Right: He *had laid* the pencil on the pad.
Right: The hen *laid* an egg.

25. Leave, let. *Leave alone* means to depart from or cause to be in solitude. *Let alone* means to be undisturbed.
Wrong: The man had pulled a gun on her but Mr. Jones intervened and talked him into *leaving her alone*.
Right: The man had pulled a gun on

471

her but Mr. Jones intervened and talked him into *letting her alone.*
Right: When I entered the room I saw that Jim and Mary were sleeping so I decided to *leave them alone.*

26. Less, fewer. If you can separate items in the quantities being compared use *fewer.* If not, use *less.*
Wrong: The Rams are inferior to the Vikings because they have *less* good linemen.
Right: The Rams are inferior to the Vikings because they have *fewer* good linemen.
Right: The Rams are inferior to the Vikings because they have *less* experience.

27. Like, as. Don't use *like* for *as* or *as if.* In general, use *like* to compare with nouns and pronouns; use *as* when comparing with phrases and clauses that contain a verb.
Wrong: Jim blocks the linebacker *like* he should.
Right: Jim blocks the linebacker *as* he should.
Right: Jim blocks *like* a pro.

28. Marshall, marshal. Generally, the first form is correct only when the word is a proper noun: John *Marshall.* The second form is the verb form: Marilyn will *marshal* her forces.
The second form is the one to use for a title: *Fire Marshal* Stan Anderson, *Field Marshal* Erwin Rommel.

29. Mean, average, median. Use *mean* as synonymous with *average.* Each word refers to the sum of all components divided by the number of components. *Median* is the number that has as many components above it as below it.

30. Nouns. There's a growing trend toward using them as verbs. Resist it.

Host, headquarters and *author*, for instance, are nouns, even though the dictionary may acknowledge they can be used as verbs. If you do, you'll come up with a monstrosity like: "Headquartered at his country home, John Doe hosted a party to celebrate the book he had authored."

31. Oral, verbal. Use *oral* when use of the mouth is central to the thought; the word emphasizes the idea of human utterance. *Verbal* may apply to spoken or written words; it connotes the process of reducing ideas to writing. Usually, it's a *verbal* contract, not an *oral* one, if it's in writing.

32. Over, more than. They aren't interchangeable. *Over* refers to spatial relationships: The plane flew *over* the city. *More than* is used with figures: In the crowd were *more than* 1,000 fans.

33. Parallel construction. Thoughts in series in the same sentence require parallel construction.
Wrong: The union delivered demands for an increase of 10 percent in wages and to cut the work week to 30 hours.
Right: The union delivered demands for an increase of 10 percent in wages and for a *reduction* in the work week to 30 hours.

34. Peddle, pedal. When selling something, you *peddle* it. When riding a bicycle or similar form of locomotion, you *pedal* it.

35. Pretense, pretext. They're different, but it's a tough distinction. A *pretext* is that which is put forward to conceal a truth: He was discharged for tardiness, but this was only a *pretext* for general incompetence.
A *pretense* is a "false show"; a more

472

overt act intended to conceal personal feelings: My profuse compliments were all pretense.

36. Principle, principal. A guiding rule or basic truth is a *principle*. The first, dominant, or leading thing is *principal*. *Principle* is a noun; *principal* may be a noun or an adjective.

Right: It's the *principle* of the thing.
Right: Liberty and justice are two *principles* on which our nation is founded.
Right: Hitting and fielding are the *principal* activities in baseball.
Right: Robert Jamieson is the school *principal*.

37. Redundancies to avoid: Easter Sunday. Make it *Easter*. Incumbent Congressman. *Congressman*. Owns his own home. *Owns his home*. The company will close down. *The company will close*. Jones, Smith, Johnson and Reid were all convicted. *Jones, Smith, Johnson and Reid were convicted*. Jewish rabbi. Just *rabbi*. 8 p.m. tonight. All you need is *8 tonight* or *8 p.m. today*. During the winter months. *During the winter*. Both Reid and Jones were denied pardons. *Reid and Jones were denied pardons*. I am currently tired. *I am tired*. Autopsy to determine the cause of death. *Autopsy*.

38. Refute. The word connotes success in argument and almost always implies an editorial judgment.

Wrong: Father Bury *refuted* the arguments of the pro-abortion faction.
Right: Father Bury responded to the arguments of the pro-abortion faction.

39. Reluctant, reticent. If he doesn't want to act, he is *reluctant*. If he doesn't want to speak, he is *reticent*.

40. Say, said. The most serviceable words in the journalist's language are the forms of the verb *to say*. Let a person *say* something, rather than declare or admit or point out. And never let him grin, smile, frown or giggle something.

41. Slang. Don't try to use "with-it" slang. Usually a term is on the way out by the time we get it in print.

Wrong: The police cleared the demonstrators with a sunrise *bust*.

42. Spelling. It's basic. If reporters can't spell and copy editors can't spell, we're in trouble. Some ripe ones for the top of your list.

It's *consensus*, not concensus. It's *restaurateur*, not restauranteur. It's *dietitian*, not dietician.

43. Temperatures. They may get higher or lower, but they don't get warmer or cooler.

44. That, which. *That* tends to restrict the reader's thought and direct it the way you want it to go; *which* is non-restrictive, introducing a bit of subsidiary information.

For instance:
The lawnmower that is in the garage needs sharpening. (Meaning: We have more than one lawnmower. The one in the garage needs sharpening.)
The lawnmower, which is in the garage, needs sharpening. (Meaning: Our lawnmower needs sharpening. It's in the garage.)
Note that *which* clauses take commas, signaling they are not essential to the meaning of the sentence.
Editorial Note: Although some prominent grammarians advocate, for the sake of clarity, using only *that* to introduce restrictive clauses, they concede that some writers, not incorrectly, use *which* in that type of clause. For an extensive discussion of the subject, see *A Dictionary of Modern*

473

English Usage, by H.W. Fowler, or *Modern American Usage,* by Wilson Follett.

45. Under way, not underway. But don't say something got under way. Say it *started* or *began.*

46. Unique. Something that is unique is the only one of its kind. It can't be very unique or quite unique or somewhat unique or rather unique. Don't use it unless you really mean unique.

47. Up. Don't use it as a verb.
Wrong: The manager said he would *up* the price next week.
Right: The manager said he would *raise* the price next week.

48. Who, whom. A tough one, but generally you're safe to use *whom* to refer to someone who has been the object of an action. *Who* is the word when the somebody has been the actor:
A 19-year-old woman, to *whom* the room was rented, left the window open.
A 19-year-old woman, *who* rented the room, left the window open.

49. Who's, whose. Though it incorporates an apostrophe, *who's* is not a possessive. It's a contraction for *who is.* *Whose* is the possessive.
Wrong: I don't know *who's* coat it is.
Right: I don't know *whose* coat it is.
Right: Find out *who's* there.

50. Would. Be careful about using *would* when constructing a conditional past tense.
Wrong: If Soderholm *would not have had* an injured foot, Thompson wouldn't have been in the lineup.
Right: If Soderholm *had not had* an injured foot, Thompson wouldn't have been in the lineup.

The 50 Most Misspelled Words

Editorial Experts, Inc., has analyzed a number of spelling tests and they find that the 50 words below are among the most frequently misspelled. In fact, many people misspell them the same way. Circle the correct spelling (a) or (b) for each word, and then check your answers below. TIP: One of the words is misspelled in both (a) and (b). (Reprinted from *The Editorial Eye*. Copyright 1978 Editorial Experts, Inc., 95 S. Bragg St., Alexandria, VA 22312.)

1. (a) grammer	(b) grammar		26. (a) liason	(b) liaison
2. (a) arguement	(b) argument		27. (a) proceed	(b) procede
3. (a) supprise	(b) surprise		28. (a) harrass	(b) harass
4. (a) achieve	(b) acheive		29. (a) perseverance	(b) perseverence
5. (a) annoint	(b) anoint		30. (a) ecstacy	(b) ecstasy
6. (a) definately	(b) definitely		31. (a) antiquated	(b) antequated
7. (a) separate	(b) seperate		32. (a) insistent	(b) insistant
8. (a) desirable	(b) desireable		33. (a) exhillarate	(b) exhilarate
9. (a) developement	(b) development		34. (a) vacuum	(b) vaccuum
10. (a) existence	(b) existance		35. (a) ridiculous	(b) rediculous
11. (a) pronounciation	(b) pronunciation		36. (a) nickel	(b) nickle
12. (a) occasion	(b) occassion		37. (a) oscilate	(b) oscillate
13. (a) assistant	(b) assisstant		38. (a) tyrannous	(b) tyranous
14. (a) repitition	(b) repetition		39. (a) drunkenness	(b) drunkeness
15. (a) privilege	(b) priviledge		40. (a) dissention	(b) dissension
16. (a) dependant	(b) dependent		41. (a) connoiseur	(b) connoisseur
17. (a) irresistible	(b) irresistable		42. (a) sacreligious	(b) sacrilegious
18. (a) consensus	(b) concensus		43. (a) battallion	(b) batallion
19. (a) accommodate	(b) accomodate		44. (a) prerogative	(b) perogative
20. (a) occurence	(b) occurrence		45. (a) iridescent	(b) irridescent
21. (a) concience	(b) conscience		46. (a) inadvertent	(b) inadvertant
22. (a) commitment	(b) committment		47. (a) geneology	(b) genealogy
23. (a) embarrass	(b) embarass		48. (a) villify	(b) vilify
24. (a) indispensible	(b) indispensable		49. (a) innoculate	(b) inoculate
25. (a) allotted	(b) alotted		50. (a) dilettante	(b) dilletante

Film Table

Words per frame of 8mm, 16mm and 35mm film.

— FILM FOOTAGE —

Time	Words	35mm	16mm	8mm	Frames
1 Sec.	2	1.5	.6	.3	24
2 Sec.	4	3	1.2	.6	48
3 Sec.	6	4.5	1.8	.9	72
4 Sec.	8	6	2.4	1.2	96
5 Sec.	10	7.5	3	1.5	120
6 Sec.	12	9	3.6	1.8	144
7 Sec.	14	10.5	4.2	2.1	168
8 Sec.	16	12	4.8	2.4	192
9 Sec.	18	13.5	5.4	2.7	216
10 Sec.	20	15	6	3	240
11 Sec.	22	16.5	6.6	3.3	264
12 Sec.	24	18	7.2	3.6	288
13 Sec.	26	19.5	7.8	3.9	312
14 Sec.	28	21	8.4	4.2	336
15 Sec.	30	22.5	9	4.5	360
16 Sec.	32	24	9.6	4.8	384
17 Sec.	34	25.5	10.2	5.1	408
18 Sec.	36	27	10.8	5.4	432
19 Sec.	38	28.5	11.4	5.7	456
20 Sec.	40	30	12	6	480
21 Sec.	42	31.5	12.6	6.3	504
22 Sec.	44	33	13.2	6.6	528
23 Sec.	46	34.5	13.8	6.9	552
24 Sec.	48	36	14.4	7.2	576
25 Sec.	50	37.5	15	7.5	600
26 Sec.	52	39	15.6	7.8	624
27 Sec.	54	40.5	16.2	8.1	648
28 Sec.	56	42	16.8	8.4	672
29 Sec.	58	43.5	17.4	8.7	696
30 Sec.	60	45	18	9	720
31 Sec.	62	46.5	18.6	9.3	744
32 Sec.	64	48	19.2	9.6	768
33 Sec.	66	49.5	19.8	9.9	792
34 Sec.	68	51	20.4	10.2	816
35 Sec.	70	52.5	21	10.5	840

Time: Indicated in seconds or minutes.
Words: Narration (average pace) number of words per second.
Footage: Indicated in 16mm feet or 35mm feet of film.
Frames: Total number at sound speed (24 frames per second).

FILM FOOTAGE

Time	Words	35mm	16mm	8mm	Frames
36 Sec.	72	54	21.6	10.8	864
37 Sec.	74	55.5	22.2	11.1	888
38 Sec.	76	57	22.8	11.4	912
39 Sec.	78	58.5	23.4	11.7	936
40 Sec.	80	60	24	12	960
41 Sec.	82	61.5	24.6	12.3	984
42 Sec.	84	63	25.2	12.6	1008
43 Sec.	86	64.5	25.8	12.9	1032
44 Sec.	88	66	26.4	13.2	1056
45 Sec.	90	67.5	27	13.5	1080
46 Sec.	92	69	27.6	13.8	1104
47 Sec.	94	70.5	28.2	14.1	1128
48 Sec.	96	72	28.8	14.4	1152
49 Sec.	98	73.5	29.4	14.7	1176
50 Sec.	100	75	30	15	1200
51 Sec.	102	76.5	30.6	15.3	1224
52 Sec.	104	78	31.2	15.6	1248
53 Sec.	106	79.5	31.8	15.9	1272
54 Sec.	108	81	32.4	16.2	1296
55 Sec.	110	82.5	33	16.5	1320
56 Sec.	112	84	33.6	16.8	1344
57 Sec.	114	85.5	34.2	17.1	1368
58 Sec.	116	87	34.8	17.4	1392
59 Sec.	118	88.5	35.4	17.7	1416
60 Sec.	120	90	36	18	1440
1 Min.	120	90	36	18	1440
2 Min.	240	180	72	36	2880
3 Min.	360	270	108	54	4320
4 Min.	480	360	144	72	5760
5 Min.	600	450	180	90	7200
6 Min.	720	540	216	108	8640
7 Min.	840	630	252	126	10080
8 Min.	960	720	288	144	11520
9 Min.	1080	810	324	162	12960
10 Min.	1200	900	360	180	14400
15 Min.	1800	1350	540	270	21600
20 Min.	2400	1800	720	360	28800
25 Min.	3000	2250	900	450	36000
30 Min.	3600	2700	1080	540	43200
40 Min.	4800	3600	1440	720	57600
50 Min.	6000	4500	1800	900	72000
60 Min.	7200	5400	2160	1080	86400

Reprinted with permission from Al Stahl's Fotomation Film Table. Copyright © 1972 Animation Productions, Inc.

Gag Submission Sample

John Doe
1234 Maple St.
Anaheim CA 90007   409A

Supermarket. Man pushing loaded shopping
cart for his wife, says to another man:

"I estimate the cost per mile to operate one of
these things is around $300!"

In his *Cartoonist's and Gag Writer's Handbook,* Jack Markow says, "Most gag men mail these
slips in an envelope 3⅝"x6½" with the same size return envelope enclosed and folded in
half. Others use a size 3½"x6" return envelope mailed flat with the gags."

Greeting Card Submission Samples

Typewritten form

                                        Birthday—Studio
                                        Feminine

    Pg. 1 We might be getting older, but at least we can still
           shake it!

    Pg. 2 . . . (the problem's getting it to stop!)

           HAPPY BIRTHDAY ANYWAY!

                                        Kreider

Dummied card form:

Don't think of it
as MIDDLE AGE . . .

Think of it as

YOUTH PARTY

HAPPY BIRTHDAY!

Editorial Note: *The dummied card would actually be a folder made of typewriter paper with the page 1 material as shown left above and the page 3 material as on the right. In the case of both typewritten ideas and dummied ideas, the writer's name and address and a code number would appear on the back. These card ideas are the property of Gibson Greeting Cards, Inc., and are reprinted with their permission.*

Jobs in Advertising

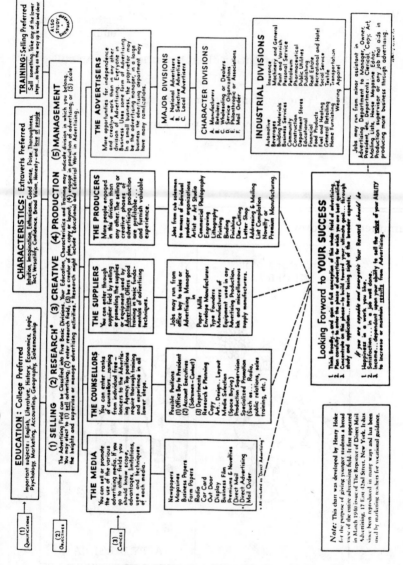

Reprinted by permission of The Reporter of Direct Mail Advertising, 224 Seventh Street, Garden City, L.I. New York 11534.

Juvenile Book Publishing Costs at Alternative Levels of Production[1] (Trade Edition)

	Number of Copies		
	7,500	10,000	15,000
Fixed and semi-fixed			
Plant costs	$4,000	$4,000	$4,000
Editorial and design	2,000	2,000	2,500
Overhead	3,000	3,500	3,500
Total fixed costs	$9,000	$9,500	$10,000
Variable			
Printing, paper, binding	7,500	10,000	15,000
Promotion, warehousing, shipping	3,800	5,100	7,700
Royalty[2] (based on 90% sold) at			
$5.95 list price	4,000	5,400	8,000
Total variable costs	$15,300	$20,500	$30,700
Total costs	$24,300	$30,000	$40,700
Fixed costs as percent			
of total	37%	32%	25%
Cost per book printed	$3.24	$3.00	$2.71

[1]Costs are for hypothetical 32-page picture book to sell at $5.95.
[2]10% royalty on list price.

Source: Children's Books and Magazines, Copyright 1979, Knowledge Industry Publications

Largest College Textbook Publishers, Estimated Revenues and Rank, 1981

1979 Rank	1981 Rank	Publisher	1979 Revenues	1981 Revenues (in millions)	% Change
1	1	Prentice-Hall	$105.0	$ 135.0	28.6%
2	2	McGraw-Hill	91.2	95.7	4.9
4	3	SFN Cos.[1]	49.1	63-66	28-34
3	4	CBS Publishing	52.0	58-60	11.5-15
6	5	John Wiley[2]	40.0	49.5	23.7
7	6	Addison-Wesley	34.8	48.0	27.5
5	7	Macmillan[3]	41.0	46.0	10.8
6	8	Harcourt Brace Jovanovich[3] (incl. Academic Press)	40.0	42.0	5.0
10	9	Wadsworth	31.0	41.8	34.8
8	10	Richard D. Irwin	33.5	41.1	22.7
9	11	Harper & Row[1]	32.2	33.5	4.0
		Total Revenues, 11 companies	$549.8	$ 658.6	19.8%
		Percent of market, 11 companies	66.6%	61.8%	-4.8%
		Total textbook market	$825.6	$1065.0	29.0%

[1] Based on publisher's projection for fiscal year ended April 30, 1982
[2] Sales for fiscal year ended April 30, 1981
[3] Estimate

© 1982 Knowledge Industry Publications, Inc.

Sales of Leading Hardcover Trade Book Publishers, 1979-1981

1981 Rank	Company	Parent Company	Sales (in millions of dollars)				Titles Published — 1982 (projected)			Titles Published — 1981		
			1979	1980	1981	% Change	Adult	Juvenile	Total	Adult	Juvenile	Total
1	Random House	Newhouse Publications	$ 73.0	$95.0	$102.0	+39.7	400	215	615	360	186	546
2	Simon & Schuster	Gulf & Western Industries	40.5	60.0-65.5	80.0[1]	+97.5	204	246	450	194	188	382
3	Harper & Row	Harper & Row Publishers, Inc.	65.5	68.8	71.8[2]	+ 9.6	264	116	380	331	141	472
4	Doubleday Publishing	Doubleday & Co., Inc.	55.0	64.0	65.0[2]	+18.2	394	28	422	489	57	546
5	Crown/Outlet	Crown Publishers, Inc.	40.0	45.0	50.0	+25.0	183	17	200	194	16	210
6	Putnam Publishing Group	MCA, Inc.	24.0	26.0	29.0	+20.8	140	86	226	192	74	266
7	Little, Brown	Time Inc.	24.0	26.0	27.0	+12.5	83[3]	42	125	86	46	132
8	William Morrow	Hearst Corp.[4]	20.0	23.0	25.0	+25.0	155	151	306	156	141	297
9	Macmillan	Macmillan, Inc.	22.0	24.2	24.2	+10.0	140	42	182	120	20	140
10	Houghton Mifflin	Houghton Mifflin Co.	15.9	19.3	22.5	+41.5	178	82	260	161	73	234
11	Grosset & Dunlap	Filmways, Inc.[5]	17.0-18.0	17.0-18.0	20.0	+11.1- -17.6	N/A	N/A	N/A	84	65	149
	Total 11 Major Companies		396.9-397.9	468.3-474.8	516.5	+29.8-30.1						
	Industry Totals (Adult and Juvenile)		1,086.2	1,271.3	1,353.7	+24.6						
	% of Domestic Market		36.6	37.3	38.2	+ 4.4						

[1] Fiscal year ended July 31, 1981. Revenues for fiscal '82 were $82.5 million.
[2] Fiscal year ended April 30, 1982.
[3] Includes 13 titles published under the New York Graphic Society imprint.
[4] Hearst Corp. acquired William Morrow from SFN Cos. in 1981.
[5] Fiscal year ended Feb. 28, 1982. The Putnam Publishing Group acquired Grosset & Dunlap in July 1982.
© 1982 Knowledge Industry Publications, Inc.

Leading Mass Market Book Publishers' Sales 1979-1981

(in millions of dollars)

Rank	Company	Parent	1979 Sales	1980 Sales	1981 Sales	% Change 1979-81	% Domestic Market Share '81
1	Bantam[1]	Bertelsmann	$ 93.0	$101.0	$115.0	+23.7%	13.9
2	Harlequin (U.S. sales)	Torstar	63-70	75-80	85-90	+31.6	10.6
3	Pocket Books[2]	Simon & Schuster/Gulf + Western	55.0	63.0[3]	81.2[3]	+47.6	9.8
4	New American Library	Times Mirror Co.	61-62	67-68	74-77	+22.8	9.1
5	Dell[4]	Doubleday & Co., Inc.	60-63	65-68	67-70	+11.4	8.3
6	Avon	Hearst Corp.	55.0	56.0	57.0	+ 3.6	6.9
7	Ballantine	Random House/Newhouse	42.0	46.0	51.0	+21.4	6.2
8	Fawcett (incl. Crest, Gold Medal and Popular Library)[5]	CBS, Inc.	54.5	54.1	49.7	- 8.8	6.0
9	Berkley/Jove	MCA, Inc.	33-35	37.0	43.5	+29.4	5.2
10	Warner	Warner Communications	33.0	34.0	40.0	+21.2	4.8
11	Ace[6]	Filmways, Inc.	18-20	17-19	20.0	+ 5.0	2.4
12	Playboy[7]	Playboy Enterprises	6.0	8.0	11.7	+95.0	1.4
13	Pinnacle	Michigan General	8.5	11.2	11.4	+34.1	1.4
	Total 13 Major Companies		$582.3-597.3	$641.3-652.3	$706.5-717.5	+20.7	85.3-86.7%
	Industry Total		673.3	739.2	827.9	+23.0%	100.0

[1] Fiscal year ends June 30. FY 82 sales were $132 million.

[2] Estimates. Fiscal year ends July 31. FY 82 sales were $94.7 million.

[3] Includes Silhouette imprint. Silhouette's FY 82 sales were about $23 million.

[4] Estimates. Fiscal year ends April 30. Figures are for FY '80, '81 and '82.

[5] Fawcett sold six of its paperback lines to Random House in January 1982. Popular Library was not included in the sale.

[6] Fiscal year ends Feb. 28. Berkley/Jove acquired Ace in May 1982.

[7] Fiscal year ends June 30. FY 82 sales were $12.3 million. Berkley/Jove acquired Playboy in June 1982.

© 1982, Knowledge Industry Publications, Inc.

Library Classification Systems

For browsing in open stacks at libraries using either the Dewey Decimal System or the Library of Congress cataloging method, here are selected references:

Subject	LC	Dewey Decimal
Agriculture	S	630
Arts, Fine	N	700
Bibliography	Z	010
Biography	CT	920
Education	L	370
General Works (encyclopedias, etc.)	A	000
Geography	G	910
History, America	E	973
History, Outside America	D	900
Language	P	400
Law	K	340
Literature	P	800
Medicine	R	610
Military Science	U	355
Music	M	780
Naval Science	V	359
Philosophy	B	100
Political Science	J	320
Religion	BL-BX	200
Science	Q	500
Social Sciences	H	300
Technology	T	600

Magazine Editorial
Reply/Agreement Form

Freelance writer Michael Major uses the following form as a means of getting a speedier reply to a query letter and establishing a clear understanding of the payment and rights involved. Readers of this encyclopedia may copy the agreement and/or adapt it for their own purposes without requesting permission from Mr. Major or Writer's Digest Books.

(Please check your preference, and, if you wish to make an assignment, sign below. Keep one form for your records and return the second in the enclosed SASE.)

☐ Yes, this looks good, and your terms are acceptable. You have an assignment. See my signature below.

☐ Sorry, this looks good and your terms are acceptable, but we're overstocked now. Try us again with this in _____ months.

☐ Sorry, we can't use this one, but we respect your professionalism and your terms are acceptable, so we encourage you to try us with another query.

☐ This is not for us.

The terms of agreement between the Author, MICHAEL J. MAJOR, and the Publication, _____ for the Author's proposed work, titled, _____ are: a payment of $_____ minimum, plus normal expenses; for the leasing of first North American serial rights only for the written work; and, if photos are included, one-time editorial use in one issue only for the photos; a response to all communications within 30 days; and the printing of the byline, "Mike Major," beneath the title of the published work. Also, it is understood that the Author's proposed work will be done on assignment, which means that the Publication will pay the Author, in full, within 30 days of its receipt of the Author's completed work, according to the terms of this agreement, and that this payment will be nonrefundable. If, within one year of the Publication's leasing the Author's work, the Publication does not publish this work, all rights revert to the Author. The Publication also agrees to send the Author three copies of the issue in which his work appears.

"I have read and agree to the above terms."

signed, _____

The Author, MICHAEL J. MAJOR, guarantees that his proposed work will meet the highest editorial standards, that, if the Editor finds the work in any way unsatisfactory, the Author will make all the necessary corrections for no added charge. Unless other arrangements are made, the proposed work will be delivered within three months of the assignment. If the Editor wants the work sooner, the Author will make every effort to comply. He will certify, in writing, the new, agreed-upon deadline. The Author affirms that he has never missed a deadline.

signed, MICHAEL J. MAJOR, PRESIDENT
MAJOR ENTERPRISES

Magazine Organization Chart

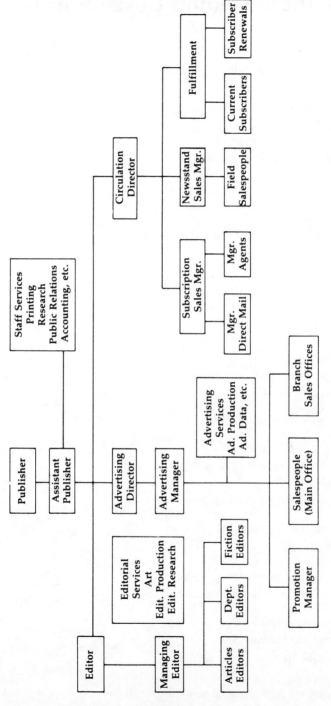

Source: *Magazine Editing and Production*, by J.W. Click and Russell N. Baird, © 1979 by Wm. C. Brown Company, Publishers.

Magazine Revenues/Costs/Profits

	Percentages of total revenue 1981
Total number of magazines reporting:	170
Revenue	
Net advertising revenues	51.08
Gross subscription revenues	33.30
Gross single copy revenues	15.62
Total magazine revenues	**100.00%**
Expenses	
Advertising	
Selling costs	5.28
Research and promotion costs	2.93
Total advertising expenses	**8.21%**
Circulation	
Commissions to subscription agencies	5.91
Other subscription promotion costs	7.66
Commissions on single copy sales	7.08
Other single copy promotion costs	1.35
Fulfillment costs	2.58
Total circulation expenses	**24.58%**
Editorial costs	7.75
Manufacturing and production	
Paper costs	16.20
Printing and bindery costs	16.25
Total manufacturing and production **expenses**	**32.45%**
Total distribution expenses	**8.62%**
Other operational expenses	
First class postage costs	1.23
Third class postage costs	1.43
Other postage & operating costs	.89
Total other operational costs	**3.55%**
Administrative costs	5.87
Total magazine costs	**91.03%**
Operating profit (before taxes)	**8.97%**

Source: Magazine Publishers Association

Manuscript Length, Average

The following table provides average word counts for each of the basic forms of writing; it gives the beginning writer the usual expected length of most manuscripts. When submitting work to magazines, though, the writer should adhere to the editor's requirements, which may be more specific than the average word count. *Writer's Market* lists individual editors' preferences as to word length.

How Long Is a . . . ?

	Average Words
Short-short story	500-2,000
Short story	2,500-5,000
Novella	7,500-40,000
Novelette	7,000-25,000
Novel—hardcover	25,000-150,000
Novel—paperback	35,000-80,000
Children's picture book	500-2,500
Juvenile book	15,000-80,000
Nonfiction book	20,000-200,000
TV script: ½-hour	25-40 double-spaced typewritten pages
TV script: 1-hour	55-70 double-spaced typewritten pages
Play: one-act	20-30 minutes playing time
	20-30 double-spaced typewritten pages
Play: three-act	1½-2 hours playing time
	90-120 double-spaced typewritten pages
Movie scenario	1½-2 hours playing time
	120-250 double-spaced typewritten pages
Radio feature copy	1 minute = 15 double-spaced lines
	3 minutes = 2 pages
Poem	2-100 lines (most mags prefer 4-16 lines)
Query letter	1 full-page, single-spaced
Speech	250 words = 2 minutes
	12-15 pages = ½ hour

Editorial Note: The average full double-spaced typewritten page contains 250 words of pica typewriter type.

Manuscript Preparation Guidelines

Jones--2

Begin the second page, and all following pages, in this

manner--with a page-number line (as above) that includes your

name, in case loose manuscript pages get shuffled by mistake.

Joe Jones
1234 My Street
Anytown, U. S. A.
Tel 123/456-7890

About 3,000 words
First Serial Rights
© 1983 Joe Jones

YOUR STORY OR NOVEL TITLE HERE

by

Joe Jones

The manuscript begins here--about halfway down the first page.
It should be cleanly typed, double-spaced, using either elite or
pica type. Use one side of the paper only, and leave a margin of
about 1-1/2 inches on all four sides.

If the author uses a pseudonym, it should be placed on the title page only in the by-line position; the author's real name must always appear in the top left corner of the title page—for manuscript mailing and payment purposes.

Reprinted from *Writer's Market '83*. Copyright 1982. Published by Writer's Digest Books.

The Music Business

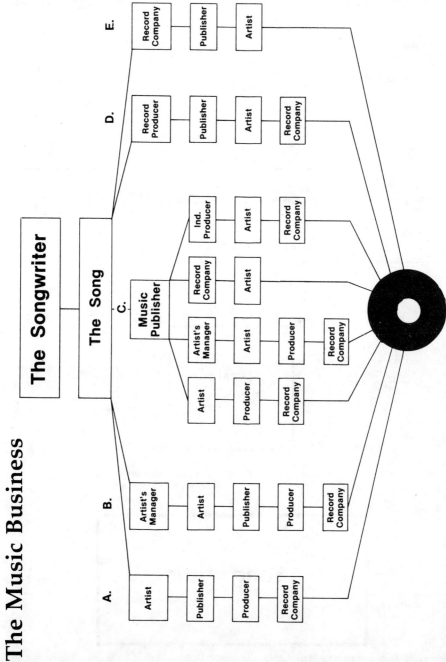

Music Royalties

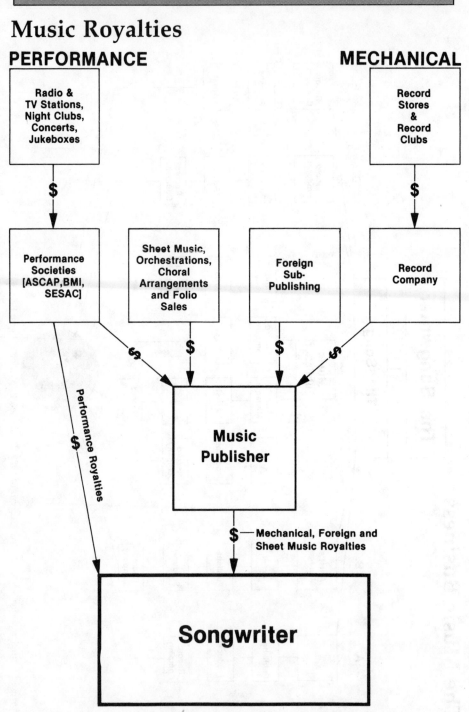

PERFORMANCE

MECHANICAL

Radio &
TV Stations,
Night Clubs,
Concerts,
Jukeboxes

Record
Stores
&
Record
Clubs

$

$

Performance
Societies
[ASCAP,BMI,
SESAC]

Sheet Music,
Orchestrations,
Choral
Arrangements
and Folio
Sales

Foreign
Sub-
Publishing

Record
Company

$

$

$

$

Music
Publisher

Performance Royalties

$

$ — Mechanical, Foreign and
Sheet Music Royalties

Songwriter

Reprinted from *Songwriter's Market 1983*. Copyright 1982. Published by Writer's Digest Books.

New Product Release Sample

BETTY CROCKER FOOD & NUTRITION CENTER

NEWS

For Release: **November, 1981**
Contact: **Pam Becker**
Telephone: **(612) 540-2470**

A bit of Mexico flavors the newest addition to the Hamburger Helper® line of products from General Mills, Inc. Hamburger Helper mix for Tamale Pie, which is completing its national introduction, is a unique addition to the Hamburger Helper line of products.

Unlike other flavors of Hamburger Helper, Tamale Pie does not contain pasta or potatoes. Instead, the mix contains a packet of tomato-based sauce mix with dried corn, which is mixed with a pound of ground beef, and a seasoned cornmeal topping which is cooked on top.

The introduction of Hamburger Helper mix for Tamale Pie will be supported by network television commercials focusing on the Mexican meal. These are scheduled for late October and November. Cents-off coupons will appear in November issues of leading women's magazines including WOMAN'S DAY, PARENTS, GOOD HOUSEKEEPING and REDBOOK, and the December issue of SUNSET. Coupons will also be included in November Sunday supplements. The advertising agency is Needham, Harper & Steers, Chicago.

A 9-ounce package of Hamburger Helper mix for Tamale Pie will retail for approximately $1.05. Combined with a pound of ground beef, it will serve five.

®Reg. T.M. of General Mills, Inc.

General Mills, Inc., P.O. Box 1113, Minneapolis, Minnesota 55440

A33377

News Release Sample

FOR IMMEDIATE RELEASE

FROM: Mayfield Senior Citizen's Center
3210 Apple Road
Cincinnati, Ohio 45209

CONTACT: Jane Doe
987-6543

Kathy White, a Cincinnati native,
is the new director of the Mayfield
Senior Citizen's Center, 3210 Apple
Road. She replaces Abby Jones,
who resigned to take a camp
position in Michigan.

Ms. White has been with the
Cincinnati Recreation Commission
as an arts specialist at both the
downtown and Eden Park Senior
Centers. She is a graduate of the
University of Cincinnati, in
Theatre Arts and Arts
Administration.

One of Ms. White's first duties will
be to coordinate Mayfield's
"Old-Fashioned Arts and Crafts
Fair." It will be held at the center
Saturday, October 20, from 10 A.M.
to 5 P.M. The public is invited.

#

Reprinted by permission from *The Publicity Handbook* of the Cincinnati Chapter of Women in Communications, Inc.

Newspaper Organizational Chart

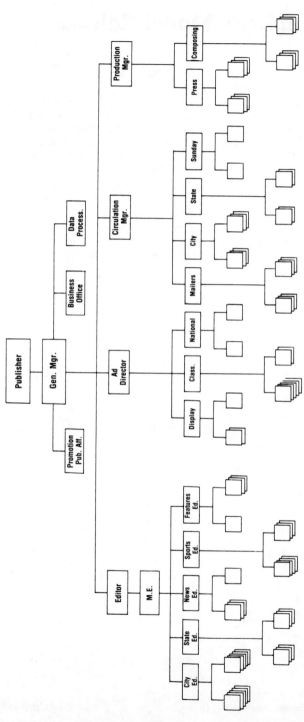

Source: American Newspaper Publishers Association, 1982

Photographer's Model Release

Model Release

In consideration for value received, I, _____, do hereby give _____ (the photographer), and parties designated by the photographer, including clients, licensees, purchasers, agencies, and periodicals, the irrevocable right to use my name (and any fictional name) and photograph for sale to and reproduction in any medium for purposes of advertising, trade, display, exhibition or editorial use. I have read this release and fully understand its contents.

I affirm that I am more than 18 (21) years of age.

Witness:_____ Signed:_____

Address:_____ Address:_____

Date:_____

Guardian's Consent

I am the parent or legal guardian of the above-named minor and hereby approve the foregoing and consent to the photograph's use subject to the terms mentioned above.

I affirm that I have the legal right to issue such consent.

Witness:_____ Signed:_____

Address:_____ Address:_____

Date:_____

Editorial Note: Writers and photographers can print their own model releases by typing a copy of this wording on their own letterheads and have them reproduced by a quick printer.

Reprinted from *Photographer's Market 1983*. Copyright 1982. Published by Writer's Digest Books.

Play Format Notes

by Martha Monigle

STYLE: follow the New York style with character names (capitalized) at center of page. English style places those names to left margin.

PAPER: use heavy bond, 20 lb. preferred. No erasable or onionskin. White 8½x11 sheets; punch two holes to left and place script in simple binder with fasteners. One-acters may be submitted without holes to publishers.

TYPING: pica preferred. Not elite or script form.

PAGE NUMBERING:

—FIRST PAGE (unnumbered) is "cover sheet" with title centered in caps; next spaces show if one or three acts; author's name and address.

—SECOND PAGE (unnumbered) has heading CHARACTERS (or CAST OF CHARACTERS) in caps. On separate lines below place character names, not caps. Age and identification may be placed beside each name.

—THIRD SHEET is numbered: I-1. Mark either at top or to right edge. Indicate each act by Roman numerals, pages by Arabic. Each of the three acts starts with p.1 to its end, as: I-1; II-1; III-1. In scene division, mark: II-2-15 for 2nd scene in act II, page 15. Note that a new scene of an act requires a new page and heading.

—One typed sheet equals about a minute's playing time. One-acts average 15-20 pp. Full plays (two or three acts) run little more than two hours, or about 115-125 pp. Children's theater ranges from 5-minute skits to full-length high school plays up to 60-90 minutes.

FORMAT: single-space for speeches and stage directions but double-space between those units. Wide margins, 1½-1" on all sides.

—Dialog starts at left margin.

—Stage directions, always in parentheses, indented 10 spaces. If brief and contained in character's speech, directions may be so enclosed in the dialog. Sometimes a directional word or phrase may be inserted between character name and speech. (See example below.)

—Capitalize character NAME at all times except when mentioned in dialog.

—Capitalize ENTRANCES and EXITS, which must be noted in script.

Note: Directions are written from actor's position; JOAN ENTERS L means "stage right" from audience view. State time and place.

OPENING PAGE EXAMPLE:

SUNDAY'S MYSTERY   I-1
ACT ONE

TIME: The present. Noon. Sunday.
PLACE: The Blairs' living room in Los Angeles.
AT RISE GEORGE is seated on couch with Sunday papers strewn about him. He wears pajamas and slippers. JOAN ENTERS L, annoyed at disorder. She is fully dressed. She picks up papers from the floor.

GEORGE

Why?
(JOAN continues to work)

497

                              JOAN
It's Sunday.

                             GEORGE
  (groaning)
Oh, Joan! I bet Scott isn't nagged by his wife.

  (EXIT JOAN in injured silence to kitchen)

PROPERTIES LISTING: Type list of properties or "props" on last page.
Objects carried or used by actors in play, as newspapers above.

Proofreader's Marks

MARK	EXPLANATION	(In margin.) **EXAMPLE** (In text.)
l	Take out character indicated.	*l* Your manuscript.
stet or ...	Let it stay.	*stet* Your manuscript.
#	Put in space.	# Your manuscript.
⌒	Close up completely.	Writer's Di gest School.
tr	Transpose; change places.	*tr* Your manuscript.
caps or	Use capital letters.	*caps* Writer's digest school. writer's digest school.
lc	Use lower-case letters.	*lc* Your Manuscript.
bf or	Use bold-face type.	*bf* Writer's Digest School. Writer's Digest School
ital or ___	Use italic type.	*ital* Writer's Digest.
⩔	Put in apostrophe.	⩔ Writers Digest School.
⊙	Put in period.	⊙ Your manuscript
,/	Put in comma.	,/ Your manuscript
:/	Put in colon.	:/ Your manuscript
;/	Put in semicolon.	;/ Writer's Digest School
⩔ ⩔	Put in quotation marks.	⩔ ⩔ He said, Yes.
?	Question to author.	? *No hyphen OK* Free lance writer.
=/	Put in hyphen.	=/ Free lance writer.
!	Put in exclamation.	! This is great
?	Put in question mark.	? Are you starting
(/)	Put in parenthesis.	(/) Your first rough draft.
¶	Start paragraph.	¶ a writer. Learn to sell
‖	Even out lines	‖ Writer's Digest and Writer's Digest School.
⊏	Move the line left	⊏ Your manuscript.
⊐	Move the line right	Your manuscript. ⊐
No ¶	No paragraph; run together	*No ¶* a writer. There are more needed
out, sc	Something missing, see copy.	*out, sc* Writer's School.
spell out	Spell it out.	*spell out* Your ms.

Public Service Announcement for Television

"Caring About Trees" Introducing SPUNKY SQUIRREL

30 Seconds   16mm   5400 K   SOF

ANNCR: (V/O) "Trees are treasures."

MAN: (V/O) "Dani...come see what just landed."

DANI: (SYNCH) "It's a squirrel...It's Spunky Squirrel!"

SPUNKY: (SYNCH) "Any home in America can have healthy trees when you follow Spunky's five point check list."

ג PLAN

ג PLANT

ג PROVIDE

ג PROTECT

ג PRUNE

ANNCR: (V/O) "Trees are treasures. People who care, care for them. To keep your trees a valuable part of your property...

American Forestry Association
P.O. Box 2000
Washington, D.C.
20013

write for a free brochure today."

Editor's Note: Public Service Directors of television stations remind local groups seeking air time that it is important to have more than one piece of video (a slide) to support a ten-, twenty-, thirty-, or sixty-second piece of copy. Only one slide makes for too static a spot, and it is useful to keep the needs of the TV station in mind when formulating a PSA to ensure air time.

Publication Consent Agreement

Publication Consent Agreement

In consideration for value received, receipt whereof acknowledged,

I hereby give ___(name of author)___ the absolute right and permission to copyright and/or publish or to have copyrighted or have published the information about me contained in the attached manuscript. I understand that the manuscript will undergo editing prior to any publication and I consent to the use of the information in revised or edited form without first seeing the revised or edited manuscript.

I also hereby waive any right to inspect and/or approve not only the final edited-for-publication versions, but also any advertising copy that may be used in connection therewith.

Date_____   Signature_____

                     Address_____

Witness_____

The usual "value received" is one dollar or whatever monetary amount the author may wish to pay or is obligated to pay. However, the "remuneration" can consist solely of the gratification derived by the signee at seeing his or her name or story or photograph in print. It could, for example, include the copy of the manuscript attached to the agreement, or in the case of a photograph it might be a copy print of that photograph.

Query Letter Sample

Judy Loveless

Ms. Bernadette Carr, Editor*
Weight Watcher's Magazine
149 Fifth Avenue
New York NY 10011

Dear Ms. Carr:

It happens eventually in the closest of families. For years, you've been dining together at the appointed hour, sharing food, feelings and conversation--then one day you ring the dinner bell, and nobody comes.

Or worse yet, they straggle in at different hours, all expecting nourishment without communication, and the one special hour of family sharing slowly dissolves into an evening marathon of exits and entrances. Tommy has a basketball game, Jill works evenings at McDonald's, your husband has racquetball court time, and you are left staring glumly at a 4-pound roast beef for 1.

My proposed article describes this phenomenon which I call the "mid-life meal crisis," in about 2500 words. Entitled "COPING WITH THE STAGGERED DINNER HOUR," the piece details the problem with various examples, and provides ways of circumventing the situation. It will cover aspects of keeping family togetherness intact, shopping, planning and cooking for staggered diners, coping with "no-shows" and how to avoid being the kitchen slave while the troops come and go.

I have published many articles in SEVENTEEN MAGAZINE, and also write frequently for NEWSDAY, MIAMI HERALD, CHICAGO TRIBUNE and various other publications. I am including some published samples, and I'd be willing to do the proposed piece for you on spec, since we have never worked together before.

Thanks for your time and interest.

Very truly yours,

Judy Loveless

Judy Loveless

---

*The current editor of *Weight Watchers* is Lee Aiken and the magazine is now at 360 Lexington Ave., New York NY 10017. This writer's letterhead, of course, carried the author's address and phone number.

Radio Commercial Script

Client	Delta Air Lines	City	CVG	Spot No.	6522

Date	6/16	Job No.		Type		Length	:60

This Spot effective **July 5**   It replaces Spot   Remarks:

MUSIC: WHEN YOU'RE READY

ANNCR:
16″   Let Delta Air Lines put you in a sunny state of mind . . . like Florida. Delta has straight lines to sandy shorelines. And low fares for good times all across the state.

SINGERS: WHEN YOU'RE READY TO GO PLACES . . . DELTA IS THE AIRLINE YOU SHOULD FLY . . . UP INTO THE SKY.

ANNCR: Delta takes you nonstop to Miami, Orlando and Tampa/St. Pete . . . thru to Ft. Lauderdale, West Palm Beach and Ft. Myers . . . and gives you fast service to Daytona Beach and Sarasota/Bradenton. What's more, when it comes to fares, every day is discount day on Delta. For convenient flights and low fares . . . call Delta or your Travel Agent.

SINGERS: DELTA IS READY WHEN YOU ARE.

Radio commercial script sample courtesy BDA/BBDO, Inc., Atlanta, Georgia.

503

Radio Drama Script Sample Page

```
never use staples in radio ms.          RADIO MS EXAMPLE - 1
use paper clip in this corner
```

```
1.   MUSIC          MAIN TITLE UP, ESTABLISH, FADE OUT UNDER

2.   MAMET          This the way you type @#$%¢&! radio manuscript?

3.   GREAT MAN      This is one common way. Mind if I smoke?

4.   SOUND          MATCH BEING STRUCK

5.   MAMET          Of course I do, Yuri, but who can stop you? I

6.                  notice this @#$%¢&! script has wide margins, is

7.                  double spaced and uses pica type.

8.   GREAT MAN      (puffing) Also notice that the lines are numbered

9.                  and that there are 24 lines per page. The cues are

10.                 typed at the left margin and the lines are

11.                 indented 15 spaces from that margin. This gives

12.                 you about a minute of playing time per page.

13.                 (puffs)

14.  MAMET          (coughing) Can I open a window?

15.  GREAT MAN      Sure, Dave.

16.  SOUND          MAMET THROWS WINDOW OPEN. OUTDOOR AMBIENCE

17.  MAMET          I also notice that @#$%¢&! dashes and elipses are

18.                 used for semi-colons, colons and parenthesis.

19.  SOUND          GREAT MAN WALKS TO WINDOW, SHUTS IT. AMBIENCE OUT

20.  GREAT MAN      It's getting cold in here....Also, note the

21.                 special argot. In stage directions, "pan" means a

22.                 movement in stereo, "fade up" means get closer to

23.                 the mike, "fade" means go away from the mike, "off

24.                 mike" means up-stage, "on mike" means downstage.
```

© 1985 Yuri Rasovsky

Regional English Expressions

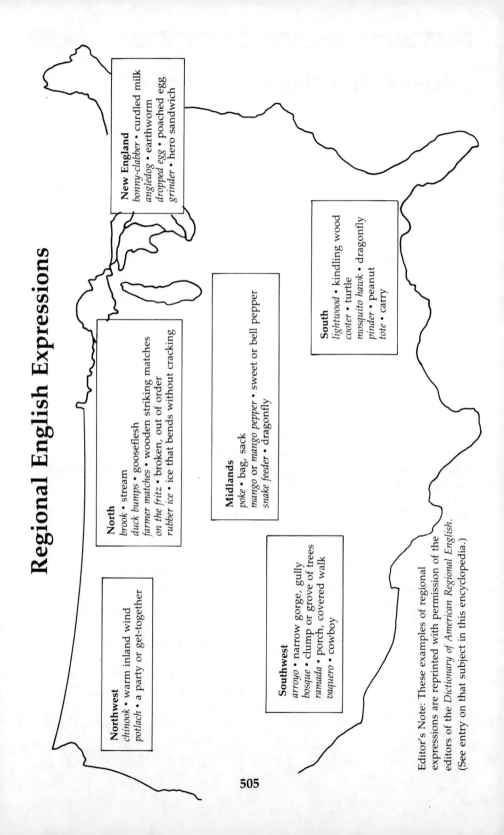

New England
bonny-clabber • curdled milk
angledog • earthworm
dropped egg • poached egg
grinder • hero sandwich

South
lightwood • kindling wood
cooter • turtle
mosquito hawk • dragonfly
pinder • peanut
tote • carry

North
brook • stream
duck bumps • gooseflesh
farmer matches • wooden striking matches
on the fritz • broken, out of order
rubber ice • ice that bends without cracking

Midlands
poke • bag, sack
mango or mango pepper • sweet or bell pepper
snake feeder • dragonfly

Northwest
chinook • warm inland wind
potlach • a party or get-together

Southwest
arroyo • narrow gorge, gully
bosque • clump or grove of trees
ramada • porch, covered walk
vaquero • cowboy

Editor's Note: These examples of regional expressions are reprinted with permission of the editors of the *Dictionary of American Regional English*. (See entry on that subject in this encyclopedia.)

505

Résumé: Functional

Shirlie Jane Doe

24 Mockingbird Terrace
Cincinnati, Ohio 45331

Single—willing to
travel and relocate

Telephone: (513)000-0000
or leave message 000-0000

Available immediately

JOB OBJECTIVE:

Field of personnel (selection and
recruitment nontechnical personnel)

WORK EXPERIENCE:
July 25, 1964 to
April 1, 1981

The Pyramid Manufacturing Company
1234 XYZ Street
Finneytown Hill,
Cincinnati, Ohio 45201

Selected personnel for executive offices. Developed a training-grant program to
guarantee an inflow of competent secretaries. Cost saving of $15,000 the first six
months, increased savings thereafter.
Worked with our public relations department and local press on series of articles
about our employees. Result: A sharp drop in turnover and an equally sharp
rise in the number of job candidates. We ran no want ads during this period.
Money saved from the advertising budget was used to implement the program
mentioned above.

June 25, 1958 to
July 25, 1964

Acme Temporary Placements
5678 ABC Street
Cincinnati, Ohio 45201

Client sales. One of my clients was Pyramid. They negotiated with my employer
when an opening developed in their personnel department.

EDUCATION:

Walnut Hills High School, graduated
1954
University of Cincinnati, 1954-56
University of Miami, Coral Gables,
Florida, 1956-1958 (B.A. in English)
University of Cincinnati Evening
College
(personnel courses including tests and
measurements, techniques of
interviewing, and communications)

506

Résumé: Simplified

NAME: Smith, John David

ADDRESS: 606 Main Street, Big City, Maine 04330

TELEPHONE: (207)000-0000
Message can be taken at (207)000-1111

JOB OBJECTIVE: If you're familiar with the employer's terminology, use it.

EDUCATION: Whichever of these two categories is the more impressive should be listed directly under the job objective.

WORK EXPERIENCE: If you hold a degree, you won't need to waste space on high school background; unless, of course, you were valedictorian or class president.

SPECIAL SKILLS/ATTRIBUTES:

This is the section where your résumé should be different. Think about the job requirements and list those skills/attributes that show how to meet them.

Each item mentioned here won a job interview for the person who listed it:
- knowledge of a foreign language (tell which one)
- knowledge of sign language
- knowledge of procedures for federal grant requests
- knowledge of a computer language (tell which one)
- ability to type sixty words per minute
- knowledge of shorthand
- knowledge of CPR (cardiopulmonary resuscitation)
- ability to handle $2/3$-axle vehicles
- willingness to travel or relocate
- have own transportation (One young man mentioned five years of accident-free driving and won a job.)

REFERENCES: If you decide to use them, be sure you include full addresses and phone numbers. Also, indicate that you have the permission of the person listed.

NOTE: The candidates I work with are outstandingly successful when they attach a letter of reference instead of listing references. My guess is that the employer responds favorably because this practice saves so much work for him or her.

Rights for Sale

This diagram shows the possibilities for a typical, successful hardcover book. The pattern does not hold true for every book, and very few books realize their potential for all uses.

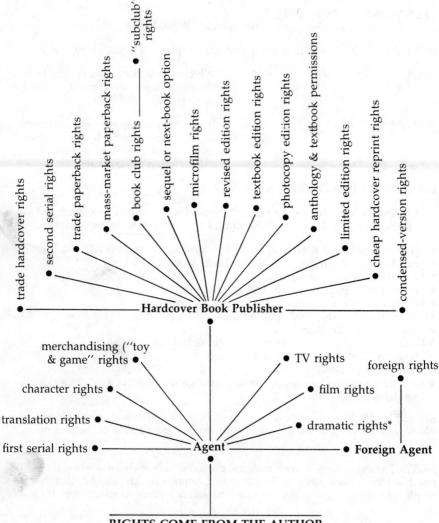

RIGHTS COME FROM THE AUTHOR

*Although dramatic rights were not included in the original chart, since they represent a right for sale by the author they are included in this reprint.

Script Release Form

Gentlemen:

I am submitting to you herewith the following material (hereinafter referred to as "said Material").

TITLE: _____

FORM OF MATERIAL

Synopsis   Screenplay   Radioplay

Treatment   Telescript   Other _____

PRINCIPAL CHARACTERS: _____

_____

BRIEF SUMMARY OF THEME OR PLOT: _____

_____

_____

_____

WGA REGISTRATION NO.: _____ NO. OF PAGES: _____

1. I request that you read and evaluate said material, and you hereby agree to do so, and you agree to advise me of your decision with respect to the material.

2. I warrant that I am the sole owner and author of said material, that I have the exclusive right and authority to submit the same to you upon the terms and conditions stated herein; and that all of the important features of said material are summarized herein. I will indemnify you of and from any and all claims, loss or liability that may be asserted against you or incurred by you, at any time, in connection with said material, or any use thereof.

3. I agree that nothing in this agreement nor the fact of my submission of said material to you shall be deemed to place you in any different position than anyone else to whom I have not submitted said material.

4. I understand that as a general rule you purchase literary properties through the established channels in the industry and not through a submission such as this. I recognize that you have access to and/or may create or have created literary materials and ideas which may be similar or identical to said material in theme, idea, plot, format or other respects. I agree that I will not be entitled to any compensation because of the use by you of any such similar or identical material which may have been independently created by you or may have come to you from any other independent source. I understand that no confidential relationship is established by my submitting the material to you hereunder.

5. You agree that if you use any legally protectible portion of said material, provided it has not been obtained by you from, or independently created by, another source, you will pay me an amount that is comparable to the compensation normally paid by you for similar material or an amount equal to the fair market value thereof as of the date of this agreement, whichever is greater. If we are unable to agree as to said amount, or in the event of any dispute concerning any alleged use of said material or with reference to this agreement, such dispute will be submitted to arbitration.

6. I have retained at least one copy of said material, and I hereby release you of and from any and all liability for loss, or damage to, the copies of said material submitted to you hereunder.

7. I enter into this agreement with the express understanding that you agree to read and evaluate said material in express reliance upon this agreement and my covenants, representatives and warranties contained herein, and that in the absence of such an agreement, you would not read or evaluate said material.

8. I hereby state that I have read and understand this agreement and that no oral representatives of any kind have been made to me, and that this agreement states our entire understanding with reference to the subject matter hereof. Any modification or waiver of any of the provisions of this agreement must be made in writing and signed by both of us.

9. If more than one party signs this agreement as submittor, the reference to "I" or "me" through this agreement shall apply to each party jointly and severally.

Very truly yours,

_____   _____
Address   Signature

_____   _____
City and State   Print Name

_____
Telephone Number

Accepted and Agreed to by

_____
Signature

Editorial Note: Some production companies may have their own versions of this standard release form. In any case, whichever form you use, be sure to write the words RELEASE FORM ENCLOSED on the envelope containing your script to avoid having the package sent back unopened. Release form reprinted from *The Complete Book of Scriptwriting*, © 1982 by J. Michael Straczynski.

Society of American Travel Writers Ethics Code

The Society of American Travel Writers has the responsibility of accenting the need for truth and accuracy in all aspects of travel journalism, while setting standards which leave no room for dishonest or distorted stories. Toward this goal, SATW will continue to serve the public interest and work for the professional needs of its diverse membership in the following specific areas of concern:

1. SATW recognizes the need for annual and ongoing scrutiny of its membership, eliminating those dilettantes who merely engage in travel journalism as a hobby, and at the same time demanding ever high professional standards for admission to membership.

2. SATW will work cooperatively with publishers, editors and broadcast media toward achieving higher rates of pay for articles, photographs, films and other travel-related materials, while stressing the economic necessity for reimbursement of legitimate travel expenses so that all members may function in travel journalism without even the appearance of compromising their integrity, so far as the public is concerned.

3. SATW will maintain liaison with those segments of the travel industry which sponsor familiarization trips, while at the same time underscoring the complete independence of the travel journalist in reporting on the negative as well as the positive results of such trips, or to decide that the material justifies no report of any kind. In this connection, SATW emphasizes the advisability of sponsors providing advance documentation as to the variety of potential story material that might be developed by a familiarization trip, and stresses the negative impact on a journalist's productivity if too much time is devoted to unnecessary social events at the expense of free time to develop story materials.

4. SATW recognizes that professional travel journalists are expected to be thoroughly professional, exercising common courtesy and respect for fellow members and for the customs and cultures of other countries. Flagrantly unprofessional conduct in this respect will not be tolerated and will be dealt with in whatever manner deemed necessary by SATW Officers and Board of Directors, as subsequently detailed in Section 6.

5. The sole responsibility of the SATW member is to provide his/her readers, listeners or viewers with objective and independent reporting. SATW calls direct attention to the fact that some members represent publications which do not accept complimentary transportation, accommodations or other necessities or amenities of travel. Prospective hosts sponsoring familiarization trips at no charge to invited journalists are requested also to state in the invitation what the full rate or the press or industry rate would be for such trips, giving those members who must pay

all or part of the cost of any trip the option to do so.

6. Formal complaints of a violation of the spirit or letter of this Statement of Ethics and Professional Responsibility by an SATW member must be made in writing, signed by the complainant(s) and sent to the Society's Ethics and Professional Practices Committee. All complaints will be promptly investigated by this committee. The member(s) complained against shall have full opportunity to respond to the complaint before the Committee's detailed report is submitted to Board of Directors.

Should the Board feel that disciplinary action is necessary, up to and including expulsion from membership, the member complained against shall be notified in advance of such action in a certified letter, signed by the President of SATW, of his or her right to make a formal reply or request a formal hearing before the next Board meeting. Said member will be required to pay his or her own expenses to be present at such a hearing, but may also have the option of designating third party representation.

7. Members shall not accept payment or courtesies for producing favorable materials about travel destinations against their own professional appraisal.

8. Members shall deal with only those destinations of which they have first-hand knowledge or have utilized reliable sources of information.

9. No member shall permit his or her by-line to appear on work not produced or fully supervised by him or her.

10. Members shall make every attempt to honor deadlines.

11. Members shall regard press trips as working opportunities and make every effort to obtain and report travel news accurately, without imposing excessive demands upon the hospitality of hosts. Any services required by a member, over and above those provided on a hosted trip, shall be paid for by the member.

12. Editor members are encouraged to pay on acceptance whenever possible and should return unaccepted manuscripts and other materials courteously and as promptly as possible.

13. Associate members shall neither accept nor pay money for acquiring new accounts, and shall not offer cash or any other form of payment to editors and writers in return for editorial coverage.

14. The Society shall discipline, as provided in Section 6, members found guilty of breach of oral or written contracts, of plagiarism, or other unethical acts.

15. SATW and its membership pledges to continue to do everything possible to attain and maintain for travel journalists a position of highest prestige and integrity in the journalistic fraternity.

Song Lead Sheet

DANCIN' LIKE LOVERS

MUSIC LARRY HERBSTRITT
LYRIC DOUG THIELE

THE MUSIC'S PLAYIN' SOFTLY IN THE SUMMER NIGHT

AND STARLIGHT'S PLAYIN' MAGIC IN YOUR HAIR

JUST YOU AND ME SURROUNDED BY THE CITY LIGHTS

IT'S GOT ME FEELIN' SOMETHING SPECIAL IN THE AIR

YOU KNOW I'VE SAID HELLO TO YOU A HUNDRED TIMES

THERE COMES A TIME YOU'VE GOTTA TAKE THE CHANCE

BUT EVEN THO' I'M FEELIN' VER-Y CLOSE TO YOU

513

Songwriter's Lyric Sheet

THE MISUNDERSTANDING

WE HAD A MISUNDERSTANDING
AND I CAN SEE YOU'RE TRYING TO SAY GOODBYE
YOU TELL ME ALL YOUR DREAMS HAVE GONE SAILING
AND YOU CAN FEEL OUR LOVE BEGIN TO DIE

(Chorus)   BUT DARLIN', WE SHOULD BE LOVERS FOREVER AND EVER
NOT JUST FROM DAY TO DAY
SO PLEASE DON'T LET THIS MISUNDERSTANDING
STAND IN THE WAY.

YOU TURN AWAY IN YOUR SORROW
AND YOU WATCH THE SUNSET FADE TO NIGHT
YOU SAY THERE'S NOTHING MORE TO ARGUE
'CAUSE YOU'RE LEAVIN' WITH THE MORNIN' LIGHT

BUT LADY, WE SHOULD BE...(Chorus)

(Bridge)   DON'T LEAVE ME DROWNIN' IN THE OCEAN
DON'T LEAVE ME STANDIN' IN THE RAIN
I'LL NEVER HOLD YOU IN MY ARMS AGAIN
IF YOU CLIMB ABOARD THAT ONE-WAY TRAIN

AND DARLIN', WE SHOULD BE...(Chorus)

words & music: Doug Thiele

@ 1982: Firelight Publishing

all rights reserved

CONTACT: Doug Thiele (213) 463-7178

514

Standard Time Zones of the United States

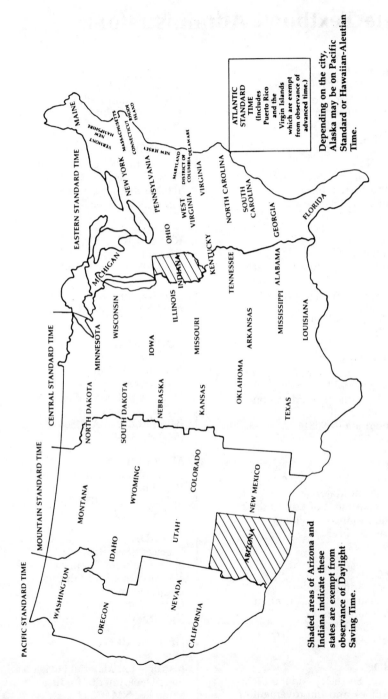

PACIFIC STANDARD TIME

MOUNTAIN STANDARD TIME

CENTRAL STANDARD TIME

EASTERN STANDARD TIME

WASHINGTON

OREGON

IDAHO

NEVADA

CALIFORNIA

UTAH

ARIZONA

MONTANA

WYOMING

COLORADO

NEW MEXICO

NORTH DAKOTA

SOUTH DAKOTA

NEBRASKA

KANSAS

OKLAHOMA

TEXAS

MINNESOTA

IOWA

MISSOURI

ARKANSAS

LOUISIANA

WISCONSIN

ILLINOIS

MICHIGAN

INDIANA

KENTUCKY

TENNESSEE

MISSISSIPPI

ALABAMA

OHIO

WEST VIRGINIA

VIRGINIA

NORTH CAROLINA

SOUTH CAROLINA

GEORGIA

FLORIDA

MAINE

VERMONT

NEW HAMPSHIRE

NEW YORK

PENNSYLVANIA

MASSACHUSETTS

CONNECTICUT

RHODE ISLAND

NEW JERSEY

DELAWARE

MARYLAND

DISTRICT OF COLUMBIA

ATLANTIC
STANDARD
TIME
(Includes
Puerto Rico
and the
Virgin Islands
which are exempt
from observance of
advanced time.)

Depending on the city,
Alaska may be on Pacific
Standard or Hawaiian-Aleutian
Time.

Shaded areas of Arizona and
Indiana indicate these
states are exempt from
observance of Daylight
Saving Time.

Source: U.S. Department of Transportation

515

State Textbook Administrators

ALABAMA
State Textbook Coordinator
State Department of Education
405 State Office Building
Montgomery, AL 36130
(205)832-3313

ARIZONA
State Department of Education
1535 West Jefferson
Phoenix, AZ 85007
(601)255-5057

ARKANSAS
Coordinator
Division of Instructional Materials
State Department of Education
Room 104B, Arch Ford Education
    Building
Little Rock, AR 72201
(501)371-2068

CALIFORNIA
Manager, Curriculum Frameworks and
    Instructional Materials
State Department of Education
721 Capitol Mall
Sacramento, CA 95814
(916)445-2731

FLORIDA
Administrator
Instructional Materials
State Department of Education
111 Miles Johnson Building
Tallahassee, FL 32301
(904)488-8184

GEORGIA
Textbook Administrator
State Department of Education
321 Education Annex
Atlanta, GA 30334
(404)656-2404

IDAHO
Executive Secretary—Idaho State
    Textbook and Improvement of
    Instruction Committee

State Department of Education
650 West State Street
Len B. Jordan Building
Boise, ID 83720
(208)384-2165

ILLINOIS
Manager, Textbook Program
Illinois State Board of Education
100 North First Street
Springfield, IL 62777
(217)782-9374

KENTUCKY
Director
Division of Free Textbook Services
State Department of Education
1535 Capitol Plaza Tower
Frankfort, KY 40601
(502)564-3913

LOUISIANA
Director
Bureau of Materials of Instruction and
    Textbooks
State Department of Education
P.O. Box 44064
Baton Rouge, LA 70804
(504)342-3464

MISSISSIPPI
Textbook Purchasing Board
P.O. Box 1075
Jackson, MS 39205
(601)354-6187

NEVADA
Executive Secretary
State Textbook Commission
c/o Department of Education
Capitol Complex
Carson City, NV 98710
(702)885-3136

NEW MEXICO
Director
Instructional Material Division
State Department of Education
Santa Fe, NM 87503
(505)827-2575

NEW YORK
Textbook Coordinator for Instructional
  Services
State Department of Education
Albany, NY 12234
(518)474-5893

NORTH CAROLINA
Director
Division of Textbooks
Department of Public Education
Education Building, Room #389
Raleigh, NC 27609
(919)733-3846

OKLAHOMA
Administrator
Textbook Division
State Department of Education
Oliver Hodge Building
2500 N. Lincoln
Oklahoma City, OK 73105
(405)521-3456

OREGON
Administrative Assistant
State Textbook Commission
700 Pringle Parkway, SE
Salem, OR 97310
(503)378-3610

SOUTH CAROLINA
Director
Office of Textbooks
State Department of Education
301 Rutledge Building
Columbia, SC 29201

TENNESSEE
Director
Textbook Services
Tennessee Department of Education
130 Cordell Hull Building
Nashville, TN 37219
(615)741-3379

TEXAS
Director, Textbook Division
Texas Education Agency
201 E. 11th Street
Austin, TX 78701
(512)475-4676

UTAH
Specialist
Utah State Board of Education
250 East Fifth South Street
Salt Lake City, UT 84111
(801)533-5572

VIRGINIA
Supervisor
School Libraries and Textbooks
State Department of Education
Box 6
Richmond, VA 23216
(804)768-7705

WEST VIRGINIA
Coordinator of Special Projects
West Virginia Department of
  Education
Capitol Complex, Building 6,
  Room B-338
Charleston, WV 25305
(304)348-7010

Stress Test for Writers

In his book, *The Stress of Life* (McGraw-Hill, 1956), Dr. Hans Selye indicated that when you experience chronic stress, your body sends off warning signals. Those physical aches and pains and emotional problems that confront us are actually telling us that unless we cope with the stressors we face, we may find ourselves very sick . . . or worse, dead.

Stress researcher Jim Creighton reviewed Dr. Selye's list of critical signs, expanded on them, and applied them to the writer. If you exhibit at least ten of these symptoms, you may be experiencing dangerously high levels of stress.

The Danger Signs:
1. You frequently worry: Will the editor be upset if I ask about my manuscript? Did I forget to sign my letter? Will someone steal my idea?
2. You are aware of a heavy pounding of your heart (a sign of high blood pressure) when racing to complete an assignment.
3. You sense dryness in your throat and mouth whenever you speak to your editor or your agent.
4. You behave impulsively, starting and stopping a writing project in midstream and going on to another.
5. You frequently take a long time to begin to concentrate on a task.
6. You have an overpowering urge to cry, run or hide when that rejection slip comes.
7. You are often bothered by weakness or dizziness.
8. You are easily fatigued when you spend even a little time on your writing.
9. You feel anxiety and dread, although you do not know what it is that you're afraid of.
10. Your muscles are tense, and you feel "keyed up" all the time.
11. You have trembling, nervous tics when you are asked to speak to an audience.
12. You are easily startled by small sounds.
13. You have a high-pitched, nervous laugh.
14. You stutter or exhibit some other speaking difficulty, although you do not have a speech defect.
15. You grind your teeth or tense up when concentrating on writing.
16. You find yourself either unable to go to sleep right away or you wake up in the middle of the night for no apparent reason.
17. You're always on the go and feel guilty if you relax.
18. You have a frequent need to urinate and use this as an excuse to repeatedly run to the bathroom during the course of your writing.

19. You have diarrhea or a queasiness in the stomach whenever you are confronted with tight deadlines or expect a call from your editor or agent.
20. You experience migraine headaches—even when you feel apparently "relaxed."
21. You tend to lose perspective of yourself and your writing. You either focus inordinate attention on minute, almost insignificant details of your writing or else focus only on the "larger picture," to the detriment of necessary detail.
22. You suffer from a sharp pain in the neck or your lower back after sitting in the same position for a while.
23. You are either constantly snacking while writing or else you become so emotionally involved with your writing that you lose your appetite.
24. You feel a strong need for a drink when you want to unwind.
25. You smoke more cigarettes while working than when relaxing.
26. Depression and/or self-doubt overcomes you soon after you turn in a major piece of writing.
27. You make many errors in judgment and feel a sense of "losing control."

Reprinted by permission of the author, Tom Mach. Copyright 1981 *Writer's Digest.*

Television Program
Material Release Form

_____, 19 _____

Title and/or Theme of Material Submitted Hereunder: _____

Gentlemen:

I am today submitting to you certain program material, the title and/or theme of which is indicated above (which material is hereinafter referred to as the "program material"), upon the following express understanding and conditions.

1. I acknowledge that I have requested permission to disclose to you and to carry on certain discussions and negotiations with you in connection with such program material.

2. I agree that I am voluntarily disclosing such program material to you at my request. I understand that you shall have no obligation to me in any respect whatsoever with regard to such material until each of us has executed a written agreement, which by its terms and provisions will be the only contract between us.

3. I agree that any discussions we may have with respect to such program material shall not constitute any agreement expressed or implied as to the purchase or use of any of such program material which I am hereby disclosing to you either orally or in writing.

4. If such material submitted hereunder is not new or novel, or was not originated by me, or has not been reduced to concrete form, or if because other persons including your employees have heretofore submitted or hereafter submit similar or identical program material which you have the right to use, then I agree that you shall not be liable to me for the use of such program material and you shall not be obligated in any respect whatsoever to compensate me for such use by you.

5. I further agree that if you hereafter produce or distribute a television program or programs based upon the same general idea, theme, or situation, and/or having the same setting or background and/or taking place in the same geographical area or period of history as the said program material, then, unless you have substantially copied the expression and development of such idea, theme or situation, including the characters and story line thereof, as herewith or hereafter submitted to you by me in writing, you shall have no obligation or liability to me of any kind or character by reason of the production or distribution of such program(s), nor shall you be obligated to compensate me in connection therewith.

6. You agree that if you use any legally protectible portion of said program, provided it has not been obtained by you from, or independently

created by, another source, you will pay me an amount that is comparable to the compensation normally paid by you for similar material or an amount equal to the fair market value thereof as of the date of this agreement, whichever is greater.

I acknowledge that but for my agreement to the above terms and conditions, you would not accede to my request to receive and consider the said program material that I am submitting to you herewith.

Very truly yours,

_____

_____

_____

This release form reprinted by permission of the author from *The Complete Book of Scriptwriting* © 1982 by J. Michael Straczynski.

Television Script Sample

TED
(puts hamster in cage)
Are you?

6   CLOSE—LIZ

presses her lips together as a wave of pain hits her. He starts toward her.

TED
(continuing)
Something wrong?

She forces a smile, shakes her head. He continues looking at her questioningly.
A beat. Then he lets it pass.

TED
(continuing)
You know what you need? Hot sun . . . warm beach
. . .

LIZ
(wanly; dreamily)
M-m-m- . . .

TED
Listen, I've got a week coming next month. I'd be
glad to pick up an extra plane ticket . . . Did you
ever see the water off Ladego Beach, Jamaica . . . it's
so blue and clear . . .

7   FAVORING LIZ

taking off her white jacket, looking into the reflection of her drawn face in a
small mirror perched on a shelf, she wearily pushes some strands of hair away
from her forehead.

TED
(continuing; watching her)
You haven't heard a word I said . . .

She looks across at him.

TED
(continuing; unhappily)
Tell me something, hun—what have these hamsters
got that I haven't got . . .?

Sample page from the Ben Casey program "Courage at 3:00 A.M." by Alfred Brenner,
produced by Bing Crosby Productions.

Television Station Organization Chart

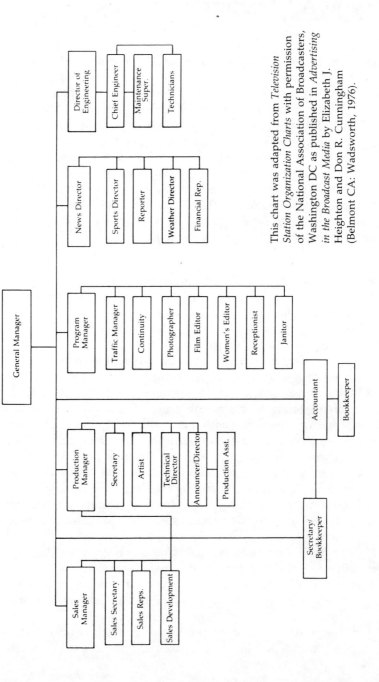

This chart was adapted from *Television Station Organization Charts* with permission of the National Association of Broadcasters, Washington DC as published in *Advertising in the Broadcast Media* by Elizabeth J. Heighton and Don R. Cunningham (Belmont CA: Wadsworth, 1976).

General Manager

- **Director of Engineering**
  - Chief Engineer
  - Maintenance Super.
  - Technicians

- **News Director**
  - Sports Director
  - Reporter
  - **Weather Director**
  - Financial Rep.

- **Program Manager**
  - Traffic Manager
  - Continuity
  - Photographer
  - Film Editor
  - Women's Editor
  - Receptionist
  - Janitor
  - Accountant
    - Bookkeeper

- **Production Manager**
  - Secretary
  - Artist
  - Technical Director
  - Announcer/Director
  - Production Asst.

- **Sales Manager**
  - Sales Secretary
  - Sales Reps.
  - Sales Development
  - Secretary/Bookkeeper

"Type A" Writers

In their book, *Type A Behavior and Your Heart* (Fawcett, 1974), cardiologists Meyer Friedman and Ray Roseman noted the strong link between specific personality characteristics and susceptibility to heart attacks. They discovered that those who chronically struggled to achieve more, tried to cram everything into a short span of time, and competed fiercely were top candidates for heart disease. These individuals they labeled "Type A." "Type B" people, on the other hand, though no less ambitious than Type A folks, were more relaxed, had little need to discuss achievements, and could engage in activities without feeling compelled to win.

Dr. Donald L. Tasto, a practicing clinical psychologist and co-author of a self-improvement book entitled *Spare the Couch* (Prentice-Hall, 1979), reviewed the list of Type A behavior patterns identified by Friedman and Roseman, and adapted them to the writer.

A Type A Writer:

- Always moves, walks, eats and writes rapidly.
- While interviewing others, finds it difficult to restrain himself from hurrying them.
- Is impatient about not hearing quickly from an agent or an editor *each and every time* he sends something out.
- Accepts a larger number of writing assignments than he knows he can cope with and tries to schedule things tighter so he can get more done.
- In a writing class or writers club with opportunity to read his own material, tends to hurry the ends of his sentences, mirroring his underlying impatience with spending even the time for his own speech.
- Feels a strong need to outperform another aggressive, compulsive writer and resents praise such a writer receives.
- Frequently finds himself doing two or more things at once, such as eating while writing or walking the dog while reading.
- Is often upset about the time it takes to research a manuscript.
- Finds that he always wants to bring the topic of social conversation to his writing.
- Believes that his success as a writer has been due in large part to his ability to get things done faster than other writers.
- Is constantly translating his accomplishments into numbers: the number of books he has published, the number of words he has written, the amount of money he has made.
- Has nervous tics that betray his impatience, such as clenching his jaw or chewing on a pencil.

Writers Guild Rates: Screenplays

WGA 1985 Theatrical and Television Basic Agreement
Theatrical Compensation

Employment,
Flat Deals +

	Effective 3/1/85-2/28/86		Effective 3/1/86-2/28/87		Effective 3/1/87-2/29/88	
	LOW	HIGH	LOW	HIGH	LOW	HIGH
A. Screenplay, Including Treatment	$22,801	$42,400	$24,169	$44,944	$25,740/25,619*	$47,865/47,641*
Installments:						
Delivery of Treatment	8,549	13,032	9,062	13,814	9,651/9,606*	14,712/14,643*
Delivery of First Draft Screenplay	10,259	19,549	10,875	20,722	11,582/11,528*	22,069/21,965*
Delivery of Final Draft Screenplay	3,993	9,819	4,232	10,408	4,5074,485*	11,084/11,033*
B. Screenplay, Excluding Treatment	14,249	29,320	15,104	31,079	16,086/16,010*	33,099/32,944*
Installments:						
Delivery of First Draft Screenplay	10,259	19,549	10,875	20,722	11,582/11,528*	22,069/21,965*
Delivery of Final Draft Screenplay	3,990	9,771	4,229	10,357	4,504/4,482*	11,030/10,979*
C. Additional Compensation for Story Included in Screenplay	3,260	6,516	3,456	6,907	3,681/3,663*	7,356/7,321*
D. Story or Treatment	8,549	13,032	9,062	13,814	9,651/9,606*	14,712/14,643*
E. Original Treatment	11,806	19,549	12,514	20,722	13,327/13,265*	22,069/21,965*
F. First Draft Screenplay, With or Without Option for Final Draft Screenplay						
First Draft Screenplay	10,259	19,549	10,875	20,722	11,582/11,528*	22,069/21,965*
Final Draft Screenplay	6,839	13,032	7,249	13,814	7,720/7,684*	14,712/14,643*
G. Rewrite of Screenplay	8,549	13,032	9,062	13,814	9,651/9,606*	14,712/14,643*
H. Polish of Screenplay	4,276	6,516	4,533	6,907	4,828/4,805*	7,356/7,321*

LOW BUDGET—Photoplay costing less than $2,500,000
HIGH BUDGET—Photoplay costing $2,500,000 or more

+ and * for explanations of these discounts and double column figures, see the "Schedule of Minimums" booklet available for $1 from the Writers Guild of America, West, Inc., 8955 Beverly Blvd., Los Angeles, CA 90048.

Writers Guild Rates: Teleplays

Network Prime Time

Length of Program: 90 minutes or less (but more than 60 minutes)

Applicable Minimums	Effective 3/1/85- 2/28/86	Effective 3/1/86- 2/28/87	Effective 3/1/87- 2/29/89
Story	$ 8,090	$ 8,575	$ 9,132/9,090*
Teleplay	$14,385	$15,248	$16,239/16,163*
Installments:			
+First Draft:	60% of Agreed Compensation but not less than 90% of minimum		
Final Draft:	Balance of Agreed Compensation		
Story & Teleplay	$21,354	$22,635	$24,106/23,993*
Installments:			
+Story:	30% of Agreed Compensation		
First Draft Teleplay:	40% of Agreed Compensation or the difference between the Story Installment and 90% of minimum, whichever is greater		
Final Draft Teleplay:	Balance of Agreed Compensation		

Length of Program: 120 minutes or less (but more than 90 minutes)

EPISODIC

Story	$10,806	$11,454	$12,199/12,141*
Teleplay	$18,459	$19,567	$20,839/20,741*
Installments:			
+First Draft:	60% of Agreed Compensation but not less than 90% of minimum		
Final Draft:	Balance of Agreed Compensation		
Story & Teleplay	$28,096	$29,782	$31,718/31,569*
Installments:			
+Story:	30% of Agreed Compensation		
First Draft Teleplay:	40% of Agreed Compensation or the difference between the Story Installment and 90% of minimum, whichever is greater		
Final Draft Teleplay:	Balance of Agreed Compensation		

+On pilots and non-episodic programs, the writer is to be paid 10% of the first installment (as an advance against such first installment) upon commencement of services. The applicable minimum for a pilot story or story and teleplay is 150% of the applicable minimum set forth above.

*For explanation of these figures, see the "Schedule of Minimums" booklet available for $1 from the Writers Guild of America, West, Inc., 8955 Beverly Blvd., Los Angeles CA 90048.

Writer's Tax Form

SCHEDULE C
(Form 1040)

Department of the Treasury
Internal Revenue Service (O)

Profit or (Loss) From Business or Profession
(Sole Proprietorship)
Partnerships, Joint Ventures, etc., Must File Form 1065.
► Attach to Form 1040 or Form 1041. ► See Instructions for Schedule C (Form 1040).

OMB No. 1545-0074

1984
09

Name of proprietor

Social security number

A   Main business activity (see Instructions) ►   Product or Service ►

B   Business name and address ► ....

C   Employer ID number

D   Method(s) used to value closing inventory:
   (1) ☐ Cost   (2) ☐ Lower of cost or market   (3) ☐ Other (attach explanation)

E   Accounting method: (1) ☐ Cash   (2) ☐ Accrual   (3) ☐ Other (specify) ► ....

	Yes	No

F   Was there any change in determining quantities, costs, or valuations between opening and closing inventory? . . . . . .
   If "Yes," attach explanation.

G   Did you deduct expenses for an office in your home? . . . .

Part I   Income

1 a Gross receipts or sales	1a	
b Less: Returns and allowances	1b	
c Subtract line 1b from line 1a and enter the balance here	1c	
2 Cost of goods sold and/or operations (from Part III, line 8)	2	
3 Subtract line 2 from line 1c and enter the gross profit here.	3	
4 a Windfall Profit Tax Credit or Refund received in 1984 (see Instructions)	4a	
b Other income	4b	
5 Add lines 3, 4a, and 4b. This is the gross income . . . . ►	5	

Part II   Deductions

6 Advertising		23 Repairs		
7 Bad debts from sales or services (Cash		24 Supplies (not included in Part III below)		
method taxpayers, see Instructions)		25 Taxes (Do not include Windfall		
8 Bank service charges.		Profit Tax here. See line 29.) . . .		
9 Car and truck expenses		26 Travel and entertainment		
10 Commissions		27 Utilities and telephone		
11 Depletion		28 a Wages . .		
12 Depreciation and Section 179 deduction		b Jobs credit		
from Form 4562 (not included in Part		c Subtract line 28b from 28a . .		
III below).		29 Windfall Profit Tax withheld in 1984		
13 Dues and publications		30 Other expenses (specify):		
14 Employee benefit programs		a		
15 Freight (not included in Part III below) .		b		
16 Insurance		c		
17 Interest on business indebtedness . .		d		
18 Laundry and cleaning		e		
19 Legal and professional services . .		f		
20 Office expense.		g		
21 Pension and profit-sharing plans . .		h		
22 Rent on business property		i		

31 Add amounts in columns for lines 6 through 30i. These are the total deductions . . . . ►	31	
32 **Net profit or (loss).** Subtract line 31 from line 5 and enter the result. If a profit, enter on Form 1040, line 12, and on Schedule SE, Part I, line 2 (or Form 1041, line 6). If a loss, you MUST go on to line 33	32	

33 If you have a loss, you MUST answer this question: "Do you have amounts for which you are not at risk in this business (see Instructions)?" ☐ Yes ☐ No
   If "Yes," you MUST attach Form 6198. If "No," enter the loss on Form 1040, line 12, and on Schedule SE, Part I, line 2 (or Form 1041, line 6).

Part III   Cost of Goods Sold and/or Operations (See Schedule C Instructions for Part III)

1 Inventory at beginning of year (if different from last year's closing inventory, attach explanation)	1	
2 Purchases less cost of items withdrawn for personal use	2	
3 Cost of labor (do not include salary paid to yourself)	3	
4 Materials and supplies	4	
5 Other costs	5	
6 Add lines 1 through 5	6	
7 Less: Inventory at end of year	7	
8 **Cost of goods sold and/or operations.** Subtract line 7 from line 6. Enter here and in Part I, line 2, above. . .	8	

For Paperwork Reduction Act Notice, see Form 1040 Instructions.   Schedule C (Form 1040) 1984

◦U.S. GPO: 1984-423-085 E.I. NO 43-1110209

BIBLIOGRAPHY

Of the thousands of sources we consulted in preparing this encyclopedia, the following are some books we came back to again and again. Within individual entries in the encyclopedia, you'll also find specialized titles cited and both they and the following books contain bibliographies which provide further resources on the art, craft, and business of writing.

The ABC of Copyright. Paris: United Nations Educational, Scientific and Cultural Organization, 1981.

Before Philosophy: The Intellectual Adventure of Ancient Man. Henri Frankfurt. New York: Viking Penguin, Inc., Penguin Books, 1949.

The Book Market: How to Write, Publish and Market Your Book. Aron Mathieu. New York: Andover Press, Inc., 1981.

The Book of Jargon: An Essential Guide to the Inside Languages of Today. Don Ethan Miller. New York: Macmillan, Inc., 1982.

Book Publishing: What It Is, What It Does. John P. Dessauer. New York: R.R. Bowker Co., 1974.

Books In Print, 6 vols. New York: R.R. Bowker Co., 1982.

Cartoonist's & Gag Writer's Handbook. Jack Markow. Cincinnati: Writer's Digest Books, 1967.

The Children's Picture Book: How to Write It, How to Sell It. Ellen E.M. Roberts. Cincinnati: Writer's Digest Books, 1981.

The Complete Book of Scriptwriting. J. Michael Straczynski. Cincinnati: Writer's Digest Books, 1982.

The Complete Guide to Editorial Freelancing, 2nd ed. Carol L. O'Neill and Avima Ruder. New York: Barnes & Noble Books, Everyday Handbook Series, 1979.

The Complete Handbook for Freelance Writers. Kay Cassill. Cincinnati: Writer's Digest Books, 1981.

Confession Writer's Handbook, rev. ed. Florence K. Palmer. Revised by Marguerite McClain. Cincinnati: Writer's Digest Books, 1980.

The Craft of Interviewing. John Brady. Cincinnati: Writer's Digest Books, 1976.

The Craft of Science Fiction. Reginald Bretnor, ed. New York: Barnes & Noble, 1976.

Creating Short Fiction. Damon Knight. Cincinnati: Writer's Digest Books, 1981.

The Creative Writer, 2nd rev. ed. Aron Mathieu, ed. Cincinnati: Writer's Digest Books, 1972.

Dictionary of American Slang, 2nd ed. Harold Wentworth and Stuart B. Flexner. New York: T.Y. Crowell, 1975.

Dictionary of Euphemisms and Other Doubletalk. Hugh Rawson. New York: Crown Publishers, Inc., 1981.

Directory of Corporate Affiliations. Bob Weicherding, ed. Skokie, IL: Standard Rate & Data Service, Inc., National Register Publishing Co., Inc., 1982.

Dun & Bradstreet Reference Book of Corporate Managements. New York: Dun & Bradstreet, Inc., 1982.

The Encyclopedia of Self-Publishing: How to Successfully Write, Publish, Promote and Sell Your Own Work. Marilyn Ross and Tom Ross. Saguache, CO: Communication Creativity, 1980.

Essentials of English. Vincent F. Hopper and Cedric Gale. Woodbury, NY: Barron's Educational Series, Inc., 1961.

The Eye of the Heart. Barbara Howes, ed. New York: The Hearst Corp., Avon Books, 1974.

Fiction Writer's Market. Jean M. Fredette and John Brady, eds. Cincinnati: Writer's Digest Books, 1982.

The Golden Bough, abr. ed. Sir James G. Frazer. New York: Macmillan, 1960.

Guide to Retention Requirements. Washington, DC: Government Printing Office, 1981.

A Guide to Writing History. Doris Ricker Marston. Cincinnati: Writer's Digest Books, 1976.

Harbrace College Handbook, 8th ed. John C. Hodges and Mary E. Whitten. New York: Harcourt Brace Jovanovich, Inc., 1977.

History of Book Publishing in the United States, 4 vols. John Tebbel. New York: R.R. Bowker Co., 1972-1981.

How to Lie with Statistics. Darrell Huff and Irving Geis. New York: W.W. Norton & Co., Inc., 1954.

How to Write a Play. Raymond Hull. Cincinnati: Writer's Digest Books, 1983.

How to Put Your Book Together and Get a Job in Advertising. Maxine Paetro. New York: Elsevier-Dutton Publishing Co., Inc., Hawthorn Books, 1979.

How to Write and Sell Your Personal Experiences. Lois Duncan. Cincinnati: Writer's Digest Books, 1979.

How to Write and Sell (Your Sense of) Humor. Gene Perret. Cincinnati: Writer's Digest Books, 1980.

How to Write Best-Selling Fiction. Dean R. Koontz. Cincinnati: Writer's Digest Books, 1981.

How to Write Short Stories that Sell. Louise Boggess. Cincinnati: Writer's Digest Books, 1980.

How You Can Make $20,000 a Year Writing (No Matter Where You Live). Nancy Edmonds Hanson. Cincinnati: Writer's Digest Books, 1980.

"International Copyright Conventions." Washington, DC: The Library of Congress, Copyright Office, 1977.

International Literary Market Place. New York: R.R. Bowker Co., 1982.

Into the Mainstream: Conversations with Latin American Authors. Luis Harss and Barbara Dohmann. New York: Harper & Row, Publishers, Inc., 1967.

Investigative Reporting and Editing. Paul N. Williams. Englewood Cliffs, NJ: Prentice-Hall, Inc., 1978.

Jobs for Writers. Kirk Polking, ed. Cincinnati: Writer's Digest Books, 1980.

Bibliography

Law and the Writer, 1st rev. ed. Kirk Polking and Leonard S. Meranus. Cincinnati: Writer's Digest Books, 1981.

Literary Market Place. New York: R.R. Bowker Co., 1982.

The Madwoman in the Attic: A Study of Women and the Literary Imagination in the Nineteenth Century. Sandra Gilbert and Susan Gubar. New Haven, CT: Yale University Press, 1979.

Magazine Writing: The Inside Angle. Art Spikol. Cincinnati: Writer's Digest Books, 1982.

Magazines in the Twentieth Century, 2nd ed. Theodore Peterson. Champaign, IL: University of Illinois Press, 1964.

Make Every Word Count. Gary Provost. Cincinnati: Writer's Digest Books, 1980.

Martin's Magic Formula for Getting the Right Job. Phyllis Martin. New York: St. Martin's Press, 1981.

Mass Media Law and Regulation, 2nd ed. William E. Francois. Columbus, OH: Grid, Inc., 1978.

National ZIP Code and Post Office Directory. Retail Operations Division, Delivery Services Department, U.S. Postal Service. Washington, DC: United States Postal Service, annually.

Opportunities in Journalism. John Tebbel. Louisville, KY: Data Courier, Inc., Vocational Guidance Manuals, 1977.

Photographer's Market. Robert D. Lutz, ed. Cincinnati: Writer's Digest Books, 1982.

The Poet's Handbook. Judson Jerome. Cincinnati: Writer's Digest Books, 1980.

Professional's Guide to Publicity, 2nd ed. Richard Weiner. New York: Richard Weiner, Inc., 1978.

Profitable Part-Time/Full-Time Freelancing. Clair Rees. Cincinnati: Writer's Digest Books, 1980.

Publish It Yourself: The Complete Guide to Self-Publishing Your Own Book. Charles Chickadel. San Francisco: Trinity Press, 1978.

The Publish-It-Yourself Handbook: Literary Tradition and How-To. Bill Henderson, ed. Yonkers, NY: The Pushcart Press, and New York: Harper & Row, Publishers, Inc., 1980.

The Relaxation Response. Herbert Benson, M.D., and Miriam Z. Klipper. New York: The Hearst Corp., Avon Books, 1976.

Religious Publishing and Communications. Judith S. Duke. White Plains, NY: Knowledge Industry Publications, Inc., 1980.

The Religious Writers Marketplace. William H. Gentz and Elaine W. Colvin. Philadelphia: Running Press, 1980.

Resume Writing: A Comprehensive, How-to-Do-It Guide, 2nd ed. Burdette E. Bostwick. New York: John Wiley & Sons, Inc., Wiley-Interscience, 1982.

The Road to Syndication. W.H. Thomas, ed. New York: Talent Information Press, 1967.

The Sacred and the Profane: The Nature of Religion. Mircea Eliade. Translated by Willard Trask. New York: Harcourt Brace Jovanovich, Inc., 1968.

Science Fiction A to Z: A Dictionary of the Great S.F. Themes. Isaac Asimov, Martin H. Greenberg, and Charles G. Waugh, eds. Boston: Houghton Mifflin Co., 1982.

Science Fiction Writer's Workshop - 1. Barry B. Longyear. Philadelphia: Owlswick Press, 1980.

The Self-Publishing Manual: How to Write, Print and Sell Your Own Book, 2nd ed. Dan Poynter. Santa Barbara: Para Publishing, 1980.

Sell Copy. Webster Kuswa. Cincinnati: Writer's Digest Books, 1979.

Silences. Tillie Olsen. New York: Doubleday & Co., Inc., Dell Publishing Co., Inc., 1979.

Songwriter's Market. Barbara Norton Kuroff, ed. Cincinnati: Writer's Digest Books, 1982.

Standard & Poor's Register of Corporations, Directors and Executives. Thomas A. Lupo, ed. New York: Standard & Poor's Corp., 1982.

Standard Directory of Advertisers: Classified Edition. Bob Weicherding, ed. Skokie, IL: Standard Rate & Data Service, Inc., National Register Publishing Co., Inc., 1982.

Writer's Encyclopedia

Standard Directory of Advertisers: Geographical Edition. Bob Weicherding, ed. Skokie, IL: Standard Rate & Data Service, Inc., National Register Publishing Co., Inc., 1982.

Standard Directory of Advertising Agencies, 3 vols. Bob Weicherding, ed. Skokie, IL: Standard Rate & Data Service, Inc., National Register Publishing Co., Inc., 1982.

The Stress of Life, 2nd ed. Hans Selye, M.D. New York: McGraw-Hill Book Co., 1978.

Stress Without Distress. Hans Selye, M.D. New York: Harper & Row, Publishers, Inc., 1974.

Subject Guide to Books In Print, 3 vols. New York: R.R. Bowker Co., 1982.

Successful Outdoor Writing. Jack Samson. Cincinnati: Writer's Digest Books, 1979.

Synopsis of the Law of Libel and the Right of Privacy, rev. ed. Bruce W. Sanford. New York: World Almanac Publications, 1981.

Teach Yourself to Write. Evelyn A. Stenbock. Cincinnati: Writer's Digest Books, 1982.

A Treasury of Tips for Writers. American Society of Journalists and Authors. Marvin Weisbord, ed. Cincinnati: Writer's Digest Books, 1981.

The TV Scriptwriter's Handbook. Alfred Brenner. Cincinnati: Writer's Digest Books, 1980.

Understanding Science Fiction. Michael A. Banks. Morristown, NJ: Silver Burdett Co., 1982.

What Color Is Your Parachute?, rev. ed. Richard N. Bolles. Berkeley: Ten Speed Press, 1982.

Where to Go for What. Mara Miller. Englewood Cliffs, NJ: Prentice-Hall, Inc., Spectrum Books, 1981.

Who Owns the Media? Concentration of Ownership in the Mass Communications Industry. Benjamin M. Compaine, ed. White Plains, NY: Knowledge Industry Publications, Inc., 1979.

Who's Hiring Who. Richard Lathrop. Berkeley: Ten Speed Press, 1977.

The Word Processing Book. Peter A. McWilliams. Los Angeles: Prelude Press, 1982.

Write on Target. Connie Emerson. Cincinnati: Writer's Digest Books, 1981.

A Writer's Guide to Book Publishing, 2nd ed. Richard Balkin. New York: Hawthorn Books, Inc., 1981.

The Writer's Manual, rev. ed. Roy E. Porter et al. Palm Springs: E T C Publications, 1979.

Writer's Market. P.J. Schemenaur, ed. Cincinnati: Writer's Digest Books, 1982.

Writer's Resource Guide. Bernadine Clark, ed. Cincinnati: Writer's Digest Books, 1983.

The Writer's Survival Guide. Jean Rosenbaum, M.D., and Veryl Rosenbaum, Psa. Cincinnati: Writer's Digest Books, 1982.

Writing and Selling Science Fiction, 1st paperback ed. Science Fiction Writers of America. Cincinnati: Writer's Digest Books, 1982.

Writing for Children and Teenagers, 2nd rev. ed. Lee Wyndham. Revised by Arnold Madison. Cincinnati: Writer's Digest Books, 1980.

Writing for Regional Publications. Brian Vachon. Cincinnati: Writer's Digest Books, 1979.

Writing for Young Children: A Handbook for Would-Be Writers and for Parents and Teachers, paperback ed. Claudia Lewis. New York: Viking Penguin, Inc., Penguin Books, 1982.

Writing Popular Fiction. Dean R. Koontz. Cincinnati: Writer's Digest Books, 1972.

Writing the Broadway Musical. Aaron Frankel. New York: Drama Book Specialists (Publishers), 1977.

Writing to Inspire. William Gentz, ed. Cincinnati: Writer's Digest Books, 1982.